THE COMPLETE BOOK OF COLLECTIBLE BASEBALL CARDS

THE COMPLETE BOOK OF COLLECTIBLE BASEBALL CARDS

BEEKMAN HOUSE
New York

Louis Weber, President
Publications International, Ltd.
3841 West Oakton Street
Skokie, Illinois 60076

Manufactured in the United States of America

10 9 8 7 6 5 4 3 2 1

Library of Congress Catalog Card Number: 86-62603

ISBN: 0-517-44815-7

This edition published by:
Beekman House
Distributed by Crown Publishers, Inc.
One Park Avenue
New York, New York 10016

Principal Author: Robert Lemke
Cover Design: Inez Smith
Photography: Sam Griffith Studio, Inc.

CONTENTS

1969–1960

1959–1950

1949–1940

1939–1930

1929–1920

1919–1910

1909–1900

19TH CENTURY

INTRODUCTION

As these words are being written, a venerable American tradition—the baseball card—approaches its 100th anniversary. To be sure, the idea of putting the hometown heroes' visages on a piece of paper had been around for a longer time. The Boston club, which won the National League pennant in 1878, is credited with the first use of tiny 1×2" photos of baseball players as a team promotional item. But the use of baseball cards to sell another product, and the distribution of such cards on a relatively widespread geographic basis, traces to 1886 and the highly competitive cigarette industry.

When machinery capable of mass-producing cigarettes was first introduced, it replaced the labor-intensive hand-rolling process used up to that time. Cigarettes could be made and sold cheaply for the first time since the Indians taught Sir Walter Raleigh to inhale the smoke from burning tobacco leaves. Virtually overnight, hundreds of small cigarette companies blossomed. To induce the smoker to choose one brand over all the others, the various cigarette makers began to use premiums. Some included in each box of cigarettes cou-pons that were redeemable for merchandise. Others borrowed an idea from the British—the inclusion of small, colorful trading cards in their cigarette packages. At first, American tobacco companies followed the British themes of military uniforms, bathing beauties and actresses, animals, flags, etc. In 1886, though, Goodwin & Company, New York, hit upon the idea of using baseball players as subject matter for the trading cards in its packages of Old Judge cigarettes. The timing was right. Just three years earlier, the second "major" league had begun play, and with teams in such cities as Cincinnati, Pittsburgh, Louisville, and St. Louis, the American Association brought big league baseball to much of the "western" U.S.

By the following year, several other tobacco companies were also using baseball cards to sell their cigarettes and an American institution had been born. Almost immediately, the candy makers followed suit, offering baseball cards in their packages of caramels, mints, and chewing gum. At that time, the West Coast played its own brand of baseball; it remained completely isolated from the major leagues for another 70 years. None-theless, the western teams were quick to pick up on the idea of baseball cards, and many regional issues were created that remain collector favorites today. Soon, wherever in the nation there was a highly competitive market in a product that attracted men or children, baseball cards became a popular method of persuading them to buy one brand over another. Over the past century, baseball cards have been issued as an inducement to buy not only cigarettes and candy but also newspapers, bread, gasoline, clothes, cookies, hot dogs, potato chips, milk, soda pop, dog food, gelatin dessert, cereal, and a wide range of other items. The popularity of baseball—and of cards with pictures of baseball players on them—as a sales tool has been undisputed for nearly 100 years.

Today, the issue of baseball cards has come full cycle; baseball cards are now a salable item in and of them-selves. There are now three principal manufacturers of baseball cards for the over-the-counter and hobby markets. While Topps still sells its baseball cards with a small stick of bubblegum, the success of Fleer and Donruss, who have sold their cards without gum since 1982, has shown that today it is the baseball cards that are being bought, not the bubblegum.

Certainly the hobby of baseball card collecting is as old as the cards themselves. After all, from the very start, baseball cards were issued in series or sets, with buyers of the products encouraged to collect full sets and thereby to keep buying the products in which they were included. By World War II, the hobby of card collecting in America had progressed to the point where a young man named Jefferson Burdick felt the need to catalog every known issue in a pioneer reference work called *The American Card Catalog*. For many years, Burdick's catalog was the "bible" of the hobby and the numbers he assigned to each card set became their official identification. Interestingly, baseball cards were only a part of Burdick's work. His catalog covered the entire field of collectible cards, of which baseball cards have been, and continue to be, just a part.

The baseball card hobby as we know it today really took off in the mid-1970s. Prior to that, the collecting of baseball cards had always been considered principally a preoccupation for children. Generations of Americans have grown up collecting baseball cards—whether from cigarette packages in the 1910s, bubblegum in the 1930s, or cereal boxes in the 1960s— but they "put away the things of a child" as they grew up. For most of the period of baseball card issue, there have been more important things to occupy young adults: World War I, the Depression, World War II, and the Korean and Vietnam conflicts. In the mid-70s, though, a peculiar set of circumstances came together that made the baseball card hobby boom—and it was tied to another boom, the post-World War II baby boom. The children who were born in the late 1940s and early 1950s, like their fathers and grandfathers before them, were collectors of baseball cards. Also like their fathers and grandfathers, they gave up baseball cards as they grew to be teenagers, discovered romance, went to school, or began their careers. When the nostalgia craze hit America in the mid-1970s—fueled by the painfully drawn-out end of the Vietnam war and the everyday problems of coping with double-digit inflation, many of this baby-boom generation

turned back to their baseball cards. At the same time, baseball was also enjoying a resurgence of public interest. The violence of professional football, which had so enthralled the nation during the Vietnam years, suddenly seemed out of place in an America finally at peace. Expansion of the major leagues to Montreal, San Diego, Seattle, and (again) Kansas City in 1969, Milwaukee in 1970, and Toronto and Seattle (second try) in 1977, and the creation of divisional play and league championship play-offs, brought new interest to the national pastime—and to baseball cards.

Large numbers of Americans in their late 20s and early 30s, their families begun and their careers underway, turned to the baseball cards they had collected in the 1940s and 1950s as a means of recreation and escape into the "Happy Days" that television told them they should remember from their youth. These born-again collectors found that the baseball card hobby had been growing along without them, quietly and without fanfare, and was waiting to welcome them back in the fold. The hard-core collectors who had kept their own hobby interest alive nonstop in the '50s and '60s had some surprises for those returning to the hobby. There were magazines and newspapers where the collector could buy, sell, trade, and keep informed. There were catalogs and checklists detailing issues of 100 years ago and those of the previous season. There were card shows where dealers and collectors set up displays of cards and related memorabilia for sale and trade. And, there was a whole generation of baseball card issues that these former collectors had missed when they went off to college or to war.

There was a lot of catching up to do, but this new generation of collectors had the time and money to do it. As their own children grew up, and evidenced their own interest in baseball cards, many of these former collectors realized that baseball card collecting was a hobby that could be shared by the whole family.

Many of those who returned to the baseball card hobby in the mid-1970s began to make contributions that resulted in further growth. Some used their education and experience in fields such as business, data process-

ing, and marketing in the hobby, creating meaningful price guides, alphabetical checklists, and a corps of professional, full-time baseball card dealers. Former collectors who now worked in the media began to give the hobby unprecedented publicity in newspapers and on television. The result was an outpouring of hoards of baseball cards and other collectible treasures from attics and basements all over the country. Demand by collectors for the now-scarce cards of their youth created higher prices for those cards, and the higher prices, in turn, brought cards out of the woodwork to fill the demand.

By the late 1970s, baseball cards had become collectible, and like many other collectibles, were being seriously considered as a hedge against inflation that had risen to 10 to 11 percent. As demand increased, prices of the "hot" cards of the 1950s began to progress by leaps and bounds; gains of 50 to 100 percent a year were common. Then speculation set in. Former collectors, now familiar with the ways of big business, began to treat baseball cards as another Wall Street commodity; there were daily quotes, buy and sell spreads, attempts to corner the market in particular issues, and a general feeling that card prices were on a never-ending spiral upward. If a Mint 1952 Topps Mickey Mantle card sold for $500 in 1979, $1,500 in 1980, and $3,000 in 1981, what in the world would it sell for in 1982?

Would you believe $1,000? Like most other "hard assets" from coins to Oriental rugs, diamonds to postage stamps, the value of collectible old baseball cards peaked in 1981—then crashed. Interest rates, which had soared to 16 percent on the back of inflation and which now seemed on the verge of being tamed by "Reaganomics," suddenly lured all of the speculative money out of baseball cards and into Treasury bills and long-term certificates of deposit. The baseball card hobby was back in the hands of the hobbyists.

You hear the word "investment" much less these days in the hobby, but that doesn't mean buying baseball cards is throwing money away. A quality collection, built with care and a bit of thought, will more than take care of itself in terms of return on the money spent. Other than hot "rookie cards," which can be bought in a pack for 2¢ today and sold for $2 tomorrow, there isn't much "easy money" in cards today, but the steady influx of new collectors, and the growing demands of established collectors, have once again put the values of many baseball card issues on an upward move. The gains are more modest—10 to 20 percent a year is not uncommon in popular collecting areas—but they are real. More importantly, though, the monetary gains of building a baseball card collection are secondary to the personal gains of enjoying a hobby that has meant so much to so many for nearly 100 years.

And today, where does the baseball card collecting hobby stand? It has never been bigger or stronger. Circulation of the hobby trade papers is at an all-time high, as is attendance at the many baseball card shows held around the country. There is more to collect, as well. Besides its main baseball card set, each of the "Big 3" card companies, Fleer, Topps and Donruss, has bombarded the market with a number of auxiliary issues in 1984, and the number of local and regional companies issuing baseball cards has never been greater, not to mention the many collector sets being produced each year. There has been an accompanying "information explosion" in the past few years, with books, magazines, and reference works to help the collector get the most out of his hobby. The baseball card hobby has never been so easy or so much fun.

HOW TO COLLECT BASEBALL CARDS

Surprise! One of the greatest things about the baseball card hobby is that there is no right or wrong way to collect. Each collector is free to follow the hobby as he sees fit. Those who are new to the hobby, though, might like a few words of advice.

Perhaps the most important thing to do when you decide to pursue the baseball card hobby is to set your goals. Nobody can collect everything. There have probably been a quarter of a million different baseball cards issued within the past 100 years, and nobody will ever live long enough or have enough money to collect them all. In truth, even the most experienced hobbyists don't know about all the cards that have been issued. There are new discoveries being made every month of cards that were previously unknown. Choose your goals carefully, with an eye toward challenging all of your resources, personal and financial. Don't make your goals so easy that they are quickly attained, or you'll lose interest in collecting in a big hurry. On the other hand, don't set your sights so high that your goal is unattainable, or you will become discouraged. Decide what you want to collect with an eye on your budget and on the time and energy you have to devote to pursuing your collection.

The traditional hobby approach has been to collect complete sets, one of every card issued in a particular year by a particular company. For relatively modern cards, since the late 1960s or so, this is a reasonable goal for many collectors, but as you get back into older cards, or scarce sets where the price per card is extremely high, it can be an impossible objective for all but the wealthiest collector. As more and more of the earlier baseball card issues have been priced out of the range of full-set collectors, the hobby has sought alternatives.

Team collecting is a fast-growing specialty in the hobby. Every card collector has his or her favorite baseball teams, whether they are currently players or one of the now-defunct teams in baseball history. A large number of collectors devote their hobby time and money to collecting just the cards of one or two teams; some will collect cards over the entire range of the team's history, while others limit themselves to the era that they remember best, often when they first became fans, and collect from that point forward.

Superstar collecting is another current favorite. Here again, each collector decides who is a superstar and whose cards to collect. One collector's favorite player may be on the bottom of the list of another, so there's plenty of room for everybody in this field. In collecting all of the issues of one player, or a small group of players, the collector is exposed to a wide range of lesser-known card issues. These issues are likely to be expensive as well as hard to find. One of the great things about superstar collecting is that a collection is almost never finished. The bigger the star, the more items he was pictured on and the greater the challenge of finding them all. Those who collect cards of current players will find new issues each year to keep their collections alive, while continuing to research older issues, such as minor league sets, for cards of their favorite players.

An outgrowth of the superstar collecting craze has been rookie card collecting. Since, speaking only in generalities, each year's cards are printed in greater quantity than the previous year, earlier cards are numerically scarcer than those that follow. Consequently, a player's first baseball card—his rookie card—will be scarcer than those that are printed in subsequent years. This has created additional demand for those premier cards and has added to their price tags. Rookie cards have become the last refuge of the baseball card speculator, many of whom accumulate stacks of a player's first card in hopes that his on-field performance will cause the cards to rise in price and make the speculator rich. In fact, that can and does happen. In 1981, for example, Robin Yount's 1975 Topps rookie card sold for a dime apiece. Today, an MVP season later, the card is a $15 item. But you can lose your shirt speculating in rookie cards. Also in 1981, for example, the hottest young player in the game was Joe Charboneau, the 1980 Rookie of the Year in the American League, and darling of the Cleveland media. His 1981 baseball cards were a 25¢ item the day they were issued. Today, you can buy all the "Super Joe" cards you need for 3¢ or a nickel apiece. Still, for the collector who likes a little action, rookie card speculation can liven up one's hobby involvement.

Another collecting specialty that is catching on in a big way is type collecting. In building a type collection, you try to assemble just one card from each set that has been issued—but again, you need to set some limits; there have been just too many sets issued. While it is possible to find a single card from each of the sets listed in this encyclopedia, there are at least as many sets not listed here—enough to keep you searching and broke for the rest of your days. You could, perhaps, limit a type collection to the 20th century, to the post-World War II years, or to the time divisional play began in 1969, or—whatever you wish. Remember, there are no rules in baseball card collecting.

A final word about building your collection concerns condition. One of the hard and fast facts of life in the baseball card hobby is that of two identical baseball cards, the one in better condition will be worth more money. Most collectors want cards that are as close as possible to the way they were issued. Cards that are in higher grades of preservation will retain their value better and will increase in value faster than cards in lower grades. In general, you should collect the highest grade your budget can stand. Baseball card grading is subject to interpretation by each individual collector. Unlike coins or diamonds, there is no single accepted grading standard for baseball cards. One of the more popular grading guides is that formulated by *Baseball Cards* magazine and *Sports Collectors Digest,* presented here:

BASEBALL CARD GRADING GUIDE

It is necessary that some sort of card grading standard be used so that buyer and seller (especially when dealing by mail) may reach an informed agreement on the value of a card. Unlike other collectible hobbies which have one fairly uniform set of grading standards, the baseball card hobby exists with nearly as many grading standards as there are collectors and dealers.

Readers are invited to make use of the following grading standards developed by the staff of *Baseball Cards.* However, no one, whether dealer or collector, is required to conform to this—or any other—standard.

The staff of this publication will cooperate in any effort designed to provide this hobby with uniform and universal grading standards; contact the editor.

Mint (Mt.) A perfect card, well-centered with four sharp, square cor-ners. No creases, edge dents, surface scratches, yellowing or fading, regardless of age. No imperfectly printed card (out of register, badly cut) or card stained by contact with gum, wax or other substances can be considered truly Mint.

Excellent to Mint (Ex.-Mt.) A nearly perfect card. May have one or two corners which are not perfectly sharp. May have minor printing imperfections. No creases or scruffiness on surface. May show hint of paper or ink aging.

Excellent (Ex.) Corners and edges no longer sharp, though not markedly rounded or dented. Centering may be off, but all borders must show. No creases. Surfaces may show slight loss of original gloss from rubbing across other cards.

Very Good (VG) A card that shows obvious handling. Corners will be rounded and perhaps creased. One or two other minor creases may be visible. Surfaces will exhibit some loss of luster, but all printing is intact. May show moderate gum, wax or other packaging stains or defects. No major creases, tape marks or extraneous markings or writing. Exhibits no damage, just honest handling.

Good (G) A card that shows excessive wear or abuse. May have thumbtack holes in or near margin, corners rounded into design, perhaps small tears. Will have one or more major creases, breaking the paper, and several minor creases. May have minor added pen or pencil writing or other stains. Back may show evidence of having been taped or pasted, with small pieces of paper missing or covered.

Fair (F) A card that has been tortured to death. Corners or other areas may be torn off. Card may have been trimmed, show holes from paper punch or have been used for BB gun practice. Major portions of front or back printing may be missing from contact with heaven-only-knows what substance. Card may exhibit added decoration in the form of moustaches or writing in the form of derogatory comments on the player's ability, ethnic heritage or legitimacy.

HOW TO USE THIS ENCY-CLOPEDIA

This volume is designed to present the most information about the baseball card hobby available between two covers anywhere, but it is not—nor can any baseball card book be—all-inclusive. The diversity of baseball card issues in the past century has been too great to allow any book to present it all.

Three of the key words in the title—Collectible Baseball Cards—explain how we have chosen to narrow the focus of this book. Of the hundreds, perhaps thousands, of baseball card issues since the 19th century, not all are collectible. Some of the older issues are too obscure, too rare, too expensive, or just simply not popular enough to be collectible. On the other hand, some of the newer issues, those which have been produced by collectors, for collectors—recent minor league sets, or retrospective sets of great teams of the past, for example—and which are subject to possible re-issue anytime in the future—do not meet the true definition of a collectible, that is, something that is produced in a limited (either by time or number) edition.

In determining which issues would appear in this book, the words "baseball cards" were also carefully considered. In general (there are exceptions for popularly collected issues), the listings in this book reflect true baseball cards: pictures of contemporary baseball players in paper or cardboard in a size generally conducive to being held in the palm of the hand. This has resulted in the exclusion of many large-format issues, particularly team-issued postcards and 5×7" or 8×10" pictures, along with the small-size strip cards of the 1920s and the various baseball coins, discs, and other odd-size or peculiarly shaped issues that have appeared over the years.

These limitations were imposed in an effort to focus the reader on what is essentially 95 percent of the popularly collected baseball card issues today. As the collector advances in the hobby, perhaps he will feel a need to move on to the more obscure issues which are beyond the scope of this book, but for the vast majority of hobbyists, this book will meet all of their collecting needs for a lifetime of hobby enjoyment. The fact that a particular baseball card issue does not appear in this book does not mean it is particularly rare or valuable. Rather, in the opinion of the editors, it is just not as popularly collected or collectible as those cards that are listed.

This volume has been arranged with the most recent baseball card issues presented first, working backward to the end of the book, where the earliest cards are chronicled. This reflects the manner in which baseball cards are collected today, and in fact, the way they have always been collected. The newer baseball card issues are simply more popular than those that have preceded them. This condition is the result of the large numbers of new collectors that swell the hobby ranks each year.

Each listing in the book is identified by the year of issue and the name by which it is most popularly known among collectors. Photographs of representative cards in many sets are presented as an aid to identification.

The SPECIFICATIONS listed for each issue include the size and a description of the method of manufacture and distribution. The sizes listed give the horizontal (width) dimension first, followed by the vertical (depth), and are expressed in inches. On many earlier issues, the cutting of cards from the sheets on which they were printed was not as automated or as perfect as it is today, and these sizes should be considered "ideal" rather than the norm. Wear and trimming of a card may also change the physical dimensions of a card from the sizes given here, invariably to the detriment of the value of the card. Descriptions of the front and back of the card are meant to correct misinformation that has been propagated within the hobby on the method of card manufacture over the years. Details of an issue's original distribution are presented where they are known, to assist the collector in understanding the particular card.

For each listing, a HISTORY of the issue is presented. It is this information that makes this book particularly valuable to the collector, because much of this has never before been available between two covers. Literally a century of baseball card lore is included here for the first time in such comprehensive fashion.

The good and bad points about each issue are summarized in the FOR and AGAINST sections of the listings. These summarize reasons for the popularity and collectibility of the set and may be of use to the hobbyist in determining whether or not the issue is suitable for his own collection.

Under the heading NOTEWORTHY CARDS in each listing, we attempt to detail the peculiarities of each set or issue. Those cards that are —accountably or inexplicably—scarce or rare, or merely expensive, are detailed in this area, as well as those cards that are different from the rest of the set.

For some of the issues we have included a listing for OUR FAVORITE CARD, to present some of the more interesting and unusual aspects of baseball card collecting—focusing on the most important part, the players themselves who appear on the cards.

Each listing ends with a discussion of current value. Since there are entire price guides dedicated to this subject, we have elected to keep the dollars and cents aspects to only what is necessary to give the collector an idea of what kind of financial commitment is called for in pursuit of any particular set, issue, or single card. In presenting the 5-YEAR PROJECTION, it has been our intent to give the collector an educated guess on how each particular issue will fare— when compared to all other baseball cards as a whole—pricewise over the long term. We have used a system roughly based on an average appreciation of 10 percent per year. That is, we feel that overall the value of a "portfolio" of collectible baseball cards, given the current economic conditions, can be expected to rise at a rate of about 10 percent per year. Naturally, some issues, and some specific cards, will do much better than that, while some issues will do worse. It is only these rough trends we are trying to indicate by the 5-year projections. Persons interested in investing or speculating in baseball cards must make their own appraisal of such factors as supply and demand before making buy or sell decisions about any baseball card or baseball card set.

RICK
SUTCLIFFE   P

Mickey Mantle

1984-
1980

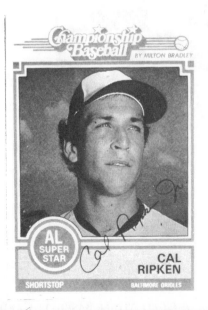

CAL
RIPKEN

SHORTSTOP   BALTIMORE ORIOLES

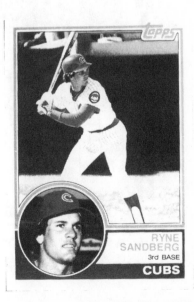

RYNE
SANDBERG
3rd BASE

CUBS

1984 TOPPS

SPECIFICATIONS

SIZE: 2½×3½". FRONT: Color photograph. BACK: Purple and red printing on gray cardboard. DISTRIBUTION: Nationally, in packages with bubblegum.

HISTORY

Compared to competing sets from Fleer and Donruss, the 1984 Topps baseball card set is not viewed by collectors as one of the company's best efforts. While Topps retained the popular concept of combining a large action photo with a smaller portrait photo on the front of the card, many collectors feel the effect was spoiled by putting the team name in large, colored block letters down the left side of the card, thereby eating up too much space that could otherwise have been used for photos. The player's name and position are printed next to the smaller portrait photo, in the same color as the team name. A Topps logo intrudes into the upper-right corner of the photo from the white top border. Instead of natural backgrounds for the portrait photos, as used in 1983, the square-framed '84 portraits have a solid color background. Card backs feature an unusual red and purple coloring, and include complete major and minor league stats,

personal data, and a few highlights from the previous season. A team logo appears in the upper-right corner on back. Set size was again set at 792 cards for '84. The first six cards feature highlights of the previous season. Other specialty cards in the '84 set include team leader cards, which feature the top pitcher and batter of each club; 1983 season leaders in major statistical categories; All-Star cards for both leagues; active leaders in career stats; and six numbered checklists. Missing from the '84 set, for the second year, were team rookie or "Future Stars" cards.

FOR

Typical Topps set.

AGAINST

Many collectors just don't like the design.

NOTEWORTHY CARDS

All the regular stars are present, but few of the hot rookies of '84; Topps was saving them for the Traded set later in the year.

VALUE

MINT CONDITION: Complete set, $18; common card, 3¢; stars, 25¢–75¢. 5-YEAR PROJECTION: Above average.

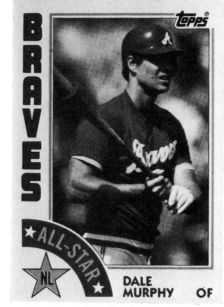

1984 Topps, Dale Murphy, All-Star

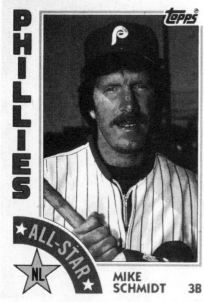

1984 Topps, Mike Schmidt, All-Star

1984 Topps, Chicago Cubs Team Leaders Card

1984 Topps, Steve Carlton

1984 Topps, Sparky Anderson

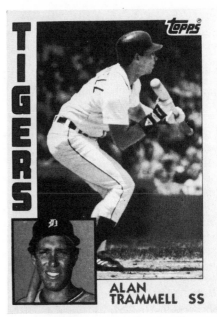

1984 Topps, Alan Trammell

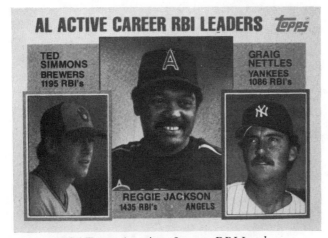

1984 Topps, American League RBI Leaders

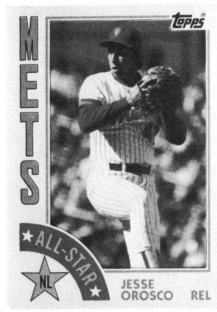

1984 Topps, Jesse Orosco, All-Star

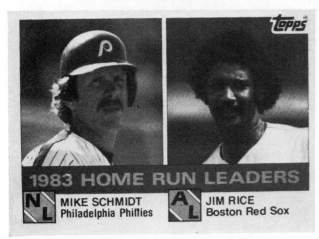

1984 Topps, 1983 Home Run Leaders

1984 TOPPS TRADED

SPECIFICATIONS

SIZE: 2½×3½". FRONT: Color photograph. BACK: Blue and red printing on white cardboard. DISTRIBUTION: Complete, boxed sets sold only through hobby dealers.

HISTORY

For the fourth year in a row, Topps produced a 132-card Traded set to supplement its regular baseball card issue in 1984. The Traded set is made up principally of players who were traded, sold, or who otherwise changed teams between the time Topps deadlined its regular '84 set and mid-summer, when the Traded set was closed out. While most collectors appreciate the chance to get cards of the current year's design featuring players in the "right" uniform, the principal attraction of the Traded set is the presence of rookie cards that were not included in the regular set. Also included in the issue are a sprinkling of cards of new managers. While most of the cards in the '84 Topps Traded set feature new photos of the players, a few cards have had new uniforms created by a Topps artist. The design of the Traded set is identical to the regular issue cards for 1984. Card backs are easier to read because the cardboard is white, whereas the regular issue cards had gray cardboard on the back. Numbers on the '84 Topps Traded cards have a "T" suffix, and go from 1-T to 132-T, the latter card being a checklist. Like the 1981–1983 Traded sets, the '84 Traded issue is sold only through hobby channels as a complete boxed set. The cards are not available from the normal retail outlets that featured 1984 Topps cards in bubblegum packs all year.

FOR

Chance for collectors to get updated cards to more accurately reflect the status of players during the 1984 baseball season.

AGAINST

Because the cards are not sold to the general public, some collectors don't feel they are "real" baseball cards. Cost per card is relatively high.

NOTEWORTHY CARDS

The inclusion of manager cards such as Yogi Berra in the Topps set is a feature that was virtually overlooked by its competitors in 1984. Future Hall of Famers Tom Seaver, Pete Rose, and Joe Morgan were included in the Traded set. However, by the time the set was released in late September, Pete Rose was no longer an Expo, so his "updated" card was already outdated. All the big-name rookies of 1984 were part of the issue.

VALUE

MINT CONDITION: Complete set, $9; common card, 3¢–5¢; stars, 25¢ and up; Pete Rose, $2, Juan Samuel, Alvin Davis, $2.50; Dwight Gooden, $3. 5-YEAR PROJECTION: Above average.

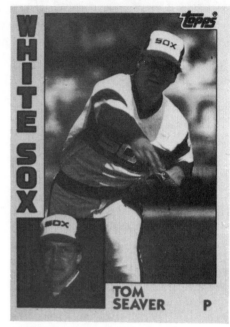

1984 Topps Traded, Tom Seaver

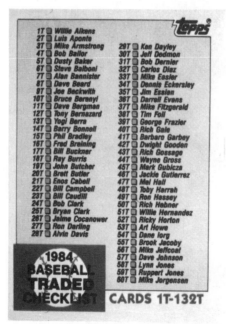

1984 Topps Traded, Checklist

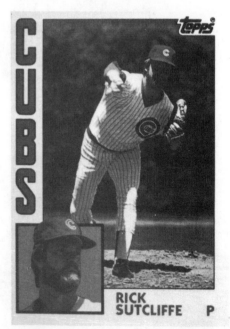

1984 Topps Traded, Rick Sutcliffe

1984 TOPPS SUPERSTAR 5×7s

SPECIFICATIONS
SIZE: 4⅞×6⅞". FRONT: Color photograph. BACK: Red and purple printing on gray cardboard. DISTRIBUTION: Limited geographic areas in cellophane packs.

HISTORY
A test issue sold in limited areas of the country, the Topps 5×7 issue of 1984 was unusual in that the 30 cards in the set were merely giant-size versions of the players' cards in the 1984 Topps set. Fronts and backs are exactly the same as the regular issue.

FOR
Something different for the superstar collector.

AGAINST
If you didn't like the design of the '84 Topps cards in the first place, you'll hate them when they're twice as big.

NOTEWORTHY CARDS
They're all superstars.

VALUE
MINT CONDITION: Complete set, $10; common cards, 25¢–35¢; super-superstars, 50¢. 5-YEAR PROJECTION: Above average.

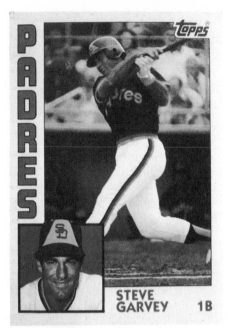

1984 Topps Superstar 5×7s, Steve Garvey (front)

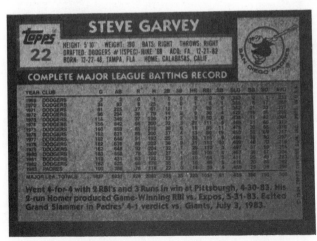

1984 Topps Superstar 5×7s, Steve Garvey (back)

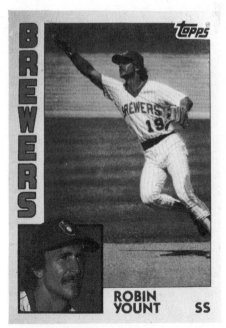

1984 Topps Superstar 5×7s, Robin Yount

1984 TOPPS ALL-STAR GLOSSIES

SPECIFICATIONS

SIZE: 2½×3½". FRONT: Color photograph. BACK: Red and blue printing on white cardboard. DISTRIBUTION: Nationally, in Topps cellophane-wrapped "rack-packs"; complete set via hobby dealers.

HISTORY

Buoyed by the collector response to its Glossies set of the previous year, Topps produced a similar specialty issue in 1984 to honor the starting All-Stars of 1983. The 22 cards in the 1984 All-Star Glossies set include the starting nines for the American and National Leagues, along with the managers and honorary team captains. Besides wholesaling the sets to baseball card dealers, Topps made single cards available by inserting them in their "rack-packs," cellophane-wrapped packages containing 36 regular cards and sold alongside the traditional wax packs with bubblegum. Card fronts feature a color photo with a special All-Star banner at the top, and a league emblem in the lower-left corner. A special glossy coating on the front of the card gives it an especially appealing appearance. Backs have no statistics or personal data on the player, just a name, team, position, card number, and description of the set as "1983 All-Star Game Commemorative Set."

FOR

Attractive set of superstars.

AGAINST

Relatively expensive per card.

NOTEWORTHY CARDS

All of the players are current superstars.

VALUE

MINT CONDITION: Complete set, $8; common card, 25¢; super-superstars, 50¢–$1. 5-YEAR PROJECTION: Above average.

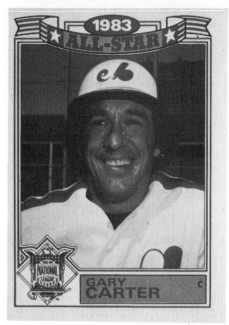

1984 Topps All-Star Glossies, Gary Carter

1984 Topps All-Star Glossies, Rod Carew

1984 Topps All-Star Glossies, Johnny Bench

1984 Topps All-Star Glossies, Carl Yastrzemski

1984 FLEER

SPECIFICATIONS
SIZE: 2½×3½". FRONT: Color photograph. BACK: Black and blue printing on white cardboard. DISTRIBUTION: Nationally, in packages with team logo and cap stickers.

HISTORY
If you want to get a feeling of what major league baseball was like in the early 1980s, look at the 1984 Fleer set, which certainly ranks as one of the finest major card sets of modern times. The design was clean and attractive. The photography was sometimes inspired and was only occasionally short of perfect. Candids were included along with the usual mix of portraits and action shots, inspiring a difference of opinion among collectors. Some collectors feel the pictures too often were not in keeping with the serious nature of baseball and baseball card collecting. Other collectors, however, feel that the inclusion of candids helps reveal what baseball and the players of the 1980s were really like. Card fronts for '84 feature a large rectangular photo in the center, bordered at top and bottom by a bright blue stripe that extends all the way across the face of the card. The sides of the photo are bordered in white, and there is a white border at top and bottom. The top blue stripe contains only the Fleer logo, in white type, while the bottom stripe has the player's name, also in white. The player's position is in small black letters in the bottom white border. A full-color team logo appears in the lower-right corner of the card, superimposed on the bottom stripe and the lower corner of the photo. Card backs for '84 are almost exact copies of '83. They have the same vertical format, same black and white player photo in the upper-right corner, same arrangement of bio, year-by-year major and minor league stats, and when space permits, a trivia question about the player. The only differences are that the card number was moved out to the upper-left corner, and the majority of the printing was in blue, instead of brown. Once again, the 660 cards in the set were arranged alphabetically by player's name within team. The teams were arranged in order of their 1983 season finish, those with the highest winning percentage being near the front of the set. There were 14 checklist cards at the end of the set, and a large group of "Super Star Special" cards, some featuring a single player, some featuring more than one. A group of four cards detailed the 1983 World Series. No major error or variation cards exist for the 1984 Fleer set.

messages in the form of equipment advertising, stadium billboards, etc. Among the "Super Star Special" cards worthy of special note are six cards meant to be viewed side-by-side as pairs. One card in each pair has no left border, the other has no right border, so that they form a continuous picture when laid together. The pairs feature Wade Boggs and Rod Carew, the 1983 American League batting champ and runner-up (there is no similar pair for the National League batting leaders); teammates Tim Raines and Al Oliver of the Expos; and the National League All-Star second baseman Steve Sax and shortstop Dickie Thon. "Retiring Superstars" Johnny Bench and Carl Yastrzemski share a card, while Gaylord Perry appears on two of the special cards, one called "Going Out in Style," the other showing him in the dugout pointing out how high George Brett is applying pine tar to a bat. That card is titled "The Pine Tar Incident, 7/24/83." Bench, Yaz, and Perry also appear on "regular" '84 Fleer cards, even though they all retired at the end of the 1983 season.

VALUE
MINT CONDITION: Complete set, $13; common card, 3¢; stars, 25¢–75¢. 5-YEAR PROJECTION: Above average.

FOR
Attractive set, perhaps destined to be a classic, at currently low price.

AGAINST
Some collectors feel there are too many cards in the set that picture players in nontraditional poses.

NOTEWORTHY CARDS
You can't mention the 1984 Fleer set without mentioning the Glenn Hubbard card (#182), on which the Braves second baseman is pictured with a big bearded smile—and a boa constrictor draped around his shoulders. On the Jay Johnstone card (#495), the Cubs outfielder is shown wearing a Budweiser umbrella-hat. Critics contend that too many of the cards in the '84 Fleer set have similar "commercial"

1984 Fleer, Tony Pena

1984 Fleer, Gary Gaetti

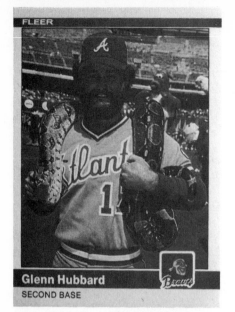

1984 Fleer, Glenn Hubbard

1984 Fleer, Backstop Stars, Super Star Special

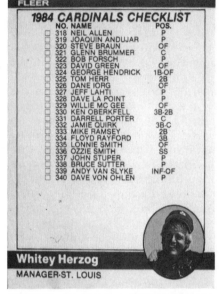

1984 Fleer, St. Louis Cardinals Checklist

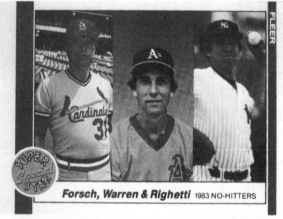

1984 Fleer, 1983 No-Hitters, Super Star Special

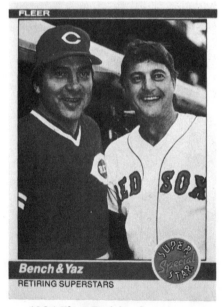

1984 Fleer, Retiring Superstars,
Super Star Special

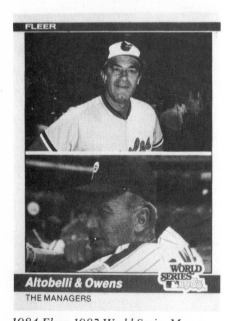

1984 Fleer, 1983 World Series Managers

1984 Fleer, Reds Reunited, Super Star Special

1984 Fleer, Jay Johnstone

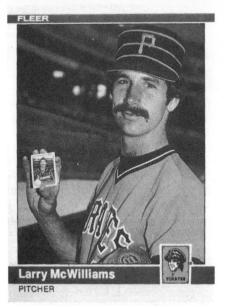

1984 Fleer, Larry McWilliams

1984 Fleer, Eddie Murray

1984 Fleer, Greg Brock

1984 Fleer, Luis Leal

1984 Fleer, Lee Smith

1984 Fleer, Don Sutton

1984 Fleer, Mookie Wilson

1984 FLEER UPDATE

SPECIFICATIONS
SIZE: 2½×3½". FRONT: Color photograph. BACK: Blue printing on white cardboard. DISTRIBUTION: Sold as complete sets only, through hobby channels.

HISTORY
Recognizing a good idea, the folks at Fleer introduced an updated version of their 1984 baseball card set in September of that year. The concept was the same as that pioneered by Topps in 1981: "updating" the year's card set by issuing new cards of players who had been traded and cards of rookies who had been overlooked in the regular set. Like the Topps Traded sets, the '84 Fleer Update issue was sold only through baseball card dealers as a complete set. It was not generally available over the counter at the traditional candy store outlets that sold the regular packs of Fleer cards all year. The 132 cards in the Fleer Update set came boxed with an assortment of the 36 team logo and cap sticker cards that were packaged with the company's card packs. Besides the new pictures of the players, the only difference between the Fleer Update cards and the regular issue cards of 1984 is the numbering system. The Update cards have numbers on the back from U-1 through U-132. There are 131 player cards in the set, numbered alphabetically; card #U-132 is a checklist card.

FOR
A well-done set, carrying through the generally excellent photography found in Fleer's regular 1984 set. Gives collectors a chance to own 1984 cards with players in the uniforms of the teams for which they played in 1984, rather than the teams from which they were traded. The set also gives collectors rookie cards of hot new stars.

AGAINST
Because the cards are not available to the public except through hobby dealers, some collectors feel they are not legitimate.

NOTEWORTHY CARDS
Fleer did a good job of updating its 1984 set until the very last possible moment. Rick Sutcliffe and Ron Hassey, who were traded to the Cubs in June, are shown in their new uniforms, although Mel Hall and Joe Carter, who went to the Indians in the deal, are not included in the set. Pete Rose, who is shown as a Phillie in the regular set, is pictured as an Expo in the updated issue, though by the time the cards had been issued, he was with the Reds. Rookie pitching sensation Dwight Gooden of the Mets is one of the new players highlighted in the set.

VALUE
MINT CONDITION: Complete set, $9; common card, 2¢; stars, 25¢–$1; superstars, $1–$2; Gooden, $3. 5-YEAR PROJECTION: Above average.

1984 DONRUSS

SPECIFICATIONS
SIZE: 2½×3½". FRONT: Color photograph. BACK: Green and black printing on white cardboard. DISTRIBUTION: Nationally, in wax packs and complete boxed sets.

HISTORY
In its fourth year, Donruss really hit its stride as a baseball card producer. The company's 1984 set was acclaimed by most collectors as the best overall of the "Big 3." The set was not without controversy though. It seems there was some confusion as to what constituted a "complete" set. If you collected the set from wax packs, you could find 660 cards. If you bought your set from the so-called "vendor cases" of complete, boxed, and sorted sets sold to baseball card dealers, you got only 658 cards. The difference was a pair of special pasteboard cards that Donruss called "Living Legends" cards. Each of the Living Legends cards featured a pair of superstars who had retired after the 1983 season; the cards were supposed to be Donruss's way of saying farewell. However, Donruss jumped the gun by including Brewers reliever Rollie Fingers on one of the cards. Fingers came back from his 1982 arm injury to make significant contributions from the bullpen in '84. Fingers shares his Legends card with Gaylord Perry. The other Living Legends card depicts future Hall of Famers Carl Yastrzemski and Johnny Bench. These two cards were distributed only in the '84 wax packs. This created immediate problems for the card dealers who had ordered dozens or hundreds of '84 Donruss sets, and now had to pass onto their customers—the collectors—sets that were "missing" two cards. While the Living Legends cards were not numbered as part of the set (they carried letter designations of "A" and "B"), collectors quickly decided that they were necessary to have a complete set. This created an instant demand for the cards pulled from the wax packs, and the Living Legends cards skyrocketed in value to a dollar apiece overnight. The Living Legends cards are not all that attractive; players' portraits are squashed onto the card so that all that is visible is a mug shot from the bill of the cap to the point of the chin. In contrast, the regular design of the '84 Donruss cards was the company's best up to that time. A large, sharp color photo covers virtually the entire card front. Down toward the bottom, four wavy yellow lines containing the team name and an '84 Donruss logo are overprinted on the photo. Below the picture is a thin colored stripe bearing the player's name and position. There is a white border around the entire design. Card backs are virtually identical to the previous two years. Year-by-year stats of the player's "recent" major league performance are in the white center section; yellow bars at the top and bottom contain the player's vital information and career highlights. Like the 1982 and 1983 sets, the '84s began with a run of 26 Diamond Kings cards, artist-painted representations of one player from each team. Donruss really catered to the collector market with the next 20 cards in the set. Called "Rated Rookies" in the red and blue banners on the front, these cards depict the young ballplayers who Donruss felt had a chance to be the hot rookie stars of 1984. In all, more than 95 rookie cards were interspersed throughout the '84 Donruss set—a real bonanza for rookie card collectors. There was

only a single multi-player feature card in the '84 Donruss set, titled, somewhat peculiarly, "Running Reds." The title was peculiar because the four players featured on the card are all St. Louis Cardinals. The mystery is cleared up a bit on the back of the card, where the "full" title, "Running Redbirds," appears. Besides the player cards, there are seven unnumbered checklists, a "Famous Chicken" card, and a card picturing the Duke Snider jigsaw puzzle, three pieces of which were inserted in each wax pack.

FOR

Nice-looking recent set. Nearly 100 rookie cards give it potential speculative appeal if some of those players make it big in the majors.

AGAINST

Donruss still had problems with color reproduction, resulting in many "sunburned" white players and purple-hued black players. There were hard feelings about the two Living Legends cards not being inserted in dealer sets.

NOTEWORTHY CARDS

Two major variations exist in the '84 Donruss set among the Rated Rookie cards. Mike Stenhouse and Ron Darling, #19 and #20 respectively, were originally printed in the wax-pack press run without their card numbers. This error was corrected in the printing for the vendor cases. On the backs of the Diamond Kings cards the art gallery that produces the player paintings, Perez-Steele Galleries, was misspelled "Perez-Steel." These cards were also corrected in the second printing. A number of cards that featured incorrect first names, misspelled names, wrong teams, or wrong positions were not corrected.

VALUE

MINT CONDITION: Complete set, $14.50; common card, 3¢; stars, hot rookies, 25¢–50¢. 5-YEAR PROJECTION: Above average.

1984 Donruss, Ron Darling, Rated Rookie (front)

1984 Donruss, San Diego Chicken (back)

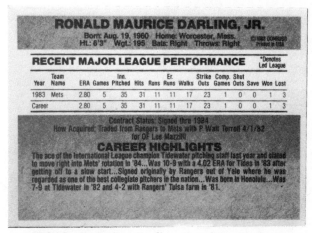

1984 Donruss, Ron Darling, Rated Rookie (back)

MICHAEL STEVEN STENHOUSE
Born: May 29, 1960   Home: Cranston, R.I.
Ht: 6'1"   Wgt: 195   Bats: Left   Throws: Right

© 1983 DONRUSS
Printed in USA

RECENT MAJOR LEAGUE PERFORMANCE

*Denotes Led League

Year	Team Name	Bat. Avg.	Games	At Bat	Hits	Runs	2B	3B	HR	RBI	Steal	Walk	SO
1982	Expos	.000	1	1	0	0	0	0	0	0	0	0	1
1983	Expos	.125	24	40	5	2	1	0	0	2	0	4	10
Career		.122	25	41	5	2	1	0	0	2	0	4	11

Contract Status: Signed thru 1984
How Acquired: Signed by Expos as their No. 1 choice in secondary phase of Jan. 1980 amateur draft.

CAREER HIGHLIGHTS
Has excellent chance to make Expos as a first baseman this season after outstanding Triple A record at Wichita last year...Named American Association Most Valuable Player in '83 when he hit .355 with 25 HR and 93 RBI at Wichita. Also had 33 doubles and scored 93 runs...Was called up to Expos briefly in midseason...Is the son of former major league pitcher, Dave Stenhouse, who hurled for Senators in '60s...Was drafted by Expos out of Harvard U. and is 1st Ivy Leaguer to play for Montreal.

1984 Donruss, Mike Stenhouse, Rated Rookie (back)

*1984 Donruss, Mike Stenhouse,
Rated Rookie (front)*

1984 Donruss, Fred Lynn, Diamond King

1984 Donruss, Hubie Brooks

*1984 Donruss, Bill Madlock,
Diamond King*

1984 Donruss, Julio Franco

1984 Donruss, Tom Brunansky

1984 Donruss, LaMarr Hoyt

1984 Donruss, Gary Carter

1984 Donruss, Lou Piniella

1984 DONRUSS ACTION ALL-STARS

SPECIFICATIONS

SIZE: 3½×5″. FRONT: Color photograph. BACK: Color photograph. DISTRIBUTION: Nationally, in cellophane packs with jigsaw puzzle pieces.

HISTORY

Following up on the success of its 1983 Action All-Stars set, Donruss repeated in 1984 with a similar issue. Again in postcard-size format, the set is unique in that it was the first major baseball card issue to feature full-color photos of the player on both card front and card back. Donruss arranged the cards in vertical format for '84, featuring a large color action photo on the front of the card, interrupted only by a small company logo in an upper corner. In a thin stripe at bottom were the player's name and position. White and burgundy borders surround the photo. On back, a portrait photo of the player appears in full color at the top of the card, with the team name printed as part of the gray background. Vital figures and career highlights are presented in red color boxes below, separated by a white band with yearly stats. Again in the '84 issue, there were 59 player cards and a checklist. The cards were sold in cello packages of six cards with three pieces of a 63-piece Ted Williams jigsaw puzzle.

FOR

Attractive follow-up of a very successful issue.

AGAINST

Some collectors don't like large-format cards.

NOTEWORTHY CARDS

Virtually all of the players in the set are stars of some stature.

VALUE

MINT CONDITION: Complete set, $7.50; common card, 5¢; superstars, 20¢–45¢. 5-YEAR PROJECTION: Above average.

1984 Donruss Action All-Stars, Bob Horner

1984 Donruss Action All-Stars, Nolan Ryan

1984 Donruss Action All-Stars, Fernando Valenzuela

1984 DONRUSS CHAMPIONS

SPECIFICATIONS

SIZE: 3½×5″. FRONT: Color photograph. BACK: Black and brown printing on white cardboard. DISTRIBUTION: Nationally, in cellophane packs with jigsaw puzzle pieces.

HISTORY

Donruss still had not given up on the idea of selling baseball cards of former players in 1984 when it issued its 60-card set of "Champions" (59 player cards and a checklist). The postcard-size cards were a mix of Hall of Famers and current players, arranged in statistical categories. The old-timers are depicted in the set in Dick Perez paintings, while the current players are shown in color photos. Color "art deco" frames surround the pictures, with a white border around the entire production. On the back there is short career and biographical information, along with a photo of the Hall of Fame plaque of the statistical leader in each category. The logic of the set is contrived and collectors have generally not paid much attention to the issue other than to acquire single cards of their favorite players if they were included.

FOR

Inexpensive large-format cards of big name past and current players.

AGAINST

The purpose of the set was confusing, and the combination of current and former players was not popular with collectors.

NOTEWORTHY CARDS

Since the cards are of statistical leaders, nearly all of them are stars or superstars.

VALUE

MINT CONDITION: Complete set, $7; common card, 5¢; superstars, 25¢–50¢. 5-YEAR PROJECTION: Average.

1984 Donruss Champions, Greg Luzinski

1984 Donruss Champions, Tom Seaver

1984 Donruss Champions, Hank Aaron (front)

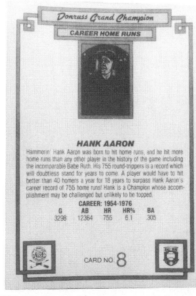

1984 Donruss Champions, Hank Aaron (back)

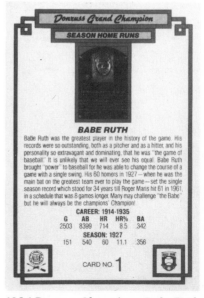

1984 Donruss Champions, Babe Ruth (back)

1984 MILTON BRADLEY

SPECIFICATIONS

SIZE: 2½×3½". FRONT: Color photograph. BACK: Black and red printing on gray cardboard. DISTRIBUTION: Nationally, in board game.

HISTORY

Dice baseball games have always been popular with young fans, and they have often contained baseball cards that became collectible. Milton Bradley continued that tradition in 1984 with a new dice board game called "Championship Baseball," which simulates a game between American and National League superstars. The 30 baseball player cards used in game play were printed by Topps for Milton Bradley. Player pictures appear on the front of the card, surrounded by blue, red, and yellow borders and designs, with a white border. Because Milton Bradley did not have an agreement with major league baseball, they were not allowed to display team logos on the caps or uniforms of the players pictured; these details have been airbrushed out. Card backs give brief biographical details on the players.

Pitchers' cards give career stats, used to play the game, while players at other positions have dice charts on the back of their cards to indicate their play performance with each roll of the dice. Stats for the previous year appear only on the back of nonpitcher cards. Milton Bradley had produced game cards previously in 1969, 1970, and 1972 baseball games, though they were not produced by Topps and were not in color.

FOR

All the cards are superstars, circa 1984, and they *are* produced by Topps.

AGAINST

Cards were not made available outside of the game. The "blank" caps and uniforms give the players the look of softball players. Game cards are not, in general, as popular with collectors as "real" cards.

NOTEWORTHY CARDS

All are superstars, including 1983 Rookie of the Year in the American League, Ron Kittle.

VALUE

MINT CONDITION: Complete set, $15; individual cards, 50¢–$1. 5-YEAR PROJECTION: Below average.

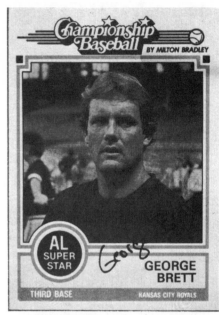

1984 Milton Bradley, George Brett

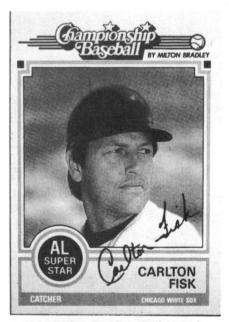

1984 Milton Bradley, Carlton Fisk

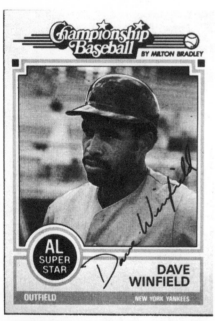

1984 Milton Bradley, Dave Winfield

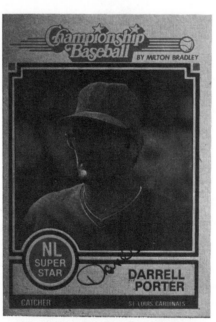

1984 Milton Bradley, Darrell Porter

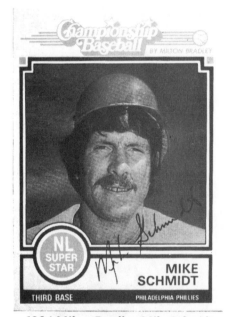

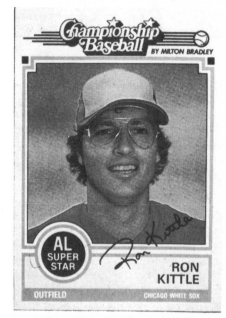

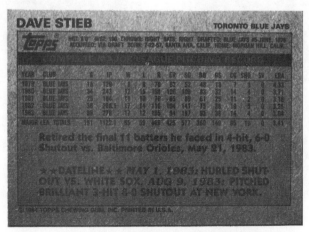

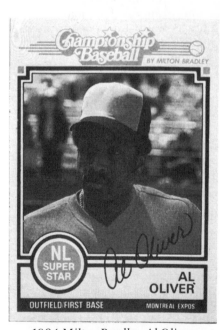

1984 Milton Bradley, Mike Schmidt (back)

1984 Milton Bradley, Ron Kittle

1984 Milton Bradley, Mike Schmidt (front)

1984 Milton Bradley, Dave Stieb (front)

1984 Milton Bradley, Al Oliver

1984 Milton Bradley, Dave Stieb (back)

1984 NESTLE DREAM TEAM

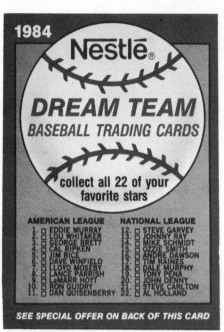

1984 Nestle Dream Team, Checklist

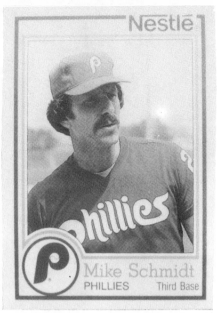

1984 Nestle Dream Team, Mike Schmidt

SPECIFICATIONS

SIZE: 2½×3½″. FRONT: Color photograph. BACK: Red and purple printing on gray cardboard. DISTRIBUTION: Nationally, three player cards and header card in candy bar packages (see following listing).

HISTORY

In 1984, when Nestle made its debut into the baseball card promotional market, it did so in a big way—with two separate collector issues produced for them by Topps. The Nestle Dream Team trading card issue was a 22-card set depicting an "all-star" team from each major league. Each league had eight starting fielders, plus left- and right-handed starting pitchers and a relief pitcher. All qualify as at least "stars," and there are a number of superstars in the line-ups. The Nestle Dream Team cards feature a color picture at center, surrounded by borders of white, orange, yellow, maroon, and white. A color team logo appears in a white circle at the lower left, and the Nestle logo is in the upper right. Card backs are almost identical to the regular issue Topps cards for 1984, except that the logo appearing over the card number is Nestle's, not Topps, and the card number has been changed. American Leaguers are cards #1 to #11; National League cards are #12 to #22.

FOR

All new pictures of current stars; limited edition promotional issue.

AGAINST

Design is a bit too gaudy; there's too much design, too little picture.

NOTEWORTHY CARDS

All are stars or superstars; none particularly worthy of special note.

VALUE

MINT CONDITION: Complete set, $7.50; individual cards, 25¢–$1. 5-YEAR PROJECTION: Average.

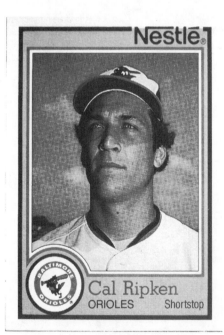

1984 Nestle Dream Team, Cal Ripken

1984 Nestle Dream Team, André Dawson

1984 NESTLE

SPECIFICATIONS
SIZE: 2½×3½". FRONT: Color photograph. BACK: Red and purple printing on gray cardboard. DISTRIBUTION: Nationally, in uncut sheets via mail-in offer.

HISTORY
As an adjunct to its Dream Team baseball card issue, Nestle made available by mail order uncut sheets of 132 Topps cards carrying the Nestle logo. A special "header" card in the Dream Team card packages offered one uncut sheet for $4.75 plus five candy bar wrappers. A special offer that accompanied the first sheet ordered allowed the collector to order the other five sheets necessary to make a complete set of 792 Nestle/Topps cards. The Nestle cards on the uncut sheets are identical to the regular 1984 Topps issue with the exception of the Nestle logo replacing the Topps logo on front and back. Card numbers are the same on both issues.

FOR
Historically, this is the largest product promotion baseball card set ever produced with Topps cooperation. They are much scarcer numerically than the virtually identical Topps cards.

AGAINST
The set is too much like the regular 1984 Topps cards. Single cards are hard to find because of the problems involved in cutting the sheets into individual cards in the aftermarket. At a total cost of $28.50 (not to mention the chocolate bars for proofs of purchase), the set is quite expensive for a current issue.

NOTEWORTHY CARDS
Since the Nestle sheet set is the same as the regular Topps set for '84, all the notable cards are the same.

VALUE
MINT CONDITION: Complete set, $35; common cards, 10¢; stars, 25¢–$1. 5-YEAR PROJECTION: Above average.

1984 RALSTON PURINA

SPECIFICATIONS
SIZE: 2½×3½". FRONT: Color photograph. BACK: Blue and red printing on white cardboard. DISTRIBUTION: Nationally, in packages of cereal, and mail-in offer.

HISTORY
The 33-card set produced by Topps for Ralston Purina was the cereal company's first baseball card issue, but probably won't be its last. A blue banner at the top of the card says, "1st Annual Collectors' Edition." Like many others among the special-edition card sets of 1984, the Ralston Purina set features only the top stars of the game. Also, like many other issues, the set could be obtained from hobby dealers almost before the specially marked boxes of cereal containing individual cards were put on store shelves. The front of the Ralston Purina cards features a close-up portrait of the player with the blue banner at top, which also includes a card number. On the sides and bottom the photo is bordered in red and yellow, and the player's name, team, and position appear at the bottom, with the name in red and the other information in black. A Topps script logo appears in the lower-right corner of the photo. In the upper left is a red and white Ralston Purina checkerboard logo and the company name. Backs of the Ralston Purina cards are different from most other Topps-printed issues. Instead of using a modification of the regular-issue Topps back, the set has at center a red and white checkerboard. Printed over this in blue is the player's vital data, statistics for 1983 and lifetime, career highlights, and a few personal facts. For Gary Carter, for example, we read: "Wife: Sandy; two daughters. Hobbies include collecting baseball cards." Above the checkerboard design are red and blue banners identifying the issue again, and including the card

1984 RALSTON PURINA

number. At bottom, in a blue box, is an advertising message. Four cards were included in each box of cereal, and the complete set could be ordered for three proofs of purchase and 50¢.

FOR
Distinctively different card issue for '84, with all the big name stars.

AGAINST
It's not so much this particular issue, but so many 1984 baseball sets were produced, and most have all the same superstars. The Ralston Purina set is much cheaper when bought from a dealer than when collected in cereal boxes.

NOTEWORTHY CARDS
All of the Ralston Purina cards feature star players; it is a bonanza for the superstar collector.

VALUE
MINT CONDITION: Complete set, $7; common card, 25¢; "super" superstar, 50¢. 5-YEAR PROJECTION: Above average.

1984 Ralston Purina, Greg Luzinski

1984 Ralston Purina, Bruce Sutter

1984 Ralston Purina, André Dawson

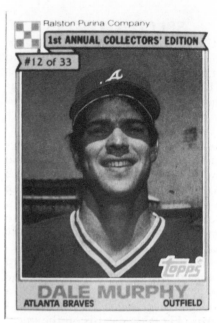

1984 Ralston Purina, Dale Murphy

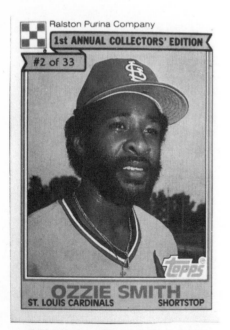

1984 Ralston Purina, Ozzie Smith

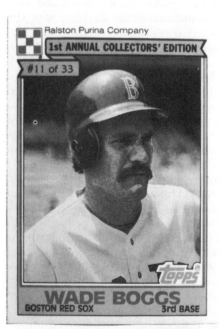

1984 Ralston Purina, Wade Boggs

1984 Ralston Purina, Dan Quisenberry

1984 DRAKE'S

SPECIFICATIONS
SIZE: 2½×3½″. FRONT: Color photograph. BACK: Red and purple ink on gray cardboard. DISTRIBUTION: East Coast, in packages of bakery products; nationally, in complete sets in the hobby market.

HISTORY
The 1984 Drake Bakeries baseball cards have a line at the top of the card that reads, "4th Annual Collectors' Edition." The 33-card "Drake's Big Hitters" set was printed by Topps, and like the previous three issues, the cards concentrate on baseball's current crop of sluggers. Every last one of the photos shows the player in a bat-swinging pose, carrying through the theme of the set. There is a fancy red, blue, and yellow frame around the photo, with a Drake's logo in the lower left hand corner. Player names are printed in red (American League) or green (National League) at lower right. There is a card number at the top. A facsimile autograph across the front completes the design. Card backs are very similar to regular-issue 1984 Topps cards, except the Drake's logo appears at upper left, in place of the Topps logo.

FOR
Many of the game's most popular contemporary figures are included in this set, which is generally inexpensive.

AGAINST
The cards are quite similar in design to those of previous years. Drake's has also acquired the reputation of "dumping" its sets on the collector market after the promotion of its bakery products is over.

NOTEWORTHY CARDS
Virtually all of the players in the Drake's set are big name stars; two of special note are second-year cards of Darryl Strawberry and Ron Kittle.

VALUE
MINT CONDITION: Complete set, $6; common card, 25¢; superstars, 50¢–$1. 5-YEAR PROJECTION: Above average.

1984 MOTHER'S COOKIES

SPECIFICATIONS
SIZE: 2½×3½″. FRONT: Color photograph (current team), color painting (San Francisco Giants All-Stars). BACK: Black (Mariners) or red and purple (Giants All-Stars, A's, Astros, Padres) printing on white cardboard. DISTRIBUTION: Home team cities, partial sets given out at ballpark on promotional days, supplemental cards available via mail-in offer.

HISTORY
The West Coast-based Mother's Cookies greatly expanded its baseball card set effort in 1984, producing five team sets, four of current teams and one of San Francisco Giants all-time All-Stars, in commemoration of the 1984 All-Star Game held at Candlestick Park. There were 28 cards in each set, for a total of 140 cards. Each set was distributed in the same manner. At special "Baseball Card Day" promotional games, partial sets of 20 cards were given out to fans as follows: A's, 30,000 sets, July 15; Astros, 25,000 sets, July 15; Giants, 30,000 sets, July 8; Mariners, 20,000 sets, July 15; Padres, 25,000 sets, July 8. Certificates good for eight more cards were either distributed with the partial sets, or made available in local media advertising. The eight cards returned for the certificate would probably not be the same eight needed to complete a set. Mother's Cookies officials felt this method of distribution would encourage trading of cards to complete sets. As usual, collectors could buy complete sets from hobby dealers who had good connections. The cards were printed on rather thin white cardboard with a high gloss finish on the front. In the manner of Mother's baseball card sets of 1952–1953, the corners of the 1984 cards were rounded. The four current-team sets feature one card each of the 25 roster players, a card for the manager, a group card of the coaches, and for the Mariners, the A's, and the Padres, a checklist card featuring the team's

stadium. The Astros set checklist card has a team logo on front. The full-color borderless photos on the front of the card are generally full-length or three-quarter poses taken in the stadium, and are exceptionally sharp and colorful. The player's name and team appear in white type in an upper corner. Backs of the four current-team sets are virtually identical, except the Mariners are printed in black, while the A's, the Astros, and the Rangers are printed in red and purple. There is a Mother's Cookies logo in the upper-right corner, with a year, team name, and card number below. At left are the player's name, position, uniform number, and vital data, including a "How obtained" line. At the bottom there is a blank line for an autograph. The Giants set differs from the others in that rather than featuring all current players, it features current and former San Francisco Giants who have appeared in All-Star Games. Fronts of the Giants cards have an artist's color painting of the player, surrounded by a wide white vignette. The player's name and "Giants All-Star" appears in black at the bottom. Backs are similar to the current-team issues, with the logo, date, team, and card number at right. At left is the player's name, position, uniform number, birthdate, batting and throwing sides, and the years he appeared in the All-Star Game. There is a blank line below, but it does not have the "Autograph" notation.

FOR
With the quality of photography and production, the '84 Mother's Cookies cards are among the most attractive of recent years. They will be especially desirable to team collectors. The cards are fairly scarce regional issues that should be somewhat hard to come by in the not-too-distant future.

AGAINST
The method of original distribution will create many incomplete sets, while the number of complete sets sold by hobby dealers will be relatively small. This could make full sets difficult to acquire as demand picks up.

NOTEWORTHY CARDS
Many of the San Francisco Giants All-Star cards are superstars of their

day: Mays, McCovey, Marichal, Cepeda. Lots of current stars in the other teams' sets: Nolan Ryan and Dickie Thon of the Astros, Rickey Henderson and Joe Morgan of the A's, and Steve Garvey and Goose Gossage of the Padres. Good rookies, too: Alvin Davis of the Mariners, and the Padres' Kevin McReynolds, for example.

VALUE

MINT CONDITION: Complete set (140), $30; common card, 10¢; superstars, 50¢–$1. 5-YEAR PROJECTION: Above average.

1984 CALIFORNIA ANGELS FOREST RANGER

SPECIFICATIONS

SIZE: 2½×3¾". FRONT: Color photograph. BACK: Black printing on white cardboard. DISTRIBUTION: Anaheim, complete sets given away to youngsters attending June 16 Angels game.

HISTORY

The California Angels were one of two major league teams to commemorate the 40th "birthday" of Smokey the Bear by issuing special baseball card sets to youngsters attending a promotional game. Unlike the San Diego Padres set, the photos on the Angels cards do not include Smokey posing with the players. A color picture of the famous bear does appear in the lower left corner of the cards, though. A blue and red Angels logo is at right above the symbols of the U.S. Forest Service and the California State Department of Forestry. The player's last name appears above the picture on the front of the card. Card backs have a fire safety quote from the player, along with his 1983 stats and a few biographical details. The Angels cards are not numbered. There are 32 cards in the set, 29 of them featuring players. Manager John McNamara

has a card and there are two "header" cards rounding out the set. One has a color portrait of Smokey and a message explaining the set, while the other card has the black and white logos of the state and U.S. forest services. Most of the player photos in the Angels/Smokey set are game-action pictures, although there are also a few portraits.

FOR

Good "theme" for a safety set, combining the popularity of Smokey the Bear with a baseball card issue.

AGAINST

About the only negative aspect of the set is that they are printed on cardboard that is thinner than collectors generally like, and this makes the cards more susceptible to creasing.

NOTEWORTHY CARDS

Good combination of young and old stars from the '84 Angels—Dick Schofield, Gary Pettis, and Daryl Sconiers, along with Reggie Jackson, Tommy John, Rod Carew, and Fred Lynn.

VALUE

MINT CONDITION: Complete set, $7.50; common card, 15¢; stars, 25¢–50¢; Jackson, 50¢–$1. 5-YEAR PROJECTION: Above average.

1984 BLUE JAYS FIRE SAFETY

SPECIFICATIONS

SIZE: 2½×3½". FRONT: Color photograph. BACK: Black printing on white cardboard. DISTRIBUTION: Ontario area, five-card groups given away at fire stations and by mail-in offer with newspaper coupon.

HISTORY

The first safety set to feature the Toronto Blue Jays, this 35-card issue was co-sponsored by the *Toronto Sun* newspaper and the Ontario Association of Fire Chiefs. Groups of five cards were available every two weeks to children who stopped in at local fire stations.

Cards could also be obtained by sending in a special coupon that appeared in the Toronto paper. Apparently recognizing the hobby demand for such cards, the makers added a note to the back of the cards that says, "These trading cards are not to be sold for any purpose." While the Blue Jays Fire Safety cards are similar in format to other recent police and fire sets, there are significant differences. Foremost, the Blue Jays cards are in the standard 2½×3½" format, rather than the larger size that is popular for most safety sets. Also, rather than the customary wide white border on the front of the cards, the Toronto set has a light blue border, similar in hue to the color of the team's road jerseys. Set into the blue border is a color action picture of the player. Black type at the bottom gives the player's name, position, and uniform number. A red, white, and blue team logo appears in the lower-right corner. Backs have the logos of the co-sponsors, abbreviated biographical details on the player, and a fire safety tip. The cards are numbered by uniform number, which appears on the back. Depicted in the set are a full complement of Blue Jays roster players, along with individual cards for the coaches and managers.

FOR

One of the more attractive of the recent safety sets, and the first to feature the Blue Jays. In fact, it is the first major regional issue of the team, and is thus popular with fans and collectors.

AGAINST

Method of distribution makes it hard for collectors outside the Toronto area to obtain a complete set.

NOTEWORTHY CARDS

Besides the well-known top performers on the team like Lloyd Moseby, Dave Stieb, Damaso Garcia, Alfredo Griffin, etc., the Blue Jays Fire Safety set was also the first to include new team members Willie Aikens, Rick Leach, and others in their new uniforms.

VALUE

MINT CONDITION: Complete set, $15; common card, 25¢–50¢; stars, $1–$2. 5-YEAR PROJECTION: Above average.

1984 ATLANTA BRAVES POLICE

SPECIFICATIONS

SIZE: 2⅝×4⅛″. FRONT: Color photograph. BACK: Red, blue, yellow, and black printing on white cardboard. DISTRIBUTION: Atlanta area, single cards distributed by local police officers.

HISTORY

The Braves were one of the first baseball teams to issue a police safety set (in 1980); the 1984 issue of 30 cards marked the team's fifth consecutive issue. Sticking pretty closely to the traditional police set format of a slightly larger-than-standard card size, the '84 Braves set features a color photo of the player on the front, along with a color team logo in the lower-right corner. In the wide white border at the top of the card are a Police Athletic League shield and an "A '84" in red. The player's name, position, and number appear in black at the lower left. Card backs are unusual in that they feature the logos of the sponsoring companies, Coca-Cola and Hostess, in full color. The rest of the card back contains a few biographical details about the player and a safety message related in baseball terms, along with credit lines for the photographer and printer. The set contains the 25 Braves on the roster, along with individual cards for the manager and coaches.

FOR

One of the easier police sets to obtain, perhaps because the Braves publicity director, who is also a baseball card collector and one of the better-known specialists in safety sets, has encouraged wide distribution.

AGAINST

Similarity in format to the previous four Braves Police set issues.

NOTEWORTHY CARDS

Besides cards for popular current Braves stars like Dale Murphy, Bob Horner, and Craig McMurtry, the '84 police set is a veritable who's who of old-timers in the manager and coaches cards. All had significant major league playing experience, from manager Torre to Hall of Fame coaches Gibson and Appling.

VALUE

MINT CONDITION: Complete set, $5; common card, 10¢; stars, 50¢–$1. 5-YEAR PROJECTION: Average, perhaps a bit below.

1984 MILWAUKEE BREWERS POLICE

SPECIFICATIONS

SIZE: 2¹³/₁₆×4⅛″. FRONT: Color photograph. BACK: Blue printing on white cardboard. DISTRIBUTION: Wisconsin, complete sets given out at stadium at "Baseball Card Day" promotional game; individual cards given out by local police departments.

HISTORY

Amazingly, if a collector were to try to assemble a "complete" set of 1984 Brewers police cards, he would need more than 1,500 different varieties. At last count, more than 50 different law enforcement agencies around the state had become involved with the team's baseball card program. The same basic 30 cards were printed with a single distinguishing change for each department. On the front of the card a different second line of type was inserted for each police agency. Reports are that some small communities had only 500 sets produced, while the Milwaukee Police Department had some 120,000. Besides those cards given out at the special promotional game, the cards were supposed to be handed out, two per week, by uniformed officers to children encountered on the beat. This manner of distribution makes complete sets of some communities very difficult to assemble. In many cases, though, complete sets of the cards were slipped out the back doors of the police stations into the waiting hands of local dealers and collectors. While it is likely that many of the varieties of this issue will be truly scarce in the future, the huge size of the issue overall makes it unlikely that it will be seriously collected by town of issue. Most collectors will content themselves with acquiring one of the more common sets. Like most recent police sets, the '84 Brewers cards are a bit larger than the standard cards, and feature a color photo surrounded by a wide white border. The front of the card, besides listing the department of issue, has the player's name, uniform number, and position. Card backs have the Brewers logo and a safety tip "authored" by the player on the front.

FOR

One of the most common and inexpensive of recent police sets—as long as you stick to the common cities.

AGAINST

The proliferation of varieties in terms of different issuing police departments makes it impossible to collect a complete set. Card photos are not uniformly high quality.

NOTEWORTHY CARDS

The set includes 27 individual player cards, a team photo, a card for manager Rene Lachemann, and a group card that pictures the team's coaches, but does not name them. All the popular Brewers stars are included: Yount, Molitor, Fingers, etc.

VALUE

MINT CONDITION: Complete set, $4.50; common card, 10¢; stars, 50¢–$1. 5-YEAR PROJECTION: Below average.

1984 GARDNER'S BREWERS

SPECIFICATIONS

SIZE: 2½×3½″. FRONT: Color photograph. BACK: Red and purple printing on gray cardboard. DISTRIBUTION: Wisconsin, single cards in packages of bread and buns.

HISTORY

In 1984, the Gardner Baking Company of Madison, Wisconsin, repeated its successful baseball card issue of the previous year, inserting one of 22 different Milwaukee Brewers cards into loaves of bread and packages of buns. The cards were printed by Topps, using a completely different design and photos than the regular-issue Topps cards of 1984. Front of the cards features a color photo at center, surrounded by a round-cornered "frame" of pink and yellow, and a blue border. In a red box below the photo, the player's name, team, and position are designated. There is a Brewers logo at lower left and a Gardner's logo at top center. Both logos are in color. A line in the yellow stripe of the frame at bottom says "1984 Series II." As in '83, card backs are virtually identical to the regular Topps cards, with the exception of changed card numbers. New Brewers manager Rene Lachemann is card #1 in the set, and the 21 players' cards are numbered alphabetically. A blue Brewers logo appears in the upper-right corner. As was the case in 1983, the Gardner's cards were not made available to hobby sources at the wholesale level, making the set among the scarcest of the year's many regional issues. Because the cards were only distributed in the Wisconsin area, collectors around the country had to buy their cards from dealers and collectors who had pulled them from the bakery's products. At a cost of 80¢ or so for a loaf of bread, this meant that on a per-card basis, the 1984 Gardner's Brewers cards were quite expensive.

FOR

Attractive regional set of a popular team with lots of big name stars.

AGAINST

Price is relatively high for a 1984 set.

NOTEWORTHY CARDS

The regular 1984 Topps set did not have a card of manager Rene Lachemann, and it pictured new Brewers' additions Jim Sundberg and Bobby Clark with the Rangers and Angels, respectively. The '84 Gardner's Brewers, however, offered these new Milwaukee favorites in the home team's uniform. All the other Brewers stars are also present in the set: Molitor, Cooper, Fingers, Yount, etc.

VALUE

MINT CONDITION: Complete set, $25; common card, $1; Fingers, Molitor, Cooper, Simmons, $2; Yount, $3. 5-YEAR PROJECTION: Above average.

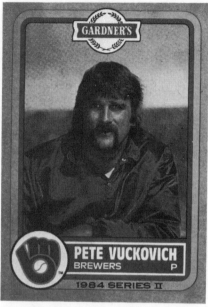

1984 Gardner's Brewers, Pete Vuckovich

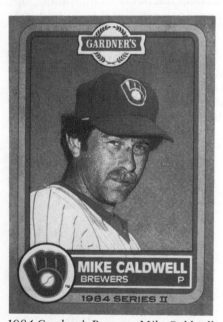

1984 Gardner's Brewers, Mike Caldwell

1984 Gardner's Brewers, Jim Gantner

1984 Gardner's Brewers, Don Sutton

1984 7-UP CUBS

SPECIFICATIONS

SIZE: 2¼×3½". FRONT: Color photograph. BACK: Black printing on white cardboard. DISTRIBUTION: Chicago, complete sets given away at special baseball card promotional game at Wrigley Field.

HISTORY

For the third straight year, the Chicago Cubs held a special "Baseball Card Day" promotional game at Wrigley Field, and for the third straight year, the team set was issued with the cooperation of a new sponsor—7-Up. In most other respects, the 1984 Cubs team-issued set was quite similar to the 1982 and 1983 offerings. The cards featured a borderless color action photo, some arranged vertically, some horizontally. The only type on the front of the cards is the player's uniform number, name, and position. Card backs feature complete minor and major league statistics, a copyright line, and a 7-Up logo. There are 26 individual player cards, a card for the manager, Jim Frey, and a group card of the team's coaching staff. Apparently because of a defect in the machinery that cut, sorted, and wrapped the cards in complete sets, many sets were packaged with duplicates of some cards, resulting in incomplete sets.

FOR

Team-issued set of one of baseball's perennially popular teams, and one of 1984's hottest contenders.

AGAINST

Cards are off-standard in size; format is almost identical to previous years. On some cards, it's hard to pick the player out from the Wrigley Field background of the photos.

NOTEWORTHY CARDS

The 7-Up Cubs set is exceptional in that it includes most of the important players acquired in mid-season trades, such as Dennis Eckersley and Rick Sutcliffe. The team's one-two punch of Bob Dernier and Ryne Sandberg are among the stars represented, along with rookie prospect Henry Cotto and old vets like Ron Cey and Larry Bowa.

VALUE

MINT CONDITION: Complete set, $8; common card, 15¢; stars, 25¢–50¢; Sandberg, 50¢–$1. 5-YEAR PROJECTION: Average or a bit above.

1984 7-Up Cubs, Scott Sanderson

1984 7-Up Cubs, Dennis Eckersley

1984 7-Up Cubs, Coaches

1984 7-Up Cubs, Larry Bowa

1984 LOS ANGELES DODGERS POLICE

SPECIFICATIONS
SIZE: 2⅞×4⅛". FRONT: Color photograph. BACK: Blue printing on white cardboard. DISTRIBUTION: Los Angeles area, single cards given to children by police officers, complete sets given away at special promotional game, June 4.

HISTORY
For the fifth year in a row, the Los Angeles Dodgers and local police cooperated in issuing a baseball card set aimed at improving rapport between police officers and local youngsters. The theme of the safety messages printed on the backs of the '84 cards is DARE (Drug Abuse Resistance Education). There are 30 cards in the set, featuring the Dodgers roster players, manager Tommy Lasorda, and the coaches. Card fronts have a color photo of the player surrounded by the wide white border that has come to be associated with police sets. At the bottom is a blue and red Dodgers logo, with the date, the player's name, and uniform number printed in black. Card backs have biographical and statistical information about the player, a drug abuse prevention message, and a small portrait photo of the player, all printed in blue. A total of five million cards was reported printed, enough for 160,000 sets.

FOR
An attractive continuation of the long-standing Dodgers police set tradition. Lots of new young players.

AGAINST
Too similar to previous issues.

NOTEWORTHY CARDS
All the regular Dodgers stars.

VALUE
MINT CONDITION: Complete set, $5; common card, 10¢; stars, 25¢–50¢; 5-YEAR PROJECTION: Average, or somewhat below.

1984 STUART EXPOS

SPECIFICATIONS
SIZE: 2½×3½". FRONT: Color photograph. BACK: Blue printing on white cardboard. DISTRIBUTION: Canada, single cards in boxes of Stuart Bakery products.

HISTORY
One of the largest single-team regional card sets in recent years, the '84 Stuart Expos cards were released in two 20-card series over the course of the baseball card season, a total of 40 cards. In similar format to the company's premier set of the previous year, the 1984 Stuart's cards feature on the front a quality color photograph of the player. The picture is surrounded by a red border, in the lower corners of which are a red Stuart's logo and an Expos team logo, along with a graphic symbol for the year of issue. Black type in the white border at bottom gives the player's name and uniform number. Card backs feature the usual combination of player biographical and statistical information in both French and English, as is often seen on card sets originating in the Province of Quebec. Unlike many of its counterparts south of the border, the Stuart Expos cards were not generally made available in complete sets to dealers or collectors, requiring the completion of sets by purchasing the company's products —which is the whole idea of issuing baseball cards with products. Besides the normal 25 roster players, the Stuart Expos set also featured cards for many of the team's young prospects, as well as the coaches, manager, and Youppi, the team mascot. The first 20 cards were among the earliest regionals in the hands of collectors in 1984, being distributed in Stuart products from May through July. The final 20 cards in the set were released beginning in August.

FOR
Good-looking, scarce regional issue.

AGAINST
Somewhat tough or expensive to acquire a complete set; the issue of the set in two series over the course of the summer kept collectors guessing on the final make-up of the issue.

NOTEWORTHY CARDS
The 1984 Stuart Expos set was the first to contain a card of Pete Rose in the uniform of his new team for '84, a feature that made the set very popular with collectors. Besides the other established Expos stars like Andre Dawson, Charlie Lea, Tim Raines, and Gary Carter, the set also includes many rookie cards of young players who had spring or late-season trials with the team.

VALUE
MINT CONDITION: Complete set, $12; common card, 25¢; stars, $1–$2; Rose, $3. 5-YEAR PROJECTION: Average.

1984 WHEATIES INDIANS

SPECIFICATIONS
SIZE: 2¹³/₁₆×4⅛". FRONT: Color photograph. BACK: Black printing on white cardboard. DISTRIBUTION: Cleveland, complete sets given out at July 22 promotional game and sold at Indians' gift shop.

HISTORY
Wheaties cereal, which has been associated with various baseball card issues as far back as the 1930s, was the co-sponsor for the third year of a baseball card set featuring the Cleveland Indians in 1984. Complete 29-card sets were given away at a promotional game on July 22 at Municipal Stadium. The remainder of the 15,000 sets printed were offered for sale at the Indians' gift shop. Once again choosing a format much like recent police sets, the 1984 Indians set features a full-color game-action photo of each player, set on a wide white background. The player's name and position appear in black at bottom-center, while team and Wheaties logos appear in color at left and right. Card backs have players' complete major league statistics, along with a card

number that corresponds to the player's uniform number. Besides individual cards for 26 players, there is a card for manager Pat Corrales and unnumbered cards for team mascot Tom-E-Hawk, and the coaches (John Goryl, Dennis Sommers, Ed Napoleon, Bobby Bonds, and Dan McMahon).

FOR

Wheaties sponsorship gives the set a tie with many past baseball card issues and may make it more desirable to collectors in coming years as part of a long-running "set."

AGAINST

Design is identical to previous years. Cardboard stock is very thin, sustains damage easily. Game-action photos are not the best way to showcase a player on a baseball card.

NOTEWORTHY CARDS

All of the Indians' crop of bright young stars is present in this set, including the players acquired in the mid-year trade with the Cubs—Mel Hall, Joe Carter, and Don Schulze.

VALUE

MINT CONDITION: Complete set, $5; common card, 25¢. 5-YEAR PROJECTION: Average, maybe a bit above.

1984 SAN DIEGO PADRES FOREST RANGER

SPECIFICATIONS

SIZE: 2½×3¾". FRONT: Color photograph. BACK: Black printing on white cardboard. DISTRIBUTION: San Diego, complete sets given to youngsters attending special Padres promotional game, May 14.

HISTORY

To commemorate the 40th anniversary of the adoption of Smokey the Bear as the fire safety spokesperson of the U.S. Forest Service, the San Diego Padres joined the California Angels in issuing promotional baseball card sets. The Padres set of 30 cards is one of the more innovative and entertaining baseball card issues ever produced. Each color photo shows the player and Smokey the Bear. Some players are shown giving or getting baseball tips, others are sitting on Smokey's lap, etc. All in all, it looks like the Padres had a good time posing for the photos used on the cards. In addition to the photo, the front of the card has a color drawing of Smokey in the lower left corner, and a brown and yellow Padres team identification and the logos of the U.S. Forest Service and the California State Department of Forestry at right. The player's last name appears above the photo. Card backs are printed in black and have a brief player biography, 1983 season record, and a fire safety message from the player. Cards are numbered by player uniform number. There are 18 player cards in the Padres/Smokey set, along with cards for manager Dick Williams and his four coaches. Former players Jerry Coleman and Dave Campbell are included in the set as members of the Padres broadcasting team, and there is a card for team VP Jack McKeon. Of special interest are cards of the famous San Diego mascot, the Chicken, and of umpire Doug Harvey, a San Diego resident. The Doug Harvey card is significant in that it is the first baseball card of an umpire issued since the 1955 Bowman set included the men in blue. A "header" card picturing Smokey the Bear and explaining the issue rounds out the 30 cards in the set.

FOR

Imaginative, enjoyable set.

AGAINST

Set is a little short of players, basically featuring just the starters, and was produced too early in the year to include notable Padres trade acquisitions Goose Gossage, Graig Nettles, and Carmelo Martinez.

NOTEWORTHY CARDS

Young Padres batting stars Kevin McReynolds and Tony Gwynn, along with long-time Southern California favorite Steve Garvey, are among the stars in the set.

VALUE

MINT CONDITION: Complete set, $7.50; common card, 15¢; stars, 25¢–50¢. 5-YEAR PROJECTION: Above average.

1984 TEXAS RANGERS

SPECIFICATIONS

SIZE: 2⅜×3½". FRONT: Color photograph. BACK: Black printing on white cardboard. DISTRIBUTION: Arlington, complete sets given away at "Baseball Card Night" promotional game on Aug. 31.

HISTORY

A total of 10,000 sets of Texas Rangers cards were printed for distribution at a special promotional game. The '84 Rangers cards are virtually identical to the 1983 issue, featuring a color action photo of the player on the front. A blue panel below the photo has the player's name, team, and position. Card backs feature a black and white portrait photo of the player. The 30 cards in the set are numbered by uniform number on the back of the cards, which also contains brief biographical and personal data and a line of major league stats. The bottom of the back features an imprint from the set's sponsor, The Jarvis Press, Inc.

FOR

A team-issued set with relatively low printing quantity.

AGAINST

Cards are printed on stock that is quite thin. Lack of format change from the previous year's issue lowers collector interest.

NOTEWORTHY CARDS

It's hard to find notable cards on a team that spent virtually the entire season in last place. However, some of the young players may eventually earn star status.

VALUE

MINT CONDITION: Complete set, $6.50; common card, 25¢; stars, 50¢–$1. 5-YEAR PROJECTION: Average.

1984 MINNESOTA TWINS

SPECIFICATIONS

SIZE: 2½×3½". FRONT: Color photograph. BACK: Red and blue printing on white cardboard. DISTRIBUTION: Minneapolis, team issue, sold at stadium and via mail order.

HISTORY

In 1984, for the second straight year, local collector Barry Fritz and Park Press created a Minnesota Twins card set for issue by the team. The 36 cards in the set feature all 25 of the roster players, the manager, coaches, and an aerial view of the Metrodome. There are also a Twins logo card and a special card honoring former Twins great Harmon Killebrew, who was elected to the Hall of Fame in 1984, the first Twin to be so honored. The 1984 cards feature a borderless posed color photo of the player taken at spring training. A Twins uniform jersey in the lower-left corner of the card has the player's uniform number. Card backs feature standard player biographical data, along with complete major and minor league statistics, a copyright line, and a card number, all printed in an attractive combination of blue and red. The baseball card set, along with a similar issue of postcards, was sold for $5 a set at the stadium and through the mail.

FOR

Reasonably priced team-issue card set, printed in relatively low numbers.

AGAINST

Format is virtually identical to the 1983 issue.

NOTEWORTHY CARDS

All of the rising young stars of the '84 Twins, plus all-time Twins favorite, "The Killer," Harmon Killebrew.

VALUE

MINT CONDITION: Complete set, $6.50; common card, 10¢; stars, 25¢–50¢; Killebrew, $1. 5-YEAR PROJECTION: Average.

1984 TRUE VALUE WHITE SOX

SPECIFICATIONS

SIZE: 2⅝×4⅛". FRONT: Color photograph. BACK: Black printing on white cardboard. DISTRIBUTION: Comiskey Park, cards given out two at a time at selected Tuesday night home games.

HISTORY

For the second year in a row, the True Value hardware company, based in Chicago, sponsored a set of White Sox cards that was given out two at a time at selected Tuesday night home games at Comiskey Park. There are 30 cards in the '84 set: 25 players, a card for manager Tony LaRussa, a group card of the coaching staff, cards for past White Sox favorites Minnie Minoso and Luis Aparicio, and—a first for any major baseball card set—a woman's card with Comiskey organist Nancy Faust. The latter three cards were not distributed at the stadium, but were given out by the individuals themselves. Like the '83 cards, the 1984 True Value White Sox issue features a full-color photo of the player (most taken at spring training in Sarasota), surrounded by a wide white border. In the bottom border, at left, is a red and blue "Chisox" logo. At right, printed in black, is the player's name, position, and uniform number. Card backs, which are unnumbered, have the player's name and uniform number in the upper corners in a black band with a True Value logo between them. Complete major and minor league stats make up the rest of the card back. The coaches' and Faust's cards have blank backs. Because of the manner of distribution of the cards, complete sets of the '84 True Value White Sox are rather difficult to acquire.

1984 True Value White Sox, Tom Seaver

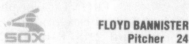

*1984 True Value White Sox,
Floyd Bannister*

FOR

Great regional item for the team colector, not widely distributed within hobby channels.

AGAINST

Complete sets are tough to find and somewhat costly because not all cards were distributed in even numbers owing to differing attendance at the various games.

NOTEWORTHY CARDS

Besides the aforementioned first card of a woman, the set features all of the White Sox stars of their division-winning 1983 team, and the first card of future Hall of Famer Tom Seaver as a White Sox pitcher.

VALUE

MINT CONDITION: Complete set (30), $25; common card, 25¢–50¢; Baines, Minoso, Hoyt, Luzinski, Fisk, $1; Seaver, Kittle, Aparicio, $3–$5. 5-YEAR PROJECTION: Above average.

SOX
CARLTON FISK
Catcher   72

1984 True Value White Sox, Carlton Fisk

1983 TOPPS

SPECIFICATIONS

SIZE: 2½×3½″. FRONT: Color photograph. BACK: Orange and black printing on gray cardboard. DISTRIBUTION: Nationally, in packs with bubblegum.

HISTORY

Topps reached back 20 years for the design inspiration of its 1983 baseball card set. Like the 1963 set, the '83 Topps cards featured a large color photograph at the top of the card, and in a circle at the bottom, a smaller portrait photo of the player. Unlike the '63 cards, the smaller photo on the '83 Topps was also in color. The top and bottom sections of the card were framed in team colors. A prominent Topps logo intruded into the photo in the upper-right corner. The team name appeared in the colored bottom border, while the player's name and position were printed in a white panel opposite the small portrait photo. Card backs were horizontal in format and featured complete major and/or minor league stats for the player on an annual basis, along with a few personal figures, and if space was available, a few 1982 season highlights. All in all, the '83 Topps design was popular with collectors, many of whom hailed it as one of the best in recent years. The regular-issue Topps set for 1983 consisted of 792 cards. For the first time since 1962, the set did not feature any "Future Stars" or other rookie cards, the company preferring to save the popular rookie cards for inclusion in the "Traded" set later in the autumn. A special and popular feature in the '83 set was a group of 34 "Super Veteran" cards, numbered in the set right after the "regular" card of the same player. The Super Veteran cards are in horizontal format and show the player in his first major league season on the left, and in a current photo on the right. There was a "Team Leaders" card for each club to honor the batting and pitching leaders. Backs of the Team Leader cards had a team checklist. The first six cards in the set honored record-breaking performances of the previous season. Other groups of specialty cards included league leaders, All-Stars, and six numbered checklists.

FOR

An unusually popular recent Topps set; all the current stars at a low price.

AGAINST

A lot of collectors felt that Topps' decision not to issue team rookie cards, as in past years, was a move intended to force collectors to buy the relatively more expensive "Traded" set later in the year.

NOTEWORTHY CARDS

All the usual stars, plus a rookie card of Wade Boggs that was selling for $2.50 right out of the pack.

VALUE

MINT CONDITION: Complete set, $20; common card, 3¢; superstars, 25¢–75¢; Boggs, $4. 5-YEAR PROJECTION: Above average.

1983 Topps,
Reggie Jackson, Super Veteran

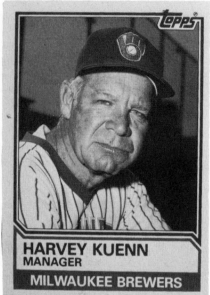

1983 Topps, Harvey Kuenn

1983 Topps, Joe Cowley

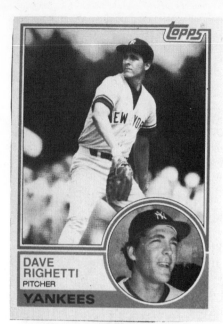

1983 Topps, Dave Righetti

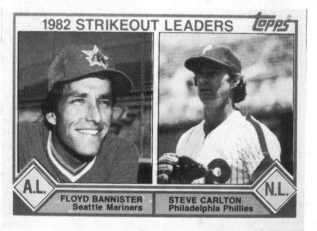

1983 Topps, 1982 Strikeout Leaders

*1983 Topps, Rickey Henderson,
1982 Record Breaker*

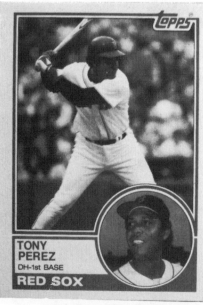

1983 Topps, Tony Perez

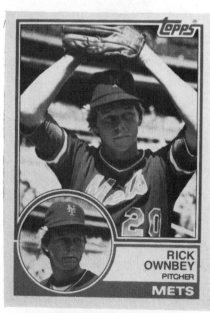

1983 Topps, Rick Ownbey

1983 TOPPS TRADED

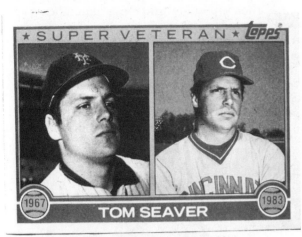

1983 Topps, Tom Seaver, Super Veteran

1983 Topps, Bruce Sutter, Super Veteran

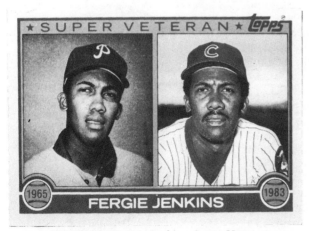

1983 Topps, Fergie Jenkins, Super Veteran

SPECIFICATIONS

SIZE: 2½×3½″. FRONT: Color photograph. BACK: Black and red printing on white cardboard. DISTRIBUTION: Nationally, in complete sets through hobby dealers.

HISTORY

For the third straight year, Topps in 1983 produced a 132-card Traded set. The cards are in the same basic design as the regular 1983 Topps set, although the backs are in a different color. The cards are numbered from 1 to 132, with a "T" after the number. Cards in the set include players who had been traded since late 1982, when production of the regular 1983 Topps set was completed. These players are pictured in their new uniforms in the Traded set. Other cards in the set are rookie cards of hot young players who did not appear in the regular set, and some of the new managers. As in previous years, the Traded cards were not sold in gum packs, only in complete boxed sets by baseball card dealers. Sets retailed for about $7 or $8, or about 5½¢ a card, compared to the 2¢ a card, or so, price of the regular 1983 cards when bought in gum packs or in complete sets from dealers. The cards in the 1983 Topps Traded series are numbered alphabetically by the player's last name, with the final card in the set being a checklist. Because the cards were sold only through hobby dealers, they were printed in far smaller quantity than the regular-issue Topps cards of the same year.

FOR

For collectors who favor Topps cards, the '83 Traded set was the only way to get cards of many favorite players in their current uniforms; also the only way to get Topps cards of the hot new rookies.

AGAINST

Some collectors feel that because the Traded set is sold only as a complete set through card dealers, it is not a "legitimate" issue, and is little more than a collector's issue.

NOTEWORTHY CARDS

It seems that the really high-demand cards in the Traded set each year are not the traded players at all, but the rookies. In the 1983 Traded set, the big money was being paid for the Darryl Strawberry card. Topps was the only one of the "Big 3" card companies to have an '83 card for the National League Rookie of the Year. There was also a card in the set for Ron Kittle, American League Rookie of the Year, and for high-demand rookies Julio Franco and Mel Hall.

VALUE

MINT CONDITION: Complete set, $10; common card, 5¢; superstars, 50¢–$1; Kittle, $3; Strawberry, $5. 5-YEAR PROJECTION: Above average.

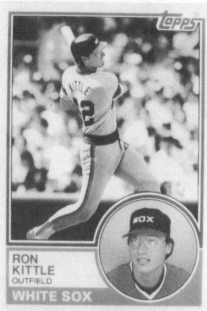

1983 Topps Traded, Ron Kittle

1983 TOPPS GLOSSIES

SPECIFICATIONS

SIZE: 2½×3½". FRONT: Color photograph. BACK: Red and blue printing on white cardboard. DISTRIBUTION: Nationally, as prizes in Topps contest; complete sets from dealers.

HISTORY

A scratch-off game card in packs of regular 1983 Topps baseball cards offered a special set of 40 cards as a "consolation prize" for accumulated losing cards. Topps called this set the "Collector's Edition All-Star Set," but collectors know it as "Glossies." With the postage and handling costs, along with the cost of packs of cards to accumulate the game cards, the cost of a set collected as a consolation prize was more than $20. Luckily, Topps also wholesaled complete sets of the Glossies to dealers, and they were widely available in hobby channels for $8 or so—still not cheap. The Glossies take their hobby nickname from the shiny surface coating applied to the front of the card, giving it a glazed appearance that collectors find extremely appealing. The basic design of the set is simple. A large color photo of the player takes up the entire face of the card and is surrounded by a yellow border. The only printing on the front is the

player's name in tiny type in the lower-left corner of the white border. There are no stats or player data on the back of the card, just a Topps identification, the player's name, team, position, and the card number.

FOR

Extremely attractive and popular specialty set; lots of stars.

1983 Topps Glossies, Jim Palmer

1983 Topps Glossies, Bill Buckner

1983 Topps Traded, Billy Martin

AGAINST

Relatively expensive.

NOTEWORTHY CARDS

All of the cards in the '83 Glossies are stars.

VALUE

MINT CONDITION: Complete set, $10; common card, 25¢; superstars, 50¢–$1. 5-YEAR PROJECTION: Above average.

1983 TOPPS FOLDOUTS

1983 Topps Glossies, Lance Parrish

1983 Topps Glossies, Gary Carter

1983 Topps Glossies, Kent Hrbek

1983 Topps Glossies, Dave Stieb

SPECIFICATIONS

SIZE: $3\frac{1}{2} \times 5\frac{5}{16}''$. FRONT: Color photograph. BACK: Color photograph. DISTRIBUTION: Limited geographic areas, in cellophane packs.

HISTORY

Late in the 1983 baseball season, Topps introduced in limited areas a test issue of "Baseball Foldouts." Much like booklets of souvenir postcards, the Foldouts are an accordion-style presentation of 9 postcard-size cards. Each of the five different Foldouts booklets (85 cards in all) has a theme of currently playing career statistical leaders in the categories of pitching wins, home runs, batting average, saves in relief, and stolen bases. Some players appear in more than one booklet. The cards themselves are unusual in that there is a player on each side of the cards, plus one on the back of the folder's cover. Each Foldout thus pictures 17 players. Cards are borderless color photos crossed by a facsimile autograph. A black strip at the bottom gives the player's name, team, and career stats in the appropriate category. While some collectors will undoubtedly cut the individual cards out of the Foldouts, it appears that the set will retain its greatest value in complete, uncut form.

FOR

Innovative concept; nice large-size cards.

AGAINST

Team or superstar collectors can't display the cards they want without cutting the folder up and greatly reducing the value of the individual cards.

NOTEWORTHY CARDS

Since most of the career leaders in these categories are stars, most of the big name players of 1983 are included.

VALUE

MINT CONDITION, COMPLETE FOLDERS: Complete set, $10; individual Foldouts, $2. 5-YEAR PROJECTION: Average or slightly below.

1983 TOPPS '52 REPRINTS

SPECIFICATIONS

SIZE: 2½×3½". FRONT: Color painting made from photo. BACK: Red and black printing on white stock. DISTRIBUTION: Nationally, sold through hobby dealers and ads in sporting magazines only.

HISTORY

Rumors that Topps was planning to reprint at least one of its early baseball card sets proved accurate in early 1983 when the Brooklyn bubblegum company announced the availability of a limited edition (10,000 sets) reprint set of its classic 1952 baseball card issue. Many dealers and hobby purists were aghast. Dealers felt the availability of replica cards would stifle demand for the genuine '52 Topps cards and cause prices to plummet. Prior to the announcement of the reprinting project, a complete Mint-condition set of '52 Topps (if one could be found) was an $8,000 item. The Mantle card alone was selling for $1,000, and each of the "commons" in the 97-card high number series was worth $35 in top grades. Even the most common card in the early series sold for $3 in Mint. Hobby purists screamed that the issue would turn collectors away from the "real thing," and that Topps was betraying them by making available to virtually every collector replicas of cards that could previously be held by only a select few. Collectors, on the other hand, seemed to be either happy with the news or unconcerned. Those newer collectors who appreciated the beauty and history of the original '52 Topps set, but could never afford to collect it, welcomed the reprints. Many modern collectors had no interest in 30-year old baseball cards and didn't know Johnny Sain from Ferris Fain, and therefore gave the news of the reprint set scant attention. For its part, Topps promised nobody would ever confuse the reprints for the original cards; they were being printed in a smaller size, on lighter-weight white cardboard, and would carry in big bold red letters on the back the notation "TOPPS 1952 RE-PRINT SERIES." What Topps didn't say quite so loudly was that only 402 of the original 407 cards in the 1952 set were being reproduced. The company had gone back to each living player and the estate of each dead player who had appeared in the 1952 set in an effort to obtain releases for the re-issue. Five such clearances could not be obtained, so the 1983/1952 Topps set was issued without reprint cards of Dom DiMaggio, Saul Rogovin, Billy Loes, Solly Hemus, and Tommy Holmes. By the time the cards were actually released, the fuss had blown over. Topps priced many collectors right out of the market by setting the wholesale price for the set so high that dealers had to get $35 to $40 retail to make a profit. Additionally, after they actually saw the reprints, many potential customers decided not to buy; the quality of the printing and color reproduction was nowhere near that of the originals and many collectors felt they'd rather have no reprint than a bad one. When Topps saw that hobby demand for the set would not eat up the inventory, they began offering them to the general public through full-page ads in *The Sporting News* and other sporting media, at $42 a set. Most collectors feel the experiment was a failure and that it will discourage Topps from reprinting others of its rare early card sets.

FOR

At about 10¢ a card, collectors who desire "the nearest thing" to rare old superstars of the 1950s may find the '52 reprints to be satisfactory.

AGAINST

Poor quality. Failure to issue a complete reprint set. Relatively high cost per card for a large 1983 issue.

VALUE

MINT CONDITION: Complete set, $37.50. 5-YEAR PROJECTION: Below average.

1983 FLEER

SPECIFICATIONS

SIZE: 2½×3½". FRONT: Color photograph. BACK: Brown and black printing on white cardboard. DISTRIBUTION: Nationally, in packages with team logo and cap stickers.

HISTORY

Fleer got back on the right track in 1983 with a near perfect baseball card set, in contrast to the errors and variations that had plagued the company's 1981 and 1982 offerings. The 660-card set was arranged in the logical numerical order of player name (alphabetically) within team. The 1982 World's Champion St. Louis Cardinals opened the set, while the Minnesota Twins, the team with the worst win/loss record of the previous season, were grouped near the end. There are 18 "Super Star Special" cards and 14 checklists at the end of the set. The special cards are a combination of multi-player feature cards and cards honoring single players for important achievements or unusual accomplishments. Design of the '83 Fleers was attractive and colorful. Round-cornered color photos in the center of the front were surrounded by thin white and black lines, which were surrounded in turn by a brownish-gray border. A full-color team logo appears in a white circle in the lower-left corner, while a red Fleer logo is in the upper-left corner. The player's name and position appear in black print below the photo. The backs of the '83 Fleers were distinguished by the appearance of a small black and white photo of the player in the upper-right corner, the first time a major card set had included a player photo on the back since 1971 Topps. In vertical format, the backs also contained a traditional mix of vital data on the player, complete major and minor league stats, and if space permitted, a "Did you know?" trivia fact about the player. Once again, because Fleer was frozen out of the bubblegum market for its baseball cards by Topps' exclusive contracts, the '83 cards were sold in packs with team logo and cap stickers. After its many problems with errors and variations in previous years' card issues, the virtual perfection of the '83 set was welcomed by collectors.

FOR

Attractive cards, low price. Good possibility for future price appreciation.

AGAINST

Fleer vastly overestimated the collector demand for its 1983 card set, and at the end of the year was selling its overruns to dealers at huge markdowns—as low as $60 per case, or less than ½¢ per card. This will keep prices on the overall set quite low for the foreseeable future, though superstars and hot rookies will climb in value.

NOTEWORTHY CARDS

Fleer had a real coup by being the first major card company to have a Ron Kittle rookie card in its '83 set. Donruss didn't have one at all that year, and Topps didn't have a Kittle card until its Traded set was distributed in September, long after Kittle had sewn up American League Rookie of the Year honors. Until the Topps card came on the market, a Ron Kittle card could be pulled out of a 30¢ Fleer wax pack and sold for $2.50 or more. Like its two competitors, the '83 Fleer set also had a rookie card of Wade Boggs. Several of the "Super Star Special" cards are worth note. Four of the cards were produced in pairs that, when laid side by side, formed a single picture, one of the cards having no left border, the other card having no border on the right. One pair showed Kansas City Royals pitchers Bud Black and Vida Blue, and was titled—groan—"Black and Blue." The other card featured Angels teammates Rickey Henderson and Reggie Jackson, titled "Speed & Power." Fleer apparently felt the need to make up for its 1982 mistake of picturing Bo Diaz with Len Barker on its "Perfect Game" card; in '83 they issued a card showing Barker with his actual catcher in that 1981 perfect game, Ron Hassey. The '83 card was titled "Last Perfect Game."

VALUE

MINT CONDITION: Complete set, $13.50; common card, 3¢; stars, 25¢–75¢; Wade Boggs, $1.50; Ron Kittle, $2.50. 5-YEAR PROJECTION: Above average.

1983 Fleer, Frank Viola

1983 Fleer, Bud Black, Super Star Special

1983 Fleer, Vida Blue, Super Star Special

1983 Fleer, Charlie Lea

1983 Fleer, Scott McGregor

1983 Fleer, Jack Morris

1983 Fleer, André Dawson

1983 Fleer, Jim Palmer

1983 Fleer, Lou Whitaker

1983 Fleer, Carlton Fisk

1983 Fleer, Ryne Sandberg

1983 Fleer, Steve Sax

1983 Fleer, Robin Yount

COMPLETE BOOK OF COLLECTIBLE BASEBALL CARDS

1983 Fleer, Ron Hassey, Len Barker, Super Star Special

1983 Fleer, Joel Youngblood, Super Star Special

1983 Fleer, Jason Thompson

1983 DONRUSS

SPECIFICATIONS

SIZE: 2½×3½". FRONT: Color photograph. BACK: Yellow and black printing on white cardboard. DISTRIBUTION: Nationally, in packages with jigsaw puzzle pieces, and in complete sets through dealers.

HISTORY

Donruss stood relatively pat in its third year of baseball card production—and collectors generally voiced disapproval. There was little innovation in the 1983 set. The cards again featured a large color photo surrounded by a stripe color co-ordinated by team. The Donruss logo and date were moved to the upper-right corner. A bat once again provided the bottom border for the photo, with the player's name inside, along with a baseball with the position abbreviation. A glove at lower right had the team name. Card backs were virtually identical to the previous year, substituting yellow boxes at top and bottom for the blue that had been used the previous year to highlight the player's vital data and career summary. Recent stats again appeared in a wide white strip at center. As in the previous year, the '83 Donruss set contained 660 cards, including seven unnumbered checklists. There were once again 26 artist-drawn Diamond King cards to open the set, one player from each team. A few multi-player feature cards were again sprinkled through the set, along with better-known coaches and managers. The final numbered card in the set was a picture of the Ty Cobb puzzle that was included, three pieces at a time out of a total of 63, in each wax pack. Donruss made a major concession to the hobby in 1983 by offering wholesale dealers full sets, already arranged by card number and boxed to save the time and expense of sorting. There were fewer errors and variations than ever in the '83 Donruss set.

FOR

Nice major set with few errors or problems.

AGAINST

Too similar to the '82 issue to suit many collectors.

NOTEWORTHY CARDS

Rookie cards of Wade Boggs and Mel Hall. Two wrong-photo cards in the set were never corrected: The Indian on Dan Spillner's card is actually Ed Whitson, and the player on Joe Pittman's card is Padres teammate Juan Eichelberger. Two team-name errors were corrected. Pascual Perez's card can be found with either the correct Braves designation or the incorrect Twins designation in the glove on the card front. Ron Jackson can be found with the correct Angels or the incorrect A's in the same place. In addition, there are two versions of the A's-Jackson card. On one, considered correct, the frame around the photo is in red, like the cards of the other Angels; on the other, considered to be the double-error, the frame is in green. Another variation pair occurs on card #88, on which Bryn Smith's name will be found spelled correctly, or incorrectly, as "Byrn." In each case, the error version is worth about 75¢.

OUR FAVORITE CARD

Many collectors were surprised to see on Mike Schmidt's card (#168) that the famed Phillies third baseman was wearing uniform number 37, instead of his familiar number 20. According to Donruss, the photo was taken in spring training, 1982, after Schmidt's jersey had been stolen.

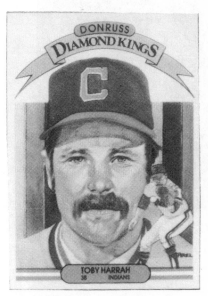

1983 Donruss, Toby Harrah, Diamond King

1983 DONRUSS

VALUE

MINT CONDITION: Complete set, $15; common card, 3¢; stars, 25¢–$1; Chicken, $1; Boggs, $2.50. 5-YEAR PROJECTION: Above average.

1983 Donruss, San Diego Chicken (back)

1983 Donruss, Joe Niekro, Diamond King

1983 Donruss, Tony Pena

1983 Donruss, Ray Burris

1983 Donruss, John Wockenfuss

1983 Donruss, Pascual Perez

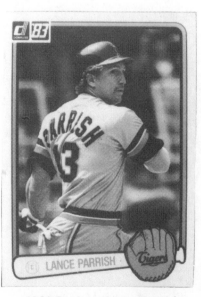

1983 Donruss, Lance Parrish

COMPLETE BOOK OF COLLECTIBLE BASEBALL CARDS

1983 DONRUSS ACTION ALL-STARS

1983 Donruss, San Diego Chicken (front)

1983 Donruss, Ryne Sandberg

1983 Donruss, Jody Davis

SPECIFICATIONS

SIZE: 3½×5″. FRONT: Color photograph. BACK: Black and red printing on white cardboard. DISTRIBUTION: Nationally, in cellophane packs with jigsaw puzzle pieces.

HISTORY

For the first time, in 1983, Donruss introduced more than a single baseball card issue, and it met with critical success for its 60-card Action All-Stars offering. The postcard-size cards provided two color photos of each player on the front of the card, a portrait at left and an action photo at right. The player's name and position were printed below the smaller action photo, and the team name was incorporated as part of the gray background design. White and wine-red borders surrounded the card. On the back, in contrast to the regular Donruss cards, the Action All-Stars present full major league stats for the player on a year-by-year basis, along with more detailed personal and career data. The stats are printed in white at the center while red boxes at top and bottom contain personal and career data. The cards were sold in cello packs, each containing six cards and three pieces of a 63-piece Mickey Mantle jigsaw puzzle, for 30 to 35 cents. The set contains 59 player cards and a checklist.

FOR

Large format gives play to exceptionally popular design. All cards are stars.

AGAINST

Some collectors don't like cards that aren't in the standard 2½×3½″ format.

NOTEWORTHY CARDS

Since all of the players in the Action All-Stars set are stars, they are all noteworthy. A back variation exists on the Reggie Jackson card. On the more scarce version, the red printing from the lower data box extends into the last few lines of season stats. On later cards the red was removed.

VALUE

MINT CONDITION: Complete set, $7.50; common card, 5¢; superstars, 25¢–50¢. 5-YEAR PROJECTION: Above average.

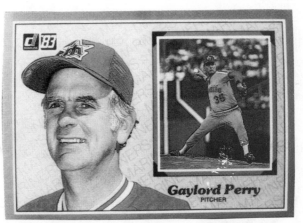

1983 Donruss Action All-Star, Gaylord Perry

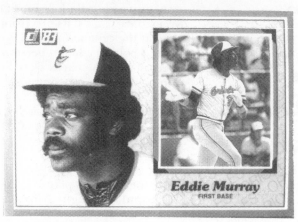

1983 Donruss Action All-Stars, Eddie Murray

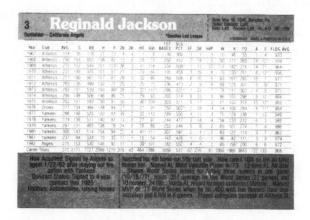

1983 Donruss Action All-Stars, Reggie Jackson (back)

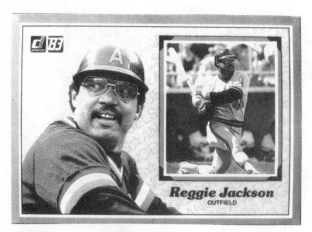

1983 Donruss Action All-Stars, Reggie Jackson (front)

1983 DONRUSS HALL OF FAME HEROES

SPECIFICATIONS

SIZE: 2½×3½″. FRONT: Color painting. BACK: Red and blue printing on white cardboard. DISTRIBUTION: Nationally, in packages with jigsaw puzzle pieces.

HISTORY

While Donruss hit a home run with its Action All-Stars set of 1983, the company struck out with its second subsidiary issue, "Hall of Fame Heroes." The first 42 cards of the 44 in the set depicted "old-timers" who had been enshrined in baseball's Hall of Fame. Rather than photos, though, the cards depicted the players as painted by Dick Perez. Frankly, the strain of producing so many player paintings is evident in the overall quality of the artwork, which is not up to par for Perez. The 43rd card in the set is a picture of the Mickey Mantle jigsaw puzzle, three pieces of which were included in each wax pack of the Hall of Fame Heroes cards. The 44th is a checklist. Card backs, in vertical format, were a colorful red, white, and blue, and featured a short biography of the player, along with pennants, bats, balls, and other baseball trappings. Donruss kept its selection to better-known Hall of Famers of the 20th Century, with a heavy concentration of players from the 1950s and 1960s, but collectors stayed away in droves. Donruss learned that retrospective sets of former players are not in big demand with either kids at the candy counter or most collectors.

FOR

Cheap cards of famous players.

AGAINST

Generally unattractive artwork of old-timers.

NOTEWORTHY CARDS

They're all Hall of Famers.

1983 KELLOGG'S

1983 Donruss Hall of Fame Heroes, Cy Young

1983 Donruss Hall of Fame Heroes, Roberto Clemente

1983 Donruss Hall of Fame Heroes, Jackie Robinson

1983 Donruss Hall of Fame Heroes, Early Wynn

SPECIFICATIONS

SIZE: 1⅞×3¼". FRONT: Color photograph, 3-D effect. BACK: Black printing on white cardboard. DISTRIBUTION: Nationally, complete sets by mail, individual cards in cereal boxes.

HISTORY

The 1983 Kellogg's set of 60 cards was the 14th, and final, annual issue by the cereal company. Kellogg's announced in 1984 that it would no longer produce card sets. In the early years of the company's issues (1970-on), Kellogg's had often been the only nationally distributed baseball card set other than Topps. By 1981, everybody and his brother were issuing baseball cards, and the value of continued use of cards to sell cereal was questioned by Kellogg's officials. The 1983 Kellogg's set was again "down-sized" from the previous year, returning in physical dimensions to the narrow 1⅞×3¼" format. The set was also reduced in number from 64 to 60 cards. As had been the case for all but one year of Kellogg's sets, the cards were produced in the "Xograph process" to give them the appearance of being three-dimensional. This visual "trick" was effected by laminating a thin piece of very finely-ribbed plastic to the front of the card. Behind the plastic, a sharp, clear photo of the player was overlaid on a blurred stadium background, giving the card the illusion of depth. The effect is quite striking and made the cards very popular among collectors. The design of the 1983 Kellogg's card was quite different from previous years. Two white stripes were incorporated within the area of the color photo, with panels at top and bottom giving the name of the set, "Kellogg's 3-D Super Stars," and the player's last name and position. The player's name and "Kellogg's" script logo are in red, the rest in black. A white border surrounds the whole design. As was the case in each Kellogg's issue, a facsimile autograph appears on the face of the card. Card backs were also quite different in the 1983 set; they were vertical in format.

1983 KELLOGG'S

Career stats and a short biography of the player appear on card backs, along with a team logo and the logos of Major League Baseball and the Major League Baseball Players Association, which gave permission for the Kellogg's issues. In its final year, Kellogg's returned to the policy of placing individual cards in cereal boxes, Sugar Corn Pops in this case. Complete sets could be obtained by sending $3.95 and a pair of box tops or proof-of-purchase seals to Battle Creek, Mich.

FOR
The final issue of Kellogg's cards has a lot going for it. The cards are attractive and inexpensive. There are a lot of superstars for the set size. A lot of room for future price appreciation.

AGAINST
The narrow card size of the 1983 Kellogg's issue makes the cards prone to curling and cracking as the plastic fac-

ing contracts with age. Cards that evidence cracks across the plastic are worth much less than undamaged cards. It is difficult to buy single superstars since most '83s are dealt in complete sets; few collectors, it seems, bought many cereal boxes to hunt for superstars.

NOTEWORTHY CARDS
A majority of the cards in the '83 Kellogg's set are legitimate stars or superstars. Lots of great young players make their first (and last) appearance in the 1983 set, most notably, Dale Murphy. There is an error on the card of Dan Quisenberry; his name is misspelled on the front, "Quiesenberry." It is spelled correctly on back.

VALUE
MINT CONDITION: Complete set, $5; common card, 10¢; stars, 25¢–50¢; Rose, Murphy, 75¢. 5-YEAR PROJECTION: Well above average.

1983 Kellogg's, Jim Rice

1983 Kellogg's, Bill Madlock,

1983 Kellogg's, Pete Vuckovich

1983 Kellogg's, Pedro Guerrero

1983 Kellogg's, Pete Rose

1983 Kellogg's, Robin Yount

1983 DRAKE'S

SPECIFICATIONS

SIZE: 2½×3½". FRONT: Color photograph. BACK: Black and orange printing on gray cardboard. DISTRIBUTION: Single cards, Northeast in packages of bakery products; sets, nationally by hobby dealers.

HISTORY

Right there at the top of the card is a banner that says this is the "3rd Annual Collectors' Edition," and so it is. In 1983, Topps produced another 33-card set for Drake's bakeries. Single cards were inserted into family-size boxes of snack cakes, but again in '83, Drake's wholesaled large numbers of the cards to baseball card dealers, who made complete sets available to collectors at reasonable prices. Format of the cards is similar to previous editions, with each photo showing the player in a game-action batting pose, in keeping with the "Big Hitters" theme of the set. All of the players are known either for being power hitters, or for compiling high batting averages. Like the previous two issues, the '83 Drake's cards feature a fancy framework around the photo, and a facsimile autograph. Backs of the cards are virtually identical to the corresponding Topps cards, with the exception of numbers that have been changed to reflect alphabetical order of the players in the set, and the addition of a Drake's logo and copyright line.

FOR

Nice inexpensive regional cards of big name players.

AGAINST

Many collectors find fault with the "busy" design of the '83 Drake's.

NOTEWORTHY CARDS

Most of the players in the set are stars or superstars. The '83 set includes Cal Ripken, Jr., for the first time.

VALUE

MINT CONDITION: Complete set, $5; common card, 10¢; superstars, 50–75¢. 5-YEAR PROJECTION: A bit above average.

1983 GRANNY GOOSE A'S

SPECIFICATIONS

SIZE: 2½×4¼". FRONT: Color photograph. BACK: Black printing on white cardboard. DISTRIBUTION: Northern California, single cards in bags of potato chips; complete sets given away at promotional ball game.

HISTORY

For the third year in a row, Granny Goose Foods issued a 15-card regional set of Oakland A's baseball cards in 1983. While the design of the cards was quite similar to the previous issues, there were two principal differences. The first was the inclusion of a tear-off coupon at the bottom of the card. The tab had a scratch-off "Instant Winner Game" box featuring valuable prizes. If a prize was won, the coupon on the back of the tab could be filled in and mailed away to collect the winnings. Cards with the tab intact and unscratched are worth twice as much as those without. The other major difference between the 1983 Granny Goose set and those of 1981 and 1982 is the inclusion of the date, "1983," in the green-on-yellow A's logo on the front of the card. The basic format of the front design was not changed from earlier years, however. A color photo is surrounded by a white border. Beneath that is a green box with yellow letters giving the player's name, uniform number, and position. Card backs feature smaller type for the minimal player information, a smaller A's logo, and for the first time, a Granny Goose logo. Single cards were once again distributed in large packages of potato chips, while complete sets (without tabs) were given away at a special "Baseball Card" promotional game in July.

FOR

Nice, relatively inexpensive regional set; great for team collectors.

AGAINST

Design too similar to earlier issues.

NOTEWORTHY CARDS

Stars in the 1983 Granny Goose set

include Rickey Henderson, Carney Lansford, and Dwayne Murphy.

VALUE
MINT CONDITION, WITH TABS: Complete set, $24; common card, $1; stars, $2; Henderson, $4. 5-YEAR PROJECTION: Average.

1983 ATLANTA BRAVES POLICE

SPECIFICATIONS
SIZE: 2⅝×4⅛″. FRONT: Color photograph. BACK: Full-color on white cardboard. DISTRIBUTION: Atlanta area, individual cards given out by local police officers.

HISTORY
The 30-card 1983 Braves Police set is similar in design to the team's two previous sets. There is a notation in the upper-right corner that the team was the 1982 Western Division Champion of the National League. Otherwise, the cards are the same basic color photo on a white border, with Police Athletic League and team logos and a player identification. The card number on the front of the card is also the player's uniform number. Backs feature the color logos of Coca-Cola and Hostess, along with a safety tip and a few lines about the player. Besides the players' cards, there is a card for manager Torre and each coach.

FOR
Nice item for team collectors.

AGAINST
Design too similar to previous years; cardboard too light.

NOTEWORTHY CARDS
Bob Gibson, Dale Murphy, Bob Horner, Phil Niekro.

VALUE
MINT CONDITION: Complete set, $12.50; common card, 35¢; stars, 50¢–$1. 5-YEAR PROJECTION: Above average.

1983 MILWAUKEE BREWERS POLICE

SPECIFICATIONS
SIZE: 2¹³/₁₆×4⅛″. FRONT: Color photograph. BACK: Blue printing on white cardboard. DISTRIBUTION: Wisconsin, individual cards by members of various police departments; complete sets given away at special baseball card promotion game.

HISTORY
A total of 28 police departments all over the state of Wisconsin cooperated in the distribution of the 1983 Brewers Police set. Multiply that by the 30 different cards in the set, and that comes to a whopping total of 840 varieties. Few collectors will attempt to assemble such a "complete" set, and most are content to acquire a basic 30-card set such as the one given away by the Milwaukee Police Department at a special Baseball Card Day promotion at the park. The other departments made the cards available to youngsters asking police officers for them. All of the cards are basically the same, with the appropriate police department's name inserted as the second line of type below the player's color photo on the front of the card. Card backs have the Brewers logo, a police shield, and a statement by the player offering a safety, anti-crime, or personal development message in a baseball context. In addition to the players cards there are four coach cards, a manager card, and a team photo card. Whether the cards of the various departments will ever take on an identity and a price structure of their own is debatable at this point, but most veteran collectors doubt it.

FOR
Nice for the team collector.

AGAINST
"Complete" set impossible to obtain.

NOTEWORTHY CARDS
Robin Yount, Rollie Fingers, all the other Brewers stars.

VALUE
MINT CONDITION: Complete set, $9; common card, 25¢; stars, 50¢–75¢. 5-YEAR PROJECTION: Above average.

1983 GARDNER'S BREWERS

SPECIFICATIONS
SIZE: 2½×3½″. FRONT: Color photograph. BACK: Orange and black printing on gray cardboard. DISTRIBUTION: Wisconsin, single cards in packages of bread and buns.

HISTORY
One of 1983's scarcest regional baseball card issues was produced by Gardner Baking Company, Madison, Wisconsin. The set consisted of 22 Milwaukee Brewers cards, 21 players and manager Harvey Kuenn. The cards were produced by Topps and inserted in "specially marked packages" of bread and hot dog and hamburger buns. Because no sets were made

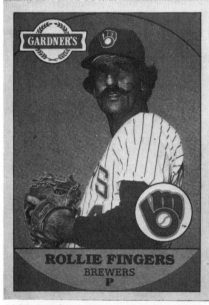

1983 Gardner's Brewers, Rollie Fingers

available to dealers or collectors, the Gardner's set has maintained high value. Often with such sets, the issuer makes quantities of the cards available to the hobbyist to offset the cost of printing. Many Wisconsin collectors chose not to buy the bread products, at a cost of 75¢ or more per loaf (and per card), waiting patiently for the cards to come on the wholesale market. When they never did, there was a scramble to purchase sets that had been assembled from the loaves. Naturally, those collectors who lived outside of Wisconsin had no choice but to buy the cards on the aftermarket. Gardner's "day-old" bakery outlets became a favorite hangout for collectors and dealers during this promotion, as a loaf of bread with a card could be bought for 25¢ or so, leaving a pretty good profit margin. The '83 Gardner's cards featured a tombstone-shaped photo of the player at center, surrounded by a frame of pink, orange, and yellow with a white border. There was a red and black Gardner's logo in the upper-left corner, and a yellow and blue Brewers logo in the lower-right corner. With the exception of the changed card number (Kuenn is card #1, the rest are numbered alphabetically by player name), backs were identical to the regular-issue Topps cards of 1983; there is not even a Gardner's logo on the back. Because the cards were inserted into packages of buns and bread, they absorbed grease from the products. There was concern at first that the cards would be permanently stained. In time, however, the stains disappeared.

FOR

Popular regional set of the reigning American League champions. Genuinely scarce and likely to maintain good value.

AGAINST

The design is a bit gaudy, but you can't say much that's bad about a regional baseball card set that's distributed the way regionals were meant to be distributed.

NOTEWORTHY CARDS

All the stars from the pennant-winning 1982 Brewers are here: Yount, Cooper, Molitor, Fingers, etc.

VALUE

MINT CONDITION: Complete set, $30; common card, $1; Fingers, Thomas, Molitor, Simmons, Cooper, $2; Yount, $3. 5-YEAR PROJECTION: Above average.

1983 Gardner's Brewers, Cecil Cooper

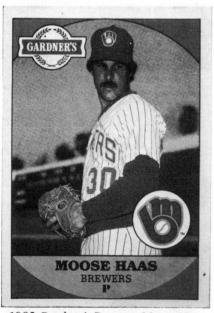

1983 Gardner's Brewers, Moose Haas

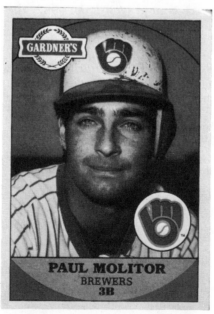

1983 Gardner's Brewers, Paul Molitor

1983 Gardner's Brewers, Don Money

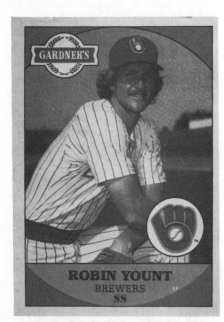

1983 Gardner's Brewers, Ted Simmons

1983 Gardner's Brewers, Robin Yount

1983 THORN APPLE VALLEY CUBS

SPECIFICATIONS

SIZE: 2¼×3½". FRONT: Color photograph. BACK: Black printing on white cardboard. DISTRIBUTION: Chicago, at special "Baseball Card Day" promotional game.

HISTORY

Similar to the Red Lobster set of the previous year, the 27-card set of Cubs cards given away at a special "Baseball Card Day" promotional game was co-sponsored in 1983 by Thorn Apple Valley, the meat company that produces the hot dogs sold at Wrigley Field. The set consists of 25 individual player cards, a team card, and a card with the manager and coaches. As in 1982, the TAV-Cubs set features borderless color photos, both game action and posed, taken at the home ballpark. A single line of type on the card has the player's name, uniform number (which is also the card number), and abbreviation for his position. Overall, the quality of the photos in the set is improved from 1982; the players stand out from the background more sharply than in the previous set. Card backs in '83 again feature year-by-year major and minor league stats, statistical totals by league (where appropriate for players who were on American League clubs), and major league stat totals. There is a small ad for Thorn Apple Valley and a copyright line for the Cubs at the bottom of the card.

FOR

Nice scarce regional set for the Cubs collector.

AGAINST

Not very professional in appearance, most of the cards are cut a fraction of an inch off the "true" dimensions.

NOTEWORTHY CARDS

Rookie cards of Ryne Sandberg, Mel Hall, Craig Lefferts, and Joe Carter.

VALUE

MINT CONDITION: Complete set, $8; common card, 25¢; stars, rookies, 50¢. 5-YEAR PROJECTION: Above average.

1983 LOS ANGELES DODGERS POLICE

SPECIFICATIONS

SIZE: 2¹³/₁₆×4⅛". FRONT: Color photograph. BACK: Blue printing on white cardboard. DISTRIBUTION: Los Angeles area, single cards given away by neighborhood police officers; complete sets given away at game.

HISTORY

While maintaining the same basic format as the previous years' issues, the 1983 Dodgers Police set has a few key differences. The fronts are simplified somewhat; the color photo has just two lines of type below, the player's name and uniform number on one line, and the date and Dodgers' script logo at bottom. Card backs feature a second, smaller photo of the player, along with his name, uniform number (card number), personal and career data, and an LAPD badge. There is no safety tip as such, just a note that the card is distributed "from your friends at the LAPD." The 30 cards in the set feature 28 players, the manager, and the coaching staff.

FOR

Attractive item for the team collector.

AGAINST

Tired format; light cardboard suffers damage too easily.

NOTEWORTHY CARDS

Valenzuela, Guerrero, Sax; rookie cards of Brock and Maldonado.

VALUE

MINT CONDITION: Complete set, $6; common card, 20¢; stars, 45¢–75¢. 5-YEAR PROJECTION: Above average.

1983 STUART EXPOS

SPECIFICATIONS
SIZE: 2½×3½". FRONT: Color photograph. BACK: Red and blue printing on white cardboard. DISTRIBUTION: Quebec area, single cards in boxes of snack cakes, complete sets by mail-in offer.

HISTORY
One of the more elusive and expensive of the 1983 regional baseball card issues was the 30-card set of Montreal Expos produced and distributed by Stuart's baking company. Single cards were distributed in the company's snack cake products during the baseball season, and a mail-in offer at the end of the year allowed complete sets to be obtained. The cards feature the players, manager, and coaches of the Expos. Card fronts have a color photo at top, with blue and red stripes beneath, surrounded by a wide white border. The player's uniform number and name appear at the center on bottom, with a color Expos logo to the left, and a red Stuart's logo to the right. The back, printed like many Canadian baseball cards in both French and English, contains a little personal data, and a short career summary. An Expos logo appears at the top and the card number at bottom. A bar at lower center has the year of issue prominently displayed. The theft of a large number of the '83 Stuart's cards made them more widely available within the hobby earlier than they might otherwise have been, and has somewhat obscured the fact that the issue is not all that common.

FOR
Good-looking and scarce regional item.

AGAINST
Set is still suffering from the bad hobby publicity connected with the theft and sale of cards on the black market.

NOTEWORTHY CARDS
All of the Expos stars of 1983 are in the set: Gary Carter, Al Oliver, Tim Raines, Andre Dawson, etc.

VALUE
MINT CONDITION: Complete set, $25; common card, 75¢; stars, $1–$2. 5-YEAR PROJECTION: Average.

1983 MOTHER'S COOKIES GIANTS

SPECIFICATIONS
SIZE: 2½×3½". FRONT: Color photograph. BACK: Red and purple printing on white cardboard. DISTRIBUTION: Team-issued, at baseball card giveaway promotional game on August 7.

HISTORY
For the first time in 30 years, Mother's Cookies sponsored a baseball card set in 1983. Featuring 20 members of the San Francisco Giants, it was the first Mother's set of major league ballplayers. Fans attending a special baseball card promotional game on August 7 were given a box containing 15 of the 20 cards, and a coupon that could be sent to Mother's Cookies for five additional cards. Since the bakery did not guarantee that the five cards received for the coupon would be the five cards missing from that collector's set, the concept encouraged the good old-fashioned baseball card art of trading—or at least that's the way it was supposed to work. In reality, dealers seemed to have an adequate stock of complete sets for sale to the hobby. The cards are printed on rather thin white cardboard in an attractive format. A sharp color photo of the player—generally a posed-action shot taken at Candlestick Park—was surrounded by a frame in the team's orange and black colors and a white border. The player's name appeared in black in the orange part of the frame, while a black and white team logo was in a circle at the lower-right corner. Card backs have no statistical information, but include the player's name, position, uniform number, card number, some personal data, and a line on how he joined the Giants. There is a Mother's logo in the upper-right corner, and at bottom, a space for the player's autograph. The 20 cards in the set include 19 players and Hall of Fame manager Frank Robinson.

FOR
Attractive regional set from a well-known name in baseball card history. The concept of issuing the cards and requiring trading to complete a set was good, even if it didn't work as well as planned.

AGAINST
Relatively expensive for a very recent issue; card stock too thin.

NOTEWORTHY PLAYERS
Manager Frank Robinson is the biggest name on the 1983 Giants, but the team was young, and some of the players may yet join him in the Hall of Fame.

VALUE
MINT CONDITION: Complete set, $15; common card, 50¢; stars, 75¢–$1; Robinson, $1.50. 5-YEAR PROJECTION: Above average.

1983 WHEATIES INDIANS

SPECIFICATIONS
SIZE: 2¹³/₁₆×4¹/₈". FRONT: Color photograph. BACK: Blue printing on white cardboard. DISTRIBUTION: Team issue, complete sets given away during promotional game and sold in gift shop.

HISTORY
In 1983, for the second time, Wheaties cereal and the Cleveland Indians worked together to issue a baseball card set. The set count was up two in '83, to 32 cards, including 27 players, the manager, and four coaches. The cards retained the same basic "police set" format of a color photo on front surrounded by a wide white border. In the space below the photo there is a color Indians logo, the player's name and position, and a Wheaties logo, in black. Backs of the manager's and

coaches' cards continue to carry nothing but a large Wheaties ad. The backs of the players' cards were changed in the 1983 set to feature complete major and minor league statistics. In an interesting innovation, the stats are broken down in American League and National League totals where appropriate, and then major league totals are given. The complete set was given away at a special baseball card promotional date at Municipal Stadium, and was subsequently placed on sale at the Indians souvenir shop. This has helped to keep the price of the set low.

FOR
Inexpensive, attractive cards for the team collector.

AGAINST
Too similar in design to 1982 issue.

NOTEWORTHY CARDS
Rookie card of Julio Franco.

VALUE
MINT CONDITION: Complete set, $5; common card, 15¢–20¢; stars, 25¢–50¢; Franco, $1. 5-YEAR PROJECTION: Above average.

1983 KANSAS CITY ROYALS POLICE

SPECIFICATIONS
SIZE: 2½×4⅛". FRONT: Color photograph. BACK: Blue printing on white cardboard. DISTRIBUTION: Ft. Myers, Florida, area, single cards given away by local police officers.

HISTORY
The ten cards in the 1983 Kansas City Royals Police set are virtually identical to the set issued in 1981. Both were issued by the Ft. Myers, Florida, Police Department. This area is the spring training base of the Royals. Fronts feature a color photo, facsimile autograph, team logo, and the player's name position, height, and weight. There is no card number. Backs fea-

ture logos for the sponsoring groups, a safety tip, and a short career summary about the player. The easiest way to tell the '83 Royals Police cards from the '81s is that the '83 cards do not have year-by-year stats.

FOR
Good set for team collectors.

AGAINST
Too much like the 1981 set.

NOTEWORTHY CARDS
George Brett, Dan Quisenberry, Willie Wilson.

VALUE
MINT CONDITION: Complete set, $10; common card, 75¢; stars, $1–$3. 5-YEAR PROJECTION: Above average.

1983 MINNESOTA TWINS

SPECIFICATIONS
SIZE: 2½×3½". FRONT: Color photograph. BACK: Red and blue printing on white cardboard. DISTRIBUTION: Minnesota, sold at souvenir stands and by mail.

HISTORY
One of the lesser-known and potentially scarcer baseball card sets of 1983 was the Minnesota Twins team issue of 36 cards. Reportedly, only 4,000 sets were prepared, and they were quickly sold out at the Metrodome concession stands and by mail order. The cards feature attractive posed photos taken in spring training. The fronts have just the photo, no border or writing. A drawing of the Twins home jersey, with the player's uniform number, appears in the lower-right corner. Card backs feature full major and minor league statistics on an annual basis, personal data including the player's team nickname, and a card number. Besides the 25 regular-roster players who have individual cards in the set, there are 11 specialty cards.

Each of the four coaches and manager Billy Gardner have their own cards, and they appear on a group card, as well. Three multi-player cards feature the Twins three-man catching corps, a trio of Minnesota-born Twins, and "The Lumber Company," the team's four big hitting stars. There is a team photo card and an aerial view of the "Humptydome" in downtown Minneapolis to round out the set.

FOR
Scarce, good-looking team-issued regional set.

AGAINST
Most collectors have never heard of it, so current demand is low.

NOTEWORTHY CARDS
Counting the team card, Twins star Kent Hrbek appears on four cards in the set. There are rookie cards of Gary Gaetti and Jim Eisenreich, and for collectors who favor the Fifties, the manager and coaches cards include former ballplayers Billy Gardner, Jim Lemon, and Johnny Podres.

VALUE
MINT CONDITION: Complete set, $12; common card, 35¢; stars, 75¢; Hrbek, $1.50. 5-YEAR PROJECTION: Above average.

1983 TRUE VALUE WHITE SOX

SPECIFICATIONS
SIZE: 2⅝×4⅛". FRONT: Color photograph. BACK: Black printing on white cardboard. DISTRIBUTION: Team issue, at special Tuesday night games.

HISTORY
To collect the 23-card set co-sponsored by the Chicago White Sox and True Value hardware stores, you theoretically had to attend the special Tuesday night games at which cards were given away. But you couldn't acquire the complete set in this way.

Rainouts forced the cancellation of a couple of games, and on rainy Tuesdays cards intended to be handed out that night were instead smuggled out the back door to collectors and dealers. Because complete sets were not made available, the True Value White Sox cards of 1983 are a rather expensive regional set to put together. The format of the cards is rather like the recent police sets, with a large color photo being set into a wide white border. A red and blue Sox logo is in the lower-left corner, while the player's name, position, and uniform number (also the card number) are in the lower right. Card backs feature year-by-year major and minor league statistics, along with league (where applicable) and career stats, and a True Value ad.

FOR

Great cards for team and superstar collectors, especially since the White Sox were the American League West pennant-winners in 1983.

AGAINST

Rather expensive modern regional issue; complete sets hard to come by. Some collectors feel that the stigma of three of the player cards entering hobby channels directly, rather than through the team, taints the set.

NOTEWORTHY CARDS

Team-issued rookie card of Ron Kittle and Cy Young Award winner LaMarr Hoyt. Three of the cards were not given out at games, but made their way into the hobby via dealers and collectors who had connections with White Sox officials; the cards of Marc Hill, Harold Baines, and Salome Barojas are thus considered scarcer than the rest of the set.

VALUE

MINT CONDITION: Complete set, $50; common cards, $1.50; Hill, Baines, Barojas, Hoyt, $3; Kittle, $5.
5-YEAR PROJECTION: Above average.

1983 True Value White Sox, Salome Barojas

1983 True Value White Sox, LaMarr Hoyt

1983 True Value White Sox, Harold Baines

1983 True Value White Sox, Dennis Lamp

1982 TOPPS

SPECIFICATIONS
SIZE: 2½×3½″. FRONT: Color photograph. BACK: Green and blue printing on gray cardboard. DISTRIBUTION: Nationally, in 30¢ and 49¢ gum packs.

HISTORY
Topps produced its biggest baseball card set ever in 1982—792 cards. The addition of 66 cards over the previous year's total allowed Topps, for the first time since 1978, to eliminate "double prints," cards printed more than once on a sheet and therefore twice as common as the others. While collectors applauded the increased number of cards, they were generally unenthusiastic about the design of the '82s. The card fronts featured a pair of color stripes down the left side. To most collectors they looked like hockey sticks and seemed to draw attention away from the player photo. Card backs were an incredibly hard-to-read combination of blue and green ink on gray cardboard. The first six cards in the '82 set highlighted great performances of the previous season. Other special subsets included runs of American and National League All-Stars, 1981 statistical leaders from each league, and 40 "In Action" cards, which depicted players in game action. The In Action cards are numbered in the set immediately after

the "regular" card of that player. Each team manager was pictured on a card, along with that team's batting and pitching leaders. The popular "Future Stars" cards were also included in the 1982 set, each card featuring three top prospects for a particular team. These cards have traditionally offered some of the most valuable "rookie cards" in hobby history; prices for some cards have literally gone from 2¢ to $2 in a single season.

FOR
Large set, no double prints, lots of potential for price appreciation.

AGAINST
Unpopular design.

NOTEWORTHY CARDS
Because of a printing foul-up, some of the George Foster All-Star cards (#342) are found without the facsimile autograph on the front of the card; this card currently carries a $2.25 value, as compared to $1 or so for the version with autograph. Currently hot "rookie cards" found in the 1982 Topps set include: Cal Ripken, Jr. ($3.50), Steve Sax–Mike Marshall ($1.50), Kent Hrbek ($1.50), Dave Righetti ($1), and Johnny Ray (75¢).

VALUE
MINT CONDITION: Complete set, $19; common card, 3¢; superstars, 25¢–50¢. 5-YEAR PROJECTION: Above average.

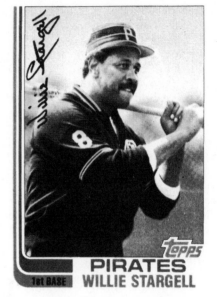

1982 Topps, Willie Stargell

1982 Topps, 1981 Victory Leaders

1982 Topps, Texas Rangers Leaders and Team Checklist

1982 Topps, 1981 Stolen Base Leaders

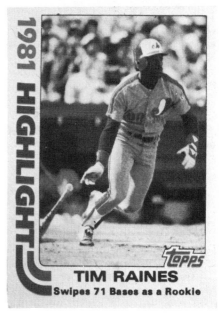

1982 Topps, Tim Raines

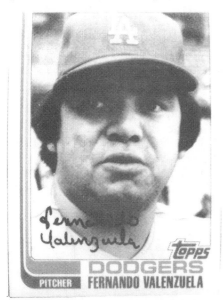

1982 Topps, Fernando Valenzuela

1982 Topps, Dave Winfield, All-Star

1982 Topps, Greg Luzinski, In Action

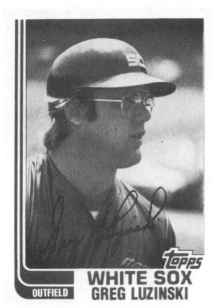

1982 Topps, Greg Luzinski

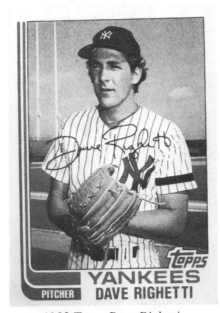

1982 Topps, Dave Righetti

1982 TOPPS TRADED

SPECIFICATIONS

SIZE: 2½×3½″. FRONT: Color photograph. BACK: Black and red printing on white cardboard. DISTRIBUTION: Nationally, sold only as complete sets through hobby dealers.

HISTORY

For the second straight year, Topps produced a 132-card update or Traded set in September of 1982. The set, sold exclusively in the baseball card hobby, rather than in gum packs, offers 1982-style cards of traded players in their new uniforms (sometimes the uniforms are created by airbrush artists), single cards of rookies who had previously appeared on "Future Stars" cards, and new cards of players who had been missed in the regular '82 Topps set, but who had become fan and collector favorites during the early part of the season. The cards themselves follow the basic design of the regular 1982 Topps issue, but overall the photographs and printing quality are not up to the same level. Card backs are printed in red, rather than green, and the cards are numbered from 1 to 132, with the letter "T" following the number. The cards are numbered in alphabetical order, with card #132T being a checklist.

FOR

The Traded sets give collectors a chance to see their favorite players on a card in the uniform of the team for which they played in 1982. They also provide each hot rookie with a card of his own, whereas in the regular Topps set each had to share a card with two other prospects.

AGAINST

Because the update series is not available through traditional retail outlets, only through baseball card dealers, some purist collectors don't feel they are "legitimate." This has given rise to discussion of which is a player's "real" rookie card, etc. Despite these objections, most collectors don't feel their '82 Topps set is complete without the Traded series.

NOTEWORTHY CARDS

Single-player rookie cards of Cal Ripken, Jr. ($3), Steve Sax ($1.75), and Kent Hrbek ($1.75), along with the first card of Reggie Jackson in the California Angels uniform and Gaylord Perry as a member of the Kansas City Royals.

VALUE

MINT CONDITION: Complete set, $8.50; common card, 10¢; superstars, 35¢–75¢. 5-YEAR PROJECTION: Above average.

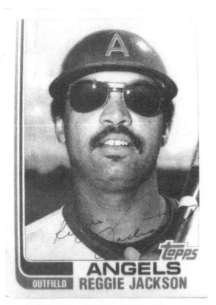

1982 Topps Traded, Reggie Jackson

1982 Topps Traded, Checklist

1982 Topps Traded, Chet Lemon

1982 FLEER

SPECIFICATIONS

SIZE: 2½×3½″. FRONT: Color photograph. BACK: Four-color printing on white cardboard. DISTRIBUTION: Nationally, in packages with team logo stickers.

HISTORY

After its acclaimed baseball card issue of 1981, Fleer really struck out in 1982. The biggest blow came in a federal court, which overturned Fleer's 1980 decision against Topps. The court reaffirmed the validity of Topps' exclusive contracts to market baseball cards with confectionery products such as bubblegum. Relatively undaunted, Fleer merely sold its "bubblegum" cards of 1982 without the gum, substituting team logo stickers in each pack of cards. That move has not gone unchallenged by Topps, which contends the use of stickers is merely a ruse to facilitate the sale of baseball cards in illegal competition. The matter is likely to be in court for many more years. Fleer also struck out with collectors in '82. To some collectors, several errors and variations in the 660-card set seemed intentional—an attempt to stimulate the same type of demand for Fleer cards that had been brought on by the "C" Nettles error card of the previous year. Many collectors boycotted the issue entirely. A more important factor in the lack of popularity for the set, though, is the generally poor quality of the photography in the set. A majority of the photos were blurred or fuzzy, giving the set a most unprofessional look. The basic design of the cards was not bad; a large photo was surrounded by a round-cornered frame using a different color for each team. A lozenge-shaped panel at the bottom of the frame contained the player's name, team, and position. Card backs were similar to the previous year's issue, in that complete major and minor league stats were presented, but they had the added touch of a color team logo in the upper-right corner. The box with the stats was printed in yellow, while the overall design of the back was in light blue. Fleer's best innovation in the '82 set was the further refinement of its numbering scheme. Cards were still arranged in team order, with the World Series Champions (Dodgers) and American League Champions (Yankees) being the first cards in the set, followed by the rest of the teams in order of winning percentage. Within each team, though, Fleer numbered the cards in alphabetical order, a simple, logical arrangement that had never before been used in a major set. Besides the individual players cards in the set, there were 19 special cards or multi-player feature cards in the '82 Fleer offering, along with 14 checklists.

FOR

Fleer had some innovative ideas for its 1982 card set; they just weren't properly executed.

AGAINST

Poor photography, contrived error/variation cards.

NOTEWORTHY CARDS

Whether or not some—or all—of the error/variation cards in the '82 Fleer set were a deliberate attempt by the company to dupe the collectors, only one of them has any real potential to retain a major portion of its premium value. As with many Fleer and Donruss cards of 1981 and 1982, there was a reversed negative card in the 1982 Fleer set, creating a card of Padres pitcher John Littlefield that looks as if he is pitching left-handed. This card was swiftly corrected early in the print run, and it is quite scarce. Whether or not collectors in the future will feel it is necessary to have the card for a "complete" set will determine how much of its current value it holds. Also corrected relatively early was a printing error on the back of card #438, Al Hrabosky of the Braves. This card, in fact, has three variations. In the first, the "double-error" card, his first name is spelled "All," and his height is listed as 5′1″. On the first "correction," the name was spelled right, but the height was still wrong. Finally, on the third try, Fleer got the card right, giving his height as 5′10″. While the first version of this card is also quite scarce, demand is limited and decreasing; it is not the type of error collectors will pay a great deal of attention to down the road. The specialty cards contained a major boo-boo, as well. Card #639, "Perfect Game," pictures Cleveland Indians battery-mates Len Barker and Bo Diaz, in honor of Barker's perfect game of May 15, 1981, when he retired all 27 Blue Jays he faced without a baserunner. The only problem was that Diaz was not the Indians catcher in that perfect game; Ron Hassey was behind the plate. Another notable card in the specialty run pictures Pete Rose and his son, Pete Jr., as a batboy, and carries the title of "Pete and Re-Pete." Many collectors thought the card was a bit too cute for a baseball card set. There is a Cal Ripken, Jr. rookie card in the set.

VALUE

MINT CONDITION: Complete set (no variations): $15; common card, 3¢; stars, 25¢–50¢; Cal Ripken, Jr., $2.50; "All" Hrabosky, $5; Littlefield "leftie," $25. 5-YEAR PROJECTION: Below average.

1982 Fleer, Johnny Bench, Tom Seaver

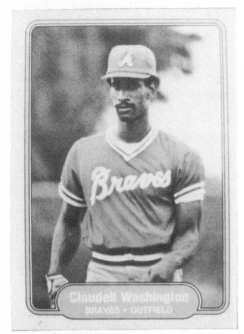

1982 Fleer, Claudell Washington

1982 Fleer, J. R. Richard

1982 Fleer, Bobby Bonds

1982 Fleer, André Dawson

1982 Fleer, Sparky Lyle

1982 Fleer, Reggie Jackson,
Dave Winfield (front)

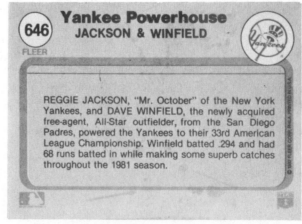

1982 Fleer, Reggie Jackson, Dave Winfield (back)

1982 Fleer, Fernando Valenzuela

1982 Fleer, Phil Niekro

1982 Fleer, Dan Driessen,
Dave Concepcion, George Foster

1982 Fleer, Gary Carter, Dave Parker

1982 Fleer, Bruce Sutter,

1982 Fleer, Len Barker, Bo Diaz,

1982 DONRUSS

SPECIFICATIONS

SIZE: 2½×3½". FRONT: Color photograph. BACK: Blue and black printing on white cardboard. DISTRIBUTION: Nationally, in packages with jigsaw puzzle pieces.

HISTORY

When federal courts upheld Topps' exclusive right to market baseball cards in conjunction with "confectionery" products (bubblegum, etc.), Donruss was undaunted. The Memphis candymaker merely created a 63-piece Babe Ruth jigsaw puzzle and inserted three pieces into wax packs with its 1982 baseball card series. After all, by 1982 kids and collectors were buying packs of baseball cards for the cards themselves, rather than for a piece of bubblegum. Donruss capitalized on the lessons learned in its premier issue, and the company's 1982 product was considerably improved. The cardboard stock was beefed up to better resist creases and more closely resemble that used by Topps and Fleer. Far fewer errors occurred in the '82 set, requiring fewer corrected variations to vex collectors. Donruss increased the size of its issue in 1982 to a total of 660 cards, including seven unnumbered checklists. A specialty group titled "Diamond Kings" was created to open the '82 Donruss cards. One well-known player was represented from each team in a painted portrait created by baseball artist Dick Perez. These artistic cards proved to be instant collector favorites. In design, the '82 Donruss series was also widely acclaimed by collectors. A large color photo dominates the face of the card, framed with a border color coordinated by team. A Donruss logo and "'82" appear in the upper-right corner. The team name appears in a baseball at the lower-left corner, while the player's name and an abbreviation for his position appear in a bat that stretches across the bottom of the card. For the back design in '82, Donruss dropped the vertical format and went with a more traditional horizontal layout. A blue box at the top contained the player's vital data, while a similar blue box at bottom featured "Career Highlights." In between was a white band containing the "Recent Major League Performance" stats. The small space allowed for these stats meant that only a few years' worth could be printed, along with career total figures. This innovation has not been widely accepted by collectors, many of whom like to see complete figures on their baseball cards. The '82 Donruss set expanded the use of multi-player feature cards to a handful, but dropped the special cards for Cy Young winners that had been part of the '81 set. Also in contrast to the previous issue, the '82 Donruss series offered one card per player, except those who appeared in the Diamond Kings group. Donruss made points with many collectors by issuing cards for managers and some coaches who were well-known as players at one time, such as Johnny Podres and Harvey Haddix. A bit more controversial was the inclusion of a San Diego Chicken card in the Donruss set. Those collectors who enjoy the Chicken's antics applauded the card, while other collectors contended that these on-field clowns have no part on a baseball card set. Whatever a collector's feelings, the card is popular and has attained a relatively high value. Overall, most collectors felt Donruss did an excellent job of improving its baseball card issue between 1981 and 1982.

FOR

A much improved major set with lots of innovative cards and concepts.

1982 Donruss, Garry Templeton

1982 Donruss, Amos Otis

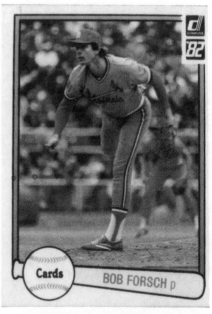

1982 Donruss, Bob Forsch

AGAINST

Again, color reproduction on the final cards was not as accurate overall as collectors have come to expect from major issues. Still a few too many errors for most collectors.

NOTEWORTHY CARDS

Rookie cards of Cal Ripken, Jr.; Steve Sax; and Kent Hrbek. Significant errors and corrected variations are: Alan Trammell regular and Diamond King cards, with name misspelled "Trammel" on the initial press run, and corrected in a second printing; Shane Rawley card with Jim Anderson photo and with correct photo; Juan Eichelberger card with Gary Lucas photo and with correct photo; Phil Garner card with reversed and correct negative; Randy Lerch card with "Braves" in ball and with correct "Brewers." The unnumbered Diamond Kings checklist will also be found with Trammell's name spelled correctly or incorrectly.

VALUE

MINT CONDITION: Complete set, $17; common card, 3¢; stars, errors, 25¢–$1; Cal Ripken, Jr., $1.50.
5-YEAR PROJECTION: Above average.

1982 Donruss, San Diego Chicken (front)

1982 Donruss, San Diego Chicken (back)

1982 Donruss, Chris Chambliss

1982 Donruss, Buddy Bell, Diamond King

1982 Donruss, Richie Zisk, Diamond King

1982 KELLOGG'S

1982 Donruss, Keith Hernandez,
Diamond King

1982 Donruss, Terry Kennedy,
Diamond King

SPECIFICATIONS

SIZE: 2⅛×3¼". FRONT: Color photograph, 3-D effect. BACK: Black printing on white cardboard. DISTRIBUTION: Nationally, complete sets available by mail.

HISTORY

"Smaller" was the key word for the 1982 Kellogg's set. The cards shrank in size to 2⅛×3¼", and the set was reduced from 66 to 64 cards. The front of the cards featured a color photo set in a scalloped blue frame with white stars up and down the sides. A script "Kellogg's" logo appears in red at the top, while the player's last name appears on the bottom, also in red. "3-D Super Stars" is in white at top, the player's position in white at the bottom. A 3-D look is imparted to the cards by laminating a piece of ribbed plastic over the photo on front. Card backs are the usual combination of player personal and career stats, and a short biography. There is no cartoon character on back; rather the script

1982 Donruss, George Foster,
Diamond King

1982 Donruss, Dave Winfield,
Diamond King

1982 Kellogg's, Carl Yastrzemski

"Kellogg's" appears over a baseball, indicating that the set could be obtained that year by sending in box tops from several brands of cereal, rather than just a single brand, along with $3.95. No cards were packaged singly in cereal boxes for the second straight year. The return to the narrower card size brought a return of the problem of the plastic facing on the card curling and/or cracking, greatly reducing the value of the card.

FOR
Inexpensive set with lots of stars and lots of room to grow in value.

AGAINST
Problem with cracking and curling; hard to find single cards because of prevalence of complete sets on the market.

NOTEWORTHY CARDS
Many of the game's new young stars make their debut in the 1982 Kellogg's set, such as Fernando Valenzuela, Tim Raines, and Ozzie Smith.

VALUE
MINT CONDITION: Complete set, $5; common card, 10¢; stars, 25¢–50¢; Rose, 75¢. 5-YEAR PROJECTION: Well above average.

1982 Kellogg's, Rickey Henderson

1982 Kellogg's, Hubie Brooks

1982 Kellogg's, Rollie Fingers

1982 Kellogg's, George Foster, Steve Carlton, Johnny Bench

1982 DRAKE'S

SPECIFICATIONS

SIZE: 2½×3½". FRONT: Color photograph. BACK: Blue and green printing on gray cardboard. DISTRIBUTION: Single cards, Northeast in packages of snack cakes; complete sets, nationally by hobby dealers.

HISTORY

Most collectors learned a valuable lesson when Drake's wholesaled its 1981 card issue to the hobby. Collectors waited in 1982 for the set to become available at a reasonable price from dealers, rather than trying to assemble it by buying family-size packages of snack cakes to get the single cards inside. The theme of the 1982 Drake's issue remained "Big Hitters," and the set once again contained 33 cards of players known for their bat-handling. Again, while the cards were produced by Topps, the design on the front was completely different from the regular Topps issue of 1982. A larger photo was used in '82 than had been the case the previous year. The player's picture gives the appearance of being an autographed snapshot "mounted" on the background by photo corners. Predominant color scheme of the National League cards is green; for the American League, red. A banner at the top of the card heralds the set as "2nd Annual Collectors' Edition," and includes a card number. There is a Drake's logo at the bottom, along with the player's name, team, and position. Card backs are quite similar to the '82 Topps, and surprisingly, do not feature a Drake's logo, though there is a Drake's copyright line at the bottom. Differing from the regular Topps set, the 33 cards are numbered alphabetically.

FOR

Good inexpensive regional set with lots of stars in different poses.

AGAINST

Design is still too busy for many collectors' taste. Otherwise, you can't find much fault with the set.

NOTEWORTHY CARDS

Virtually everybody in the set is a star. Padres catcher Terry Kennedy's card uses the same photo as his regular 1982 Topps card.

VALUE

MINT CONDITION: Complete set, $5; common card, 10¢; superstars, 50¢–75¢. 5-YEAR PROJECTION: Average or slightly above.

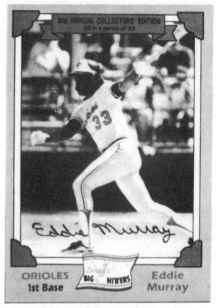

1982 Drake's, Eddie Murray

1982 Drake's, Bill Madlock

1982 Drake's, Jack Clark

1982 Drake's, Dave Winfield

1982 SQUIRT

1982 Drake's, Gary Carter

1982 Drake's, Buddy Bell

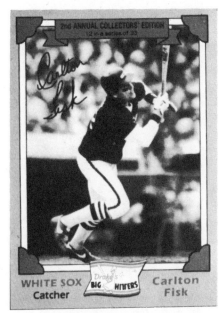

1982 Drake's, Carlton Fisk

1982 Drake's, Bill Buckner

SPECIFICATIONS

SIZE: Card: 2½×3½″, Panel: 2½×9″. FRONT: Color photo on red/yellow/green background. BACK: Black and yellow printing on white cardboard. DISTRIBUTION: Nationally, in cartons and six-packs of soda.

HISTORY

Buoyed by the success (?) of their 1981 issue, Squirt was back at it in 1982 with another Topps-produced baseball card issue. This time they really went overboard. The 22 cards in the set were distributed in four different types of arrangements—and collectors don't seem to care for any of them. As with the 1981 cards, virtually the entire issue immediately went out the back doors of soda warehouses into the hands of card dealers. The hobby seems to find the whole 1982 Squirt issue too much to fathom. Putting it into its simplest terms, the cards were issued in four ways: 1) One card on a ring-tab panel, with scratch-off contest; 2) Two cards on a ring-tab panel, no contest; 3) One card on a can-hanger panel, with scratch-off contest; and 4) One card on a can-hanger panel, no contest. Most collectors seem content to acquire any one set of panels that gives them the complete set of 22 individual cards. There are indications that several of these panel types are much scarcer than others, but nobody seems to know—or care. Certainly they don't care enough to pay more money for one than another.

FOR

It's a nice group of recent superstar cards at a reasonable price. Someday somebody may sort out the whole mess and find out some of these are really scarce. Whether collectors will give a darn is another story. You'd think, though, that someday collector demand would start to pick up on the better-known superstars.

AGAINST

The whole issue was so totally confusing it turned collectors off. Besides, the cards are too gaudy.

VALUE

MINT CONDITION: Complete set of panels, any type, $5–$7.50. 5-YEAR PROJECTION: Above average.

1982 K-MART

SPECIFICATIONS

SIZE: 2½×3½". FRONT: Color photo. BACK: Red and blue printing on gray stock. DISTRIBUTION: Nationally, sold in K-Mart discount department stores.

HISTORY

This set is probably the least popular item from the great baseball card flood of 1982. Topps and K-Mart conspired to produce a 44-card set marking the 20th anniversary of the discount department store chain. The "Limited Edition Collectors' Series" came in a cardboard box with a stick of bubblegum. Original price was $1.97, then $1, then two for $1, and finally, K-Mart was selling the sets for a dime apiece. The problem was simply overproduction: too many sets, not enough buyers. Forty-one of the cards honor the American League and National League winners of the Most Valuable Player award from 1962–1981 (the odd number comes because there were co-winners in the National League in 1979, Keith Hernandez and Willie Stargell). On the front these cards depict a full-color mini version of the regular issue Topps baseball card from the year of the award. Backs recap the season's performance for the player that led to the MVP award. The three cards that round out the set are season highlights cards of Don Drysdale (1968, 58⅔ scoreless innings), Hank Aaron (1974, 715 career home runs), and Pete Rose (1981, 3,631 career hits). The sets remain a glut on the collector market and they are still readily available for 25¢ to 50¢ apiece. Some card dealers use them as giveaways when you make a $5 or $10 purchase.

FOR

For half a buck there are a lot of superstars in the 44-card set. There's also a certain charm in seeing familiar cards reproduced in miniature.

AGAINST

Design is gaudy. There's too much advertising on the cards. Demand will probably never catch up with supply.

NOTEWORTHY

Two of the K-Mart cards are of special interest because they don't depict actual Topps cards in the years those players received the MVP. The cards of Fred Lynn (American League, 1975) and Maury Wills (National League, 1962) are mock-ups of what the cards would have looked like if they had been issued. In Topps' regular 1975 set, Lynn was just one of four small pictures on a "Rookie Outfielders" card. Since it wouldn't do to reproduce a multi-player card in the special K-Mart set, Topps artists gave Lynn his own 1975 rookie card after the fact. A similar situation arose with Maury Wills. Wills never appeared on a Topps baseball card until 1967. He

1982 K-Mart, Mickey Mantle

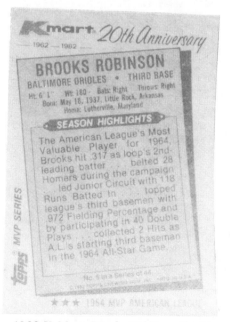
1982 K-Mart, Pete Rose

1982 K-Mart, Zoilo Versalles

1982 K-Mart, Brooks Robinson (back)

was miffed that the company had thought so little of his chances to make the big time when he was starting out in the minor leagues that he refused to allow the company to use his picture until he had been a major league star for eight years.

VALUE
MINT CONDITION: Complete set, 50¢. 5-YEAR PROJECTION: Above average.

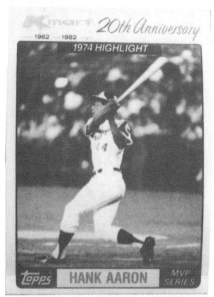

1982 K-Mart, Hank Aaron

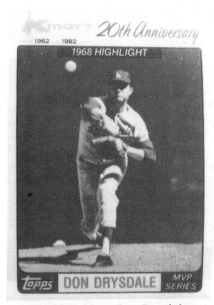

1982 K-Mart, Don Drysdale

1982 CRACKER JACK

SPECIFICATIONS
SIZE: 2½×3½″. FRONT: Color photograph. BACK: Red, blue, and black printing on gray cardboard. DISTRIBUTION: Nationally, via mail-in offer.

HISTORY
In 1982, in conjunction with its sponsorship of the first annual Old-Timers Classic game to benefit the former major league players' relief fund, Cracker Jack issued a 16-card set of "All Time Baseball Greats" from the 1940s through the 1970s. The cards were printed on sheets with eight player cards and a Cracker Jack advertising card at the center. Eight National League players were on one sheet, eight American Leaguers on the other. The cards were printed by Topps. Sets of the Cracker Jack cards could be obtained by sending in box tops and 50¢. Some dealers were apparently able to make connections that allowed them to obtain quantities of the sheets, as well. Most of the sheets ordered by collectors directly

from Cracker Jack were beat up in the mail and arrived in creased condition; collectors who desired Mint cards almost had to buy them from hobby sources. Design of the Cracker Jack cards is interesting and attractive. The player's photo is set against a background of the actual Cracker Jack product. A banner at the bottom of the card (red for American League, green for National League) had the player's name and position in white type. The name of the team with which the player is most often associated is printed in black script to the lower left of the photo, while the famous Cracker Jack logo of the sailor boy and dog appears to the right. Card backs give personal information about the players, a career summary, and lifetime batting or pitching record. There is also a color Cracker Jack logo on the back of the cards. The cards are separated on the sheets by black dotted lines. They can be cut into individual cards, but few collectors do so. Value of the set is greatest in complete sheet form. It is interesting to note that Topps generally chose photos or artwork of the players as they appeared later in their careers. Some of the pictures used on the '82 Cracker Jack cards appeared on earlier Topps cards. The paintings of Bob Feller and Ralph Kiner were used on 1953 Topps cards, while the photo of

1982 Cracker Jacks, National League All Time Baseball Greats (uncut sheet, back)

Brooks Robinson appears—in black and white—on a Topps Deckle-Edge card of 1969. It is interesting to note that not all of the players who have cards in the Cracker Jack card set played, or even made an appearance, at the old-timers' game.

FOR
Nice uncut mini-sheet. Unique design. Lots of stars.

AGAINST
Sheet format makes it tough to get single cards of desired players.

NOTEWORTHY CARDS
Virtually everybody in the set is a Hall of Famer—or should be.

VALUE
MINT CONDITION: Uncut sheets, complete set, $8; single cards, 25¢–50¢. 5-YEAR PROJECTION: Above average.

1982 GRANNY GOOSE A's

SPECIFICATIONS
SIZE: 2½×3½". FRONT: Color photograph. BACK: Black printing on white cardboard. DISTRIBUTION: Northern California, single cards in bags of potato chips; complete sets at Oakland A's game.

HISTORY
The 1982 Granny Goose Oakland A's set is nowhere near as rare as the 1981 issue. While the cards continued to be issued in twin-bags of potato chips, complete sets of 15 were also given away at the Fan Appreciation Day ballgame in Oakland. The '82 Granny Goose set is identical in design to the previous year's issue; you have to read the write-up on the back of the card to determine which year is which. The front features a color photo of the player surrounded by a white border. A green box at the bottom has the player's name, position, and uniform number. A green-on-yellow A's team logo appears in the lower-left corner. Backs are printed in black, on thin white cardboard, and contain just a

few personal statistics, along with an A's logo. The cards given away at the stadium were not in contact with potato chips, and because they have no grease stains, collectors prefer them.

FOR
Good, relatively inexpensive regional set for the team collector.

AGAINST
Design is identical to the previous year, which can be confusing.

NOTEWORTHY CARDS
Besides manager Billy Martin, high-demand players in the '82 Granny Goose set include Rickey Henderson, Tony Armas, and Dwayne Murphy.

VALUE
MINT CONDITION: Complete set, $12.50; common card, 50¢; stars, $1.50–$2. 5-YEAR PROJECTION: Average.

1982 ATLANTA BRAVES POLICE

SPECIFICATIONS
SIZE: 2⅝×4⅛". FRONT: Color photograph. BACK: Full-color on white cardboard. DISTRIBUTION: Atlanta area, individual cards given out by police officers.

HISTORY
In the same mold as its 1981 police set, the 1982 Atlanta Braves Police issue features cards of 24 players, five coaches, and manager Joe Torre. Front has a color photo at center. In the wide white border are team and Police Athletic League logos, and a notation of the team's record-setting 13-game winning streak at the beginning of the season. The player's uniform number on front is the card number, as well. Card backs feature the Coke and Hostess logos, a write-up on the player, and a safety or anti-crime tip.

FOR
Good item for team collectors.

AGAINST
Same old design; cardboard is too light.

NOTEWORTHY CARDS
Pitching coach Bob Gibson, Dale Murphy, Phil Niekro, Bob Horner, rookie cards of Brett Butler and Steve Bedrosian. Bob Watson card is supposedly scarcer than the others in the set.

VALUE
MINT CONDITION: Complete set, $12.50; common card, 25¢; stars, 50¢–$1. 5-YEAR PROJECTION: Above average.

1982 MILWAUKEE BREWERS POLICE

SPECIFICATIONS
SIZE: 2¹³/₁₆×4⅛". FRONT: Color photograph. BACK: Blue printing on white cardboard. DISTRIBUTION: Milwaukee area, single cards given away by police officers, complete sets given out at ball game.

HISTORY
The 1982 Milwaukee Brewers Police set began a trend toward having different police jurisdictions hand out the same team's cards, the only difference being the name of the police agency on the front of the card. The 1982 Brewers Police cards can be found with the names of the Milwaukee, New Berlin, or State Fair Police Departments as the third line of type on the front of the card. Like most other police sets, the cards were designed to build better rapport between the police department and local children, who had to approach the neighborhood cop and ask for the cards. The Brewers Police sets were also given away at a special Baseball Card Day promotion at County Stadium to kids 14 and under. Card

fronts feature the familiar color photo in a wide white frame, with the player's name, position, and uniform number. The uniform number is also the card number in the Brewers set. Backs have a background badge, the Brewers logo, and a safety or anti-crime tip. There are 30 cards in the '82 Brewers set: 25 different player cards, a team card, and separate cards for manager Buck Rodgers, the coaches, and general manager Harry Dalton.

FOR
Nice item for team collectors.

AGAINST
Odd size, compared to the now-standard 2½×3½″ format for most modern baseball cards. Cardboard is extra light, making the cards susceptible to damage.

NOTEWORTHY CARDS
Robin Yount, Rollie Fingers.

VALUE
MINT CONDITION: Complete set, $10; common card, 25¢; stars, 50¢–75¢. 5-YEAR PROJECTION: Above average.

1982 RED LOBSTER CUBS

SPECIFICATIONS
SIZE: 2¼×3½″. FRONT: Color photograph. BACK: Black printing on white cardboard. DISTRIBUTION: Chicago, team issue, at "Baseball Card Day" promotional game.

HISTORY
Red Lobster seafood restaurants and the Chicago Cubs combined in 1982 to issue a special 28-card set given away at a Baseball Card Day promotional game on August 20. Each of the players on the 25-man roster is pictured in the set, which also includes a team photo card, a card for manager Lee Elia, and a card with the five coaches. Slightly narrower than the standard modern card width of 2½″, the Red Lobster Cubs set has a border-

less color action photo (taken at Wrigley Field) on the front, with a facsimile autograph and a single line of type with the player's name, uniform (card) number, and abbreviation for his position. Backs have complete major and minor league stats, along with play-off and World Series stats, where applicable—that means when the player was with a team other than the Cubs—and an ad for Red Lobster. The cards are printed on relatively thin cardboard, and were not cut evenly—most cards are a fraction of an inch off their nominal dimensions. The cards are not all that common, and represent a true regional issue.

FOR
Great limited edition set for the team collector.

AGAINST
Rather unprofessional appearance; single cards are hard to find, nearly always sold as a complete set.

NOTEWORTHY CARDS
None to speak of.

VALUE
MINT CONDITION: Complete set, $8; common card, 25¢; stars, 50¢. 5-YEAR PROJECTION: Above average.

1982 Red Lobster Cubs, Lee Elia (front)

1982 Red Lobster Cubs, Lee Elia (back)

1982 LOS ANGELES DODGERS POLICE

SPECIFICATIONS

SIZE: $2^{13}/_{16} \times 4^{1}/_{8}$". FRONT: Color photograph. BACK: Blue printing on white cardboard. DISTRIBUTION: Los Angeles area, individual cards given out by police officers; complete sets available at special ball game.

HISTORY

Containing 30 cards, the 1982 Dodgers Police set presents more than just 25 individual players. Special cards commemorate the team, the Western Division, and National League and World Series victories. There are also a trophy-checklist card and one for manager Tommy Lasorda. Fronts follow the basic police card format of a color photo surrounded by a wide border and a few lines of type below. The cards are numbered by player uniform number on the front of the card. Backs have biographical and career information on the player along with a safety tip. Individual cards were given out by officers to neighborhood children, and complete sets were available at a special Baseball Card Day promotion at the ballpark.

FOR

Great item for team collector.

AGAINST

Cheap cardboard, prone to damage.

NOTEWORTHY CARDS

Rookie card of Steve Sax, plus cards of Garvey, Guerrero, and Valenzuela.

VALUE

MINT CONDITION: Complete set, $7.50; common card, 20¢; stars, 50¢–75¢. 5-YEAR PROJECTION: Above average.

1982 HYGRADE EXPOS

SPECIFICATIONS

SIZE: 2×3". FRONT: Color photograph. BACK: Black printing on white cardboard. DISTRIBUTION: Quebec area, single cards in packages of meat products; complete sets by mail-in offer.

HISTORY

Collectors who are too quick to jump on every new issue really got burned with the Hygrade meats set of 24 Montreal Expos players in 1982. While single cards were issued in packages of the company's meat products, there was a mail-in offer by which the complete set, plus a display album, could be obtained for $3. Before most U.S. collectors had heard of the mail-in offer, the frenzy to obtain the newest regional set had driven prices to near $45, and Canadian dealers and collectors with sources of the cards were selling all they could get. The cards, printed on very thin cardboard, are smaller than the current baseball card standard and feature rounded corners. The top half of the card front contains a borderless color photo of the Expo player, with a yellow-and-red Hygrade logo in the corner. A white strip at the bottom of the card contains the player's name and uniform number. There is no card number other than the uniform number on front. Card backs, written entirely in French, contain an offer for the album to house the set.

FOR

While the set is not as rare as was first thought, it is quite scarce, and a nice item for the Expos team collector.

AGAINST

The fact that many collectors were burned on the price of the set has turned off a lot of other hobbyists. Besides, the cards are too small and have rounded corners, neither of which is favored by most modern collectors. The thin stock on which they are printed is also a handicap since it makes the cards prone to damage.

NOTEWORTHY CARDS

All the Expos stars of 1982 are present: Gary Carter, Tim Raines, Andre Dawson, Al Oliver, etc., along with a rookie card of Terry Francona.

VALUE

MINT CONDITION: Complete set, $18; common card, 75¢; stars, $2–$3. 5-YEAR PROJECTION: Average.

1982 ZELLERS EXPOS

SPECIFICATIONS

SIZE: Three-card panel, 7½×3½"; single card, 2½×3½". FRONT: Color photograph. BACK: Blue printing on white cardboard. DISTRIBUTION: Canada, three-card panels at Zellers department stores.

HISTORY

The 1982 Montreal Expos card set produced and distributed by Zellers department stores in Canada is one of the largest regional sets of modern times. The set consists of 60 individual cards in the form of 20 three-card panels. Each panel is numbered, and each card on the panel is lettered, as "1A, 1B, 1C." The cards feature baseball playing tips from 11 different Expos players and coach Billy Demars. The front of the card has a circular photo of the player at center, surrounded by red, white, and blue rings, on a yellow background. There is a red Zellers logo at top center, flanked by a pair of circles, also in red, announcing that the cards contain "Baseball Pro Tips" in English and French. The player's name and the name of the lesson appear below the photo. On back, the playing tip is explained, again in both languages, along with another Zellers logo and the player's name. Because the cards were originally distributed as three-card panels, they are most valuable when they are in that form. Cards that have been separated have considerably less value.

FOR

An interesting set for the team collector; unusual format.

AGAINST

Collectors don't generally favor cards that offer playing tips; in general the hobbyists want cards that are a picture of the player, and nothing more.

NOTEWORTHY CARDS

Star catcher Gary Carter is featured on 15 of the 60 cards; other Expos stars like Tim Raines and Andre Dawson are also among the "instructors" in the set.

VALUE

MINT CONDITION: Complete set (in panels), $10; common player panel, 50¢; star player panel, $1; single cards, 20¢–25¢. 5-YEAR PROJECTION: Below average.

1982 Zellers Expos, Gary Carter (front)

1982 Zellers Expos, Gary Carter (back)

1982 Zellers Expos, Scott Sanderson

1983 Zellers Expos, Terry Francona

1982 Zellers Expos, André Dawson

1982 Zellers Expos, Tim Raines

1982 WHEATIES INDIANS

SPECIFICATIONS
SIZE: $2^{13}/_{16} \times 4^{1}/_{8}''$. FRONT: Color photograph. BACK: Blue printing on white cardboard. DISTRIBUTION: Cleveland team issue, given away at special games and sold at souvenir shop.

HISTORY
For the first time in 30 years, Wheaties cereal produced a baseball card set in 1982. Unlike earlier issues, which featured players of many sports and teams, the 1982 issue included only Cleveland Indians. The 30-card set includes 25 players, individual cards for the four coaches, and one card for the manager. The cards were given out ten at a time during three special promotional games (May, June, July), and the set was subsequently placed on sale at the team gift shop. In design, the '82 Wheaties Indians closely resemble recent police sets. The cards feature color photos (many of them game-action) surrounded by a wide white border. The player's name and position appear below, at center. There is a color Indians team logo in the lower-left corner and a Wheaties logo in black at right. Card backs have only a Wheaties advertisement. The cards are unnumbered, and printed on relatively thin cardboard.

FOR
Attractive regional set for the team collector; inexpensive.

AGAINST
Lack of stats; the fact that the set continued to be sold in the Indians' gift shop after it was issued made it impossible for the price to rise.

NOTEWORTHY CARDS
Rookie card of Von Hayes. All the stars of the Cleveland Indians.

VALUE
MINT CONDITION: Complete set, $5; common card, 15¢–20¢; stars, 25¢–50¢; Hayes, 75¢. 5-YEAR PROJECTION: Above average.

1982 COCA-COLA REDS

SPECIFICATIONS
SIZE: $2\frac{1}{2} \times 3\frac{1}{2}''$. FRONT: Color photograph. BACK: Red and black printing on gray cardboard. DISTRIBUTION: Cincinnati area, in cartons of Coca-Cola.

HISTORY
In contrast to the 1981 Coke cards, the 1982 issue is a true regional set, produced by Topps for distribution in the Cincinnati area with purchases of soda. The 22 player cards all feature Cincinnati Reds. A "header" advertising card, which was distributed with each cello pack of three player cards, offered uncut sheets of Topps cards. While the design of the '82 Coke Reds is virtually identical to the regular Topps set, seven of the cards feature different photos. Six of those players —Cedeno, Harris, Hurdle, Kern, Krenchicki, and Trevino—were traded to the Reds and appear in the regular '82 Topps set in different uniforms, while Paul Householder appeared in the '82 Topps set on a "Reds Future Stars" card. Otherwise, the only difference on the card fronts is the addition of a red and white square Coke logo in the upper corner. On back, rather than the green and blue of the regular Topps issue, the Coca-Cola Reds have red and gray colors. There is also a card number, Coke logo, and trademark information on the back. Cards are numbered alphabetically in the group.

FOR
A nice regional set that few collectors realize is as scarce as it actually is. Once they do, expect prices to rise.

AGAINST
Too similar in design and most photos to the '82 Topps regular issue to attract the average collector.

NOTEWORTHY CARDS
Besides the different poses in the set, the '82 Coke Reds contain regional cards of Tom Seaver and Johnny Bench.

VALUE
MINT CONDITION: Complete set, $4.50; common card, 10¢; Soto, 25¢; Seaver, Bench, 75¢. 5-YEAR PROJECTION: Above average.

1982 COKE-BRIGHAM'S RED SOX

SPECIFICATIONS
SIZE: $2\frac{1}{2} \times 3\frac{1}{2}''$. FRONT: Color photograph. BACK: Red and black printing on gray cardboard. DISTRIBUTION: Boston area, with soda and ice cream purchases; nationally, through hobby dealers.

HISTORY
Here's another case where a large portion of what was supposed to be a regional baseball card premium issue was diverted to hobby dealers. Co-sponsored by Coca-Cola and Brigham's ice cream stores, and produced by Topps, this 22-card issue of Boston Red Sox players was intended to be distributed at the soda fountains in three-card cello packs with a purchase of Coke or ice cream. An advertising "header" card in each pack offered uncut sheets of 1982 Topps cards for sale. The set soon became widely available through hobby channels. Photos on the cards, and the basic design, are the same as the regular-issue 1982 Topps cards. On the front, a Brigham's logo in the upper-left corner and a Coca-Cola logo in the upper-right corner are the only discernible differences, though most collectors say the printing and color quality on these cards is superior to the regular '82 Topps cards. On back, the color scheme has been changed from the green and blue of the regular Topps set to red and gray. Card numbers were also changed, and are presented alphabetically. Brigham's and Coke logos also appear on the back.

FOR
Somewhat different variety for Red Sox collectors. Plus, they are, after all, Topps cards.

AGAINST
They're not different enough to excite most collectors.

NOTEWORTHY CARDS
Carney Lansford, Jim Rice, Carl Yastrzemski.

VALUE
MINT CONDITION: Complete set, $3; common card, 8¢; Lansford, 25¢; Rice, 50¢, Yaz, $1. 5-YEAR PROJECTION: Average.

1981 TOPPS

SPECIFICATIONS
SIZE: 2½×3½″. FRONT: Color photograph. BACK: Red and black printing on gray cardboard. DISTRIBUTION: Nationally, in 30¢ and 49¢ gum packs.

HISTORY
Once again in 1981, the Topps baseball card set contained 726 different cards. Because the set was printed in six sheets of 132 cards each, there were again 66 double-printed cards in the '81 set. That is, each sheet featured one row of 11 cards that was printed twice, making the cards in those rows twice as common as the cards on the rest of the sheet. Among the double-printed cards are Mike Schmidt, and the rookie card of Rich Dotson. The front of the '81 Topps cards featured a nice big photo of the player, surrounded by a thin border in one of several colors. All cards of a particular team shared the same color border. In the lower left, a baseball cap in team colors contained the player's team and position. Card backs featured complete major and minor league year-by-year stats, along with a headline and/or cartoon panels highlighting some aspect of the player's career, if there was room. The first six cards in the set feature statistical leaders of the 1980 season. Record-breakers of the previous season are also highlighted in a special run of cards, as are the 1980 Play-offs and World Series. Team photo cards are included in the set for the last time, with the manager's photo in the upper corner and a team checklist on the back. Once again,

three "Future Stars" of each team share a card in the 1981 Topps set.

FOR
Nice design; all the stars, lots of currently hot rookies and the game's newest stars.

AGAINST
After a year without featuring its logo on the front of the card, and faced with national gum-pack competition for the first time since 1963, Topps once again added its name to the front of the cards in 1981, in a small white baseball in the lower right-hand corner. Most collectors feel these logos are an unnecessary design element that just clutters the card. Because of the competition from Fleer and Donruss, the 1981 Topps cards were issued earlier than ever before, making their appearances in some areas prior to the first of the year. This meant that few of the post-season trades could be reflected in the issue, and it set the stage for the first of Topps' recent Traded sets (see following listing).

NOTEWORTHY CARDS
Rookie cards of Fernando Valenzuela, LaMarr Hoyt, Al Holland, Kirk Gibson, Leon Durham, Harold Baines, Mike Boddicker, Britt Burns, Tim Raines, Tony Pena, and Lloyd Moseby (50¢–$2 apiece).

VALUE
MINT CONDITION: Complete set, $24; common card, 4¢; superstars, 50¢–$1. 5-YEAR PROJECTION: Above average.

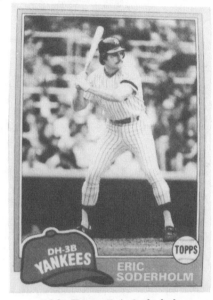
1981 Topps, Eric Soderholm

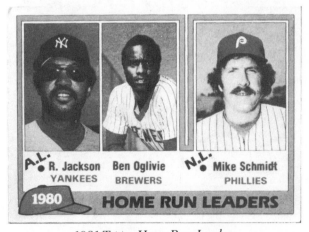
1981 Topps, Home Run Leaders

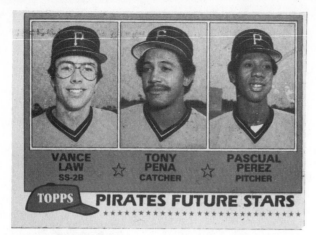

1981 Topps, Pittsburgh Pirates Future Stars

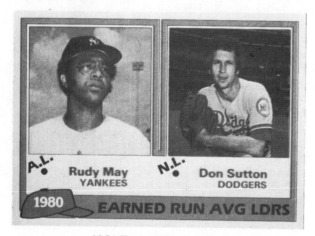

1981 Topps, ERA Leaders

1981 Topps, St. Louis Cardinals Team Checklist

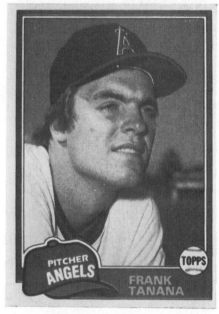

1981 Topps, Frank Tanana

1981 Topps, Darrell Porter

1981 TOPPS TRADED

1981 Topps, Joe Rudi

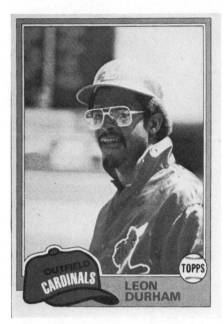

1981 Topps, Leon Durham

1981 Topps, Rollie Fingers

1981 Topps, Gaylord Perry

SPECIFICATIONS

SIZE: 2½×3½". FRONT: Color photograph. BACK: Red and black printing on gray cardboard. DISTRIBUTION: Nationally, complete sets sold only through baseball card dealers.

HISTORY

Faced with its first major baseball card competition since 1963, Topps scrambled for a competitive edge in 1981. They found it in their Traded set, which is more popularly known among collectors as the "'81 Updates." Unlike subsequent years, when the Traded sets would be numbered with a letter "T" and would feature different color printing on the back, the 1981 update series is a real extension of the 726-card "regular" issue of 1981. The 132 cards in the '81 Traded set are numbered from 727 to 858, and feature back designs identical in format to the rest of the 1981 issue. For this reason, many collectors think of the cards as the "high numbers" of the 1981 set (the first high numbers since Topps began issuing its cards all at one time in 1973). Rather than packaging the cards in gum packs for over-the-counter sales at traditional retail outlets, Topps boxed the 132-card Traded set in a red carton and made them available only through baseball card dealers. This infuriated many collectors because the issue price was quite high in comparison to the regular issue '81 cards. Cards #1–#726 could be bought for about 2¢ apiece in gum packs, but the 132-card Traded set was priced around $9, or about 7¢ a card. Still, it has proven to be a good investment; two years later the set was selling in the $14 range, a return of about 25 percent a year. By no means did all collectors dislike the set. Many praised it as being the only way that players could be pictured in their current team's uniform after a mid-season trade. In addition, the Traded set gave the season's newest "phenoms" a card of their own, to replace the "Future Stars" card they shared with two teammates.

FOR

A couple of years from now, collectors are going to overlook the fact that these cards were separately issued. They are, after all, in the same style as the rest of the 1981 Topps set, and are consecutively numbered. The set features a large number of stars and hot rookies. Being issued in far fewer numbers than the regular Topps cards of 1981, these will continue to be scarce and demand will increase as future collectors seek "complete" 1981 sets.

AGAINST

Some collectors are never going to give the Traded set their personal stamp of legitimacy. They feel that if a card set isn't available to the general public it is only a "collector's issue," regardless of whether Topps' name is on it.

NOTEWORTHY CARDS

Single-player rookie cards of Danny Ainge (who opted for pro basketball over a baseball career), Fernando Valenzuela, Tim Raines, Leon Durham, and Joe Lefebvre. Also, cards of superstars in their "new" 1981 uniforms: Dave Winfield, Gaylord Perry, Rollie Fingers, Don Sutton, Ted Simmons, Fred Lynn, Greg Luzinski, Carlton Fisk, Bruce Sutter, and Joe Morgan.

VALUE

MINT CONDITION: Complete set, $15; common card, 8¢; Hot rookies, 75¢–$1.25; Raines, $3; Valenzuela, $3.50. 5-YEAR PROJECTION: Above average.

1981 Topps Traded, Darrell Porter

1981 Topps Traded, Ken Kravec

1981 Topps Traded, Dennis Lamp

1981 Topps Traded, Leon Durham

1981 TOPPS
5x7s

SPECIFICATIONS
SIZE: 4⅞×6⅞". FRONT: Color photograph. BACK: Blue printing on white cardboard. DISTRIBUTION: Limited geographic areas in cellophane packs.

HISTORY
For the second straight year in 1981, Topps test-marketed baseball cards in the 5x7" format, and again they found only limited success. Two different designs were tried. The first consisted of 102 cards offered as "Home Team Photos." These cards featured a large color photo on the front, with a facsimile autograph and a white border. Nothing else. Backs had the player name, team, and position, and at bottom, a box with the checklist for the cards in that "home team" area. The cards were sold in limited geographic areas, corresponding to the eleven teams involved in the issue. In some cities, only one team was included: the Cincinnati Reds, the Boston Red Sox, and the Philadelphia Phillies—each of these sets had 12 cards. In other areas, two teams were included in the "home team" set. In the New York area, the set contained a dozen Yankees and six Mets; in Chicago, collectors found nine Cubs and nine White Sox; in Southern California, the grouping consisted of twelve Dodgers and half a dozen Angels; while in Texas, there were six each from the Astros and the Rangers. Mail-in offers on the cellophane packaging offered complete team sets. The second oversize issue by Topps in '81 is known to collectors as the "National Photo Issue." The 15 cards in this group were sold in areas not served by the Home Team sets. The cards were essentially the same in format, but did not have a checklist on the back. Ten of the cards in the "National" issue were the same photos as found in the Home Team set, but there were five players unique to the national set: George Brett, Cecil Cooper, Jim Palmer, Dave Parker, and Ted Simmons. The issue was widely distributed among hobby dealers and is not particularly scarce or in strong demand.

FOR
Attractive large-format cards for superstar or team collectors.

AGAINST
Many collectors will not buy oversize cards.

NOTEWORTHY CARDS
Many of the cards in the issue are better-known stars and superstars.

VALUE
MINT CONDITION: Complete set (102 "Home Team," 15 "National"), $35; common card, 25¢; superstars, 50¢–$1. 5-YEAR PROJECTION: Average.

1981 Topps 5×7s, Steve Carlton

1981 Topps 5×7s, Reggie Jackson

1981 Topps 5×7s, Ron LeFlore

1981 Topps 5×7s, Dave Kingman

1981 FLEER

SPECIFICATIONS

SIZE: 2½×3½". FRONT: Color photograph. BACK: Yellow and black printing on white cardboard. DISTRIBUTION: Nationally, in packages with bubblegum.

HISTORY

In 1980, a series of court entanglements of some 20 years' standing came to a head when a Pennsylvania court ruled that Topps Gum Company did not have exclusive rights to market baseball cards with bubblegum. This ruling opened the door for the Fleer Company of Philadelphia to make its own contracts with major league baseball and the Players' Association. In 1981, for the first time in 18 years, Fleer produced its first set of baseball cards featuring current players. Throughout the 1970s, Fleer had produced a number of baseball card sets, but they did not feature current players, or even photos of old-timers. Those cards featured drawings by Robert Laughlin and were incorporated in series like "World Series Highlights," "All-Star Games," etc. They were sold with bubblegum, but were not at all popular with kids or collectors. The 1981 Fleer set, on the other hand, was a hit with both groups, and Fleer has been a major force in the hobby ever since. Fleer's 1981 set is widely known for the large number of error and corrected cards. Most collectors feel the set is complete at 660, while others attempt to acquire each of the variations, another 40 cards, for a nice round total of 700. The '81 Fleer in all its variations was produced in three distinct press runs. The first contains all of the error cards; the second and third printings were undertaken to correct those errors. The range of Fleer error and variation cards in 1981 is too broad to describe here; a detailed checklist is a necessity. A few of the more prominent error/variation cards will be mentioned in the "Noteworthy Cards" section of this listing. For its first current-player set since 1963, Fleer came up with the remarkably reasonable idea of grouping the players by team and numbering them consecutively. Further, the order of

card groupings was determined by the team's winning percentage of the previous season. Thus, the first 27 cards in the 1981 Fleer set are the 1980 World's Champion Philadelphia Phillies. The next 23 cards are the American League Champion Kansas City Royals, and so on down the line through the Texas Rangers. There are some exceptions to this system, but by and large it was followed closely. Besides the regular players' cards, there were a number of specialty cards in the set, most of them being second poses of superstars with titles like "Mr. Baseball" (Reggie Jackson) and "Home Run King" (Mike Schmidt). There are 15 numbered checklists in the series; 14 detail the listings of two teams each, with the last one checklisting the specialty cards. A single multi-player feature card is present in the 1981 Fleer set, a card called "Triple Threat," and featuring Phillies Mike Schmidt, Pete Rose, and Larry Bowa. Design of the '81 Fleers is clean and attractive. The player's photo on the front of the card is surrounded by a round-cornered, colored stripe, with the stripe generally (but not always) the same color for each player on the same team. At the lower-left corner the team name is printed in script inside a baseball. The player's name and position are printed in a yellow panel below the photo. A white border surrounds the whole thing. On back, the cards feature a gray border. A large white panel at center gives complete major and minor league stats on a year-by-year basis. This panel is surrounded by a round-cornered yellow frame. Wording at the top of the frame describes these figures as "Complete Major and Minor League Batting Record," even on the pitchers' cards. This is one error in the Fleer set that was not corrected on any of the cards. Below the stats are a few bits of personal data on the player. His name, team, and position appear in a black panel at the top of the card. At the left of that panel is the card number in a white circle, while a corresponding circle at right has the player's cumulative major league batting average, or in the case of pitchers, earned run average. Despite the problems with the errors and variations, and the fact that the photography is not as good as that of Topps, the set has remained popular with collectors.

FOR

You've got to give Fleer credit for breaking Topps' virtual monopoly in the baseball card market. This set was a creditable effort. With one exception, the error and variation cards are not expensive, and if a collector is so inclined, they make an interesting challenge.

AGAINST

Most collectors are not interested in a lot of error cards, and such cards do reflect poorly on the set's issuer. Overall, the photography on the '81 Fleers is not as sharp as that of its principal competitor, Topps.

NOTEWORTHY CARDS

The most notable card in the 1981 Fleer set is one of the error cards. In fact, it was the first one of the error cards to be discovered and corrected, even before the so-called first printing had been completed. Thus, it is also the scarcest and most expensive of the '81 Fleer cards. The error occurred when Fleer made the understandable mistake of spelling Yankee third baseman Graig Nettles' name as "Craig" on the back of the card. The corrected version is far more com-

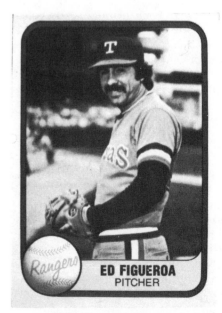

1981 Fleer, Ed Figueroa

mon. While there are more than three dozen other variations in the set, the more significant cards, those that will probably retain some measure of collectibility and premium value down the road, include: #382, Kurt Bevacqua, whose card can be found with a reversed negative (so that the "P" on his Pirates cap reads backward), and with a correct-reading negative; #493, Tim Flannery, on which a similar flopped negative shows him batting right-handed on the error card, leftie on the corrected version; #514, Jerry Augustine or Billy Travers, the photo on the card is actually Travers, though it is identified as Augustine; card front and back were corrected in the second printing; #547, Pete Vuckovich or Don Hood, in the same situation, the photo actually being Hood in both cases; and #645, Triple Threat, which can be found with or without the card number on the back.

VALUE
MINT CONDITION: Complete set (without variations), $20; common card, 3¢; stars, 25¢–75¢; Fernando Valenzuela rookie card, $2; "C" Nettles, $12. 5-YEAR PROJECTION: Average.

1981 Fleer, Graig Nettles

1981 Fleer, Dan Spillner

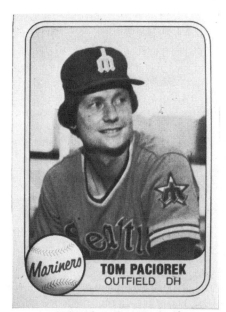

1981 Fleer, Tom Paciorek

1981 FLEER STAR STICKERS

SPECIFICATIONS
SIZE: 2½×3½". FRONT: Color photograph. BACK: Black and yellow printing on white cardboard. DISTRIBUTION: Nationally, in packs with bubblegum.

HISTORY
In general, this book will not detail the many recent issues of stickers, stamps, and other noncard issues. However, because of the size and collector popularity of the 1981 Fleer Star Stickers, they are a worthy exception. Not content to publish just a major baseball card set in 1981, Fleer came out with a subsidiary issue called "Star Stickers." Unlike other baseball player stickers and stamps of the early 1980s, the '81 Fleer issue was in the standard 2½×3½" format that card collectors have come to favor. There are 125 different player cards in the 128-sticker set; the three checklists that complete the set have sticker fronts of Reggie Jackson, Mike Schmidt, and George Brett. Pictures and design of the Star Stickers differ from those used on the Fleer baseball cards of the same year. Photos are set in the center of the sticker in an ornate yellow frame, surrounded by a deep blue border. Thumb notches at the corners with the direction "PEEL" facilitate stripping the gum-backed picture from the slick sticker backing to allow the photo to be attached to some other object. Stickers that have been thus separated are worth little or nothing to collectors. Sticker backings were identical to the backs of the players' cards in the Fleer baseball card set, except for a change in card numbers.

FOR
These are the only large-format baseball stickers of recent years; they were produced in relatively limited quantities and are really not all that common today. If demand ever picks up, the values of the '81 Fleer stickers could move upward rapidly, perhaps more rapidly than prices for Fleer's regular 1981 issue.

AGAINST

Many hobbyists do not collect items such as stickers and stamps; usually because of their odd size, but often just because most baseball card collectors are an unusual bunch who feel that "real" cards shouldn't "do" anything—like stick to other objects.

NOTEWORTHY CARDS

Most of the 125 players in the '81 Fleer stickers were stars or at least minor stars. Besides the individual player stickers, there is a "Triple Threat" sticker with Pete Rose, Mike Schmidt, and Larry Bowa.

1981 Fleer Star Stickers, Don Sutton

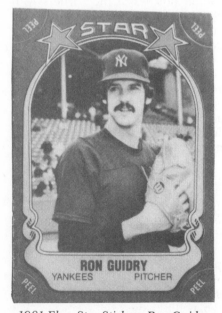

1981 Fleer Star Stickers, Ron Guidry

VALUE

MINT CONDITION, "UN-PEELED": Complete set, $35; common sticker, 20¢; stars, 50¢–$2. 5-YEAR PROJECTION: Average, perhaps a bit better.

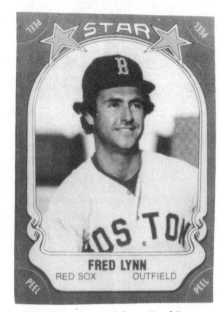

1981 Fleer Star Stickers, Fred Lynn

1981 Fleer Star Stickers, Lou Piniella

1981 DONRUSS

SPECIFICATIONS

SIZE: 2½×3½". FRONT: Color photograph. BACK: Black and red printing on white cardboard. DISTRIBUTION: Nationally, in packages with bubblegum.

HISTORY

The Memphis-based Donruss candy company, a subsidiary of General Mills, immediately took advantage of Fleer's temporary victory over Topps, which allowed competitors to market baseball cards with bubblegum. Donruss entered the 1981 "Card Wars" with a set of 605 cards. The effort was Donruss' first major sports card project, though the company had previously marketed nonsports cards with its bubblegum products, and would continue to do so. The premier Donruss baseball card effort was not particularly well-received by collectors. The cards were printed on very thin cardboard, making them easily susceptible to damage. The color reproduction was not the greatest; many of the white players looked like they had a case of raging sunburn, while many of the blacks had a purplish tint in their portraits. Donruss also had great difficulty mixing its cards in packs and boxes, and collectors often complained of getting two or more of the same card in a single pack, and handfuls of the same card in a single box. While that's not bad if you're getting Pete Rose or the latest rookie phenom, nobody wants to find two or more Joe Ferguson cards in their wax pack. Finally, and most importantly, the 1981 Donruss set is noted for the more than three dozen error/correction variation pairs in the set. The Donruss cards exhibited virtually every kind of error to which baseball cards are prone. There were wrong photos, reversed negatives, misspelled names, incorrect statistics, rewritten biographies, etc. There are so many errors that collectors need a detailed checklist to keep track of them. In all, 38 errors to player cards and four out of the five unnumbered checklists were corrected in a second print run.

While the first run errors are generally the scarcer of the two varieties, few of these variations have any appreciable degree of premium value. Certainly some of them, like the wrong or reversed photos, will probably attain higher value in the future, but most will merely become curiosities. Donruss did a few things right in 1981, as well. They reintroduced the idea of multi-player feature cards, which had last been seen in a Topps set in 1969. Their card #537, "Best Hitters," featured George Brett and Rod Carew. Donruss also featured more than one card for major superstars like Pete Rose, Reggie Jackson, and Steve Garvey. There were special cards for MVPs George Brett and Mike Schmidt and for 1980 Cy Young Award winners Steve Carlton and Steve Stone. Overall, the design of the 1981 Donruss cards was attractive. A large color photo dominated the card, surrounded by thin black and white lines and then a thick colored line, with a white border all around. A Donruss logo and the year "'81" appear in the upper-left corner, while the team name is in heavy shadowed type in the lower right. The player's name and position appear on a single line at the bottom. Backs of the '81 Donruss are a departure from what Topps had been doing. Vertical in format, they featured stats for just the previous year and lifetime cumulative. Most of the back was devoted to a "Career Highlights" section, presented chronologically. There were the usual personal data such as full name, birthplace, residence, height, weight, bats, throws, etc., along with a card number and a rather large design at the top incorporating another Donruss logo, bats, a ball, banners, and other elements, plus the line at top, "First Edition Collector Series." An interesting note: a large majority of the photos in the set were taken at Chicago's two major league parks, Wrigley Field and Comiskey Park.

FOR

Overall, an attractive premier effort for a new baseball card company.

AGAINST

Card stock too thin, easily damaged. Lots of error cards create confusion. Photo reproduction is not the best.

NOTEWORTHY CARDS

All the big stars are in the set, along with rookie cards of Tim Raines, LaMarr Hoyt, Rich Dotson, and others.

VALUE

MINT CONDITION: Complete set, $22; common card, 3¢; stars, 25¢–75¢; Rose, Best Hitters, $1; Raines, $1.50. 5-YEAR PROJECTION: Average.

1981 Donruss, Bucky Dent

1981 Donruss, Rick Cerone

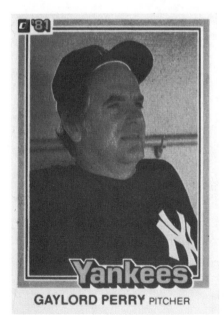
1981 Donruss, Gaylord Perry

1981 Donruss, Tony Perez

1981 KELLOGG'S

SPECIFICATIONS

SIZE: 2½×3½″. FRONT: Color photograph, 3-D effect. BACK: Black printing on white cardboard. DISTRIBUTION: Nationally, complete sets by mail.

HISTORY

There were several significant changes in the Kellogg's baseball cards for 1981. For the only time in the series, the cards were produced in the 2½×3½″ format that has been the standard for baseball cards since 1957. Also for the first time, the cards were not packaged individually in boxes of cereal. Collectors had to mail in two box tops from Sugar Frosted Flakes and $3.95 in cash to receive the complete set, which at 66 cards was the largest in number since 1971. The color photo on front of the 1981 Kellogg's cards is surrounded by a yellow frame with red stars. A white border, in turn, surrounds the whole design. Kellogg's used the expanded size of the card to greatly increase the biographical and career data appearing on the back of the card. There is a cartoon figure of Tony the Tiger on back, along with logos of the player's team, the Major League Baseball Players Association, and Major League Baseball. The change in size to a wider card seems to have licked the traditional problem of curling and cracking of the plastic "face" on the Kellogg's cards. A sheet of finely ribbed plastic is used to create a three-dimensional effect on the cards; it is a visual trick caused by setting a sharp photo of the player against an indistinct stadium background.

FOR

Large, attractive format. No problem with curling or cracking cards. Lots of stars at a low price.

AGAINST

Since the '81s were only available as complete sets, it is hard to buy desired single cards. Few dealers want to break up sets.

NOTEWORTHY CARDS

Most of the big names are here—Rose, Jackson, Yastrzemski, Schmidt, Garvey, Carlton, etc.—but there are a lot of "common" stars, too. Interesting to note that no players from the two Canadian teams, Montreal Expos and Toronto Blue Jays, are included in the 1981 set.

VALUE

MINT CONDITION: Complete set, $5; common card, 10¢; stars, 25¢–50¢; Rose, 75¢. 5-YEAR PROJECTION: Average.

1981 Donruss, Dan Petry

1981 Donruss, Dave Stieb

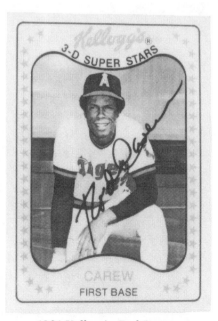

1981 Kellogg's, Rod Carew

1981 Kellogg's, Davey Lopes

1981 DRAKE'S

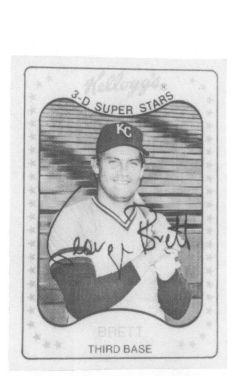

1981 Kellogg's, Steve Garvey

SPECIFICATIONS

SIZE: 2½×3½″. FRONT: Color photograph. BACK: Black and red printing on gray cardboard. DISTRIBUTION: Metropolitan Northeast in packages of bakery products; nationally by hobby dealers.

HISTORY

A lot of collectors and dealers got stung with early purchases of the 33-card "Big Hitters Collector's Edition" from Drake's. The cards, produced by Topps, were originally inserted in family-size boxes of snack cake products in the Northeast section of the country. Because 1981 was the first big year for regional card issues in a long time, collectors and dealers assumed that buying the product was the only way cards could be obtained. Wrong-o! Drake's wholesaled huge quantities in hobby channels. Early in the summer, collectors had been paying $8 for the set; by late autumn, sets could be had for $2. Drake's continued this wholesale policy within the hobby in its subsequent issues, but by then collectors had been forewarned and didn't pay big money to buy sets that had been collected from bakery boxes. The set itself is innovative, featuring well-known—both for average and power—hitting stars of the major leagues. The photo chosen for each card is a game-action picture, showing the player at bat. The photo occupies the upper two thirds of the card, has a facsimile autograph across it, and is framed in a rather gaudy series of borders, panels, banners, etc. Predominant color scheme on American League player cards is red and yellow, while National Leaguers are presented on cards with a heavy blue emphasis. A large panel below the photo has the player's name, team, and position, and a pennant with the Drake's logo. There is a card number on top, in a yellow banner. Card backs are quite similar to the regular '81 Topps cards for these players, although a Drake's logo, a new card number, and a batting tip "What Makes a Big Hitter?" are presented at the top of the card. The 1981 Drake's set was actually a return to the baseball card market for the bakery. In 1950,

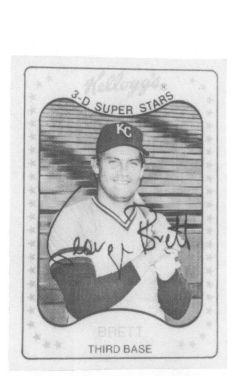

1981 Kellogg's, George Brett

the company had issued a 36-card set that has become quite valuable.

FOR

Different poses of lots of stars on a set that is at least nominally a regional issue.

AGAINST

Drake's cards still suffer somewhat from the fact that many collectors paid too much in their haste to get them. Design a bit too loud for many collectors.

NOTEWORTHY CARDS

Most of the players in the set are stars or superstars. The 1980 Rookie of the Year, Joe Charboneau, is included.

VALUE

MINT CONDITION: Complete set, $5; common card, 10¢; superstars, 50¢–75¢. 5-YEAR PROJECTION: Average.

1981 Drake's, Al Oliver

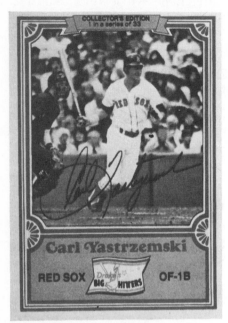

1981 Drake's, Carl Yastrzemski

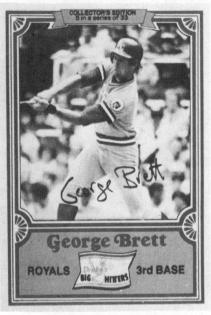

1981 Drake's, George Brett

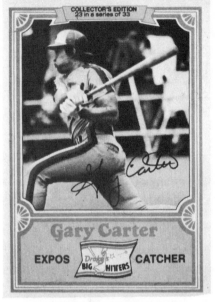

1981 Drake's, Gary Carter

1981 Drake's, Pete Rose

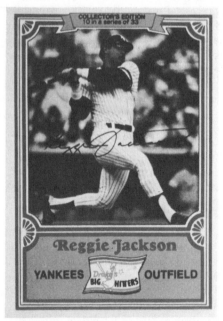

1981 Drake's, Reggie Jackson

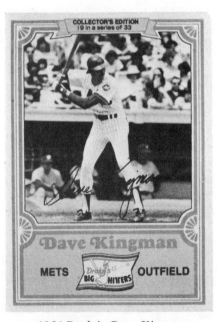

1981 Drake's, Dave Kingman

1981 SQUIRT

1981 Drake's, Jack Clark

1981 Drake's, Tony Armas

SPECIFICATIONS

SIZE: Single card, 2½×3½"; panel, 2½×10½". FRONT: Color photograph on red/white baseball, on yellow/green background. BACK: Black and red printing on gray stock. DISTRIBUTION: Nationally, one two-card panel in each carton of soda.

HISTORY

Squirt soda joined more than a dozen other relatively major issuers of baseball cards in 1981 in an attempt to boost sales. The pop maker had the right idea, getting Topps to print the cards, but the whole program fell through on the retail level. The two-card vertical panels with the ring tab at top were supposed to be found, one each, hanging on six- and eight-packs of soda. The cards, however, seldom found their way to the store shelves. Soda distributors sold the cards out the back door to local dealers and collectors, and if by chance the distributor didn't, the individual retailer did. The net result was that collectors saved a lot of money. Rather than having to search out and buy 22 cartons of Squirt at $1.50 to $2.00 apiece, the collector could pick up the complete set through hobby channels for $6 to $8. The 1981 Squirt set consists of 33 different player cards, available in 22 different panel combinations. Cards #1–#11, generally the bigger name stars, were each paired with two different cards. The cards were perforated for easy separation, but any collector who separated them probably ruined the cards' value; buyers seem to want the 1981 Squirts only as two-card panels.

FOR

They're cheap, considering they're "real" Topps cards and virtually every player is a big name. And they're not as common as you'd think for being just a couple of years old.

AGAINST

They're too gaudy for most collectors' taste. The way dealers glommed onto the cards left a bad impression on many hobbyists.

NOTEWORTHY CARDS

Virtually every player in the 1981 Squirt set is a star, or was in 1981. The set contains a card of Joe Charboneau, who went on to be named Rookie of the Year in the American League that year. He washed out of major league baseball two years later.

VALUE

MINT CONDITION: Set of panels, $17.50; set of individual cards, $10; common card, 50¢. 5-YEAR PROJECTION: Average.

1981 COCA-COLA

SPECIFICATIONS

SIZE: 2½×3½". FRONT: Color photograph. BACK: Black and red printing on gray cardboard. DISTRIBUTION: Limited areas in cartons of Coke; nationally through hobby dealers.

HISTORY

Intended as a premium with the purchase of Coca-Cola, the 132 cards in the 1981 Coke set produced by Topps rarely reached the store shelves. Dealers and collectors bought up most of the supply from distributors and put them directly into hobby channels. Eleven teams are represented in the issue, with 11 player cards and a "header" card for each team. The back of the header card offered collectors a chance to buy uncut sheets of regular 1981 Topps cards for $4, the first time uncut sheets of a major baseball card set were made available to collectors. The 11 teams represented in the '81 Coke issue are: the Astros, the Cardinals, the Cubs, the Mets, the Phillies, the Pirates, the Reds, the Red Sox, the Royals, the Tigers, and the White Sox. The cards are virtually identical to the regular issue Topps cards of 1981. The principal difference on the front is the addition of a red and white Coke logo in one of the upper corners of the photo. Backs are essentially the same as the regular cards of the same players, though a different card number has been used, a Coke logo substituted for the Topps logo in the upper-left corner, and Coca-Cola trademark information added to the bottom of the card. Because so many of these cards were bought up in case lots by dealers, they are nationally quite common for what would otherwise have been a regional issue. Some teams, though, are scarcer than others, and the '81 Coke cards are usually sold in team sets, rather than as a complete set of 132.

FOR

Scarcer variations of a major national issue.

AGAINST

Too common to have much status as a real regional issue; use of same photos as on regular '81 Topps cards gives collectors little incentive to want the cards.

NOTEWORTHY CARDS

Generally, because only 11 players per team were chosen, they are better-known players and stars.

VALUE

MINT CONDITON: Complete set, $15; common card, 5¢; superstars, 25¢-75¢. 5-YEAR PROJECTION: Average

1981 Coca-Cola, Bill Buckner

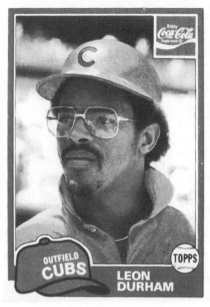

1981 Coca-Cola, Leon Durham

1981 Coca-Cola, Ed Farmer

1981 Coca-Cola, Wayne Nordhagen

1981 Coca-Cola, Rick Reuschel

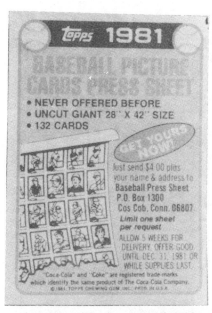

1981 Coca-Cola, Cover Card (front)

1981 Coca-Cola, Cover Card (back)

1981 GRANNY GOOSE A'S

SPECIFICATIONS

SIZE: 2½×3½". FRONT: Color photograph. BACK: Black printing on white cardboard. DISTRIBUTION: Northern California, in packages of potato chips.

HISTORY

A classic example of a modern regional set, the 15-card Granny Goose Oakland A's issue was given away one card at a time in bags of potato chips. No cards were made available to dealers or collectors. Since the cards were included only in the big $1.20 bags of chips, it was an expensive set to collect. One dealer literally bought a truckload of chips, opened each bag to acquire the card, and then gave the chips away. It was not an unprofitable venture, though, since he was selling the cards in *Sports Collectors Digest* for $5.75 apiece for commons, with stars selling for $8 to $12, and the rare Revering card (see below) at $79. The cards featured a large color photo of the player, surrounded by a white border. Below the photo was a green box containing the player's name, uniform number, and position in yellow letters. A round green and yellow A's logo appears in the lower-left corner. Card backs have a short write-up of the player's 1980 season performance, a few vital statistics, and another A's logo. The cards are unnumbered, unless you consider the player's uniform number, which appears on front and back, to be the card number. The Granny Goose cards are printed on thin cardboard and are quite susceptible to damage. Because they were packaged right in the bags with the potato chips, most of the cards picked up grease stains that detract from their appearance. Cards without the stains are worth a bit of a premium.

FOR

A truly scarce regional issue, great for the team collector.

AGAINST

Tough to find really Mint cards; an expensive set.

NOTEWORTHY CARDS

While Rickey Henderson and manager Billy Martin are the "stars" of the 1981 Granny Goose set, they are not the most valuable cards. That honor goes to the Dave Revering card. In true regional set fashion, the Revering card was withdrawn from distribution when he was traded to the Yankees on May 20. The card is one of the scarcest baseball cards of the 1980s.

VALUE

MINT CONDITION: Complete set, $145; common card, $5; Martin, $10; Henderson, $12; Revering, $90. 5-YEAR PROJECTION: Below average.

1981 ATLANTA BRAVES POLICE

SPECIFICATIONS

SIZE: 2⅝×4⅛". FRONT: Color photograph. BACK: Full-color on white cardboard. DISTRIBUTION: Atlanta area, individual cards given out by police officers.

HISTORY

The 27-card Atlanta Braves Police set of 1981 was co-sponsored by local Coca-Cola and Hostess distributors, whose color logos appear on the back of the cards. Fronts feature a color photo of the player surrounded by a wide white border. An Atlanta Police Athletic League logo appears in the upper-left corner, and—for some reason—a green bow in the upper-right. The Braves logo appears in the lower-right corner, while the player's name, uniform number, position, height, and weight are printed in the lower-left corner. Backs feature a sentence about the player and a safety or anti-crime tip. Like other police sets, the '81 Braves cards were designed to be given away to neighborhood kids by police officers in the hope of fostering better relations between the kids and the cops.

1981 ATLANTA BRAVES POLICE

FOR
Good set for team collectors.

AGAINST
Flimsy cardboard.

NOTEWORTHY CARDS
Dale Murphy, Hank Aaron (coach), Phil Niekro, Bob Horner, Gaylord Perry. The Terry Harper card is scarcer than the rest of the set.

VALUE
MINT CONDITION: Complete set, $10; common card, 25¢; stars, 50¢–$1.
5-YEAR PROJECTION: Above average.

1981 Atlanta Braves Police,
Claudell Washington

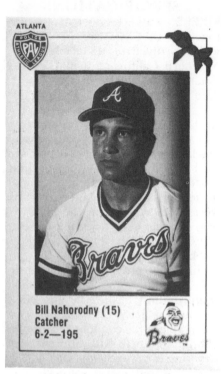

1981 Atlanta Braves Police,
Bill Nahorodny

1981 Atlanta Braves Police,
Rafael Ramirez

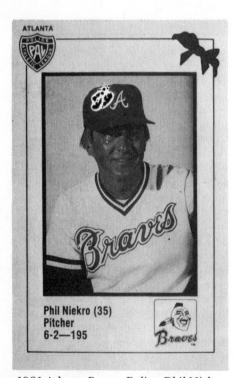

1981 Atlanta Braves Police, Phil Niekro

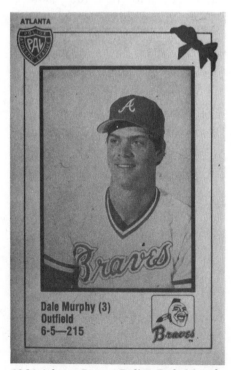

1981 Atlanta Braves Police, Dale Murphy

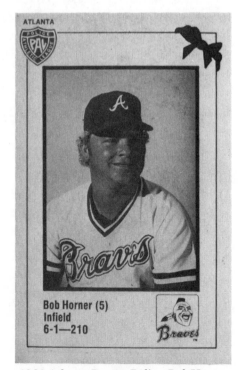

1981 Atlanta Braves Police, Bob Horner

COMPLETE BOOK OF COLLECTIBLE BASEBALL CARDS

1981 LOS ANGELES DODGERS POLICE

SPECIFICATIONS

SIZE: $2^{13}/_{16} \times 4^{1}/_{8}''$. FRONT: Color photograph. BACK: Blue printing on white cardboard. DISTRIBUTION: Los Angeles area, individual cards given away by police officers, complete sets at ball game.

HISTORY

The 32-card Los Angeles Dodgers Police set continued the basic format begun by the team a year earlier. In addition to the individual players' cards, there were cards for manager Tommy Lasorda, the coaching staff as a group, and the team. The cards combine a color photo on the front with a Dodgers script logo. The player's name, position, and uniform number (also card number) appear under the photo, along with a dateline. Card backs contain a miniature LAPD badge at the bottom along with a safety tip ostensibly written by the player. Sets are quite common in the hobby, because complete sets were given away at baseball card night festivities at the ballpark in addition to the cards being distributed by neighborhood police officers.

FOR

Nice item for team collectors.

AGAINST

Cheap cardboard, prone to damage. Odd size.

NOTEWORTHY CARDS

Rookie card of Fernando Valenzuela, also cards of Steve Garvey, Pedro Guerrero. Cards of Ken Landreaux and Dave Stewart somewhat scarcer than rest.

VALUE

MINT CONDITION: Complete set, $9; common card, 25¢; stars, 50¢–75¢; Valenzuela, $1. 5-YEAR PROJECTION: Above average.

1981 Los Angeles Dodgers Police, Coaches

1981 Los Angeles Dodgers Police, Tom Lasorda

1981 Los Angeles Dodgers Police, Rick Sutcliffe

1981 Los Angeles Dodgers Police, Team Card

1981 SEATTLE MARINERS POLICE

SPECIFICATIONS

SIZE: 2⅝×4⅛". FRONT: Color photograph. BACK: Red and blue printing on white cardboard. DISTRIBUTION: Seattle area, individual cards given away by local police officers.

HISTORY

The one and only Seattle Mariners Police set, this contained 16 cards and was co-sponsored by local Kiwanis, Coca-Cola, and Ernst Home Centers, all of whose logos appear on the back of the card, along with a card number and a safety or anti-crime tip. Front of the cards is a common design for police sets, a large color photo on a wide white border. The player's name and position appear below the photo, with a team logo at bottom.

FOR

One-year set, great for team collectors.

AGAINST

Odd size, only 16 players represented, flimsy cardboard.

NOTEWORTHY CARDS

Floyd Bannister, Maury Wills (manager).

VALUE

MINT CONDITION: Complete set, $5; common card, 25¢; stars, 50¢. 5-YEAR PROJECTION: Above average.

1981 KANSAS CITY ROYALS POLICE

SPECIFICATIONS

SIZE: 2½×4⅛". FRONT: Color photograph. BACK: Dark blue printing on white cardboard. DISTRIBUTION: Ft. Myers, Florida, area, individual cards given away by police officers.

HISTORY

At only 10 cards, this is the smallest of modern major league baseball police sets. The Royals set was distributed by the Ft. Myers, Florida, Police Department in conjunction with a local bank and a trucking company. The Royals conduct spring training in the Ft. Myers area. Card fronts follow the tried and true format of a color photo surrounded by a wide white border. There is a facsimile autograph on the face of the card, along with a team logo, and player name, position, and personal data. The cards are unnumbered. Card backs of the Royals set are unusual in that they contain recent seasons' stats for the player, along with a safety message and sponsors' logos.

FOR

Good item for team collectors.

AGAINST

Small set, odd size; lightweight cardboard is prone to damage.

NOTEWORTHY CARDS

George Brett, Willie Wilson.

VALUE

MINT CONDITION: Complete set, $12.50; common card, 75¢–$1; Wilson, $2; Brett, $4. 5-YEAR PROJECTION: Above average.

1980 TOPPS

SPECIFICATIONS

SIZE: 2½×3½". FRONT: Color photograph. BACK: Black and blue printing on gray cardboard. DISTRIBUTION: Nationally, in packages with bubblegum.

HISTORY

In basic design, the 1980 Topps set is quite close to the 1974 issue. A round-cornered photo at center of the card is framed in the upper left and lower right by colored pennants. The flag at top carries the player's position, with the player's name in the white border to the right. The lower pennant has the team name. The Topps logo does not appear on the front of the 1980 cards, as it has done every other year since 1979. There is a facsimile autograph across the face of the card. Card backs are a traditional mix of major league stats, personal information, a few headlines about the player's best performances, and a cartoon drawing at left about the player. The Topps set for 1980 again numbered 726 cards. Since Topps prints its cards on six sheets of 132 cards each, this meant that one row of 11 cards on each sheet was printed twice. Among the superstars who populate the 1980 double-prints are Fred Lynn, Mike Schmidt, Rod Carew, and Carl Yastrzemski. Specialty runs in the 1980 set include a seven-card group of statistical leaders from the American and National Leagues in 1979, and cards featuring highlights of the previous season. Rookie cards in 1980 were again arranged by team, three players to a card, this year in color.

FOR

The set represents good value for the current price tag. The design is attractive and there are probably some superstar rookie cards yet to be found.

AGAINST

There's not too much bad you can say about the set; a typical Topps effort in the days before Fleer and Donruss became competitors.

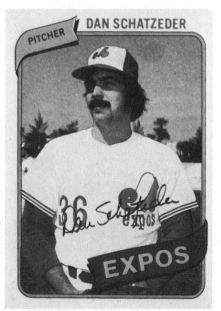

1980 Topps, Dan Schatzeder

1980 Topps, Kansas City Royals Future Stars

1980 Topps, Home Run Leaders

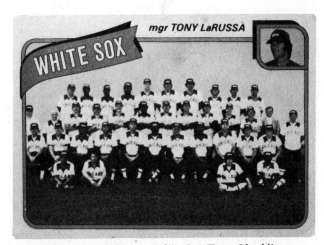

1980 Topps, Chicago White Sox Team Checklist

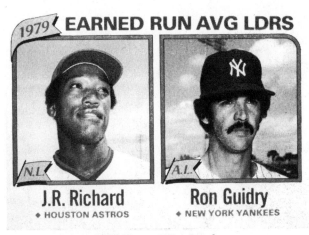

1980 Topps, ERA Leaders

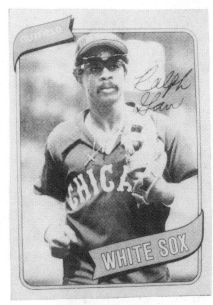

1980 Topps, Ralph Garr

NOTEWORTHY CARDS

Topps was known to use old photos on its team cards, but in the 1980 set, they really reached for one, using a 1977 picture of the White Sox to represent the current year's team. The best rookie cards of 1980 weren't on the three-player "Prospects" cards; Rickey Henderson and Dave Stieb had their premier cards all to themselves. Among the team prospect cards, the big names are Dickie Thon on the Astros and Dan Quisenberry on the Royals.

VALUE

MINT CONDITION: Complete set, $30; common card, 5¢; superstars, $1–$2; Henderson, $4. 5-YEAR PROJECTION: Above average.

1980 TOPPS SUPERSTAR PHOTOS

SPECIFICATIONS

SIZE: 4⅞×6⅞". FRONT: Color photograph. BACK: Black printing on gray or white stock. DISTRIBUTION: Test-marketed in different manners in selected geographic areas.

HISTORY

A very recent example of how market hype can stimulate demand, the 1980 Topps "Superstar Photo" issue was ostensibly a test issue to determine the extent of demand for large-format cards. Dealers, however, quickly gobbled up available supplies, and as with many Topps test issues of the time, the gum company never really had a chance to gauge demand among the youth market toward whom they claim to target most of their offerings. The 60 cards (mostly stars and superstars) have an attractive white-bordered color photo on the front, with only a facsimile autograph in blue ink to identify the player. Backs of all cards have the player's name, team, position, and card number. The set was issued on two different cardboard stocks. The first issue was on thick cardboard with a white back; the second version is on thinner cardboard

with a gray back. The backs of the latter version carry a large Topps logo at center. Six of the biggest names in the set were triple-printed, making them much more common than the remaining 54 cards, but no less valuable. There was considerable agitation in the hobby at the time of issue, and for a while thereafter, to price the supposedly scarcer "white backs" significantly higher than the "gray backs." This seems to have died down now and few collectors are willing to differentiate between the two versions, or pay a premium for one of them.

FOR

Extremely attractive large-format photos of superstars at an extremely low price; cheaper by far than the regular issue Topps card of the same year.

AGAINST

Dealers who are buried in these cards probably bought them at inflated levels and have been reluctant to sell at the prices collectors are willing to pay. This oversupply may hang over the hobby for quite some time until the demand catches up with supply.

1980 Topps Superstar Photos, Mike Schmidt

1980 Topps Superstar Photos, Willie Stargell

1980 Topps Superstar Photos, Rod Carew

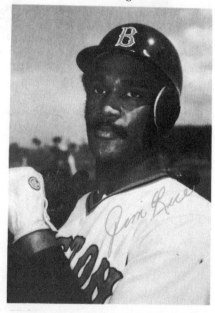

1980 Topps Superstar Photos, Jim Rice

VALUE

MINT CONDITION: Complete set, $10; common card, 10¢; star, 25¢; superstar, 50¢. 5-YEAR PROJECTION: Above average.

1980 KELLOGG'S

SPECIFICATIONS

SIZE: 1⅞×3¼". FRONT: Color photograph, 3-D effect. BACK: Blue printing on white cardboard. DISTRIBUTION: Nationally, single cards in cereal boxes, complete sets by mail.

HISTORY

The 1980 Kellogg's cards were just a bit narrower than those of the previous year. A blue border with white highlights surrounds the color photo on front. A Kellogg's script logo appears in red at the top, and "3-D Super Stars" at the bottom. Diagonal yellow stripes at upper left and lower right contain the player's position and last name. The effect of depth is created on the card by use of a piece of ribbed plastic overlaying the photo. Card backs contain personal and career stats, along with a team logo and a cartoon representing the Raisin Bran cereal in which single cards were packaged. The complete 60-card set could also be obtained by sending in box tops and cash.

FOR

Attractive, inexpensive set with lots of room for future value growth.

AGAINST

Most collectors don't like the narrow format. Plastic facing on the cards is prone to curling and cracking.

NOTEWORTHY CARDS

There is a very high percentage of superstars and potential superstars in the 1980 Kellogg's set.

VALUE

MINT CONDITION: Complete set, $7.50; common card, 10¢–15¢; stars, 25¢–50¢; Rose, $1. 5-YEAR PROJECTION: Well above average.

1980 BURGER KING ALL-STARS

SPECIFICATIONS

SIZE: 2½×3½". FRONT: Color photograph. BACK: Blue and black printing on gray cardboard. DISTRIBUTION: Nationally, given away with food purchases at Burger King restaurants.

HISTORY

Finally in 1980 Burger King and Topps produced a baseball card set that was made available nationwide. It was known to many collectors as the "Pitch, Hit & Run" set partly because of the Burger King advertising on the back of the cards. The set consists of 33 player cards and an unnumbered checklist card. There are three basic subsets of cards in the 1980 Burger King set, 11 each of well-known pitchers, hitters, and speedy runners/fielders. While the set is basically styled after the regular Topps issue of 1980, there are differences. As mentioned, the backs have a Burger King ad instead of a player cartoon, and the card numbers are different from those in the regular Topps set. On the front of the cards, for the first time, a Burger King logo appears, in the upper-right corner, along with the words, "Collector's Series." Most of the photos used in the set are the same as those used on the 1980 Topps set, but a few have been changed. Since most of the players in this set are of All-Star caliber, the 1980 Burger King Pitch, Hit & Run set is in demand by superstar collectors. The set is readily available today because of hoards acquired by collectors and dealers during the promotion, but—because of the stars in the set—it is not particularly inexpensive.

FOR

A "real" specialty set with the Burger King logo to differentiate it from the Topps cards of the same year. Lots of stars. Good value at current prices.

AGAINST

Usually sold as a set; it's tough to find single cards of a particular superstar.

NOTEWORTHY CARDS

Almost all of the cards in the 1980 set are stars.

VALUE

MINT CONDITION: Complete set, $9; common card, 15¢; stars, 25¢–75¢. 5-YEAR PROJECTION: Above average.

1980 BURGER KING PHILLIES

SPECIFICATIONS

SIZE: 2½×3½". FRONT: Color photograph. BACK: Blue and black printing on gray cardboard. DISTRIBUTION: Philadelphia area, given away with food purchases at Burger King restaurants.

HISTORY

The Philadelphia Phillies were the only team to have a special Burger King regional set produced by Topps in 1980, although there was a nationally distributed All-Star set issued elsewhere (see previous listing). Finally in 1980, Burger King used a logo on the back of the card to identify its Phillies issue as being different from the regular 1980 Topps cards. Otherwise, except for the card numbers on back, the 23 Topps and Burger King cards were identical. Lots of '80 Burger King Phillies went out the back doors of the restaurants, so they are plentiful today, though certainly less numerous than their Topps counterparts.

FOR

Good regional items for Phils collectors or superstar collectors. Burger King logo on back gives cards a separate identity from Topps' issue of the same year.

AGAINST

Nothing bad to say about the set.

NOTEWORTHY CARDS

Big name Philly stars of 1980 who appear in the Burger King team set are Rose, Schmidt, Luzinski, and Carlton.

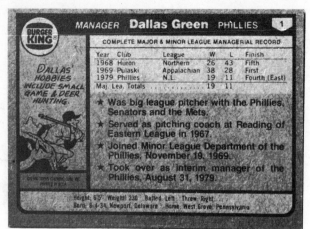

1980 Burger King Phillies, Dallas Green (back)

NOTEWORTHY CARDS

Steve Garvey, Don Sutton, Pedro Guerrero.

VALUE

MINT CONDITION: Complete set, $7.50; common card, 25¢; stars, 50¢–75¢. 5-YEAR PROJECTION: Above average.

1980 SAN FRANCISCO GIANTS POLICE

SPECIFICATIONS

SIZE: 2⅝×4⅛″. FRONT: Color photograph. BACK: Orange and black printing on white cardboard. DISTRIBUTION: San Francisco area, individual cards given out by police officers, sets given away at ball game.

HISTORY

The 1980 set is very similar in design and format to the 1979 Giants Police set, and the easiest way to tell the difference between the two is that the 1979 cards have a "#" symbol in front of the player's uniform number on the front of the card; the 1980 cards do not have the symbol. Otherwise, design is much the same: a color photo surrounded by a wide white border. Back has a combination of advertising logos, and safety and baseball tips. Like most police sets, the 31-card San Francisco Giants issue of 1980 has found its way into the hobby in good numbers.

FOR

Good set for team collectors.

AGAINST

Thin cardboard makes cards susceptible to damage.

NOTEWORTHY CARDS

Willie McCovey, Jack Clark.

VALUE

MINT CONDITION: Complete set, $7.50; common card, 25¢; stars, 50¢. 5-YEAR PROJECTION: Above average.

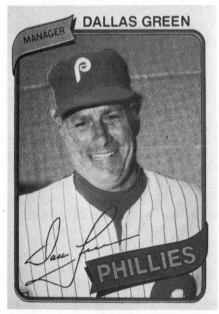

1980 Burger King Phillies, Dallas Green (front)

1980 LOS ANGELES DODGERS POLICE

SPECIFICATIONS

SIZE: 2¹³/₁₆×4⅛″. FRONT: Color photograph. BACK: Blue printing on white cardboard. DISTRIBUTION: Los Angeles area, single cards distributed by local police officers, sets given away at ball game.

HISTORY

The first issue of baseball cards by the Los Angeles Police Department, the 1980 Dodgers Police set contains 30 cards. They follow the basic format of a color photo set in a wide white border. Below the photo are the player's name, uniform number (which is also the card number), position, and a few vital stats. Card backs feature the Dodgers script logo, along with a baseball tip and a message on safety or against crime. An LAPD badge appears in the background. Besides the individual players' cards in the set, there is a team photo card.

FOR

Nice item for team collectors. Cards readily available.

AGAINST

Thin cardboard is prone to damage.

VALUE

MINT CONDITION: Complete set, $5; common card, 20¢; stars, 50¢. 5-YEAR PROJECTION: Above average.

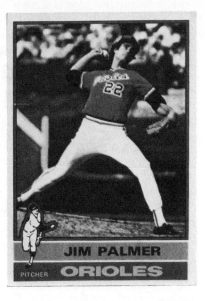

1979- 1970

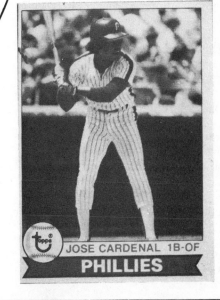

1979 TOPPS

SPECIFICATIONS

SIZE: 2½×3½". FRONT: Color photograph. BACK: Black and green printing on gray cardboard. DISTRIBUTION: Nationally, in packages with bubblegum.

HISTORY

There were no major modifications to the Topps baseball card set for 1979. The size of the set remained constant at 726 cards, and the design was little changed from the previous year. Card fronts featured a large photo at the top. At the bottom in a space only a fraction of an inch wide, the player's name and position appeared on one line, with the team name in a color banner at the very bottom. One design element disliked by most collectors made its premier appearance in 1979: Topps placed its logo on the front of the card, in a white baseball at lower left. With the exception of the ink colors, the backs of the 1979 Topps cards were about the same as in '78. The panel at right was changed from a baseball game situation to a quiz called "Baseball Dates"—questions about famous days in baseball history. In 1979 Topps weighted its double-printed cards heavily with superstars such as Joe Morgan, Steve Garvey, Tom Seaver, Johnny Bench, Jim Hunter, Buddy Bell, and Reggie Jackson. Several groups of cards within the '79 set marked record-setting performances of the previous season. Cards #1–#8 noted the league-leading performers in batting, home runs, RBIs, stolen bases, wins, strikeouts, ERA, and relief pitching. Other subsets noted major league records set during the season by current players, and there was an eight-card run marking career records, mostly by retired ballplayers. For the first time in 1979, rookie cards were arranged by team, each "Prospects" card featuring three black-and-white photos of up-and-coming players.

FOR

Nothing special to point out.

AGAINST

Use of the Topps name on the front of the card.

NOTEWORTHY CARDS

One of the more popular and valuable variation cards of recent years pops up in the Topps set of 1979. In the earliest printings of the set, Texas Rangers shortstop Bump Wills' team is identified in the banner at bottom as "Blue Jays," a team for which he had never played. The error was corrected later in the press run with the correct "Rangers" designation. It was once thought that the earlier, Blue Jays, version was the scarcer of the two, but now most collectors have swung around to the opinion that the correct version, Rangers, is scarcer. Demand for the variation has cooled somewhat in the last couple of years, but the cards still sell in the $4 area. Notable rookies making their premier baseball card appearance in the 1979 Topps set include: Ozzie Smith, Willie Wilson, Bob Horner, Pedro Guerrero, Lonnie Smith, Dale Berra, and Terry Kennedy.

VALUE

EX.-MT. CONDITION: Complete set, $40; common card, 5¢; superstars, $1–$3; Horner, Guerrero, $3–$4. 5-YEAR PROJECTION: Average, or a bit above.

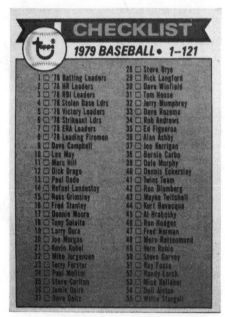

1979 Topps, Checklist

1979 Topps, Philadelphia Phillies Team Card

1979 Topps, Lance Parrish

1979 Topps, Claudell Washington

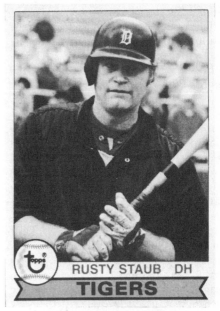

1979 Topps, Rusty Staub

1979 Topps, Jim Rice

1979 Topps, Darrell Porter

1979 Topps, Buddy Bell

1979 HOSTESS

SPECIFICATIONS

SIZE: Single card, 2¼×3¼", three-card panel, 7¼×3¼". FRONT: Color photograph. BACK: Black printing on white cardboard. DISTRIBU-TION: Nationally, a three-card panel on the bottom of snack cake boxes.

HISTORY

In 1979, ITT Continental Baking Company of Rye, New York produced the last of five consecutive baseball card issues as part of the packaging for its Hostess snack cakes. Three cards were printed on the bottom of each family-size box. The cards were meant to be cut off the boxes, but large numbers were saved by collectors in complete box form or as three-card panels. Cards left on the original packaging have traditionally attained a greater degree of value than cards removed from the boxes. In the case of three-card panels, the premium is worth some 10 to 15 percent more than the combined value of the three individual cards; for boxes, a 25 to 33 percent premium should be added to the total value of the three individual cards. To be considered in top grade a '79 Hostess card cut from the box should be neatly trimmed with even margins. Most collectors prefer the card to be cut right on the dotted line, rather than inside it. The '79 Hostess set numbers 150 cards. Hostess used much the same format as the previous year: a large square color photo and a white panel with the player's name, team, and position. In '79, however, the photo is at the bottom of the card, with the white panel at top. Card backs are virtually identical to the four previous years: a large card number in a black circle at upper left and a few lines of biographical information and career statistics. Some cards, originally on boxes of less popular snack products, or distributed in parts of the country with few collectors, are somewhat more difficult to find today.

FOR

Because they are numerically scarcer than the Topps baseball cards of the same year, common players' cards in the Hostess set are two to three times more expensive. Stars and superstar cards, however, are priced significantly lower than the corresponding Topps issue. These represent a good bet for future price appreciation. The cards are attractive, contain a high proportion of stars, and provide a collecting challenge, as they can seldom be bought as a complete set.

AGAINST

It is sometimes tough to buy a particular superstar from the Hostess series as a single card. Because of the prevalence of uncut panels and boxes, the superstar collector often has to pay for two unwanted cards to get the one desired.

NOTEWORTHY CARDS

Most of the game's big name players are included in the 1979 Hostess set, a notable exception being Carl Yastrzemski. There is a card of Yankees catcher Thurman Munson, who died in a plane crash on August 2 of that year.

VALUE

EX.-MT. CONDITION, NEATLY CUT FROM BOX: Complete set, $45; common card, 15¢–20¢; stars, $1–$2; Rose, $3. 5-YEAR PROJECTION: Above average.

1979 KELLOGG'S

SPECIFICATIONS

SIZE: 1¹⁵/₁₆×3¹/₄". FRONT: Color photograph, 3-D effect. BACK: Blue printing on white cardboard. DIS-TRIBUTION: Nationally, single cards in cereal boxes, complete sets by mail.

HISTORY

In its tenth year of baseball card production, Kellogg's made its set bigger and the individual card smaller. The magic number was three: the cards were made three sixteenths of an inch narrower, and the set was made three cards larger for a total of 60. Kellogg's continued to give its 3-D look by placing a layer of ribbed plastic over the photo. The color picture was topped by a red and yellow panel with a big "Kellogg's" logo, while a smaller yellow panel at bottom gave the player's last name and position. Blue stripes with white stars formed a frame at the sides of the pictures. The whole design was surrounded by a white border. Card backs continued to offer player biography and stats, along with a team logo and picture of Tony the Tiger. Like many of its predecessors, the 1979 Kellogg's set could be obtained by sending in box tops and cash, or the collector could buy many boxes of Sugar Frosted Flakes to get the individual cards packed inside.

FOR

Low price, good growth potential.

AGAINST

Many collectors don't like the narrow format. Cards tend to curl and crack.

NOTEWORTHY CARDS

Many of the game's current stars make their first Kellogg's appearance in the 1979 set: Ron Guidry, Paul Molitor, and Jason Thompson, to name a few. The set also includes stars who had been skipped a year or two, such as Pete Rose and Carl Yastrzemski.

VALUE

EX.-MT. CONDITION: Complete set, $10; common card, 15¢; stars, 50¢–$1; Rose, $2. 5-YEAR PROJECTION: Above average.

1979 BURGER KING

SPECIFICATIONS

SIZE: 2½×3½". FRONT: Color photograph. BACK: Black and green printing on gray cardboard. DISTRIBUTION: Philadelphia and New York areas, given away with purchases at Burger King restaurants.

HISTORY

Only two Burger King team sets were produced by Topps for 1979, the Yankees and the Phillies. Each set featured 23 player cards and an unnumbered checklist card. Although the cards of a few players had different photos on the Burger King issue, the 1979 hamburger chain's set was virtually identical to the regular-issue 1979 Topps cards—with the exception of card numbers on the backs. The cards were given away with purchases at Burger King stores in the New York and Philly areas, and collectors and dealers managed to get their share. None of the 1979 Burger King cards is scarce; though as a whole, they are harder to find than their '79 Topps counterparts.

FOR

Nice regional cards, good item for team collectors. A few superstars.

AGAINST

Being identical to the Topps cards, for the most part, the set is confusing to collectors.

NOTEWORTHY CARDS

No hot rookie cards among the '79 Burger Kings, but a few superstars: Pete Rose, Mike Schmidt, Steve Carlton, Greg Luzinski, Thurman Munson, Catfish Hunter, Ron Guidry, Tommy John, Rich Gossage, Reggie Jackson.

VALUE

EX.-MT. CONDITION: Complete set, $5–$7 per team; common card, 25¢; superstars, 50¢–$1. 5-YEAR PROJECTION: Above average.

1979 Burger King, Rich Gossage

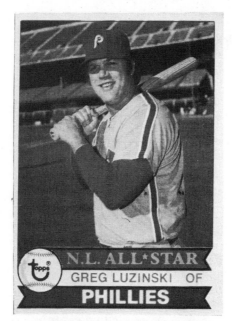

1979 Burger King, Greg Luzinski

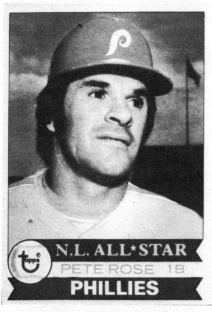

1979 Burger King, Pete Rose

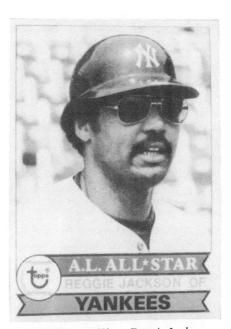

1979 Burger King, Reggie Jackson

*1979 Burger King,
New York Yankees Cover Card*

1979 SAN FRANCISCO GIANTS POLICE

SPECIFICATIONS

SIZE: 2⅝×4⅛". FRONT: Color photograph. BACK: Orange and black printing on white cardboard. DISTRIBUTION: San Francisco area, single cards given out by police officers, 15-card groups given away at ball game.

HISTORY

The 30-card 1979 San Francisco Giants police set was the first such issue by a major league club since the relatively little-known Baltimore Orioles set of 1972. Following the pattern set by the basketball card issue of the Portland Trailblazers in 1977 and 1978, the Giants cards were meant to foster better relations between local police and neighborhood children. Cards were made available, one or two at a time, to kids who walked up to the cop on the beat on their street and asked for them. Local police community relations officers felt this would encourage rapport between kids and cops. A starter set of 15 cards was also available at a special baseball card day at Candlestick Park during the 1979 season. The San Francisco Giants police set follows what has become something of a standard design for police sets. A color photo of the player is set in a rather wide white frame. A facsimile autograph appears in blue on the face of the card. Uniform number, name, and position are printed below the photo, along with a color team logo. The back contains a logo for KNBR radio, a baseball tip, and a safety or anti-crime tip. The '79 Giants police cards are numbered by player uniform number on the card front. Like most police sets, the '79 Giants cards found their way into dealer and collector hands in relatively large numbers.

FOR

Regional issue, great for team collectors. First of the modern major league baseball police sets.

AGAINST

Printed on relatively thin cardboard, prone to damage.

NOTEWORTHY CARDS

All 25 roster players, the coaches, and manager are featured in the set; big names include Willie McCovey, Jack Clark, and Bill Madlock.

VALUE

EX.-MT. CONDITION: Complete set, $15; common card, 25¢; stars, 50¢–75¢. 5-YEAR PROJECTION: Above average.

1978 TOPPS

SPECIFICATIONS

SIZE: 2½×3½". FRONT: Color photograph. BACK: Blue and orange printing on gray cardboard. DISTRIBUTION: Nationally, in packs with bubblegum.

HISTORY

In 1978, Topps added 66 cards to its 1977 total, bringing the set to 726 cards, the biggest issue since 1972. But 66 cards equal only half of one press sheet, so Topps began double-printing certain cards in 1978. One row of 11 cards on each sheet was repeated, making those cards twice as common as the rest of the cards on the sheet. There were a number of big names among the 1978 double-prints, but that doesn't seem to have held prices down too much for stars like Pete Rose, Tony Perez, Cecil Cooper, Ron Guidry, and Graig Nettles. Once again in '78, there were several subsets of special cards in the Topps issue. The first seven cards in the set honored baseball records set by Lou Brock, Sparky Lyle, Willie McCovey, Brooks Robinson, Pete Rose, Nolan Ryan, and Reggie Jackson. Statistical leaders of both leagues shared a run of eight cards in the set, while there was a three-card group marking the league play-offs and World Series. Toward the end of the set the "rookie cards" appeared, again grouping four players per card by position rather than team. Design of the 1978 Topps set was certainly one of its finest in recent years. Maximum space was devoted to the player's photo. In a wide white border at the bottom of the card, the team name appeared in script at lower left, while the player's name was in relatively small type at the right. A white baseball in an upper corner held the abbreviation for the player's position. On cards of the previous season's starting All-Stars, the baseball was replaced with a red, white, and blue shield (except for Richie Zisk, who started the All-Star Game in left field for the American League—they forgot his shield on the '78 card). Year-by-year career stats dominated the back of the cards, and at right was a baseball situation play, allowing the cards to be used to play a game of baseball.

FOR

Attractive design, good bunch of rookie cards, decent value for the current price.

AGAINST

Topps' decision to return to double-printing some cards within a set was to plague collectors for the next four years. There's no card more common than a recent Topps double-print common.

NOTEWORTHY CARDS

You could make a virtual All-Star team of the rookies who make their first appearance in the 1978 Topps set. Principal collector interest currently is on the premier card of Eddie Murray, the most expensive single card in the set. Other notable rookies include Mario Soto, Floyd Bannister, Jack Morris, Lou Whitaker, Lance Parrish, and, sharing a "Rookie Shortstops" card, Alan Trammell and Paul Molitor. Though Dale Murphy appears on card #708, "Rookie Catchers," it is not his rookie card. He appeared on a similar card in the 1977 set.

VALUE

EX.-MT. CONDITION: Complete set, $45; common card, 6¢; superstars, $1–$3; Molitor-Trammell, Parrish-Murphy, $4; Murray, $8. 5-YEAR PROJECTION: Above average.

1978 Topps, Phil Niekro

1978 Topps, Nolan Ryan

1978 Topps, Jack Clark

1978 Topps, Eddie Murray

1978 Topps, Pete Rose

1978 Topps, Promotion Panel

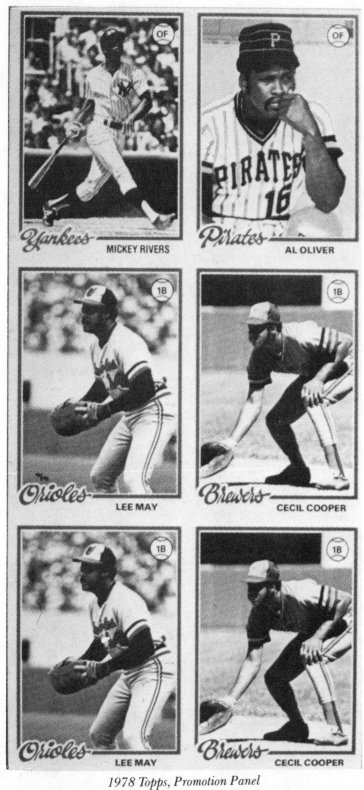

1978 Topps, Promotion Panel

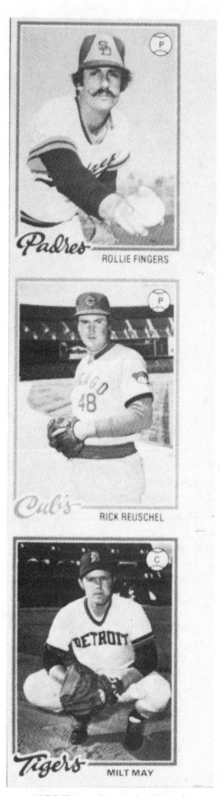

1978 Topps, Promotion Panel

1978 Topps, Promotion Panel

1978 Topps, Promotion Panel

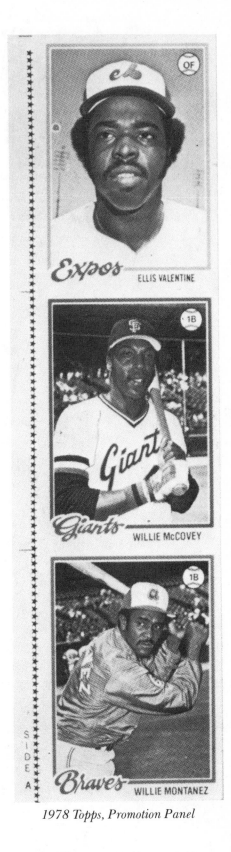

1978 Topps, Promotion Panel

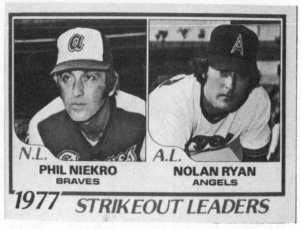

1978 Topps, Strikeout Leaders

1978 Topps, Tom Seaver

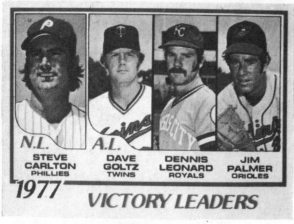

1978 Topps, Victory Leaders

1978 HOSTESS

SPECIFICATIONS

SIZE: Single card, 2¼×3¼", three-card panel, 7¼×3¼". FRONT: Color photograph. BACK: Black printing on white cardboard. DISTRIBUTION: Nationally, a three-card panel on the bottom of snack cake boxes.

HISTORY

In its fourth year of issuing baseball cards, Hostess continued to run with its successful format. Again in 1978, the bakery products company issued a 150-card set in the form of three-card panels printed on the bottoms of family-size packages of its snack cakes. For 1978, the type in the white panel at the bottom of the card—which designated the player's team and position—was made smaller, resulting in room for a larger photo. The cards are bordered by a dotted line, meant to provide a guide for cutting out the cards. Because the collecting hobby was in full swing by 1978, many collectors did not cut the cards off the boxes or panels. Traditionally, cards issued in this form retain a premium value if left uncut. Complete Hostess boxes from 1978 are worth some 25 to 33 percent more than the individual values of the three cards if they are removed from the box. Three-card panels, cut off the box but not cut into separate cards, have a 10 to 15 percent premium value. As with the other Hostess issues, some panels are more difficult to find because they were originally distributed on the bottoms of less popular brands or in parts of the country where there are few collectors. Overall the '78 Hostess set is a bit more challenging than the company's other issues.

FOR

Good-looking set with lots of superstars at low prices.

AGAINST

Sometimes difficult to find single specimens of superstars in high grade.

NOTEWORTHY CARDS

Many of today's current superstars are present in the 1978 Hostess set, as well as a "rookie card" of Eddie Murray.

VALUE

EX.-MT. CONDITION, NEATLY CUT FROM BOX: Complete set, $45; common card, 15¢–25¢; stars, $1–$2; Murray, Rose, $3–$4. 5-YEAR PROJECTION: Above average.

1978 KELLOGG'S

SPECIFICATIONS

SIZE: 2⅛×3¼". FRONT: Color photograph, 3-D effect. BACK: Blue printing on white background. DISTRIBUTION: Nationally, single cards in cereal boxes, complete sets by mail.

HISTORY

In its 1978 card set, Kellogg's gave itself plenty of advertising. The company name appears in big script in the upper-left card front, and a cartoon of Tony the Tiger appears on the back in the space which had traditionally held a small photo of the player. The photograph on the front of the card is bordered at top and bottom by large red and yellow banners; the top one reading "Kellogg's 3-D Super Stars," the bottom banner giving the player's last name and position. The photo is bordered on the sides by stripes of light and dark blue in a neon effect. The '78 cards had Kellogg's characteristic three-dimensional look—achieved by laminating a piece of finely ribbed plastic over the photo. Combined with the fuzzy stadium background against which the player's picture is set, the visual effect is one of depth. The set size remained at 57 cards for 1978. Single cards came wrapped in envelopes in cereal boxes. Hobbyists could obtain a complete set by mailing in box tops and money to Kellogg's. The set is not scarce.

FOR

Usual attractive format, low price.

AGAINST

Hard to obtain single cards; almost always sold as a complete set. Plastic coating on face of cards is prone to contract with age, causing the card to curl from top to bottom and cracking the plastic. Such damaged cards are worth significantly less than uncracked cards.

NOTEWORTHY CARDS

There are not a great number of superstars in the 1978 Kellogg's set, though there is a "rookie card" of Eddie Murray. Pete Rose is noticeably absent, the only year he doesn't appear in the Kellogg's set.

VALUE

EX.-MT. CONDITION: Complete set, $12.50; common card, 15¢–20¢; stars, 50¢–75¢; Murray, $1. 5-YEAR PROJECTION: Above average.

1978 BURGER KING

SPECIFICATIONS

SIZE: 2½×3½". FRONT: Color photograph. BACK: Blue and orange printing on gray cardboard. DISTRIBUTION: Houston, Dallas, Detroit, and New York areas, given away with food purchases at Burger King restaurants.

HISTORY

Following the 1977 use of baseball cards as a promotional giveaway in New York area Burger King outlets, the company expanded the program in 1978 to include four teams: the Astros, the Rangers, the Tigers, and the Yankees. A total of 92 player cards and four unnumbered checklists were issued in 1978, 23 players and a checklist card for each team. As with the 1977 cards, none of the 1978 cards have any Burger King advertising, nor do any logos appear. Some of the player photos are different than those found on the regular 1978 Topps cards, but the only difference on most of the cards is the card number on the back, which will be different from the number in the regular Topps set. Otherwise, the cards are identical, front and back. There are no rarities among the 1978 Burger King cards to compare to the '77 Piniella. All '78 Burger King team sets are in decent supply, collectors and dealers having been able to obtain them in quantity when they were issued.

FOR

Regional cards that are numerically scarcer than the regular Topps issue, but not a great deal more expensive. Nice item for the team collector.

AGAINST

Their similarity to regular Topps cards of 1978 is confusing. Unless the card is one of the few with different pictures, even superstar collectors don't bother to get the Burger King cards.

NOTEWORTHY CARDS

High-demand cards found in the 1978 Burger King sets are: Joe Niekro, J.R. Richards (Astros); Ferguson Jenkins, Al Oliver (Rangers); Mark Fidrych, Alan Trammell (rookie card), Lou Whitaker (Tigers); Billy Martin, Thurman Munson, Ron Guidry, Rich Gossage, Reggie Jackson (Yankees).

OUR FAVORITE CARD

An excellent bet for collectors who like to dabble in "superstar futures" is the 1978 Burger King set for the Detroit Tigers. Two of the fastest-rising infield stars in the American League are represented in the set as "rookie cards"—second baseman Lou Whitaker and shortstop Alan Trammell—as is pitcher Jack Morris. What makes these cards special is that while this talented double-play combination and the premier pitcher were represented in the regular Topps issue of 1978, each had to share his rookie card with three other guys. The much scarcer Tigers regional Burger King cards feature Morris, Whitaker, and Trammell on cards of their own. In the next year or two, when these youngsters really get the credit that's due them, these cards are going to be in big demand. Too bad the Burger King people missed another Tigers rookie phenom of 1978, Lance Parrish.

VALUE

EX.-MT. CONDITION: Complete set, $7–$10 each team; common card, 25¢–35¢; superstars, 75¢; Morris, Whitaker, Trammell, $2–$3. 5-YEAR PROJECTION: Above average.

1977 TOPPS

SPECIFICATIONS
SIZE: 2½×3½″. FRONT: Color photograph. BACK: Green printing on gray cardboard. DISTRIBUTION: Nationally, in packs with bubblegum.

HISTORY
In comparison to the designs of the five preceding years, the 1977 Topps set was a clean, attractive effort. A large, square color photo of the player appeared at the bottom of the card, with a facsimile autograph overprinted. In the wide white border at top were the player's team, name, and in a banner at upper right, position. When space permitted, card backs included personal and career stats, a few career highlights in headline style, and a cartoon about baseball or another player. What nobody has yet explained about the backs of the 1977 Topps cards is what those little figures at the bottom are; they look like fence gates overgrown with weeds. For the fifth straight year, Topps set the size of its annual issue at 660 cards. The set opened with eight cards featuring the American and National League leaders in several major statistical categories. Later on in the set, record-setting 1976 performances by George Brett, Minnie Minoso, Jose Morales, and Nolan Ryan were featured. There were five feature cards in the set titled "Turn Back the Clock," which recalled great baseball moments of the past. Another novelty subset of the 1977 Topps issue was a quartet of "Big League Brothers" cards, depicting George and Ken Brett, Bob and Ken Forsch, Lee and Carlos May, and Paul and Rick Reuschel (the Reuschels are misidentified in the front of the card; that's Rick on the left). Most team cards combined a team photo with the picture of the current manager, though in the case of the Mariners and the Blue Jays, in their first year of major league play, the coaches were also included on the card. Rookie cards in the 1977 set continued to group players by position, rather than team.

FOR
Nice set. Lots of the photos were taken during the 1976 season, so collectors get to see some of the special Bicentennial uniforms adopted by the teams.

AGAINST
Can't really find anything major wrong with it.

NOTEWORTHY CARDS
Despite all the special cards in the '77 set, the really notable cards are the rookie cards, particularly what is today one of the hottest cards in the hobby, #477, Rookie Catchers, featuring Dale Murphy. Other in-demand rookie cards in the set are Bruce Sutter, Jason Thompson, Andre Dawson, Jack Clark-Lee Mizzilli, and Steve Kemp-Tony Armas. Besides the misidentified Reuschels, there are two other wrong photos in the 1977 set: card #431, Dave Collins, actually has a photo of Paul Splittorff, while the picture identified as Gil Patterson on card #472 is actually Sheldon Gill. Talk about luck: Gil Patterson, who was 1-2 for the Yankees that year—his only season in the major leagues—never did appear on a baseball card. Sheldon Gill never appeared on another card, either—but then again, he never played an inning of major league ball. The 1977 set also featured the last regular-issue card of Brooks Robinson during his playing career; he retired in 1977.

VALUE
EX.-MT. CONDITION: Complete set, $75; common card, 7¢; superstars, $1–$3; Rose, $5; Murphy, $25. 5-YEAR PROJECTION: Average, or just a bit better.

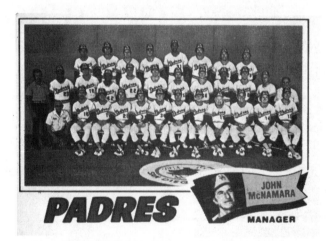

1977 Topps, San Diego Padres Team Card

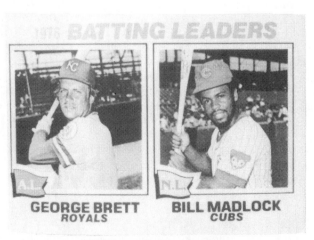

1977 Topps, Batting Leaders

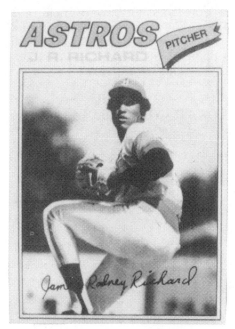

1977 Topps, J. R. Richard

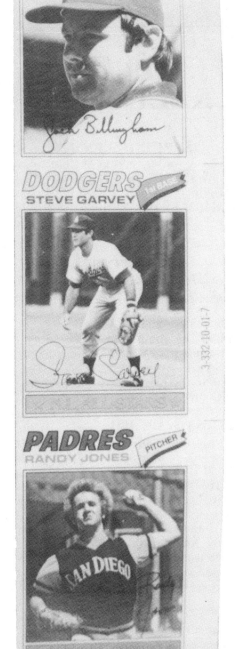

1977 Topps, Mike Schmidt

1977 Topps, Nolan Ryan, Record Breaker

1977 Topps, Promotion Panel

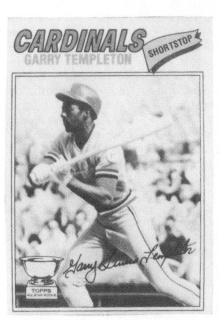

1977 Topps, Garry Templeton

1977 HOSTESS

SPECIFICATIONS

SIZE: 2¼×3¼", three-card panel, 7¼×3¼". FRONT: Color photograph. BACK: Black printing on white cardboard. DISTRIBUTION: Nationally, a three-card panel on the bottom of bakery product boxes.

HISTORY

In its third year of issuing baseball cards, Hostess continued to produce a 150-card set, printing three cards on the bottom of each family-size box of its snack cakes. Because the baseball card hobby was quite well established in 1977, many of the Hostess cards were saved on their original boxes or at least in the complete three-card panel that comprised the bottom of the box. There is a premium on these items over and above the cumulative value of the three individual cards. The premium for complete boxes is around 25 to 50 percent; panels are worth 10 to 15 percent more. If the cards have been cut into single specimens, it is important that they be neatly trimmed, with even borders. Most collectors prefer those cards that have been cut exactly on the dotted line, rather than inside it. Certain of the three-card panels of '77 Hostess cards, notably those printed on the bottoms of less popular items, are scarcer today than the rest of the series. The back design for 1977 remained unchanged and the front was not changed drastically. A color photo with a rounded bottom rests atop a white panel which contains the name, team, and position of the player, in red and blue letters.

FOR

An attractive, easy to collect set that has good potential for future price appreciation, especially in the star cards.

AGAINST

Because of the prevalence of uncut boxes and panels, it is sometimes hard to buy a superstar card from the Hostess series without having to pay for the two other cards with which it was issued.

NOTEWORTHY CARDS

All the superstars of 1977 are in the set.

VALUE

EX.-MT. CONDITION, NEATLY CUT FROM BOX: Complete set, $45; common card, 15¢–20¢; stars, $1–$2; Rose, $3–$4. 5-YEAR PROJECTION: Above average.

1977 KELLOGG'S

SPECIFICATIONS

SIZE: 2⅛×3¼". FRONT: Color photograph, 3-D effect. BACK: Blue printing on white background. DISTRIBUTION: Nationally, single cards in cereal boxes, complete sets by mail.

HISTORY

Considered one of the most attractive Kellogg's sets, the 1977 offering also had the 3-D look—achieved by placing a sheet of ribbed plastic over the photo on front. In combination with the indistinct stadium photo in the background and the sharp player photo, the plastic gives the cards the illusion of depth. The player's photo on the 1977 set is framed by a radiant red and gold oval. The player's name and position appear at the bottom of the card in an oval yellow panel outlined in red. The whole package is surrounded by a wide white border. Card backs were once again printed in blue ink and featured a team logo, personal and career information and stats, and a small photo of the player. This is the last time the player photo appears on the Kellogg's card backs. The set is complete at 57 cards.

FOR

One of the most attractive of the Kellogg's issue, good value for the currently low price.

AGAINST

Prone, as are all Kellogg's 3-D issues, to curl and crack across the plastic lamination on front; such damage lowers card value.

NOTEWORTHY CARDS

Stars making their first appearance on a Kellogg's card in 1977 include George Brett and Dave Winfield. The Lyman Bostock card can be found with the correct photo on back or with a photo of Doc Ellis on back, the Ellis photo being the scarcer of the pair.

VALUE

EX.-MT. CONDITION: Complete set, $15; common card, 15¢–20¢; stars, 75¢–$1; Rose, $1–$2. 5-YEAR PROJECTION: Above average.

1977 BURGER KING YANKEES

SPECIFICATIONS

SIZE: 2½×3½". FRONT: Color photograph. BACK: Green printing on gray cardboard. DISTRIBUTION: Metropolitan New York area, with food purchases at Burger King.

HISTORY

One of very few regional issues of the late 1970s, the 1977 Burger King Yankees set was produced by Topps. The cards were given out in the fast food chain's restaurants in the New York City area. Because the cards carry absolutely no advertising for Burger King, they are sometimes confused with the regular Topps cards of 1977—and with good reason. Except for the card numbers on the back, about half of the '77 Burger King Yanks are identical to their counterparts in the '77 Topps set. Some cards, however, have different photos. The Reggie Jackson card, for instance, has a real photo of Jackson in his Yankees uniform, while his "regular" Topps card for 1977 showed him in a faked Yankees uniform painted on by a Topps artist after he had been traded from the Orioles. In all, there are 23 player cards in the Burger King Yankees set, plus an unnumbered checklist card. While the '77 Burger King cards were a true regional baseball card issue, they are widely available around the country. Soon after the promotion began, collectors and card dealers managed to obtain large quantities of the cards from contacts in the Burger King chain. With the exception of the Lou Piniella card (see below), the set is not at all scarce.

FOR

A quality, one-team regional set. Some cards are desirable because their photos are different from the regular Topps issue. Overall, the set is an excellent value.

AGAINST

Lack of Burger King advertising makes them confusing.

NOTEWORTHY CARDS

Lots of Yankees superstars in the set: Jackson, Munson, Guidry, Hunter, Nettles, Piniella, manager Billy Martin.

OUR FAVORITE CARDS

The scarce Lou Piniella card in the 1977 Burger King Yankees set is one of very few baseball cards to be written up in recent baseball literature. In his popular book *The Bronx Zoo,* Yankees relief pitcher Sparky Lyle tells why the Piniella card is so scarce and expensive today. According to Lyle, Piniella was not originally part of the set. Indeed, all the subsequent Burger King team sets of 1978–1980 are complete at 22 player cards and a checklist, so it *is* unusual that the '77 Yankees set has 23 players and a checklist. Lyle says that when the set was issued, Piniella became upset because he had been ignored and went to see George Steinbrenner. Lyle says that because Piniella was a "pet" of the Yankees' owner, Steinbrenner pressured Burger King into adding a Piniella card to the promotion. But by the time the card was printed, it was too late for it to get much circulation. Today it is one of the more expensive baseball cards of the late 1970s, currently selling in the $15 to $20 range in top grade. This is one case, though, where the confusion about regular Topps cards for 1977 and the Burger King set for '77 can be used to the collector's advantage. Since the photo of Piniella is identical on both cards, a lucky collector going through a dealer's stack of '77 commons may be able to come away with the $20 Burger King ver-

sion (#23 on back) rather than the 10¢ Topps version (#96).

VALUE

EX.-MT. CONDITION: Complete set, $25; common card, 25¢–50¢; Munson, Jackson, $1–$1.50; Piniella, $15–$20. 5-YEAR PROJECTION: Above average.

1976 TOPPS

SPECIFICATIONS

SIZE: 2½×3½". FRONT: Color photograph. BACK: Black and green printing on gray cardboard. DISTRIBUTION: Nationally, in packs with bubblegum.

HISTORY

After several years of card designs in which the border sometimes overwhelmed the photo, the 1976 Topps set began a trend toward simpler design with greater emphasis on the player photo. Sharp color photos occupy the major part of the card front, with the player's name and team written in a pair of colored strips at the bottom. The player's position is indicated in the lower-left corner in small type beneath a drawing of a player representing that position. Cards of the starting National and American League All-Stars are designated by a star in the lower left-hand corner, with the league and position indicated in writing. The 1976 card back design was among Topps' best. A bat and ball appear at the left side, with the card number inside the ball. Neatly arranged to the right are personal and statistical data on the player and a few career highlights in text form. There were a number of specialty subsets among the 660 cards in the 1976 Topps set. Certainly the most significant was the 44-card "Traded" group issued later in the season. These cards featured photos (usually with the new team's uniform painted on by Topps artists) of 43 players who had been traded after the printing deadline for the regular issue. The cards are in the same basic style as the regular 1976 issue, but feature at the bottom a

"Sports Extra" headline in newspaper clipping format announcing the trade or movement that sent the player to a new team and including the date of the transaction. The back of the card continues the newspaper clipping format and presents the details of the deal. The '76 Topps Traded cards carry card numbers identical to those of the player's earlier card in the set, followed by the "T" suffix. There is a separate checklist for the Traded group. Opening the 1976 Topps issue was a group of six cards recounting the past season's record-setting performances. The statistical leaders of 1975 are featured in a series of 15 cards, one card for each league in seven categories, while the last card honors the top relief pitchers in both leagues. The first 14 cards generally feature the league's three leaders. There are two cards dedicated to the League Championship Series and the World Series. A 10-card run in the set is labeled "The Sporting News All-Time All-Stars" and pictures a line-up of baseball's greatest players—Ruth, Cobb, Gehrig, Wagner, Williams, etc. The cards feature black-and-white photos of the old-timers; lifetime stats are on the back. For collectors, the most interesting subset in the 1976 series is the "Father & Son" cards, on which former major league players are pictured with their currently-playing major league sons. The fathers are depicted on miniature versions of their old baseball cards. The dad/lad combinations are Gus and Buddy Bell, Ray and Bob Boone, Joe Coleman Sr. and Jr., Jim and Mike Hegan, and Roy Smalley Sr. and Jr. Team cards were issued in two versions in 1976. A regular group was released with the set on the same cardboard stock, while an identical set printed on much thinner, white cardboard was available in uncut sheet form directly from Topps. Rookie cards are included in the set, four players to a card, grouped by position.

FOR

There is a pleasing diversity to the 1976 Topps set, with the specialty cards generally being better-conceived than most. The cards are attractive and the set features no outrageously expensive items, though the value of the set overall is respectably high.

AGAINST

About the worst thing you can say about the 1976 Topps set is that there are no outstanding rookie cards.

NOTEWORTHY CARDS

Hank Aaron's final regular card as a player appears in the 1976 set. He is also honored on card #1 for establishing the career RBI mark of 2,262. One of few notable rookies in the set is Ron Guidry.

VALUE

EX.-MT. CONDITION: Complete set, $80; common card, 8¢; superstars, $1–$3; Rose, $5.25; Guidry, $6. 5-YEAR PROJECTION: Average.

1976 Topps, National League and American League Championship Play-off

1976 Topps, Phil Niekro

1976 Topps, St. Louis Cardinals Checklist

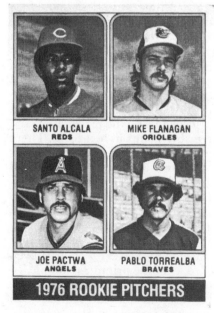

1976 Topps, Rookie Pitchers

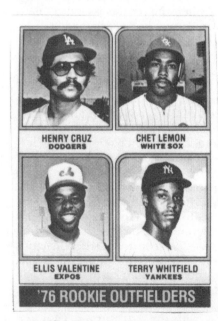

1976 Topps, Rookie Outfielders

1976 HOSTESS

1976 Topps, John Candelaria

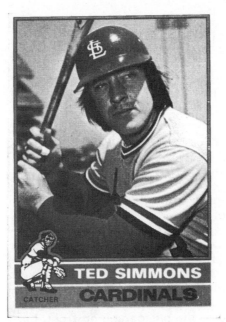

1976 Topps, Ted Simmons

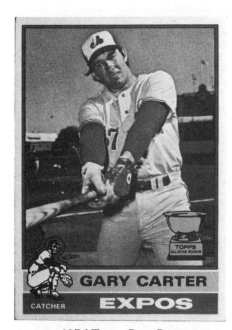

1976 Topps, Gary Carter

1976 Topps, Robin Yount

SPECIFICATIONS

SIZE: Single card, 2¼×3¼", three-card panel, 7¼×3¼". FRONT: Color photograph. BACK: Black printing on white cardboard. DISTRIBUTION: Nationally, a three-card panel on bakery product boxes.

HISTORY

In format, the 1976 Hostess cards were similar to the bakery company's premier issue of the year before. The 150 cards were issued in three-card panels, one panel comprising the bottom of a family-size box of such goodies as Hostess Twinkies, Cupcakes, Ding Dongs, etc. The cards have the greatest collector value when they are still on the original box (as much as 25 to 50 percent over the total value of the three individual cards). Three-card panels, which are not uncommon among the Hostess issue, are worth 10 to 15 percent over the total value of the cards themselves. The design for 1976 was changed little from 1975. Perhaps in keeping with the Bicentennial theme that swept the nation that year, the bottom of the card consists of red, white, and blue stripes in which are found the player's name, team, and position. Card backs again include brief biographical details and career stats. The 1976 Hostess cards are quite attractive and in fairly strong demand. While common cards are priced more than twice as high as the same players in the 1976 Topps set, it should be remembered that there are far fewer existing Hostess cards than Topps cards of the same year. Superstars, on the other hand, are a much better buy in the Hostess series than the Topps. As with the 1975 issue, some of the three-card panels which were included on boxes of less popular products are correspondingly harder to find today.

FOR

Attractive cards, reasonable set size, and low price.

AGAINST

It's almost impossible to find something bad to say about the 1976 Hostess set. How about that they're a quarter-inch smaller than the currently standard 2½×3½"?

NOTEWORTHY CARDS

Superstars in the series include Brock, Garvey, Carew, Seaver, Brooks Robinson, Rose, Ryan, Schmidt, Aaron, Brett, Jackson, and Yastrzemski, many of whom who were not included in 1975 set.

VALUE

EX.-MT. CONDITION, NEATLY CUT FROM BOX: Complete set, $45; common card, 15¢–20¢; stars, $1–$2; Rose, Aaron, $3–$5. 5-YEAR PROJECTION: Above average.

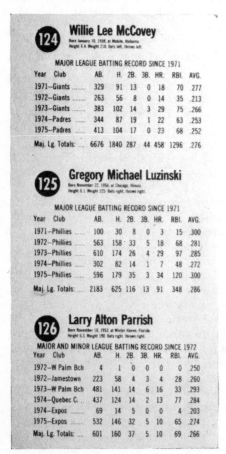

1976 Hostess, Willie McCovey, Greg Luzinski, Larry Parrish (back)

1976 KELLOGG'S

SPECIFICATIONS

SIZE: 2⅛×3¼". FRONT: Color photo, 3-D effect. BACK: Blue printing on white cardboard. DISTRIBUTION: Nationally, one card in boxes of cereal, complete set by mail.

HISTORY

While Kellogg's retained the basic 2⅛×3¼" card size, 57-card set format, and 3-D look for 1976, the cards underwent a major design change for the first time in several years. Instead of blue and white borders surrounding the photo on front, the 1976 cards have alternating blue, red, and blue stripes around the photo, with a wide white border. The cards have a three-dimensional effect caused by laminating a piece of ribbed plastic over the photograph on front. Card backs combine the player's biographical details and major league career stats with a photo and team logo. The first three cards in the set are believed to have been printed separately from

1976 Kellogg's, Willie Stargell

the other 54, and are considered somewhat scarcer. Collectors could either try to assemble a set of 1976 cards by buying boxes of cereal in which they were packaged, or could obtain the complete set by mailing in the required amount of money and a couple of box tops.

FOR

Cards are attractive, so is price.

AGAINST

When the plastic lamination on these cards contracts and curls with age or is bent by misuse, it can crack, leaving a very unsightly and unsalable card.

NOTEWORTHY CARDS

There are far fewer big name players in the 1976 Kellogg's set than in most previous years. Thurman Munson makes his premier appearance for Kellogg's. The card of Clay Carroll comes in two variations, with Reds or White Sox logo on back.

VALUE

EX.-MT. CONDITION: Complete set, $20; common card, 20¢–25¢; stars, $1; cards #1–#3, $1.50; Rose, $2. 5-YEAR PROJECTION: Above average.

1975 TOPPS

SPECIFICATIONS

SIZE: Regular cards, 2½×3½"; minis, 2¼×3⅛". FRONT: Color photograph. BACK: Green and red printing on gray cardboard. DISTRIBUTION: Nationally, in packages with bubblegum.

HISTORY

In 1975 Topps produced two card sets identical in every way except for size. In limited areas of the Midwest and West Coast, Topps test-marketed its 1975 cards in a size that was some 20 percent smaller than the traditional 2½×3½" format which the company had adopted in 1957. It's doubtful that Topps learned much from the experiment, though, because collectors snapped up virtually the entire issue. Prices on the 660 "minis" (as they are known in the hobby) are generally quoted at exactly double those of

1975 Topps, Willie McCovey

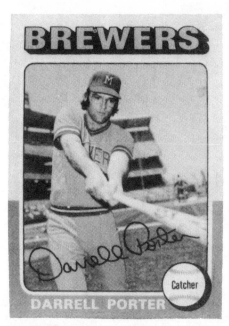

1975 Topps, Darrell Porter

1975 Topps, Mike Schmidt

the same card in regular size. This is currently the most popular Topps set of the 1970s, but it is hard to say whether that is because of the card design or in spite of it. Collectors either love or hate the 1975 design. It was a real eye-popper. A color photo at the center of the card is framed in a round-cornered white border. Around that is a distinctive two-color border in a wide spectrum of bright, "mod" colors. The team name is printed at top in bold, colorful letters. The player's name is at the bottom, with his position abbreviated in a baseball at lower right. The only word to describe the overall effect is—loud. Card backs are presented in vertical format, an unusual choice for Topps. Besides the usual personal and career figures, there is a baseball trivia quiz question on the back. The '75 set opens with seven cards dedicated to stellar or record-setting performances of the previous season. A long subseries of 24 cards presents the American and National League MVPs since 1951. The award-winners are pictured on these cards in miniature versions of their Topps cards from their MVP season. The 1974 season statistical leaders in each league share a run of special cards in the 1975 set, and there

is an eight-card series detailing the League Championship and World Series. Rookie cards are presented in the format of four players sharing a card by position.

FOR
In terms of dollar value this has been the fastest-rising baseball card set of the 1970s. It seems that each year one of the many rookie cards in the set gets hot as that player reaches the level of superstardom. Some people see the design of the set as being a major point in its favor.

AGAINST
Some people see the design as the set's only major drawback.

NOTEWORTHY CARDS
There are two wrong-photo cards in the 1975 set: card #120, Steve Busby, is really Fran Healy; #626, Larry Haney, is really Dave Duncan. The last regular-issue card of Hall of Fame slugger Harmon Killebrew appears in the '75 set. The real stars of the 1975 Topps set, though, are the incredible number of high-demand rookie cards. The players who made their initial baseball card appearance in 1975 could take the field as an all-star team.

They include: Robin Yount, George Brett, Jim Rice, Gary Carter, John Denny, Fred Lynn, and Keith Hernandez.

OUR FAVORITE CARD
Topps cheated a bit in creating three of the cards in the subset picturing the MVP Award winners from 1951 through 1974. The cards for the 1951 and 1955 MVPs include representations of Topps Roy Campanella cards for those years, and the 1962 MVP card shows a Topps Maury Wills card. But Topps never issued any of those cards. Campy was one of many stars of the early Fifties who jumped between Topps and Bowman card sets in different years, sometimes appearing in both, sometimes in one or the other. Wills was miffed at Topps for not signing him to a baseball card contract when he was a minor leaguer and refused to appear for Topps until 1967.

VALUE
EX.-MT. CONDITION: Complete set $175; common card, 10¢; superstars. $1–$4; Aaron, $6; Schmidt, $7; Rose, $9; rookie cards, Carter, Lynn, Hernandez, Rice, $7–$9; Yount, Brett, $15. 5-YEAR PROJECTION: Above average.

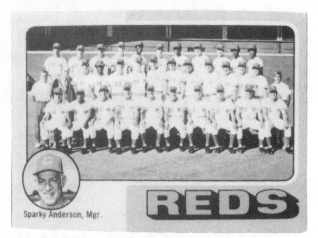

1975 Topps, Cincinnati Reds Team Card (front)

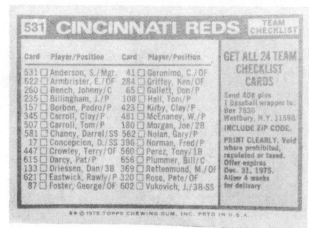

1975 Topps, Cincinnati Reds Team Card (back)

1975 Topps, 1958 MVP Players

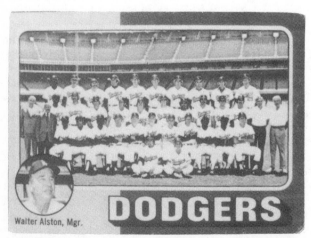

1975 Topps, Los Angeles Dodgers Team Checklist

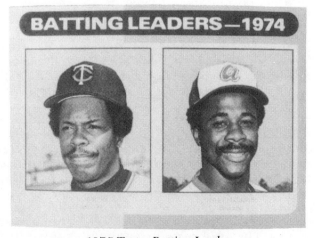

1975 Topps, Batting Leaders

1975 HOSTESS

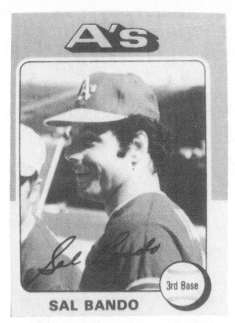

1975 Topps, Sal Bando

1975 Topps, National League Championship Play-off

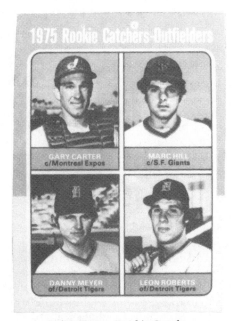

1975 Topps, Rookie Catchers

SPECIFICATIONS

SIZE: Single card, 2¼×3¼″; three-card panel, 7¼×3¼″. FRONT: Color photograph. BACK: Black printing on white cardboard. DISTRIBU-TION: Nationally, a three-card panel on the bottom of bakery product boxes.

HISTORY

In 1975 Hostess issued the first of what would become five consecutive annual baseball card sets. The 150 cards in the premier Hostess issue contained most of the big name stars of the game that year. Like many other baseball cards issued in connection with food products, the '75 Hostess cards were printed right on the bottom of the package box. Unlike most other box-package cards, the Hostess cards had player statistics printed on the backs. To print on the backs of such cards requires a second trip through the printing press, and since it is a relatively expensive proposition, most issuers elect to skip it. Also unlike many "cut on the dotted line" cards, the '75 Hostess cards do not share a common border between cards. This makes it easier to cut the cards apart neatly and evenly, an important consideration in determining card value. As with all cards issued as part of a package design, the Hostess cards are more valuable when uncut. Complete boxes are more desirable; they're worth perhaps 25 to 50 percent over and above the total value of the three cards taken as individuals. Original panels which have been cut from the box, but not separated into single cards, carry a 10 to 15 percent premium. Because the baseball card collecting hobby was fairly popular by the time these first Hostess issues were released, many uncut boxes were saved. It is entirely possible to build a complete collection in either form. The 1975 Hostess cards themselves are quite attractive: maroon corners frame each of the color photos, and the player's name and position are printed in blue in the white space below; beneath that, the team name is printed in red. Not all of the '75 Hostess cards are easy to find. Some panels were printed on less popular products and were naturally sold in smaller quantities. Even so, these scarcer cards are not priced at so high a level as to be prohibitive.

FOR

While the 1975 Hostess cards can be considered more numerically scarce than the Topps issue of the same year, they are priced much lower per card, especially for the stars. A 1975 Topps Robin Yount "rookie" card, for example, is a $12.50 card in top grade, but you can buy a complete 1975 Hostess box and get a different scarcer Yount rookie card for $5 and you get cards of Al Oliver and Andy Messersmith in the bargain. Demand is just starting to pick up on these cards and it is quite likely prices will follow.

AGAINST

Cards that have been cut off the box in sloppy fashion have little collector value. All cards should have neat, even, white borders, or be trimmed outside of the "dotted line."

NOTEWORTHY CARDS

Variations exist for three of the '75 Hostess cards. Misspelled cards include Burt Hooton's, which can be found with his name spelled "Hooten"; and Doug Rader's, which is sometimes found with his name spelled "Radar." Bill Madlock's card comes with two positions indicated, "Infield" (correct) and "Pitcher." There is also a wrong-photo card in the set—the picture on the "Milt May" card is Lee May.

VALUE

EX.-MT. CONDITION, NEATLY CUT FROM BOX: Complete set, $50; common card, 15¢–20¢; stars, variations, $1–$2; Rose, Yount, $3–$5. 5-YEAR PROJECTION: Well above average.

1975 KELLOGG'S

SPECIFICATIONS

SIZE: 2⅛×3¼". FRONT: Color photograph, 3-D effect. BACK: Blue

1975 Kellogg's, Ken Singleton

printing on white cardboard. DISTRIBUTION: Nationally, one card in cereal boxes, complete sets by mail.

HISTORY

The 1975 Kellogg's set was much lke many of its predecessors in appearance. A color photograph of the player was overlaid on a blurry stadium background and a ribbed plastic sheet was laminated over the whole thing to give it a three-dimensional appearance. The effect is very pleasing, and the cards have been quite popular. A blue border with white stars surrounds the photo on the 1975 set, and it, in turn, is surrounded by a white border. Red panels at the bottom of the card and upper right contain the player's last name and position, respectively. The back of the card features a small photo of the player, a team logo, biographical information, and major league career stats. The size of the 1975 set was increased slightly, to 57 cards from 54. Individual cards were found packaged in Kellogg's Raisin Bran and selected other types of cereal, or the complete set could be ordered directly from the company by sending in a combination of cash and box tops.

FOR

These cards are attractive and inexpensive. The 3-D look is especially

popular with superstar collectors, and these cards really jazz up a display of "normal" cards.

AGAINST

The cards curl and the plastic lamination cracks as the result of age or misuse, greatly lowering the value of a card. In this, as in other later Kellogg's sets, it is sometimes difficult to find single cards of superstar or other players, as the cards are usually sold in complete sets.

NOTEWORTHY CARDS

Steve Garvey, Carl Yastrzemski, and Mike Schmidt make their first appearance in the Kellogg's series with the 1975 set. The Jim Hunter card is found with either the Yankees or A's logo on the back of the card; he was traded to New York prior to the opening of the 1975 season.

VALUE

EX.-MT. CONDITION: Complete set, $20; common cards, 25¢; stars, $1–$1.75; Rose, $2–$3. 5-YEAR PROJECTION: Above average.

1975-1976 TWINKIES

SPECIFICATIONS

SIZE: 2¼×3¼". FRONT: Blank (yes, that's right, blank). BACK: Black printing on white cardboard. DISTRIBUTION: West Coast, one card on bottom of snack cake packages.

HISTORY

Why anybody would want to collect the Twinkies cards is a real mystery—they are the only baseball cards in history without a picture of the player! Some collectors say this was a "test issue" limited to the West Coast area, where the cards were printed on the bottom of 25-cent Hostess Twinkies packages. It is much more likely that these "cards" were simply scrap cardboard that was being recycled from the printing of the regular 1975 and 1976 Hostess issues. Nobody in their right mind would issue baseball cards without pictures, would they? Yet that's what the Twinkies cards purport to be, just the back printing from the Hostess cards. Nevertheless, those who desire to collect a full set of 60 Twinkies cards will find the common cards somewhat more expensive and the star cards about the same price as the regular Hostess issue—even without the pictures on front. Like all box-package baseball cards, value is greatest if the cards are still attached to the rest of the original package. Those cards that have been cut from the package should be neatly trimmed. Each year Twinkies cards have the same card numbers as the corresponding Hostess issue. The 1975 Twinkies series includes all of the first 36 of the Hostess cards, but is skip-numbered thereafter, from card #40 to #136. Steve Garvey, Robin Yount, and Hank Aaron are among the stars included in the last 24 cards of the Twinkies set for 1975. The 1976 Twinkies are the first 60 numbers from the Hostess set of that year.

FOR

These cards really don't have a thing going for them.

AGAINST

Everything. Why would anybody want to collect a baseball card without a picture on it?

VALUE

EX.-MT. CONDITION, NEATLY CUT FROM PACKAGE: Complete set, $45; common card, 50¢; Brock, Garvey, $1.50; Aaron, $2.50; Rose, Yount, $3–$5. 5-YEAR PROJECTION: Well below average.

1974 TOPPS

SPECIFICATIONS

SIZE: 2½×3½″. FRONT: Color photograph. BACK: Black and green printing on gray cardboard. DISTRIBUTION: Nationally, in packages with bubblegum.

HISTORY

In 1974, for the first time, Topps released all of its cards at one time—in the beginning of the year—but they probably wish they hadn't. Prior to the opening of the season there was a lot of talk that the San Diego Padres were going to be sold and moved to Washington, D.C. Everybody in baseball was so sure the deal would go through that Topps prepared most of the Padres cards with a team designation that said "Washington, Nat'l League" on the front. When the sale fell through, and the team opened the season in San Diego, Topps went back to press to correct the cards, but the error version had already been issued in gum packs. The scarce Washington variations are priced at several times the value of the San Diego-designated cards. In all, 15 cards were affected by the error, including the team card and #599, "Rookie Pitchers," on which Dave Freisleben can be found with one or the other team shown. The Dave Winfield rookie card is not one of the variations. The basic design of the 660 '74 Topps cards was again good, but the set is plagued by the same overuse of action photos that marked the 1973 set. All too often, players are depicted as small figures in a giant stadium or with too many other players. The 1974 issue featured a record number of specialty card subsets for Topps. Since Hank Aaron was just two home runs short of breaking Babe Ruth's career homer record, Aaron was featured on the first six cards in the set; card #1 being a special career summary card, while cards #2–#6 pictured miniature versions of Aaron's Topps cards from 1954–1973, four cards at a time. Backs of those cards had a running story of Aaron's distinguished career. Team managers again share a card with their coaches (except Tigers manager Ralph Houk, who has card #578 to himself). There are the traditional runs of cards honoring the previous season's statistical leaders, league play-offs, and the World Series. The starting All-Star lineups appear on a nine-card subset, each card featuring the starters, by position, of both leagues. The rookie cards are arranged by position, rather than team, with four players per card. Once again in 1974, Topps issued a group of 24 unnumbered team checklist cards. Like those in 1973, there is a team name and year at top, a panel of facsimile autographs below, and a team checklist on the back. The '74 team checklist cards are bordered in red. Later in the season, Topps produced a 44-card "Traded" set, including the cards in regular gum packs. There are 43 players cards and a checklist. The cards are similar in format to the rest of the 1974 cards on the front, except that there is a big panel below the player's photo with "TRADED" on it. Most of the uniforms shown on the traded cards are the work of Topps artists; rarely did Topps obtain actual photos of the players in their new uniforms. Backs of the Traded cards feature a "Baseball News" newspaper presentation, giving the details of the trade. Card numbers in the Traded series correspond to the players' numbers in the regular set, except there is a "T" suffix after the number. The only really notable player in the Traded set for 1974 is Juan Marichal.

FOR

For the collector who likes relatively new cards, but still wants a challenge, assembling a complete set of 1974 cards, with all variations, can be an interesting undertaking.

AGAINST

"Busy" photos; confusing variations.

NOTEWORTHY CARDS

Besides all the current stars who appear in the 1974 set, and the aforementioned Padres/Washington variations, there are two well-known error cards to be found. Jesus Alou (#654) was originally printed without his position being designated in the upper-right corner. This card, without the word "OUTFIELD," is a $7.50 item, while the corrected version is worth about 50¢. For card #608, "Rookie Pitchers," there are also two versions. The correct card will have Bob Apodaca's name spelled properly, while the incorrect card has it spelled "Apodaco," with an "o" at the end. The right card is worth 50¢ or so, the error, $2. Big name rookie cards found in '74 include: Dave Parker, Dave Winfield, Ken Griffey, Bill Madlock, and Gorman Thomas.

VALUE

EX.-MT. CONDITION: Complete set, $145; common card, 10¢; "Washington" players, $2.50; Aaron #1, $6; Aaron specials, $1.50; stars, $1–$3; McCovey "Washington," Schmidt, Rose, Winfield, $6–$8. 5-YEAR PROJECTION: Average.

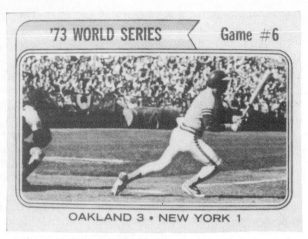

1974 Topps, World Series Game #6

1974 Topps, Home Run Leaders

1974 Topps, Dick Allen

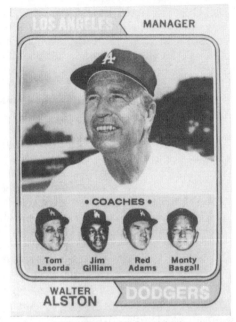

1974 Topps, Walter Alston

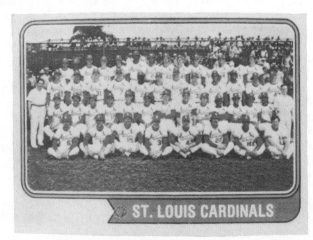

1974 Topps, St. Louis Cardinals Team Card

1974 Topps, California Angels Team Card

1974 TOPPS DECKLE-EDGE

1974 Topps, Rusty Staub

1974 Topps, Oakland A's Team Card (front)

1974 Topps, Frank Robinson

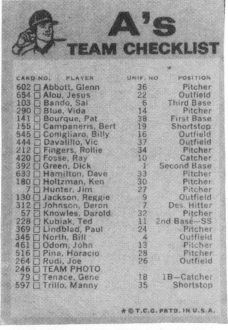

1974 Topps, Oakland A's Team Card (back)

SPECIFICATIONS

SIZE: 2⅞×5″. FRONT: Black-and-white photo. BACK: Black printing on gray cardboard. DISTRIBUTION: Test basis in limited areas of the East Coast, in packages with bubblegum.

HISTORY

One of the more popular and scarce Topps test issues of the mid-1970s is the 72-card "Deckle-Edge" set. The cards feature a borderless black-and-white photo on the front, with the only writing being a blue facsimile autograph at the bottom. The cards get their nickname from the unique manner in which they were cut, which gave the edges a scalloped appearance. Card backs have at bottom a mocked-up newspaper clipping giving a detail from the player's career. At top, in handwritten script, are the player's name, team, and position, as well as the date and location of the picture—something quite unusual on a baseball card. Many of the photos were taken at spring training the previous year. The '74 Deckle-Edges are a true test issue, having been sold only in limited areas on the East Coast. Like many Topps test issues, proof versions in uncut sheet form will sometimes be found, as will cards cut from those sheets with straight edges. Such items were usually "rescued" from the garbage at Topps' printing plant. The '74 Deckle-Edge cards are quite scarce, and the stars among them are in high demand.

FOR

One of the better-known test issues. Attractive addition to team or superstar collections.

AGAINST

Quite scarce and expensive.

NOTEWORTHY CARDS

Hall of Fame caliber players in the set are: Bob Gibson, Steve Carlton, Thurman Munson, Catfish Hunter, Tom Seaver, Pete Rose, Lou Brock,

Willie McCovey, Willie Stargell, Rod Carew (twice, cards #32 and #36), Nolan Ryan, Carl Yastrzemski, Jim Palmer, Hank Aaron, Reggie Jackson, Carlton Fisk, Brooks and Frank Robinson, and Johnny Bench.

VALUE

EX.-MT. CONDITION: Complete set, $750; common card, $8–$10; stars, $12–$15; superstars, $20–$40; Rose, $60. 5-YEAR PROJECTION: Below average.

1974 KELLOGG'S

SPECIFICATIONS

SIZE: 2⅛×3¼″. FRONT: Color photograph, 3-D effect. BACK: Blue printing on white cardboard. DISTRIBUTION: Nationally, one card in cereal boxes, complete sets by mail order.

HISTORY

After a one-year experiment with "regular" baseball cards, Kellogg's in 1974 returned to its successful and popular 3-D look. This 3-D look was achieved by laminating a piece of ribbed plastic over the photograph on the front of the card to create an image of depth. Card size returned to the smaller format that had been used in 1972, while the set size remained at 54 cards. Back designs continued to be a typical arrangement of biography and stats, along with a small player photo. Blue and white borders surround the player photo on front. The player's last name appears in a yellow banner at the bottom of the card, while his position is printed in a yellow shield at top. Again in 1974, complete sets could be obtained by sending in the proper amount of money and box tops. Individual cards could also be found in certain brands of Kellogg's cereal.

FOR

Popular 3-D look.

AGAINST

Return to 3-D brought back the problem of curling and cracking of the plastic lamination on the front of the card as it contracts with age.

NOTEWORTHY CARDS

Johnny Bench returned to the 1974 Kellogg's set after a three-year absence.

VALUE

EX.-MT. CONDITION: Complete set, $20; common cards, 25¢; stars, $1–$2; Rose, $3. 5-YEAR PROJECTION: Above average.

1973 TOPPS

SPECIFICATIONS

SIZE: 2½×3½″. FRONT: Color photograph. BACK: Black and yellow printing on gray cardboard. DISTRIBUTION: Nationally, in packages with bubblegum.

HISTORY

After Topps had produced its largest set ever in 1972 (787 cards), it cut back a bit in 1973, to the 660 cards which would remain the company's standard for half a decade. The 1973 set was also the last that Topps issued in different series. Beginning in 1974, all Topps cards were released at one time early in the year. This means that the 1973 set contains the last of the "high numbers"—until 1981, when Topps began issuing Traded sets. In the '73 set, cards #529–#660 are the high numbers, and they are considerably scarcer than the rest of the set. The '73 cards were well-designed, with a large photo occupying the top of the card. A silhouette of a player in action, set against a colored circle at bottom, depicted the position of the player on the card. The position was also spelled out in the white border at bottom, as were the player's name and team. Card backs were vertical, the first time Topps had used this arrangement on its regular-issue set since 1968. A player cartoon appears at top, with personal information in a black panel at center, and a career summary and stats printed in a gold box below. The choice of photos for the 1973 Topps set was overall the worst job ever seen on a major baseball card set. Topps opted for "action" photos for far too

many cards. The result was too often a tiny picture of a player who could barely be identified, set against a huge, distracting stadium. On other cards, there are so many players pictured, it is hard to tell who is featured. In only a few cases are the action photos at all effective. There are a number of specialty runs in the 1973 Topps set. Card #1 depicts Ruth, Aaron, and Mays as all-time home run kings; league leaders in various statistical categories are pictured together on a group of eight cards; a 10-card run depicts action in the League Championship Series and World Series; there is a group of "All-Time" leader cards, picturing Cobb, Ruth, Gehrig, etc.; and, for the second year in a row, pictures of current big leaguers when they were kids (too cute for words—gag me with a Louisville Slugger!). The "Boyhood Photos" cards in the 1973 set are Jim Palmer, Gaylord Perry, Chris Speier, Sam McDowell, Bobby Murcer, and Catfish Hunter. Rookie cards in 1973 combine a trio of player photos by position, rather than team. Another interesting specialty group in the 1973 set are the manager/coaches cards. The manager of each team is pictured in color at the left of the horizontal-format card, and there are insect-size black-and-white photos of the coaches on the right side. The inclusion of the coaches, for the first time in many years, allows collectors to have such "old-timers" as Johnny Podres, Ernie Banks, Elston Howard, Lew Burdette, Ted Kluszewski, Larry Doby, Warren Spahn, Bill Mazeroski, Jim Gilliam, and Tommy Lasorda on 1973 cards.

FOR

Overall, the design is good, even if the photos are not always so hot.

AGAINST

Too many bad photos, too many specialty cards that collectors don't find special.

NOTEWORTHY CARDS

The only really "hot" card in the 1973 Topps set has been the rookie card of Mike Schmidt, one of three players featured on card #615, "Rookie Third Basemen." It's scarce, and a $45 to $50 item. A few other rookie cards worth mention are Buddy Bell, Rich Gossage, Gary Matthews, Al Bumbry, and

Dwight Evans. There are a couple of wrong photos in the '73 set. The photo on the Elly Rodriguez card is John Fleske; the photo on the Joe Rudi card is Gene Tenace. The last regular-issue card of Willie Mays as a player is found in the set, as is the last regular card of Roberto Clemente, killed in a plane crash on Dec. 31, 1972. There is a little known specialty series in the 1973 Topps set, a series of unnumbered team checklist cards that was included, probably among the high numbers. The cards have the team name at top and a white panel with facsimile autographs at the bottom of the front. There is a blue border around the front of the card. Card backs present a checklist for that team. These cards are not usually listed in the price guides, and few collectors have them in their "complete" 1973 sets.

VALUE

EX.-MT. CONDITION: Complete set, $175; common card, low numbers, 10¢; common card, #529–#660, 40¢; stars, $1–$3; Clemente, Mays, Aaron, Jackson, Yastrzemski, $5; Rose, $10; Schmidt, $45–$50. 5-YEAR PROJECTION: Average.

1973 Topps, Larry Bowa

1973 Topps, Pittsburgh Pirates Team Card

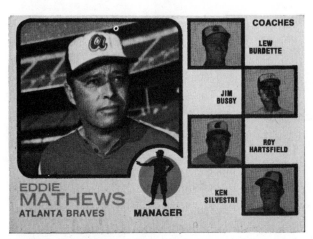

1973 Topps, Atlanta Braves Manager and Coaches

1973 Topps, Luis Aparicio

1973 Topps, Felix Millan

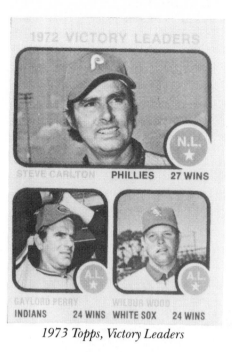

1973 Topps, Victory Leaders

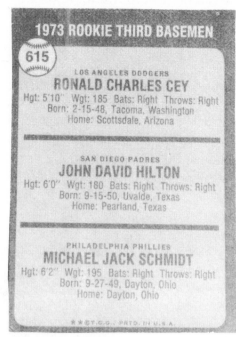

1973 Topps, Rookie Third Basemen (back)

1973 Topps, National League Play-off

1973 Topps, Reggie Jackson

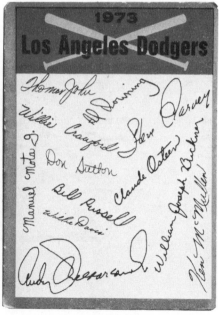

1973 Topps,
Los Angeles Dodgers Team Checklist

1973 KELLOGG'S

VALUE

EX.-MT. CONDITION: Complete set, $35; common card, 50¢; stars, $1–$2; Rose, $3–$4. 5-YEAR PROJECTION: Average.

SPECIFICATIONS

SIZE: 2¼×3½″. FRONT: Color photograph on blue, red, and yellow background. BACK: Blue printing on white cardboard. DISTRIBUTION: Nationally, one card in each cereal box, sets available by mail.

HISTORY

Collectors call this the Kellogg's 2-D set because it was the only issue from the cereal company without the three-dimensional visual effect. The cards featured a player's color photo set in a blue and white shield on a red background. There was a white border all around with a row of nine blue stars at top and bottom. The player's last name appeared in a yellow banner below the photo, with his position in the red field above it. A small photo of the player continued to be part of the back design, along with biographical information and career stats. The 1973 Kellogg's cards returned to the slightly larger 2¼×3½″ format for that year. The set size remained at 54 cards. Cards continued to be available in boxes of cereal, but a new offer was made in 1973. By sending in a specified amount of cash and box tops, a collector could receive a complete set by mail. This mail-in offer has been continued and has resulted in fairly steady supplies of Kellogg's cards from 1972 on.

FOR

The 1973 set is not prone to the type of curling and cracking found on the earlier and later Kellogg's issues with the plastic lamination.

AGAINST

Because the '73 set lacks the 3-D effect of the rest of the Kellogg's issues, it is considered "different" by collectors, and sometimes spurned for this reason.

NOTEWORTHY CARDS

Biggest names in the set are Rose, Carlton, Gibson, Ryan, Palmer, Perry, Brock, Seaver, Jackson, Kaline, and Carew. No Aaron, Yastrzemski, or Robinsons.

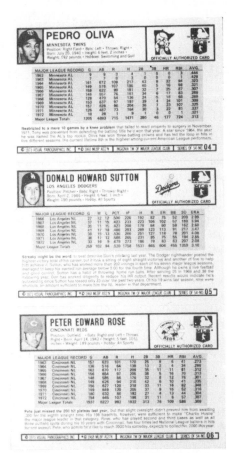

*1973 Kellogg's,
Tony Oliva, Don Sutton, Pete Rose (back)*

1973 Kellogg's, Tony Oliva, Don Sutton, Pete Rose (front)

1972 TOPPS

SPECIFICATIONS

SIZE: 2½×3½″. FRONT: Color photograph. BACK: Black and orange printing on gray cardboard. DISTRIBUTION: Nationally, in packages with bubblegum.

HISTORY

In 1972, Topps issued its largest card set—at 787 cards—to date. The 1972 issue was also Topps' gaudiest. "Psychedelic" is the word most often heard in describing the issue. The color photo of the player at the center of the card is shaped like a tombstone and is surrounded by two different colored borders (sometimes the colors harmonize, sometimes they clash awfully) inside the outermost white border. The team name is presented at the top of the card in "superhero" type in a variety of colors. The player's name is in a white panel below the picture. The '72 cards are unique for Topps in that the player's position is not indicated anywhere on the front of the card. Card backs are a much more traditional blend of personal and career stats, along with a baseball trivia question. Collectors generally concede four levels of scarcity to the '72 Topps set. Most common are cards #1–#394, followed by #395–525, then #526–#656, and finally the "high numbers," #657–#787. The high numbers are probably much scarcer than current price levels would indicate, but the current lack of collectors attempting to complete full sets of the 1972 issue helps keep prices low. The high-number superstars Rod Carew and Steve Garvey and the Steve Carlton "Traded" card are certainly priced more in line with true scarcity. Topps filled in the extra numbers in its '72 set with a record number of specialty runs. One of the largest and most innovative was the more than six dozen "In Action" cards. This concept allowed Topps to get into its set at least two baseball cards of each of the then-popular superstars or current heroes. The card number of the "In Action" cards immediately followed the "regular" portrait card of those players. It is a concept that Topps has used often in recent years. Curiously, most collec-

tors have an aversion to the "In Action" type of cards. There is a feeling widespread in the hobby that any card other than a player's "regular" card is less desirable. This translates into lower values for the "In Action" cards on all but the most common players. For stars in the 1972 set, the "In Action" cards are generally valued at just about half the value of the regular card of the same player. In its statistical leader subset for the 1971 season, Topps combined pictures of the top ranked player and the two runners-up, one from each league, on each card. There was a 10-card series summarizing the League Championship and World Series action of 1971 (Orioles-Pirates), and the World's Champion Pirates had the honor of having their team card as the #1 card in the 1972 set. Topps may have gotten a bit too cutesy-pie with its specialty series of 16 "Boyhood Photo" cards of current stars. Still, some collectors have always wondered what guys like Tom Seaver and Brooks Robinson looked like in short pants. There was a short series of cards depicting various major baseball award winners of 1971. The final specialty was a group of seven "Traded" cards. Unlike later Topps Traded cards, which were usually numbered outside the regular set, the '72 Traded series is numbered as part of the regular issue (#751–#757). The cards are similar in design to the rest of the set, but feature a large stenciled "TRADED" across the front of the card, with details of the transaction on the back. Four fairly big names are involved in the Traded group, Steve Carlton, Frank Robinson, Denny McClain, and Joe Morgan. Rookie cards for 1972 are presented either with three teammates per card or three players at the same position from different teams.

FOR

Large, colorful set; lots of specialty cards if that's your preference.

AGAINST

Too gaudy for most people's taste. The high numbers are a serious impediment to completing a set.

NOTEWORTHY CARDS

Two error cards appear in the '72 set, both on "specialty" cards. On the Brewers Rookies card, the pictures of

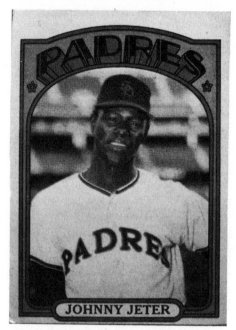

1972 Topps, Johnny Jeter

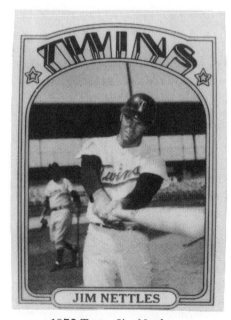

1972 Topps, Jim Nettles

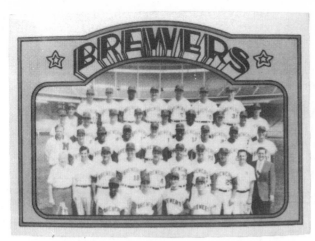

1972 Topps, Milwaukee Brewers Team Card

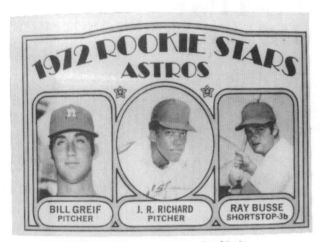

1972 Topps, Houston Astros Rookie Stars

Jerry Bell and Darrell Porter have the names mixed up. On the National League ERA leaders card, the player identified as Dave Roberts (2.10 ERA in '71) is really Danny Coombs (6.21 ERA in '71). Best rookie card in the set is Red Sox Rookies, with both Cecil Cooper and Carlton Fisk. Most of the other rookie cards in '72 are stars of lesser stature: Toby Harrah, Chris Chambliss, Dave Kingman, George Hendrick, and Ben Oglivie-Ron Cey (same card).

OUR FAVORITE CARD

Many of the "In Action" cards in the '72 set give the viewer a real insight into the player pictured. Certainly one such card is that of Billy Martin, the only manager to have an "In Action" card. Then-Tigers skipper Martin is shown "In Action" in a very characteristic pose, beefing with an umpire.

VALUE

EX.-MT. CONDITION: Complete set, $300; common card, #1–#525, 15¢; #526–#656, 25¢; #657–#787, 75¢; superstars, $1–$4; Mays, Yastrzemski, Aaron, Carlton, Jackson, Robinson Traded, Oglivie-Cey rookie, $5–$7; Cooper-Fisk rookie, Rose In Action, $9–$10; Carlton Traded, Carew In Action, $13–$15; Rose, $22–$25; Carew, Garvey, $35. 5-YEAR PROJECTION: Average.

1972 Topps, World Series

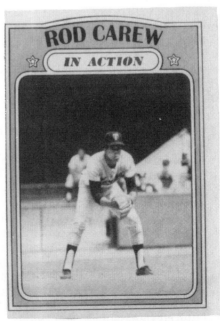

1972 Topps, Rod Carew, In Action

1972 KELLOGG'S

SPECIFICATIONS

SIZE: 2⅛×3¼". FRONT: Color photograph, 3-D effect. BACK: Blue printing on white cardboard. DISTRIBUTION: Nationally, one card in each box of cereal.

HISTORY

There were some changes in the 1972 Kellogg's set. The issue was made smaller: the individual cards were made ¼" smaller all-around, and the set was reduced from 75 cards to 54. Still featuring the 3-D effect (achieved by laminating a piece of ribbed plastic to a color photo of the player set against an indistinct stadium backdrop), the cards of 1972 are identifiable at first glance by the diagonal red stripes across the upper-left and lower-right corners. The player's last name and position are printed on the stripes. Blue and white borders surround the photo area. Backs of the 1972 Kellogg's cards once again feature a small player photo, and a short biography has been added to the personal and career stats. In 1972, collectors rushed to store shelves to buy boxes of cereal, not wanting to be left out as many had been in 1971 when no surplus cards were made available at the end of the promotion. Instead of buying Corn Flakes, in '72 they had to buy Raisin Bran. Kellogg's surprised them again, however. At the end of the 1972 season the cereal company made large quantities of the cards available to selected dealers. Net result is that the '72 set is much easier to complete than the '71, and much less expensive.

FOR

Nice-looking cards, attractive price.

AGAINST

Tendency for the cards to curl as the ribbed plastic lamination contracts with age. This, or rough handling of the cards, can result in cracking of the plastic layer.

NOTEWORTHY CARDS

The number of superstars in the '72 Kellogg's set was reduced right along with the overall set size. The only Hall of Fame caliber players among the 54 cards are Seaver, Rose, McCovey, Palmer, Jackson, Catfish Hunter, Bob Gibson, Marichal, Brock, Clemente, Stargell, and Mays.

VALUE

EX.-MT. CONDITION: Complete set, $35; common card, 35¢; stars, $1–$2; Rose, $3–$4. 5-YEAR PROJECTION: Average, or slightly better.

1972 KELLOGG'S ALL-TIME GREATS

SPECIFICATIONS

SIZE: 2¼×3½". FRONT: Color-tinted black-and-white photograph, 3-D effect. BACK: Blue printing on white cardboard. DISTRIBUTION: Nationally, one card in each package of toaster pastry.

HISTORY

While most collectors know and identify these 15 cards as "1972 Kellogg's All-Time Greats," they were in reality first issued two years before, in bags of Rold Gold pretzels. Only the copyright date has been changed—to 1972 for the Kellogg's cards. Because there is nothing on the cards that mentions the pretzel company (or the cereal company, for that matter), they are best known for having been distributed in packages of Kellogg's Danish-Go 'Rounds. The All-Time Greats cards are in the same basic format as the Kellogg's 3-D issues, and the cards were produced by the same company, Xograph, in Texas. For this series, black-and-white—rather than color—player photos have been used. These were color tinted and placed in front of blurred stadium backgrounds, and then covered by a lamination of ribbed plastic to give a 3-D look. The player's name is printed in a yellow banner at bottom, while his position, either as "Greatest" or "Finalist," appears in a yellow shield in the upper corner. Backs feature an-

other photo of the player, a short biography, and a career summary with lifetime stats.

FOR

Collectors of All-Time Greats issues have a unique format in the Kellogg's/Rold Gold series; the cards are quite attractive and make the old-timers seem to "come alive."

AGAINST

There is still the problem that most collectors don't like cards of players issued after their careers are over; they don't seem "legitimate." Beyond that, there is the usual problem of the Xograph-process cards cracking and curling as a result of handling or age. This greatly reduces card value.

NOTEWORTHY CARDS

The 15-card "All-Time Baseball Greats" set features 14 Hall of Fame players (Babe Ruth has two cards in the set). Gehrig and Cobb, Wagner and Johnson, all the big names are included. There are no bench-warmers in this set.

VALUE

EX.-MT. CONDITION: Complete set, $8.50; common card, 50¢; Ruth, $1. 5-YEAR PROJECTION: Below average.

1971 TOPPS

SPECIFICATIONS

SIZE: 2½×3½". FRONT: Color photograph. BACK: Green and black printing on gray cardboard. DISTRIBUTION: Nationally, in packages with bubblegum.

HISTORY

Topps' 1971 set—at 752 cards—was its biggest ever. And its design and format was one of the company's finest. A large color photo at the bottom of the card was bordered in white, and a pitch-black border surrounded the whole. The player's name, team, and position were reversed out of the black border in bright colors at the top of the card. A facsimile autograph over the photo completed the front design. The back design was a major innovation in that a second photo of the player appeared, in a 1½″-square black-and-white "snapshot" at the left, the first time a baseball card had ever carried the player's photo on the card front and back. Naturally, the photo left little room for other information on the back, so stats were limited to the previous season and cumulative lifetime figures. Another interesting feature of the '71 backs is a little line giving the year of the player's first pro game and his first major league game. In addition, there is a short player biography and a few personal statistics. While the black-bordered 1971 Topps set is extremely attractive when the cards are found in Mint condition, they show wear very easily, the black ink chipping or flaking off the corners and edges with little provocation. This makes Mint cards hard to come by. Some unscrupulous persons will touch up the corners or edges with a black crayon to make a slightly worn card appear better than it is. In comparison to other 1970s Topps sets, there were few specialty subsets in the 1971 issue. The winners and runners-up in various important statistical categories were featured by league on a group of 12 cards; there was an eight-card run depicting action in the American and National League play-offs; and a six-card grouping recounted the Orioles' victory over the Reds in the World Series. There were a large number of rookie cards in the 1971 set, a few of individual players, some showing two or three to a team, and a few grouped by position. Because the 1971 set was released series by series as the baseball season progressed, there are several levels of scarcity among the 752 cards. Cards #1–#523 are the most common, there is a "semi-high" series in #524–#643, and the "high numbers," #644–#752, are quite challenging.

1971 Topps, American League Play-off

1971 Topps, Bob Lemon

FOR
One of Topps' most attractive card sets. Lots of superstars as well as little-known players to delight team collectors.

AGAINST
Extremely hard to find Mint cards.

NOTEWORTHY CARDS
Lots of good rookie cards in the '71 set, most notably, Steve Garvey. Others are: Dave Concepcion, Ken Singleton, Ted Simmons, George Foster, Greg Luzinski, and, on the same "Rookie Outfielders" card, Dusty Baker and Don Baylor.

OUR FAVORITE CARD
Pete Rose collectors can find a "hidden" Pete Rose card in the 1971 set. That Cincinnati Reds baserunner on second, behind Phillies pitcher Chris Short on Short's card (#511), is ol' Charlie Hustle himself.

VALUE
EX.-MT. CONDITION: Complete set, $300; common cards, #1–523, 12¢; #524–#643, 40¢; #644–#752, 60¢; superstars, $2–$6; Clemente, Aaron, Yastrzemski, $7–$9; Rose, $13–$15; Garvey, $17.50–$20. 5-YEAR PROJECTION: Average, perhaps above.

1971 Topps, World Series Game #3

1971 Topps, Steve Garvey

1971 Topps, RBI Leaders

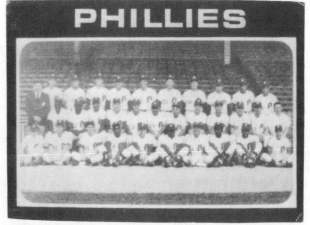

1971 Topps, Philadelphia Phillies Team Card

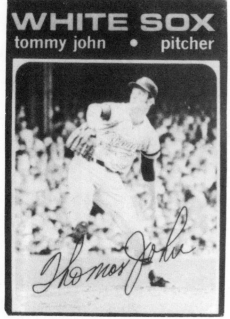

1971 Topps, Tommy John

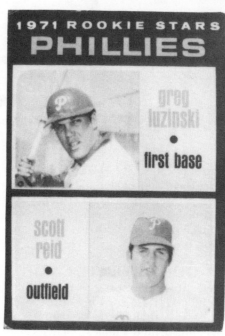

1971 Topps, Philadelphia Phillies Rookie Stars

1971 Topps, Gaylord Perry

COMPLETE BOOK OF COLLECTIBLE BASEBALL CARDS

1971 TOPPS SUPERS

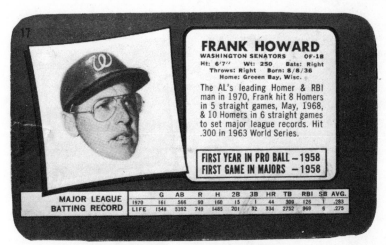

1971 Topps Supers, Frank Howard (back)

SPECIFICATIONS

SIZE: 3⅛×5¼″. FRONT: Color photograph. BACK: Green and black printing on gray cardboard. DISTRIBUTION: Nationally, in packages with bubblegum.

HISTORY

In 1971, for the second straight year, Topps produced a separate set of oversize baseball cards called Supers. These large-format cards featured borderless color photos on the front, with only a facsimile autograph for identification. The corners of the cards are rounded, so they tend to hold up well without looking used. Backs of the cards are enlarged versions of the same player's card in the regular Topps set for 1971; only the card number has been changed. There are 63 cards in the 1971 Super set, compared to 42 the previous year. The 63-card set size meant there were no short-printed cards in the '71 Supers, and hence no real scarcities. Naturally, most of the players in this special set were stars, so it is not an inexpensive set to collect, and the cards themselves are far scarcer than the regular Topps issue for 1971.

FOR

Attractive, large-size cards. Great for the superstar collector, and priced reasonably, considering their scarcity as a whole.

AGAINST

Many collectors don't like oversize cards, or cards with rounded corners.

NOTEWORTHY CARDS

Virtually all Hall of Fame caliber players active in 1971 are present in the Supers set.

VALUE

EX.-MT. CONDITION: Complete set, $90; common card, 50¢–75¢; stars, $1–$3; Brock, Bench, Seaver, Kaline, Brooks Robinson, Killebrew, $5; Clemente, Jackson, Aaron, Mays, Yastrzemski, $7–$10; Rose, $15–$17.50. 5-YEAR PROJECTION: Above average.

1971 Topps Supers, Frank Howard (front)

1971 Topps Supers, Luis Aparicio

1971 Topps Supers, Fritz Peterson

1971 Topps Supers, Rich Allen

1971 Topps Supers, Bert Campaneris

1971 TOPPS GREATEST MOMENTS

SPECIFICATIONS

SIZE: 2½×4¾". FRONT: Color and black-and-white photos. BACK: Black and white. DISTRIBUTION: Limited geographic areas on test basis, in packages with bubblegum.

HISTORY

One of the scarcer and more popular Topps test issues of the early 1970s, the Greatest Moments set of 1971 is quite a challenge for a card set less than 15 years old. The 55 cards in the set depict a career highlight for then-current players. A portrait photo of the player appears in color at the left end of the card front. A black-and-white deckle-edge action photo at right takes up the majority of the card. There is a small headline in the white border of the photo. The whole front is surrounded by a black border, a design which presents the problems of chipping and flaking as in the regular 1971 Topps issue. Card backs, also bordered in black, feature a detail from the front photo and present the story of the particular "Greatest Moment" in newspaper format. It is interesing to note that the news-paper-style accounts appear under the name and general logotype of real hometown newspapers in the different cities.

FOR

Unusual format helps spice up a superstar collection; virtually every player in the set is a star.

AGAINST

Cards are really quite scarce, also expensive.

NOTEWORTHY CARDS

Virtually everybody in the set is a star; when the "commons" in a set include Jim Perry, Bill Freehan, Rico Petrocelli, and Jim Wynn, you know it's loaded with stars.

VALUE

EX.-MT. CONDITION: Complete set, $550; common card, $4; Hall of

Famers, $10–$20; Mays, Yastrzemski, $20–$25; Rose, $40–$45. 5-YEAR PROJECTION: Average, perhaps a bit below.

1971 BAZOOKA

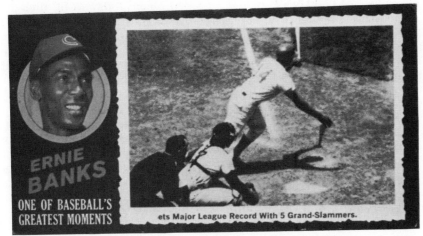

1971 Topps Greatest Moments, Ernie Banks (front)

1971 Topps Greatest Moments, Ernie Banks (back)

SPECIFICATIONS

SIZE: Single card, $2 \times 2^5/_8''$; three-card panel, $5^5/_{16}'' \times 2^5/_8''$. FRONT: Color photograph. BACK: Blank. DISTRIBUTION: Nationally, a three-card panel on each bubblegum box.

HISTORY

The final Bazooka bubblegum cards were issued by Topps in 1971, reverting to the same basic formula used since the second Bazooka set was issued in 1960. A strip of three baseball cards was printed on the bottom panel of each 25-piece box of 1¢ Bazooka bubblegum (the box generally retailed for about 19¢ to 21¢ back then). In all, there were a dozen different bottom panels in 1971—36 different cards. The cards were meant to be cut off the box on the familiar "dotted lines." Because most kids weren't too careful with the scissors, well-cut cards with nice even borders are somewhat scarce. Collectors will pay a premium for cards still in uncut strips of three (generally 10 to 15 percent over the total value of the three cards priced individually). Complete boxes command a 25 to 50 percent premium. Like many of the earlier Bazooka sets, the 1971 issue contains a high percentage of Hall of Famers and soon-to-be Hall of Famers. The format of the cards is little changed from the early years, a full-color photo of the player, surrounded by a white border. On the 1971 issue, the player's name, team, and position are printed in a red oval at the bottom of the card. The '71 Bazookas are unnumbered.

FOR

The 1971 set returned to Bazooka's successful format of individual cards of current players. There are lots of stars in the set. Prices are reasonable, considering scarcity in relation to the much more common regular-issue Topps cards of the same year.

AGAINST

Card size is too small to suit most collectors, who prefer the standard of $2^1/_2 \times 3^1/_2''$.

NOTEWORTHY CARDS

Hall of Famers: Killebrew, Clemente, Mays, Marichal, Aparicio, Brooks Robinson, Aaron, Gibson. Superstars: Reggie Jackson, Rose, Yastrzemski.

VALUE

EX.-MT. CONDITION, NEATLY CUT FROM BOX: Complete set, $75; common card, $1; Hall of Famers, $3–$5; Aaron, Mays, Yastrzemski, Jackson, $7.50–$10; Rose, $15. 5-YEAR PROJECTION: Average.

1971 KELLOGG'S

SPECIFICATIONS

SIZE: 2¼×3½". FRONT: Color photograph, 3-D effect. BACK: Blue printing on white cardboard. DISTRIBUTION: Nationally, one card in each cereal box.

HISTORY

Collectors had been burned in 1970: they'd bought their Kellogg's cards in cereal boxes, one at a time, only to find complete sets available later that year. These same collectors thought they would play it smart in 1971 and wait for the complete-set offer at season's end, rather than buying cases of Corn Flakes. Kellogg's outsmarted them again, however; the 1971 cards were issued only in the cereal boxes. They were never made available in complete sets. By the time the hobby realized this, the "specially-marked boxes" were off store shelves. The result was a mad scramble to complete sets, with resulting increases in card value. The 1971 set is the most difficult Kellogg's set to complete, and the most valuable of the company's 14 issues. There are again 75 cards in the 1971 issue, produced in the same three-dimensional look as the 1970 cards. A blue border with white highlights surrounds the color photo on the front of the card, and it, in turn, is surrounded by a white border. Overall, this results in a much smaller picture area. The player's last name and position appear in a red star in an upper corner. On card backs, a small photo of the player has been included

in the upper left, along with an official team logo.

FOR

A good-looking set, genuinely challenging to complete, good future potential for price appreciation.

AGAINST

Cards have a tendency to curl from top to bottom. This, or rough handling, can result in cracks in the ribbed plastic lamination on the card's front. Such damaged cards are greatly reduced in value.

NOTEWORTHY CARDS

There are fewer big names in the 1971 Kellogg's set than in previous sets. Notably absent among those who appeared the previous year are Hank Aaron, Brooks Robinson, Reggie Jackson, and Johnny Bench. Still no Yastrzemski card. Superstars who do appear in the set are Seaver, Clemente, Frank Robinson, Gaylord Perry, Mays, Brock, McCovey, Kaline, Killebrew, Banks, Palmer, and Rose.

VALUE

EX.-MT. CONDITION: Complete set, $250; common card, $2–$3; stars, $5–$7.50; Rose, $15. 5-YEAR PROJECTION: Well above average.

1971 MILK DUDS

SPECIFICATIONS

SIZE: 1¹³/₁₆×2⅝". FRONT: Sepia photograph on light tan cardboard. BACK: Blank. DISTRIBUTION: Nationally, on the back of 5¢ boxes of Milk Duds candy.

HISTORY

Perhaps one of the more underrated baseball cards of the early 1970s, the Milk Duds issue of 1971 contains a high percentage of superstar players among its 69 cards. Surprisingly for a card which was issued on the back of a box, the Milk Duds cards are seldom found cut off their original container. It's a good thing, too, because most collectors would not recognize them; there is no identification on the card

itself, just the player's picture, his name, and a short line about his 1970 performance. The cards are usually found on empty boxes, and they apparently made their way into the hobby channels directly from the printer or the Holloway candy company. However, since it would be no problem today to fill such a leftover box and glue it shut, there is no premium value attached to a full box. Cards which have been cut from the box are worth only about half of the value of a complete box.

FOR

Good value in terms of rarity; Milk Duds are priced just a bit over the price of the same player's card in the much more common 1971 Topps set. Complete boxes make nice shelf display items.

AGAINST

Cards are too small, not in full color. Storing lots of flattened boxes takes up a lot of space.

NOTEWORTHY CARDS

Hall of Famers Aparicio, Killebrew, Frank and Brooks Robinson, Aaron, Banks, Clemente, Gibson, Mays. Future Hall of Famers Hunter, John, Palmer, Bench, Brock, McCovey, Perry, Rose, Seaver. Also, Thurman Munson.

VALUE

EX.-MT. CONDITION, COMPLETE BOX: Complete set, $300; common card, $1.50; Hall of Famer or future Hall of Famer, $3–$4; Aaron, Mays, $10; Rose, $12.50. 5-YEAR PROJECTION: Above average.

1970 TOPPS

SPECIFICATIONS

SIZE: 2½×3½". FRONT: Color photograph. BACK: Blue and yellow printing on white cardboard. DISTRIBUTION: Nationally, in packages with bubblegum.

HISTORY

Because it was issued at the beginning of a decade, the 1970 Topps set is a popular "starting point" for many modern baseball card collectors. At 720 cards, the issue was the largest produced by Topps up to that point. The design is simple, yet attractive. A color photo at the top of the card is overprinted with the team name in big red, yellow, or white block letters, and the whole photo is framed with a thin white border. The player's name is in script at bottom left, and his position in the lower right. A gray border surrounds the entire package. Compared to the black border which Topps would use the next year, the gray border is not especially susceptible to damage and does not show wear as easily. Card backs are bright and easy to read, combining a cartoon about the player with a short career summary, personal data, and major/minor league stats. The 1970 cards were issued in series as the year progressed, and the set is one of many Topps issues in which the cards are progressively tougher to find. Cards #1–#459 are the easiest; #460–#546 are a little more difficult; #547–#633 are harder still; and #634–#720 are the hardest. The most expensive card in the set is Johnny Bench, who appears in the high numbers along with Nolan Ryan, Frank Robinson, and Al Kaline. A three-year tradition began in 1970 when Topps made the team card of the World Series winner—the Amazin' Mets—card #1 in the set. The Mets also featured prominently in two of the specialty subsets of 1970: eight cards recapping the 1969 American and National League play-offs, and the six-card World Series highlights cards. There were also special cards for 1969's statistical leaders in major categories. The winner in each league shared a card with the two runners-up, creating some three- and four-player cards with a lot of superstars. Topps also ended a three-year tradition in 1970 by issuing the last separate set of *Sporting News* All-Star cards until 1982 (such cards were also issued 1958–1962). Like most of its predecessors, the 1970 All-Star issues were of a somewhat different design than the rest of the set. The '70 All-Star cards feature a color portrait of the player "tearing through" a newspaper bearing the *Sporting News* logo and a January 24, 1970 dateline, along with—curiously—a headline that says something about the Sharks, a forfeit, and the Caribbean Series. All-Star card backs feature a large cartoon portrait of the player. Like most All-Star cards (unless they appear in rare high number series), the 1970s are worth less than the "regular" cards in the set which feature the same players. There are 20 cards in the '70 All-Stars, eight starting fielders for each league and left- and right-handed pitchers. The rookies are arranged by team, featuring either two or three players.

FOR

A good place to start a modern collection. The 1970 set has many of the best old features of the 1960s, without a lot of the gimmick cards that would be seen later in the '70s. There are lots of older Hall of Famers still playing or managing, as well as some of what are the better-known veterans of the game today. Considering its age and the scarcity of high number cards, the price is reasonable.

AGAINST

There's not much that can be said that's negative about the 1970 set, except that eagle-eyed error hunters will have a field day with card backs and some "strange" photos.

NOTEWORTHY CARDS

The 1970 Topps set was one of many in that era that devoted specialty subsets to league play-offs and the World Series. Topps was not always so careful, though, in choosing the photos that they used on those cards. Never one to let an incorrect photo get in the way of a good baseball card, the company frequently used game-action photos from different games to represent the play-off and World Series contests. Probably Topps' worst year in this respect was 1970, when three of the eight league play-off cards had wrong photos. Cards #195 and #196, purporting to show Games 1 and 2 of the National League pennant series, which were played in Atlanta, actually show action from Game 3, at New York. The giveaway is that in the photos, the Mets are wearing home uniforms. On card #201, which claims to show the deciding game of the Orioles-Twins play-offs, Baltimore catcher Andy Etchebarren is pictured, but he only played in the first and second games of that series. The 1970 set also contains a number of "equipment errors" among the player photos. When the Topps photographer stopped players from whatever they were doing on the field and asked them to strike an "action" pose for the camera, some details were overlooked. Grant Jackson (#6) is shown "pitching" while wearing a batting glove, and Steve Huntz is shown throwing the ball, also with a batting glove. Outfielder Bob Watson posed

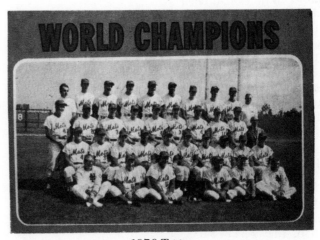

1970 Topps,
New York Mets World's Champions Team Card

1970 Topps, Bobby Murcer

1970 Topps, Al Oliver

for card #407 with a catcher's mitt, and Cardinals shortstop Dal Maxvill is shown in a fielding pose—but he's wearing a batting helmet. The hot rookie card in 1970 is Thurman Munson; others of note are Vida Blue-Gene Tenace, Jerry Reuss, and Bill Buckner.

OUR FAVORITE CARD

It's a toss-up. How can you choose between these two? Card #59, Dick Ellsworth, shows the Cleveland Indians pitcher in a Cubs uniform. Ellsworth last played for the Cubs in 1966, and in between times had been with the Phillies and the Red Sox. Card #74, "Angels Rookies," features pitcher Wally Wolf. That's actually Wolf's second "rookie card," he appeared on card #208, "Rookie Stars," seven years earlier! Actually, Wolf's 1963 debut card was a bit premature, because Wolf didn't appear in the major leagues until 1969. He owns a lifetime 0-0 record in 7.1 innings of major league play, with a 7.36 ERA.

VALUE

EX.-MT. CONDITION: Complete set, $275; common card, #1–#459, 12¢; #460–#546, 18¢; #547–#633, 30¢; #634–#720, 50¢; superstars, $2–$6; Aaron, Kaline, Yastrzemski, $7–$8; Mays, $10; Ryan, Munson, $13–$15; Rose, $20–$25; Bench, $30–$35. 5-YEAR PROJECTION: Average, or somewhat better.

1970 Topps, Hank Aaron, All-Star (back)

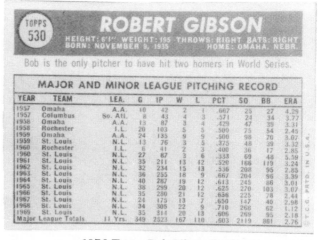

1970 Topps, Bob Gibson (back)

1970 TOPPS SUPERS

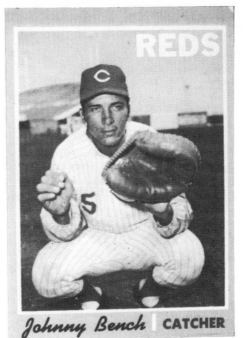

1970 Topps, Johnny Bench

1970 Topps, Hank Aaron, All-Star (front)

1970 Topps, Jim Spencer

1970 Topps, Bob Gibson (front)

SPECIFICATIONS

SIZE: 3⅛×5¼". FRONT: Color photograph. BACK: Blue and yellow printing on yellow cardboard. DISTRIBUTION: Nationally, in packages with bubblegum.

HISTORY

The 1970 "Super Baseball" card issue from Topps was an expansion on the format begun a year earlier. The principal difference was in the size of the cards. While the '69 Supers had been about the same size as the regular issue baseball cards, the 1970 Supers were produced in postcard-size format. The cards were printed on heavy, white glossy stock and then trimmed to give them rounded corners. Card fronts were borderless color photos with no other design element but a facsimile autograph. Card backs were just an enlarged version of the same player's card from the regular 1970 Topps set. There were 42 cards in the 1970 Supers, and it is believed that the press sheet configuration to arrive at that number resulted in three "short-printed" cards, which are scarcer than the rest. Cards #36 and #37, Ollie Brown and Frank Robinson, are somewhat scarcer than the other 39 cards in the set, while #38, Boog Powell, is the scarcest of all. Overall, the '70 Supers were distributed in larger quantities than the '69s, so they are not as expensive.

FOR

Attractive large-format cards. They make nice additions to superstar or team collections.

AGAINST

A lot of collectors don't like oversize cards or round corners.

NOTEWORTHY CARDS

Proportionately, there are a lot of stars in the '70 Supers; also lots of hometown favorites from the early '70s.

VALUE

EX.-MT. CONDITION: Complete set, $100; common card, 75¢; stars, $1–$3; Seaver, Bench, Brock, Brown,

Killebrew, Aparicio, $5; Aaron, Mays, Jackson, Frank Robinson, $7; Yastrzemski, $10; Rose, $15–$20; Powell, $35–$40. 5-YEAR PROJECTION: Above average.

1970 KELLOGG'S

SPECIFICATIONS
SIZE: 2¼×3½". FRONT: Full-color photo, 3-D effect. BACK: Blue printing on white cardboard. DISTRIBUTION: Nationally, one card per cereal box; complete sets through selected dealers at the end of the season.

HISTORY
In 1970, Kellogg's began a 14-year run of baseball card issues. These cards are important in the overall history of baseball cards because in many of those years, the Kellogg's cards were the only nationally distributed issue besides Topps. The cards feature a sharp color photo of the player set against a blurred stadium background, surrounded by a blue border. A layer of ribbed plastic laminated over the picture gave a three-dimensional effect. Card backs featured a few biographical and career details, along with major league stats, all printed in blue. This was the first widespread baseball card issue to utilize the 3-D look, which Topps had tried on a test basis in 1968. The cards were produced by Xograph Company of Irving, Tex. One of the 1970 "3-D Super Star" cards was packaged in each box of Kellogg's Corn Flakes. A lot of collectors ate a lot of corn flakes trying to find all 75 cards—at a cost that could run to $50 or more. Kellogg's had a surprise in store at the end of the season, though, when hobbyists were shocked to find Kellogg's had dumped its leftover cards into the market by selling them to selected dealers and certain toy store outlets.

The price of the set plummeted to $5, though it has since regained its lost market value.

FOR
Attractive cards, reasonable price.

AGAINST
The 3-D process in which the Kellogg's cards are produced causes them to curl upward, bottom to top, as they get older. This, or rough handling, also causes the plastic overlay to crack, greatly reducing the value of the cards.

NOTEWORTHY CARDS
About every third card in the 1970 Kellogg's set is a major star of Hall of Fame proportions; all the names you'd expect to see are there, with the exception of Carl Yastrzemski.

VALUE
EX.-MT. CONDITION: Complete set, $50; common card, 35¢–50¢; stars, $1–$2; Aaron, Mays, Clemente, Jackson, $2–$3; Rose, $3–$5. 5-YEAR PROJECTION: Above average.

1970 TRANSO-GRAM

SPECIFICATIONS
SIZE: 2⁹/₁₆×3¹/₂". FRONT: Color photograph. BACK: Blank. DISTRIBUTION: Nationally, on bottom of boxes of toy baseball player statues.

HISTORY
The 1970 Transogram cards were produced in two series. There was a 45-card group of players from all teams, and a special 15-card series honoring "The Amazin' Mets," 1969 World's Champions. While the cards themselves were little changed for 1970 (they were one-sixteenth inch wider than in 1969), they were issued differently. Instead of one card per box, with one toy player figure inside, the boxes in 1970 contained three statues and had three cards printed on the bottom. Bordered by a dotted line on which to cut them, the '70 Transograms featured a color portrait photo with a white frame and yellow border. Player names were in red below the picture, with team, position, and a few biographical details in black. There is no card number. Backs are blank. All of the cards that appeared in both 1969 and 1970 Transogram sets feature the same photos, with the exception of Joe Torre and Johnny Callison (whose reversed photo from '69 was corrected in '70). The 1970 Transogram cards are most valuable when still attached to the complete box, with statues inside. Value of such an item is double the total value of the three cards as individuals. Cards still attached in panels of three would be worth some 50 percent more than the cards' cumulative value. Cards which have been cut from the box in sloppy fashion are least desirable.

FOR
Something different for the superstar collector. The Mets cards are especially nice for the team collector.

AGAINST
Hard to find in nice condition. Cards are really not that attractive.

NOTEWORTHY CARDS
Again, lots of stars and Hall of Famers.

VALUE
EX.-MT. CONDITION, NEATLY CUT FROM BOX: Complete set, $275; common card, $2.50; stars, $3–$5; McCovey, Banks, Gibson, Frank Robinson, Kaline, Killebrew, Ryan, $10–$15; Mays, Seaver, Aaron, Clemente, Jackson, Yastrzemski, $18–$22; Rose, $25–$30. 5-YEAR PROJECTION: Below average.

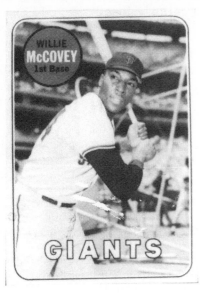

SANDY KOUFAX

PITCHER L.A. DODGERS

1969-1960

DON
DRYSDALE

1969 TOPPS

SPECIFICATIONS

SIZE: 2½×3½". FRONT: Color photograph. BACK: Black and pink printing on white cardboard. DISTRIBUTION: Nationally, in packages with bubblegum.

HISTORY

The 1969 set is unusual in many ways, all of which make it popular and collectible. For one thing, Topps again set a record—664—for the number of cards. Distribution of the series was also unusual. There are four levels of scarcity in the '69 set, but the "high numbers" (#514–#664) are not generally considered the scarcest; that honor goes to cards in the range #219–#327. Cards #1–#218 and #328–#512 are considered the most common. There are enough collectible (and valuable) variations in the 1969 set to keep you busy for some time assembling a complete set. The 1969 set featured the last Topps multi-player feature cards, and was missing the team cards that had been a staple of its issues since 1956. The three specialty subseries of the previous year returned in '69: a 12-card rundown of the statistical leaders in each league; a group of eight World Series special cards detailing the Tigers' win over the Yankees; and a *Sporting News* All-Star group of 20. Rookies were grouped two or three to a card, by team or league. Design of the 1969 set is somewhat similar to the 1967 set. A large color photo, bordered in white, occupies most of the card front. As on the 1967 cards, the team name is printed in colored block letters at the bottom. The player's name and position are contained in a circle in one of the upper corners. Card backs returned to a horizontal orientation in 1969, again combining (where space permitted) complete major and minor league stats, a cartoon, a short biography, etc.

FOR

In its basic form, the 1969 set is inexpensive and relatively easy to collect.

AGAINST

If you really want a complete set, you've got to do some studying to learn what actually constitutes a complete set. You've got to go out and find the variation cards, some of which can be quite expensive.

NOTEWORTHY CARDS

Let's start with the easy stuff, the rookie cards; Reggie Jackson has his own card in 1969, and it's the hottest card in the set. Other "name" rookies in the set are Amos Otis, Al Oliver, Graig Nettles, and Rollie Fingers. Now the tough stuff—the variations. The largest and most expensive group of variety cards in the 1969 set are the so-called "white letter" cards. Now, lots of cards in the set have the player or team name in white letters, but some cards in the area of #440–#511 come with these elements in either yellow (common) or white (scarce). Only the following cards are affected and are thus more valuable: 440, 441, 444, 447, 451, 452, 461, 464, 468, 470, 471, 473, 476, 482, 485, 486, 491, 493, 500, 501, 505, 511. Among common players in this group, the yellow-letter varieties are worth 20¢ or so and the white-letter cards are in the $1.50–$2 range. There are, however, three superstars in the group whose cards are worth considerably more. Willie McCovey (#440) with his last name in white is a $20 card as opposed to $4.50 with yellow name. Gaylord Perry (#485) with last name in white is $12; in yellow, $2.50. The big money in the white/yellow letter variations is in card #500, Mickey Mantle. A $16.50 item with the last name in yellow, the card featuring his name in white letters retails for $45–$50 in top condition. (This is also the last regular-issue Mickey Mantle card of his career; he had retired at the end of the previous season.) Next in collectibility are a pair of team/pose variations: cards #151, Clay Dalrymple and #208, Donn Clendenon. The Dalrymple card can be found with a portrait and the team specified as Orioles, or with the player in a catching position and the team listed as Phillies. The first is a 20¢ card; the second is worth $4–$5. Clendenon is seen with either "Houston" on the front (20¢), or "Expos" ($4–$5). There is a wrong-name variation on card #49, Royals Rookies: on the common type, Elly Rodriguez's name is spelled correctly (20¢); the scarcer variety has the name spelled "Rodriquez" and is a $4–$5 card.

There are two cards on which the player can be found with and without a team logo on his helmet or cap, the "without" version having had the logo airbrushed off the card to reflect a trade. These cards are #47, Paul Popovich ("C" for Chicago Cubs) and #77, Ron Perranoski ("LA" for Los Angeles Dodgers). On both cards, the version with the team emblem is a $4–$5 card, while the no-logo cards are worth 20¢. Checklist 2 (card #107) shows either "Jim Purdin" or "John Purdin" (correct) as card #161; the correct card being a $2 item, the error worth about 75¢. In the "photo problems" area for 1969, we have one flopped negative, #209, Larry Haney; one "hidden ball trick," card #465, on which Tommy John is shown following through on his pitching motion—with the ball still in the glove; and three "Let's fool the photographer" cards. On two of those, Gary Geiger (#478) and Mack Jones (#625) are shown batting the wrong way. The third is one of the classic baseball cards of all time, card #653, purporting to be the rookie card of Aurelio Rodriguez but actually picturing the Angels batboy.

OUR FAVORITE CARD

While on the subject of rookie cards, there is a Lou Piniella "rookie card" in the 1969 Topps set, #394, "Pilots

1969 Topps, Milt Pappas

Rookies." Actually, Piniella never played for Seattle; he was traded to Kansas City before the beginning of the season. Also, it isn't even Piniella's "real" rookie card; he appears in the 1968 set on card #16, "Indians Rookies." But that's not Piniella's true rookie card, either. The real Lou Piniella rookie card is in the 1964 Topps set, where he appears on card #167, "Senators Rookies." If you think three rookie cards is some kind of record, you're wrong. However, the real record for rookie card appearances *is* set in the 1969 Topps set, where Bill Davis appears on his *fifth* rookie card in as many years. Davis was on Indians rookie cards in 1965 through 1968, and a Padres Rookies card in 1969. Davis never appeared on a regular Topps card. In parts of three major league seasons, 43 games with the Indians in 1965 through 1966 and 31 with the Padres in 1969, Davis amassed a lifetime .181 batting average, striking out 28 times in 64 at bats.

VALUE

EX.-MT. CONDITION: Complete set, $275; common card, 15¢–25¢; superstars, $1–$4; Clemente, Oliver, Bench, Aaron, Yastrzemski, Mays, Carlton, Carew, Ryan, Fingers, $5–$10; Rose, Mantle, $15–$20; Jackson, $45. 5-YEAR PROJECTION: Average.

1969 Topps, The Sporting News *All-Stars, Ken Harrelson*

1969 Topps, Earl Wilson

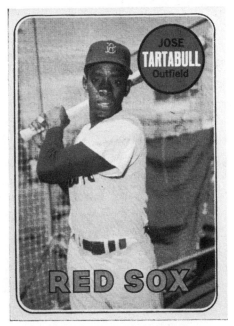

1969 Topps, Jose Tartabull

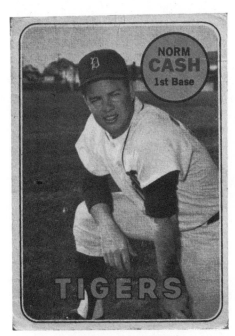

1969 Topps, Norm Cash

1969 Topps, Gil Hodges

1969 TOPPS SUPERS

SPECIFICATIONS
SIZE: 2¼×3¼". FRONT: Color photograph. BACK: Black printing on white cardboard. DISTRIBUTION: Nationally, in limited numbers.

HISTORY
Topps called them "Super Baseball Cards" on the back, a name that stuck with collectors and is also applied to the similar-format postcard-size issues of 1970 and 1971. The 1969 Topps Supers, though, weren't bigger than the regular-issue cards of that year. In fact, they were an eighth-inch smaller on each side. What was super about the cards was the high gloss finish that really enhances the bright color photo on the front of the card. The only other design element on the front is a black facsimile autograph. Card backs contain only a rectangular box at bottom with the player's name, team, and position, a copyright line, and a card number. The cards feature rounded corners. Superstars abound in the '69 Super set, and even the common cards are relatively scarce. The set was distributed in very limited numbers and is an expensive challenge for the collector today. Because of the high quality of the cards and the attractive photos, however, these cards are the highlight of many superstar collections.

FOR
Extremely attractive, scarce, and valuable; lots of superstars.

AGAINST
High dollar value of even common cards and high demand for stars make it a tough set to collect.

NOTEWORTHY CARDS
Most of the big name stars of 1969 are in the Super set. There is a "last" card of Mickey Mantle, and a rookie card of Reggie Jackson; about a dozen other Hall of Famers and future HOFers are sprinkled throughout the set.

VALUE
EX.-MT. CONDITION: Complete set, $2,000; common card, $7.50; stars, $10–$15; Morgan, Wills, $25, Drysdale, Marichal, McCovey, Gibson, Seaver, Frank Robinson, Killebrew, $50–$75; Brooks Robinson, Clemente, $100–$125; Aaron, Mays, Reggie Jackson, Yastrzemski, $150–$175; Mantle, Rose, $300. 5-YEAR PROJECTION: Average, perhaps a bit below.

1969 TOPPS DECKLE-EDGE

SPECIFICATIONS
SIZE: 2¼×3¼". FRONT: Black-and-white photo. BACK: Blue printing on white cardboard. DISTRIBUTION: Nationally, in packs of regular 1969 Topps cards.

HISTORY
Designed to resemble the popular wallet-size photos of movie stars of the 1950s, the Topps Deckle-Edge set of 1969 takes its name from the peculiar scalloped effect on the white border of the cards. Photos are black-and-white, and the only other feature on the front of the card is a facsimile autograph of the player, printed in light blue ink. The same blue ink is seen on the back, where the player's name and card number are shown in a small rectangular box at bottom of the card. Although the back of the card says there are 33 photos in the set, there are actually 35; card #11 can be found as either Jim Wynn (scarce) or Hoyt Wilhelm (more common); and card #22 can be seen as either Joe Foy (scarce) or Rusty Staub (more common). The Deckle-Edge 1969s were inserted in regular packs of '69 Topps cards, and are not particularly rare today; all the same, collecting a complete set is still a challenge.

FOR
Inexpensive, unusual cards for a superstar collection.

AGAINST
They're black-and-white with a "funny" edge.

NOTEWORTHY CARDS
Most of the 35 players in the set are stars or minor stars of the era. The big name players include Brooks Robinson, Yastrzemski, Aparicio, Carew, Clemente, Rose, Gibson, McCovey, Marichal, and Mays.

VALUE
EX.-MT. CONDITION: Complete set, $35; common card, 25¢–50¢; stars, $1.25–$2.50; Wynn, Foy, Rose, $4–$5. 5-YEAR PROJECTION: Above average.

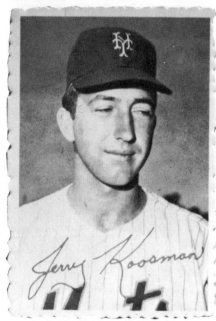

1969 Topps Deckle-Edge,
Jerry Koosman

*1969 Topps Deckle-Edge,
Luis Aparicio*

*1969 Topps Deckle-Edge,
Ken Harrelson*

1969 Topps Deckle-Edge, Rodney Carew

*1969 Topps Deckle-Edge,
Carl Yastrzemski*

1969 Topps Deckle-Edge, Pete Rose

1969 KAHN'S

SPECIFICATIONS
SIZE: $2^{13}/_{16} \times 3^{1}/_{4}''$ and $2^{13}/_{16} \times 3^{15}/_{16}''$. FRONT: Color photograph. BACK: Blank. DISTRIBUTION: Chicago, Ohio, Pittsburgh, and St. Louis areas; single cards in packages of meat products, complete sets available by mail.

HISTORY
The 15-year history of baseball card issues came to an end for the Kahn's meat company in 1969. While the later Kahn's sets certainly have their fans, the issues are too similar and too confusing for many collectors who would otherwise be attracted to these scarce regional issues. A total of 22 players make up the final Kahn's card issue, drawn from six teams, the Cubs, the White Sox, the Reds, the Indians, the Pirates, and the Cardinals. Again, as in the previous year, Kahn's 1969 cards come in two sizes; the smaller cards measure $2^{13}/_{16} \times 3^{1}/_{4}''$ with the advertising tab, and $2^{13}/_{16} \times 1^{7}/_{8}''$ without the tab. The larger cards measure $2^{13}/_{16} \times 3^{15}/_{16}''$ with the tab, and $2^{13}/_{16} \times 2^{11}/_{16}''$ without the tab. The two sizes were apparently issued for insertion in meat product packages of different sizes. Only three players—Aaron, Maloney, and Perez—appear in the smaller format for 1969. The cards keep the same basic design used by Kahn's since 1966. The upper portion of the card is an advertising tab with a red Kahn's rose logo, separated from the actual baseball card by a dotted line. While collectors prefer their Kahn's cards with the ad tab, the cards are more often found without it and values quoted below are for cards without tabs. Cards with the ad tab are worth some 15 to 20 percent more. The actual baseball card is a color photo set against a border of alternating colored stripes. The player's name is printed at the top, and a facsimile autograph appears across the front of the card. Backs of the 1969 Kahn's cards are blank and, like all Kahn's cards, the 1969s are unnumbered. Because the same players appeared in some or all of the identical-format 1966–1969 cards, a detailed checklist is necessary to date positively any particular player's card that appeared in

more than one year. The Kahn's cards were inserted individually in packages of the company's hot dogs or other meat products, or could be purchased as a complete set directly from the company. These cards carry a wax coating to protect the meat from absorbing ink off the cards. Because the later Kahn's issues are so confusing, they are not as popular as they might otherwise be considering that they are really fairly scarce regional cards.

FOR
Nice regionals; lots of appeal for team or star collectors.

AGAINST
Too confusing; the stripes make the cards a bit too gaudy.

NOTEWORTHY CARDS
The only really big name in the 1969 Kahn's set is Henry Aaron.

VALUE
EX.-MT. CONDITION: Complete set, $100; common card, $3; minor stars, $4–$5; Aaron, $15–$20. 5-YEAR PROJECTION: Average or a bit below.

Frank Robinson—OF
Baltimore Orioles

1969 Nabisco Team Flakes, Frank Robinson

1969 NABISCO TEAM FLAKES

SPECIFICATIONS
SIZE: $1^{3}/_{4} \times 3''$. FRONT: Color photograph. BACK: Blank. DISTRIBUTION: Nationally, on back of cereal boxes.

HISTORY
Taking a cue from the Post cereal cards of the early 1960s, Nabisco produced a 24-card set in 1969, printing the cards on the backs of its Team brand cereal boxes. The cards were printed eight to a box, and three different panels were produced. The cards are not all that common, especially in uncut panels, which are worth some 50 percent more than the cumulative value of the cards taken as

individuals. The value of these cards is affected to a great degree by the manner in which they were cut from the box. Cards that were neatly cut right on the traditional "dotted line" will be worth more than those that were cut sloppily, with the borders trimmed into the margin. The full-color photos on the cards do not feature any team insignia on caps or jerseys, a sure sign that Nabisco did not pay royalties to Major League Baseball for such use. Most players shown are stars, many are HOFers. The photos are bordered in black, with the player's name, team, and position appearing in the bottom border. Between the black frame of the photo and the cutting line is a yellow outer border that varies in width, causing some cards to be slightly larger than others. The 1969 Nabisco Team Flakes cards are blank-backed and have no numbers.

1969 TRANSO-GRAM

1969 Nabisco Team Flakes, Bob Gibson

SPECIFICATIONS
SIZE: 2½×3½″. FRONT: Color photograph. BACK: Blank. DISTRIBUTION: Nationally, on boxes containing toy baseball player statue.

HISTORY
The Transogram toy company produced a 60-card set in conjunction with its line of toy baseball player statues in 1969. The cards were printed on the bottoms of the toy boxes. While the players shown on the cards were stars of the day, the statues inside were generic and not really identifiable as any specific player. Decals were included to make the uniform look like the player on the box. The cards featured a color photo at top, surrounded with a white, round-cornered border. Below the photo the player's name was printed in red, and the team and a few personal details were printed in black. There is no card number. All of this was on a yellow background separated from the rest of the box by a black dotted line on which the card was to be cut off the box. Naturally, collectors today prefer to find the cards still on the box—or better yet—the complete box with statue inside. Complete boxes with the toy inside are worth double the values listed below. The '69 Transogram cards are not extremely popular with collectors, so even though they are really quite scarce the price is not particularly high.

FOR
For superstar and team collectors, the cards offer something different.

AGAINST
As with all cut-out cards, the original scissors-work of the kid who bought the statue in 1969 is important in determining the value of the card. Too often they are poorly cut.

NOTEWORTHY CARDS
Lots of stars and Hall of Famers, too numerous to mention. The Johnny Callison card features a reversed negative.

VALUE
EX.-MT. CONDITION, NEATLY CUT FROM BOX: Complete set, $300; common card, $2.50; minor stars, $4–$5; Killebrew, Frank Robinson, Brock, Marichal, Gibson, McCovey, Banks, $10–$15; Seaver, Mays, Aaron, Clemente, Yastrzemski, $20–$22.50; Mantle, Rose, $25–$30. 5-YEAR PROJECTION: Below average.

FOR
One of the scarcer national issues of the late 1960s, lots of stars.

AGAINST
Cards are smaller than standard size and the lack of team logos diminishes their popularity.

NOTEWORTHY CARDS
The Nabisco Team set is loaded with stars of the day, about half being of Hall of Fame caliber.

VALUE
EX.-MT. CONDITION, NEATLY CUT FROM BOX: Complete set, $150; common card, $3; minor stars, $8–$10; Brock, Clemente, Gibson, Kaline, Brooks Robinson, Frank Robinson, Seaver, $10–$20; Aaron, Mays, $20–$25; Rose, $30. 5-YEAR PROJECTION: Below average.

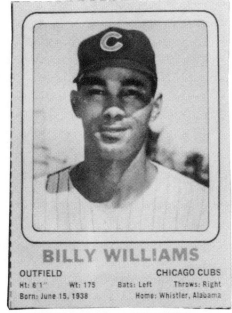

1969 Transogram, Billy Williams

1969–1970 BAZOOKA ALL-TIME GREATS

SPECIFICATIONS
SIZE: Side-panel card, 1¼×3⅛″, bottom-panel card, 3×6¼″, complete box 5½×6¼″. FRONT: Black-and-white photograph, gold plaque and scroll. BACK: Blank. DISTRIBUTION: Nationally, a five-card panel on each box of bubblegum.

HISTORY
In producing its second All-Time Greats set on Bazooka gum boxes,

Topps adopted a style similar to that used for its 1968 Bazooka issue. The bottom of the box was taken up with a large "Baseball Extra" card, made to resemble a newspaper account of a famous baseball accomplishment. A contemporary photo of the player involved is included. Each side of the box features a pair of tall, narrow "All-Time Greats" cards of Hall of Famers. As with the 1963 set, the photos are generally those taken later in the players' lives, so they tend to look old. Many of the same photos from the 1963 All-Time Greats set were recycled in the 1969–1970 effort. While collectors generally prefer to obtain this set in 12 complete boxes, the better-known players are also avidly collected in the small side-panel cards and large "Baseball Extra" bottom panels. Although a full set of 12 bottom panels will contain 48 side-panel cards, there are only 30 different All-Time Great cards. Several of the cards appear with two different bottom panels.

FOR

These are inexpensive cards of some of baseball's greatest players.

AGAINST

A lot going against the set. The cards are either too large (bottom panel) or too small (side panel); All-Time Greats cards are not particularly popular with collectors, who prefer cards actually issued during the career of the player, and, if a card *is* issued after the fact, it should at least have a picture of the player as he looked during his heyday.

NOTEWORTHY CARDS

They're all Hall of Famers, and the expected big names—Ruth, Cobb, Gehrig, etc.—are all there.

VALUE

EX.-MT. CONDITION, NEATLY CUT FROM BOX: Complete set, $100; common bottom-panel card, $2–$3; Cobb, Gehrig bottom-panel card, $5–$7.50; Ruth bottom-panel card, $10; common side-panel card, 50¢–75¢; "star" Hall of Famer, $1–$3; Cobb, Gehrig, $5; Ruth, $7.50. Add 25 percent premium to card totals for complete box. 5-YEAR PROJECTION: Below average.

1968 TOPPS

SPECIFICATIONS

SIZE: 2½×3½". FRONT: Color photograph. BACK: Black and yellow printing on white cardboard. DISTRIBUTION: Nationally, in packages with bubblegum.

HISTORY

There's no telling how popular the 1968 Topps set would be if the design weren't so unusual in appearance. The best way to describe it is to say that it looks as though a color photo had been laid on top of a burlap sack. The player's name is printed below the photo, on the brown-mesh background, while a colored circle at lower right contains the player's team and position. The design is not really unattractive, it's just . . . different. Card backs retained the vertical format of the previous year, but the elements are rearranged so that the cartoon appears on the bottom and the stats in the middle. After the 1967 high of 609 cards, the 1968 set returned to the 598 cards that had been the norm in 1965 and 1966. Besides the National League and American League statistical leader cards (the first 12 in the set) and the World Series specials (eight

cards on the Cardinals' win over the Red Sox in seven games), the 1968 set marks the return of an All-Star subseries—20 players chosen by *The Sporting News*. Other than a few multiplayer feature cards and the usual checklists and rookie cards, these were the only special cards in the 1968 set. While the last several series in 1968 (cards #458–#598) are nominally considered high numbers, they are not really much more scarce or expensive than the first 457 cards.

FOR

One of the easier late-'60s sets to assemble owing to lack of rare high numbers. Lots of stars; some good rookie cards and a reasonable price.

AGAINST

Some people don't like the "burlap look" of the set.

NOTEWORTHY CARDS

All the usual stars, plus rookie cards of Nolan Ryan and Jerry Koosman (on the same card) and Johnny Bench. Last player cards of Roger Maris and Eddie Mathews. Card #66, Casey Cox, can be found with the team name in white (20¢) or yellow ($4) letters. Pitcher Steve Hamilton is shown on card #496 wearing a first baseman's glove.

1968 Topps, Jack Hiatt (front)   *1968 Topps, Jack Hiatt (back)*

VALUE

EX.-MT. CONDITION: Complete set, $250; common card, #1–#457, 15¢; #458–#598, 25¢; superstars, $1.50–$4; Seaver, Mays, Carew, Aaron, Clemente, $5–$10; Carlton, Mantle, Yastrzemski, $12–$15; Bench, Ryan, Rose, $15–$17.50.
5-YEAR PROJECTION: Above average.

1968 Topps, Minnesota Twins Team Card

1968 Topps, Los Angeles Dodgers Rookie Stars

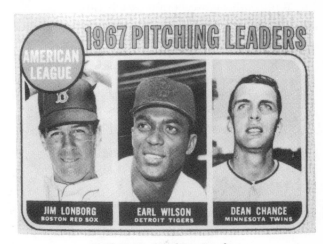

1968 Topps, Pitching Leaders

1968 Topps, Jerry Adair

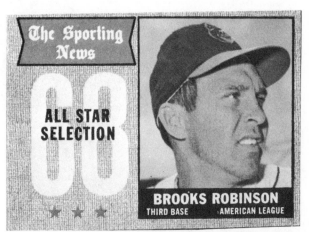

*1968 Topps, The Sporting News All Stars,
Brooks Robinson*

1968 TOPPS GAME

SPECIFICATIONS
SIZE: 2¼×3¼". FRONT: Color photograph. BACK: Blue printing on white cardboard. DISTRIBUTION: Nationally, in packages of 1968 Topps baseball cards and in boxed sets.

HISTORY
The idea of issuing baseball cards that could be used to play a game was not new for Topps; they had done the same thing with their Red Backs and Blue Backs sets of 1951. The 33 1968 game cards follow the same concept. Besides a color head-and-shoulders portrait of the player and a facsimile autograph at the bottom, each card has a baseball situation: "line out," "error," "single," etc. Backs of the round-cornered cards feature a baseball motif. The set is not very popular with collectors, who don't as a rule like baseball cards that are intended for any other purpose than to be worshipped. Because of that lack of demand, it is relatively tough, though inexpensive, to assemble a complete set.

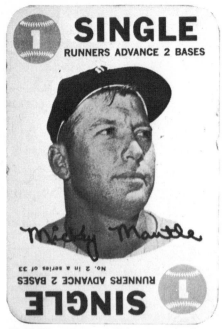

1968 Topps Game, Mickey Mantle (front)

1968 Topps Game, Mickey Mantle (back)

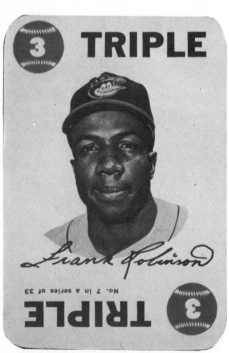

1968 Topps Game, Frank Robinson

1968 Topps Game, Willie Mays

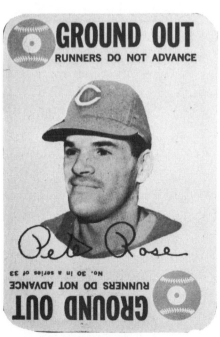

1968 Topps Game, Pete Rose

FOR

The big names in the set make cheap additions to a superstar collection.

AGAINST

They're too small, they have rounded corners, and they were intended to be used as a game—strike three, they're out.

NOTEWORTHY CARDS

A large percentage of the 33 game cards in this insert set are stars, or at least were considered stars in 1968. Hall of Famers include Kaline, Frank and Brooks Robinson, Mantle, Clemente, Aaron, Killebrew, and Mays. Also in the set are Yastrzemski, Carew, Staub, and Rose.

VALUE

EX.-MT. CONDITION: Complete set, $25; common card, 30¢; stars, $1.50–$2.50; Rose, $3. 5-YEAR PROJECTION: Below average.

1968 TOPPS 3-D

SPECIFICATIONS

SIZE: 2¼×3½". FRONT: Color photograph, 3-D effect. BACK: Blank. DISTRIBUTION: Limited geographic areas on test basis.

HISTORY

Two years before Kellogg's began its lengthy run of 3-D baseball cards, Topps experimented with such an issue. The cards were given a three-dimensional look by a layering process; the technique was perfected by the Xograph Company of Dallas. An indistinct color stadium photo provided the background of the card. This was printed with a special screen that imparted subtly wavy vertical lines across the photo. In front of this backdrop, a normal color photo of the player was stripped, along with his name and, in a circle at upper left, his position and team. Over this composite photo was laminated a layer of plastic formed with hundreds of fine vertical "ribs." The lines in the plastic and the wavy lines of the background photo gave the illusion of depth when

the card was tilted or moved. Topps produced just 12 cards in this limited edition test set. The cards are unnumbered and have a blank back. They were sold in a generic plain white wrapper with a color sticker identifying the issue. Because of extremely limited printing quantities and distribution, these cards are very rare today, and command a high price. The Topps 3-D cards represent the most expensive baseball card for every player in the set.

FOR

Extremely rare and very valuable if you happen to find one in an old shoe box or at a rummage sale. An attractive Topps test issue.

AGAINST

Extreme rarity and high dollar value make them impractical for most collectors.

NOTEWORTHY CARDS

The only Hall of Famer in the 3-D Topps test set is Roberto Clemente. Three others of special note are Rusty Staub, Tony Perez, and Boog Powell.

VALUE

EX.-MT. CONDITION: Complete set, $2,250; common card, $150–$200; Staub, Powell, Perez, $250; Clemente, $500. 5-YEAR PROJECTION: Below average.

1968 BAZOOKA

SPECIFICATIONS

SIZE: Side-panel card, 1¼×3⅛", bottom-panel card, 3×6¼", complete box, 5½×6¼". FRONT: Color photograph. BACK: Blank. DISTRIBUTION: Nationally, on boxes of bubblegum.

HISTORY

Topps radically changed the nature of Bazooka baseball cards in their 10th year of issue. The 1968 Bazooka set consists of 15 numbered boxes. The bottom of each box has a player photo and a series of baseball instruction drawings called "Tipps from the

Topps." Each side of the box contains two tall and narrow players cards. Since four of the side-panel cards were repeated (Agee, Rose, Santo, and Drysdale are found on the sides of box #6, featuring Orlando Cepeda, and box #15, featuring Lou Brock), there are 71 different cards in the 1968 Bazooka set: 15 bottom-panel cards and 56 side-panel cards. These cards are most often collected as complete boxes, which are worth 25 to 50 percent more than the total value of the five individual cards that make up the box.

FOR

Lots of big name players, reasonably priced.

AGAINST

Unusual format and card size make the set unpopular. Except for the superstars, there is little demand for '68 Bazookas, especially the "Tipps" cards; collectors have traditionally shunned this type of card.

NOTEWORTHY CARDS

Hall of Famers Kaline, Frank and Brooks Robinson, Marichal, Aaron, Drysdale, Killebrew, Gibson, Mantle, Mays, Clemente. Lots of potential Hall of Famers like Seaver, Yastrzemski, Rose, Carew, Brock.

VALUE

EX.-MT. CONDITION, NEATLY CUT: Complete set, $125; common card, $1.50–$2; stars, $4–$7.50; Mays, Aaron, Yastrzemski, $10; Mantle, $15; Rose, $20. 5-YEAR PROJECTION: Below average.

1968 KAHN'S

SPECIFICATIONS

SIZE: 2¹³/₁₆×3¹/₄" or 2¹³/₁₆×3⁷/₈". FRONT: Color photograph. BACK: Blank. DISTRIBUTION: Various areas according to the teams that appear, single cards in packages of meat products; complete sets by mail.

HISTORY

Things really get confusing with the 1968 Kahn's set. The cards are in the same basic format as the 1966 and 1967 issues, which can cause confusion when collectors try to attribute correct dates to cards of players who appear in two or three of those years. In addition, there are two different sizes of cards in the 1968 set and a number of variations within each group. A record number of teams is represented in the '68 issue: the Cubs, the White Sox, the Braves, the Reds, the Pirates, the Indians, the Tigers, and the Mets. Perhaps the easiest way to begin to describe the 1968 set is to say that there is a total of 50 cards of 38 different players. The two sizes of cards were created to better fit them into meat products packages of different sizes. The smaller size set contains 12 cards; the larger size has the same 12 cards plus 26 others. Like the Kahn's sets of 1966 and 1967, the format is a two-part card, separated by a dotted line. Naturally, collectors prefer their cards with both halves intact, but the values quoted below are for cards that have had the top part removed. Kahn's cards with the ad tab are worth about 20 percent more. The lower portion of the two-part card is a player photo bordered by alternating stripes of different colors. The player's name is printed in the upper border, and a facsimile autograph appears across the front of the card. The top portion of the card continues the striped format, and has a red Kahn's rose logo. With the advertising tab, the smaller cards measure $2^{13}/_{16} \times 3^{1}/_{4}$"; without the tab, they are $2^{13}/_{16} \times 1^{7}/_{8}$". The larger cards measure $2^{13}/_{16} \times 3^{7}/_{8}$" with the ad tab; $2^{13}/_{16} \times 2^{11}/_{16}$" without the tab. Again, to discern the exact year of issue between the large-size 1968 cards and the same players' cards that may appear in the 1966 or 1967 sets requires a detailed checklist. Besides the size differences, the colors of the background stripes vary. Because of all this confusion, the later Kahn's cards are not as popular with collectors as they might be otherwise.

FOR
Reasonably priced regional cards.

AGAINST
Too confusing for the average collector.

NOTEWORTHY CARDS
Johnny Bench makes a rookie card appearance in the 1968 Kahn's set. Henry Aaron is the only other superstar in the set; Rose, Clemente, and Stargell are absent.

VALUE
EX.-MT. CONDITION: Complete set, $200; common card, $3–$4; minor stars, $5–$7; Aaron, Bench, $18–$22. 5-YEAR PROJECTION: Average or a bit below.

1967 TOPPS

SPECIFICATIONS
SIZE: $2^{1}/_{2} \times 3^{1}/_{2}$". FRONT: Color photograph. BACK: Green and black printing on white cardboard. DISTRIBUTION: Nationally, in packages with bubblegum.

HISTORY
One of the most popular sets of the 1960s, Topps' 1967 effort combines attractive cards with the real challenge of assembling a set that contains some very tough cards. More so than in most years, the high numbers in the '67 set (#534–#609) are considerably scarcer than the other series. Part of the scarcity in the '67 highs comes from the fact that some of the 76 cards in that group are double-printed, but collectors can't yet agree on which. Since there are a Hall of Famer (Brooks Robinson), several potential HOFers (Tommy John, Rocky Colavito, Maury Wills, Jim Bunning), and the rookie cards of two future Hall of Famers (Rod Carew, Tom Seaver) in the high-numbered series, the value of these cards, and of the set as a whole, is considerable. The set, at 609 cards, was Topps' largest to that date. Design of the set is simple but effective. A large color photo of the player is bordered in white. Within the area of the photo, the player's name and position are printed in small letters at the top, while the team name is printed in color block letters at bottom. Except for the Milt Pappas card, #254, there is a facsimile autograph on the photo. The 1967 issue was the first for which Topps had adopted a vertical format for card backs; however, all the old familiar elements are there: cartoon, year-by-year stats, paragraph about the player, biographical details, and card number.

After a year's absence, the subseries devoted to the previous year's World Series returned in the 1967 set, recounting the Orioles' four-game sweep of the Dodgers. League leaders in the various major statistical categories were the only other subset in the issue. Rookie cards were printed in a horizontal format with two players per card on a team or league basis.

FOR
Popular design; some scarce cards; a few varieties to keep things interesting.

AGAINST
Relatively expensive for cards that aren't yet 20 years old.

NOTEWORTHY CARDS
The Seaver and Carew rookie cards mentioned earlier are the only premier appearance worthy of special note in the 1967 set. All the big name stars are present and accounted for, with Whitey Ford making his final appearance in a regular baseball card set that year. Two of the 1967 cards, Bob Priddy (#26) and Mike McCormick (#86), will be found with or without information on the back indicating trades to other teams. As in 1959, the cards without the traded line are most valuable; they're worth about $4, as compared to 20¢ for the common variety. Checklist 3 (card #191) will be found with card #214 listed as Tom Kelley or Dick Kelley, the latter being correct. The first version is worth $1 or so, the second, $3. The 1967 set contains Topps' first card of Maury Wills. The Brooklyn bubblegum company apparently snubbed Wills when handing out baseball card contracts to minor leaguers in the mid-1950s, and Wills held a grudge against them until he was traded to the Pirates in '67. The Wills card appears in the high number series.

OUR FAVORITE CARD
The Tigers rookie cards are really messed up. Card #72 purports to show "John Matchick" and "George Korince." Actually, it shows Matchick, who played under the name "Tommy" but who was born John Thomas Matchick (and who turned an unassisted triple-play with Syracuse of the International League in 1966), with

Ike Brown (who didn't get his own rookie card until 1970). To make up for the mistake, Topps gave Korince another chance, and pictured him on card #526 (where he is paired with Pat Dobson, Brewers pitching coach and Lite beer commercial partner of Sparky Lyle). So Korince had a pair of rookie cards, right? Wrong! He had three. His only other baseball card is in the 1968 Topps set, card #447, "Tigers Rookies." Not bad for a guy with a lifetime pitching record of 1-0 and a 4.24 ERA.

VALUE

EX.-MT. CONDITION: Complete set, $600; common card, #1–#457, 20¢; #458–#533, 40¢; #534–#609, $1.60; superstars, $2–$4; Carlton, Clemente, Bunning, Colavito, Mays, Aaron, $7.50–$10; Mantle, Yastrzemski, $15; John, Rose, $22–$25; Carew, Wills, $40–$45; Seaver, Brooks Robinson, $70–$75. 5-YEAR PROJECTION: Above average.

1967 Topps, Al Kaline

1967 Topps, Hank Aaron

1967 Topps, Willie McCovey

1967 Topps, Steve Carlton

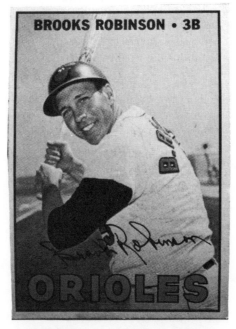

1967 Topps, Brooks Robinson (front)

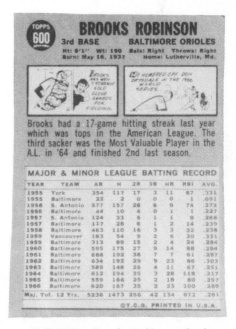

1967 Topps, Brooks Robinson (back)

1967 BAZOOKA

SPECIFICATIONS
SIZE: Single card, $1^9/_{16} \times 2^1/_2''$, three-card panel, $4^{11}/_{16} \times 2^1/_2''$. FRONT: Color photograph. BACK: Blank. DISTRIBUTION: Nationally, a three-card panel on the bottom of each bubblegum box.

HISTORY
In 1967, its ninth year of issuing baseball cards as part of Bazooka gum boxes, Topps got a little lazy. Besides recycling the format and design of the previous four years' sets, a total of 38 out of the 48 cards in the '67 set were exactly the same cards issued the previous year—same picture, same card number, and all. As might be expected, you have to have an original, complete gum box to figure out whether one of these 38 cards is a 1966 or 1967—a fine distinction that is, nevertheless, very important to most people who collect these cards. Naturally, such boxes are scarce; the cards, after all, were meant to be cut off the box in the first place. Complete boxes are worth some 25 to 50 percent more than the total value of the three cards on the panel. There is also a premium (10 to 15 percent or so) value to uncut three-card panels. In all cases, the condition of the cards depends primarily on how well they were originally cut from the box.

FOR
Lots of big name players, nice photos.

AGAINST
Nonstandard size, confusion between 1966 and 1967 issues.

NOTEWORTHY CARDS
Mantle, Mays, Aaron, Yastrzemski, Rose, and a few other Hall of Famers are all back from earlier years; the best-known players among the 10 "new" cards in the 1967 set are Jim Kaat and Denny McClain.

VALUE
EX.-MT. CONDITION, NEATLY CUT: Complete set, $125; common card, $2; Hall of Famers, $5–$10; Aaron, Mays, Yastrzemski, $12.50– $15; Mantle, $20; Rose, $25. 5-YEAR PROJECTION: Average.

1967 KAHN'S

SPECIFICATIONS
SIZE: $2^{13}/_{16} \times 4''$. FRONT: Color photograph. BACK: Blank. DISTRIBUTION: Georgia, New York, Ohio, and Pittsburgh areas, in packages with meat products; complete sets available by mail.

HISTORY
The 1967 Kahn's set is almost identical to the 1966 set, and can therefore cause identification problems among the cards of players who appear in both sets. The cards were issued in the same two-part format, a $2^{13}/_{16} \times 2^{11}/_{16}''$ picture card at bottom, with a $2^{13}/_{16} \times 1^5/_{16}''$ advertising tab at top. The two are separated by a dotted line. Like the '66 set, the 1967 cards feature a color photo with a facsimile autograph across the front, and the player's name is printed in the top border. Also like the 1966 cards, the '67s feature a border design of alternating color stripes. Several different color pairs were used in 1967 in addition to the yellow and white stripes found in 1966. Cards with stripes other than yellow or white can easily be attributed to 1967, but when a card is found with yellow and white stripes it takes a detailed checklist by photo pose to differentiate the two years. Card backs are blank and the cards are unnumbered, so no clues as to date are offered here. The 41 cards in the 1967 set are made up of players from the Reds, the Indians, the Pirates, the Braves, and, for the first time, the New York Mets.

FOR
Nice cards for regional or team collectors; they are a good value for the current price.

AGAINST
Confusion over which year's cards are which.

NOTEWORTHY CARDS
Aaron, Rose, and Stargell, along with many minor stars of the era.

VALUE
EX.-MT. CONDITION: Complete set, $200; common card, $4; minor stars, $6–$8; Stargell, $15; Aaron, $25; Rose, $50. 5-YEAR PROJECTION: Average, or a bit below.

1966 TOPPS

SPECIFICATIONS
SIZE: $2^1/_2 \times 3^1/_2''$. FRONT: Color photograph. BACK: Black and orange printing on white cardboard. DISTRIBUTION: Nationally, in packages with bubblegum.

HISTORY
One of the more underrated Topps sets of the 1960s, the 598-card issue of 1966 is a much more challenging set than most collectors realize. The high numbers (#523–#598) are—as in many years—considerably scarcer than the previous several series, and the "semi-highs" (#447–#522) are a lot tougher to find than their current price tags would indicate. The first 110 cards in the set are the most common, followed by cards #111–#446, which are just a bit more difficult. While there is nothing spectacular about the design of the 1966 set, the cards are attractive. A large color photo at center dominates the front of the card. In the upper-left corner, a diagonal stripe of color carries the team name, while a band of the same color at bottom has the player's name and position. Backs are not much different from the previous year, combining year-by-year major and minor league stats with a short career summary, a cartoon, and the usual biographical statistics. Though a handful of multi-player feature cards were included in the set, after having been suspended the previous year, there was only one specialty subset in '66: this was a group of 12 cards honoring the league leaders in various major statistical categories for 1965. Each of the dozen cards pictures the winner and two runners-up. Most of the team managers had their own cards in '66; the Houston Astros had two—Lum Harris and Grady Hatton. Rookie cards were generally arranged by team, two or three players per card.

FOR

An attractive, challenging set that has not yet been subjected to any great run-up in price because it lacks hot rookie cards.

AGAINST

There are no readily apparent negative aspects to collecting the 1966 set.

NOTEWORTHY CARDS

The mix of cards in the 1966 Topps set is a fascinating blend of old-time baseball history, baseball as it was in the 1960s, and baseball as it is today. Managers' cards offer such stars of the 1940s and 1950s as Hank Bauer, Eddie Stanky, Harry Walker, Red Schoendienst, and Gil Hodges. Superstars still active in 1966 include Mantle, Mays, and Aaron. And, finally, the 1966 set included rookie cards of several players still active today, Jim Palmer and Don Sutton foremost among them. Other rookie cards in

'66 include Ferguson Jenkins and Bobby Murcer. Like the 1959 set, the 1966 set offers some cards that can be found both with and without notice of sale or trade to another team. Unlike '59, though, it is the cards with the added lines that are more valuable in the 1966 set. The four cards with the variations are Merritt Ranew (#62), Bob Uecker (#91), Dick Groat (#103), and Alex Johnson (#104). In addition to several minor varieties (which few collectors bother with) among the checklist cards, checklist card #2 (card #101) can be found with either Bill Henry (correct) or Warren Spahn listed as card #115. While the common varieties of these five cards are valued at about 20¢ to 35¢ each (75¢ for Uecker), the scarcer varieties sell in the range of $4 to $5 in top condition. Because of the configuration of cards on press sheets of the high number (#523–#598) series, it is assumed that some cards were single-

printed and some cards double-printed. This has affected the prices of the presumably single-printed McCovey and Perry cards.

OUR FAVORITE CARD

The "ghost" of Chicago Cubs second baseman Ken Hubbs, who was killed when his light plane crashed near Provo, Utah, on February 15, 1964, appears in the 1966 Topps set. Hubbs' photo appears on card #447, which was supposed to be Dick Ellsworth.

VALUE

EX.-MT. CONDITION: Complete set, $450; common card, #1–#446, 29¢; #447–#522, 50¢; #523–#598, $1.90; superstars, $2–$4; Koufax, Jenkins, Sutton, Clemente, Billy Williams, $5–$7; Aaron, Robin Roberts, McClain, Yastrzemski, Mantle, $10–$15; Palmer, Mays, $17–$20; Rose, McCovey, $25–$30; Perry, $45. 5-YEAR PROJECTION: Average.

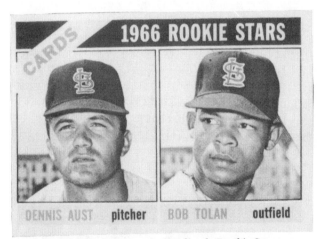

1966 Topps, St. Louis Cardinals Rookie Stars

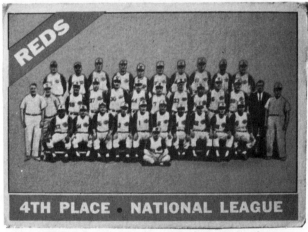

1966 Topps, Cincinnati Reds Team Card

1966 Topps, Home Run Leaders

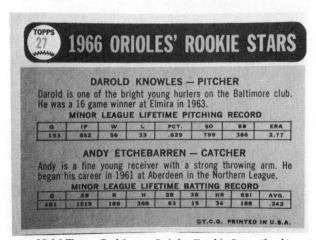

1966 Topps, Baltimore Orioles Rookie Stars (back)

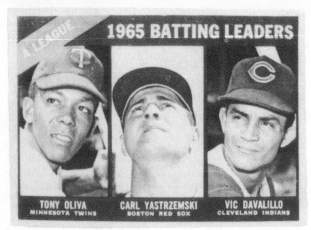

1966 Topps, Batting Leaders

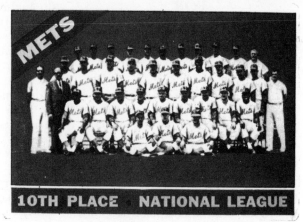

1966 Topps, New York Mets Team Card

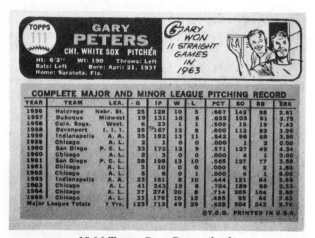

1966 Topps, Gary Peters (back)

1966 Topps, Curt Flood (back)

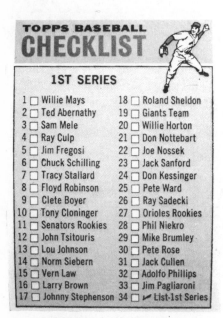

1966 Topps, Checklist Card

1966 Topps, Bert Campaneris

1966 Topps, Curt Flood (front)

1966 BAZOOKA

1966 Topps, Harry Walker

1966 Topps, Jim Gentile

1966 Topps, Jim Hunter

1966 Topps, Rocky Colavito

SPECIFICATIONS

SIZE: Single card, 1⁹/₁₆×2¹/₂″, three-card panel, 4¹¹/₁₆×2¹/₂″. FRONT: Color photograph. BACK: Blank. DISTRIBUTION: Nationally, a three-card panel on the bottom of each box of bubblegum.

HISTORY

In 1966 Topps at last did something different so that collectors today can tell the 1966 Bazooka cards from those of identical design (and sometimes even identical card numbers) issued from 1963–1965; they changed the size of the set from 36 to 48 cards. The small line of type in the white border at bottom now reads: "NO. ____ OF 48 CARDS." But wait, there's still a problem; 38 of the 48 cards in the 1966 Bazooka set also appear in the 1967 set, with the very same card number *and* photo. You have to have complete three-card panels or, better yet, boxes, to tell the difference between most 1966 and 1967 Bazookas. Because many collectors find the most desirable way to collect this type of baseball cards is on the original packaging, a premium of 25 to 50 percent is attached to a complete box, over and above the values of the three cards taken as individuals. Panels of three cards, cut off the box but not separated into single cards, are worth 10 to 15 percent above the total value of the three cards. Badly cut cards are quite common and in little demand; collectors want cards of this kind to be neatly cut with even borders.

FOR

Good photos and lots of star players; relatively inexpensive.

AGAINST

Cards are not a popular size; the difficulty of assembling them into a complete year-set makes it too challenging a project for most collectors.

NOTEWORTHY CARDS

First Bazooka card for Pete Rose. Yastrzemski is back after a year's absence from the Bazooka series. Hall of Famer players in the set are Koufax,

Mantle, Marichal, Killebrew, Mays, Gibson, Clemente, Aaron, Frank and Brooks Robinson, Drysdale, and Kaline.

VALUE

EX.–MT. CONDITION, NEATLY CUT: Complete set, $125; common card, $2; Hall of Famer, $5–$10; Aaron, Mays, Yastrzemski, $15–$17.50; Mantle, $20; Rose, $25. 5-YEAR PROJECTION: Average.

1966 KAHN'S

SPECIFICATIONS

SIZE: 2¹³/₁₆×4″. FRONT: Color photograph. BACK: Blank. DISTRIBUTION: Ohio, Pittsburgh, Atlanta areas, in packages of meat products; complete sets available by mail.

HISTORY

With the 1966 set things begin to get a bit confusing among the Kahn's cards. The issue includes 32 players from the Reds, the Pirates, the Indians, and the Atlanta Braves in their first year in Georgia. There was a radical format change in the '66 set: the cards now come in two parts. The basic card, 2¹³/₁₆×2¹¹/₁₆″, is separated by a dotted line from a 2¹³/₁₆×1⁵/₁₆″ advertising tab at the top. A color photograph of the player dominates the card, flanked and bordered at bottom by yellow stripes. At top are alternating yellow and white stripes, which continue on the ad tab where they are joined by a red rose and Kahn's logo. Cards with the advertising tab still attached are more desirable than those without it. Values quoted below are for cards without the tab; add 20 percent for cards with the tab. The card portion features a facsimile autograph across the front, and the player's name printed at top. Backs of the '66 Kahn's cards are blank and the cards are unnumbered. As in many previous years, single cards could be found in meat packages, or the set could be obtained through a mail-in offer. Because the '66 Kahn's cards are so similar to the 1967 issue, collectors will need a visual checklist detailing each year's cards to differentiate the two issues.

FOR

Scarcer regional cards at a good price for the team or star collector.

AGAINST

Distracting "Circus Stripes" design, lack of dating on card.

NOTEWORTHY CARDS

Roberto Clemente rejoined the Kahn's line-up in 1966, but Frank Robinson was gone, traded to the Baltimore Orioles. Still around are Aaron, Rose, and Stargell.

VALUE

EX.–MT. CONDITION: Complete set, $200; common card, $4; minor stars, $5–$8; Stargell, $15; Clemente, $20; Aaron, $25–$30; Rose, $50. 5-YEAR PROJECTION: Average, perhaps a bit below.

1966 PEPSI TULSA OILERS

SPECIFICATIONS

SIZE: Single card, 2½×3¼″; panel, 5½×6¾″. FRONT: Sepia-tone photograph. BACK: Black printing on white cardboard. DISTRIBUTION: Oklahoma area, one two-card panel hung by ring tab on bottle in each carton of soda.

HISTORY

The last of three Pepsi-Cola baseball card issues for the Tulsa Oilers minor league team, the 1966 set again featured farmhands of the St. Louis Cardinals. By 1966, however, the Tulsa team had moved up a class, to AAA ball, as a member of the expanded Pacific Coast League (which stretched inland that year as far as Indianapolis!). The 24 cards in the set were not evenly printed on the two-card panels in which they were issued; eight cards were double prints and can be found with either of two "partners" on panels. Card backs were the usual mix of stats and bio, and the detachable part of the panel at top gave details on how card owners could redeem them (along with specially

marked bottle caps) for a $24 bounty or tickets to Tulsa ballgames. Like all cards issued in panels, the cards are worth significantly more intact than separated.

FOR

Since this is a high minor league set, more of the players are recognizable than would be the case with most minor league teams. The issue is relatively common in collector circles, but not as common as their currently low price would indicate.

AGAINST

Limited demand for minor league sets that don't contain any current superstars.

NOTEWORTHY CARDS

Being a Triple-A level team, the 1966 Tulsa Oilers had many players who had been or would be major league ballplayers. Names that come immediately to mind are Alex Johnson, Coco Laboy, Charlie Metro, Ted Savage, Robert Tolan, and Walt "No Neck" Williams.

VALUE

EX.–MT. CONDITION: Complete set, $30; common card, $1.50; someone whose name you recognize, $2.50–$3. 5-YEAR PROJECTION: Below average.

1965 TOPPS

SPECIFICATIONS

SIZE: 2½×3½″. FRONT: Color photograph. BACK: Black and blue printing on white cardboard. DISTRIBUTION: Nationally, in 1¢ and 5¢ packages with bubblegum.

HISTORY

A relatively straightforward Topps set from the mid-'60s, the issue returned to the set size of 598 cards, a Topps record set in 1962. The extra 11 cards in the '65 set were additional player cards, not specialty subsets. For the first time since 1957 there were no multi-player feature cards in the 1965 set. The first 12 cards in the set represented American and National League statistical leaders for the 1964 season, and an eight-card group highlighted the '64 World Series victory of the Cardinals over the Yankees. Rookie cards in 1965 were shared by between two and four players, generally arranged by team, but also including a pair of "Rookie Stars" cards for the National League and the American League. The usual team cards and numbered checklists were part of the set. The design of the 1965 Topps cards featured a large color photo at the center of the card, surrounded by a colored, round-cornered frame and a white border. The frame widens at the bottom of the card to carry the player's name and position at the lower right. At the lower left is a pennant with a color team logo and the team name. Card backs feature annual major and/or minor league statistics and, space permitting, a cartoon and headline about the player. The usual biographical details are there as well. While the cards numbered #523–#598 are considered high numbers, they are not all that much more scarce than the rest of the issue.

FOR
A high quality Topps set without a great deal of challenge or, for that matter, anything spectacular about it.

AGAINST
While there is nothing spectacular to point to in favor of the '65 set, there are no glaring problems with the issue either.

NOTEWORTHY CARDS
There are a good number of rookie cards in the 1965 set that feature players who have good Hall of Fame potential, including Joe Morgan, Catfish Hunter, Tug McGraw, Tony Perez, and Steve Carlton (the premier rookie card of 1965). Other notable rookie cards that year are Luis Tiant and Denny McClain. The Jim Kaat card of 1965 (#62) features a misspelling of his name on front, as "Katt." The Lew Krausse card (#462) has a photo of Pete Lovrich.

OUR FAVORITE CARD
The '65 set contains another example of a player having a joke at the expense of the Topps photographer. Noted baseball funnyman Bob Uecker is pictured on card #519 batting left-handed. Since he only managed to compile a lifetime .200 batting average hitting right-handed, it's unlikely he was experimenting in front of the camera. Besides, the grin on his face shows he's enjoying the ruse.

VALUE
EX.-MT. CONDITION: Complete set, $350; common card, #1–#446, 15¢–20¢; #447–#522, 35¢; #523–#598, 65¢; superstars, $2–$5; Morgan, Clemente, Koufax, Banks, Hunter, Brock, Perez, $7–$9; Aaron, Mays, Mantle, Yastrzemski, $12–$17; Rose, $45; Carlton, $80. 5-YEAR PROJECTION: Average.

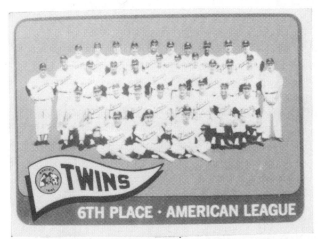
1965 Topps, Minnesota Twins Team Card

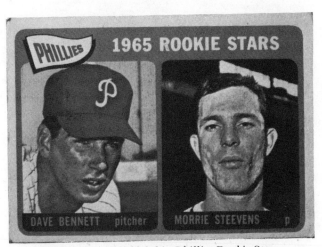
1965 Topps, Philadelphia Phillies Rookie Stars

1965 Topps, Tony Cloninger

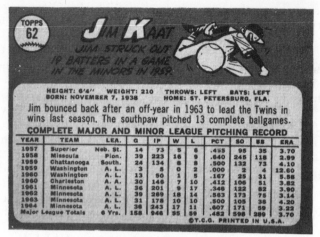

1965 Topps, Jim Kaat (back)

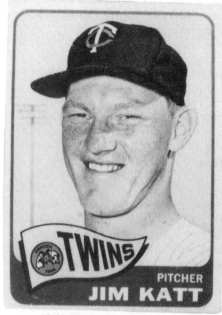

1965 Topps, Jim Kaat (front)

1965 Topps, St. Louis Cardinals Team Card

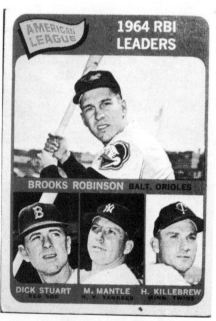

1965 Topps, RBI Leaders

1965 Topps, Jim Bouton

1965 Topps, Don Wert

1965 TOPPS EMBOSSED

1965 Topps, Robin Roberts

SPECIFICATIONS

SIZE: 2⅛×3½″. FRONT: Gold-foil embossment. BACK: "Framed" card number. DISTRIBUTION: Nationally, in packages of 1965 Topps baseball cards.

HISTORY

The 72 cards of the 1965 Topps Embossed set were inserted individually in packs of the regular 1965 Topps baseball cards. The cards are unique in the history of the hobby in that they feature an embossed profile portrait of the player on gold foil-like cardboard. There are 36 embossed cards for each league: the embossments on the American League cards are framed in blue, and the oval portraits on the National League players' cards are surrounded in red. There is a gold border on the outside of the card. The player's name appears in white below the picture, with his team and position on a bottom line. Card backs are blank except for a decorative rectangle at

bottom with the card number and copyright line. These cards are not particularly popular, which in some ways is good because they are extremely tough to find in true Mint condition. The high-relief areas of the embossed portraits tended to lose their gold ink when rubbed, leaving white spots.

FOR

A real challenge for the condition-conscious collector who doesn't want to spend a lot of money. Since the players are mostly stars, they are nice additions to a superstar collection.

AGAINST

The pictures don't look anything like the players they are supposed to represent.

NOTEWORTHY CARDS

Virtually all of the players are stars, or at least were considered above-average in 1965.

VALUE

EX.-MT. CONDITION: Complete set, $40; common card, 35¢; superstars, $1–$3; Mantle, $4. 5-YEAR PROJECTION: Below average.

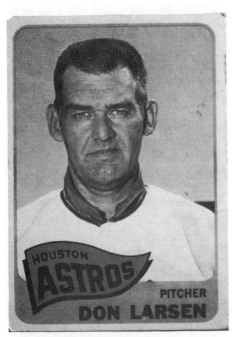

1965 Topps, Don Larsen

1965 Topps Embossed, Ernie Banks

1965 BAZOOKA

1965 Topps Embossed, Frank Robinson

1965 Topps Embossed, Carl Yastrzemski

1965 Topps Embossed, Rocky Colavito

SPECIFICATIONS

SIZE: Single card, $1^9/_{16} \times 2^1/_2''$; three-card panel, $4^{11}/_{16} \times 2^1/_2''$. FRONT: Color photograph. BACK: Blank. DISTRIBUTION: Nationally, a three-card panel on the bottom of each box of bubblegum.

HISTORY

Topps really created problems for collectors with its 1965 issue of Bazooka cards. Besides using the same design as in 1963 and 1964, exactly half the set—18 of 36 cards—carry the same card numbers as they did in 1964. Sure, the pictures are different, but you have to compare original three-card panels and checklists to find out what year's cards you have. As you approach the higher numbers in the set, the situation gets worse; the last two panels—#31–#33 (Frank Robinson, Sandy Koufax, Rocky Colavito) and #34–#36 (Al Kaline, Ken Boyer, Tommy Davis)—are the same players and numbers as in the previous year. If you have any of these cards from 1964 or 1965, you'll need complete original boxes to tell which year is which. All of this is too much for the average collector today, and it has kept the Bazooka issues from becoming really popular. Because the cards were issued as part of the package and had to be cut off, they are often found poorly cut. Original three-card panels and—especially—complete boxes are worth a decent premium, perhaps 10 percent more than the individual cards in the case of the panel and 25 to 50 percent for a box.

FOR

There are lots of big name players in the set, and collectors find the photos attractive.

AGAINST

The confusion over the same design and same card numbers makes the set too tough to figure out for all but the devoted specialist. Again, the cards are too small to be really popular; most collectors today aren't attracted to cards that aren't the standard $2\frac{1}{2} \times 3\frac{1}{2}''$.

NOTEWORTHY CARDS

Lots of Hall of Famers are back from previous years, along with some new stars—Boog Powell and recently elected Hall of Famers Bob Gibson and Juan Marichal.

VALUE

EX.-MT. CONDITION: Complete set, $125; common card, $2; Hall of Famers, $5–$10; Aaron, Mays, $15; Mantle, $20. 5-YEAR PROJECTION: Average.

1965 KAHN'S

SPECIFICATIONS

SIZE: 3×3½". FRONT: Color photograph. BACK: Black printing on white cardboard. DISTRIBUTION: Upper Midwest, in packages of meat products; complete sets by mail.

HISTORY

The 1965 Kahn's set features the largest number of players of the entire 15-year series. Forty-five cards are included in the Kahn's set, representing players from the Reds, the Indians, the Pirates, and the Milwaukee Braves—it was the Tribe's last year in the beer city. The format for the 1965 set remained the same as that used the previous year. The entire front of the card is a borderless color photo, with only a facsimile autograph added. The card back features brief career information and annual statistics through the 1964 season. The cards are unnumbered. Like other later Kahn's sets, the 1965 issue was available in two ways. Single cards could be collected in individual packages of Kahn's hot dogs and other meat products, or the complete set could be bought by mail. The addition of the Milwaukee Braves helps make the '65 issue one of Kahn's more popular sets.

FOR

Lots of good players and great teams for the regional and team collector. The '65 Kahn's are attractive cards at attractive prices.

AGAINST

It's hard to say anything bad about the '65 Kahn's.

NOTEWORTHY CARDS

Joining the all-star line-up of Frank Robinson and Pete Rose in the '65 set is Henry Aaron. Roberto Clemente is curiously absent from the set. Willie Stargell and Joe Torre also appear for the first time in 1965.

VALUE

EX.-MT. CONDITION: Complete set, $250; common card, $4–$5; minor stars, $6–$8; Robinson, Stargell, $15–$20; Aaron, $50; Rose, $75. 5-YEAR PROJECTION: Average or a bit above.

1964 TOPPS

SPECIFICATIONS

SIZE: 2½×3½". FRONT: Color photograph. BACK: Orange printing on white cardboard. DISTRIBUTION: Nationally, in 1¢ and 5¢ packages with bubblegum.

HISTORY

Hard on the heels of its attractive 1963 card design, Topps came up with another winner in 1964. A large color photo at the center of the card bleeds into a white top panel that contains the team name in large, color block letters. A colored panel at the bottom of the card contains the player's name and position. The layout is clean, simple, and attractive. Card backs featured an innovative "hidden" baseball quiz question. When a white panel at the bottom of the card was rubbed with a coin, the answer to a trivia question appeared. Most of the rest of the card back is devoted to yearly major and minor league career statistics, with minimal biographical details at top. Also unusual for the back design is that it is printed entirely in orange ink, rather than in two colors as had been done in most past years. While the traditional high numbers series of 1964 (#523–#587) are scarcer than the rest of the set, they are not all that uncommon. Cards #371–#522 are just a bit tougher to find than the first 370 cards in the set. Topps continued to downplay specialty subsets in 1964, following the '63 pattern of including just two: a 12-card group of 1963's statistical leaders, and a five-card run

detailing the Dodgers' four-game sweep of the Yankees in the 1963 World Series. Rookie cards are generally arranged by team, two players per card. The set contains several multi-player cards, featuring star players.

FOR

Attractive design, reasonable cost, lots of stars, no gimmicky specialty cards.

AGAINST

High price of the Pete Rose card.

NOTEWORTHY CARDS

Pete Rose got his own card in the 1964 Topps set. Interestingly, the photo on the '64 Rose card is an enlarged version of the same photo used on his rookie card. The '64 Rose card, valued at around $80 in top grade, has currently thrown off the value of the rest of the set, which catalogs list at around $300. Surely, the other 586 cards in the set are worth more than the $220 you get after subtracting the Rose card. Card #550 is an "In Memoriam" card of Cubs second baseman Ken Hubbs, who was killed February 13, 1964. Significant rookie cards in '64 include Lou Piniella, Tommy John, and Phil Niekro. The photo representing Bud Bloomfield on card #532 is actually Jay Ward, who also appears on card #116. Unfortunately for Bloomfield, he never did appear as a major leaguer on a baseball card. One of the greatest card-back writing goofs occurs on the card of Phillies rookie (#213) Dave Bennett—"The 19-year-old right-handed curveballer is just 18 years old. . . ."

OUR FAVORITE CARD

You'd think that after Topps had been taken in by Lew Burdette pretending to be a left-handed pitcher on his 1959 card, they'd be more careful. But not only is Joe Koppe (#279) pictured in the '64 set with a glove on the wrong hand, but Lew Burdette is shown pitching "leftie" once again!

VALUE

EX.-MT. CONDITION: Complete set, $300; common card, #1–#522, 20¢–25¢; #523–#587, 65¢; stars, $2.50–$5; Brock, John, Koufax, Clemente, Niekro, $7–$10; Aaron, Yastrzemski, Mays, Mantle, $15–$18; Rose, $80. 5-YEAR PROJECTION: Above average.

1964 Topps, Detroit Tigers Team Card

1964 Topps, World Series Game #4

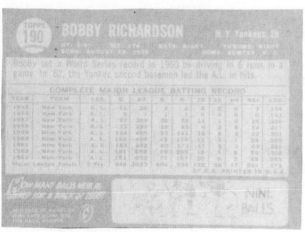

1964 Topps, Bobby Richardson (back)

1964 Topps, World Series Game #1

1964 Topps, Home Run Leaders

1964 Topps, Harmon Killebrew

1964 Topps, St. Louis Cardinals Team Card

1964 Topps, Bob Friend

1964 Topps,
Carl Yastrzemski, Chuck Schilling

1964 Topps, Roger Maris

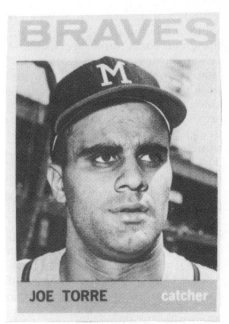

1964 Topps, Joe Torre

1964 TOPPS STAND-UPS

SPECIFICATIONS

SIZE: 2½×3½". FRONT: Color photograph. BACK: Blank. DISTRIBUTION: Nationally, in packages with bubblegum.

HISTORY

For several years beginning in 1960, Topps had marketed, on a test basis or otherwise, a variety of baseball player novelties in addition to its regular annual card set—things like tattoos, rub-offs, stick-ons, coins, etc. In 1964, two separate sets of baseball cards were added to the regular set. Each was packaged and sold separately. The scarcest of these is the 77-card "Stand-up" set. The first (and last) die-cut cards produced on a widespread basis by Topps since its All-Stars of 1951, the Stand-up set of 1964 features a full-color, full-length photo of the player at the center of the card. There is a yellow background on the top half of the card and a green background on the bottom. Directions for punching out the player and folding down the yellow background to make the card stand are printed along the left edge of the yellow top. When so folded, only the player's picture and the green background are visible. A yellow rectangle on which the player "stands" contains his name, team, and position. There is a black facsimile autograph across the front. The cards are unnumbered. Naturally, collectors prefer to own these cards in unpunched and unfolded condition. The values quoted below are for such cards; cards that have been folded are worth about half the figures mentioned. There are 22 scarcer cards among the Stand-ups, the result of double-printing of the other 55 cards in the set. Hall of Famers Warren Spahn, Juan Marichal, and Don Drysdale, as well as two potential Hall of Famers, Carl Yastrzemski and Willie McCovey, are among the 22 players single-printed in the set. The set has a certain degree of popularity, but if it ever really became a high-demand item collectors would quickly find out how scarce and underpriced the cards are.

FOR

Scarce, interesting Topps issue in the "standard" size; a challenge to collect.

AGAINST

Collectors don't like cards that are designed to be folded, spindled, or mutilated.

NOTEWORTHY CARDS

Besides Drysdale, Marichal, and McCovey, Hall of Famer quality players in the Stand-up set include Aaron, Banks, Clemente, Kaline, Killebrew, Mantle, Mathews, Mays, and Frank and Brooks Robinson.

VALUE

EX.-MT. CONDITION: Complete set, $550; common cards, $1.25; single-prints, $6–$8; superstars, $8–$12; Aaron, Marichal, Mathews, Drysdale, Mays, McCovey, Spahn, $17–$20; Mantle, $30–$35; Yastrzemski, $60–$75. 5-YEAR PROJECTION: Above average.

1964 TOPPS GIANTS

SPECIFICATIONS

SIZE: 3⅛×5¼". FRONT: Color photograph. BACK: Black printing on white cardboard. DISTRIBUTION: Nationally, in packages with bubblegum.

HISTORY

The third Topps baseball card issue for 1964 (in addition to its regular card set and the Stand-ups), the Topps Giants were the company's first issue in postcard-size format. The 60 cards in the set (generally stars and minor stars) feature large color photos surrounded by a white border. The only other design element on the front of the card is a white baseball in the lower-right corner with the player's name at center, position at top, and team at bottom. Card backs contain a second photo of the player, at the center of the card, surrounded by a newspaper-style write-up of a high point in his career. The '64 Giants are something of the Rodney Dangerfield of Topps' early '60s baseball cards.

They "don't get no respect." While it is true that they were distributed in huge quantities, these supplies have been virtually absorbed by increasing numbers of collectors in the past couple of years. Though the hobby generally doesn't flock to buy cards in postcard-size, the superstars in this set are favorite—and inexpensive—targets for collectors.

FOR

Attractive, large-format cards; lots of cards; low price.

AGAINST

Oversize; generally perceived as being common as dirt.

NOTEWORTHY CARDS

Lots of Hall of Famers, future Hall of Famers, and players who probably deserve to be Hall of Famers.

VALUE

EX.-MT. CONDITION: Complete set, $30; common card, 15¢; stars, $1; Yastrzemski, Mays, Aaron, Mantle, Koufax, $2–$3. 5-YEAR PROJECTION: Well above average.

1964 Topps Giants, Camilo Pascual

5 WHITEWASHING EXPERT ©T.C.G. PRINTED IN U.S.A.

PAPPAS HURLS 16TH CAREER SHUTOUT

The ace righthander of the Baltimore Orioles, Milt Pappas completed the 1963 campaign in fine form as he hurled his 16th big league shut-out and won his 81st ball-game. His sixteen victories were a new personal high for him as he surpassed his old mark of 15 wins set back in 1959 & 1960. Among his finer games of 1963 were his three 3-hitters vs. American League competition. Milt is an unusual hurler in that he pitched only eleven innings of minor league ball before he was brought up for keeps with the Orioles. In his first full year in the majors, the righty curve-baller was a 10 game winner. He has hit the double figure in wins every season with Baltimore.

1964 Topps Giants, Milt Pappas (back)

1964 Topps Giants, Milt Pappas (front)

1964 Topps Giants, Jim Fregosi

1964 Topps Giants, Harmon Killebrew

9 ROCKY'S HOT BAT ©T.C.G. PRINTED IN U.S.A.

COLAVITO SMASHES 4 HOME RUNS

Rocky Colavito tied a major league record in 1959 when he crashed four consecutive home runs in a game. Then a member of the Cleveland Indians, Rocky was only the sixth big leaguer ever to accomplish this feat. Rocky's booming bat has also seen action with the Detroit Tigers and the Kansas City Athletics. In 1951, the righthanded power hitter began playing ball with Daytona Beach and he won his first home run title. Two years later, Rocky led the Eastern League at Reading as he connected for 28 circuit clouts. His 38 circuit clouts at Indianapolis, which earned the slugger another home run title in the American Association, convinced the experts that Rocky was coming to the majors. Feared for his strong, accurate throwing arm, Rocky was a part time pitcher in the minor leagues, too.

1964 Topps Giants, Rocky Colavito (back)

1964 Topps Giants, Rocky Colavito (front)

1964 Topps Giants, Ron Santo

1964 Topps Giants, Ken Johnson

1964 BAZOOKA

SPECIFICATIONS

SIZE: Single card, $1^9/_{16} \times 2^1/_2''$; three-card panel, $4^{11}/_{16} \times 2^1/_2''$. FRONT: Color photograph. BACK: Blank. DISTRIBUTION: Nationally, a three-card panel on the bottom of each box of bubblegum.

HISTORY

The problem of differentiating the various Bazooka issues returns with the 1964 cards. The '64 Bazookas were in exactly the same design and format as the 1963 cards. To make matters worse, 19 of the 36 cards have the same card numbers as the previous year (some even carried the same card number in 1965). Luckily the pictures are different. If you really want to know what year card you have, you have to have it in the original three-card panel and compare the other cards on it to a checklist for each year. Again, because the cards were issued on the bottom of gum boxes, they are as often as not found roughly cut. Cards in the original panel or still attached to the box are worth a premium over the total value of the three individual cards, perhaps 10 to 15 percent for panels, 25 to 50 percent for boxes. Cards that are poorly cut, especially when cut into the picture, can be considered in Very Good condition, at best.

FOR

Lots of stars; nice photos.

AGAINST

Small size; the aggravation of trying to figure out what year cards you have.

NOTEWORTHY CARDS

Lots of the big names from earlier years were back in '64; Willie McCovey makes his first appearence on a Bazooka card.

VALUE

EX.-MT. CONDITION, NEATLY CUT: Complete set, $125; common card, $2–$3; Hall of Famers, $5–$10; Aaron, Mays, Yastrzemski, $17.50–$20; Mantle, $25. 5-YEAR PROJECTION: Average.

1964 KAHN'S

SPECIFICATIONS

SIZE: $3 \times 3^1/_2''$. FRONT: Color photograph. BACK: Black printing on white cardboard. DISTRIBUTION: Ohio-Western Pennsylvania area, in packages of meat; complete sets available by mail.

HISTORY

In 1964 Kahn's finally made a major change in the format of its baseball card set. Smaller in size than the previous nine years' cards, the '64s featured a full-color borderless photo on the front of the card. The only other design element on the front was a black facsimile autograph. The familiar ad message, "Compliments of Kahn's 'The Wiener the World Awaited,'" appeared on the back of the card at bottom. Card backs also contained brief biographical information and career stats. The 31 cards in the 1964 Kahn's set are unnumbered. Only three teams—the Reds, the Indians, and the Pirates—are represented in the '64 set.

FOR

Attractive new format; in demand by team collectors.

AGAINST

Nothing negative to note.

NOTEWORTHY CARDS

Pete Rose makes his debut for Kahn's cards in the 1964 set, joining Roberto Clemente and Frank Robinson in the superstar ranks.

VALUE

EX.-MT. CONDITION: Complete set, $175; common card, $4–$5; Robinson, $20–$25; Clemente, $30–$35; Rose, $75. 5-YEAR PROJECTION: Average.

1963 TOPPS

SPECIFICATIONS

SIZE: $2^1/_2 \times 3^1/_2''$. FRONT: Color photo. BACK: Black and yellow printing on yellow cardboard. DISTRI-

BUTION: Nationally, in 1¢ and 5¢ packages with bubblegum.

HISTORY

This is probably the only large modern baseball card set in which one card accounts for 40 to 50 percent of the set's value. The set price of the 576-card Topps set of 1963 is largely determined by the fortunes of card #537, "Rookie Stars." And the value of *that* card is largely determined by the current on-field performance of one of the four players whose nickel-size photos appear on the card—that skinny-looking kid in the lower left, Pete Rose. Currently the hottest investment or speculation card in the hobby, the 1963 Topps Pete Rose rookie card has overshadowed the rest of what is really an excellent and highly collectible set. For '63, Topps pulled in its horns and dropped the number of cards in the issue to 576 (598 cards had been issued in 1962). One of Topps' most highly acclaimed designs, the 1963 cards feature a large color photo at the top, while in a colored circle at the bottom right of the card is a smaller black-and-white picture. In a wide band of color below the color picture are listed the player's name, team, and position. Card backs in 1963 once again featured full major and/or minor league stats on a year-by-year basis. These are combined with a traditional combination of a cartoon, a career summary, and short biographical details. Like all Topps sets between 1952 and 1973, the 1963 set was issued in series. The first few series, cards #1–#288, were issued during the early spring, when interest in baseball and baseball cards was at its peak. As the year progressed and the novelty wore off, fewer and fewer cards were sold; the result was smaller printing quantities of cards #289–#446, smaller still of the "semi-highs," #447–#506, and perhaps the smallest of all, cards #507–#576, the "high numbers." As high numbers go, the '63 cards really are quite scarce. While this has contributed to the $350+ price tag on the Pete Rose card in their midst, it is really the demand for that particular card that supports the price. By contrast, a common player's card in the 1963 highs is a $1.25 item. Some students of the 1963 set, and dealers who handle a lot of cards, contend that it is really the semi-highs in the set that are the scarcest, but they have yet to convince the hobby as a whole. One of the reasons the 1963 set is so popular is that there are far fewer specialty cards. The first 10 cards in the set honor the American and National Leagues' statistical performers of 1962, with the winner in each league sharing a card with the four runners-up. The only other subset in '63 is the seven-card group recounting the 1962 World Series. The various "Rookie Stars" cards of 1963 are unusual in that they are not arranged by team or by position.

FOR

The set is attractive, challenging, and —discounting the Pete Rose rookie card—relatively inexpensive. Lack of gimmicky specialty cards compared to most years is a big plus.

AGAINST

The extremely high demand and price for the Pete Rose rookie card makes building a complete set the most expensive project among 1960s Topps sets.

NOTEWORTHY CARDS

Naturally, the Pete Rose rookie card is the best-known card in the set. Collectors should be aware that the card was counterfeited in 1982. The counterfeit is relatively easy to spot: if held up to a strong light it will appear somewhat transparent and you can see the shadow of your fingers behind it. This resulted from printing the card on thinner cardboard than the original. If a genuine 1963 card is held to the strongest light, no light penetrates. Two of the other "Rookie Stars" cards in 1963 contain the only significant variations in the set. The common versions of cards #29 and #54 have the date 1963 in yellow at top, while the scarcer variety have the date 1962 in white. All seven of the checklist cards exist with subtle variations, but few collectors bother with them. Besides the Rose rookie, two other significant rookie cards appear in the 1963 set, Rusty Staub and Willie Stargell. Though Gaylord Perry appears on a "Rookie Stars" card, it is not his rookie card; he appeared on his own card in the 1962 set. Some photo errors in the 1963 set are worth mentioning. On card #113, Don Landrum, both photos are of Ron Santo; on card #231, Eli Grba, the large color photo is actually Ryne Duren. The photo of Ray Herbert on card #8 is reversed. The 1963 Topps set features the last contemporary baseball card issue of Stan Musial.

VALUE

EX.-MT. CONDITION: Complete set, $750; common card, #1–#288, 20¢; #289–#446, 25¢–30¢; #447–#506, $1.25; #507–#576, $1.15–$1.25; stars, $2–$4; Musial, Berra, Frank and Brooks Robinson, Drysdale, Banks, Gibson, Ford, Killebrew, Staub, $5–$10; Koufax, Snider, $12–$15; McCovey, $17; Yastrzemski, Mays, Aaron, Stargell, $20–$25; Mantle, $25–$27.50; Brock, $30; Rose, $350. 5-YEAR PROJECTION: Above average.

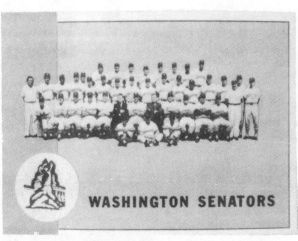

1963 Topps, Washington Senators Team Card

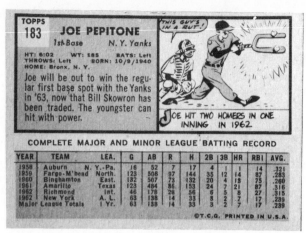

1963 Topps, Joe Pepitone (back)

1963 Topps, Joe Pepitone (front)

1963 Topps, Minnesota Twins Team Card

1963 Topps, Strikeout Leaders

1963 Topps, World Series Game #4

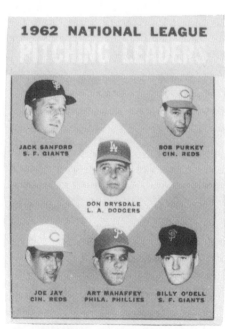

1963 Topps, Pitching Leaders

1963 FLEER

1963 Topps, Ryne Duren

1963 Topps, Jim Gilliam

1963 Topps, Frank Robinson

1963 Topps, World Series Game #6

SPECIFICATIONS

SIZE: 2½×3½″. FRONT: Color photograph. BACK: Black and yellow-green printing on white cardboard. DISTRIBUTION: Nationally, in packages with a cookie.

HISTORY

The 66-card 1963 Fleer set was another round in the early battles of the "Card Wars." In 1959 Fleer had issued its Ted Williams set; in 1960 and 1961 the Philadelphia-based bubblegum company had issued a set of old-timers. By 1963, Fleer apparently felt ready to take on Topps in the market for current players' cards. In a ploy to avoid Topps' monopoly on issuing baseball cards with "confectionery" products, Fleer packaged its 1963 cards in a wax gum-style wrapper with a "cookie." Topps' lawyers challenged this evasion in court and won. It is not known whether Fleer had intended to issue more than the 66 cards that year or not. Regardless, the court order kept Fleer out of the market for current players' cards for another 18 years. The 1963 Fleer cards are not unlike the '63 Topps in design. The top of the card is dominated by a large color photo of the player, either a portrait or posed action shot. In the lower-left corner, where Topps had a black-and-white photo of the player, Fleer had a line drawing of a player representing the position of the player on the card. The name, team, and position were to the right, in the wide white bottom border. Backs of the '63 Fleers were vertical in format and featured a short write-up on the player plus stats for the 1962 season and lifetime totals. Card number is in a circle at lower center, in front of a pair of crossed bats. Cards in the '63 Fleer set are generally numbered by team, though a few players at the end of the set do not follow this sequence. The 1963 Fleer cards were widely distributed before the court order took them out of the ball game, and surviving cards are not particularly scarce, with two exceptions noted below. In terms of sheer numbers of each card issued, the 1963 Fleer cards are not in the same league with Topps, but current prices do not really reflect this overall difference in scarcity. The Fleer set is picking up new followers regularly, though, and it is expected to be one of the better performers pricewise over the next several years.

FOR

An important set in terms of baseball card history. Short enough to complete easily; lots of stars; decent quality.

AGAINST

You can't say much against the '63 Fleers; they were in there pitching to break up Topps' virtual monopoly.

NOTEWORTHY CARDS

Fleer had an ace card or two up its sleeve in the 1963 set. Most important, the first nationally distributed baseball card of Maury Wills appeared in this set. That was quite a coup for Fleer, because Wills had been named the National League MVP in 1962, an award that is noted on the front of his card. Because Topps had snubbed Wills when handing out baseball card contracts to minor leaguers in the early 1950s, Wills refused to appear on a Topps card until 1967. Other major stars in the 1963 Fleer set include Willie Mays, Carl Yastrzemski, Brooks Robinson, Sandy Koufax, Warren Spahn, Bob Gibson, and Roberto Clemente. The most valuable cards,

though, are the unnumbered checklist and card #46, Joe Adcock. It is surmised that somewhere toward the end of the printing run, the Adcock card was replaced on the press sheet with the checklist card, making both of them scarce today.

VALUE

EX.-MT. CONDITION: Complete set, $150; common card, 50¢; superstars, $4–$8; Adcock, checklist, $25–$30. 5-YEAR PROJECTION: Above average.

1963 POST

SPECIFICATIONS

SIZE: 3½×2½". FRONT: Color photograph. BACK: Blank. DISTRIBUTION: Nationally, on backs of cereal boxes.

HISTORY

The 200-card set issued with Post cereals in 1963 is one of the most challenging baseball card sets of the 1960s. The method of distribution, printing cards as part of the cereal box design, produced some very scarce cards to tease today's collectors. Many cards were printed on only one or two different brands or sizes of cereal. If those brands were not very popular—Post Oat Flakes is the classic example—the cards on those boxes were not widely distributed. Consequently, they are rare and expensive today. Be-

sides the basic 200 cards in the set there are also numerous variations—most frequent variation was in the color—the photo background. Some collectors specialize in these variations. A detailed checklist will be necessary for the collector to determine what he wants to collect and how much he can afford to collect. The cards were printed with thin black lines separating them on the package, and it was very easy for the kids of 20 years ago to make a mess of cutting the cards off the box. Well-trimmed cards, therefore, are especially desirable among collectors, and the accuracy of the trim must be taken into consideration when grading a card. While they are not common, complete panels, comprising the entire back of a cereal box, or even complete cereal boxes are not all that unusual. Such premium items have a value one-and-a-half to two times the total value of the individual cards on the panel. The '63 Post cards have a color photo of the player at the left end of the card, and a biography on the right. A pale yellow panel at the bottom of the card carries the player's statistics for the 1962 season and his career totals. Backs are blank. The 200 cards in the 1963 set were numbered by team, the first 11 cards being the Minnesota Twins, the next 12 cards being New York Yankees, etc. The 1963 Post cereal cards were reproduced in a slightly smaller size for boxes of Jell-O (see listing).

FOR

An extremely challenging modern set. Old accumulations of these sets

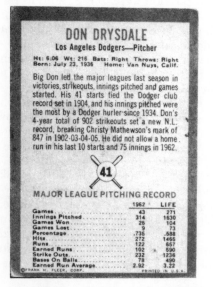

1963 Fleer, Don Drysdale (back)

1963 Post, Leon Wagner

can often yield cards worth lots of money—depending on what cereal the owner ate 20 years ago.

AGAINST

Rarity of some cards makes this an extremely difficult set to complete. It's hard to find cards in top condition.

NOTEWORTHY CARDS

Virtually all of the big stars of 1963 are present in the Post set except Stan Musial, then in the final year of his career. The photos of Los Angeles Angels teammates George Thomas and Lee Thomas are mixed up. The most noteworthy cards are those seemingly common players that are worth a lot of money because of their scarcity. Some of the most valuable cards are listed below.

VALUE

EX.-MT. CONDITION, NEATLY CUT FROM BOX: Complete set, $1,350; common card, 50¢; superstars, $2–$5; Al Smith, Dick McAuliffe, Chuck Cottier, Marty Keough, Don Hoak, Willie Mays, Del Crandell, Ken Hubbs, Dick Bertell, Norm Larker, $10–$20; Lenny Green, Lee Thomas, Floyd Robinson, Jim Bunning, Jerry Lumpe, Manny Jiminez, Tom Haller, Willie Davis, Hank Aaron, Curt Flood, Billy Williams, $25–$50; Roger Maris, Jerry Adair, Eddie Kasko, Frank Thomas, $60–$90; Mickey Mantle, Carl Yastrzemski, Bob Aspromonte, $100. 5-YEAR PROJECTION: Average.

1963 JELL-O

SPECIFICATIONS

SIZE: 3¼×2½". FRONT: Color photograph. BACK: Blank. DISTRIBUTION: Upper Midwest, one card on back of each box of Jell-O.

HISTORY

The 200 cards in the 1963 Jell-O set are nearly identical to those issued by Post cereals. The only difference between the two issues is that the Jell-O cards are a quarter-inch narrower than their Post counterparts. Type size on the Jell-O cards is also a bit smaller, but a card would have to be examined side by side with a Post card to tell the difference by type size alone. The '63 Jell-O cards were printed as part of the back of packages of the gelatin dessert. A solid black line around the card was to be used as a guide in cutting it from the box. Whether or not a card has been neatly trimmed from the box is a major factor in its grading. Some collectors prefer cards that have been trimmed outside the black guide line; some prefer the lines to have been cut off. While they are not common, it's possible to find some uncut boxes and some complete boxes still filled with 20-year-old Jell-O. These premium items command prices corresponding to two to three times the value of an individual card. The Jell-O set was numbered consecutively within team groupings. While the usual demand for superstars is an important factor in pricing 1963 Jell-O cards, there is also a scarcity factor to be considered. Because some of the cards were printed on the backs of the less popular 6-oz. family size, or on less popular flavors of Jell-O, they were not sold in the same quantities as cards on the 3-oz. boxes of popular flavors. Consequently, fewer have survived, and they are often more valuable as a result. Values of such cards can range from $6 to $15; but a detailed checklist is necessary to determine which are the scarce cards. This factor makes the '63 Jell-O set a challenge to collect, though it is not nearly as tough as the '63 Post issue. There are many color variations in the set, usually associated with the background behind the player's picture. They have little effect on price and most collectors do not concern themselves with these variations.

FOR

A challenging but by no means impossible set.

AGAINST

Easily confused with the '63 Post issue. Because of sloppy scissors-work by the kids who originally cut them off the boxes, it is sometimes hard to find cards in top condition. It is expensive for a 20-year-old set.

NOTEWORTHY CARDS

The photos of Los Angeles Angels teammates George Thomas and Lee Thomas are mixed up. All the big name stars of 1963 are in the set, except for Stan Musial.

VALUE

EX.-MT. CONDITION, NEATLY CUT FROM BOX: Complete set, $1,000; common card, $1; scarce cards, $6–$15; Yastrzemski, Mays, McCovey, Gibson, Aaron, $20–$25; Mantle, $40. 5-YEAR PROJECTION: Below average.

1963 BAZOOKA

SPECIFICATIONS

SIZE: Single card, 1⁹⁄₁₆×2½"; three-card panel, 4¹¹⁄₁₆×2½". FRONT: Color photograph. BACK: Blank. DISTRIBUTION: Nationally, a three-card panel on the bottom of each box of bubblegum.

HISTORY

After three years of nearly identical card issues, Topps changed the format and design slightly for its 1963 Bazooka series. The company also returned to a 36-card set, as opposed to the 45-card set issued in 1962. The cards were still distributed as a three-card panel comprising most of the bottom of a 20-piece box of bubblegum. They were meant to be cut off the box and cut into individual cards. Naturally, cards that are still attached to the original box, or at least in three-card panel form, have premium value above the total values of the three individual cards on the panel. In the case of panels, the extra value is in the area of 10 percent or so; whole boxes would be worth some 25 to 50 percent extra. As with all baseball cards that have to be cut off a box, top grade '63 Bazookas are somewhat hard to find; many of the youngsters who originally bought the cards had trouble cutting in a straight line. For 1963, the Bazooka cards were made a quarter-inch smaller all around, and the colored rectangular strips that had carried the player information in the 1959–1962 issues were replaced with white ovals at the bottom of the cards. Within the oval, the player's name appears in red; his team name and position are in black. The card numbers returned in the '63 Bazookas, again in small black type in the white border below the picture. Unlike some other Bazooka card issues, there are no known scarcities among particular panels in the 1963 set.

FOR

Inexpensive, attractive cards; lots of big name players.

AGAINST

Unpopular size. Difficult to find in good condition.

NOTEWORTHY CARDS

There continued to be a fairly high proportion of star players in the 1963 Bazooka offering. Hall of Famers Stan Musial (in his last season) and Brooks Robinson appear on a Bazooka card for the first time in the 1963 set, as does Carl Yastrzemski, a sure bet for Hall of Fame honors and currently the hottest card in the set. Other superstars represented in the set include Mantle, Banks, Spahn, Killebrew, Aaron, Mays, Clemente, Drysdale, Frank Robinson, and Kaline.

VALUE

EX.-MT. CONDITION, NEATLY CUT FROM BOX: Complete set, $150; common card, $2; Hall of Famers, $7.50–$15; Mays, Aaron, $17.50; Yastrzemski, $20; Mantle, $25. 5-YEAR PROJECTION: Average.

1963 BAZOOKA ALL-TIME GREATS

SPECIFICATIONS

SIZE: $1^{9}/_{16} \times 2^{1}/_{2}''$. FRONT: Black-and-white bust photo in ornate gold "frame," white border. BACK: Black printing on yellow background. DISTRIBUTION: Nationally, in boxes of bubblegum.

HISTORY

When you plunked down your 19¢ for a 20-piece box of Topps' Bazooka brand bubblegum in 1963, you got a lot of baseball cards along with the thick, hard wad of gum. Besides the three cards of current players on the bottom of the box, there were five "Golden Edition" baseball cards stuffed inside. Known generically as All-Time Greats cards, sets that featured old-time stars were a popular gimmick for baseball card issuers in the early 1960s (and have been, off and on, since then). The Bazooka old-timers cards seem to have been a response to similar issues by Fleer in 1960 and 1961. The '63 Bazooka All-Time Greats numbered 41 cards, all Hall of Famers. They were the same size as the cards on the bottom of the box, but did not have to be cut off anything or cut apart. The cards were not particularly popular with youngsters, because other than Babe Ruth, Ty Cobb, Lou Gehrig, and a few others, most of the players in the set were unknown to the average kid in 1963. Because many of the photos used on these cards were taken long after the player's career was over, a lot of baseball's great stars of the early years just look like old men in this issue.

FOR

These cards offer a look at yesterday's stars at a reasonable price.

AGAINST

They share the same unpopular size as the other Bazooka cards of the '60s. Collectors have never been particularly attracted to cards of baseball players issued after their playing days; many hobbyists don't consider them quite legitimate. The '63 Bazooka All-Time Greats are also a fairly difficult set to collect because they were not apparently saved in great numbers. Even so, they remain inexpensive.

NOTEWORTHY CARDS

They're all Hall of Famers, how much more noteworthy can you get?

VALUE

EX.-MT. CONDITION: Complete set, $95; common card, $2; Cobb, Gehrig, $7.50; Ruth, $10. 5-YEAR PROJECTION: Below average.

1963 KAHN'S

SPECIFICATIONS

SIZE: $3^{1}/_{4} \times 4''$. FRONT: Black-and-white photograph. BACK: Black printing on white cardboard. DISTRIBUTION: Eastern, Midwestern U.S., in packages of meat products; complete sets by mail.

HISTORY

After eight years with the same design, Kahn's changed the format of its baseball card issue for 1963—but only a little. The black-and-white photo that occupies most of the front of the card now has a white border all the way around. Still there are the facsimile autograph and the advertising strip at bottom. Card backs once again feature year-by-year stats and career information. There were five teams in the 1963 Kahn's line-up: the Reds, the Pirates, the Indians, the Cardinals, and, for the first time, the New York Yankees. A total of 30 cards was issued, with no variations. The cards are not numbered. As in the previous few years, cards were available singly in packages of meat, or in a complete set as a mail-in offer.

FOR

Adding the Yankees expanded the roster of teams; low price, considering relative scarcity.

AGAINST

Kahn's didn't change the design enough to make the cards really different from previous years. Also cards are not really attractive compared to contemporary issues.

NOTEWORTHY CARDS

The addition of Yankee players in the '63 set gives Kahn's collectors such well-known players as Bobby Richardson, Tony Kubek, and Elston Howard, along with the familiar big name stars Frank Robinson and Roberto Clemente.

VALUE

EX.-MT. CONDITION: Complete set, $150; common card, $4–$5; minor stars, $6–$7.50; Robinson, $30; Clemente, $40–$45. 5-YEAR PROJECTION: Below average.

1963 PEPSI COLT .45s

SPECIFICATIONS

SIZE: Single card, 2⅜×3¾"; panel, 2⅜×9⅛". FRONT: Black-and-white photo; miscellaneous blue and red printing. BACK: Black printing on white cardboard. DISTRIBUTION: Houston, Texas, area, one card/panel in each carton of soda.

HISTORY

This is a relatively recent regional major league issue on which the value is being held artificially low by the rarity of a couple of cards in the issue. In other words, since few collectors can hope to complete the set—which chronicles the two-year-old predecessor of today's Houston Astros—they're unwilling to start. Distribution on these cards varied widely when they were placed on store shelves in cartons of Pepsi. It appears today that the card of John Bateman was never publicly distributed. A similar situation seems to have occurred with the Carl Warwick card, but some small number of them nevertheless made their way into the hobby's commercial channels. The cards themselves (styled, not unconsciously, after the 1961 Topps issue) are perforated at top and bottom and could be detached from a long strip that offered a Colt .45s schedule for the 1963 season. On the back of the card is a typical biographical and statistical summary of the pictured player.

FOR

Truly scarce regional major league issue of a popular expansion team. A must for Astros team collectors.

AGAINST

It's almost impossible to complete a set without a large outlay of cash for the rare Bateman card.

NOTEWORTHY CARDS

A rookie card of Rusty Staub is included in this set; also current Astros manager Bob Lillis in his playing days.

OUR FAVORITE CARD

Naturally, John Bateman. For whatever reason the Bateman card was never distributed, it is undeniably rare today. A collector desiring an example could search the hobby publications and every card show within driving distance for a full year without ever seeing one for sale. It ranks as one of the legitimate great rarities in the hobby, but has yet to be priced as such. Still, at $200–$250, it is out of reach for most collectors.

VALUE

EX.-MT. CONDITION, COMPLETE PANEL: Complete set, $400; common card, $2.50; Staub, $10; Warwick, $25–$40; Bateman, $200–$250. Cards removed from panel are worth about half as much. 5-YEAR PROJECTION: Above average.

1963 SUGARDALE

SPECIFICATIONS

SIZE: 5⅛×3¾". FRONT: Black-and-white photo. BACK: Black and red printing on white cardboard. DISTRIBUTION: Cleveland-Pittsburgh areas, in packages of hot dogs.

HISTORY

The second and final year of baseball card production by the producers of Sugardale hot dogs consisted of a 31-card set virtually identical in format to the previous year's issue. The 25 Cleveland Indians players in the set are skip-numbered between 1 and 28, while the six Pirates are lettered A–E rather than numbered. Like the '62 Sugardales, the 1963 issue has a player photo on the front of the card, along with a biography. A facsimile autograph appears above the bio. Ads for the company and the team appear at the bottom of the horizontal-format cards. On the backs there is a line drawing and a baseball playing tip from the player pictured on the front of the card. A Sugardale logo appears at the bottom. The Sugardale cards have rounded corners. To differentiate the '63 cards from the '62 issue it is necessary to read the biography on the front for mention of the 1962 season.

FOR

Important issue for team and regional collectors.

AGAINST

The cards are too large to suit most collectors; they're not particularly attractive and are quite expensive. If they were at all popular there's no telling how much they would cost.

NOTEWORTHY CARDS

There are no big stars in the 1963 Sugardale set. The cards of Jim Perry and Bob Skinner are scarcer than the others because they were withdrawn from distribution when those players were traded in mid-season.

VALUE

EX.-MT. CONDITION: Complete set, $650; common card, $20; Perry, Skinner, $45–$60. 5-YEAR PROJECTION: Below average.

1963 PEPSI TULSA OILERS

SPECIFICATIONS

SIZE: Single card, 2½×3½"; panel, 5×7". FRONT: Sepia-tone photograph. BACK: Black and white. DISTRIBUTION: Tulsa, Oklahoma, area, with cartons of soda.

HISTORY

In 1963, for the second straight year, Pepsi-Cola sponsored a minor league baseball card set for the Cardinals' farm team in the Texas League. Two-card panels, perforated for easy separation, were attached by means of a ring tab to one of the bottles in each carton of Pepsi. The detachable tab challenged collectors to assemble a complete collection of 24 cards, and match the names with those found under the cork liners of bottle caps. A complete matched set of cards and bottle caps could be sent to the bottling plant for a $24 reward—and you got the cards back! Any ten of the Pepsi Oilers cards shown at the gate were good for free admission on certain Pepsi Nights at the ballyard.

FOR

Relatively inexpensive, indicating that collectors or dealers obtained large quantities of the uncut panels during or after the promotion. One of few minor league sets of the 1960s.

AGAINST

Generally little demand for minor league cards unless they portray a current or former superstar. Inclusion of two bat boy cards in the set.

NOTEWORTHY CARDS

The '63 Pepsi Tulsa Oilers set contains the last contemporary card of famed 1930s St. Louis Cardinals shortstop "Pepper" Martin, who was managing the Tulsa team. Martin died in 1965 in McAlester, Oklahoma, at the age of 61.

VALUE

EX-MT. CONDITION: Complete set, $30; common card, $1.25; Martin, $4. 5-YEAR PROJECTION: Below average.

1962 TOPPS

SPECIFICATIONS

SIZE: 2½×3½". FRONT: Color photograph. BACK: Black and red printing on gray cardboard. DISTRIBUTION: Nationally, in 1¢ and 5¢ packages with bubblegum.

HISTORY

While the Topps set for 1962 is numbered through card #598, a number of significant photo variations push the total for a complete set to more than 600 cards. Even at 598 cards, the '62 issue was Topps' biggest ever to that date. Design of the '62s is one of those Topps creations that an individual either loves or hates. The photo on the front of the card is set against a woodgrain background. The lower-right corner of the picture has been airbrushed to make it look as if it is curling away from the wood background. In that exposed corner, the player's last name is printed in white capital letters. The player's first name, team, and position are indicated in black lettering. Card backs feature a return to abbreviated statistics, giving only the previous season's perform-

ance and the cumulative career record. There is a short paragraph about the player's career, a pertinent cartoon, and the usual biographical details. In that year after his historic record-breaking 61 home runs, Roger Maris opens the 1962 Topps set as card #1. Virtually all of the specialty series within the 1962 set are copies of those done in 1961. There are subsets for league statistical leaders of the previous year (four per card), a number of multi-player feature cards, a series detailing the Yankees' victory over the Reds in the 1960 World Series, and the usual checklist and team photo cards. All-Star cards, which had traditionally been issued at the end of the set, are in the middle of the 1962 issue. There are some new specialty cards in the 1962 set. The most significant is the first of the multi-player rookie cards. Topps utilized the concept of grouping five player photos by position, regardless of team, on each of eight "Rookie Parade" cards, the last eight cards of the set. Nine of the stars of 1962 are featured on second cards within the set, usually in a sequence of photos showing action on the field. These are the ancestors of the "In Action" cards that would come in later years. The final specialty card group is a run of 10 "Babe Ruth Special" cards, tracing his baseball career. As with most specialty cards in recent sets that depict old-time players, demand for the Ruth specialty cards is much less than the beginning collector would expect. The 1962 set can be carved up into three degrees of scarcity. Cards

#1–#370 are the most common; cards #371–#522 are somewhat tougher; and the high numbers, #523–#598, are scarcer still. Because 1962 was the first year for the New York Mets and the Houston Colt .45s, most of their players are shown without caps and in uniforms of their previous teams, sometimes airbrushed to hide details.

FOR

The unusual design of the '62s is quite popular with some collectors. There are enough variation cards, major and minor, to keep the avid collector busy for years—and more probably will be discovered. Price is currently quite low in comparison to other early 1960s sets.

AGAINST

If you don't like the '62 design, you probably hate it enough to keep you from collecting the cards. The varieties, some of them very minor in nature, can drive a collector crazy.

NOTEWORTHY CARDS

Let's look at the major varieties in the '62 set, ignoring the numerous color-tint differences that some collectors cherish. All of the popularly collected variations occur between #129 and #190, and involve pose or card number variations. In the following descriptions, the more common card is listed first. Lee Walls, #129, will be found facing either right or left. The Angels team card, #132, will be found without or with two small portraits in

1962 Topps, Cleveland Indians Pitchers

the upper corners. Billy Hoeft, #134, can be found facing slightly right or facing straight out. Card #139 can be found three ways, as "Babe Hits 60," with Hal Reniff's portrait, or with Reniff in a pitching pose. Bill Kunkel, #147, can also be found in portrait or pitching variations. Carl Willey, #174, is seen without and with a cap. And, finally, Eddie Yost, #176, and Wally Moon, #190, can be found in portrait or batting poses. Two other variations that are just a bit less popular are cards #458 and #462, Bob Buhl and Willie Tasby. In the more common version, the pair are shown with Braves and Senators caps on their heads. In the scarcer type, the logos have been air-brushed from the caps, reflecting trades. Notable rookie cards in the 1962 set include Gaylord Perry and Lou Brock, who have their own cards, and the following players who appear on the multi-player rookie cards: Sam McDowell, Jim Bouton, Joe Pepitone, and Bob Uecker. Also worth special mention is the fact that 1962 Topps cards are sometimes seen with the backs printed in Spanish. These cards were originally issued in Venezuela.

OUR FAVORITE CARD

In terms of number of stars gathered on a single baseball card, it would be hard to beat card #18 in the 1962 set, "Manager's Dream." The card features Mickey Mantle and Willie Mays facing the camera and smiling. However, if you look in the background, you'll see another group of players posing for a different photographer. In that group are Elston Howard, Hank Aaron, and George Altman, whose eighth inning pinch-hit home run in the 1961 All-Star Game was the margin of victory for the National League. The photo is one of many taken at All-Star Games that appear on Topps multi-player feature cards.

VALUE

EX.-MT. CONDITION: Complete set, $375; common card, #1–#522, 25¢–35¢; #523–#598, $1.25; scarce variations, $3–$5; stars, $3.50–$7; Bouton, Uecker, Pepitone, McDowell, $4–$5; Maris, Koufax, Clemente, Musial, $8; Perry, Mays, Aaron, $15; Mantle, Brock, Gibson, McCovey (latter two in high numbers), $20. 5-YEAR PROJECTION: Average or slightly below.

1962 Topps, Los Angeles Angels Team Card

1962 Topps, Warren Spahn,
National League Left-Handed Pitcher All-Star

1962 Topps, Victory Leaders

1962 Topps, Elston Howard,
The Sporting News *All-Stars*

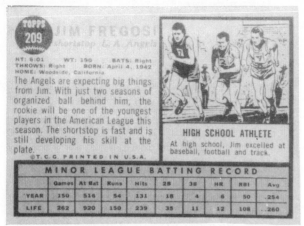

1962 Topps, Jim Fregosi (back)

1962 Topps, Jim Fregosi (front)

1962 Topps, Los Angeles Dodgers Team Card

*1962 Topps,
American League Strikeout Leaders*

1962 Topps, Vernon Law

1962 Topps, Ryne Duren

1962 BAZOOKA

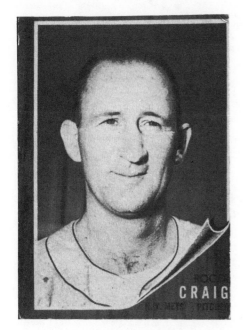

1962 Topps, Roger Craig

1962 Topps, Frank Robinson,
The Sporting News *All-Stars*

SPECIFICATIONS

SIZE: Single card, $1^{13}/_{16} \times 2^{3}/_{4}''$; three-card panel, $5^{1}/_{2} \times 2^{3}/_{4}''$. FRONT: Color photograph. BACK: Blank. DISTRIBUTION: Nationally, a three-card panel on the bottom of each box of bubblegum.

HISTORY

Not one to tamper with success—even to the point of going stagnant—Topps left the design of the 1962 Bazooka cards unchanged from that of 1960 and 1961. A three-card panel would again be found on the bottom of each 20-piece box of bubblegum. In many cases, these panels were gleefully hacked off by the young buyer. Since few of the original owners were skilled with scissors, many of these Bazooka cards are found poorly trimmed, a condition that reduces their value considerably. By contrast, cards still attached to the complete gum box are worth 25 to 50 percent above what the single cards would sell for. Three-card strips cut from the boxes but not separated into individual cards are also worth a small premium (maybe 10 percent or so) over the total value of the three cards as singles. While at first glance the 1962 cards seem exactly like the 1960 and 1961 issues, there is an important difference. They are not numbered. (SPECIAL NOTE: That's not entirely true; some 1962 Bazookas have surfaced in recent years with card numbers. It is speculated that these are printer's proofs, rather than actually issued cards, but the question is unresolved currently. Numbered 1962 Bazookas sell for several times the value of the unnumbered versions, but that situation may change.) The other big change in 1962 was the expansion of the set from 12 panels (36 cards) to 15 panels (45 cards). This seems principally to have been done as a result of National League expansion that season; the 1962 Bazooka set features players of the new Houston Colt .45s and the New York Mets. Distribution of three of the 15 panels seems to have been somewhat uneven, and the Allison-Mathews-Pinson, Romano-Banks-Siebern, and Zimmer-Killebrew-Woodling panels are quite scarce, valued at around $100 apiece in nice condition.

FOR

Nice, manageable, attractive set. Not too expensive, but with a few scarce cards to keep it challenging. Lots of stars, and the "new" Mets and Colts.

AGAINST

Same old design as on the 1960 and 1961 cards; same old problem, too small to be attractive to most collectors, who prefer the $2^{1}/_{2} \times 3^{1}/_{2}''$ size.

NOTEWORTHY CARDS

Aaron is back in '62, and two other Hall of Famers, Sandy Koufax and Whitey Ford, make their first Bazooka appearance in this set. Lots of other stars, but also lots of lesser-known players—who was Don Schwall, anyway? Hard to find in top grade.

VALUE

EX.-MT. CONDITION, NEATLY CUT FROM BOX: Complete set, $450; common card, $2.50; minor stars, $4–$6; Hall of Famers, $7.50–$15.00; Aaron, Mays, $20; Mantle, $25; Mathews, Banks, Killebrew, $30–$45. 5-YEAR PROJECTION: Average.

1962 POST

SPECIFICATIONS

SIZE: $3^{1}/_{2} \times 2^{1}/_{2}''$. FRONT: Color photograph. BACK: Blank. DISTRIBUTION: Nationally, on back of cereal boxes.

HISTORY

The most attractive and easiest to complete set of the 1960–1963 Post cereal issues is the 200-card 1962 set. Unlike the '61 set, which could be obtained directly from the company by a mail-in offer, the 1962 cards were only available on the backs of cereal boxes. Single cards were printed on the backs of the small serving-size cereal boxes, while panels of eight cards made up the back of family-size boxes of most

Post brands. Because black lines dividing the cards were shared by two cards, it is difficult to find '62 Posts with a complete black border, though some collectors do try. Most will settle for a card that is neatly trimmed inside the black line, with straight edges. Cards that have ragged edges, or that have been cut into the photo or colored part of the design, are worth much less than neatly cut cards. The most valuable form for the '62 Post cards is on complete boxes or complete back panels. Such uncut card panels are worth two to three times the total value of the individual cards on the panel. Once again in '62, the Post set was numbered by teams, with the American League preceding the National League. There are far fewer error and variation cards in the 1962 set, most of them being color variations of little interest to most collectors. Design of the 1962 set is similar, though more attractive, than the 1961 cards. The player color photo appears on the right of the card in '62. The card number is printed in red in the upper-left corner, while the player's name is in blue script letters. There are some personal figures and a career summary printed in a yellow panel to the left of the photo, and a red and white Post logo appears in the lower-right corner of that panel. The player's 1961 and lifetime total statistics are printed in a white box at the bottom of the card. This box is surrounded by a heavy red border on the National League cards and blue border on the American League cards. Backs are blank. NOTE: A virtually identical set of 200 cards was printed and distributed in Canada on Post cereals. The photos on these cards are slightly smaller, to accommodate the bilingual French and English text. All card numbers and photos are the same; the layout has just been slightly rearranged. The 1962 set is the only Post set to have a Canadian version. The Canadian Post cards are worth about twice what a U.S. card will bring.

FOR
Attractive, relatively inexpensive national set of the early Sixties. Lots of big name stars and just enough scarce cards to make it interesting.

AGAINST
Hard to find an Ex.–Mt. or better set.

1962 Post, Willie Mays

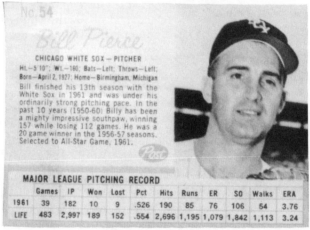
1962 Post, Bill Pierce

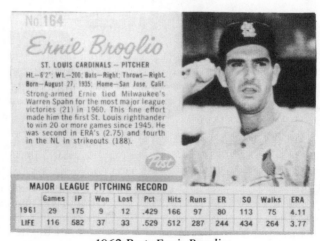
1962 Post, Ernie Broglio

NOTEWORTHY CARDS

There are a lot of interesting cards in the '62 Post set, in addition to the usual big name superstars and Hall of Famers. Two of the cards, Mantle and Maris, were printed on thin cardboard with an advertising back and were inserted into early spring issues of several national magazines to promote the set. They are valued about the same as the regular card, though the complete ad insert or magazine is a highly prized item. Two of the most popularly collected variations in the set are the Joe Adcock (#145) and Jim Gentile (#27) cards. The former can be found with the script-lettered name spelled correctly, or incorrectly as "Adock," the error version being a $15 item in top grade, while the card with the correct spelling brings 75¢ or so. On the Gentile card, the more common variation lists his home as Baltimore, Maryland, while the scarcer type gives his home as San Lorenzo, California. Value of the California address is about $4, compared to 75¢ for the Maryland listing. The 1962 Post set also features a handful of scarce cards that were distributed on the backs of less popular cereals, and are much in demand today. They are (value listed in Ex.–Mt. condition): #55–Early Wynn, $12; #69–Marty Keough, $12; #92–Norm Siebern, $22; #101–Gil Hodges, $25; #113–Norm Larker, $15; #116–Gordy Coleman, $30; #125–Jim Brosnan, $12; #127–Jerry Lynch, $18; #131–Willie McCovey, $30; #140–Juan Marichal, $35; and #158–Bill White, $15.

VALUE

EX.-MT. CONDITION: Complete set, $400; common card, 50¢–75¢; stars, $2–$8; Aaron, Mays, Yastrzemski, Mantle, $12. 5-YEAR PROJECTION: Average, or a bit better.

1962 JELL-O

SPECIFICATIONS

SIZE: 3½×2½". FRONT: Color photograph. BACK: Blank. DISTRIBUTION: Upper Midwest, one card on back of each Jell-O box.

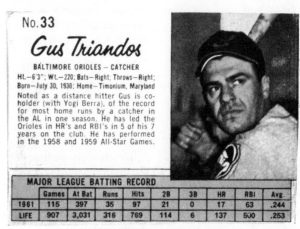

1962 Jell-O, Gus Triandos

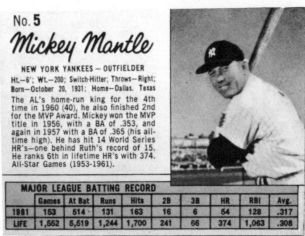

1962 Jell-O, Mickey Mantle

HISTORY

The 1962 Jell-O set is a direct spin-off of the 1962 Post cereal set, and it was originally intended to feature the same 200 cards. Both companies were part of the General Foods conglomerate. The Jell-O version contains only 197 cards (#29, Brooks Robinson; #82, Ted Kluszewski; and #176, Smokey Burgess, were not issued in the Jell-O set), and has one card, #19, which is a different player, Ken Aspromonte in the Jell-O set, Rocky Colavito in Post. The Jell-O cards were issued only in the Upper Midwest, one card on the back of each box of Jell-O. Because each card was printed only on certain sizes and flavors of the gelatin dessert, those cards that appeared on the 6-oz. size or on the less popular flavors are today scarcer than other cards in the set. A detailed checklist is necessary to

sort them out. Overall, the 1962 Jell-O cards are much scarcer than their Post counterparts. The Jell-O cards are virtually identical in design to the Posts, but for three elements. The red Post logo is missing to the left of the photo on the Jell-O version; the red or blue color stripes that surround the statistical box at the bottom of the card do not appear on the Jell-O set; and the stats are printed in a yellow box, rather than white. Like the Post cards, the backs of the Jell-O cards are blank. Because the Jell-O cards were printed one to a box, it is not too difficult to find them bordered by a complete black line, and cards are generally worth more that way. Whether they were cut inside or outside the black line, most collectors want them to have straight edges. Complete boxes are worth three to five times the value of the card alone.

FOR

Scarce regionally issued version of a popular set.

AGAINST

The cards are not as attractive as their Post counterparts, are much harder to assemble into a complete set, and are much more expensive.

NOTEWORTHY CARDS

All the same stars and superstars as the Post issue.

VALUE

EX.-MT. CONDITION, NEATLY CUT FROM BOX: Complete set, $1,750; common card, $3–$4; stars, $10–$50; scarce cards, $15–$50; Mantle, $100. 5-YEAR PROJECTION: Below average.

1962 KAHN'S MAJOR LEAGUE

SPECIFICATIONS

SIZE: 3¼×4″. FRONT: Black-and-white photograph. BACK: Black printing on white cardboard. DISTRIBUTION: Upper Midwest, individual cards in packages of Kahn's meats; complete sets available by mail.

HISTORY

A new team joined the Kahn's league in 1962, the Minnesota Twins. With representatives from the Pirates, the Reds, and the Indians, a total of 38 players comprise the set, three of them having two variation cards apiece. The tried and true design which Kahn's had used since 1955 was retained for 1962. The front of the card was dominated by a borderless black-and-white photo, on which was printed a facsimile autograph. Under the photo was a half-inch white strip bearing a Kahn's advertisement. The back of the unnumbered card carried career information about the player. Like other Kahn's issues, the 1962 cards had a protective wax coating to prevent damage to either the cards or the hot dogs with which they were packaged. Besides the single cards in meat packages, the company also made complete sets available via a mail-in offer. This has helped keep the price of '62 Kahn's reasonable.

FOR

Nice regional cards, relatively inexpensive considering they aren't all that common.

AGAINST

The design remained unchanged from eight years earlier.

NOTEWORTHY CARDS

Three of the 1962 Kahn's cards exist with variations. The card of Gus Bell comes with and without what the hobby has come to call "the fat man" included in the photo. Bob Purkey's card can be found missing the facsimile signature. Vic Power is seen in the '62 Kahn's cards as a member of the Twins or the Indians. Roberto Clemente and Frank Robinson are the only Hall of Fame players represented in the set.

VALUE

EX.-MT. CONDITION: Complete set, $450; common card, $5; minor stars, $6–$8; common variation, $15; Robinson, $30–$40; Clemente, $50–$60; Power (Indians), Bell (with fat man), $75; Purkey without autograph, $100. 5-YEAR PROJECTION: Below average.

1962 BELL BRAND DODGERS

SPECIFICATIONS

SIZE: 2⁷/₁₆×3½″. FRONT: Color photograph. BACK: Black printing on white cardboard. DISTRIBUTION: Southern California, inserted into packages of snack chips.

HISTORY

While the design of the fourth and final Bell Brand chips issue was identical to the 1960 and 1961 sets, the cards were printed on a thicker cardboard stock with a glossy surface, giving the cards overall a better appearance. There were again 20 cards in the 1962 Bell set, all Los Angeles Dodgers. On the front of the card, player photos in full color with facsimile autographs overprinted were surrounded by a white border. At the bottom, the player's name, team, and position were printed. Card backs were similar to the previous design; they combined a statistical review of the player's 1961 performance with a Dodgers home schedule and a Bell advertisement. Cards were numbered with the player's uniform number. There are no especially scarce cards in the 1962 Bell set.

FOR

Least expensive of the Bell sets, a good item for the regional collector and Dodgers team fan.

AGAINST

Design is the same as previous two years, creating confusion among collectors.

NOTEWORTHY CARDS

Hall of Famers Duke Snider, Walt Alston, Sandy Koufax, and, for the first time since the 1958 premier set, Don Drysdale.

VALUE

EX.-MT. CONDITION: Complete set, $125; common card, $5–$7; Alston, $10; Snider, Drysdale, Koufax, $15. 5-YEAR PROJECTION: Average.

1962 SUGARDALE

SPECIFICATIONS

SIZE: 5⅛×3¾″. FRONT: Black-and-white photograph. BACK: Black and red printing on white cardboard. DISTRIBUTION: Cleveland-Pittsburgh areas, inserted in packages of hot dogs.

HISTORY

This large-format set contains 22 cards showing the Cleveland Indians and the Pittsburgh Pirates. The Indians cards are numbered 1 to 19, though no card #6 was issued; the

Pirates cards are designated by the letters A to D. Horizontal in format, with rounded corners, the Sugardale cards feature on the front a black-and-white photo of the player with biographical data below. At right is a short career summary, with a facsimile autograph above. The bottom of the card carries advertisements for the hot dog company and the team. Card backs feature baseball tips, ostensibly written by the player depicted on the front of the card, along with a line drawing demonstrating the principle. Another Sugardale ad is at the bottom. The cards are quite scarce, but because they are not popularly collected, their value is not as high as it might otherwise be—though the cards are plenty expensive as is.

FOR

Scarce regional cards for team or single-player collectors. Much rarer than their current price tag would indicate.

AGAINST

The cards are really in too large a format to please most collectors. They are also rather unattractive. Their scarcity makes completion of a full set a real tax on the patience and pocketbook.

NOTEWORTHY CARDS

Card #10, Bob Nieman, was only recently discovered, and is currently priced quite high. The only superstar in the set is Roberto Clemente.

VALUE

EX.-MT. CONDITION: Complete set, $500; common card, $20; Clemente, Nieman, $100–$125. 5-YEAR PROJECTION: Below average.

1962 PEPSI TULSA OILERS

SPECIFICATIONS

SIZE: Single card, 2½×3½"; two-card panel, 5½×7". FRONT: Black-and-white photograph. BACK: Black

printing on white cardboard. DISTRIBUTION: Oklahoma, with carton of soda.

HISTORY

These cards were originally issued in two-card panels. A ring tab at the top of the panel allowed it to be placed over the neck of a soda bottle. The cards were perforated and could be detached from the panel. As with virtually all baseball cards issued in panels or with tabs, the cards are more valuable when still attached as a pair to the original ring tab. The 24 cards consist of players, coaches, the manager, and the bat boy of the Tulsa Oilers, a Class AA Texas League farmclub of the St. Louis Cardinals. Quite similar in appearance to subsequent 1963 and 1966 issues, the premier 1962 set can be differentiated by the angled bottle cap to the right of the player's name and the "Pepsi-Cola" in script.

FOR

The set is readily available today, apparently because collectors and/or dealers were able to secure undistributed quantities during or after the local promotion. The association with Pepsi-Cola helps the set's popularity.

AGAINST

There is virtually a complete lack of "name" players in this minor league set. Most of the cards would not be recognized by anybody but the most fervent Cardinals fan. Inclusion of bat boy cards is also a negative factor; other than the kids' mothers, nobody wants cards of nonplayers (with the possible exception of managers and coaches *if* they were once players).

NOTEWORTHY CARDS

The best card in the set is that of manager "Pepper" Martin, famed sparkplug of the St. Louis Cardinals "Gashouse Gang" of the late 1930s. Also included in the set is former major league (1962-1975) shortstop Dal Maxvill, recently a coach for the St. Louis Cardinals and currently coaching for the Los Angeles Dodgers.

VALUE

EX.-MT. CONDITION: Complete set, $30; common card, $1.25; Pepper Martin, $3.50. 5-YEAR PROJECTION: Below average.

1962 KAHN'S ATLANTA CRACKERS

SPECIFICATIONS

SIZE: 3¼×4". FRONT: Black-and-white photograph. BACK: Black printing on white cardboard. DISTRIBUTION: Atlanta area, in packages of Kahn's wieners and other meat products.

HISTORY

A separate issue for Kahn's in 1962 was a 24-card set of the Atlanta Crackers of the International League, a Class AAA affiliate for the St. Louis Cardinals. This was Kahn's only minor league set, and though the cards are really quite scarce, there is less demand for them than for the meat company's major league card sets. The Atlanta Crackers cards followed the standard Kahn's format, a large black-and-white photo, with a white strip along the bottom carrying a Kahn's advertising message. There is no facsimile autograph on the cards. Card backs carry an abbreviated career summary of the player and an offer for free Atlanta tickets. The cards are unnumbered. Like other Kahn's cards, the Atlanta series was issued in packages of the company's hot dogs and other meat products in the home area of the team.

FOR

Of interest to minor league collectors and St. Louis Cardinals fans. Relatively inexpensive, considering their scarcity.

AGAINST

It's a minor league set in a not particularly attractive format.

NOTEWORTHY CARDS

No big name stars in the set, but there are a few former major leaguers as well as a young Tim McCarver on his way up.

VALUE

EX.-MT. CONDITION: Complete set, $100; common card, $4–$5; McCarver, $7.50. 5-YEAR PROJECTION: Below average.

1961 TOPPS

SPECIFICATIONS
SIZE: 2½×3½″. FRONT: Color photograph. BACK: Black and green-gold printing on gray cardboard. DISTRIBUTION: Nationally, in 1¢ and 5¢ packages with bubblegum.

HISTORY
After holding the line at a 572-card set for two years, Topps raised the limit for 1961 to 589 cards, but they actually issued only 587 cards—with 586 numbers. Card #426, which was checklisted as the Braves team card, was not issued. Instead, Topps issued a Braves team card and a player card of Jack Fisher and designated both #463. Cards #587 and #588, which fall in the range of the All-Star cards, were also not issued. There are, however, a full complement of 10 All-Star player cards and a manager card for each league. The design of the 1961 cards is straightforward. A large color photo dominates the top 90 percent of the card. Below are two rectangular colored boxes, the left one with the player's name and position, the right with the team name. Card backs have a black band at the top with the player's biographical information. Complete major and/or minor league statistics are given below. If there is room, a three-panel cartoon highlights some part of the player's career. For the first time, in 1961, checklists were issued as numbered cards within the Topps set. Also introduced in '61 was the concept of issuing cards for various statistical category leaders of the previous season. In the '61 set, Topps had each league's statistical winner share a card with three runners-up. The categories in which the leaders were honored were batting average, home runs, ERA, winning percentage, and strikeouts. Multi-player feature cards were continued in 1961, as was the subseries recounting the previous season's World Series. In 1961 the latter comprised eight cards, detailing the Pirates' win over the Yankees in seven games. There is a series of 10 "Baseball Thrills" cards, recounting dramatic games, plays, and individual records from the distant and not-so-distant past. These cards have newspaper-

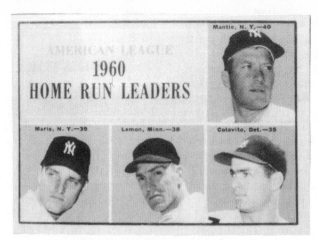

1961 Topps, Home Run Leaders

1961 Topps, Detroit Tigers Team Card

1961 Topps, Al Lopez

1961 Topps, Jim Gilliam

style backs. Another innovation in the 1961 set was a 16-card series honoring players who have won the Most Valuable Player award in each league since 1951. Finally, the set closed with a 22-card group of *Sporting News* All-Star selections. These cards featured a player photo "busting out" of a mock-up of the paper. There are really only two levels of scarcity in the 1961 set: the low numbers, 1–522, and the high numbers, 523–589. The '61 high numbers are among the scarcest of such series in the years through 1973, when Topps began issuing all its cards at one time. Luckily the only superstars in the '61 highs are the All-Star cards, and they are not in as great a demand as the regular cards of the same players. Three other high number cards command a $7 to $10 price: the team cards of the expansion Minnesota Twins and the Pittsburgh Pirates, and the card of potential Hall of Famer Hoyt Wilhelm.

the A's and Yankees as a relief pitcher, adding four saves to his credit. His 4.29 ERA is nothing to brag about. Kunkel's "rookie card" as a player appears in the 1961 Topps set, where he is shown in a heavily retouched photo taken in a minor league park, but which purports to show him wearing the uniform of the Kansas City A's.

VALUE

EX.-MT. CONDITION: Complete set, $675; common card, #1–#522, 25¢; #523–#589, $4.50; stars, $2.50–$5; Maris, Musial, Koufax, Mantle MVP, Mays MVP, Aaron MVP, McCovey, $5–$7.50; Mays, Clemente, Aaron, Wilhelm, following All-Stars: Frank and Brooks Robinson, Banks, Maris, Kaline, Ford, Spahn, $10–$15; Marichal, Mantle, Yastrzemski, $20–$25; Aaron and Mays All-Stars, $35; Mantle All-Star, $45–$50. 5-YEAR PROJECTION: Average or a bit below.

1961 Topps, Ted Kluszewski (front)

FOR

The 1961 set is popular, attractive, and with the scarce high number series, as challenging as any regular Topps set of the 1960s.

AGAINST

The overall scarcity of the high numbers makes the set too formidable for some collectors, as well as too expensive.

NOTEWORTHY CARDS

No shortage of Hall of Famers in the '61 set. Good rookie cards are a bit lean, though, with only Juan Marichal's premier card being worth noting. There are two wrong-photo cards in the set. The Sherman Jones card actually pictures Eddie Fisher. The Dutch Dotterer card is also wrong, but it's all in the family, because the player pictured is Dutch's brother, Tommy. That was a good deal for Tommy—he never made the major leagues or had a card of his own, while Dutch had three other cards.

OUR FAVORITE CARD

One of baseball's better-known umpires today, Bill Kunkel, is a former major league pitcher—though not a great one. Kunkel lost the only two games he ever started, with Kansas City in 1961, but brought his lifetime record up to 6-6 in 1962 and 1963 with

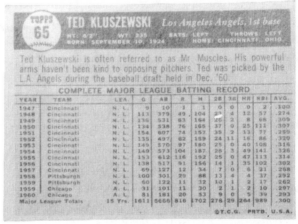

1961 Topps, Ted Kluszewski (back)

1961 Topps, World Series Game #4

1961 Topps, Frank Howard

1961 Topps, Harvey Kuenn

1961 Topps, Cincinnati Reds Team Card

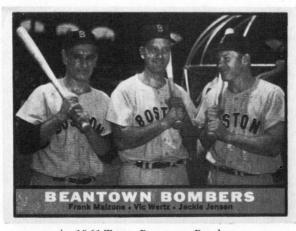

1961 Topps, Beantown Bombers

1961 BAZOOKA

SPECIFICATIONS

SIZE: Single card, $1^{13}/_{16} \times 2^{3}/_{4}$"; three-card panel, $5^{1}/_{2} \times 2^{3}/_{4}$". FRONT: Color photograph. BACK: Blank. DISTRIBUTION: Nationally, a three-card panel on each bubblegum box

HISTORY

You'd need a pair of checklists to tell the 1961 Bazooka baseball cards from the 1960 issue. The cards were identical in size and design. While the player photos were different each year, a number of players appeared in both sets; luckily each card has a different number in 1960 and 1961. Again in '61, there is a small line of type at the very bottom of the cards that states: "NO. __ OF 36 CARDS." The 1961 Bazookas were issued in a three-card panel on the bottom of the 20-piece box of Topps' bubblegum sold under the Bazooka name. The strip of three could be cut from the box and then cut into individual cards. Intact boxes have a premium value of 25 to 50 percent over the individual cards, while three-card strips are worth just a fraction over the total individual values.

FOR

Attractive set with lots of "name" players of the early 1960s.

AGAINST

Cards are too small to be popular; collectors prefer issues that are close to the now-standard $2^{1}/_{2} \times 3^{1}/_{2}$" size. Because the cards were usually cut off the original boxes by children, it is difficult for the condition-conscious collector to find true Mint specimens.

NOTEWORTHY CARDS

There are proportionately fewer Hall of Famers and superstars in the 1961 issue than in Bazooka's 1959 and 1960 efforts—even Hank Aaron is absent—and a lot more cards with players today's fans may not recognize: Chuck Estrada, Ernie Broglio, Frank Herrera, etc. Hall of Famers to be found include Mantle, Mathews, Banks, Kaline, Mays, Drysdale, Spahn, Frank

Continued on page 225.

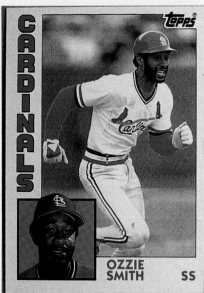

1984 Topps, Ozzie Smith

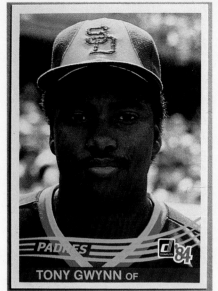

1984 Donruss, Tony Gwynn

1984 Fleer, Richard Dotson

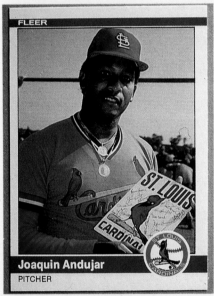

1984 Fleer, Joaquin Andujar

1984 Topps, Rick Sutcliffe

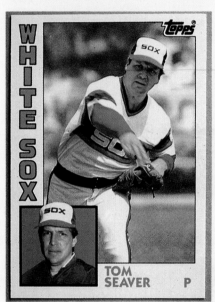

1984 Topps, Tom Seaver

1984 Gardner's Brewers, Rene Lachemann

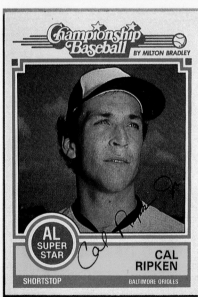

1984 Milton Bradley, Cal Ripken

1984 Donruss, San Diego Chicken

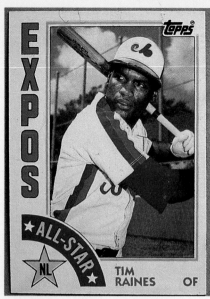

1984 Topps, All-Stars, Tim Raines

1984 Topps All-Star Glossies,
André Dawson

1984 Ralston Purina, Tom Seaver

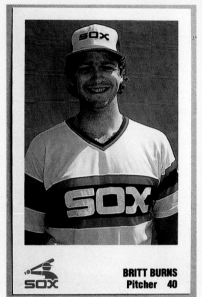

1984 True Value White Sox, Britt Burns

1984 7-Up Cubs, Gary Matthews

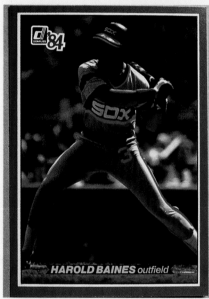

1984 Donruss Action All-Stars,
Harold Baines

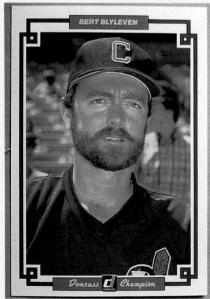

1984 Donruss Champions, Bert Blyleven

1984 Donruss Champions, Babe Ruth

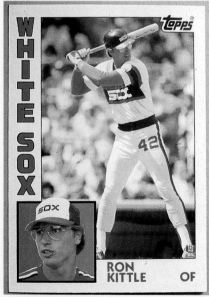

1984 Topps, Ron Kittle

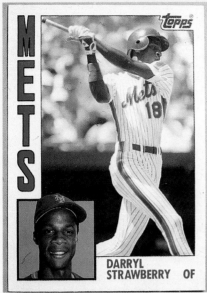

1984 Topps, Darryl Strawberry

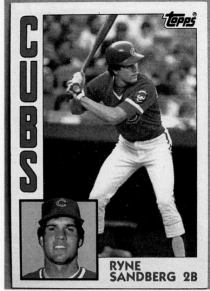

1984 Nestle, Eddie Murray

1984 Topps, Ryne Sandberg

*1984 Donruss, Living Legends,
Carl Yastrzemski, Johnny Bench*

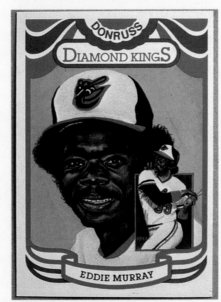

*1984 Donruss, Diamond Kings,
Eddie Murray*

1984 Fleer Update, Goose Gossage

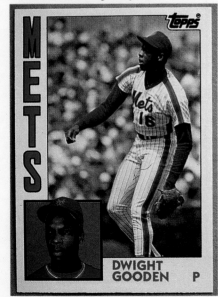

1984 Topps Traded, Dwight Gooden

1984 Topps Traded, Alvin Davis

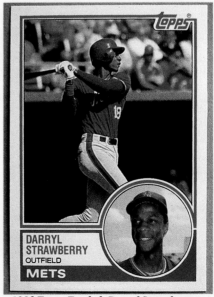

1983 Topps Traded, Darryl Strawberry

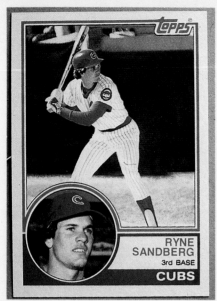

1983 Topps, Ryne Sandberg

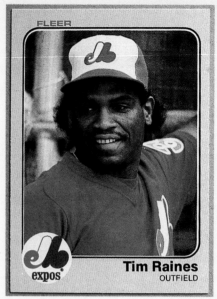

1983 Fleer, Alan Trammell

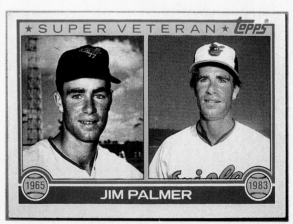

1983 Fleer, Tim Raines

1983 Topps Glossies, Bob Horner

1983 Fleer, Super Star Special, "Smith Bros."

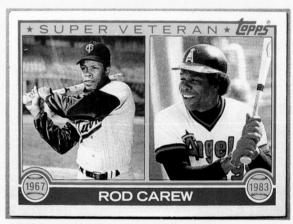

1983 Topps, Rod Carew Super Veteran

1983 Drake's, Cal Ripken

1983 Donruss Hall of Fame Heroes, Mickey Mantle

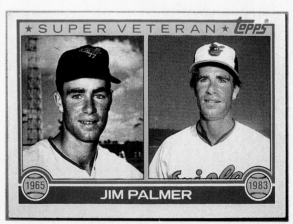

1983 Topps, Jim Palmer Super Veteran

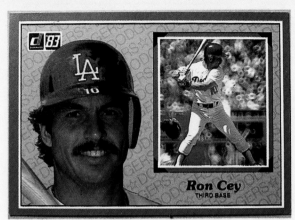

1983 Donruss Action All-Stars, Ron Cey

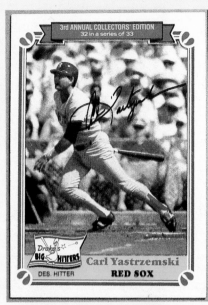

1983 Drake's, Carl Yastrzemski

1983 Kellogg's, Dave Winfield

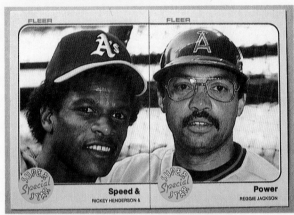

1983 Fleer, Super Star Special, Rickey Henderson;
1983 Fleer, Super Star Special, Reggie Jackson

1983 True Value White Sox, Marc Hill

1983 Gardner's Brewers, Harvey Kuenn

1983 Fleer, Super Star Special, Bud Black;
1983 Fleer, Super Star Special, Vida Blue

1983 Thorn Apple Valley Cubs, Ryne Sandberg

1982 Kellogg's, Kirk Gibson

1982 Red Lobster Cubs, Leon Durham

1982 Topps Traded, Ross Baumgarten

1982 Topps Traded, Cal Ripken

1982 Donruss, Diamond Kings, Nolan Ryan

1982 Fleer, Steve Carlton, Carlton Fisk

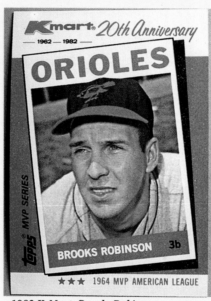

1982 K-Mart, Brooks Robinson

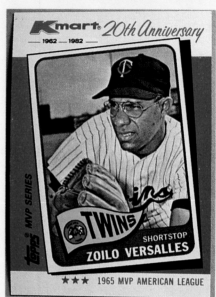

1982 K-Mart, Zoilo Versalles

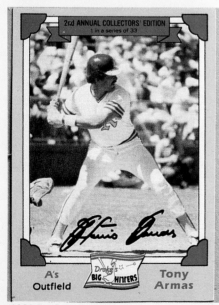

1982 Drake's, Tony Armas

*1982 Cracker Jack, National League
All-Time Baseball Greats*

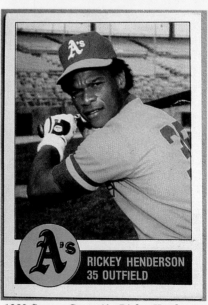

1982 Granny Goose A's, Rickey Henderson

1982 Zellers Expos, Gary Carter

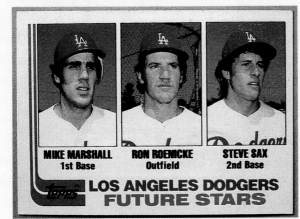

1982 Topps, Los Angeles Dodgers Future Stars

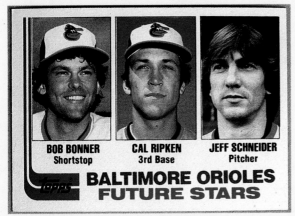

1982 Topps, Baltimore Orioles Future Stars

1982 Donruss, Diamond Kings,
Dale Murphy

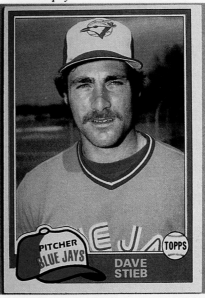

1981 Topps, Dave Stieb

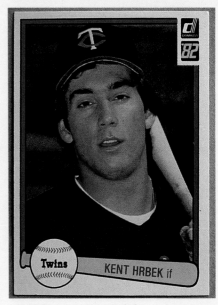

1982 Donruss, Kent Hrbek

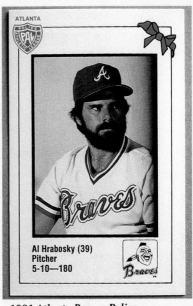

1981 Atlanta Braves Police,
Al Hrabosky

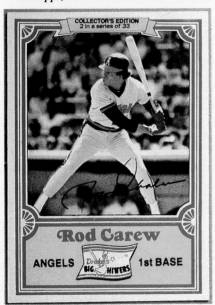

1981 Drake's, Rod Carew

1981 Los Angeles Dodgers Police,
Steve Yeager

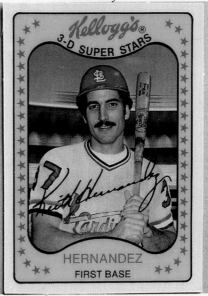

1981 Kellogg's, Keith Hernandez

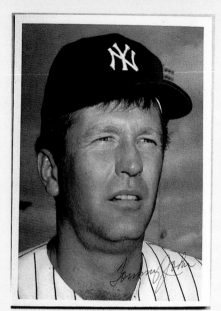

1981 Topps 5×7s, Tommy John

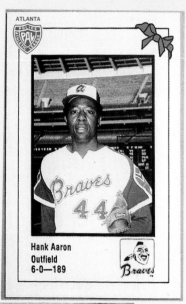

1981 Atlanta Braves Police,
Hank Aaron

1981 Atlanta Braves Police,
Gene Garber

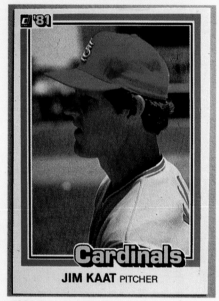

1981 Donruss, Jim Kaat

1981 Kellogg's, Garry Templeton

1981 Donruss, Joe Charboneau

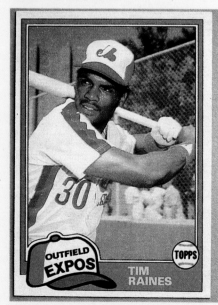

1981 Topps Traded, Tim Raines

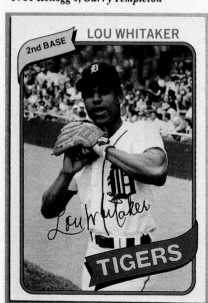

1980 Topps, Lou Whitaker

1980 Kellogg's, Claudell Washington

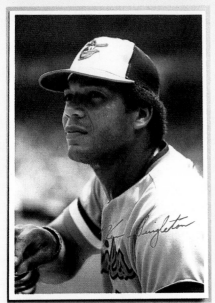

1980 Topps Superstar Photos,
Ken Singleton

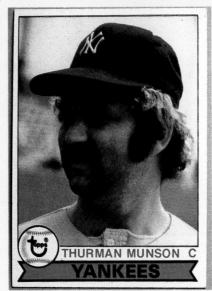

1979 Burger King, Thurman Munson

1979 Hostess, Rick Manning, Mark Fidrych, Mario Guerrero

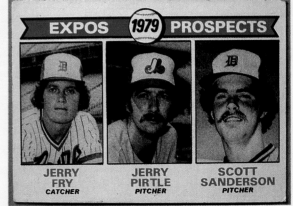

1979 Topps, Expos Rookies

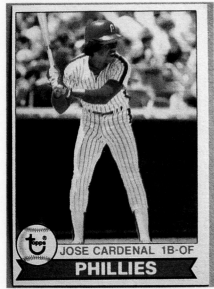

1979 Burger King, José Cardenal

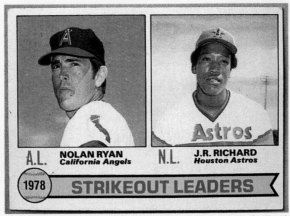

1979 Topps, Strikeout Leaders, Nolan Ryan, J. R. Richard

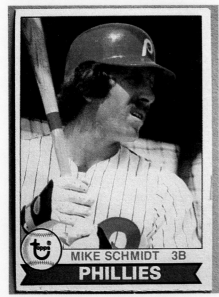

1979 Burger King, Mike Schmidt

1979 Topps, Bump Wills, Rangers

1979 Topps, Bump Wills, Blue Jays

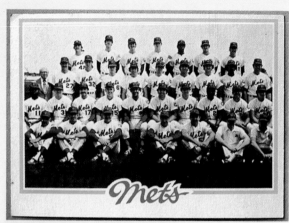

1978 Topps, New York Mets Team Card

1978 Kellogg's, Ron Cey

1977 Kellogg's, Jerry Koosman

1978 Hostess, Tommy Hutton, John Candelaria, Jorge Orta

1977 Hostess, Don Sutton, Mark Belanger, Dennis Leonard

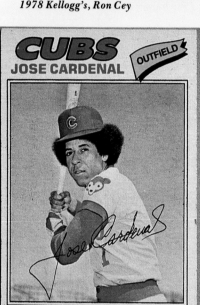

1977 Topps, José Cardenal

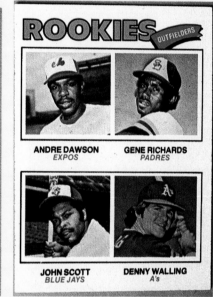

1977 Topps, Rookie Outfielders

1977 Topps, Bruce Sutter

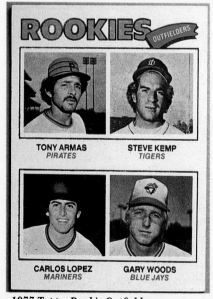

1977 Topps, Rookie Outfielders

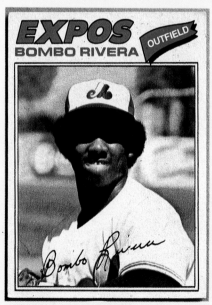

1977 Topps, Bombo Rivera

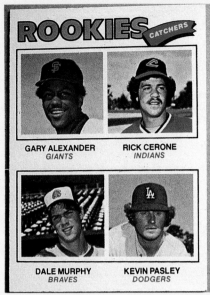

1977 Topps, Rookie Catchers

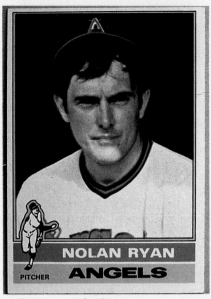

1976 Topps, Nolan Ryan

1976 Topps, Jim Palmer

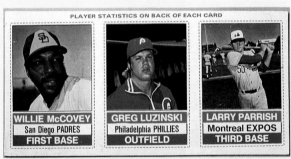

1976 Hostess, Willie McCovey, Greg Luzinski, Larry Parrish

1976 Topps, Billy Williams

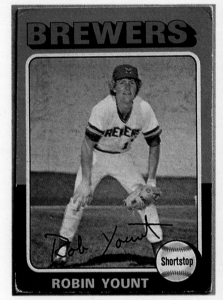

1975 Topps, Robin Yount

1975 Topps, 1953 MVP

1975 Hostess, Bert Campaneris, Pete Rose, Buddy Bell

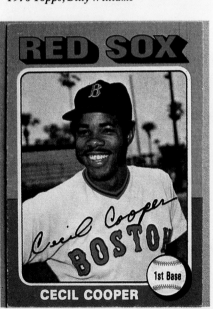

1975 Topps, Cecil Cooper

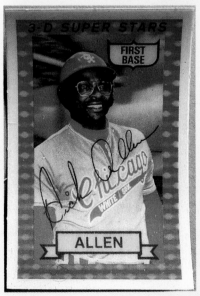

1974 Kellogg's, Dick Allen

1974 Topps Traded, Jim Wynn

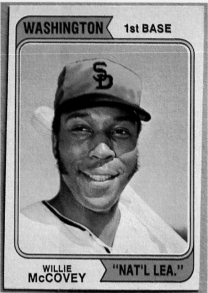

1974 Topps, Willie McCovey

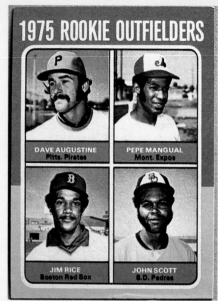

1975 Topps, Rookie Outfielders

1974 Topps, Washington "National League" —
San Diego Padres

1974 Topps, Hank Aaron Special

1973 Kellogg's, Mickey Lolich

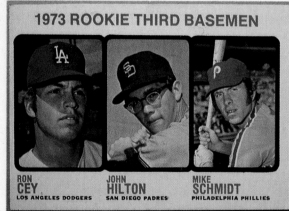

1973 Topps, Rookie Third Basemen

1973 Topps, Rich Gossage

1973 Topps, All-Time Home Run Leaders

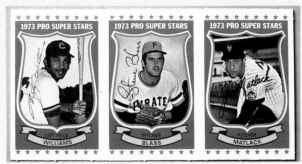

1973 Kellogg's, Billy Williams, Steve Blass, Jon Matlack

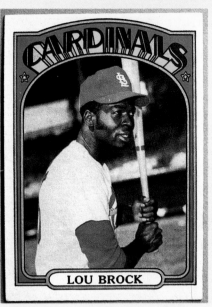

1972 Topps, Lou Brock

1972 Kellogg's, Wilbur Wood

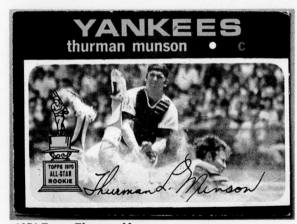

1972 Topps, Brewers Rookie Stars

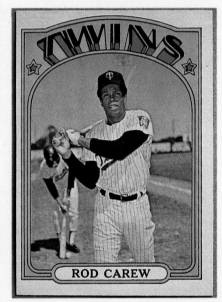

1972 Topps, Rod Carew

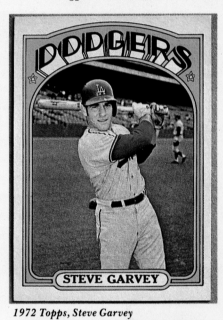

1972 Topps, Steve Garvey

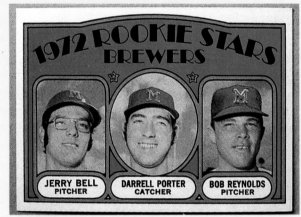

1971 Topps, Thurman Munson

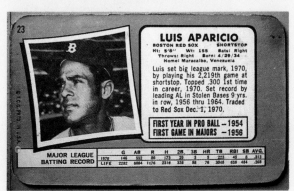

1971 Topps Supers, Luis Aparicio

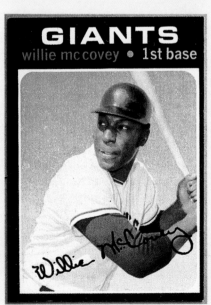

1971 Topps, Willie McCovey

1971 Kellogg's, Pete Rose

1981 Topps, Reggie Jackson

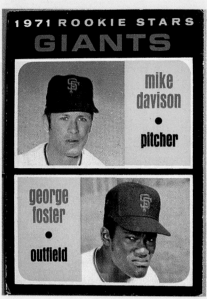

1971 Topps, Mike Davison, George Foster

1971 Topps Supers, Robert Gibson

1971 Topps, Juan Marichal

1970 Topps, Rollie Fingers

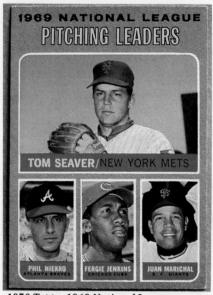

1970 Topps, 1969 National League Pitching Leaders

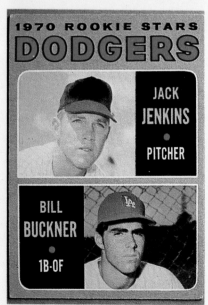

1970 Topps, Jack Jenkins, Bill Buckner

1970 Kellogg's, Bert Campaneris

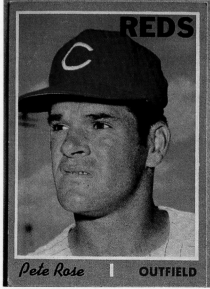

1970 Topps, Pete Rose

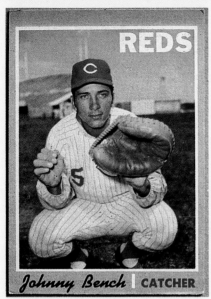

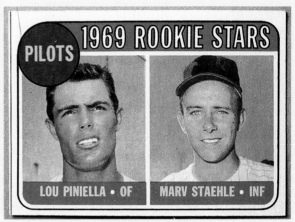

1970 Topps, Johnny Bench

1969 Nabisco Team Flakes, Al Kaline

1969 Topps, Lou Piniella, Marv Staehle

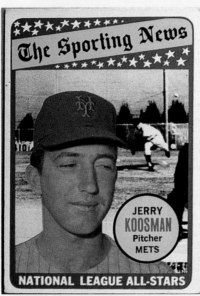

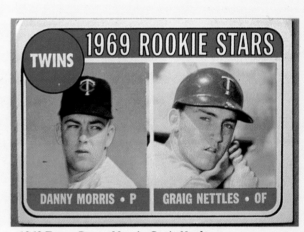

1969 Topps Supers, Tony Oliva

*1969 Topps, The Sporting News All-Stars,
Jerry Koosman*

1969 Topps, Danny Morris, Graig Nettles

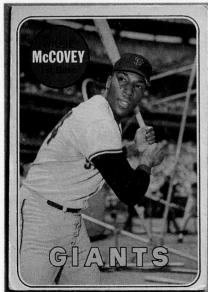

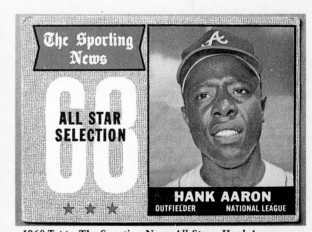

1968 Topps, The Sporting News All-Stars, Hank Aaron

1969 Topps, Willie McCovey

1969 Topps, Willie Stargell

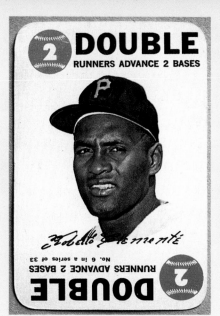

1968 Topps, Lou Piniella, R. Scheinblum

1968 Topps Game, Roberto Clemente

1968 Topps Game, Willie Mays

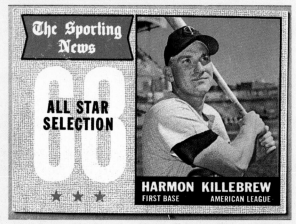

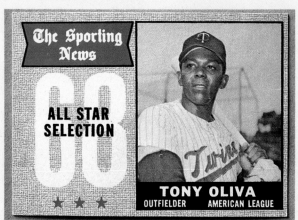

1968 Topps, The Sporting News *All-Stars, Harmon Killebrew*

1968 Topps, The Sporting News *All-Stars, Tony Oliva*

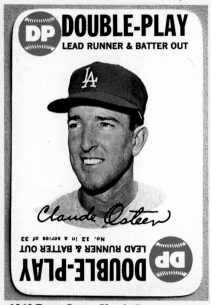

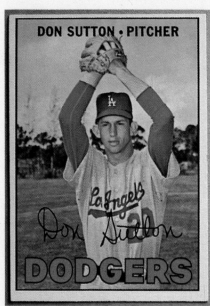

1968 Topps Game, Claude Osteen

1967 Topps, Don Sutton

1967 Topps, Dave Nicholson

1967 Topps, Maury Wills

1967 Topps, American League Rookie Stars

1966 Topps, Buc Belters

1966 Topps, Rusty Staub

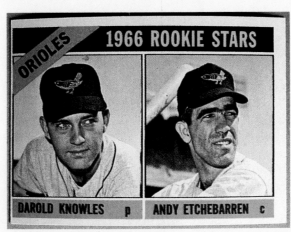

1966 Topps, Orioles Rookie Stars

1966 Topps, Gary Peters

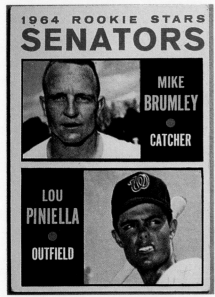

1964 Topps, Mike Brumley, Lou Piniella

1964 Topps, Bobby Richardson

1964 Topps Giants, Bob Bailey

1964 Topps Giants, Tony Oliva

1964 Topps Stand-Ups, Bob Clemente

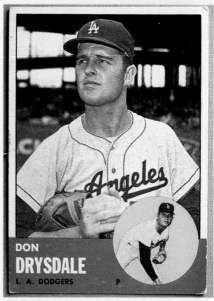

1963 Topps, Don Drysdale

1963 Post, Dean Chance

1963 Bazooka All-Time Greats, Cy Young

1963 Bazooka All-Time Greats, Connie Mack

1963 Topps, Tiger Twirlers

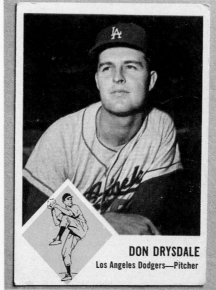

1963 Fleer, Don Drysdale

1963 Kahn's, Roberto Clemente

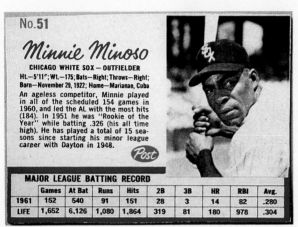

No.51

Minnie Minoso

CHICAGO WHITE SOX — OUTFIELDER

Ht.—5'11"; Wt.—175; Bats—Right; Throws—Right; Born—November 29, 1922; Home—Marianao, Cuba

An ageless competitor, Minnie played in all of the scheduled 154 games in 1960, and led the AL with the most hits (184). In 1951 he was "Rookie of the Year" while batting .326 (his all time high). He has played a total of 15 seasons since starting his minor league career with Dayton in 1948.

Post

MAJOR LEAGUE BATTING RECORD

	Games	At Bat	Runs	Hits	2B	3B	HR	RBI	Avg.
1961	152	540	91	151	28	3	14	82	.280
LIFE	1,652	6,126	1,080	1,864	319	81	180	978	.304

1962 Post, Minnie Minoso

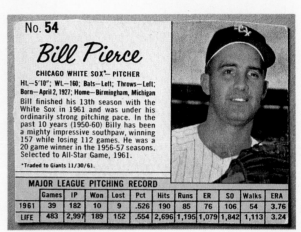

No.54

Bill Pierce

CHICAGO WHITE SOX*— PITCHER

Ht.—5'10"; Wt.—160; Bats—Left; Throws—Left; Born—April 2, 1927; Home—Birmingham, Michigan

Bill finished his 13th season with the White Sox in 1961 and was under his ordinarily strong pitching pace. In the past 10 years (1950-60) Billy has been a mighty impressive southpaw, winning 157 while losing 112 games. He was a 20 game winner in the 1956-57 seasons. Selected to All-Star Game, 1961.

*Traded to Giants 11/30/61.

MAJOR LEAGUE PITCHING RECORD

	Games	IP	Won	Lost	Pct	Hits	Runs	ER	SO	Walks	ERA
1961	39	182	10	9	.526	190	85	76	106	54	3.76
LIFE	483	2,997	189	152	.554	2,696	1,195	1,079	1,842	1,113	3.24

1962 Jell-O, Billy Pierce

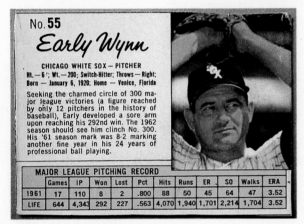

No.55

Early Wynn

CHICAGO WHITE SOX — PITCHER

Ht.—6'; Wt.—200; Switch-Hitter; Throws—Right; Born — January 6, 1920; Home — Venice, Florida

Seeking the charmed circle of 300 major league victories (a figure reached by only 12 pitchers in the history of baseball), Early developed a sore arm upon reaching his 292nd win. The 1962 season should see him clinch No. 300. His '61 season mark was 8-2 marking another fine year in his 24 years of professional ball playing.

MAJOR LEAGUE PITCHING RECORD

	Games	IP	Won	Lost	Pct	Hits	Runs	ER	SO	Walks	ERA
1961	17	110	8	2	.800	88	50	45	64	47	3.52
LIFE	644	4,343	292	227	.563	4,070	1,940	1,701	2,214	1,704	3.52

1962 Jell-O, Early Wynn

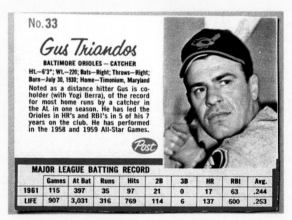

No.33

Gus Triandos

BALTIMORE ORIOLES — CATCHER

Ht.—6'3"; Wt.—220; Bats—Right; Throws—Right; Born—July 30, 1930; Home—Timonium, Maryland

Noted as a distance hitter Gus is co-holder (with Yogi Berra), of the record for most home runs by a catcher in the AL in one season. He has led the Orioles in HR's and RBI's in 5 of his 7 years on the club. He has performed in the 1958 and 1959 All-Star Games.

Post

MAJOR LEAGUE BATTING RECORD

	Games	At Bat	Runs	Hits	2B	3B	HR	RBI	Avg.
1961	115	397	35	97	21	0	17	63	.244
LIFE	907	3,031	316	769	114	6	137	500	.253

1962 Post, Gus Triandos

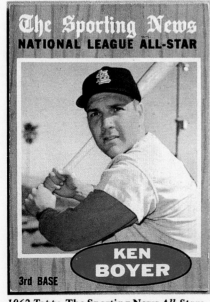

The Sporting News
NATIONAL LEAGUE ALL-STAR

KEN BOYER

3rd BASE

*1962 Topps, **The Sporting News** All-Stars, Ken Boyer*

DUKE SNIDER
Outfield
Los Angeles Dodgers

1961 Topps, Duke Snider

RALPH HOUK
Mgr.   New York Yankees

1961 Topps, Ralph Houk

1961 Topps, 1953 MVP American League,
Al Rosen

1961 Fleer, Charles Comiskey

1961 Topps, Robin Roberts

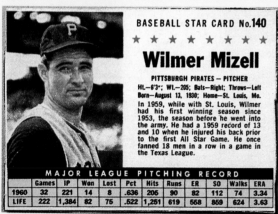

BASEBALL STAR CARD No. **140**

★ ★ ★ ★ ★ ★ ★ ★

Wilmer Mizell

PITTSBURGH PIRATES — PITCHER

Ht.—6'3"; Wt.—205; Bats—Right; Throws—Left
Born—August 13, 1930; Home—St. Louis, Mo.
In 1959, while with St. Louis, Wilmer
had his first winning season since
1953, the season before he went into
the army. He had a 1959 record of 13
and 10 when he injured his back prior
to the first All Star Game. He once
fanned 18 men in a row in a game in
the Texas League.

MAJOR LEAGUE PITCHING RECORD

	Games	IP	Won	Lost	Pct	Hits	Runs	ER	SO	Walks	ERA
1960	32	221	14	8	.636	205	90	82	112	74	3.34
LIFE	222	1,384	82	75	.522	1,251	619	558	859	624	3.63

1961 Post, Wilmer Mizell

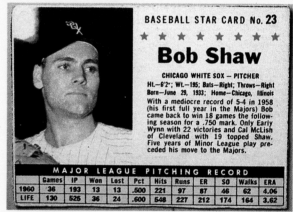

BASEBALL STAR CARD No. **23**

★ ★ ★ ★ ★ ★ ★ ★

Bob Shaw

CHICAGO WHITE SOX — PITCHER

Ht.—6'2"; Wt.—195; Bats—Right; Throws—Right
Born—June 29, 1933; Home—Chicago, Illinois
With a mediocre record of 5-4 in 1958
(his first full year in the Majors) Bob
came back to win 18 games the following season for a .750 mark. Only Early
Wynn with 22 victories and Cal McLish
of Cleveland with 19 topped Shaw.
Five years of Minor League play preceded his move to the Majors.

MAJOR LEAGUE PITCHING RECORD

	Games	IP	Won	Lost	Pct	Hits	Runs	ER	SO	Walks	ERA
1960	36	193	13	13	.500	221	97	87	46	62	4.06
LIFE	130	525	36	24	.600	548	227	212	174	164	3.62

1961 Post, Bob Shaw

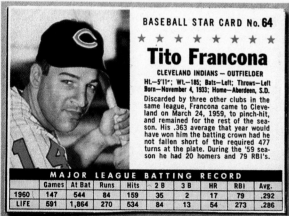

BASEBALL STAR CARD No. **64**

★ ★ ★ ★ ★ ★ ★ ★

Tito Francona

CLEVELAND INDIANS — OUTFIELDER

Ht.—5'11"; Wt.—185; Bats—Left; Throws—Left
Born—November 4, 1933; Home—Aberdeen, S.D.
Discarded by three other clubs in the
same league, Francona came to Cleveland on March 24, 1959, to pinch-hit,
and remained for the rest of the season. His .363 average that year would
have won him the batting crown had he
not fallen short of the required 477
turns at the plate. During the '59 season he had 20 homers and 79 RBI's.

MAJOR LEAGUE BATTING RECORD

	Games	At Bat	Runs	Hits	2 B	3 B	HR	RBI	Avg.
1960	147	544	84	159	35	2	17	79	.292
LIFE	591	1,864	270	534	84	13	54	273	.286

1961 Post, Tito Francona

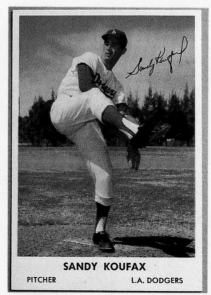

1961 Bell Brand Dodgers,
Sandy Koufax

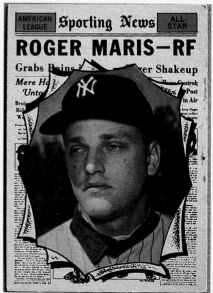

1961 Topps, The Sporting News All-Stars,
Roger Maris

1961 Topps, The Sporting News *All-Stars*,
Nellie Fox

1960 Fleer, Clark Griffith

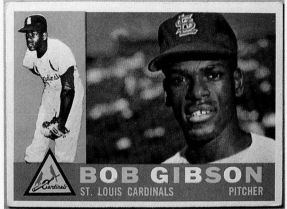

1960 Topps, Bob Gibson

1960 Topps, Ryne Duren

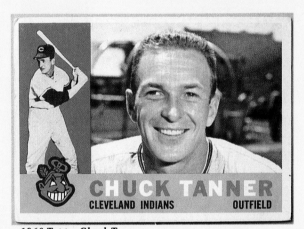

1960 Topps, Chuck Tanner

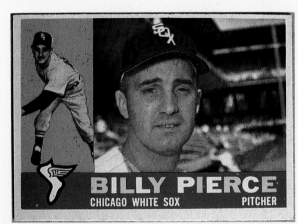

1960 Topps, Billy Pierce

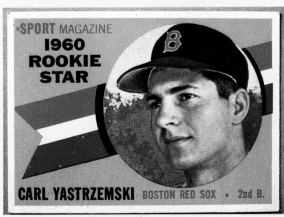

1960 Topps, Carl Yastrzemski

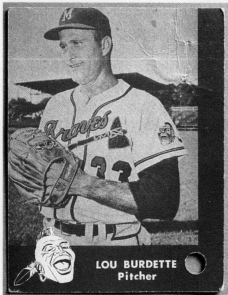

1960 Lake to Lake Braves, "Lou" Burdette

1960 Fleer, Chief Bender

1959 Topps, Jim Piersall

1959 Fleer Ted Williams

1959 Bazooka, Willie Mays

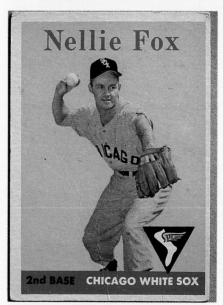

1958 Topps, Nellie Fox

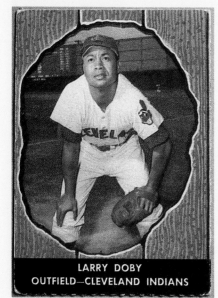

1958 Hires Root Beer, Larry Doby

1958 Bell Brand Dodgers, Roy Campanella

1957 Topps, Jim Piersall

1957 Topps, Brooks Robinson

1957 Topps, Sandy Koufax

1956 Topps, Ray Boone

1956 Topps, Chicago Cubs Team Card

1955 Topps Double Headers, Don Hoak

1956 Topps, Bob Feller

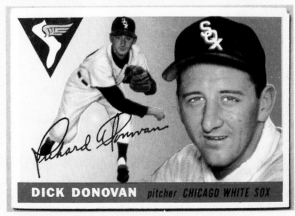

1955 Topps, Dick Donovan

1955 Bowman, Al Kaline

1955 Bowman, Phil Rizzuto

1955 Topps Double Headers,
Jackie Robinson

1955 Red Man, Hoyt Wilhelm

1955 Topps, Willie Mays

1954 Bowman, Gil Hodges

1954 Bowman, Enos Slaughter

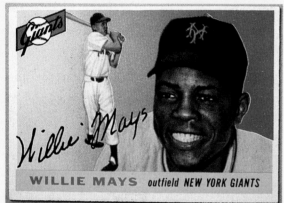

1955 Bowman, Lou Boudreau

1955 Bowman, Dick Groth

1954 Johnston Cookie Braves,
Robert Buhl

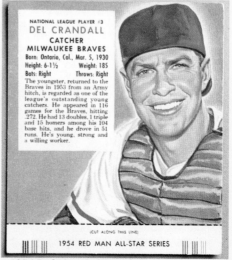

1954 Red Man, Del Crandall

1954 Topps, Jackie Robinson

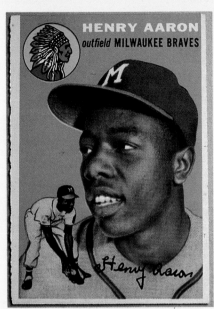

1954 Topps, Henry Aaron

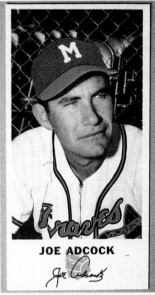

*1954 Johnston Cookie Braves,
Joe Adcock*

1954 Dan-Dee Potato Chips, Bob Feller

1954 Red Man, Roberto Avila

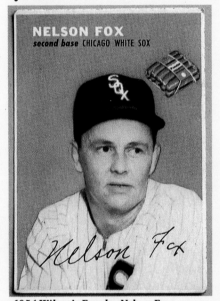

1954 Wilson's Franks, Nelson Fox

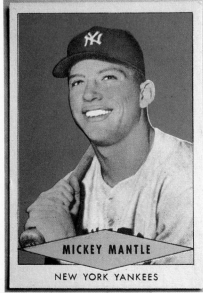

1954 Red Heart, Mickey Mantle

1954 Bowman, Ed Matthews

1954 Topps, Tom Lasorda

1953 Bowman, Mel Parnell

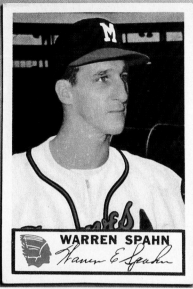

1953 Johnston Cookie Braves, Warren Spahn

1953 Bowman, Pee Wee Reese

1953 Topps, Satchell Paige

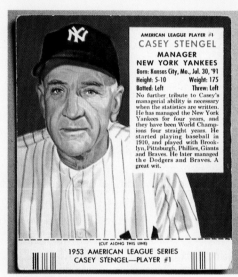

1953 Red Man, Casey Stengel

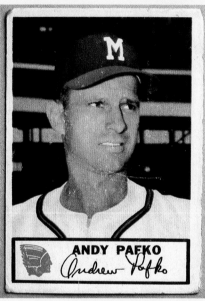

1953 Johnston Cookie Braves, Andy Pafko

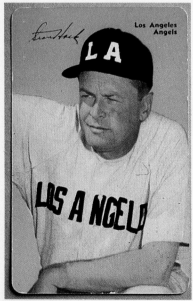

1953 Mother's Cookies Pacific Coast League, Stan Hack

1953 Bowman, Billy Martin, Phil Rizzuto

1953 Topps, Mickey Mantle

1952 Topps, Vernon Law

1952 Bowman, Willie Mays

1952 Bowman, Mickey Mantle

1952 Bowman, Casey Stengel

1952 Bowman, Roy Smalley

BOB LEMON
PITCHER, CLEVELAND INDIANS

1952 Wheaties, Bob Lemon

LARRY "YOGI" BERRA
CATCHER, NEW YORK YANKEES

1952 Wheaties, Yogi Berra

ROY CAMPANELLA
CATCHER, BROOKLYN DODGERS

1952 Wheaties, Roy Campanella

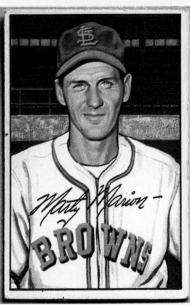

1952 Bowman, Marty Marion

1951 Bowman, Phil Cavaretta

1951 Bowman, Bill "Swish" Nicholson

1951 Bowman, Joe Garagiola

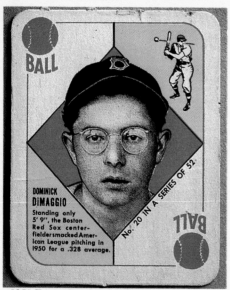

1951 Topps, Dominick DiMaggio

1950 Bowman, Casey Stengel

1950–1956 Callahan Hall of Fame,
Cy Young

1949 Bowman, Lou Boudreau

1949 Remar Baking Company,
Chuck Dressen

1948 Babe Ruth Story

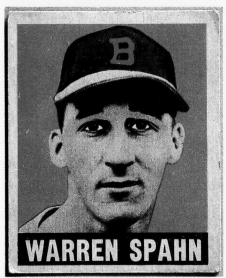

1948 Leaf, Warren Spahn

1948 Leaf, Paul Trout

1948 Bowman, Yogi Berra

1947 Signal Oil, Dario Lodigiani

1947 Tip Top Bread, Enos Slaughter

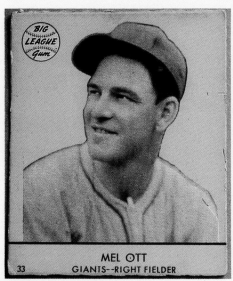

1941 Goudey, Mel Ott

1939 Play Ball—America, Carl Hubbell

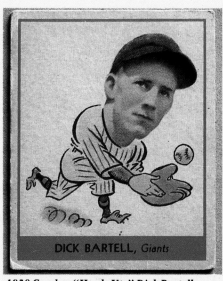

1938 Goudey, "Heads Up," Dick Bartell

1935–1936 Wheaties, Lou Gehrig (back panel)

1934–1936 Diamond Stars, Lloyd Waner

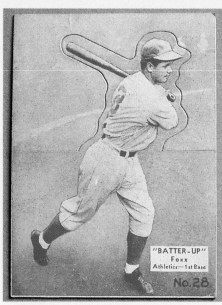

1934–1936 Batter-Up, Jimmy Foxx

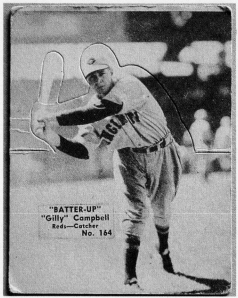

1934–1936 Batter-Up, "Gilly" Campbell

1934 Goudey, George Watkins

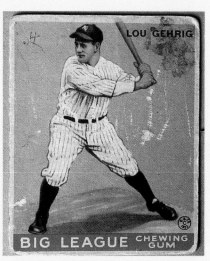

1933 Goudey, Lou Gehrig

1933 Delong, Harold "Pie" Traynor

1933 Sport Kings, Babe Ruth

1933 Goudey, Eppa Rixey

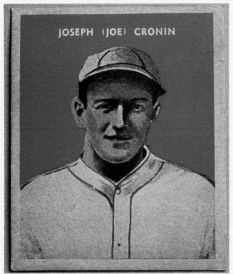

1932 U.S. Caramel, Joseph "Joe" Cronin

1922 American Caramel, Ty Cobb

1922 American Caramel, Eddie Collins

*1912 T-207 "Brown Backgrounds,"
Walter Johnson*

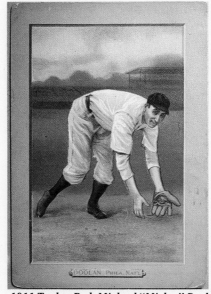

1911 Turkey Red, Michael "Mickey" Doolan

1911 Turkey Red, Napoleon Lajoie

1911 Mecca Doublefolders, Frank Chance

*1911 Mecca Doublefolders,
Johnny Evers*

*1911–1912 T-205 "Gold Borders,"
A. W. Marquard*

1911–1912 T-205 "Gold Borders,"
Walter Johnson

1909–1911 T-206, Ty Cobb

1909–1911 T-206, Tris Speaker

1909–1911 T-206,
Glenn Liebhardt

1909 Ramly, Mordecai Brown

1887 Allen & Ginter,
Charles Comiskey

1886 Old Judge, Charles Comiskey

1886 Old Judge, Tom Daly

1886 Old Judge, Bill Collins

Continued from page 192.

Robinson, and Aparicio. Also of note, Roger Maris appears in the year he hit 61 home runs to break Babe Ruth's long-standing record.

VALUE

EX.-MT. CONDITION, NEATLY CUT FROM BOX: Complete set, $125; common card, $3–$4; Hall of Famers, $7.50–$15; Maris, $12.50; Mays, $20; Mantle, $25. 5-YEAR PROJECTION: Average.

1961 POST

SPECIFICATIONS

SIZE: 3½×2½". FRONT: Color photograph. BACK: Blank. DISTRIBUTION: Nationally, on backs of cereal boxes and by mail-in offer.

HISTORY

In its second year of baseball card production, Post cereal adopted the basic method of issue that it would follow through 1963. In 1961 Post printed its 200-card set on the backs of cereal boxes. Single cards were printed on the backs of the single-serving "Post Tens" boxes, while the normal, family-size boxes carried seven cards. In addition, 10-card sheets printed on slightly thinner cardboard and featuring players from one team could also be obtained directly from the cereal company through a mail-in offer. Ironically, to obtain a complete set, cards from the mail-in offer are necessary—some of the cards on those sheets were never printed on the cereal boxes. The Post sheets were perforated for easy separation, while the cards printed on the cereal boxes had to be cut apart on heavy black lines. Since two cards often shared the same dividing line, it took very careful cutting to separate the cards neatly. Collectors today want cards that have been well cut. Some collectors prefer cards with the black lines showing, others prefer cards without any trace of the line. Whichever the preference, all want cards that are cut straight, with the trimming not intruding into the photo or statistical box. The cards are even more valuable when still attached to

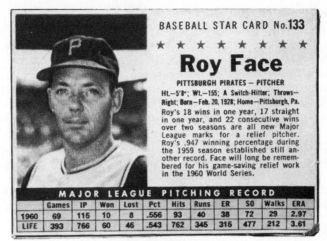

1961 Post, Roy Face

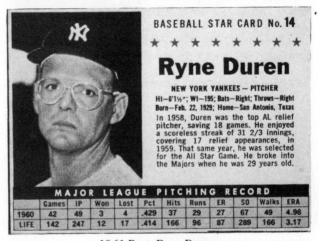

1961 Post, Ryne Duren

the original box, as a complete panel sent from the company, or a full panel taken from the back of the box. Value of complete boxes starts at more than three times the total value of the individual cards shown; complete panels are worth roughly twice as much as the cards would be singly. The '61 Post cards feature a color portrait of the player at left. In a white panel at right is the card number; at top, a row of eight red stars; the player's name, team, position, and personal data; and a career summary. At the bottom of the card is a black bar and below it, in three yellow strips, are statistics from the 1960 season and the player's cumulative major league record. Backs are blank. The cards are numbered in team sequence, with the American League teams coming first, followed by the National League. Two cards are out of sequence for no apparent reason: #62, Paul Foytack, a Detroit Tiger, is numbered with the

Cleveland Indians, while #163, Mel Roach, of the Milwaukee Braves, is numbered among the Los Angeles Dodgers. There are a great number of variation cards in the '61 Post set. Some involve changes in team designation, others show color variations of caps and uniforms, and others have lines indicating sales or trades to different teams. Many of the variations will be found on either company-mailed sheets or the box-back issues, usually not on both. Most of the variations have no great degree of value, and most collectors consider their set complete at 200 cards, regardless of variation. Serious collectors will need a checklist.

FOR

An exciting, endlessly challenging baseball card set of the '60s. The condition-conscious collector can be driven crazy looking for a high-grade set, while the variety collector has much to choose from. Overall, the set is not all that expensive.

AGAINST

The variations confuse many collectors. Design-wise, the cards are not as attractive as the later sets. It's hard to find cards in top condition.

NOTEWORTHY CARDS

By general consensus, collectors agree that at least nine of the 1961 Post cereal cards are significantly scarcer and more valuable than most of the others. This is probably based on the fact that the cards were printed in smaller numbers, on the single-serving size packages, or perhaps on less popular brands of Post cereal. The scarce '61s are: #10–Gil McDougald, #23–Bob Shaw, #70–Gene Woodling, #73–Chuck Estrada, #94–Chuck Stobbs, #113–Chuck Cottier, #135–Bill Virdon, #163–Mel Roach, and #183–Roy McMillan.

VALUE

EX.-MT. CONDITION, NEATLY CUT FROM BOX: Complete set, $600; common card, 50¢–75¢; stars, $2–$12; scarce cards, $15–$45. 5-YEAR PROJECTION: Average, perhaps a bit below.

1961 FLEER

SPECIFICATIONS

SIZE: 2½×3½". FRONT: Color photograph or hand-colored black-and-white photograph. BACK: Red and black printing on white cardboard. DISTRIBUTION: Nationally, in 5¢ packages with bubblegum.

HISTORY

Although Fleer had only limited success with its old-timers set in 1960, they were undaunted and issued a follow-up set the next year. The 1961 "Baseball Greats" set even expanded on the idea, growing in number to 154 cards. The set is divided into two series with differing degrees of scarcity, #1–#88 being the more common, with #89–#154 being more scarce and about twice as expensive on a card-for-card basis. The first card in each series is a checklist card. Card #1

features on the front a group photo of Frank Baker, Ty Cobb, and Zack Wheat; card #89 has George Sisler and Pie Traynor on the front. In both series, the cards are numbered alphabetically. Most card fronts again feature photos of the players as they appeared after their careers were over. Some photos are color pictures, but most are black-and-white with color added. The player pictures are flanked by a white border, with five blue stars on each side at the top. The player's name appears in a blue pennant below the photo, superimposed on alternating red and white stripes. On the horizontally arranged backs, a red box at the top of the card contains the player's name, birth date, and where applicable, date of death. The card number appears in a trophy design at the upper left. At the bottom of the card, a career summary appears at the left, with lifetime major league record at right. Some collectors recall that the 1961 Fleer old-timers set was issued into 1962, and the fact that the company did not have a separate 1962 issue prior to its current-players set in 1963 may indicate that the '61 Fleers were, indeed, released over a two-year period. This could explain why there are two distinct series in the set.

1961 Fleer, Heinie Manush

1961 Fleer, Hack Wilson (front)

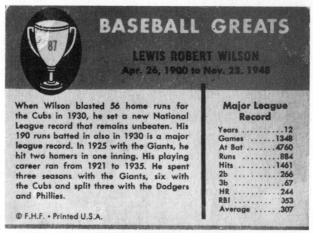

1961 Fleer, Hack Wilson (back)

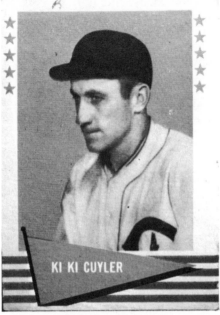

1961 Fleer, Kiki Cuyler

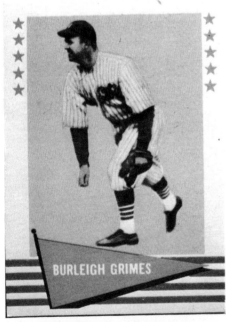

1961 Fleer, School Boy Rowe

1961 Fleer, Burleigh Grimes

1961 Fleer, Billy Evans

FOR
Even more old-timers on relatively inexpensive cards.

AGAINST
Collectors didn't like then, and don't like now, cards that are issued after the player's career is over.

NOTEWORTHY CARDS
Because Ted Williams remained under contract to Fleer, he appears in the 1961 Fleer old-timers set, though he was still actively playing that season, his last in the majors. This card may be one of the more underrated of the 1960s cards, since it sells for only $7 or so in top condition.

VALUE
EX.-MT. CONDITION: Complete set, $150; common card #1–#88, 50¢; #89–#154, $1; super-superstars, $1–$2; Cobb, Gehrig, Wagner, checklists, $4–$5; Ruth, Williams, $6–$8. 5-YEAR PROJECTION: Below average.

1961 KAHN'S

SPECIFICATIONS
SIZE: 3¼×4". FRONT: Black-and-white photograph. BACK: Black printing on white cardboard. DISTRIBUTION: Ohio-Western Pennsylvania area, in packages of Kahn's meats, and by mail-in offer.

HISTORY
For the first time in 1961, Kahn's made complete sets of its baseball card issue for that year available through a mail-in offer. Individual cards continued to be packaged in wieners and other meat products. While the set size was increased by one card in 1961, to 43, the number of teams was decreased from six to three, with only the Pirates, the Reds, and the Indians being represented. The card fronts continued to closely resemble the first Kahn's issue back in 1955. There was a borderless black-and-white photo with facsimile autograph on top of a white strip bearing a Kahn's ad. Backs of the unnumbered cards featured vital player data as well as major league statistics. Because of the

availability by mail order of complete sets, the 1961 issue marks the beginning of relatively inexpensive Kahn's cards.

FOR
Nice cards for team collectors.

AGAINST
After seven years, the design was decidedly stale.

NOTEWORTHY CARDS
Hall of Famers Roberto Clemente and Frank Robinson are the only big names in the set, but those who followed these teams in that era will find lots of familiar faces.

VALUE
EX.-MT. CONDITION: Complete set, $250; common card, $5; stars, $7–$9; Robinson, $30–$35; Clemente, $45–$50. 5-YEAR PROJECTION: Average, or a bit below.

card must be consulted. Backs of the 1961s have a statistical record of the player's 1960 season performance, along with a Dodgers home schedule, a Bell ad, and a card number. Unlike the 1960 cards, the 1961 Bell set is skip-numbered by the player's uniform number, from #3 (Willie Davis) to #51 (Larry Sherry). There are no known scarcities in the 1961 Bell set.

FOR
Good-looking Dodgers team set; good value in early 1960s regional set.

AGAINST
Similarity to the 1960 set is confusing to most collectors.

VALUE
EX.-MT. CONDITION: Complete set, $150; common card, $6–$8; Hodges, Wills, Alston, $10; Snider, Koufax, $15–$20. 5-YEAR PROJECTION: Average.

ders of the 1960 issue may have been stuffed in meat packages alongside the six new 1961 cards. In any event, the 1961 Morrells are not particularly scarce, though the fact that five of the six players can be considered stars makes them expensive.

FOR
The same things the company had going in 1959 and 1960: beautiful photography, a regional issue, and popular players/team.

AGAINST
The low number of cards.

VALUE
EX.-MT. CONDITION: Complete set, $75; Larker, Davis, $8–$10; Wills, Howard, $12.50; Drysdale, Koufax, $20. 5-YEAR PROJECTION: Above average.

1961 BELL BRAND DODGERS

SPECIFICATIONS
SIZE: 2⁷/₁₆×3¹/₂″. FRONT: Color photograph. BACK: Black printing on white cardboard. DISTRIBUTION: Southern California, in packages of snack chips.

HISTORY
For its third baseball card set exclusively featuring the Los Angeles Dodgers, the Bell Brand snack chip company made only minor changes from its 1960 issue. The size was again set at 20 cards, and the design was virtually identical to the previous year. A color photo of the player appears on the front, surrounded by a wide white border. There is a facsimile autograph across the photo, and the player's name, team, and position appear at the bottom. While the cards are one-sixteenth of an inch narrower than the 1960 version, most collectors would hardly notice the difference. To tell the two years apart, the back of the

1961 MORRELL DODGERS

SPECIFICATIONS
SIZE: 2¹/₄×3¹/₄″. FRONT: Color photograph. BACK: Brown printing on white cardboard. DISTRIBUTION: Southern California, one card in each package of Morrell meat products.

HISTORY
Only six cards were issued in the third and final year of Morrell's Los Angeles Dodgers issues. The cards are slightly smaller in size than the previous two years' offerings, but the basic format remained unchanged from 1960. A full-color posed-action photo appeared on front; player stats and a small ad on back. Of the six cards in the 1961 issue, only two are players who also appeared in the 1960 set: the Dodgers' ace pitching pair, Don Drysdale and Sandy Koufax. The inclusion of just four new players' cards—Frank Howard, Tommy Davis, Norm Larker, and Maury Wills—has led to some speculation that remain-

1961 PETERS' MEATS TWINS

SPECIFICATIONS
SIZE: 4⁵/₈×3¹/₂″. FRONT: Hand-colored black-and-white photograph. BACK: Blank. DISTRIBUTION: Minneapolis, on bottom of hot dog packages.

HISTORY
Peters, a St. Paul packaged meat products company, welcomed the old Washington Senators to Minneapolis-St. Paul as the Minnesota Twins with a 26-card issue in 1961. The set featured most of the Twins' roster, along with both men who managed the team that year, Cookie Lavagetto and Sam Mele. The cards were printed on heavily waxed cardboard as part of the packaging for the company's hot dogs and "porkettes." The cards have a photo of the player at the right end of the card. In the upper left was a white panel with a red card number; below was the player's name, also in red, flanked by color versions

of the Peters and Twins logos. A baseball biography takes up most of the space, and the player's age, height, and weight appear at the bottom. Cards are sometimes found which have not been cut from the hot dog packages, and these are worth 25 to 50 percent more than prices listed below for individual cards. Like all baseball cards that had to be cut off a package, many of the 1961 Peters' Twins will be found poorly trimmed. Value is greatly reduced when cards have been cut into the white panel at left or the photo at right. Cards are blank-backed and were protected from grease stains (and from getting ink on the hot dogs) by a heavy coating of wax.

FOR

Great first-year regional issue for collectors of Minnesota Twins cards. Quite scarce, but not that expensive.

AGAINST

Nonstandard size.

NOTEWORTHY CARDS

Hall of Famer Harmon Killebrew is the big star in the set; also appearing is long-time major league pitcher Jim Kaat.

VALUE

EX.-MT. CONDITION, NEATLY CUT FROM PANEL: Complete set, $150; common card, $5; Kaat, $15; Killebrew, $40. 5-YEAR PROJECTION: Average, perhaps a bit above.

1961 UNION OIL PACIFIC COAST LEAGUE

SPECIFICATIONS

SIZE: 3×4". FRONT: Sepia-toned photograph. BACK: Blue printing on white cardboard. DISTRIBUTION: West Coast, given away with purchases at gas stations.

HISTORY

The 67-card set of Pacific Coast League players issued by Union Oil Company in 1961 was the largest of the company's three card sets. Previous issues in similar format had been limited to players of a single team (Sacramento in 1958, Seattle in 1960). There were six teams represented in the 1961 Union issue, offering players and managers. The cards feature borderless sepia-toned photographs, generally posed-action shots. On back, printed in blue ink, is a short baseball biography of the player, along with ads for a local radio station and Union 76. The cards are not numbered. Cards from each team's home town were distributed at gas stations in that area. The six teams represented in the set include Hawaii, Portland, San Diego, Sacramento, Spokane, and Tacoma. The Spokane, and, to a lesser extent, Hawaii cards are considered more difficult to obtain than the cards from other cities.

FOR

Low-priced regional issue, with lots of former and future major leaguers.

AGAINST

Odd size; generally hard to find outside of original distribution areas on the West Coast.

NOTEWORTHY CARDS

The '61 Union Oil set contains a number of former and future major league players, including managers. The most notable former player in the set is Herb Score, who appears in the San Diego team group. The best-known of the soon-to-be major leaguers who appeared in the set is Gaylord Perry, who was then pitching for Tacoma. Two of the cards in the set, Preston Gomez (Spokane) and George Prescott (Hawaii), were withdrawn from distribution early and are scarcer than the rest of the set. The card of Norman Hershberger (San Diego) also pictures Bobby Knoop.

VALUE

EX.-MT. CONDITION: Complete set, $250; common card, Portland, San Diego, Sacramento, Tacoma, $2–$3; Hawaii, $5–$6; Spokane, $7–$8; Score, $15; Prescott, Gomez, $25–$30; Perry, $40. 5-YEAR PROJECTION: Average, perhaps below.

1961 GOLDEN PRESS HALL OF FAME

SPECIFICATIONS

SIZE: 2½×3½". FRONT: Color painting or color-added black-and-white photograph. BACK: Black printing on white cardboard. DISTRIBUTION: Nationally, 33 cards in a 29¢ booklet.

HISTORY

Another "retrospective" look at early Hall of Famers issued in the early 1960s, the Golden Press cards were originally published in the form of a booklet. The 33 cards inside were perforated and could be punched out. Each of the cards depicts a Hall of Fame player, and those chosen certainly reflect the best-known players. Card fronts are generally attractive renderings of contemporary black-and-white photos; the player's name and position appear in a white panel at the bottom. Backs recap the player's career and include a line of lifetime stats and the date of his induction into the Hall of Fame. The original books still exist in sufficient quantity for the collector who is willing to do a little digging.

FOR

These are attractive, inexpensive cards of baseball's greatest players of the first half of the 20th century. Great for the superstar collector.

AGAINST

Collectors don't particularly care for cards issued after a player's career is over.

NOTEWORTHY CARDS

All the expected players are here: Babe Ruth, Ty Cobb, Lou Gehrig, Joe DiMaggio, etc.

VALUE

EX.-MT. CONDITION: Complete book, $40; complete set, $25; common card, 50¢; Gehrig, Dean, DiMaggio, Cobb, $2–$2.50; Ruth, $4. 5-YEAR PROJECTION: Average.

1961 Golden Press Hall of Fame

1961 Golden Press Hall of Fame

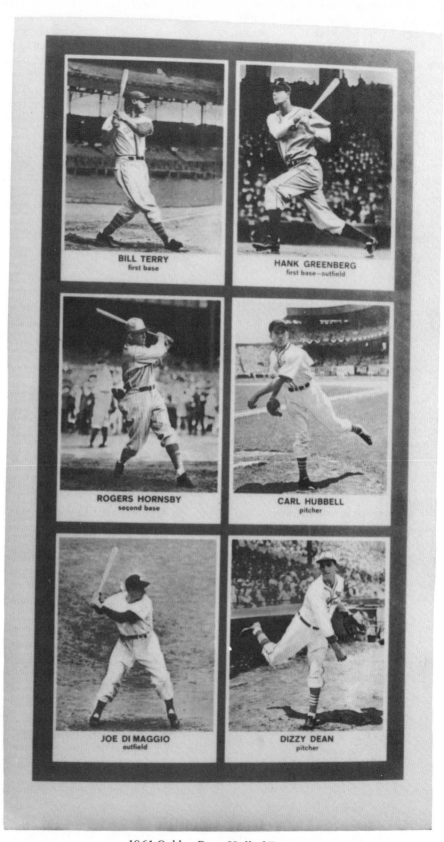

1961 Golden Press Hall of Fame

1961 NU-CARD BASEBALL SCOOPS

SPECIFICATIONS

SIZE: 2½×3½". FRONT: Black-and-white photograph. BACK: Red and black printing on white cardboard. DISTRIBUTION: Nationally.

HISTORY

In its second year of baseball "great moments" card production, Nu-Card sensibly chose to go with the more popular 2½×3½" format preferred by collectors. Otherwise the set continued to use the same basic premise and even most of the same "great moments." There are 80 cards in the 1961 Scoops set, numbered from 401 to 480 in the upper left of the simulated newspaper front page that makes up the front of the card. There is a large black-and-white photo on front, along with a big headline and a dateline that gives the date and location for this bit of baseball history. The front is printed in black, white, and red, as are the card backs. Card backs also contain a card number, along with a newspaper-style write-up of the event on the front. As mentioned, many of the card themes in the 1961 set were also used in the 1960 set. While the subject matter of the '60 Scoops issue spans most of baseball history, the 1960 issue concentrates on the period from 1950 to 1961. This has made the set a bit more popular with collectors. NOTE: In recent years this set has been reprinted; photos on the reproduction cards are not as clear as those on the orginals.

FOR

Novel format, lots of good cards for superstar collectors.

AGAINST

Collectors don't much like "in action" cards, especially those that reach back into baseball history for their subject matter. The Nu-Card sets are generally considered little more than collector issues.

NOTEWORTHY CARDS

Most of the great moments memorialized in the Nu-Card Scoops set of 1961 involve stars.

VALUE

EX.-MT. CONDITION: Complete set, $50; common card, 25¢–30¢; super-superstars, $1–$3. 5-YEAR PROJECTION: Below average.

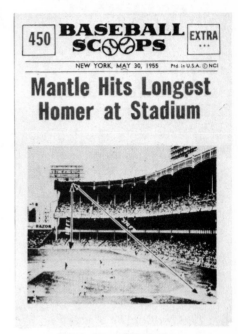

1961 Nu-Card Baseball Scoops, Mickey Mantle

1961 Nu-Card Baseball Scoops, Nellie Fox (back)

1961 Nu-Card Baseball Scoops, Nellie Fox (front)

1960 TOPPS

*1961 Nu-Card Baseball Scoops,
Hank Aaron*

*1961 Nu-Card Baseball Scoops,
Gene Autry*

*1961 Nu-Card Baseball Scoops,
Harmon Killebrew*

SPECIFICATIONS

SIZE: 2½×3½″. FRONT: Color photograph. BACK: Black and gold printing on gray or white cardboard. DISTRIBUTION: Nationally, in 1¢ and 5¢ packages with bubblegum.

HISTORY

Holding the line at 572 cards for the second year in a row, the 1960 Topps set is a collector favorite. There are enough specialty cards to make them "special" without being gimmicky, the format is unusual, and there are lots of good rookie cards and big name stars. Besides, as the first set of the decade, it is a popular starting point for collectors of recent Topps cards. The most notable feature of the '60 Topps set is that the cards are horizontal in format, the only current-size Topps cards in that configuration. A portrait photo occupies the right two-thirds of the card, while a black-and-white "action" pose is set against a solid-color background on the left end of the card. A color team logo is at bottom left, and in a solid-color band at bottom are the player's name, team, and position. The players' names are printed in two different colors, alternating with each letter. Card backs in '60 revert to use of stats for just the previous season and lifetime totals. There are a cartoon and short career summary, or on some cards, previous season highlights on a "diary" basis. Multi-player feature cards continued to be a part of the 1960 set, as were team cards with series checklists on back. A new group of specialty cards, a type which would continue off and on for many years in Topps sets, was a seven-card subset recounting the 1959 World Series victory of the Dodgers over the White Sox. Team managers and coaches got their own cards in the '60 set, both appearing on vertical-format cards. Each manager has his own card while the coaches share a card, each appearing as a "head" photo on an orange background. Lots of Hall of Famers appear among these manager and coaches cards. There are two different subsets of "rookie cards" in the 1960 set. Cards #117 to #148 are the *SPORT* magazine "1960 Rookie Star" cards. These cards have an orange background with red and black lettering and a red, white, and blue ribbon running diagonally. Set on the ribbon is a round color photo of the player. One of the hobby's hottest cards, the premier issue of Carl Yastrzemski, is in this subset, along with rookie cards of Jim Kaat and Frank Howard. The second rookie subset is a group of 10 called "Topps All-Star Rookie" cards. These feature a team of rookies "Selected by the Youth of America," according to the cards. On these, the player photo appears at left, and there is a picture of the Topps rookie trophy at right. Most of the players in this group had appeared on baseball cards previously, but the Willie McCovey card is his true rookie appearance. Backs of both rookie series are quite similar to the rest of the cards in the set. Again in 1960, the set closes out with a series of 20 All-Star cards. On these cards, the player's picture is featured in front of the large numerals "60" on a white background. The 1960 set exists in three levels of scarcity. The common cards are #1 to #440; there is a semi-high series, #441 to #506; and a group of high numbers, #507 to #572. Because of the large number of stars in the set and the currently high-demand Yastrzemski card, the price of the 1960 cards has been moving upward strongly in the last two years.

FOR
Unusual format; collectible, yet challenging set. Lots of specialty and good rookie cards.

AGAINST
The horizontal format does not allow for the best presentation of a baseball player's photo.

NOTEWORTHY CARDS
Important rookie cards in the '60 Topps set are Yastrzemski, McCovey, Kaat, and Howard. All the other big name players of the era are present and accounted for. A photo mix-up put the portraits of White Sox pitchers Gary Peters and J. C. Martin on each other's cards, though the small black-and-white pictures at left are correct.

OUR FAVORITE CARD
Topps really reached into the archives for a picture of Charlie Grimm for his Cubs' manager card. The photo used is a hand-colored version of a black-and-white picture of Jolly Cholly that appears in the 1948 Cubs yearbook—12 years earlier.

VALUE
EX.-MT. CONDITION: Complete set, $350; common card, #1–#440, 25¢; #441–#506, 50¢; #507–#572, $1.25; stars, $3–$5; Musial, Clemente, Koufax, McCovey All-Star, $7–$9; Mays, Aaron, Mantle All-Star, Mays All-Star, Aaron All-Star, $10–$15; McCovey, $22; Mantle, $25; Yastrzemski, $75. 5-YEAR PROJECTION: Average, or a bit above.

1960 Topps, Cleveland Indians Sluggers

1960 Topps, Detroit Tigers Coaches

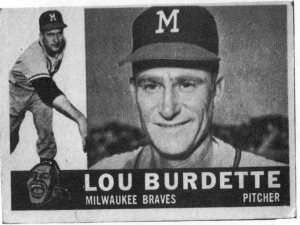

1960 Topps, "Lou" Burdette

1960 Topps, Danny Murtaugh

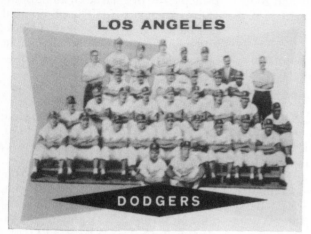

1960 Topps, Los Angeles Dodgers Team Card

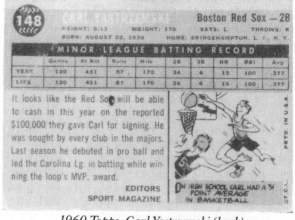

1960 Topps, Carl Yastrzemski (back)

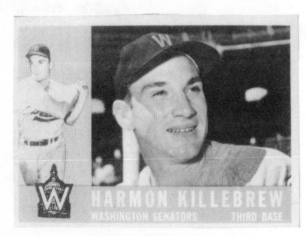

1960 Topps, Harmon Killebrew

1960 Topps, Detroit Tigers Team Card

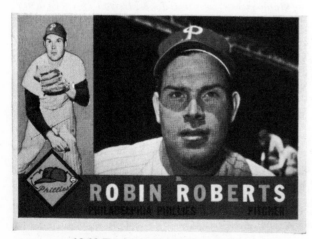

1960 Topps, Robin Roberts (front)

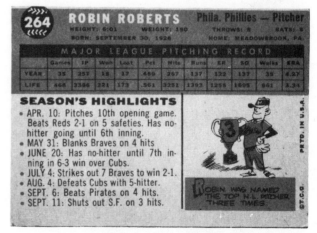

1960 Topps, Robin Roberts (back)

1960 BAZOOKA

SPECIFICATIONS

SIZE: Single card, $1^{13}/_{16} \times 2^{3}/_{4}''$; three-card panel, $5^{1}/_{2} \times 2^{3}/_{4}''$. FRONT: Color photograph. BACK: Blank. DISTRIBUTION: Nationally, three-card panel on the bottom of each bubblegum box.

HISTORY

Apparently feeling that three cards on the bottom of its Bazooka gum boxes would offer more incentive to buy than did the single large-format card of 1959, Topps, in 1960, expanded the Bazooka set to 36 cards, but reduced the cards in size and issued them in three-card panels on the bottom of each package. The 1960 issue retained the basic design of a color photo with multi-colored stripes at bottom containing the player's name, team, and position. In tiny type below that was a card number and notation that the set contained 36 cards. All 12 of the 1960 Bazooka panels seem to have received about equal distribution, and today value is affected only by condition of the cards and the popularity of the players depicted. Complete boxes are quite scarce and are worth 25 to 50 percent above the total value of the cards. Three-card panels, however, exist in remarkably large numbers, and so rate only a very slight premium over the total value of the single cards. Naturally, cards which have been cut from the boxes, either individually or in strips of three, are worth top money only if they are neatly cut on or close to the dotted lines. Whoever at Topps planned the composition of the panels did a great job of mixing superstars, stars, and lesser-known players; only two of the 12 panels do not have a Hall of Famer depicted (Cepeda-Triandos-Malzone and Kuenn-Antonelli-Crandall).

FOR

Attractive cards with a lot of superstars. It's not too hard or too expensive to complete a set.

AGAINST

Collectors don't generally like cards that are too large or too small, and these are too small (at least by current $2^{1}/_{2} \times 3^{1}/_{2}''$ standards). Also, any cards which had to be cut from a package were subjected to a lot of abuse in the process and are difficult to find in Mint condition.

NOTEWORTHY CARDS

Too many superstars to name; the 36 cards contain 13 Hall of Famers—better than 33 percent—and another six or eight who may someday be so enshrined (or at least should be).

VALUE

EX.-MT. CONDITION, NEATLY CUT FROM BOX: Complete set, $175; common card, $3–$5; Hall of Famers, $7.50–$15.00; Aaron, Mays, $20; Mantle, $25; 5-YEAR PROJECTION: Average.

1960 FLEER

SPECIFICATIONS

SIZE: $2^{1}/_{2} \times 3^{1}/_{2}''$. FRONT: Color photo and hand-colored black-and-white photo. BACK: Red and blue printing on white cardboard. DISTRIBUTION: Nationally, in 5¢ packages with bubblegum.

HISTORY

Effectively blocked out of the market for producing baseball cards of current players by Topps' exclusive contracts, Fleer tried a different approach in 1960. The Philadelphia company's 1959 Ted Williams set had met with only limited success. After all, if a kid wasn't a Ted Williams fan, he wasn't going to buy the cards. The 1960 Fleer set was an old-timers issue called "Baseball Greats." At the time, the idea was novel. It had never been tried before, but would be widely copied in the years to follow. Unfortunately, the old-timers set was not a raging success either. Fleer found out that kids buying bubblegum cards wanted to find pictures of current players, not past heroes whose names they didn't recognize. Because Fleer still had Ted Williams under contract, they included him in the set, but it still wasn't enough to make much of a dent in Topps' popularity or sales dominance. Part of the problem was that most of the photos on the cards were of old men. The pictures showed most of the players as they appeared in later years, either as managers or coaches, or as participants in old-timers games or similar events. Some were even in street clothes. Only a few of the pictures were contemporary with the player's career. Some of the photos used were current color pictures, others were originally black-and-white but had color added by hand. The photos appeared octagonal on the cards, as the result of being framed by four brightly colored "corners." The player's name appears in white at the bottom of the card, and there is a white border around the whole design. Card backs are arranged horizontally. Card numbers appear at upper left, in the familiar Fleer "crown." At right are the player's name, nickname, birth date (sometimes date of death, too), and positions played. There is a career summary in biographical form, as well as lifetime statistics and, where applicable, World Series stats. Bottom of the card contains a copyright line and photo credit. The '60 Fleer old-timers set is complete at 79 cards, though it is apparent that a card #80—Pepper Martin—was intended to be issued. A card back for the Martin card will occasionally be found with Joe Tinker or Lefty Grove on the front. These "wrong back" cards are worth some $20 to $25.

1960 Fleer, Napoleon Lajoie

1960 Fleer, Bob Feller (front)

1960 Fleer, Carl Hubbell

BASEBALL GREATS

#26 ROBERT WILLIAM ANDREW FELLER

(Rapid Robert)—Nov. 3, 1918

Right-handed Pitcher—Cleve (AL)—1936-1956

Feller holds many modern strike-out records, including 18 in one game against Detroit, and 348 strike-outs in one season (1946). He also holds the Major League record for most one-hit games (12) and is tied for most no-hitters with three, pitching one against the White Sox on opening day, 1940. In his only World Series appearance he failed to win despite a two-hit performance in one game.

		MAJOR LEAGUE TOTALS			
Games	Won	Lost	Pct.	S.O.	ERA
570	266	162	.621	2581	3.25
		WORLD SERIES TOTALS			
2	0	2	.000	7	5.02

©F. H. Fleer   Printed in U.S.A.   World Wide Photo

1960 Fleer, Bob Feller (back)

1960 Fleer, Judge Landis

1960 Fleer, Connie Mack

FOR

Inexpensive cards of baseball's greats from Cap Anson through Ted Williams.

AGAINST

There's little demand for old-timer cards and these are not especially attractive.

NOTEWORTHY CARDS

Along with all the expected big names of baseball's past, the Ted Williams card stands out as being the only card in the set of a still-active player. This card may be vastly underrated as a collectible card. Now quoted at a value of $4 or so in top grade, compare that price with the last Topps card of Williams, 1958, which is a $40 card (although it is card #1 in the 1958 set).

VALUE

EX.-MT. CONDITION: Complete set (79 cards), $60; common card, 50¢; super-superstars, $1–$2; Williams, Gehrig, Cobb, $4–$5; Ruth, $7. 5-YEAR PROJECTION: Below average.

1960 LEAF

SPECIFICATIONS

SIZE: 2½×3½″. FRONT: Black-and-white photograph. BACK: Black printing on white cardboard. DISTRIBUTION: Nationally, in limited numbers, in packages with marbles.

HISTORY

Since Topps had a lock on the bubblegum baseball card market, the Leaf gum company of Chicago issued its 144-card black-and-white baseball card set in a wax package with a marble. Naturally, this made the packs hard to store and they were easily torn, but it was a good try. The '60 Leafs were the company's second and last baseball card issue, the previous set having been a 98-card effort in 1948–1949. The 1960 Leaf cards were widely distributed geographically, but not in very large numbers compared to their competitor, Topps. The cards feature a black-and-white studio portrait of the players (the backlighting of the photo gives the players the ap-

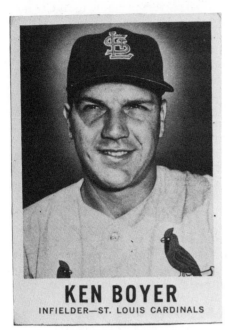

1960 Leaf, Ken Boyer

1960 Leaf, "Jim Grant"

1960 Leaf, Duke Snider (front)

pearance of having a halo), surrounded by a white border. The player's name, team, and position appear in black type beneath the photo. On back, the card number appears in a baseball at the upper left, and there is the traditional card-back information of the player's vital data, a brief career summary, and previous season and lifetime statistics. Like the 1948–1949 set, the 1960 Leaf issue is equally divided into two series, cards #1 to #72 being considered the more common, with cards #73 to #144 being considerably more scarce. While the 1960 Leaf cards are not nearly as common as their Topps counterparts, they are also not as popularly collected, possibly because by 1960 a black-and-white card set looked outdated.

FOR
Scarce nationally distributed issue. High numbers keep it challenging.

AGAINST
High numbers are really quite scarce, and priced at nearly 10 times the value of the low numbers, they add greatly to the cost of assembling a full set.

1960 Leaf, Camilo Pascual

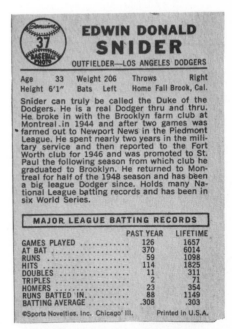

1960 Leaf, Duke Snider (back)

1960 Leaf, Glen Hobbie

NOTEWORTHY CARDS

A "wrong photo" error in the '60 Leaf set was later corrected, creating a collectible variation. Card #25, Jim Grant, was originally issued with the picture of Brooks Lawrence. The difference, if you don't recognize the players on sight, is that on the correct card, Grant is wearing a dark cap with a light "C" (for Cleveland). On the error card, Lawrence is wearing a white pin-striped cap with the dark "C" (for Cincinnati). The handful of superstars in the '60 Leaf set includes Luis Aparicio, Brooks Robinson, and Duke Snider.

VALUE

EX.-MT. CONDITION: Complete set, $350; common card, #1–#72, 50¢; #73–#144, $4–$5; minor stars, $1; Aparicio, $4; Snider, Robinson, $6. 5-YEAR PROJECTION: Average, or a bit below.

1960 POST

SPECIFICATIONS

SIZE: 7×8¾". FRONT: Color photograph. BACK: Blank. DISTRIBUTION: Nationally, on back of boxes of Post Grape Nuts and Grape Nuts Flakes cereal.

HISTORY

The first of four annual baseball card issues by Post cereals, the 1960 set is the smallest, the largest, and the rarest. It's smallest in the number of cards it contains—nine. And not all of them are baseball players; there are two basketball and two football players in the set, along with five baseball players. The '60 issue is the largest of the Post cereal cards in physical size. The cards measure 7×8¾", and comprised almost the entire back of a cereal box. The cards feature a large color photo of the player set against a solid color background, around which is printed a wood-look picture frame. On a simulated brass plate printed on the bottom piece of the frame, the player's name and team appear. A facsimile autograph appears across the face of the photo. The cards are unnumbered and the back is blank. The 1960 Post cards are decidedly rare and quite valuable, the baseball players being more expensive than the football players, and the basketball players bringing up the rear of the value structure. Because they were part of the box design, meant to be cut off, the quality of the trimming is important to the condition, and value, of these cards. A surprising number of the cards are found with portions of the box still attached. Since this allows the collector to carefully cut out the card portion if he wishes, the '60 Posts are most valuable in this state of preservation. A card that has been neatly cut from the box, straight on the outer lines of the picture frame, also carries full value. Cards which have been cut off in sloppy fashion, so that the edges are trimmed into the wooden frame, are worth considerably less. These cards are also sometimes found with the wooden-look frame cut off completely, greatly reducing the value. Tack holes, evidence that the cards were once hung on a wall, will also reduce the value of such cards, but not as greatly as bad cutting.

FOR

The historical "first" issue from Post, whose issues of the early 1960s are a collector favorite today. Large-format cards make attractive additions to superstar collections.

AGAINST

The large size of the cards makes them hard to fit into standard collecting patterns. The cards are also very expensive and rare.

NOTEWORTHY CARDS

The entire set consists of superstars. Since there are only nine, we'll list them. BASEBALL: Don Drysdale, Al Kaline, Harmon Killebrew, Ed Mathews, Mickey Mantle (each one a Hall of Famer); FOOTBALL: Frank Gifford, John Unitas; BASKETBALL: Bob Cousy, Bob Pettit.

VALUE

EX.-MT. CONDITION, NEATLY CUT FROM BOX: Complete set of five baseball players, $1,100; Drysdale, Kaline, Killebrew, Mathews, $150; Mantle, $500; Gifford, Unitas, $125; Cousy, Pettit, $75. 5-YEAR PROJECTION: Below average.

1960 Leaf, Brooks Robinson

1960 KAHN'S

SPECIFICATIONS

SIZE: 3¼×4". FRONT: Black-and-white photograph. BACK: Black printing on white cardboard. DISTRIBUTION: Midwest, in packages of Kahn's meat products.

HISTORY

Kahn's greatly enhanced the scope of its baseball card issue in 1960, to 42 players representing six teams. Besides the Reds, the Pirates, and the Indians, which had been in the previous year's set, the 1960 issue included players from both Chicago teams and the St. Louis Cardinals. Front of the cards continued to follow the format established in 1955. A borderless black-and-white photo was over-printed with a black facsimile autograph. Beneath is a half-inch wide strip with a Kahn's ad. Instead of the player stories which had been featured on the backs of the 1958 and 1959 Kahn's cards, the 1960 set contained player career stats and biographical details. Once again, the cards were packaged with Kahn's meats, and have a waxy coating on them. Cards of each team were sold in and around that team's hometown.

FOR

The 1960 Kahn's cards offer an expanded range of interest for team collectors. Value per card is significantly lower than earlier issues.

AGAINST

Same old format.

NOTEWORTHY CARDS

Pitcher Ron Kline appears as either a Pirate or Cardinal. Harvey Kuenn's card can be found with a blank back, and is quite scarce that way. Hall of Famers in the '60 set are Frank Robinson and Roberto Clemente.

VALUE

EX.-MT. CONDITION: Complete set, $500; common card, $10–$12; stars, $12–$20; Robinson, $40; Clemente, blank-back Kuenn, $75–$100. 5-YEAR PROJECTION: Below average.

1960 BELL BRAND DODGERS

SPECIFICATIONS

SIZE: 2½×3½". FRONT: Color photograph. BACK: Black printing on white cardboard. DISTRIBUTION: Southern California, inserted in packages of snack chips.

HISTORY

After a one-year layoff, Bell Brand snack chips followed its 1958 baseball card issue with a 20-card set in 1960. According to the ad on the back of the card, single cards were inserted into packages of potato chips priced from 39¢ to 59¢, and into bags of corn chips priced from 29¢ to 49¢. Because the cards often came into contact with the chips, they are sometimes found today with grease stains, and are worth less in that condition than without such defect. Once again, all cards in the '60 Bell set are Los Angeles Dodgers. The design of the 1960 set is quite different from the company's earlier effort. The size of the 1960s is the now-standard 2½×3½". Card fronts featured a full-color photo of the player, surrounded by a white border. The player's name, team, and position appear at the bottom of the card, and there is a facsimile autograph over the photo. Half of the card back has a 1960 Dodgers home game schedule, while the other half is taken up with a recap of the player's 1959 season performance, a Bell logo, and, in the upper-left corner, a card number. Distribution of the 1960 Bell cards was much better than that of the '58s, and there are no confirmed scarcities, though the Labine, Alston, Klippstein, and Koufax cards may be somewhat tougher.

FOR

Nice regional set; not too expensive.

AGAINST

There's really nothing to be said against the set.

NOTEWORTHY CARDS

Lots of the popular Dodgers stars of the early 1960s, including Hall of

Famers Sandy Koufax, Duke Snider, and Walt Alston, and the "rookie card" of Maury Wills. Unaccountably, there is no Don Drysdale or Gil Hodges card in the 1960 set.

VALUE

EX.-MT. CONDITION: Complete set, $175; common card, $6–$8; Labine, Klippstein, Alston, Wills, $15; Koufax, Snider, $20. 5-YEAR PROJECTION: Average.

1960 MORRELL DODGERS

SPECIFICATIONS

SIZE: 2½×3½". FRONT: Color photograph. BACK: Black and red printing on white stock. DISTRIBUTION: Southern California, one card in each package of Morrell meat products.

HISTORY

The second of three annual issues featuring Los Angeles Dodgers players exclusively, the 1960 Morrell Meats set again contains 12 unnumbered cards. The format remained basically unchanged, a borderless full-color photo occupying the entire face of the card, unmarred by any written elements. The backs for 1960 were a bit different than those for the previous year, however. The advertising portion was greatly reduced and player stats for previous seasons were added. While there were no incorrect photos in the 1960 set, three of the cards are inexplicably scarcer than the other nine: Furillo, Hodges, and Snider—at least it's hard to explain why the Hodges and Snider cards are scarce. The Furillo card was probably withdrawn from distribution early in the season when Skoonj surrendered his right fielder job to Frank Howard.

FOR

Attractive regional set, popular both with Dodgers team collectors and with superstar collectors. The common cards are reasonably priced, and the three scarce cards are challenging.

AGAINST

Can't think of a thing, except maybe they could have issued "rookie cards" of Frank Howard and Tommy Davis.

NOTEWORTHY CARDS

Dodgers manager Walt Alston joins Drysdale, Koufax, and Snider as Hall of Famers in the 1960 Morrell set.

VALUE

EX.-MT. CONDITION: Complete set, $250; common card, $7.50–$10; Alston, $15; Drysdale, Koufax, $20–$25; Furillo, Hodges, Snider, $45–$60. 5-YEAR PROJECTION: Above average.

1960 LAKE TO LAKE BRAVES

SPECIFICATIONS

SIZE: 2½×3¼″. FRONT: Blue and white photograph. BACK: Red printing on white cardboard. DISTRIBUTION: Northeastern Wisconsin, one card stapled onto each milk carton.

HISTORY

One of the more challenging sets for the really condition-conscious collector—the method of distribution of the 1960 Lake to Lake Milwaukee Braves set offered two chances for the card to be damaged before it made its way into collector hands. The first damage, staple holes in the blue border at upper right, occurred when the cards were attached to cartons of milk. The second type of damage commonly found on these cards occurred because of a redemption offer. This offer on the back of the cards stated that Braves' premium prizes could be obtained by saving up the cards and redeeming them at the local dairy office. The cards were punch-cancelled in the lower-right corner upon redemption and were then returned to the owner along with the prize. For 20 cards the collector could obtain a Braves' pen-and-pencil set; for 100 cards, a pair of tickets to a Braves game. Actually, though they didn't know it then, the original owners of

the cards would have been much better off keeping the cards unpunched and selling them to collectors—they're quite valuable today. The condition preferred by collectors is unstapled and unpunched, which would mean the cards were never circulated at all. Since they are quite difficult to find in that condition, most collectors will accept cards with staple holes. Those cards that have been punch-cancelled, however, have a rather difficult time finding buyers. The Lake to Lake card fronts have a square blue and white photo of the player that is borderless on the top and left. The bottom and right edges are bordered by a reverse "L" figure, also in blue. The player's name and position appear in the bottom border, along with a Braves logo at lower left. There is no number on the cards. The 28-card set features the principal Braves roster for 1960, along with the manager and coaches.

FOR

Scarce regional set of a popular team.

AGAINST

Hard to find in Mint condition.

NOTEWORTHY CARDS

The Billy Bruton card in this set is unaccountably scarce. While Bruton was traded to the Tigers early in the season, it does not seem likely that his card was withdrawn for that reason. Half a dozen other Braves who appear in the set were traded before Bruton, and their cards are not especially scarce. To a lesser extent, Ray Boone is also considered tough. Two of the three Braves Hall of Famers from that era, Hank Aaron and Warren Spahn, are part of the set, but Ed Mathews does not appear. The 1960 Lake to Lake set contains the only baseball card of Braves pitcher Bob Giggie, who played parts of the 1959 and 1960 seasons with Milwaukee, was traded to Kansas City in 1960, and played part of that year and part of 1962 with the A's. Giggie owns a lifetime 3-1 record and 5.18 ERA.

VALUE

EX.-MT. CONDITION, WITH STAPLE HOLES, BUT NOT PUNCH-CANCELLED: Complete set, $300; common card, $4; Burdette, Schoendienst, Adcock, Crandall, $7–$8; Spahn, $15–$20; Boone,

$30; Aaron, $75; Bruton, $100. 5-YEAR PROJECTION: Below average.

1960 UNION OIL

SPECIFICATIONS

SIZE: 3⅛×4″. FRONT: Color photograph. BACK: Black printing on white cardboard. DISTRIBUTION: Seattle area, cards given away with purchases at gas stations.

HISTORY

After taking a year off between baseball card issues, Union Oil Company issued a second set of cards. The 1960 set features nine members of the Seattle Rainiers of the Pacific Coast League. The gas company's 1958 issue had been of Sacramento players only. The following year, in 1961, the company would issue a larger set of six Pacific Coast League teams. The '60 Union cards, distributed at Seattle area gas stations, featured on the front a full-color, posed-action borderless photo of the player. Card backs offer some personal data on the player, uniform number, and a "Thumb-Nail Sketch" biography, along with a Union 76 ad and a photo credit. It is unusual for a one-team minor league set of this era to feature full-color cards.

FOR

Attractive, scarce regional set.

AGAINST

Oversize cards, no former or future major leaguers of special interest.

NOTEWORTHY CARDS

The Ray Ripplemeyer card was withdrawn from distribution early in the promotion and is much rarer than the rest of the series. The most notable player in the set is Gordy Coleman, who went on to a nine-year career with the Indians and the Reds as a first baseman.

VALUE

EX.-MT. CONDITION: Complete set, $60; common card, $3; Coleman,

$4; Ripplemeyer, $30–$35. 5-YEAR PROJECTION: Below average.

1960 DARIGOLD FARMS SPOKANE INDIANS

SPECIFICATIONS
SIZE: 2³/₈×2⁹/₁₆″. FRONT: Black-and-white photograph. BACK: Black printing on white cardboard. DISTRIBUTION: Spokane area, single cards with cartons of milk.

HISTORY
In its second and final year of baseball card production, the Darigold Farms dairy company produced a 24-card set of Spokane Indians players. The fact that the Indians were the Class AAA Pacific Coast League farm club of the then-World's Champions Los Angeles Dodgers helps make the set popular with collectors today. The set is also popular because it is a scarce regional issue, distributed with cartons of the company's milk. Design of the '60 Darigold cards was changed somewhat from the previous year. Card fronts continue to offer a black-and-white photo of the player, set against a solid-colored background. Added to the 1960 issue, though, are a white border around the card, and a facsimile autograph across the photo. An ad message appears in the bottom border. Card backs are quite similar to the 1959 set, with a Spokane Indians logo appearing in the upper left, with personal data on the player to the right. Career highlights and an abbreviated record of 1959 season performance appear toward the bottom, along with a card number. The 1960 Darigold set features several cards of former and future major league players, including a few that don't appear on any other baseball card issue. This makes the cards especially popular with those team collectors who want to get as many cards as possible of those who played with the Dodgers in the early 1960s.

FOR
Scarce regional issue of a top minor league team.

AGAINST
Some collectors won't collect minor league cards.

NOTEWORTHY CARDS
Three notable Dodgers stalwarts of the 1960s make their baseball card debuts in this set, Frank Howard, Willie Davis, and Ron Fairly.

VALUE
EX.-MT. CONDITION: Complete set, $350; common card, $15; Howard, Davis, Fairly, $25–$30. 5-YEAR PROJECTION: Below average.

1960 NU-CARD BASEBALL HI-LITES

SPECIFICATIONS
SIZE: 3¼×5⅜″. FRONT: Black-and-white photograph. BACK: Red and black printing on white cardboard. DISTRIBUTION: Nationally.

HISTORY
This novelty issue contains 72 cards depicting great moments in baseball history. The roughly postcard-size cards use a black-and-white photo on a simulated newspaper front page to tell the story. The fronts are printed in red and black. A card number appears in the upper-left corner, and there is a "dateline" at the top to indicate the date and place of the baseball feat. The featured bits of history run the gamut from the game's early days right through 1959, and are written up in some detail in story form at the bottom of the card. Card backs, also in red and black, have a baseball trivia question that is tied to another of the cards in the set. While the set is not popularly collected, a lot of collectors who specialize in superstar players seek out the particular cards in the set that are pertinent to their collection. NOTE: This set has been reprinted in recent years; photos on the reproduction cards are darker than on the originals.

FOR
Novel format, a bit more baseball history than most cards impart.

AGAINST
Collectors don't like "retrospect" cards or those in oversize format.

NOTEWORTHY CARDS
Since most of the great moments in baseball history that are presented in the set featured better players, the set is full of big name stars.

VALUE
EX.-MT. CONDITION: Complete set, $75; common card, 50¢–75¢; super-superstars, $2–$4. 5-YEAR PROJECTION: Below average.

1959-1950

LARRY DOBY
OUTFIELD—CLEVELAND INDIANS

1959 TOPPS

SPECIFICATIONS

SIZE: 2½×3½". FRONT: Color photograph. BACK: Red and green (low numbers) or black and red (high numbers) printing on gray or white cardboard. DISTRIBUTION: Nationally, in 1¢ and 5¢ packages with bubblegum.

HISTORY

In expanding its 1959 set to 572 cards, the largest ever to that date, Topps added a number of specialty subseries to the "regular" player cards. The basic cards in the '59 set featured a nearly round color photo at the center of the card, with a solid-color background at top and bottom, and a white border all around. A facsimile autograph appears across the photo. The player's name is printed all in lower-case letters at the top of the card on an angle. There is a color team logo in the lower left-hand corner, and two lines of type at lower right with the player's team and position. Card backs have major and/or minor league stats on a year-by-year basis, along with a cartoon and short write-up on the player, plus the usual biographical details. On the low number cards (#1–#506), this information is printed in red and green ink, with the card number in white at the upper-left corner, in a square green box. On the high number cards (#507–#572), the printing is in black and red, with the card number in a black box. As mentioned earlier, a number of specialty series dot the 1959 Topps checklist. Topps has continued to use these subsets off and on right up to the present. There were several multi-player cards, picturing more than one player, sometimes from the same team, sometimes from opposing teams. Checklists were once again printed on the backs of team cards. One of several specialty groups that was new to the 1959 set was a ten-card run of highlights from the last few seasons, mostly featuring big name players. A second type of specialty card that debuted in 1959 was the "Rookie Stars" series of 31 cards chosen by the editors of *The Sporting News*. These cards, all numbered alphabetically from 116 to 146, featured a radically different design from the regular '59 cards. The players were pictured against a background of red, white, and blue stripes on a black shield. Lettering was in yellow and white, and there was a white border. Backs were similar to the regular cards in the set. The very first of the rookie cards, Bob Allison, was an excellent choice, because he went on to win the American League Rookie of the Year award with the Washington Senators, but most of the other 30 rookies never really made it big in the major leagues, and several never played an inning of big league ball. The final 22 cards of the 1959 set, in the high number series, are *The Sporting News* "All-Star Selection" players. Players in the All-Star cards are pictured in a shield-shaped device at the center of the card. There is a fancy eagle design behind the shield, on a blue (American League) or red (National League) background. Interestingly, the shields and eagles are of different design on the A.L. and N.L. cards. Though the 1959 Topps set was released in several series over the course of the summer, only the final 66 cards, the "high numbers," are more scarce than the rest—but they are significantly more scarce. Besides the All-Star cards, these high numbers feature the unique Roy Campanella card (see below) and the rookie cards of Bob Gibson and fellow Hall of Famer Harmon Killebrew.

FOR

Interesting and varied set with lots of historic innovations that would shape Topps cards for years to come. Set is collectible, but challenging, and certainly the price is reasonable for cards that are more than 25 years old.

AGAINST

Few collectors don't like the '59 set.

NOTEWORTHY CARDS

Let's start with the first card in the set. It's the only Topps card ever to picture the Commissioner of Baseball, at that time, Ford C. Frick. Toward the end of the set, card #550 is also special; it depicts former Brooklyn Dodgers catcher Roy Campanella in a wheelchair, the result of a tragic December, 1957, accident that left him permanently crippled. Back of the card features an inspirational message from

1959 Topps, Pittsburgh Pirates Pitchers

1959 Topps, Sandy Koufax

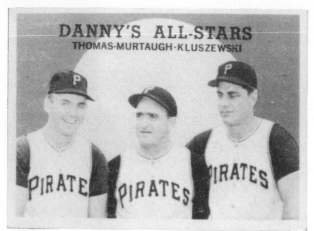

1959 Topps, Pittsburgh Pirates Manager and Stars

1959 Topps, St. Louis Cardinals Team Card

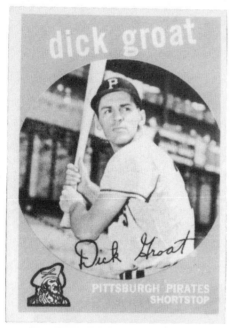

1959 Topps, Dick Groat

1959 Topps, Rocco Colavito

1959 Topps, Al Kaline

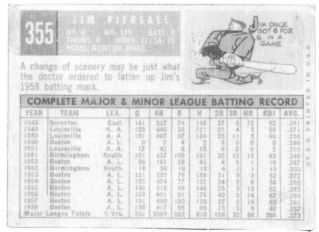

1959 Topps, Jim Piersall (back)

National League president Warren Giles. The card is titled "Symbol of Courage," and the card back talks of Campy's fight to overcome the effects of the accident and his return to baseball as a coach for the Los Angeles Dodgers. There is a wrong-photo card in the '59 set: Camilo Pascual is pictured on Ralph Lumenti's card. Pascual has his own card, as well, but the name is misspelled on the front of that one, "Camillo." Despite the fact that it's the wrong photo on front, the Lumenti card can be quite valuable— if it doesn't have a small line added to the back indicating Lumenti was sent down to the minor leagues in mid-season. Seven '59 Topps cards in the number range of 316 to 362 are known to exist with and without such added lines indicating trades or options. These variations were produced in mid-season press runs when the lines were added to the card backs. The early printings, without these notations, are worth $10 to $12 apiece, compared to the 35¢ common card price for cards with the line. The cards to look for are #316, Ralph Lumenti; #321, Bob Giallombardo; #322, Harry Hanebrink; #336, Billy Loes; #342, Ray Jablonski; #359, Bill White; and #362, Dolan Nichols. If you're a rookie card collector, besides the aforementioned Bob Gibson card, you're out of luck on big name players. Stan Musial, whose only previous Topps card was in the '58 All-Star series, appears on a regular Topps card for the first time in 1959.

OUR FAVORITE CARD

The earliest known example of a ballplayer fooling the Topps photographer appears in the 1959 set, on card #440, Lew Burdette. When the photographer showed up to take card pictures, Burdette grabbed a left-hander's glove and posed in the wind-up. Thing is, Burdette is a right-hander.

VALUE

EX.-MT. CONDITION: Complete set, $400; common card, #1–#506, 35¢; #507–#572, $1.50; stars, $3–$6; Koufax, Musial, Clemente, Killebrew, $9–$12; Aaron All-Star, Mays All-Star, Mantle All-Star, Campanella, Mays, Aaron, $15; Gibson, $20; Mantle, $25. 5-YEAR PROJECTION: Average.

1959 Topps, San Francisco Giants Team Card

1959 Topps, Bob Turley, The Sporting News *All-Stars*

1959 Topps, Don Larsen, Casey Stengel

1959 BAZOOKA

SPECIFICATIONS
SIZE: 2¾×5″. FRONT: Color photograph. BACK: Blank. DISTRIBUTION: Nationally, on bottom of bubblegum boxes.

HISTORY
Bazooka was the brand name under which Topps sold bubblegum without baseball cards for a number of years. It was traditionally marketed in a small, thick square, wrapped in wax paper with a cartoon insert. It sold for 1¢. In 1959, Topps began using baseball cards, incorporated as part of the box packaging, to sell its 25-piece box of Bazooka gum. The first issue, in 1959, was a 23-card set. The cards were issued one to a box and comprised virtually the entire bottom panel. They could be "cut on the dotted lines" and removed from the boxes, though like all baseball cards issued as part of an overall package, cards that are still intact, box and all, are worth a considerable premium— 25 to 50 percent—over neatly trimmed cards removed from the package. There are two levels of scarcity among the 1959 Bazooka cards. Nine cards were initially released and are more common than a subsequent group of 14 which came later. The cards are not numbered and have blank backs. They are considered legitimately scarce by hobbyists. It's especially hard to find them in nicely trimmed condition.

1959 Topps, Johnny Antonelli

1959 Topps, Warren Giles

1959 Bazooka, Del Crandall

FOR

Nice, colorful large-format cards. Generally, the players depicted are of star or superstar caliber. A most challenging collecting project for the hobbyist who specializes in the '50s and '60s.

AGAINST

Hard to find in top grade because of sloppy scissors-work by kids 25 years ago. There are some color variations in the strips at bottom which contain the player's name, position, and team.

NOTEWORTHY CARDS

Virtually all of the cards in the '59 Bazookas are stars, or at least they were when the cards were issued. Hall of Famers include Aaron, Banks, Drysdale, Mantle, Mays, and Snider.

OUR FAVORITE CARD

Unless he is an avid fan of the Fifties, the average collector today may wonder what Yankees pitcher Bob Turley is doing in the 1959 Bazooka set along with the superstars of the day. If you remember the 1958 baseball season, however, you don't have to ask. Bullet Bob Turley was *the* dominant pitcher in major league baseball in 1958. His 21-7 season led the American League in number of wins and winning percentage (.750); not incidentally, it helped lead the New York Yankees to a World Series grudge match against the Milwaukee Braves. His 19 complete games and 128 strikeouts were also league-topping statistics. Not content with getting the Yankees into the Series, Turley handed them the World's Championship with two wins and a save—after the Yanks had lost the first two games to Milwaukee. It was one of the most exciting World Series contests ever, and Turley's performance for the season was capped by receipt of the Cy Young Award, major league pitching's highest honor. Turley's card is priced with the least expensive of the 1959 Bazooka set.

VALUE

EX.-MT. CONDITION, NEATLY CUT FROM BOX: Complete set, $1,750; common nonstar card, $25; scarce group nonstars, $40; scarce group stars, $50–$75; Aaron, Banks, Mays, Snider, $100–$125; Mantle, $150. 5-YEAR PROJECTION: Above average.

1959 KAHN'S

SPECIFICATIONS

SIZE: 3¼×4″. FRONT: Black-and-white photograph. BACK: Black printing on white cardboard. DISTRIBUTION: Ohio-Western Pennsylvania area, in packages of Kahn's meats.

HISTORY

In its fifth year, the Kahn's wieners set once again features three teams, but the Phillies were gone. Joining the Pirates and the Reds in the '59 set of 38 cards were the Cleveland Indians. Card fronts remained little changed from previous years. The dominant feature was a black-and-white borderless photo with a facsimile autograph. Below the picture was a half-inch white strip with an ad for Kahn's. Card backs in 1959 again contained a short story purportedly written by the player. The paragraphs on the backs of '59 Kahn's cards were titled "The Toughest Play I Had to Make" or (for pitchers) "The Toughest Batter I Have to Face." The cards are not numbered.

FOR

Nice cards for the regional or team collector. Some big name stars.

AGAINST

Format is virtually unchanged from five years earlier. Cards are quite expensive on a per-card basis.

NOTEWORTHY CARDS

The Dick Brodowski card is in short supply, as, to a lesser degree, are the cards of Harvey Haddix, Woody Held, and Cal McLish. Hall of Famers in the set are currently limited to Frank Robinson and Roberto Clemente. Billy Martin is pictured in the set, a memento of his only year with the Indians.

VALUE

EX.-MT. CONDITION: Complete set, $950; common card, $20; stars, $30–$40; Robinson, $65; Clemente, $75; Haddix, Held, McLish, $100; Brodowski, $250. 5-YEAR PROJECTION: Below average.

1959 FLEER TED WILLIAMS

SPECIFICATIONS

SIZE: 2½×3½″. FRONT: Color-tinted black-and-white or color photograph. BACK: Red and blue printing on gray cardboard. DISTRIBUTION: Nationally, in 5¢ packages with bubblegum.

HISTORY

Effectively shut out of the baseball card market by Topps' monopoly on player contracts for bubblegum card appearances, Fleer tried a bold new idea in 1959, issuing an entire baseball card set featuring one player—the immortal Ted Williams. Rather crude by contemporary baseball card standards, Fleer's set made the best of the material at hand. Color photos appear in the set alongside black-and-white photos which have had color added. The 80 cards in the set trace the life and baseball career to that point of "The Splendid Splinter." There is little to obscure the picture on the front of the card besides a bat and ball that has his name, and a caption in the white border below the

Ted's Idol — Babe Ruth

1959 Fleer Ted Williams

1959 FLEER TED WILLIAMS

photo. Problems with printing or distribution of the set created a scarcity in card #68, "Ted Signs for 1959." While virtually all the rest of the cards in the set are valued at 50¢ or so, the rare card #68 is a $50–$60 item. Some years back a counterfeit of this card was produced. It can usually be detected by the overall pinkish tint of the photo, along with a *moire* pattern over the face of the card, a screen-like effect that results from making printing plates from an already printed item, rather than a new negative. Many of these counterfeits have now been stamped "Reproduction" on the back, and are sold to collectors for a couple of bucks to fill in their sets until they can buy the real thing.

FOR
If you're a Ted Williams fan, you'll love this set.

AGAINST
If you're not a Ted Williams fan, you won't. Quality is not great, many of the cards are nonbaseball in nature, like those featuring his military career. The rarity of the "Ted Signs for 1959" card makes collecting a complete set difficult.

NOTEWORTHY CARDS
There is extra demand for the second card in the Ted Williams set, "Ted's Idol—Babe Ruth," because it pictures Ruth and Williams together.

VALUE
EX.-MT. CONDITION: Complete set, $100; common card, 50¢; Williams/Ruth, $1; Ted Signs for 1959, $50–$60. 5-YEAR PROJECTION: Below average.

1959 Fleer Ted Williams

1959 Fleer Ted Williams

1959 Fleer Ted Williams

1959 Fleer Ted Williams

COMPLETE BOOK OF COLLECTIBLE BASEBALL CARDS

1959 MORRELL DODGERS

1959 Fleer Ted Williams (#68, front)

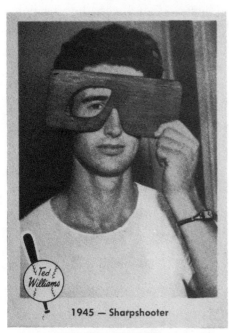

1945 — Sharpshooter

1959 Fleer Ted Williams

Ted Williams & Jim Thorpe

1959 Fleer Ted Williams

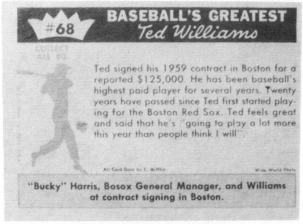

1959 Fleer Ted Williams (#68, back)

SPECIFICATIONS

SIZE: 2½×3½". FRONT: Color photo. BACK: Black printing on white cardboard. DISTRIBUTION: Southern California area, one card in each package of Morrell meat products.

HISTORY

One of several companies to welcome the Dodgers to Los Angeles in their early years, Morrell Meats issued the first of three consecutive baseball card sets in 1959, the year the Dodgers captured the World's Championship. In the popular 2½×3½" size, the card fronts feature nothing less than a gorgeous full-color borderless photo of one of 12 Dodgers pictured in the Coliseum. Two thirds of each '59 Morrell card back is advertising for the company's "Wieners, Smokees, Cheesefurters, and Polish Sausages." Player information was limited to name, birth date, and birthplace. The "Mirro-Krome" cards were produced for Morrell by the Los Angeles firm of H.S. Crocker & Company. The 1959 Dodgers set was not really Morrell's very first baseball card issue—John Morrell & Company was also the issuer of the 1954 Red Heart dog food cards, which are also still being collected.

FOR

Beautiful regional cards of a popular team with lots of stars.

AGAINST

They're fairly expensive for 1959-vintage cards. Two player identification errors (see below) detract from the quality level of the set.

NOTEWORTHY CARDS

There are lots of stars and superstars in the '59 Morrell Dodgers: Drysdale, Hodges, Koufax, Snider, etc. Two error cards in the set have photos of Stan Williams and Joe Pignatano misidentified on the cards' backs as Clem Labine and Norm Larker, respectively.

VALUE

EX.-MT. CONDITION: Complete set, $400; common card, $25; Hodges, Drysdale, Koufax, Snider, $45–$60. 5-YEAR PROJECTION: Above average.

1959 DARIGOLD FARMS SPOKANE INDIANS

SPECIFICATIONS

SIZE: 2½×2⅜″. FRONT: Black-and-white photograph. BACK: Black printing on white cardboard. DISTRIBUTION: Spokane area, single cards on cartons of milk.

HISTORY

One of the reasons for the popularity of this minor league issue is that the Spokane Indians of the Pacific Coast League were the top farm club of the Los Angeles Dodgers in 1959. Another reason is that the cards are a genuinely scarce regional issue. The 22 cards in the set were issued with cartons of milk. Card fronts feature a black-and-white photo of the player set against a solid-color background. A white stripe beneath the photo has the player's name and position, while a dark colored stripe has the message, "Compliments of Darigold Farms." Card backs, which are not numbered, feature a Spokane Indians logo in the upper left. To the right is the player's personal data, including nickname, marital status, and children's names. Toward the bottom are career highlights, lifetime major and/or minor league batting or pitching totals, and an abbreviated record for the previous season.

FOR

A scarce regional set for the top farm club of a popular team.

AGAINST

Because it's a minor league set, many collectors just aren't interested.

NOTEWORTHY CARDS

There are several players in the Darigold issue who had the proverbial "cup of coffee" in the major leagues, but never appeared on a major league baseball card. This makes their minor league cards popular with team collectors. Other players in the set are former or future major leaguers. Most noteworthy of that group is Tommy Davis, who was spending his last full season in the minors before heading up to an 18-year major league career. Perennial minor league star Steve Bilko is also part of the set.

VALUE

EX.-MT. CONDITION: Complete set, $350; common card, $15; "name" players, $20–$25; Davis, $30. 5-YEAR PROJECTION: Below average.

1958 TOPPS

SPECIFICATIONS

SIZE: 2½×3½″. FRONT: Color photograph. BACK: Red and black printing on gray cardboard. DISTRIBUTION: Nationally, in 1¢ and 5¢ packs with bubblegum.

HISTORY

The 1958 Topps set is popular and can be quite challenging, depending on how it is collected. For '58, Topps once again increased the number of cards in the set—to 494. The set is actually numbered to 495, but card #145 was not issued. Early series checklists show that card was to have been Phillies first baseman Ed Bouchee. The card was pulled from distribution, though, after Bouchee was suspended from baseball early in the season for off-field misconduct. Later checklists just show a blank after card #145. Speaking of checklists, there are two types in the 1958 set. Rather than issuing checklists as separate, unnumbered cards like those of 1956 and 1957, Topps used the backs of team cards to present checklists in 1958. While most of the checklists were by number and series, the backs of some Braves, Tigers, Orioles, and Redlegs team cards will be found with checklists arranged in alphabetical order. One of the most interesting features of the 1958 Topps set is the existence of what collectors call "yellow-letter variations" on 33 cards between #2 and #108. These variations were apparently created midway through the printing of the first series. These 33 variation cards show either the player's name at the top of the card or the team name at the bottom printed in yellow, rather than the more common white. Many other cards in the set have yellow lettering in these places, but only the 33 known cards in the first series are found in both yellow- and white-letter types. In the case of common players, which may have a value of 50¢ or so in the more numerous white-letter style, the yellow-letter cards are a $5 item. On the several Hall of Famers and superstars found with the variation, the price is about double for the yellow-letter type: Luis Aparicio, Early Wynn, and Bob Lemon going from about $3.75 to $8; Al Kaline from $10 to $24; Roberto Clemente from $15 to $30; and Hank Aaron from $25 in the white-letter style to $50 as a yellow-letter type. The card numbers which will be found with yellow- and white-letter types are 2, 8, 11, 13, 20, 23, 24, 30, 32, 33, 35, 46, 50, 52, 53, 57, 58, 60, 61, 65, 70, 76, 77, 78, 79, 81, 85, 92, 97, 98, 100, 101, 108. Most collectors either love or hate the basic design of the 1958 Topps set. The

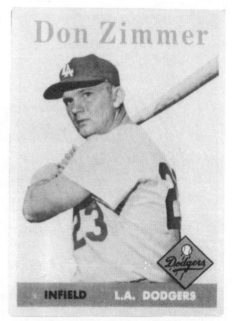

1958 Topps, Don Zimmer

front of the card features a portrait or posed-action photo of the player set against a plain, brightly colored background. A color team logo is in the lower corner and there is a contrasting color strip at the bottom with player position and name. Topps greatly increased the number of multi-player feature cards in the set. These cards usually feature the players photographed in a stadium setting. A major innovation in the '58 Topps set was the inclusion at the end of 20 "All-Star" cards selected by *The Sporting News*. These cards feature different photos of the chosen players, set against star-studded blue (National League) or red (American League) backgrounds. A 21st All-Star card shows 1957 World Series (and 1958, for that matter) managers Casey Stengel and Fred Haney together. Card backs in 1958 were quite similar in style to 1956, presenting cartoon-style highlights from the player's career, along with the usual bio and stats. Topps dropped the season-by-season stats in 1958, returning for one year to the "Year" and "Life" figures as had been used from 1952 to 1956.

FOR

The '58 Topps cards do not feature any really scarce series, so if the collector opts to collect just the basic 494 cards, the set can be assembled rather easily. Those desiring a challenge, though, can dig into the yellow-letter and checklist variations. The set is generally considered to be attractive in format, though some collectors do not like it. The 1958 Topps set is one of the better bargains in the hobby today if it can be purchased as a set in top grade.

AGAINST

Nothing to speak of.

NOTEWORTHY CARDS

Besides all the usual superstars, Stan Musial makes his first appearance on a Topps baseball card in 1958, as part of the "All-Star" series. Ted Williams makes his last appearace on a Topps card, as the #1 card in the set. Notable rookie cards for the year include Roger Maris, Orlando Cepeda, Vada Pinson, and Curt Flood. Because of the construction of printing plates for the later series, four of the higher-numbered cards are numerically quite a bit scarcer than the cards around them. While other common cards in their number range are 35¢ items, the cards of Billy Harrell, Carroll Hardy, Preston Ward, and Gary Geiger will usually be found sporting a price tag of eight to ten times that. There are a couple of "wrong photo" cards in the

'58 Topps: the picture on the Mike McCormick card is really Ray Monzant, while the photo on Milt Bolling's card is really Lou Berberet.

OUR FAVORITE CARD

While there had been multi-player feature cards in recent baseball card history, none had ever featured players from different teams on the same card until 1958. In that set, Topps photographers took advantage of photo opportunities at the World Series and All-Star Games to picture rival players on the same card. Certainly the best of these in 1958 is card #418, "World Series Batting Foes," featuring Mickey Mantle and Hank Aaron posing in their slugging stances for the photographer. In a set in which the single-player cards of Mantle and Aaron command prices of $30 and $20, respectively, surely the combination of the two on the same card is going to be worth far more someday than its current $8.50 price.

VALUE

EX.-MT. CONDITION: Complete set, $400; common card, 35¢; Hall of Famers, $4–$8; Clemente, Maris, Koufax, $12–$14; Mays, Aaron, $20; Williams, $25–$27; Mantle, $30.
5-YEAR PROJECTION: Above average.

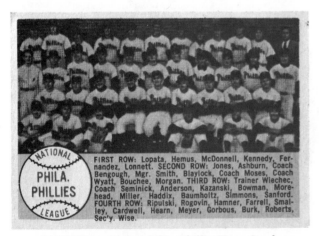

1958 Topps, Philadelphia Phillies Team Card

1958 Topps, Whitey Ford (back)

1958 Topps, Whitey Ford

1958 Topps, Harvey Kuenn, Al Kaline

1958 Topps, Warren Spahn, All-Star

1958 Topps, Ed Mayer

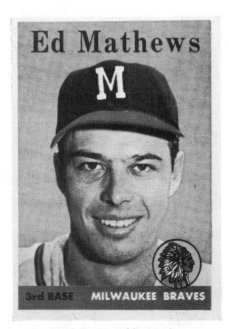

1958 Topps, Eddie Mathews

1958 Topps, Tony Kubek

1958 HIRES ROOT BEER

1958 Topps, Alex Grammas

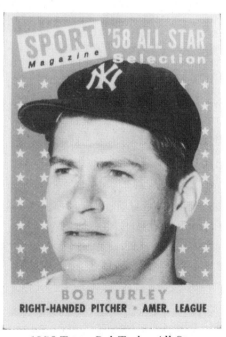

1958 Topps, Don Bessent

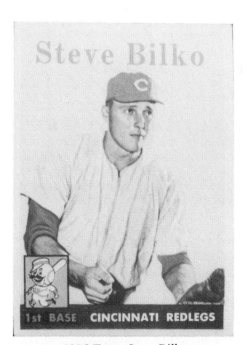

1958 Topps, Steve Bilko

1958 Topps, Bob Turley, All-Star

SPECIFICATIONS

SIZE: Card without tab, 2⁵/₁₆×3¹/₂″; card with tab, 2⁵/₁₆×7″. FRONT: Color photograph. BACK: Black printing on gray cardboard. DISTRIBUTION: Nationally, in cartons of root beer.

HISTORY

The Hires root beer set is one of the more interesting and unusual baseball card issues of the late 1950s. A long, tapering tab, attached to the card at a perforation line at the bottom of the card, was designed to hold the card in a carton of root beer. The tab offered, for a dime and two bottle caps, membership in the Hires Baseball Club, with a book of major league baseball tips and a "valuable membership card." Cards with the tab still attached are considerably more scarce—and more desirable—than cards without. For cards with the tab intact, a premium value of about 33 percent can be added to the prices quoted below. The design of the card itself is novel, featuring a photograph of the player as if viewed through the knothole in a fence. The photos are quite heavily retouched, to accentuate the colors. A black strip below the "fence" contains the player's name, team, and position. Card backs feature a Hires root beer bottle at left, and a bottle cap with the card number in the upper right. A player biography appears at center, and in a box to the right are personal data on the player. The Hires root beer set is peculiarly numbered, with card numbers from 10 to 76. Since card #69 was not issued, the complete set consists of 66 cards.

FOR

Though it was a nationally distributed set, the '58 Hires cards were produced in limited numbers, making it a popular and challenging collecting goal. The design is novel and attractive.

AGAINST

Cards are hard to find in original condition with tabs.

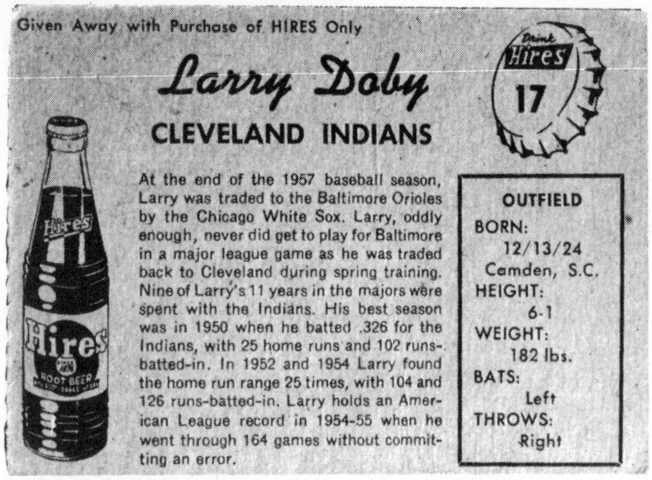
Given Away with Purchase of HIRES Only
Larry Doby
CLEVELAND INDIANS
Drink Hires
17
At the end of the 1957 baseball season, Larry was traded to the Baltimore Orioles by the Chicago White Sox. Larry, oddly enough, never did get to play for Baltimore in a major league game as he was traded back to Cleveland during spring training. Nine of Larry's 11 years in the majors were spent with the Indians. His best season was in 1950 when he batted .326 for the Indians, with 25 home runs and 102 runs-batted-in. In 1952 and 1954 Larry found the home run range 25 times, with 104 and 126 runs-batted-in. Larry holds an American League record in 1954-55 when he went through 164 games without committing an error.
OUTFIELD
BORN: 12/13/24 Camden, S.C.
HEIGHT: 6-1
WEIGHT: 182 lbs.
BATS: Left
THROWS: Right
Hires
ROOT BEER
1958 Hires Root Beer, Larry Doby (back)

NOTEWORTHY CARDS
Though there are only a handful of superstars—Duke Snider, Pee Wee Reese, Don Drysdale, Willie Mays, and Hank Aaron—in the Hires set, many of the popular home team players of the era are represented.

VALUE
EX.-MT. CONDITION: Complete set, $400; common card, $4; minor stars, $6–$8; Snider, Reese, Drysdale, $10–$15; Mays, Aaron, $75. 5-YEAR PROJECTION: Average.

1958 HIRES ROOT BEER TEST SET

SPECIFICATIONS
SIZE: Card without tab, $2\frac{5}{16}\times3\frac{1}{2}''$; card with tab, $2\frac{5}{16}\times7''$. FRONT: Sepia-toned photograph. BACK: Black printing on gray cardboard. DISTRIBUTION: Limited geographic areas, in cartons of soda.

HISTORY
Collectors generally refer to this distinctly separate baseball card issue by the Charles E. Hires Company in 1958 as a test issue. The eight-card set was released only in selected cities, probably corresponding to the team of the players pictured. The test set has the same physical characteristics as the regular 66-card Hires set of 1958 and was distributed the same way—in soda cartons. The cards were issued with a long, tapering tab at the bottom, which was separated from the card itself by a perforation. The tab was designed to be stuck into a soda carton. The tab offered membership in the Hires Baseball Club. Test-issue cards with the tab intact are considerably rarer than cards without the tab, and have a value 50 percent higher than the prices quoted below, which are for cards without tab. On the whole, the '58 Hires test set is considerably scarcer than its regular-issue counterpart. Card fronts feature a sepia-toned photograph of the player set against a solid yellow or orange background. The player's name appears in brown script lettering at the top of the card, while the team and position are printed below the photo. Card backs are similar in layout to the regular-issue Hires set, with a box of personal data on the right and a player biographical sketch on the left. There is no card number on the test cards, or any Hires logos or other identification. The Hires name appears only on the detachable tab.

FOR
A rare nationally issued test set.

AGAINST
Hard to find in original condition, with tab.

NOTEWORTHY CARDS
There is only one really big name in the '58 Hires test issue, Willie Mays. The other players in the set are Johnny Antonelli, Jim Busby, Chico Fernandez, Bob Friend, Vernon Law, Stan Lopata, and Al Pilarcik.

VALUE
EX.-MT. CONDITION: Complete set, $400; common card, $45; Mays, $150. 5-YEAR PROJECTION: Below average.

1958 KAHN'S

SPECIFICATIONS
SIZE: 3¼×4". FRONT: Black-and-white photograph. BACK: Black printing on white cardboard. DISTRIBUTION: Ohio-Pennsylvania area, in packages of Kahn's meats.

HISTORY
A third team was added to the Kahn's line-up in 1958, with the Phillies joining the Pirates and the Reds in a 29-card issue. Card fronts remained virtually identical to those of the previous years: a borderless black-and-white photograph with facsimile autograph, above a white strip with a Kahn's advertisement. Card backs, for the first time, had printing on them, a few short paragraphs titled "My Greatest Thrill in Baseball." Once again, cards were unnumbered. Like other Kahn's issues, the cards have a wax coating to protect them from the meat (or protect the meat from the ink on the cards). The cards were inserted in packages of Kahn's wieners and other meat products.

FOR
Scarce regional cards for team collector.

AGAINST
Lack of originality in design. High cost per card.

NOTEWORTHY CARDS
Three of the 1958 Kahn's cards are somewhat scarcer than the rest of the set: Wally Post, Charlie Rabe, and Frank Thomas. Hall of Famers Roberto Clemente and Frank Robinson are part of the set.

VALUE
EX.-MT. CONDITION: Complete set $650; common card, $20–$25; stars, $30–$40; Post, Rabe, Thomas, $45–$50; Robinson, $75; Clemente, $100. 5-YEAR PROJECTION: Below average.

1958 BELL BRAND DODGERS

SPECIFICATIONS

SIZE: 3×4″. FRONT: Sepia-toned photograph. BACK: Black printing on white cardboard. DISTRIBUTION: Southern California, inserted in packages of Bell Brand snack chips.

HISTORY

The first and rarest of four baseball card issues by the Bell Brand snack chip company of Los Angeles, the 1958 set consisted of 10 cards. The Bell cards were just one of several regional issues welcoming the Dodgers' and the Giants' delivery of major league baseball to California in 1958. All 10 of the '58 Bell cards feature Los Angeles Dodgers, including Roy Campanella, who was critically injured in an off-season auto accident in 1957 and never played for the team in California. Distribution of the 1958 cards was erratic, and several of them are considered scarce today. Because they feature members of one of baseball's most popular teams of the 1950s, all of the cards are popular. Design of the 1958 Bells is interesting and somewhat unusual for a baseball card. A sepia-toned photograph of the player is "framed" in a green woodgrain border. A facsimile autograph, also in green, is printed across the face of the photo. The player's name is printed in brown in a white plate at the bottom of the frame. Card backs feature a traditional mix of player personal information, year-by-year major league statistics, and a short career summary. A Bell logo appears at the bottom of the card. The Bell issue carries no card numbers.

FOR

Scarce regional issue of a popular team.

AGAINST

Cards are quite expensive and elusive. Odd size is a problem.

NOTEWORTHY CARDS

Virtually all 10 of the '58 Bell Dodgers cards feature star players. Value,

1958 Bell Brand Dodgers,
Roy Campanella (back)

though, is based more on scarcity. Distribution of the cards was evidently not equal, and some are scarcer than others. At the top of the scarcity list is Gino Cimoli, who was traded to the St. Louis Cardinals in mid-1958. As was often the case with one-team regional cards, when Cimoli was traded, his card was withdrawn from distribution, creating an instant rarity. Johnny Podres and Duke Snider are also considered quite scarce.

VALUE

EX.-MT. CONDITION: Complete set, $450; common card, $20–$35; Koufax, Campanella, Drysdale, $50; Cimoli, Snider, Podres, $75. 5-YEAR PROJECTION: Average.

1958 SAN FRANCISCO CALL-BULLETIN GIANTS

SPECIFICATIONS

SIZE: 2×4″. FRONT: Black and orange photograph. BACK: Black printing on orange cardboard. DIS-

TRIBUTION: San Francisco area, in daily newspaper.

HISTORY

The *San Francisco Call-Bulletin,* a daily newspaper, issued this 25-card set to welcome the San Francisco Giants upon their move from New York in 1958. The cards were inserted into issues of the paper early in the spring. Printed on rather thin orange cardboard, the cards feature on the front a black and orange photograph of the player, with his name and position in a black strip on the bottom. The lower third of the card is a detachable numbered stub used in playing a lottery-type giveaway game sponsored by the newspaper. Cards with the tab still attached are worth a premium of 35 percent or so over the values quoted below, which are for cards without the game stub. Backs of the Call-Bulletin set feature a San Francisco Giants home schedule. Backs of the stub portion of the card advertise the giveaway game and a local radio station.

FOR

A rather scarce regional issue that's popular with Giants collectors.

AGAINST

The cards are really quite unattractive, and somewhat expensive.

NOTEWORTHY CARDS

There is a rookie card of Orlando Cepeda in the set, as well as Giants star Willie Mays, but the real rarity in the set is the Tom Bowers card. Bowers was a hot pre-season pitching prospect for the Giants, but actually spent the 1958 season in the minor leagues. In fact, Bowers never pitched an inning of major league baseball and this is the only baseball card on which he appears. Knowledgeable collectors believe the Bowers card was never actually issued in the newspaper, the surviving examples having come from sources at the paper. Bobby Thomson appears in the set, though he spent the '58 season with the Chicago Cubs.

VALUE

EX.-MT. CONDITION: Complete set, $250; common card, $6–$8; Thomson, Cepeda, $12–$15; Bowers, $20–$25; Mays, $60. 5-YEAR PROJECTION: Below average.

1958 UNION OIL

SPECIFICATIONS
SIZE: 2½×3½". FRONT: Black-and-white photograph. BACK: Black printing on white cardboard. DISTRIBUTION: Sacramento area, cards given away with purchases at gas stations.

HISTORY
The Union Oil Company, through its Union 76 gas stations, has a long history of baseball memorabilia issues, including cards, posters, pin-ups, and booklets for both minor league and major league baseball. The company's first baseball card issue was in 1958 and was a modest ten-card effort representing players on the Sacramento Solons team of the Pacific Coast League. The cards feature a borderless, black-and-white posed-action photo of the player, under which, in a white strip at the bottom of the card, were the player's name, team, and position. Card backs repeat the name and position, and include the player's age, height, and weight, along with abbreviated statistics of the previous season, a "Union 76 Sports Club" pennant ad, and a notice that the card is good for admission to a Solons game on a specified date. Cards are unnumbered. The cards are quite scarce, but since they depict minor league players, are not extremely costly.

FOR
Scarce regional issue with lots of former major leaguers.

AGAINST
Minor league cards are just not very popular with collectors.

NOTEWORTHY CARDS
Most of the players in the '58 Union set are former major leaguers—Dick Cole, Jim Greengrass, Nippy Jones, Carlos Paula, Kal Segrist, and Sibbi Sisti; three of the others would soon play in the majors—Marshall Bridges, Al Heist, and Joe Stanka; of all the Sacramento Solon players in the 1958 Union Oil set, only one, Bud Watkins, never played baseball in the major leagues.

VALUE
EX.-MT. CONDITION: Complete set, $90; common card, $9. 5-YEAR PROJECTION: Below average.

1958 BOND BREAD BUFFALO BISONS

SPECIFICATIONS
SIZE: 2½×3½". FRONT: Black-and-white photograph. BACK: Black printing on white cardboard. DISTRIBUTION: Buffalo, N.Y., area with Bond bakery products.

HISTORY
One of the smaller minor league baseball card sets of the late 1950s, the nine-card Bond bread issue is still popularly collected. This is because all of the players in the set were former or future major league performers. All of the players in the '58 Bond set are depicted as members of the Buffalo Bisons, the Class AAA (International League) farm club of the Kansas City A's. The cards have an interesting touch for TV trivia fans, because they carry an ad for the old adventure series *Casey Jones* in the bottom margin on the front. Above the ad is a black-and-white photo of the player, while his name and position appear in the margin at top. The bottom half of the card back features an ad for the Bond bakery, and shows a loaf of bread and a box of pastry. The top half of the card has personal data on the player and what is, for baseball cards, an extremely personal write-up on the player, including his home address and the names and ages of his children.

FOR
Nice little minor league set, much more difficult to find than it is to pay for.

AGAINST
It's a minor league set, in black-and-white at a time when most cards were in color.

NOTEWORTHY CARDS
The best-known player in the set is Luke Easter, former Negro league standout who played half a dozen seasons with the Cleveland Indians in the 1940s and 1950s and then played another several seasons of minor league ball. Most collectors feel the '58 Bond card of Easter was not distributed in as large a number as the other eight cards in the set. Also in the set is manager Phil Cavaretta, whose playing career stretched from 1934 through 1955 and who had managed the Chicago Cubs from 1951 to 1953.

VALUE
EX.-MT. CONDITION: Complete set, $75; common card, $5; Cavaretta, $8; Easter, $25. 5-YEAR PROJECTION: Below average.

1957 TOPPS

SPECIFICATIONS
SIZE: 2½×3½". FRONT: Color photograph. BACK: Blue and red printing on gray cardboard. DISTRIBUTION: Nationally, in 1¢ and 5¢ packs of bubblegum.

HISTORY
What has become today's sandard size for baseball cards—2½×3½"—was adopted by Topps as the format for its 1957 set. Though the cards were reduced in size by some 11 percent from the Topps issues of 1952–1956, the set size was increased from 340 cards to 407 cards, a 20 percent jump. The 1967 set also marked the first use for Topps of "real" color photos, rather than the hand-colored black-and-white photos that had been used on previous issues. The set contained a pleasing mix of portrait and posed-action shots among the players, all set in various stadiums. There was no fancy design to the '57 Topps, just big sharp photos over which the player's name, team, and position were printed in various combinations of yellow, white, red, and blue. All of this was surrounded by a white border. There was a major innovation on the back of the '57 set; for the first time, Topps included complete major league (or minor league, in the case of "rookie cards") statistics on a year-by-

year basis rather than just stats for the previous season and cumulative lifetime figures. Baseball card collectors have been taking this feature for granted for more than 25 years, but it was not until 1957 that it was first used. On those cards which had room above the stats there was a baseball quiz cartoon. The rest of the back contained biographical details of the player, a short career sketch, and the familiar baseball with card number inside. There are three levels of scarcity in the 1957 Topps set. Interestingly, in 1957, the final series was not the most scarce, as is generally the case. In '57 the fourth series turned out to be the scarce one. Cards #265–#352 are much less often encountered than those of the first three series (#1–#264), or the fifth series (#353–#407). Consequently, they are much more expensive, costing about five times as much as cards in the other series. Fifth series cards are priced just a bit above those in the first three series, but they are actually harder to find than the small price difference would indicate. Again in 1957, Topps produced team cards. A slightly bigger photo was used than in previous years, and it was set in a gold frame with a "plaque" giving the team name on front. A color team logo appears in the lower-right corner. Identification of the players in the photo is on the back of the card. For the second straight year, American and National League presidents William Harridge and Warren Giles appeared in the '57 Topps set, though this year they were joined together on a single card.

Topps produced four unnumbered checklist cards for its 1957 set, and today they are among the most sought-after cards of the 50's, but generally only in unmarked condition. Each checklist covers two consecutive series of cards, but they overlap, covering Series 1–2, Series 2–3, Series 3–4, and Series 4–5. Each is successively scarcer than those before it, and an Ex.-Mt. unchecked Series 4–5 list is the most valuable card in the 1957 Topps set.

FOR

Clean design; big, clear photos; and the challenge of completing a set that includes 88 scarce cards have made the 1957 Topps set a great collector favorite. As the first of the now-standard 2½×3½″ cards, it is a popular starting point for collectors of modern card sets. In relation to some more recent cards, the prices of 1957 Topps cards are quite moderate.

AGAINST

From a collector's standpoint, the set is perfect; it has no faults.

NOTEWORTHY CARDS

Again in 1957, with Topps having a virtual monopoly in the baseball card field, all of the game's big stars were present—except Stan Musial. Hall of Famers Brooks and Frank Robinson, and Don Drysdale had their "rookie cards" in the 1957 Topps set, as did well-known players Jim Bunning, Bill Mazeroski, Rocky Colavito, and Tony Kubek. The scarce fourth series contains high-demand cards of Brooks Robinson and Sandy Koufax, along with the popular New York Giants and Brooklyn Dodgers team cards in their last years in the Gotham area. Two of the superstar cards in the 1957 Topps are worth noting. Card #20, Hank Aaron, is an error card; a reversed printing negative makes it look like Aaron is batting left-handed. If you look at the famous #44 on his uniform, though, you can see "Hammerin' Hank" wasn't trying to fool the photographer; the numbers are backwards. A different sort of thing makes Mickey Mantle's card #95 especially interesting. When Mantle's photo was taken, there was a man in sport shirt and slacks standing behind him, and the end of Mantle's bat appears at about the man's belt line. In an effort not to distract from the picture of Mantle on the card, Topps artists tried to airbrush the man out of the picture, by blending him into the background. The effort wasn't as effective as hoped in the early printing; the man remained too visible and Topps went back to the airbrush to obscure him some more. Today '57 Topps Mantle cards can be found with and without the man in the background. There is also a wrong-photo card in the '57 set: the picture on the Jerry Snyder card (#22) is actually a photo of teammate Ed FitzGerald,

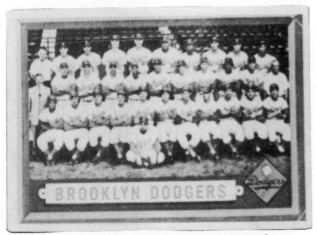

1957 Topps, Brooklyn Dodgers Team Card

1957 Topps, New York Yankees Hitters

who also appears on his own card, #367.

OUR FAVORITE CARD

It's a tie between the two multi-player feature cards which returned to Topps sets for the first time since 1954. Two of the fifth series cards depict more than one player. "Dodger Sluggers" shows an awesome array of batting power: Carl Furillo, Gil Hodges, Roy Campanella, and Duke Snider. The quartet was photographed kneeling and leaning on their bats before the familiar advertising fences of Ebbets Field. "Yankees' Power Hitters" gives us a glimpse into the Yankee dugout, where Mickey Mantle and Yogi Berra stand on the steps, bats on shoulders. These two cards were extremely popular with the youngsters in 1957, and remain popular with collectors today, worth about $15 each in top grade.

VALUE

EX.-MT. CONDITION: Complete set, $700; common card, 75¢; common card #265–#352, $2.50; Hall of Famers, $4–$10; Williams, Mays, Aaron, Frank Robinson, $30; Mantle, $45; Brooks Robinson, Sandy Koufax, $60; Checklists 1–2, 2–3, $20; Checklist 3–4, $45; Checklist 4–5, $75. 5-YEAR PROJECTION: Above average.

1957 KAHN'S

SPECIFICATIONS

SIZE: 3¼×4″. FRONT: Black-and-white photograph. BACK: Blank. DISTRIBUTION: Cincinnati-Pittsburgh areas, in packages of Kahn's meats.

HISTORY

The Kahn's baseball card set was expanded to 29 cards in 1957 with the addition of Pittsburgh Pirates players to the Cincinnati Reds in the set. Format of the cards was identical to the previous year: a black-and-white photo with facsimile autograph on the front, with a white strip at bottom carrying a Kahn's ad. To distinguish the 1957 Reds players from the 1956 cards you need a visual checklist. Once again in 1957, card backs are blank and the cards are unnumbered. Cards were inserted in packages of wieners and other Kahn's meat products.

FOR

Nice early regional sets for the team collector.

AGAINST

Relatively high cost per card precludes set collecting by all but the most serious collector.

NOTEWORTHY CARDS

With the inclusion of Pirates players in the 1957 Kahn's set, cards were produced of Roberto Clemente and other Buc stars, including a "rookie card" of Bill Mazeroski. The Dick Groat card can be found with a facsimile autograph reading "Richard Groat," or with the name "Dick Groat" printed.

VALUE

EX.-MT. CONDITION: Complete set, $750; common card, $20–$25; stars, $30–$40; Frank Robinson, $50–$75; Clemente, $100. 5-YEAR PROJECTION: Below average.

1956 TOPPS

SPECIFICATIONS

SIZE: 2⅝×3¾″. FRONT: Color-added black-and-white photos. BACK: Red, black, and green ink on white or gray cardboard. DISTRIBUTION: Nationally, in 1¢ and 5¢ packs of bubblegum.

HISTORY

For the second year in a row, Topps produced a horizontal-format card set in 1956. Somewhat similar in design to the '55s, the 1956 set features a portrait photo of the player with an "action" shot in the background. Unlike the 1955 issue, however, on which the player pictures were set against a plain colored background, the 1956 cards featured a stadium setting (sometimes cleverly faked or using two different photos). A white outline around the portrait photo separated the player from the background. Both of the photos used on the 1956 cards are black-and-white shots which have been hand-tinted by Topps artists to look like color photography. The smaller player photos make an interesting study. Some of them were used on more than one card; for instance, card #110, Yogi Berra, shows the Yankees catcher at home plate,

1957 Topps, Bob Lemon

1956 Topps, William Harridge (front)

waiting for a throw, while a Cleveland Indian slides in safely. On card #163, Gene Woodling, there is a closer view of the sliding Indian—Woodling—from the same photo, but Berra has been airbrushed out of the picture. Some of the larger player portraits are exactly the same as those on their 1955 cards, and even in some cases, on the 1954 issue. A two-color rectangular panel in one of the upper corners displays the player's name, team, and position. Card backs feature a three-panel cartoon picturing details from

the player's career. Biographical data appears above, and career stats, below. Cards #1 to #180 will be found with either white or gray backs, but few collectors differentiate between the two in terms of value or collectibility. Cards #181 to #260 are considered somewhat more scarce and a bit more valuable than the rest of the set. This was Topps' first year of producing baseball cards without competition from Bowman (whom they had bought out the previous year) or any other national issuer, but the company was not resting on its laurels. They had increased the number of cards in the set from the 206 of the previous year to 340 cards in '56.

FOR

A nice, large set with virtually all of the game's big stars. Cards are attractive and not excessively scarce or expensive.

AGAINST

Few collectors have anything bad to say about the '56 Topps set; it is almost always in the top 10 sets when collectors are polled as to their favorites. The cards do have a tendency to lose their surface shine or "gloss" rather easily, though, and condition-conscious collectors may find it a challenge to complete a set without some scruffed cards.

NOTEWORTHY CARDS

Without major competition in the baseball card field, Topps had the

superstars all to itself in 1956. Almost. Stan Musial does not appear in the '56 Topps set. There is a Mantle card, though, for the first time since 1953. Topps "sweetened" its 1956 set with three types of cards that were new to the hobby. The most significant from the standpoint of collectors today are the team cards, the first time team cards had been issued as part of the regular set. Sure, the pictures were so small you couldn't identify anybody, but Topps did identify the players at the bottom of the card. Six of the team cards can be found in three different collectible variations: 1) with the team name centered in the black band in the middle of the card, 2) with team name to the left in the black band, and 3) with the date 1955 included in the black band. The six team cards found this way are the Braves, the Cubs, the Phillies, the Orioles, the Indians, and the Redlegs. Another innovation, one that was significant to the kids who originally collected the cards, was the issue of two unnumbered checklist cards. For the first time in 1956, collectors knew early on how many cards would be in a complete set and which players they were missing. Unfortunately for today's collectors, the checklist cards weren't too important to kids in 1956. You only needed two of them, and they were only good to be marked on in the little boxes to indicate who you had and who you didn't. After you had both checklist cards, you threw them away when you found them in gum packs, because

1956 Topps, William Harridge (back)

1956 Topps, Robin Roberts

1956 Topps, John "Windy" McCall

they were no good for trading. Today, the checklist cards are the scarcest of the 1956 Topps series, and in much demand by collectors, especially in unchecked condition. Another pair of cards that was unpopular with kids in 1956 (and collectors today, for that matter) were cards #1 and #2 in the set, the presidents of the American and National League, William Harridge and Warren Giles. These cards also tended to be the first inserted in the spokes of kids' bicycles.

OUR FAVORITE CARD

The 1956 Topps card of Hank Aaron. The portrait photo is the exact same picture which Topps used on its 1954 and 1955 Aaron cards, but that isn't unique among 1956 cards. What is special about the Aaron card is that you get two superstars on one card. The small "action" photo actually is of Willie Mays. In changing the photo from black-and-white to color, the Topps artist merely painted a Braves uniform on Mays, shown as he prepares to slide into home plate. The photo is a rather well-known picture of Mays, and had been used by Dell in its 1955 *Who's Who in Baseball* book.

VALUE

EX.-MINT CONDITION: Complete set, $600; common card, 75¢; team card (no date) $2.50; dated team card, $6; superstars, $8–$25; Aaron, Mays, Williams, $30; Mantle, $60; checklists, $20. 5-YEAR PROJECTION: Above average.

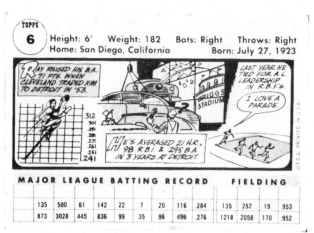

1956 Topps, Ray Boone (back)

1956 Topps, Bill Wight

1956 Topps, Dave Philley

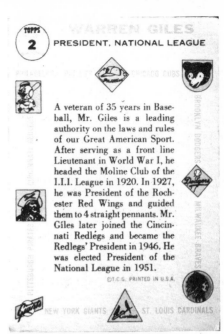

1956 Topps, Warren Giles (back)

1956 Topps, Ruben Gomez

1956 Topps, Bob Feller (back)

1956 Topps, Warren Giles (front)

1956 KAHN'S

SPECIFICATIONS

SIZE: 3¼×4″. FRONT: Black-and-white photograph. BACK: Blank. DISTRIBUTION: Cincinnati area, in packages of Kahn's meat products.

HISTORY

In its second season, Kahn's adopted the format and distribution that it would follow into the late 1960s with its baseball card issues. The set was expanded to 15 cards in 1956, each featuring a black-and-white photo of the player in a posed-action shot. A half-inch white band below the photo contained a Kahn's ad. A facsimile autograph on the front of the card was the only identification. Backs were blank, and the cards were unnumbered. Once again in 1956, only Cincinnati Redlegs players were included in the set. The 1956 Kahn's cards were inserted into packages of wieners and other meat products. They are not nearly as scarce as the '55 issue, but are a challenging set, nonetheless.

FOR

A scarce and valuable regional set of special interest to Reds team collectors.

AGAINST

High cost per card makes assembling a complete set tough.

NOTEWORTHY CARDS

The 1956 Kahn's set has the true "rookie card" of Frank Robinson. Robinson won the National League Rookie of the Year award in 1956, but didn't debut on a Topps baseball card until 1957. All the other well-known Reds of the mid-1950s are in the set.

VALUE

EX.-MINT CONDITION: Complete set, $400; common card, $25; stars, $30–$35; Robinson, $75–$100. 5-YEAR PROJECTION: Average, or a bit below.

1956 RODEO MEATS KANSAS CITY A'S

SPECIFICATIONS

SIZE: 2½×3½″. FRONT: Color photograph. BACK: Black printing on gray cardboard. DISTRIBUTION: Kansas City area, in packages of hot dogs.

HISTORY

In 1956, for the second and last year, Rodeo Meats company of Kansas City, Missouri, issued a baseball card set of the Kansas City A's. Unlike the previous year's issue, which had 38 different players, the 1956 Rodeo set is limited to 13 cards. All 13 of the players on the '56 cards also appeared in the '55 set, and since neither set is dated, an examination of the card backs is necessary to determine the year of issue. Backs of the 1956 issues do not have an advertisement for a card album. Otherwise, both years' cards are virtually identical. Fronts of the 1956 Rodeo cards have a heavily retouched photo of the player at center. There is a white strip with the player's name printed in the lower center of the photo. At left is a blue-and-white Rodeo logo. The photo is surrounded by a narrow white border. The cards are unnumbered and contain no player data or stats.

FOR

Smaller issue than the '55, with no confusing variations. Team collectors like it.

AGAINST

Too similar to the 1955 set in design. Cards are also quite expensive.

NOTEWORTHY CARDS

In trimming the 1956 issue to 13 cards, only about one third of the 1955 effort, Rodeo kept most of the team's better-known stars, including manager Lou Boudreau and such local favorites as Enos Slaughter, Vic Power, Bobby Shantz, and Gus Zernial.

VALUE

EX.-MINT CONDITION: Complete set, $400; common card, $30; Boudreau, Slaughter, $60. 5-YEAR PROJECTION: Below average.

1955 TOPPS

SPECIFICATIONS

SIZE: 3¾×2⅝″. FRONT: Color. BACK: Black, red, and green on white stock. DISTRIBUTION: Nationally, with bubble gum.

HISTORY

The smallest regular-issue Topps set, the 1955 offering, at only 206 cards, was originally intended to have at least 210 cards. Cards #175, #186, #203, and #209 were never issued. It is believed that ongoing litigation between Topps and Bowman over contracts for use of certain players' photos accounts for the missing four cards; they were probably players whom the courts "awarded" to Bowman on an exclusive basis. Since this was a year before Topps introduced its first checklist cards, the omission of these four cards drove kids crazy in 1955 looking for the quartet of cards that could never be found. It is unknown whether Topps limited its regular 1955 set to 210 cards because it was concurrently issuing the 66-card (132-player) "Double Header" set, or whether the set was prematurely cut off by Topps' "card wars" victory over Bowman that year. Their subsequent purchase of the Philadelphia-based company eliminated the only major competition Topps had. The set is generally regarded to contain three levels of difficulty, cards #1 to #159 being the most common, cards #151 to #160 being less common, and the "high numbers," #161 to #210, being scarce.

FOR

Topps' first horizontal-format player cards, the 1955 issue was essentially a rearrangement of the popular and successful 1954 design. The three levels of scarcity make it a challenging set for collectors to complete, though none of the cards is so rare as to make the set unattainable.

AGAINST

Topps recycled many of the portraits and/or action photos from its 1954 issue in creating the 1955 set. In addition, many of the portraits would be seen once again in 1956. Some portraits, like that of Henry Aaron, were used three years in a row. As luck would have it, superstar collectors will find many of the high-demand cards are in the scarce high number series, including Hall of Famers Roberto Clemente, Willie Mays, Yogi Berra, and Duke Snider, as well as Phil Rizzuto and Gil Hodges. Snider, as the last card in the set (#210), was easily damaged when cards were rubber-banded in stacks, and is thus hard to find in true Mint condition.

NOTEWORTHY CARDS

Rookie cards of Sandy Koufax, #123, worth about $30; Harmon Killebrew, #124, $15; and Roberto Clemente, #164, $75. Card #152 in the 1955 Topps set is the only baseball card ever issued of college football star Harry Agganis. The "Golden Greek" was an All-American (1951) quarterback at Boston University, but opted for a career in professional baseball upon graduation, signing with the Boston Red Sox for a reported $35,000 in 1953. In his second season of pro ball (1954), he was the starting first baseman for Boston. His career was ended on June 27, 1955, when he died of pneumonia complications at age 25.

OUR FAVORITE CARD

Jack Parks (#23). Though he appeared in both Topps' regular-issue and "Double Header" sets in 1955, Jack Parks never played an inning of major league baseball. A perpetual understudy to Milwaukee Braves catcher Del Crandall, Parks was never able to crack the line-up. Dozens of similar examples of players appearing on baseball cards without ever making the major leagues can be found in Topps sets from the early 1950s through the early 1970s.

VALUE

EX.-MINT CONDITION: Complete set, $500; common card, #1–#150, 75¢; #151–#160, $1.25; #161–#210, $3. 5-YEAR PROJECTION: Above average.

1955 Topps, Willie Mays (back)

1955 Topps, Tom Qualters (front)

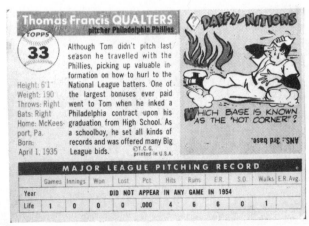

1955 Topps, Tom Qualters (back)

1955 Topps, Billy Gardner

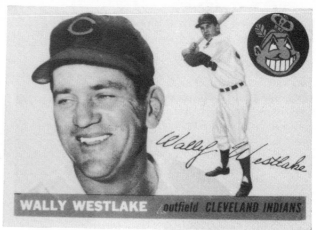

1955 Topps, Wally Westlake

1955 Topps, Bob Miller

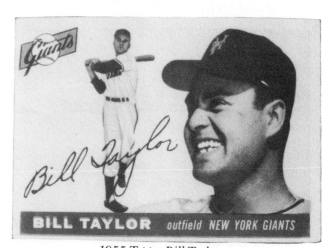

1955 Topps, Bill Taylor

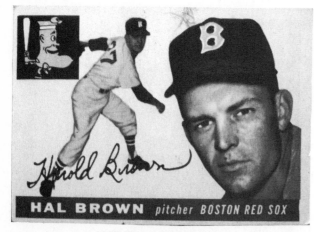

1955 Topps, Hal Brown

1955 Topps, Bob Milliken

1955 TOPPS DOUBLE HEADERS

SPECIFICATIONS

SIZE: $2^1/_{16} \times 4^7/_8$". FRONT: Color painting. BACK: Black, red, and blue printing on white cardboard. DISTRIBUTION: Nationally, in 1¢ packs of bubblegum.

HISTORY

Never reluctant to borrow a good baseball card idea from the past, Topps issued a second set of baseball cards in 1955 called "Baseball Double Headers." The idea was "borrowed" from a Mecca cigarette card set of 1911. The Topps '55 Double Headers set consists of 66 cards and 132 different players, all of whom appeared in the "regular" '55 Topps set, as well. The cards are perforated about one third of the way up, allowing them to be easily folded over, as they were when they were inserted into penny bubblegum packs. When the card is open to its full $2^1/_{16} \times 4^7/_8$" size, there is a color painting of a baseball player, set against a stadium background. When the top of the card is folded down over the painting, the upper body of a second player appears over the lower legs and feet of the first painting, but with a different stadium background. In both configurations, a small white rectangular panel in the upper left contains the player's name in black, and his position and team in red. Card backs give short career summaries for both players, as well as 1954 and lifetime stats for each. A unique feature of the Double Header cards is that when cards are placed side by side in reverse numerical order (card #21–#22, #19–#20, #17–#18, etc.), the stadium backgrounds form a continuous scene, making it look as if the players are all on the same baseball diamond. The stadium background bears a strong resemblance to old Ebbets Field in Brooklyn. While the 1955 Topps Double Headers are significantly more scarce than regular-issue '55 Topps cards, they do not command as high a premium as might be expected. The cards are simply not that popular.

*1955 Topps Double Headers,
Jackie Robinson, Don Hoak*

FOR

In 1955, when there were very few baseball card collectors and most of them had never seen a 1911 Mecca Doublefolder, the Topps Double Header cards represented a unique concept. Back then, few kids realized that you could put the backgrounds together to form stadium scenes, but the idea of two players sharing common body parts was interesting. The cards are a real challenge to collect today, but, surprisingly, they can sometimes be found in complete sets of un-perforated cards, just as they were printed 30 years ago.

AGAINST

The paintings on the cards are really rather crude, and the necessity of players sharing feet and legs sometimes results in pictures that are out of perspective. If the original owners of the cards played with them too much, the perforations frequently tore, resulting in a lack of high-grade examples of the cards for today's collectors. For a set that was nationally distributed just 30 years ago, the Double Headers are quite expensive per card.

NOTEWORTHY CARDS

Since the Double Headers contain only players who appeared in the lower-numbered series of '55 Topps cards, such superstars as Mays, Clemente, Snider, and Berra are not included. Hall of Famers who do appear in the set are Jackie Robinson, Ernie Banks, Warren Spahn, Henry Aaron, Monte Irvin, Ted Williams, Harmon Killebrew, and Al Kaline.

OUR FAVORITE CARD

Because of the predominance of right-handed hitters in baseball, a left-handed catcher is a rarity—his throwing arm would often be blocked by the batter when he attempted to pick off a base stealer. Nevertheless, there is a left-handed catcher pictured in the 1955 Topps Double Headers—Dale Long, of the Pittsburgh Pirates. Long is best remembered for creating a major league record by hitting home runs in eight consecutive ball games in 1956. The short write-up on back of the card says, "They were thinking of making a catcher out of left-handed Dale—thus this rare picture of him. He's a top prospect for the Buc First Base job this year." Even though he is pictured as a catcher on the Double Header card, his position is given as "1st base." Eventually, Dale Long did play two games as catcher, for the Chicago Cubs in 1958.

VALUE

EX.-MINT CONDITION: Complete set, $1,000; common card, $10; Irvin, $15; Banks, Kaline, Killebrew, Spahn, $38–$42; Williams, Robinson, $65–$70; Aaron, $100. 5-YEAR PROJECTION: Below average.

1955 BOWMAN

SPECIFICATIONS

SIZE: 3¾×2½". FRONT: Color photograph. BACK: Red and black printing on gray cardboard. DISTRIBUTION: Nationally, in 1¢ and 5¢ packages with bubblegum.

HISTORY

The 1955 Bowmans are an example of a baseball card set that collectors either like or dislike almost solely on the basis of its design. The cards, Bowman's only horizontal-format set, feature a gorgeous color photo of the player set into a simulated television screen border. A "plate" at the bottom of the screen says, "Color TV." The issue trades on the natural affiliation between baseball and television, and the rise in popularity of both televised baseball and color television in the mid-1950s. Many collectors don't realize that the idea of using a TV set as a baseball card design was not new with Bowman in 1955. Drake's bakery had used the concept in its regionally issued, 1950 black-and-white set. Eleven years later, Topps resurrected the idea for its 1966 football card issue. The only other design element on the front of the '55 Bowman cards is a small white stripe somewhere on the bottom half of the photo that contains the player's last name in black type. There are two distinctively different "wood finishes" on the TV cabinets that form the card's border. On cards #1 to #64, the wood is a light blonde color, while cards #65 to #320 have a darker wood tone. Photos on the cards are sharp and clear, and the color reproduction in the set was as good as any that would come along for many years, even though this was only the second major baseball card set to use actual color photos. It's interesting to note that all of the pictures in the 1955 Bowman set were shot in Philadelphia's Shibe Park, which in 1954 served as the home ball park for both the National League Phillies and the American League Athletics. Philadelphia, of course, was Bowman's home base. Card backs are also horizontal in arrangement. The card number appears in a baseball glove in the upper-

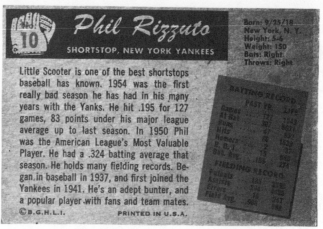

1955 Bowman, Phil Rizzuto (back)

1955 Bowman, Dee Fondy

1955 Bowman, Al Smith

COMPLETE BOOK OF COLLECTIBLE BASEBALL CARDS

left corner. To the right, in a black box are the player's name (in script type), position, and team. At right, in a gray-pink panel is the player's vital data. A red box at the lower right has—on most cards—statistics for the previous season and lifetime career. On other cards, notably the managers, coaches, umpires, and rookies, the box contains a baseball trivia question and answer. The large gray panel at left contains the traditional short baseball biography on many cards. On other cards, however, there is a short essay by the player in categories such as "My Biggest Thrill in Baseball," "My Advice to Youngsters," and "The Best Hitter (Pitcher, Fielding Play, etc.) I've Ever Seen." Some of these make for very interesting reading. There are two major degrees of scarcity within the set, cards #1 to #224 being relatively common, while the "high numbers," cards #225 to #320, are considerably scarcer. It is in these high numbers that one of the '55 Bowmans' most distinctive features appears—umpire cards. This was the first time in the 20th century that a baseball card set contained umpires. Umpires don't often appear in card sets for two principal reasons. First and foremost is that kids, who are the principal market for baseball cards, don't want to find umpire cards in their gum packs. The second reason is that umpires are forbidden by their contracts from accepting money or other considerations for commercial endorsements. The 31 umpire cards in the set contain one Hall of Famer (Jocko Conlon) and several former players. Bowman again used an innovative number system for its 1955 set. Basically, the cards are numbered in pairs by team, although there were numerous breakdowns in the plan. For example, cards #1 and #2 are New York Giants, cards #21 and #22 are Brooklyn Dodgers, etc. Overall, this scheme was followed throughout the low numbers, although there were exceptions. Why the system was chosen, though, is unclear. The 1955 Bowman set was the company's last. Before their planned 1956 baseball card set could be produced, the company had been bought out by Topps, their principal competitor. Topps thus achieved a virtual baseball card monopoly which went without serious challenge until 1963, and without successful challenge until

1981. The '55 Bowman set remains quite popular today and is relatively inexpensive to collect.

FOR
Collectors who don't find the concept of using a television set as a baseball card border to be too cutesy really like the set. It is well done and not too hard to complete.

AGAINST
Some collectors just don't like the format of the set. Besides, by 1955, Bowman had lost a large number of the game's stars to exclusive Topps baseball card contracts, and they did

not have the hot rookie cards that Topps did that year: Clemente, Koufax, and Killebrew.

NOTEWORTHY CARDS
About the only really big name Bowman had on an exclusive basis in its '55 set was Mickey Mantle, though they did have other Hall of Famers all to themselves that year: Bob Lemon, Ralph Kiner, George Kell, Robin Roberts, Bob Feller, Whitey Ford, Pee Wee Reese, Early Wynn, and Roy Campanella. There are a number of collectible variations in the set. Cards of big league brothers Milt (Red Sox) and Frank (Tigers) Bolling can be

1955 Bowman, Clyde Vollmer

1955 Bowman, Hobie Landrith

found with their numbers 48 and 204 interchanged. On the basis of Bowman's numbering scheme, the correct versions are #48, Milt Bolling, and #204, Frank Bolling. A similar error pair exists for nonbrother pitchers Don and Ernie Johnson. All cards #101 have the back of Orioles pitcher Don Johnson, though some have Ernie Johnson's picture on the front; the reverse is true on card #157, which features, in all cases, the Ernie Johnson back, but sometimes will be found with Don Johnson's picture on the front. The Erv Palica card, #195, can be found with (scarce) or without (common) a final line in the biography on back that reads, "Sent to Baltimore when Preacher Roe retired." Harvey Kuenn's card, #132, can be found with his name spelled correctly on the back (scarce), or incorrectly, as "Kueen." For all four of these error/variation pairs, the scarcer cards are worth about $4 in top grade, while the more common versions will bring $1 or so.

OUR FAVORITE CARD

Again it's a toss-up. You've got to love the write-up on the back of card #4 Eddie Waitkus. In his essay, "My Biggest Thrill in Baseball," the Baltimore Orioles first baseman begins, "In 1949 I was shot by a deranged girl...." Naturally, being gut-shot was not Waitkus' biggest thrill, but he goes on to say how he won the "Comeback Player of the Year" award. Another favorite card is one of the umpires, #267, Jim Honochick. For many years his card was priced right along with the rest of the umpires in the set, but then—almost as if the TV set design of the '55 Bowmans had been some kind of omen—Honochick landed a part in one of the more popular Lite Beer commercials . . . "Hey, you're Boog Powell!" Since then, the value of his card has been on the rise, and is now worth about twice the value of the "common" umps.

VALUE

EX.-MINT CONDITION: Complete set, $500; common card, #1–#224, 55¢; #225–#320, $2.25; common umpire, $4; minor stars, $4–$7; Hall of Famers, $5–$10; Campanella, Berra, $10–$15; Mays, Aaron, $25–$30; Mantle, $35; Banks, $45.
5-YEAR PROJECTION: Average.

1955 Bowman, Ed Rommel

1955 Bowman, William Summers

1955 RED MAN

1955 Red Man, Hoyt Wilhelm (back)

SPECIFICATIONS

SIZE: 3½×4″. FRONT: Color painting. BACK: Red printing on gray cardboard. DISTRIBUTION: Nationally, one card in each box of Red Man chewing tobacco.

HISTORY

Red Man failed to make any big changes in the fourth and final year of production of its baseball card sets. The 1955 Red Mans were the last baseball cards to be issued in conjunction with a tobacco product. Today it seems unlikely that baseball cards will ever again be associated with chewing or smoking tobacco; no company would want to face the howl of protest from parents who thought the company was trying to lure children to the use of tobacco by giving away baseball cards, and few players are so regardless of their public image as to allow their picture to be used on such a card. Thus, the '55 Red Mans mark the end of an era that had begun almost a century ago when the first baseball cards were inserted into packages of cigarettes in 1886. The real popularity of the Red Man cards, though, is that they are a rather scarce national issue of the 1950s, with plenty of stars and superstars in the set. Most collectors view the Red Mans as regional issues, and to the extent that chewing tobacco is much more popular in some sections of the country than others—the South and rural areas, for example— that is true. The cards were available nationwide, however, and they are quite popular with collectors. Though they are much less common than the 1955 cards of Topps or Bowman, the superstars in the Red Mans are priced much lower. While the common Red Mans are priced higher, fewer of them are needed to complete a set. Like the 1954 issue, the 1955 Red Man set has 50 cards, with no variations. J. Taylor Spink, editor of *The Sporting News*, selected 25 players from each of the major leagues to compose the "All-Star Series." Because of conflicting contracts with Bowman and Topps, there are fewer big name stars in the 1955 set than in some years, but most of the players are better-known performers of the Fifties. Design of the cards did not change at all in 1955. The basic format was still a borderless color painting—sometimes the same painting used in previous years' cards. In such cases, the background color was changed, or perhaps a stadium scene substituted for a blank background. A white box on one side of the card contains the card number ("American League Player" or "National League Player" #1–#25), player's name, personal data, and a career summary. The last year mentioned in the biography will identify the year of issue on cards that have had the tab removed from the bottom. The "tab" on a Red Man card is a white stripe, seven-sixteenths of an inch deep, that was designed to be cut off the card and mailed in with 49 others for a free replica major league cap. The popularity of this offer is attested to by the fact that so many Red Man cards are found today without their tabs. This is a problem for many collectors, because they generally like to find the Red Mans as they were issued—with tabs—and will usually pay an extra 25 percent to get them that way. Other collectors feel the tab was designed to be removed and since it doesn't affect the main portion of the card, those cards without tabs are perfectly acceptable. The only important information conveyed on the tab is the year of issue, which was put there because the offers for the free baseball caps expired each year, and Red Man apparently didn't want to redeem outdated tabs. All in all, the Red Man series is a popular and currently budget-priced specialty.

FOR

Cards are relatively low-priced, considering their scarcity. The paintings used are an attractive alternative to the photos that had become commonplace on other issues by that time—sort of a throwback to baseball cards' earlier days. Lots of stars on a nice big format.

AGAINST

Collecting Red Mans is tough for the condition-conscious hobbyist who insists on cards with tabs. The use and re-use of the same pictures makes the set somewhat unappealing for collectors of superstar cards. The nonstandard size of the cards is also a point against them.

NOTEWORTHY CARDS

There are only a few really big names among the eight Hall of Famers in the 1955 Red Man set: Willie Mays, Yogi Berra, and Duke Snider. Lots of home team favorites, though.

VALUE

EX.-MINT CONDITION: Complete set, $250; common card, $4; Hall of Famers, $8–$12; Berra, Snider, $15–$20; Mays, $30. 5-YEAR PROJECTION: Above average.

1955 STAHL MEYER

SPECIFICATIONS

SIZE: 3¼×4½". FRONT: Color added to black-and-white photograph. BACK: Red printing on white cardboard. DISTRIBUTION: Metropolitan New York area, single cards inserted in packages of hot dogs.

HISTORY

It's harder to tell the 1955 Stahl Meyer cards from the 1954s than it is to tell the 1954s from the 1953s. Both the 1955 and 1954 cards had a bright yellow border on the front of the card, and the players that appeared in both sets had the same pictures in each. To tell the difference, the card backs have to be consulted. The 1955 Stahl Meyers have a drawing of Mickey Mantle in the upper left, with an offer for a big league cap and pennant. The bottom half of the back of the 1955 cards is like the '54s; it offers a few vital statistics about the player, along with his career stats and those of the previous season. There is no card number. Card fronts, as mentioned, have a bright yellow border around the player's picture. The photos on the card were black-and-white pictures to which colors were added, a popular technique for baseball cards in the early 1950s. Below the photo is a box with the player's name printed and in facsimile autograph form. The Stahl Meyer set for 1955 again contains 12 cards, with four players from each of the major league teams then in the New York area.

FOR

Attractive and scarce regional cards of popular teams and players.

AGAINST

The cards are too much like the 1954 set, and too expensive.

NOTEWORTHY CARDS

The checklist for the 1955 Stahl Meyer set is identical to that for 1954, except the Willie Mays card has been replaced by a card of Dusty Rhodes. Today that may seem like an unusual switch; but Rhodes had been the hero of the 1954 World Series, with pinch-hit home runs and timely hits to provide the Giants with wins in the first three games of their four-game sweep against the Indians.

VALUE

EX.-MT. CONDITION: Complete set, $1,350; common card, $75; Hodges, Irvin, Rizzuto, $100; Snider, $150; Mantle, $500. 5-YEAR PROJECTION: Below average.

1955 KAHN'S

SPECIFICATIONS

SIZE: 3¼×4". FRONT: Black-and-white photograph. BACK: Blank. DISTRIBUTION: Cincinnati area, given away at amusement park.

HISTORY

The first of a long string of baseball card issues by Kahn's meat company, the 1955 set contained only six cards. An unusual feature of the '55 Kahn's is that the players—all Cincinnati Reds—are pictured in street clothes, rather than baseball uniforms, on the cards. Players are identified by a facsimile autograph on the front of the card. A white panel below the photo contains an ad for Kahn's. Backs are blank and the cards are unnumbered. Unlike later Kahn's issues, the 1955 cards were given away in a promotion at an amusement park in Cincinnati. This premier Kahn's set is very scarce, but, because players are shown in mufti, it's not as popular or as expensive as might otherwise be the case.

FOR

Rare cards for the team collector.

AGAINST

The players are not in uniform; the cards are very expensive.

NOTEWORTHY CARDS

Why not name all the players? There are only six: Gus Bell, Ted Kluszewski, Roy McMillan, Joe Nuxhall, Wally Post, and Johnny Temple.

VALUE

EX.-MT. CONDITION: Complete set, $1,250; common card, $200; Kluszewski, $300. 5-YEAR PROJECTION: Below average.

1955 JOHNSTON COOKIE BRAVES

SPECIFICATIONS

SIZE: 2⅞×4¹⁄₁₆". FRONT: Color added by hand to black-and-white photograph. BACK: Blue and red printing on white cardboard. DISTRIBUTION: Wisconsin, six-card panels in packages of cookies.

HISTORY

The third, and final, annual set of Milwaukee Braves baseball cards was produced by the Johnston cookie company in 1955. The set again is complete at 35 cards, including the players, manager, coaches, team doctor, trainer, and even the traveling secretary. The '55 Johnstons were distributed in an unusual manner. They were printed in strips of six cards, in an accordion-folder form, with self-covers. One strip of six cards was inserted into family-size boxes of Johnston cookies, and each folder had an ad to send in for the other series for 5¢ and a Johnston label or end flap. There are six strips of six cards each, for a total of 36 cards, but only 35 of them were different. Card #48, Andy Pafko, was included in both Series 2 and Series 4. The '55 Johnston cards were printed in a larger than standard size, on uncoated cardboard. Since they were meant to be cut apart from their original strips, they can be found today with a wide range in the degree of accuracy to which they were cut. Cut cards are most valuable when they are cut right on the blue dotted lines that divided the cards on the panel. Sloppy cutting greatly reduces the value of single cards. The '55 Johnston cards are most valuable when still in uncut panel form, though a surprising number of these folders have survived intact. To figure the premium value on an uncut strip, add 25 percent to the total value of the individual cards. Card fronts again featured color-tinted black-and-white photos taken at spring training, though the variety of poses is much improved over the 1954 cards. A box below the photo has a red Indian logo at left, and the player's name in printed and facsimile signature form. Card backs are quite similar to the 1953 and 1954 sets. Player personal data appears in a pink box at the top. An Indian silhouette at right has the card number (player's uniform number), while a strip nearly across the card has the team name. A player biography is in the center, while the stats from the previous two seasons are toward the bottom. A Johnston ad appears at the very bottom of the card. The '55s are the scarcest of the three Johnston sets.

FOR

Large-format, attractive cards of a popular team with lots of stars.

AGAINST

Hard to find in Mint condition because of low quality of cardboard and fact the cards had to be cut off panels.

NOTEWORTHY CARDS

Hall of Famers Henry Aaron, Warren Spahn, and Eddie Mathews.

OUR FAVORITE CARD

The 1955 Johnston cookie card of Braves traveling secretary Duffy Lewis is unique in baseball card history. Few of the kids collecting cards back then from boxes of Johnston cookies realized, though, that Lewis was a well-known player from the turn of the century. George "Duffy" Lewis was part of the Boston Red Sox famed outfield trio with Tris Speaker and Harry Hooper. He played with Boston from 1910 to 1917. He spent two more years with the Yankees and one with the Senators before retiring from the majors in 1921 with a lifetime .284 average. Lewis didn't look much like a big league ballplayer on his 1955 Johnston card, sitting in an office in an extremely loud red paisley-print shirt, but his card probably would have received more respect from young collectors in 1955 if they'd known that Duffy Lewis was the only man ever to pinch-hit for Babe Ruth.

VALUE

EX.-MT. CONDITION, NEATLY CUT FROM FOLDER: Complete set, $400; common card, $9; Mathews, Spahn, $17.50; Aaron, $75. 5-YEAR PROJECTION: Below average.

1955 HUNTER'S WIENERS CARDINALS

SPECIFICATIONS

SIZE: 2×4¾". FRONT: Full-color photo. BACK: Blank. DISTRIBUTION: St. Louis area, two cards per hot dog package.

HISTORY

The last of the Hunter's Wieners baseball cards featured an all-new format for 1955. Two photos of each player were included on each card, a posed-action shot and a smaller portrait. The player's facsimile autograph appears in a white panel below the photos, and below that, in white printing on red background, the player's name and short biographical details are included. As with the '54 issue, this last panel is sometimes found cut off the card to make it more like the size of then-current Topps and Bowman cards. Once again the company printed two cards per package, a total of 30 cards. Because the '55 Hunter's cards have square corners, they are more often found well cut than either of the two earlier issues. Still, well-trimmed cards, not cut into the design of the borderless photo, are worth considerably more than cards that were hacked off the package. In terms of specimens surviving in the hobby today, the 1955 Hunter's Wieners cards are the scarcest of the company's three issues.

FOR

Attractive format, all new photos, lots of lesser-known players to delight the team-collecting specialist.

AGAINST

Too often found poorly cut. High cost discourages complete set collecting.

NOTEWORTHY CARDS

Musial, Raschi, Schoendienst; rookie cards of Ken Boyer, Bill Virdon.

OUR FAVORITE CARD

Typical of many regional issues, the 1955 Hunter's set contains several

cards which are the sole baseball card appearance of little-known players. One of special interest is "Preacher Jack" Faszholz. Faszholz pitched in just four games for the Cardinals, allowing 16 hits and a walk in 11.2 innings. To his credit, he struck out seven batters. In his own three major league at bats, he struck out twice and grounded out. None of this is particularly distinguishing, except that it all happened in 1953—two years before Faszholz appeared in the 1955 Hunter's set. He never pitched another inning in the major leagues. Why he was chosen to appear in the '55 set is a mystery.

VALUE

EX.-MT. CONDITION, NEATLY TRIMMED: Complete set, $1,750; common card, $50; Boyer, Raschi, Schoendienst, Virdon, $70–$100; Musial, $350. 5-YEAR PROJECTION: Above average.

1955 RODEO MEATS KANSAS CITY A'S

SPECIFICATIONS

SIZE: 2½×3½". FRONT: Color photograph. BACK: Black printing on gray cardboard. DISTRIBUTION: Kansas City area, in packages of hot dogs.

HISTORY

The 1955 Rodeo wieners set of Kansas City A's players (their first year in K.C. after moving from Philadelphia) is one of the largest single-team regional issues in baseball card history. The basic set features virtually the entire roster of the team as well as manager Lou Boudreau and the coaches. The '55 Rodeo cards were issued in two forms. Single cards, wax-coated to prevent card ink from staining the hot dogs, were packaged with the company's hot dogs. Posters on unwaxed cardboard showing a number of cards were also distributed. Individual cards could then be cut off. A surviving poster is worth a premium of 25 percent or so over the value of the individual cards on it. These two separate printings of the cards resulted in a number of color variations in the backgrounds behind the players' pictures. In all, a complete set of 1955 Rodeo Meats Kansas City A's cards, with all variations, totals 47 cards. To assemble one card of each player issued that year requires 38 cards. Rodeo cards feature on the front a portrait or posed-action photo of the player, heavily retouched to accentuate the color. A white strip at the bottom of the card has the player's name, and a blue-and-white Rodeo logo appears at the lower left. There is a white border around the photo. Card backs, which are not numbered, have an offer of a scrapbook for the Rodeo set, which was available for 25¢ and a label. The scrapbook lists two cards that were never actually issued in the set, coach Burleigh Grimes and first baseman Dick Kryhoski. The Rodeo Meats A's cards are quite scarce and high-priced.

FOR

Large, attractive regional set with lots of better-name players.

AGAINST

Color variations and the high cost of the cards make it tough to complete a set.

NOTEWORTHY CARDS

Besides the color variations, there is another variation in the '55 Rodeo set; on pitcher Bobby Shantz's card his name is misspelled "Schantz." That error was corrected. Bobby's battery-mate and brother, Wilmer Shantz, is found only with the correct spelling.

VALUE

EX.-MINT CONDITION: Complete set (38 cards), $1,200; common card, $30; Boudreau, Slaughter, "Schantz" error, $60. 5-YEAR PROJECTION: Below average.

1954 TOPPS

SPECIFICATIONS

SIZE: 2⅝×3¾". FRONT: Color photo. BACK: Green, red, and black printing on white cardboard. DISTRIBUTION: Nationally, in 1¢ and 5¢ packs of bubblegum.

HISTORY

Once again, in 1954, Topps reduced the size of its baseball card set—to 250 cards. The '54 Topps are among the company's most attractive and popular issues of the '50s. The issue was the first of many to use two different pictures of the same player on a single card. The '54s combine a color head-and-shoulders portrait of the player with a small black-and-white posed-action shot. The pictures are set against a solid-color background in one of several bright colors. A full-color team logo appears in one of the upper corners, along with the player's name, team, and position. Card backs feature much the same data as previous years—stats, biography, and short career summary. An interesting feature of the 1954 cards, though, is the "Inside Baseball" cartoon which appears at the bottom of the card and tells the story of an incident in the player's career. Many of them make interesting reading. The back of Tigers pitcher Dick Weik's card says, "Senator owner Clark Griffith got a tip on Weik from a friend! The friend had spotted Weik pitching for a Peoria high school team! Dick signed with the Senators for $4,000—plus a free sight-seeing trip to Washington for his Mom!" Like the earlier Topps sets, the 1954 issue exists today in several levels of scarcity, reflecting original printing quantities and distribution 30 years ago. Cards #1 to #50 are considered the most common (good thing, because there are eight Hall of Famers and half a dozen potential candidates among those 50 cards); followed by #76 to #250, and then #51 to #75. The price difference is not great among the three groups, but there is a measurable difference in the ease with which the various series can be found today.

FOR

Attractive and popular set, no real rarities, lots of big stars.

AGAINST

There probably isn't a bad word to be said of the 1954 Topps cards.

NOTEWORTHY CARDS

From beginning to end, there are many notable cards in the '54 Topps set. For one thing, cards #1 and #250 are both of Ted Williams. That was Topps' way of celebrating their signing Williams to an exclusive five-year baseball card appearance contract. In between, there are a number of significant "rookie cards," like Henry

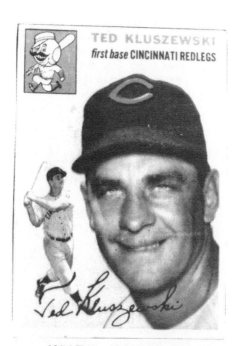

1954 Topps, Ted Kluszewski

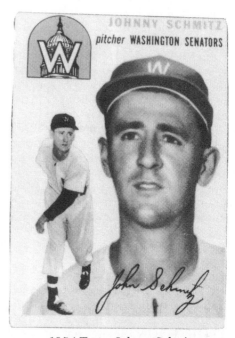

1954 Topps, Johnny Schmitz

Aaron, Ernie Banks, Al Kaline, and Tommy Lasorda (the only major league baseball card issued during his playing career). Another feature of the 1954 Topps set was the inclusion of more than a dozen managers and coaches, most of them former players. While a few major card sets had issued manager cards in the past, no modern set had ever depicted the coaches. Some of the former players who appeared as coaches in the '54 Topps set never appeared on another baseball card.

OUR FAVORITE CARD

One of the most memorable cards in the '54 Topps set is #139, Ed & John O'Brien. The O'Briens were the only twin brothers ever to play on the same major league team at the same time. They are pictured together on the 1954 Topps card, kneeling, with bats on shoulders. It marked the first time Topps featured more than one player on the same baseball card. The O'Brien twins had appeared in Topps' 1953 set, but each was on his own card. They would appear off and on, sepa-

rately and together, on Topps cards through 1959. The O'Briens played together at Pittsburgh from 1953 until mid-1958, when Eddie was sent down to the minors and Johnny was dealt to the Cardinals.

VALUE

EX.-MT. CONDITION: Complete set, $750; common card, $1–$1.50; Hall of Famers, $10–$25; Lasorda, $5; Williams, Kaline, Banks, $40–$50; Mays, $75; Aaron, $125. 5-YEAR PROJECTION: Above average.

1954 Topps, Ray Boone

1954 Topps, Ed McGhee

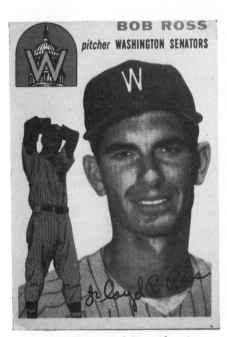

1954 Topps, Bob Ross (front)

1954 Topps, Henry Aaron (back)

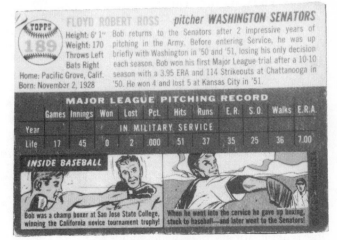

1954 Topps, Bob Ross (back)

1954 BOWMAN

SPECIFICATIONS

SIZE: 2½×3¾". FRONT: Hand-colored black-and-white photograph. BACK: Black and red printing on gray cardboard. DISTRIBUTION: Nationally, in 1¢ and 5¢ packages with bubblegum.

HISTORY

It's a mystery why, after its highly popular and successful color photo set of 1953, Bowman reverted to a less sophisticated production technique for its 1954 baseball card set. The 224 cards in the set are hand-colored black-and-white photographs. A pastel-colored rectangular panel in one of the lower corners carries a facsimile autograph or, in the case of a handful of cards, the player's name set in type. A white border surrounds the entire design. Backs are arranged in a horizontal format. At top is a red box with a copyright line in the upper-left corner. An outline of a bat contains the player's name, while the card number is contained in a ball at right. Below the bat is the player's team, position, birthplace, birth date, height, weight, and batting/throwing preference. A short biography appears in a gray panel to the left, while a corresponding box on the right has previous season and lifetime statistics. At bottom left is a baseball trivia question, while a red box at bottom right carries the answer. The 1954 Bowman set is best known for having two cards with #66. The more common is Jimmy Piersall; the scarcer is Ted Williams. Williams appeared in a Topps set for the first time in 1954 (he was the first and the last cards in that set), and it is believed that his contract with Topps prohibited Bowman from further use of his picture on baseball cards. When Topps pressed the issue, Bowman was forced to withdraw the Williams card and issue a new #66. Piersall also appears as card #210 in the '54 Bowman set. While the '54 Bowman Ted Williams card is quite expensive, it is not as rare as some sources would have you believe. Bowman used an interesting numbering scheme for its 1954 issue. While

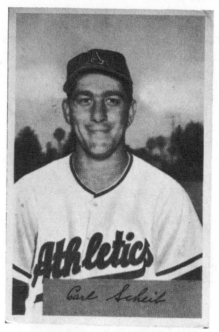

1954 Bowman, Carl Scheib

1954 Bowman, Delbert Rice, Jr.

1954 Bowman, Curt Simmons

1954 Bowman, Smokey Burgess

there were certain inconsistencies due to trades, etc., in general the set was made up to consist of 14 cards each from the 16 major league teams. Each team's cards were then numbered in increments of 16. Thus, Phil Rizzuto, a New York Yankee, is card #1 in the set. Card #17 is also a Yankee, Tom Gorman; as is card #33, Vic Raschi; card #49, Harry Byrd, etc. The Red Sox have cards #2, #18, #34, etc. The Baltimore Orioles cards in the set are interesting because Bowman artists had to create uniforms for the team on the cards, and they came up with a number of different variations. The problem was that the Orioles became a major league team in 1954, after many years in the American League as the St. Louis Browns. When the Bowman set was being produced, though, nobody yet knew what the new team's uniforms would look like. The '54 Bowman set is also well known for having errors in the statistics of a large number of cards, many of which were corrected in later printings. Few—very few—collectors concern themselves with these statistical variations, however, and neither version seems to carry any premium value.

FOR

The '54 Bowman set is attractive enough, but it suffers in comparison with those produced in 1953 and 1955. With the exception of the Williams card, it is not an expensive set to complete.

AGAINST

Not up to the same standards as the 1953 and 1955 Bowman sets, the Bowman issue of 1954 lost the "battle" that year to the Topps set, which is much more popular among collectors today. The high cost of the Williams card makes completing a set difficult for many collectors.

NOTEWORTHY CARDS

In the battle for star players, the 1954 Bowman set has a few players that do not appear in Topps, most notably Mickey Mantle, but also including Pee Wee Reese, Roy Campanella, Robin Roberts, Bob Feller, and others. There are three variations in the Bowman set that collectors do find interesting enough to place a decent premium value on. Later printings of the Vic Raschi and Dave Philley cards mention in the player biography trades to St. Louis and Cleveland, re-

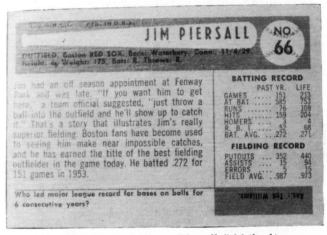

1954 Bowman, Jimmy Piersall #66 (back)

1954 Bowman, Art Houtteman

1954 Bowman, Willard Marshall

1954 Bowman, Jimmy Piersall #66 (front)

spectively; while the corrected version of Jim Greengrass' card gives his birthplace as "Addison, N.Y.," rather than "Addison, N.J." The scarcer later printings are $5 cards in top grade, while the earlier printings sell for common card price. Card #222, Memo Luna, is interesting because rather than a touched-up photograph of the player, the card has a rather crudely done painting of the Cardinals pitcher. The Willie Mays card contains an interesting error in his facsimile signature on the front of the card. The autograph reads "Willie May." Apparently, because Mays signed his name with the "s" at end detached, it was somehow omitted.

VALUE

EX.-MT. CONDITION: Complete set (#66, Piersall), $550; common card, $1; minor stars, $3–$5; Hall of Famers, $8–$12; Rizzuto, Campanella, Feller, Berra, Snider, $15–$20. Piersall, #66, $50; Mays, $65; Mantle, $80; Williams, $550. 5-YEAR PROJECTION: Average.

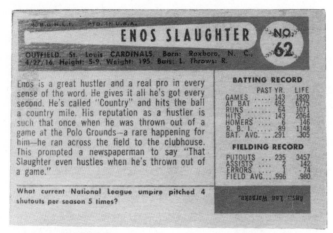

1954 Bowman, Enos Slaughter (back)

1954 Bowman, Bill Pierce

1954 Bowman, Ralph Kiner

1954 RED MAN

SPECIFICATIONS

SIZE: 3½×4″. FRONT: Color painting. BACK: Black printing on gray cardboard. DISTRIBUTION: Nationally, single cards in boxes of chewing tobacco.

HISTORY

In their third year as a giveaway in boxes of chewing tobacco, the Red Man baseball cards of 1954 show little change from the design of the 1952 and 1953 cards. The basic format is still a borderless color painting of the player at the top of the card. Beneath the picture is a thin white stripe, or "tab." Red Man cards are frequently found without the tab, which was actually a redeemable coupon. Fifty tabs collected from the cards entitled the owner to send for a major league replica cap of his favorite team. Most collectors prefer the Red Mans with the tab, as they were originally issued, so a premium value of 25 percent or so is attached to cards with the tab, over and above what a card of the same player in the same condition will bring without the tab. For the first time, in 1954, the tab on the Red Man cards did not have the card number, just the year of issue. The card number appears in the top of a white box in one of the upper corners of the card, along with the player's name, personal data, and a career summary. On cards which have had the tabs removed, the year of issue can be determined by reading the career summary to see the last year mentioned, which would be the previous season. Cards are numbered in two series, American League and National League, #1 to #25 in each. There were only 50 cards in the 1954 Red Man set (at least there were supposed to be, see below). The manager cards which had been a staple of the 1952 and 1953 issues were gone. Again in 1954, *The Sporting News* editor, J. Taylor Spink, chose the players who appeared in the "All-Star Series" for Red Man. Backs of the '54 Red Mans have an advertisement for the tobacco and details of the free cap offer. The bottom line (above the tab) reads "Red Man 'Chewers'—start a collection for your boys." In reality, at least as much of the nasty stuff was being bought and chewed by young boys to get the free baseball cards as it was by their fathers.

FOR
Relatively inexpensive for 30-year-old cards that were distributed in far smaller quantity than the contemporary Topps or Bowman issues. Lots of big stars, attractive portraits.

AGAINST
Some of the players in the 1954 Red Man set were appearing on their third consecutive card in the same pose, with only a background change. This makes the issue confusing and not as attractive to superstar collectors as it might otherwise be.

NOTEWORTHY CARDS
Few collectors—other than those who have been trying to find the cards for many years without success—realize just how scarce some of the variation cards in the 1954 Red Man set are. If it were more widely known how rare these cards are, the prices would be much, much higher. The scarce variations are a trio of American League players who were traded and appear in the '54 set in the uniform of their new and old teams. The least scarce of the trio is Dave Philley, who was traded prior to the beginning of the season from the A's to the Indians. Much tougher are the George Kell and Sam Mele variations, both of whom were dealt in mid-season. Kell appears in the set with the Red Sox and the White Sox; Mele appears with the Orioles and the White Sox. In the latter two cases, it is the White Sox version which is the scarcer of the pair. The Philadelphia card is the tougher of the Dave Philley varieties. There is also a variation among the National League cards, where two different players can be found as #19, Gus Bell and Enos Slaughter. Slaughter was the first of the two to be printed, as a St. Louis Cardinal, but he was traded to the Yankees in April, 1954, and the Gus Bell card replaced him in the National League numbering. The Bell card is the scarcer in this duo. Willie Mays returned to the Red Man set in 1954, but Stan Musial was gone. Still, there is no lack of Hall of Famers or popular home team heroes of the day.

VALUE
EX.-MT. CONDITION, WITH TAB: Complete set (no variations), $275; common card, $4; Hall of Famers, $8–$15; common variations, $12; scarce variations, $20; Mays, $30. 5-YEAR PROJECTION: Above average.

1954 RED HEART

SPECIFICATIONS
SIZE: 2⅝ × 3¾". FRONT: Color-added black-and-white photograph. BACK: Black printing on gray cardboard. DISTRIBUTION: Nationally, by mail-in offer with dog food labels.

HISTORY
One of the better-kept secrets of the hobby was that until just a few years ago, collectors could still write to the Red Heart dog food company and get an assortment of its 1954 baseball cards for a couple of dollars. That "trade secret" resulted in large numbers of the cards being available today in top condition—but they still aren't cheap. Back in 1954, Red Heart issued the 33-card set as just one of more

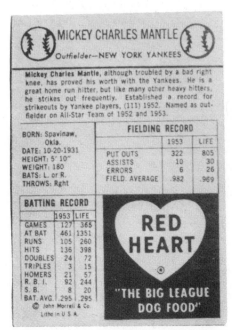

1954 Red Heart, Mickey Mantle (back)

than half a dozen baseball-related premiums that could be obtained by sending in Red Heart dog food can labels. There were caps, T-shirts, scarves, pen and pencil sets, etc. To get a series of 11 baseball cards, you had to send in two labels and a dime. Each of three series had a different color background behind the photo of the player—red, blue, or green. Since far fewer of the red-background cards were sent to collectors in later years, it is assumed that they were printed in shorter supply. There are still enough to satisfy most collectors, though, and there is no real price difference between those cards and the other two series. The photos on the cards are heavily retouched to add color to the faces and uniforms. The artwork isn't all that good, and some of the players' eyes look positively alien. At the bottom of the photo, the player's name is printed inside a colored diamond. The team name is printed in the white border at bottom. The Red Heart cards are unnumbered. Card backs are vertical in format. There are a couple of baseballs up at the top, flanking the player's name, team, and position. A short biography appears below that. In the center are personal data and a review of the past season's and career stats. At the bottom is a black box with a Red Heart logo and a copyright line for the John Morrell Meat Company. Though the Red Heart set was a one-year issue, the Morrell name would be seen again on later baseball card issues (1959–1961 Los Angeles Dodgers). There are a number of big name stars in the Red Heart set, and the cards are popularly collected.

FOR
A scarce, nationally distributed set of the 1950s that has luckily been preserved for collectors in decent numbers. This helps keep the price down.

AGAINST
Some collectors who were left out of the direct-purchase plan secret of a few years back are reluctant to pay the current price for cards they know were obtained for only a few cents apiece.

NOTEWORTHY CARDS
Stan Musial appears in the "scarce" red-background series, his only na-

tionally distributed baseball card in 1954. Mickey Mantle is in the blue series, and there are a few other Hall of Famers and potential HOFers scattered throughout the set.

VALUE

EX.-MT. CONDITION: Complete set, $300; common card, $7; Hall of Famers, $9–$12; Snider, $15–$20; Mantle, Musial, $45–$50. 5-YEAR PROJECTION: Average.

1954 WILSON'S FRANKS

SPECIFICATIONS

SIZE: 2⅝×3¾". FRONT: Black-and-white photograph, color added by hand. BACK: Black printing on gray cardboard. DISTRIBUTION: Nationally, in packages of Wilson hot dogs.

HISTORY

One of the rarest, most expensive, and most popular of the baseball card sets issued with hot dogs in the 1950s is the 20-card Wilson's Franks set of 1954. Unlike most other hot dog sets that concentrated on one or two teams, the Wilson's set featured players from more than a dozen clubs. The cards are quite attractive, featuring on the front a color-added black-and-white photograph of the player against a solid-color background. The players name, team, and position appear at the top, and there is a facsimile autograph across the front of the card. Along with these elements is a color picture of a package of Wilson's Franks, suspended somewhere above or to the side of the player's photo. These "flying hot dogs" are sometimes positioned to look as if the player is going to hit them with a swinging bat, or catch them in an outstretched glove, or, more often, get hit in the back of the head. It is one of the few instances in baseball card design where the product is pictured right on the front of the card. Card backs have the usual assortment of player personal data, a short career summary, and stats from the 1953 season and career cumulative figures. Like many of the regional card issues of the mid-1950s, the Wilson's cards are not numbered. While most collectors classify the Wilson's Franks cards as "regionals," they were, in fact, distributed nationwide, although in limited quantities. The cards were packaged right in with the hot dogs, and so are commonly found with grease stains, or even purple ink blots from the packaging. They are so scarce, however, that most collectors are willing to overlook a little grease on the card.

FOR

Unusual and attractive design. Some popular players. A real challenge.

AGAINST

A lot of lesser-known players and managers among the 20 cards in the set. Very expensive on a per-card basis. Hard to find in true Mint condition.

NOTEWORTHY CARDS

The big name in the '54 Wilson's set is Ted Williams, who is joined by fellow Hall of Famers Roy Campanella and Bob Feller. At least half a dozen others in the set will probably be enshrined at Cooperstown some day.

VALUE

EX.-MT. CONDITION: Complete set, $1,500; common card, $40; minor stars, $50–$75; Campanella, Feller, $100; Williams, $600. 5-YEAR PROJECTION: Below average.

1954 STAHL MEYER

SPECIFICATIONS

SIZE: 3¼×4½". FRONT: Color added to black-and-white photograph. BACK: Red printing on white cardboard. DISTRIBUTION: New York City area, single cards in packages of hot dogs.

HISTORY

In its second year of baseball card production, the Stahl Meyer hot dog company increased the size of its set to 12 cards, adding one player from each of the major league teams then in New York. The format for the set stayed about the same, with a yellow border replacing the white on the front of the card. Pictures were once again black-and-white photos to which color was artistically added. A panel below the picture has the player's name printed, along with a facsimile signature. Some of the same photos were used as in the 1953 set, but the color of the border makes it easy to tell the two years apart. The card backs were changed significantly on the '54 Stahl Meyer set. They are arranged vertically, with the top half offering "Johnny Stahl Meyer's Baseball Kit," which included posters, banners, and tickets to set up a make-believe ball game. Bottom of the card had the player's name and personal data, along with stats from the previous year and career cumulative figures. There is no biography or

1954 Wilson's Franks, Jacob Nelson Fox (back)

card number on the back. Overall, the '54 Stahl Meyer cards are a bit scarcer than the 1953 version.

FOR

Scarce regional cards of popular players.

AGAINST

Many collectors don't like round-cornered cards. The combination of rarity and popular players makes the '54 Stahl Meyer cards expensive.

NOTEWORTHY CARDS

Since most of the players are quite well known, we'll name all 12. Yankees: Hank Bauer, Mickey Mantle, Gil McDougald, Phil Rizzuto. Dodgers: Carl Erskine, Gil Hodges, Don Newcombe, Duke Snider. Giants: Monte Irvin, Whitey Lockman, Willie Mays, Don Mueller.

VALUE

EX.-MT. CONDITION: Complete set, $2,250; common card, $75; Irvin, Hodges, Rizzuto, $100; Snider, $150; Mays, $500; Mantle, $600. 5-YEAR PROJECTION: Below average.

1954 DAN-DEE POTATO CHIPS

SPECIFICATIONS

SIZE: 2½ × 3⅝". FRONT: Color added to black-and-white photograph. BACK: Blue and red printing on white cardboard. DISTRIBUTION: Selected geographic areas, individual cards in bags of potato chips.

HISTORY

One of the scarcer and more popular multi-team regional baseball card sets of the mid-1950s is the 29-card issue by Dan-Dee potato chips. The similarity of the cards' design to the Johnston cookie cards of the era, and the use of some of the same photos by the Dan-Dee, Briggs, and Stahl Meyer sets indicate that one company, probably an advertising agency, created all of these

sets for the various issuers. Players from the Indians, the Pirates, the Dodgers, the Yankees, the Giants, and the Cardinals are included in the '54 Dan-Dee set. The cards feature what appears to be a color photo on the front, but it is actually a black-and-white picture to which color details have been added. Beneath the photo is a box containing the player's name in type and in the form of a facsimile autograph. A red logo is at left. Card backs are a traditional mix of personal data, a short biography, and stats from the previous two seasons. A Dan-Dee ad appears at bottom, and there is no card number. Because the cards were packed in bags of potato chips, they are sometimes found with grease stains, a blemish that affects their value negatively.

FOR

Good-looking cards with lots of popular stars of the early 1950s. Scarce and valuable.

AGAINST

The sharing of the Yankee player photos among Dan-Dee, Briggs, and Stahl Meyer makes the cards less desirable to team or superstar collectors than they might otherwise be.

NOTEWORTHY CARDS

The Dan-Dee set contains many cards of the pennant-winning 1954 Cleveland Indians. The cards of Walker Cooper and Paul Smith were withdrawn in the midst of the promotion; Smith had been sent down to the

minors in the pre-season, and Cooper was dealt to the Cubs in mid-season. Hall of Famers are Feller, Irvin, Lemon, Lopez, Mantle, Snider, and Wynn.

VALUE

EX.-MT. CONDITION: Complete set, $1,350; common card, $20; Hall of Famers, $30–$50; Smith, Cooper, $150–$200; Mantle, $300. 5-YEAR PROJECTION: Below average.

1954 Dan-Dee Potato Chips, Robert Feller (back)

1954 Dan-Dee Potato Chips, Hank Bauer

1954 NEW YORK JOURNAL AMERICAN

SPECIFICATIONS

SIZE: 2×4″. FRONT: Black-and-white photograph. BACK: Black printing on white cardboard. DISTRIBUTION: New York area, cards given away with purchase of daily newspaper.

HISTORY

The Hearst newspaper empire had a reputation for innovation when it came to selling newspapers. One of those ideas provided a legacy for collectors when, in 1954, the Hearst papers created a "Lucky Baseball Cards" contest. Newsstand vendors were given boxes of baseball cards to hand out to purchasers of the *New York Journal American* newspaper. Each card had a serial number printed in red at the bottom. Each day winning numbers were printed in the paper and $1,000 in cash was given away; as much as $200 was given for each winning card. Because the cards are really quite unattractive and were "worthless" if they didn't have a winning number, they were often thrown away quickly. Those that have survived have generally done so in large lots from boxes of cards that newsstand vendors took home to the kids instead of giving to paper buyers. The 59 cards in the set represent players from all three of the New York major league teams in 1954, and those teams are quite popular with collectors and have lots of superstars. But the New York Journal American cards are not popular collector favorites, and their value is quite low, except for those big name stars for which collectors are willing to pay high prices because of their genuine scarcity. The front of the card has a player photo in black-and-white at the top. A black strip under the picture has the player and team names. The entire lower half of the front is an ad for the contest. Card backs provide home game schedules for the appropriate team. The cards are unnumbered.

FOR

The commons are quite inexpensive for really scarce regional issues.

AGAINST

The cards are really unattractive, and the really desirable cards—the superstars—are quite high-priced.

NOTEWORTHY CARDS

All the popular Dodgers, Giants, and Yankees of the era are included in the set: 20 Giants and Yankees, 19 Dodgers. The Erv Palica card is somewhat scarce because it was withdrawn when he was traded from the Dodgers to the Orioles in mid-season.

VALUE

EX.-MT. CONDITION: Complete set, $600; common card, $5; Hall of Famers, $7–$12; Campanella, Snider, Berra, Palica, $25; Robinson, $50; Mays, $75; Mantle, $100. 5-YEAR PROJECTION: Below average.

1954 JOHNSTON COOKIE BRAVES

SPECIFICATIONS

SIZE: 2×3⅞″. FRONT: Color added to black-and-white photograph. BACK: Blue and red printing on cream-colored cardboard. DISTRIBUTION: Wisconsin, single cards in packages of cookies.

HISTORY

For the second of three annual baseball card issues, the Johnston baking company increased the size of the set to 35 cards. The cards include the entire roster of the Milwaukee Braves, the manager, the coaches, and even the team's trainer and doctor. The '54 Johnstons are formatted in an unusual tall and narrow size. Photos for the set were taken at the team's spring training facility in Bradenton, Florida. Nearly all of the cards show the players posing in front of a chain link fence with metal folding chairs in the background. Once again, the photos

1954 Johnston Cookie Braves, Del Crandall

used were originally black-and-white, but had color added by hand, a common practice on cards in the early Fifties. The player's name was printed in a wide white border beneath the photo, and a facsimile autograph appears below that, superimposed on a red logo of an Indian chief's profile. Card backs are arranged horizontally, and contain the same basic information as the '53 set: a short biography, a section of personal data, stats from the 1952 and 1953 seasons, and a Johnston typographic logo. The card number in 1954 was contained in an Indian chief silhouette. The 1954 Johnstons were skip-numbered with the player's uniform numbers. The cards of the trainer and doctor are unnumbered. An ad in tiny type at the right end of the card offers a wall-hanging display sheet for the cards for a quarter. The sheets are quite rare today, and they make interesting sidelights to this set, as do uncut sheets of the cards themselves. The '54 Johnstons are considerably scarcer than the premier issue of 1953, but a

*1954 Johnston Cookie Braves,
Charles Grimm*

1954 Johnston Cookie Braves, Joey Jay

*1954 Johnston Cookie Braves,
Lew Burdette*

large hoard turned up in 1983 and has temporarily glutted the market.

FOR

Another great set for Braves collectors, in an unusual format. Quite scarce and features some players not seen in other sets.

AGAINST

Card photos have a certain boring sameness about the background.

NOTEWORTHY CARDS

There are two cards in the 1954 Johnston set that are much more ex-pensive than the rest. One of the cards, Henry Aaron, is scarce because of unusually high demand; the other, Bobby Thomson, is scarce because of limited distribution. The Aaron card in the '54 Johnston set is Hammerin' Hank's rookie card, and that makes the all-time home run king's Johnston issue especially popular with collectors. It's unusual to see Aaron as card number 5 in the set, but that's the uniform number he had for a time before adopting the familiar number 44. The Bobby Thomson card in the '54 set was withdrawn from distribution very early in the issue. Thomson broke his ankle in a pre-season exhibition game and was out for most of the season. Existing uncut sheets show that in lieu of the Thomson card the Warren Spahn or Jim Wilson card was double-printed on later press runs. The inclusion of cards for the team doctor and trainer was very unusual for a major league regional set.

VALUE

EX.-MT. CONDITION: Complete set, $275; common card, $5; Spahn, Mathews, $15; Thomson, $75; Aaron, $90. 5-YEAR PROJECTION: Below average.

1954 HUNTER'S WIENERS CARDINALS

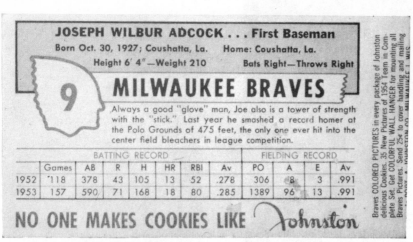

JOSEPH WILBUR ADCOCK . . . First Baseman
Born Oct. 30, 1927; Coushatta, La.   Home: Coushatta, La.
Height 6' 4"—Weight 210   Bats Right—Throws Right

9 **MILWAUKEE BRAVES**

Always a good "glove" man, Joe also is a tower of strength
with the "stick." Last year he smashed a record homer at
the Polo Grounds of 475 feet, the only one ever hit into the
center field bleachers in league competition.

| BATTING RECORD | | | | | | | FIELDING RECORD | | | |
	Games	AB	R	H	HR	RBI	Av	PO	A	E	Av
1952	'118	378	43	105	13	52	.278	306	8	3	.991
1953	157	590	71	168	18	80	.285	1389	96	13	.991

NO ONE MAKES COOKIES LIKE *Johnston*

1954 Johnston Cookie Braves, Joe Adcock (back)

ANDY PAFKO

1954 Johnston Cookie Braves, Andy Pafko

SPECIFICATIONS
SIZE: 2¼×3½". FRONT: Full-color
photo. BACK: Blank. DISTRIBU-
TION: St. Louis area, one player card
and one stat card per package of hot
dogs.

HISTORY
Hunter's upped the ante a bit with its
1954 baseball card set. While you
could have collected a complete set the
previous year by buying only 13 packages of wieners, it took 30 packages to
complete a set in 1954. Besides increasing the number of cards in the set
from 26 to 30, the hot dog company
printed just one player card per package. The photos used for the '54
Hunter's set were the same ones used
in 1953. Instead of the player's name
and bio in the white bottom panel,
however, there was printed, "WHAT'S
MY NAME? WHAT'S MY REC-
ORD?" The accompanying card on
the hot dog package—which looks
something like a normal baseball card
back—provided the answers. Far
fewer of the "answer" cards have survived to this day, so many collectors
are faced with "anonymous" '54
Hunter's cards. You have to know
your St. Louis Cardinals of 30 years
ago to successfully collect this set. For
this reason, demand is more limited
than it might otherwise be. Like the
'53 issue, the 1954 cards were round-
cornered and usually were not neatly
cut off the package by the kids who
were the original owners. Additionally, they are often found with the bottom white panel cut off, a condition
which greatly reduces the value of the
card, especially to condition-conscious
collectors.

FOR
The expanded 30-card set for 1954
means more of the marginal Cardinal
players, as well as the coaches, were
included. This is a bonus for team collectors as some of these players don't
appear on any other baseball cards.

AGAINST

The fact that it takes two pieces to make a "complete" card, and that few of the statistical cards have survived, makes it extremely difficult to complete a set, not to mention the fact that the picture cards themselves are scarce and expensive.

NOTEWORTHY CARDS

Because he did not appear in either the Topps or Bowman issue for 1954, the Hunter's Wieners card of "The Man" is highly sought-after, especially because it is a "Home Team" issue. Well-known Cardinals of yesterday are also in the set: Vic Raschi, Enos Slaughter, and Red Schoendienst. Also noteworthy is the card of Tom Alston, the first black player on the Cardinals.

OUR FAVORITE CARD

Tom Burgess made his only major league baseball card appearance in the set. Burgess was the epitome of the career minor league player of the 1950s. He began pro ball at the age of 19 in 1946, playing for a succession of Cardinals farm teams for three years. He voluntarily retired from 1949 to 1951, and then returned to the dugout in 1952. He finally got his chance at the beginning of the 1954 season when he was called up as a reserve outfielder and pinch hitter. A pinch hitter who goes 0-for-11 doesn't stay long in the majors, so Burgess took his .048 batting average back to the bush leagues, where he was a consistent .280 hitter at the AAA level. Burgess' major league career wasn't quite over, though. In 1962 he was drafted by the expansion Los Angeles Angels of the American League and played 87 games as a first baseman, outfielder, and pinch hitter—eight years after his previous big league stint. He still couldn't hit major league pitching, though, and a .196 average wasn't even good enough for the Angels that season. Burgess later turned up as a minor league manager in the late 1970s-early 1980s.

VALUE

EX.-MT. CONDITION, NEATLY TRIMMED: Complete set, $1,500; common card, $45; Raschi, Slaughter, Schoendienst, $60–$75; Musial, $350. 5-YEAR PROJECTION: Average.

1954–1955 ESSKAY ORIOLES

SPECIFICATIONS

SIZE: 2¼×3½". FRONT: Color photograph. BACK: Blank. DISTRIBUTION: Baltimore area, two cards as part of hot dog package.

HISTORY

"You can't tell the players without a scorecard," is an often-heard sales pitch at the ball park. The same situation exists with the Esskay hot dog cards of 1954 and 1955. You can't tell the year of issue without a scorecard—or even with one. The first two years that the Baltimore Orioles were members of the American League (after moving from St. Louis, where the team was known as the Browns), the Esskay meat company issued baseball cards of the Orioles players as part of its hot dog package, two cards per package. The problem was, the company made it extremely difficult to tell which year was which, and the players that happened to be in both sets (there were a lot of those) are impossible to tell apart. A total of 36 different cards was issued in 1954, and 27 were issued in 1955, but there are only 52 different players in all. It doesn't matter much that the cards from both years are so similar, though, because few people attempt to collect full sets. The cards are so rare and so expensive that collecting all cards of both years is prohibitive. What's even tougher is collecting cards in top condition. Because they were actually printed on the bottom of the hot dog package, and had to be cut out with scissors, and because kids with scissors are not known for being particularly neat, many of the Esskay cards are found with uneven edges. The manner in which the card was cut has a definite effect on the value—the neater, the better. The best Esskay cards are those which are still attached to the original package. Such an original panel is worth some 50 percent more than the total value of the two cards as individuals. The cards are quite similar in design to the Hunter's Wieners St. Louis Cardinals cards of the previous

year, almost as if the 1954–1955 Esskay cards robbed the Cardinal nest for the idea. The player is shown in a borderless color photo. Beneath the photo is a white strip that has the player's name, position, birth date, home town, and his batting and throwing preferences. There is a facsimile autograph in light blue ink in the background. There is no card number. Backs of the cards are blank, except for grease stains left from contact with the hot dogs. Naturally, cards with few, or no, grease stains are worth more than cards that are heavily affected. When a player appeared in both sets, the same photo was used. A comparison of a detailed checklist or a roster of the 1954 and/or 1955 Orioles will reveal whether a player could be from either set, or both.

FOR

Valuable cards from an expansion team's first year in a new city.

AGAINST

The cards are too similar to tell apart by year of issue, and that frustrates collectors who think complete set collecting is the only way to go. They're hard to find, harder yet to find in nice condition, and hardest of all to pay for.

NOTEWORTHY CARDS

Many of the players in the 1954–1955 Esskay set are eminently forgettable, while a few, most notably Don Larsen and Bob Turley, went on to greater fame a few years later with the New York Yankees. It's a great set for team collectors, though.

OUR FAVORITE CARD

One of the names least likely to be remembered from the roster of the 1954 Baltimore Orioles is Jehosie Heard, a veteran of the dying Negro leagues. He was a minor league player in the Browns-Orioles organization, but his physical tools were against him: he was 29 years old in 1954, he was only 5'7", 147 lbs., and for a pitcher, that's just not big enough to get anything on the ball—at least not in the majors. Heard pitched in just two major league games, both in 1954, and for a total of only 3.1 innings. In that short big league career, he gave up six hits and walked three, while striking out two, for an unenviable 13.50 ERA.

Heard knocked around the minor leagues and went on some of the Latin American circuits for several more years before dropping out of sight completely. Heard is one of the few ballplayers of modern times whose current whereabouts are unknown. Surprisingly, he not only appeared in the "Home Team" Esskay card set of 1954, but was also on a Topps card that year.

VALUE
EX.-MT. CONDITION, NEATLY TRIMMED: Complete set (52), $3,500; common card, $75; Turley, Larsen, $100. 5-YEAR PROJECTION: Below average.

1953 TOPPS

SPECIFICATIONS
SIZE: 2⅝×3¾". FRONT: Color painting. BACK: Red and black printing on gray cardboard. DISTRIBUTION: Nationally, in 1¢ and 5¢ packs of bubblegum.

HISTORY
In the midst of continuing legal wrangles with Bowman over rights to produce players' pictures on gum cards, Topps dramatically cut back the size of its baseball card set in 1953. It's '53 issue numbered only 274 cards, compared to the 407 of the previous year. So hotly contested were the players' contracts that Topps apparently lost six of them after production on the 1953 set had begun. Thus, there were no cards #253, #261, #267, #268, #271, or #275. Naturally, the fact that six cards didn't exist in the set's 1–180 numbering range didn't hurt Topps' sale of bubblegum packs. In those days before checklist cards, the average kid on the street would have no way of knowing that no matter how much bubblegum he bought, he would never get the cards he needed to fill that half-dozen gaps in his set—so he kept right on trying. The '53 Topps cards are painted portraits of the individual players, usually rendered from team publicity photos. The artists then added stadium backgrounds to the portraits. A color team logo appeared at the bottom of the card near a red (American League) or black (National League) panel which contained the player's name, team, and position in some combination of red, white, and yellow letters. A white border surrounded the card up to the border of the panel. Card backs offered brief statistics for the previous year and lifetime record of the player, along with biographical details and a short career summary. There was a facsimile autograph in red across the upper part of the card. In 1953, Topps made the first use of a baseball trivia question on the back of its cards. That year, it was called "Dugout Quiz." It was a device the company would use frequently over the years. The '53 Topps cards exist in three degrees of scarcity. Cards #166 to #220 are the most common, the first 165 cards in the set being less so, and then, scarcest of all by far, cards #221 to #280. The "high numbers" in the '53 Topps set contain the "key" card in the series, #244, Willie Mays.

FOR
The '53 Topps cards are an attractive set that offers collectors a decent challenge at lower cost than the 1952 set. The high-numbered series is scarce enough to keep a collector busy for quite some time.

AGAINST
The reduced number of players in the '53 Topps set means that many of the game's great stars are absent.

NOTEWORTHY CARDS
As mentioned earlier, the Willie Mays card in the high number series is the key card in the '53 Topps set. In strong demand and short supply, it is more than twice as valuable as the Mickey Mantle card in the low number series. Actually, Topps cheated a bit by issuing a '53 Mays card at all; Willie spent the entire season in military service. The '53 Mays has long been recognized as one of the hobby's more expensive recent cards, and it was the victim of one of the first modern baseball card counterfeit schemes. The fake '53 Mays isn't too tough to detect, though. Somebody forgot to tell the printer that the panel at the bottom of the card should be black, not red. The set features "rookie cards" of Dodgers Jim Gilliam and Johnny Podres. Card #1, the toughest to find in true Mint condition, is Jackie Robinson. The portrait on card #219, Pete Runnels, is actually that of his 1952 Senators teammate, Don Johnson. Johnson didn't play in the majors in 1953 and didn't have his own baseball card that year.

1953 Topps, Early Wynn

1953 Topps, Whitey Ford

OUR FAVORITE CARD

Most collectors who want a "legitimate" (actually issued during his career) baseball card of Hall of Fame pitching legend Satchel Paige have little choice but to obtain his 1953 Topps card. Satch appeared on only one other major baseball card issue in his short major league career, a rare series Leaf card from the 1948–1949 issue valued at some $225. By contrast, a top-grade example of his '53 Topps card will set you back only about $30. Paige was the most famous of the Negro leagues' ballplayers, and one of the oldest to successfully make the transition to the major leagues after Jackie Robinson's debut with the Dodgers in 1947. Paige was pitching for the St. Louis Browns when he appeared in the '53 Topps set. In the 1952 season he was 12-10 with a 3.07 ERA, and he had led the American League with eight wins and eight losses in relief. Though he often made a game of not revealing his true age, it is generally acknowledged that Paige was 46 years old when he appeared in the 1953 Topps set. Paige played part of the following season for the Brownies before moving down to the minor leagues and on to coachinng and instructing pitchers for various teams. In 1965—at the age of 59—

Satchel Paige took the major league mound once again as a starting pitcher, in the uniform of the Kansas City A's, and pitched three innings, giving up a single hit and striking out one. Paige was elected to the Hall of Fame on the basis of his long and successful career in the Negro leagues.

VALUE

EX.-MT. CONDITION: Complete set, $1,500; common card, #1–#220, $1.50–$2; #221–#280, $8.50; Hall of Famers, $10–$20; Paige, Robinson, $30; Mantle, $145; Mays, $300.
5-YEAR PROJECTION: Above average.

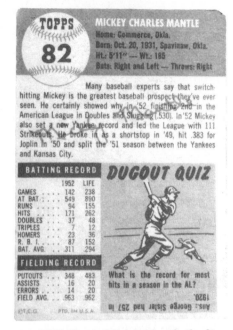

1953 Topps, Mickey Mantle (back)

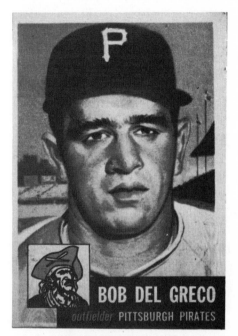

1953 Topps, Bob Del Greco

1953 Topps, Eddie Mathews

1953 Topps, Roy Face

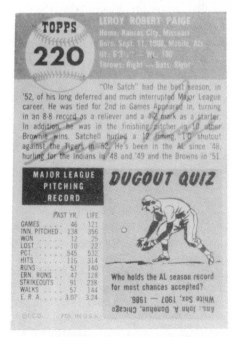

1953 Topps, Leroy Paige (back)

1953 BOWMAN COLOR

1953 Bowman Color, Pee Wee Reese (back)

SPECIFICATIONS

SIZE: 2½×3¾". FRONT: Color photograph. BACK: Red and black printing on cream-colored cardboard. DISTRIBUTION: Nationally, in 1¢ and 5¢ packages with bubblegum.

HISTORY

Nobody can ever say that Bowman sat back passively and let Topps steal the baseball card market from them. They responded to the Topps challenge of 1952 with a set that is consistently rated as the most popular of modern times in collector polls. Bowman pulled out all the stops in 1953. To match Topps' larger-format cards, Bowman increased the size of its own cards from the 2¹/₁₆×3¹/₈" size of 1951 and 1952, to a big 2½×3¾". Bowman brought Joe DiMaggio out of retirement to plug its set by picturing him on the wrapper, telling kids to "Collect them, trade them, save them." But best of all, Bowman gave kids in 1953 something no other baseball card had ever done, actual color photographs. All previous color cards had been artists' paintings or retouched photos, but the '53 Bowmans were actual color photographs. (There was also a similar Bowman black-and-white set in '53; see next listing.) Collectors then and now have responded to the '53 Bowman color set in record numbers. Because of the high cost of producing the set in those days, Bowman trimmed the number of cards back from the 252 of the previous year to just 160, but managed to retain a good number of the stars. Design of the 1953 Bowmans is straightforward; there is nothing on the front of the card except the gorgeous color photo. Bowman knew better than to minimize the impact of this baseball card milestone by cluttering the front with type or other design elements. A black line and a white border surround the photo. Card backs also show that Bowman recognized the challenge from Topps. For the first time, in 1953, Bowman included statistics on the back of the card offering major league stats from the previous season and lifetime cumulative totals. An interesting innovation—one that no one else ever tried—was a blank line beneath those two lines of stats. Labeled "This Year," it was space for the card's owner to write in the current year's stats for the player. Surprisingly, for all the millions of cards issued, they are very seldom found today with this line filled in—which is a good thing as far as collectors are concerned. Added writing on a card, even writing intended to be put there, is considered damage that lowers the collector value. The rest of the card back is the usual combination of personal information and a short career summary. The card number was placed in the upper-left corner in a representation of a baseball diamond. Even the back of the 1953 Bowman set is considered a classic, and the format is often chosen to be copied in modern-day collector issues. While no uncut sheets of 1953 Bowman cards are known to exist in the hobby, it seems likely that the set was produced in 16-card sheets, or at least 16-card increments on larger sheets. There are generally acknowledged to be three degrees of scarcity in the set, cards #1 to #112 being the most common, cards #113 to #128 being the toughest, and cards #129 to #160 being slightly less scarce than the preceding group.

FOR

The '53 Bowmans have virtually everything going for them. Gorgeous color photos, attractive backs, large size.

AGAINST

Are you kidding?

NOTEWORTHY CARDS

While Bowman suffered the loss of many stars to Topps and others, the 1953 set did have the last nationally issued Stan Musial bubblegum card until 1958. Another major innovation Bowman unveiled to fight the Topps threat was the multi-player feature card, which was last used in the 19th century. The idea was so simple, it's a wonder nobody had done it for such a long time. If a baseball card with one player on it is popular, why not have two or more players on the same card? Bowman had two such cards that year, featuring a total of five New York Yankees. One card pictured the double-play combination of Phil Rizzuto and Billy Martin, while on the other card, Yankee sluggers Mickey Mantle, Yogi Berra, and Hank Bauer were pictured in the dugout. While this pair of

1953 Bowman Color, Joe Ginsberg (front)

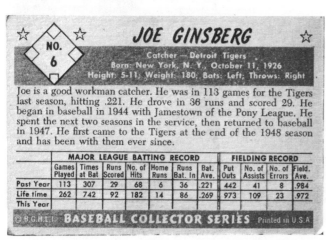

1953 Bowman Color, Joe Ginsberg (back)

1953 Bowman Color, Allie Reynolds

special cards was well received by collectors, Topps went on to overdo the idea in later years, and in general, collectors do not place as high a value on the multi-player feature cards as might be expected. There is a "wrong photo" card in the set; card #159, "Mickey Vernon," is actually a photo of Floyd Baker (who appears on his own card in the '53 Bowman black-and-white set).

OUR FAVORITE CARD

Through his appearance on a 1953 Bowman baseball card—he was never on another card—the major league career of Jack Daniels has been preserved forever. Known to his teammates as—naturally—"Sour Mash," the outfielder had a single-season major league career with the Boston Braves in 1952. By the time his '53 Bowman card had been issued, he was back in the minors for good. Daniels' one-line entry in the *Baseball Encyclopedia* shows him to have been a .187 hitter, but with a great name like that, he deserved at least one baseball card.

VALUE

EX.-MT. CONDITION: Complete set, $1,650; common card, #1–#112, $4; #113–#128, $12; #129–#160, $8; minor stars, $6–$10; Hall of Famers, $8–$15; Rizzuto, Reese, Mathews, Spahn, Hodges, Wynn, $15–$25; Rizzuto-Martin, $35; Bauer-Berra-Mantle, $45; Campanella, Martin, $30–$35; Musial, Ford, Feller, $50–$60; Berra, $110; Snider, $130; Mantle, $175. 5-YEAR PROJECTION: Above average.

1953 Bowman Color, Joe Nuxhall

1953 Bowman Color, Lou Boudreau

1953 Bowman Color, Bobby Shantz

1953 Bowman Color, Gil Hodges

1953 Bowman Color, Vic Raschi

1953 BOWMAN BLACK-AND-WHITE

SPECIFICATIONS
SIZE: 2½×3¾". FRONT: Black-and-white photograph. BACK: Red and black printing on cream-colored cardboard. DISTRIBUTION: Nationally, in 1¢ and 5¢ packages with bubblegum.

HISTORY
There's probably a great story behind Bowman's issue of two separate, but virtually identical, baseball card sets in 1953, but the hobby will probably never know the true answer. Suffice it to say that the two issues—one in color and the other in black-and-white—do exist and are both popularly collected. The 1953 Bowman black-and-white set is, indeed, a separate issue from the color cards of the same year. They came in their own differently designed wrapper and are numbered from 1 to 64. In format, however, the cards are identical to the '53 Bowman color issue. There is a large photo on the front of the card, with a black line and a white border around it; no other printing or design appears on the card front. Card backs are identical to the colored '53, with player information, stats, and a space to write in the 1953 season's performance at the bottom. The big difference between the two is that the photo on the front is in black-and-white. Another major difference is that, card for card, the 1953 Bowman black-and-whites are somewhat scarcer than the color cards, and they are about twice as expensive per card. There are no known scarcities or variations in the set.

FOR
An interesting and highly collectible version of the hobby's most popular set. While they suffer in comparison to the '53 color Bowmans, the black-and-white set is attractive in its own right.

AGAINST
Relatively expensive per card for a 1950s set.

NOTEWORTHY CARDS
There are only four Hall of Famers in the '53 Bowman black-and-white: Casey Stengel, Bob Lemon, Bucky Harris, and Johnny Mize. Another player in the set, Hoyt Wilhelm, may yet make it to Cooperstown. There are, however, lots of popular "minor stars" in the set, such as Jimmy Piersall, Ralph Branca, Billy Cox, Andy Pafko, Johnny Sain, and Preacher Roe. The Stengel card is by far the most popular and valuable.

VALUE
EX.-MT. CONDITION: Complete set, $850; common card, $9; stars, $12–$18; Mize, Lemon, $25; Stengel, $125. 5-YEAR PROJECTION: Average.

1953 Bowman Black-And-White,
Rocky Bridges

1953 Bowman Black-And-White,
Casey Stengel

1953 RED MAN

SPECIFICATIONS

SIZE: 3½×4″. FRONT: Color painting. BACK: Red printing on gray cardboard. DISTRIBUTION: Nationally, one card in each box of chewing tobacco.

HISTORY

Red Man made a few subtle changes in its 1953 baseball card set, but retained the same basic format as its premier issue of 1952. There were again 52 cards in the set: 25 players from the American League, along with 1952 World Series manager Casey Stengel, and 25 players from the National League, along with World Series manager Charlie Dressen. The players on the two "Red Man All-Star" squads were chosen by J. Taylor Spink, editor of *The Sporting News.* Spink's selections look impressive to today's hobbyists because the 52 cards in the 1953 Red Man issue contain a high percentage of superstars and Hall of Famers. The design of the '53 Red Mans follows closely the format adopted in 1952. A color painting of the player appears at the top. There is no border except at the bottom, where the picture is interrupted by a dotted line. Below the line is a white strip, or "tab," seven-sixteenths of an inch wide and containing the year, player name, and card number. Once again, the cards are numbered by league, from 1 to 26. The tab was part of an offer spelled out on the back of the cards. Fifty of the strips, when cut off the cards and mailed in to Red Man, entitled the sender to receive a replica cap from any major league team. Naturally, these caps were quite popular and resulted in a lot of the 1953 Red Man cards being relieved of their tabs. Just as naturally, collectors today prefer to have their Red Man cards with the tab, as originally issued, and are willing to pay a premium for such items. Generally, a 1953 Red Man card with the tab is worth 25 percent more than the same card in the same condition without the tab. Because the tab indicated the year of issue and because Red Man's design changed little from '52 to '53, it is a little difficult to date a card without a tab. One design change in 1953 was that the card number was printed in the white information box in the upper corner of the card front along with data and a baseball biography of the pictured player. It is possible to tell the date of a Red Man by the mention of the previous season's performance in the write-up. Some of the same paintings used in the 1952 set reappeared in the 1953 issue, though the background color was changed, or in some cases, a stadium background was used.

FOR

The 1953 Red Mans are a low-priced, attractive set with lots of superstars—it's no wonder they're popular.

AGAINST

Hard to find with tabs. Collectors don't like recycled pictures. Cards are in a nonstandard size.

NOTEWORTHY CARDS

Ted Williams and Willie Mays were both in the service in 1953, and neither appear in the Red Man set. The biggest name in the set is Stan Musial, and there are many new faces in the issue. A total of 13 Hall of Famers are included, along with at least a half dozen more who will probably be elected to the Hall of Fame.

VALUE

EX.-MT. CONDITION, WITH TAB: Complete set, $275; common card, $4; Hall of Famers, $7–$12; Campanella, $20; Musial, $30. 5-YEAR PROJECTION: Above average.

1953–1954 BRIGGS' HOT DOGS

SPECIFICATIONS

SIZE: 2¼×3½″. FRONT: Color added to black-and-white photograph. BACK: Blank. DISTRIBUTION: Washington, D.C., area, two cards as part of hot dog package.

HISTORY

It is generally accepted that the 37 cards in the Briggs hot dog set were issued over a period of two years, though details of the issue remain unclear. What is known 30 years after the fact is that the issue of unnumbered, blank-backed cards contains 25 Washington Senators cards and 12 players from the three New York teams, the Giants, the Yankees, and the Dodgers. It is interesting to note that the pictures of the New York players are the same as those found on the Dan-Dee potato chip cards of 1954 and the Stahl Meyer hot dog cards of 1953–1955. The Briggs cards were issued two to a panel as the bottom of a hot dog package. Cards still in panel form are worth about one-third more than the combined value of the individual cards. Cards that were trimmed from the box in sloppy fashion are worth considerably less than neatly cut cards. The Briggs cards are in two styles. Both feature a borderless color picture of the player at top. In a white panel below the photo, the Senators cards have the player's name, position, birth date, birthplace, and batting/throwing preference, along with a light blue facsimile autograph (exactly like the 1953 Hunters and 1954 and 1955 Esskay cards). The cards of the New York players have only the player's printed name and a black facsimile autograph in the white box.

FOR

In demand by team collectors; scarce cards, especially the Senators, who were the subject of few regional issues.

AGAINST

The use of shared photos with other sets makes the New York players' cards less desirable and less valuable than they would otherwise be.

NOTEWORTHY CARDS

Among the Senators, Jackie Jensen and Mickey Vernon are the only names the average collector is likely to know. The New York cards contain lots of the popular stars.

VALUE

EX.-MT. CONDITION, NEATLY CUT FROM BOX: Complete set, $3,300; common card, $50; Irvin, Newcombe, Hodges, Rizzuto, $100; Snider, $250; Mays, $500; Mantle, $700. 5-YEAR PROJECTION: Below average.

1953 STAHL MEYER

SPECIFICATIONS

SIZE: 3¼×4½". FRONT: Color added to black-and-white photograph. BACK: Red printing on white cardboard. DISTRIBUTION: Metropolitan New York area, one card inserted into packages of hot dogs.

HISTORY

Three of the most popular players from each of the New York teams—the Yankees, the Dodgers, and the Giants—comprise the entire baseball card set from the Stahl Meyer meat company in 1953. The cards, featuring rounded corners, were inserted into packages of hot dogs. A photograph of the player appeared on the front of the card. While these photos may appear at first glance to be in color, in reality they are black-and-white pictures to which color details have been added by an artist. The work is excellent. Below the photo is a rectangular box with a facsimile autograph of the player and a printed version of his name. A white border surrounds the front of the card. The back of the card is divided into halves in a horizontal format. There is no card number. On the left is a biography of the player, along with previous season (1952) and lifetime batting and fielding statistics. On the right is an offer for free tickets to specified New York ballgames. To get one pair of tickets, a 25-word essay had to be sent along with two of the Stahl Meyer baseball cards; the most original essays won one of 200 pairs of tickets.

FOR

Scarce, good-looking cards of some of the game's better-known players of the 1950s.

AGAINST

The combination of scarcity and popular players adds up to high cost.

NOTEWORTHY CARDS

Since all of the players are of some note, and there are only nine, we'll name them all. Yankees: Hank Bauer, Mickey Mantle, Phil Rizzuto. Dodgers: Roy Campanella, Gil Hodges, Duke Snider. Giants: Monte Irvin, Whitey Lockman, Bobby Thomson.

VALUE

EX.-MT. CONDITION: Complete set, $1,350; Lockman, Bauer, Thomson, $50–$60; Irvin, Rizzuto, Hodges, $100–$125; Campanella, Snider, $150; Mantle, $500. 5-YEAR PROJECTION: Below average.

1953 JOHNSTON COOKIE BRAVES

SPECIFICATIONS

SIZE: 2⁹/₁₆×3⁵/₁₆". FRONT: Color added to black-and-white photograph. BACK: Blue and red printing on gray cardboard. DISTRIBUTION: Wisconsin, single cards in packages of cookies.

1953 Johnston Cookie Braves, George Crowe

HISTORY

The move of the Boston Braves to Milwaukee in 1953 was an immediate success; fans all over Wisconsin embraced their new major league team. One of several companies to welcome the Tribe to Beertown with a baseball card issue was the Johnston baking company, whose Milwaukee factory lies within sight of fans at County Stadium. In 1953, Johnston issued a 25-card set featuring two dozen of the Braves players and manager Charlie Grimm. The card fronts featured attractive black-and-white photos, to which color had been artistically added. In a box below the photo, the player's name was printed along with a facsimile autograph. At the left end of the box was a red Indian chief logo of the Braves. Card backs had the traditional mix of player personal information, statistics from the two previous seasons, and a baseball biography taken right out of the Braves' yearbook. The outline of a tomahawk, like those the Braves wore on their jerseys that year, had the team name and the card number. Cards in the '53 Johnston set were numbered pecu-

1953 Johnston Cookie Braves, John Antonelli

1953 JOHNSTON COOKIE BRAVES

liarly. Card number 1 was manager Grimm; cards #2 to #12 were the pitchers, in alphabetical order; card #13 was utility player Sibby Sisti; and cards #14 to #25 were the fielders, by position. At the very bottom of the card back was a Johnston ad. The card backs were attractive and unusual in their use of two colors of ink, red and blue. The '53 Johnstons were distributed by inserting one card into each package of cookies, and they are, by far, the most common of the three sets issued by the firm.

FOR

Attractive, relatively inexpensive early 1950s regional set of a very popular team.

AGAINST

Not a thing.

NOTEWORTHY CARDS

Hall of Famers Warren Spahn and Eddie Mathews highlight the 1953 Johnson Cookie set.

VALUE

EX.-MT. CONDITION: Complete set, $120; common card, $4; Burdette, Adcock, Crandall, $6; Mathews, Spahn, $12. 5-YEAR PROJECTION: Average.

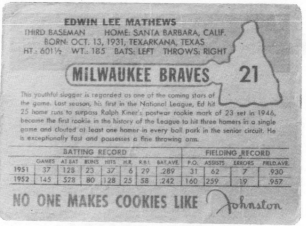

1953 Johnston Cookie Braves,
Ed Mathews (back)

1953 Johnston Cookie Braves,
Ed Mathews (front)

1953 Johnston Cookie Braves,
Warren Spahn (front)

1953 Johnston Cookie Braves,
Bob Buhl

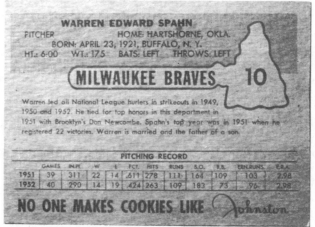

1953 Johnston Cookie Braves, Warren Spahn (back)

1953 HUNTER'S WIENERS CARDINALS

SPECIFICATIONS

SIZE: 2¼×3½". FRONT: Full-color photo. BACK: Blank. DISTRIBUTION: St. Louis area, two cards per panel on each hot dog package.

HISTORY

The early 1950s were the Golden Age for regional baseball card issues, and what could be more natural than using baseball cards to sell hot dogs? Hunter's Wieners was one of many meat companies that printed baseball cards right on the cardboard used to package hot dogs—two cards of the 26-card set were printed on each package. Kids could then cut the cards off and start a collection. The '53 Hunter's are the first of three successive issues by the company, all exclusively featuring photos of the St. Louis Cardinals. They are also the most common of the three issues, but even at that, they are plenty scarce. It is especially uncommon to encounter Hunter's cards in nice condition. Like most hot dog cards, they picked up stains from the meat in the package. Also, the cards had to be cut from the bottom of the package, and they are often found hacked up as the result of sloppy scissors-work by youngsters. The fact that the cards were issued with round corners didn't make them any easier to cut out neatly. The player's name and brief biographical details appear in a white panel at the bottom front of the card; a facsimile autograph is overprinted in light blue ink. Card backs are blank. While cards still found attached to the package would be more valuable, they are seldom encountered this way. Prices quoted are for single cards.

FOR

Great for team collectors. Cards feature excellent, unique color photos.

AGAINST

Hard to find in neatly trimmed condition. Quite expensive per card.

NOTEWORTHY CARDS

With a price nearly 10 times that of a common card in the set, Stan Musial is the premier card among the '53 Hunter's.

VALUE

EX.-MT. CONDITION, NEATLY TRIMMED: Complete set, $1,250; common card, $35–$40; Schoendienst, Slaughter, $75; Musial, $300. 5-YEAR PROJECTION: Above average.

1953 GLENDALE MEATS TIGERS

SPECIFICATIONS

SIZE: 2⅝×3¾". FRONT: Color added to black-and-white photoraph. BACK: Blue and red printing on white cardboard. DISTRIBUTION: Detroit area, single cards in packages of hot dogs.

HISTORY

The Glendale Meats set consists of 28 cards, all members of the Detroit Tigers. For some reason, most hobbyists persist in dating the cards to 1954, when in reality all the evidence points to issue in 1953, with perhaps the remainder cards being distributed the next year. None of the players traded to the Tigers in late 1953 or early 1954 are included in the set, and the statistics on the backs of the cards only go through 1952. In any event, the set is popular with Tigers team collectors and is quite scarce. One of the cards, in fact, is among the most valuable of modern baseball cards (see below). Card fronts feature a color-enhanced player photo above a white box with his name, facsimile autograph, and a color Tigers logo. On the backs of the unnumbered cards are personal data and career statistics, along with an ad offering prizes in a drawing to those who mailed in the cards at the end of the year. That probably explains why surviving 1953 Glendale Meats Tigers cards are so scarce today.

FOR

Scarce and valuable regional issue. Great for team collectors.

AGAINST

The rarity of the Houtteman card makes completing a set virtually impossible.

NOTEWORTHY CARDS

The Tigers didn't have many stars in 1953; about the only "name" in the set is Harvey Kuenn, in his rookie card debut. The Art Houtteman card was apparently withdrawn or never issued when he was traded in June, 1953, and it is one of the rarest of modern baseball cards. To a lesser extent, the cards of Joe Ginsberg and Billy Hoeft are also scarcer than normal.

VALUE

EX.-MT. CONDITION: Complete set, $2,200; common card, $40; Kuenn, Hoeft, $100; Ginsberg, $150; Houtteman, $900. 5-YEAR PROJECTION: Below average.

1953 MOTHER'S COOKIES PACIFIC COAST LEAGUE

SPECIFICATIONS

SIZE: 2¼×3½". FRONT: Color added to black-and-white photograph. BACK: Black printing on white cardboard. DISTRIBUTION: West Coast, single cards in packages of cookies.

HISTORY

The 1953 set of 63 Pacific Coast League players was the last set issued by Mother's Cookies for 30 years. It is very similar to the 1952 issue, though most of the players in the set are different. The '53 cards retained the rounded corners and the same basic format of a player photo set against a solid-color background. The back-

1952 TOPPS

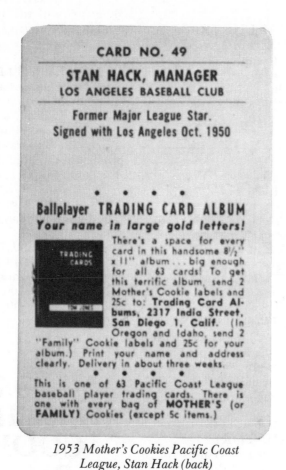

1953 Mother's Cookies Pacific Coast League, Stan Hack (back)

ground color was different for each team. Instead of the player's name being printed in the upper-left corner, it appeared in the form of a facsimile autograph. The team name was printed in the upper right. There is no border on the cards; the colored background is prone to chipping. The 1953 Mother's cards were distributed in bags of Mother's and Family cookies all over the West, and it is presumed that there was some type of offer for complete sets—complete sets are frequently found today. Card backs differ from the 1952 issue in that an album for the cards is offered, along with previous season stats for the player and the card number. Overall, the 1953 Mother's cards are much less scarce than the '52s, with no known rarities in the issue.

FOR

Attractive cards of the high minor leagues in the early 1950s.

AGAINST

Format too similar to the 1952 cards, few real big name stars.

NOTEWORTHY CARDS

While many of the players and managers in the 1953 Mother's set were former or future major leaguers, there are few big names among them. George Bamberger, Stan Hack, and Lefty O'Doul are the best known.

VALUE

EX.-MT. CONDITION: Complete set, $200; common card, $3; O'Doul, Hack, Bamberger, $7. 5-YEAR PROJECTON: Average, or a bit below.

SPECIFICATIONS

SIZE: $2\frac{5}{8} \times 3\frac{3}{4}$". FRONT: Color painting. BACK: Red and black, or just black, printing on gray cardboard. DISTRIBUTION: Nationally, in 1¢ and 5¢ packages of bubblegum.

HISTORY

When Topps came out with its first major baseball card set in 1952, the Brooklyn-based bubblegum company went right for the throat of its Philadelphia competitor, Bowman. Collectors then and now could argue which set was best, but there was no doubt that Topps was bigger. At 407 cards, the Topps set was 61 percent bigger than Bowman's 252 cards. And the physical dimensions of the Topps cards were bigger as well—$2\frac{5}{8} \times 3\frac{3}{4}$". Compared to Bowman's $2\frac{1}{16} \times 3\frac{1}{8}$" format, the Topps card was a whopping 50 percent bigger overall. In the long run, the 1952 Topps set proved to be the more valuable, also. Not all 407 Topps cards were issued in equal numbers or distributed as widely. The most common of the '52 Topps are cards #81 to #252. Only a bit more difficult to find are the first 80 cards in the set. Cards #253 to #310, called the "semi-highs" by collectors, are really quite elusive today, while cards #311 to #407, known to collectors as "high numbers," are decidedly scarce. The cards after #252 were printed and issued later in the year, when the annual spring "rush" of kids buying baseball cards was over. Most retail store owners did not restock with the higher-numbered cards. This situation is even more evident in the "high numbers," cards #311 to #407. They were issued so late in the summer that most kids and retailers were already thinking about football cards. The geographic distribution of the high numbers was extremely limited, with many of the cards being released in Canada. The elusiveness of these high-numbered cards makes collecting the 1952 Topps set a challenging—and very expensive—endeavor. Because Topps cards were printed on press sheets of 100 cards, certain baseball cards through most of the company's history have been "double-printed." That means some cards were printed twice as often as others in the same series. In the first series of 1952, for instance, cards #1 to #80, there were 20 double-prints to fill out the press sheet at 100 cards. The high numbers, by contrast, featured 97 different cards (#311 to #407), with only three double-prints. The three double-prints in the high number series are the famous Mickey Mantle card, the Jackie Robinson, and the Bobby Thomson. Even today, because of the rarity of full or partial uncut sheets of early Topps issues and the total reluctance of the company to discuss the history of its issues, most collectors have no idea which, if any, cards in a particular year or series are double-printed, and are thus more common than others. Surprisingly, there is virtually no price difference between single- and double-printed cards in a set or series; the value still depends mostly on the condition of the card and the name of the player on it. A major variety exists within the 1952 Topps set in the color of the back printing on the first 80 cards. Those cards can be found with backs printed entirely in black, or in red and black. The black-back cards are scarcer than those with red backs, but few collectors today place any price variable on the two; they are collected interchangeably. A significant innovation displayed by the '52 Topps cards was the use of the team logo in color on the front of the cards, the first time this was ever done in a major set. The 1952 Topps set is so popular with collectors that Topps reprinted the set in 1983 (see separate listing).

FOR

Most collectors consider the 1952 set to be Topps' first "real" baseball card, and it is widely collected as such. The large-format cards allowed for attractive designs and decent write-ups and stats on the backs of the cards. The set includes all varieties of players, from the superstars of the 1950s to those obscure players who only appeared on one baseball card in their entire career—there are some 18 cards of such players in the '52 Topps. The set is challenging enough to keep even the most avid collector searching for a long time. Yet, with enough time— and money—it can be completed. The '52 Topps set has proved itself to be among the finest investments among

all baseball cards, and will probably continue to be so.

AGAINST

The other side of the "challenging" coin is that, for a large number of collectors, particularly newer collectors, completion of the '52 Topps set is little more than a fantasy. The higher-numbered cards in the set are truly scarce-to-rare, and they are expensive, especially in top condition. Completion of an Excellent or Mint condition set could easily require an outlay of $7,500, and the cards aren't getting any cheaper.

NOTEWORTHY CARDS

Naturally, the most famous and expensive card in the 1952 Topps set is card #311, Mickey Mantle. While not Mantle's actual rookie card (he was in the 1951 Bowman set), it is his first Topps card, and some collectors collect nothing but Topps. While it is part of the high number series, the Mantle card is a double-print, which means it is twice as common as most of the other 96 cards in the series. However, it is more than twice as popular as the other cards, so the value continues to climb. In the midst of the baseball card "boom" in 1980, Mint examples

1952 Topps, Fred Marsh

1952 Topps, Virgil Stallcup

of the Mantle card sold for as much as $3,000. The value of the card dropped over the next couple of years, but, like the value of most '50s cards, it is again climbing. There are dozens of other superstars in the '52 set. One major variation pair in the set involves cards #48 and #49. Due to a mistake in preparing the printing plates, those cards were first printed with wrong backs, #48 Joe Page with a Johnny Sain back, and #49 Johnny Sain with a Joe Page back. The cards are also found with the correct backs. The error versions are worth $50 to $75 in top grade. The portrait on card #391, Ben Chapman, is actually Sam Chapman.

OUR FAVORITE CARD

There is a significant phenomenon in baseball cards which manifests itself in the '52 Topps set, as well as most other Topps and Bowman issues of the '50s and '60s. That is the real rarity of high-grade examples of the #1 card in each set. In the days before plastic sheets, most kids who collected baseball cards kept them in stacks bound with a rubber band, usually in numerical order. The top card of such stacks, usually card #1 in the set, tended to receive the most abuse in terms of bent corners and creases. Also, the rubber band which held the cards had a tendency to dig into the cardboard at the points of contact, creating indentations that collectors call "notching." In the 1952 Topps set, particularly, the #1 card, Andy Pafko, is a rare item in true Mint condition (four sharp corners, no creases, no scruffiness on the front of the card). While most baseball card price guides list a catalog value for the '52 Topps Pafko card at $30–$40 in top grade, several major card dealers are willing buyers of truly Mint cards at up to $75 each.

VALUE

EX.-MT. CONDITION: Complete set, $7,500; common card, #1–#252, $3; #252–#310, $7.50; #311–#407, $35; Hall of Famers, low numbers, $7.50–$15; Yogi Berra, $30; Early Wynn, Bob Lemon, $40; Willie Mays, $250; Jackie Robinson, Roy Campanella, Eddie Mathews, Pee Wee Reese, $250–$300; Mickey Mantle, $950. 5-YEAR PROJECTION: Above average.

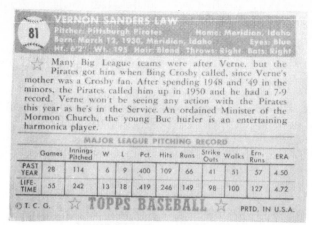

1952 Topps, Vernon Law (back)

1952 Topps, Earl Torgeson

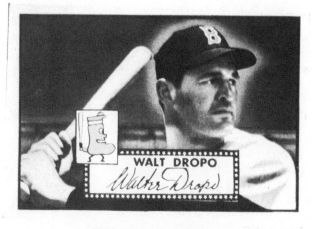

1952 Topps, Walt Dropo

1952 Topps, Bob Friend

1952 Topps, Mel Parnell

1952 Topps, Bill Rigney

1952 Topps, Fred Hutchinson

1952 Topps, Wally Westlake

1952 Topps, Yogi Berra

COMPLETE BOOK OF COLLECTIBLE BASEBALL CARDS

1952 BOWMAN

SPECIFICATIONS

SIZE: 2¹/₁₆×3¹/₈". FRONT: Color painting. BACK: Black printing on gray cardboard. DISTRIBUTION: Nationally, in 1¢ and 5¢ packages with bubblegum.

HISTORY

The 1952 Bowman set follows a format similar to the 1951 issue. Players on the cards are depicted in artists' paintings taken from actual photographs. Unlike the 1951 set, none of the paintings in the '52 set are repeats from previous years. For that reason, the '52 set has a greater collector appeal than the 1951 issue. The only discernible difference between the card fronts of those two years (other than the paintings themselves) is the fact that the player's name on the 1952 cards is in the form of a black facsimile autograph, rather than typography. Card backs of the '52s are also quite similar to the 1951s. The player's name and vital information appears at top, and there is a short career biography at center. The card number appears in three lines of type, reading, "No. ___ in 1952 SERIES/ BASEBALL/PICTURE CARDS." Beneath that is a premium offer, making baseball caps of major league teams available for 50¢ and five gum wrappers. A copyright line is at the bottom. Speaking of copyright, there is a registered trademark symbol behind the word "BASEBALL" on the backs of the cards. That little circled-R symbol figured prominently in the early "Card Wars" between Bowman and its new competitor, Topps. Bowman went to court contending that only it had the legal right to use the word "baseball" in conjunction with bubblegum cards. The court disagreed, and Topps was allowed to advertise its product as "baseball cards" also. The size of the 1952 Bowman set was cut back considerably from the previous year's high of 324 cards to 252 cards. Like many sets of the last three decades, the "high numbers" in the '52 Bowman set, cards #217 to #252, are scarcer than the rest of the issue, and more expensive.

FOR

Appealing set of well-done, all new paintings. No confusing variations.

AGAINST

There's nothing bad to be said.

NOTEWORTHY CARDS

Ted Williams and Jackie Robinson are two players who are notably absent from the 1952 Bowman set. Williams appeared that year in the Red Man tobacco card issue, and Robinson in the '52 Topps set. This would be the last year when Bowman had virtually uncontested use of players' pictures in its card sets. From 1953 to 1955, they would have to fight with Topps for exclusive rights to the big name stars.

OUR FAVORITE CARD

One of baseball's great nicknames is preserved in the facsimile autograph on card #20 in the 1952 Bowman set. Willie Jones' signature is reproduced on the card as "Puddin Head Jones." Jones' card is one of a relative handful in the '52 Bowman issue in a horizontal format.

VALUE

EX.-MT. CONDITION: Complete set, $925; common card, #1–#216, $2; #217–#252, $4.50; minor stars, $4–$8; Hall of Famers, $10–$15; Feller, Campanella, Snider, Stengel, $15–$25; Berra, $45; Musial, $55; Mays, $150; Mantle, $175. 5-YEAR PROJECTION: Above average.

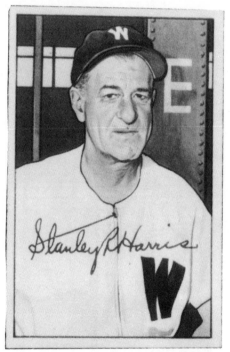

1952 Bowman, Stanley Harris

1952 Bowman, George Metkovich

1952 Bowman, Randall Gumpert

1952 Bowman, Bill Hitchcock

1952 Bowman, Howard Pollet

1952 Bowman, Ned Garver

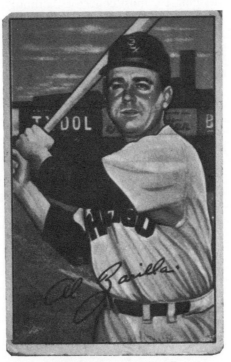

1952 Bowman, Al Zarilla

1952 Bowman, Bruce Edwards

1952 RED MAN

SPECIFICATIONS

SIZE: 3½×4″. FRONT: Color painting. BACK: Green printing on gray cardboard. DISTRIBUTION: Nationally, one card inserted into packages of chewing tobacco.

HISTORY

More than 40 years after the last baseball card issues with tobacco products had died out, the Red Man chewing tobacco "All-Star" sets began making their appearance in 1952. Each cellophane-wrapped box of Red Man contained one of 52 cards issued in the 1952 set. There were 25 player cards each from the National and American Leagues, plus a card for each of the 1951 World Series managers, Casey Stengel and Leo Durocher. According to the wording on the back of the card, the players for the set were selected by J. Taylor Spink, editor of *The Sporting News*. One of the most prominent features of the Red Man cards—one which profoundly affects their value—is a narrow white "tab" at the bottom of the card beneath the player's picture. The tab, which had the card number printed on it, was designed to be cut off and mailed in to receive "a big league style baseball cap" of the chewer's favorite team. Fifty of the tabs had to be collected for each cap, and the offer has left the majority of Red Man cards today tab-less. Many collectors feel that since there is little besides the card number on the tab of the 1952 issue, cards without the tab are just as collectible. It is a fact, though, that cards with the tab still intact are worth some 25 percent more than cards without. The values quoted below are for complete cards, that is, with tabs. Card fronts feature a borderless color painting of the player, sometimes with a blank background, sometimes with a stadium scene in the background. On some cards, the same portrait was used in several years, with the color of the background being the only change from year to year. In a white box in one of the upper corners the player's name appears in red, along with a couple of lines of personal data and a career summary. Since the tab contains the year of issue for the Red Man cards, those without it can only be dated by referring to the previous season's performance in the write-up. The Red Man cards are numbered by league, from 1 to 26. Card backs have Red Man advertising and details of the baseball cap offer. Though the Red Man cards are frequently considered to be regionals, they were, in fact, issued virtually nationwide. They were especially abundant in the South and rural areas where tobacco chewers were more prevalent.

FOR

Because of the variety of teams represented, and the relatively high percentage of big name stars, the Red Man set is one of the more popular "regional" sets of the '50s. Portraits are well-done and something different from the usual photos found on cards of the era. Considering their scarcity, in comparison to Topps or Bowman cards of the same year, they are quite inexpensive.

AGAINST

There are so few '52 Red Mans "with tabs" still available that collecting a complete set in this form is too challenging for most collectors, although the cost is certainly not prohibitively high. Use of the same pictures for successive years' issues makes the cards unpopular with some collectors.

NOTEWORTHY CARDS

Ted Williams' best baseball card from 1952 is his appearance in the Red Man issue; he didn't appear in Topp's or Bowman's set that year, and the Williams card in the Berk Ross set is downright ugly. In comparison to later Red Man issues, the 1952 set is somewhat lean on superstars, but does include more than a dozen Hall of Famers.

VALUE

EX.-MT. CONDITION, WITH TAB: Complete set, $300; common card, $4; Hall of Famers, $8–15; Mays, Musial, $35; Williams, $40. 5-YEAR PROJECTION: Above average.

1952 WHEATIES

SPECIFICATIONS

SIZE: 2×2¾″. FRONT: Blue line drawing on orange and white. BACK: Blank. DISTRIBUTION: Nationally, on backs of cereal boxes.

HISTORY

Though Wheaties had been issuing sports card sets, usually including baseball players, on the backs of cereal boxes since 1935, the 60-card set produced in 1952 is the only really widely collected Wheaties issue. There are 30 athletes in the '52 Wheaties set, each having both a portrait and an action card. Among the 30 are 10 baseball players. The cards have rounded corners and a white border surrounding a blue line drawing on an orange background. The player's name, team, and position appear at the bottom. Backs are blank. Cards are unnumbered.

FOR

Inexpensive cards for the superstar collector.

AGAINST

Unpopular size; the line drawings make the cards look antiquated and collectors generally don't like sets in which baseball players are mixed with other athletes.

NOTEWORTHY CARDS

Of the baseball players in the 1952 Wheaties set all but two are Hall of Famers: Phil Rizzuto and Preacher Roe. The HOFers are Berra, Campanella, Feller, Kell, Kiner, Lemon, Musial, and Williams. There are many better-known football players and women athletes among the rest of the cards in the set.

VALUE

EX.-MT. CONDITION, NEATLY CUT FROM BOX: Complete set (10 baseball players, 20 cards), $225; common card, $5; Hall of Famers, $7.50–15; Williams, $20. 5-YEAR PROJECTION: Below average.

1952 BERK ROSS

SPECIFICATIONS

SIZE: 2×3″. FRONT: Color-tinted black-and-white photograph. BACK: Black printing on white cardboard. DISTRIBUTION: Nationally (?), two cards in a small cardboard box.

HISTORY

In its second (and final) year of baseball card production, the New York firm of Berk Ross continued to "copycat" the more established and better-known Bowman gum company of Philadelphia. Bowman moved from a $2^1/_{16} \times 2^1/_2″$ card in 1950 to a $2^1/_{16} \times 3^1/_8″$ card in 1951. Berk Ross moved from a $2^1/_{16} \times 2^1/_2″$ card in 1951 to a 2×3″ card in 1952. Little else changed for Berk Ross in 1952 except they dropped the idea of combining all sports in their issue—the 72-card set featured all baseball players. Actually, there were only 71 players in the set. There are two cards of Phil Rizzuto; one shows him bunting, one shows him swinging. Backs of the '52 Berk Ross cards are almost identical to their previous year's effort, just a few lines of type with the player's name, team, position, and a few personal and previous season's stats. The set is un-numbered. Again in 1952, the cards were sold two to a small box for 1¢. Unlike the 1951 series, however, the '52s were not assembled in perforated, attached pairs. In comparing the 1952 Berk Ross cards with the Bowman cards of the same vintage, they come off a poor second. While in many cases the very same photos of players were used in both companies' sets, the Berk Ross method of tinting the photos resulted in a dull-looking card.

FOR

The 72-card Berk Ross set has more of 1952's superstars than either Bowman or Topps. There is an abundance of players from the 1951 World's Champion New York Yankees.

AGAINST

The cards are unattractive and there is little demand for them, even for the superstars.

NOTEWORTHY CARDS

Even though he retired before the 1952 season, Joe DiMaggio appears in the 52 Berk Ross set, as one of many New York Yankees. Also in the set are second-year cards of Mickey Mantle and Willie Mays. Stan Musial appears in the set again, and there are cards of Ted Williams and Jackie Robinson. There is a pair of error cards in the set: Ewell Blackwell's card has the back printing for Nellie Fox, and Fox's card has Blackwell's back.

VALUE

EX.-MT. CONDITION: Complete set, $750; common card, $4–$6; Hall of Famers, $10–$25; Musial, Robinson, $50–$60; Mays, Williams, $75–$100; Mantle, DiMaggio, $100–$125. 5-YEAR PROJECTION: Below average.

1952 MOTHER'S COOKIES PACIFIC COAST LEAGUE

SPECIFICATIONS

SIZE: 2¼×3½″. FRONT: Color added to black-and-white photograph. BACK: Black printing on white cardboard. DISTRIBUTION: West Coast, single cards in packages of cookies.

HISTORY

One of the last of the great Pacific Coast League baseball card sets, the Mother's Cookies issue consisted of 64 cards from all teams in the league. The cards were distributed in bags of cookies and are often found with grease stains which diminish their value. The Mother's cards feature rounded corners, an unusual feature for baseball cards in the 1950s, and they are borderless, which often leads to "chipping" of the colored backgrounds behind the players' photos. The colored background on each card is coded to a specific team; all the Portland Beavers, for example, have purple backgrounds. The photos on the cards are black-and-white pictures that have been retouched to add color, a common practice for cards in the '50s. The player's name appears in small type at the upper left, his team in the upper right. Card backs feature a card number at top and a few bits of player data. Most of the card back is taken up by an offer to send away for stamp approvals.

FOR

Attractive, scarce, and valuable cards that feature lots of players who were once, or were soon to be, in the major leagues. Some of them don't appear on any other baseball card issue.

AGAINST

Collectors don't like round-cornered cards.

NOTEWORTHY CARDS

Several cards in the '52 Mother's set are numerically scarce, probably because they were withdrawn at some time during the season when the players were traded or demoted. Joe Erautt and Buddy Peterson are the scarcest. Some well-known former big leaguers appear in the set as managers, including Frank O'Doul, Mel Ott, and Stan Hack.

OUR FAVORITE CARD

The most sought-after card in the '52 Mother's set is #4, Chuck Connors. Connors went on to greater fame as a TV and movie star (*The Rifleman*, *Yellow Rose*, etc.), but he was well known in the Pacific Coast League as the first baseman for the Los Angeles Angels. Connors played briefly with the Cubs and the Dodgers in the major leagues before leaving baseball for Hollywood.

VALUE

EX.-MT. CONDITION: Complete set, $750; common card, $9; Hack, O'Doul, $15; MacCawley, Talbot, Gordon, $20; Welmaker, Ott, $40; Connors, $75; Peterson, Erautt, $100. 5-YEAR PROJECTION: Average, perhaps a bit below.

1952 FROSTADE

SPECIFICATIONS
SIZE: 2×2½″. FRONT: Black-and-white photograph. BACK: Red printing on white cardboard. DISTRIBUTION: Limited Canadian areas, in packages of soft drink mix.

HISTORY
One of the few regional baseball card sets issued in Canada, the 1952 Frostade set contains 100 cards and features players of Canada's three teams in the International League: the Montreal Royals, the Ottawa Athletics, and the Toronto Maple Leafs, which were, respectively, Class AAA farm clubs of the Dodgers, the Phillies, and the Cardinals. The set contains many players who had been, or would be, major leaguers. An unusual aspect of the set is that besides the player cards, there is a group of 22 playing tips cards and a card of the Toronto stadium. Card fronts feature a black-and-white photo surrounded by a black line and a white border. Card backs, printed in red, have a few facts about the player, a mail-in offer for various toys, and an ad for Frostade. Cards are unnumbered.

FOR
Challenge of a "foreign" card set; minor league cards of many well-known players.

AGAINST
Cards are hard to find in the U.S.

NOTEWORTHY CARDS
Certainly the most popular card in the Frostade set is that of current Dodger manager Tommy Lasorda when he was a minor league pitcher for Montreal in the Dodgers' organization. Other well-known players include Walter Alston (manager for Montreal at the time), Jim Gilliam, Jim Pendleton, Gino Cimoli, and Johnny Podres.

VALUE
EX.-MT. CONDITION: Complete set, $525; common card, $5; minor stars, $6–$8; Alston, Lasorda, $15–$20. 5-YEAR PROJECTION: Average.

1952 NUM NUM INDIANS

SPECIFICATIONS
SIZE: 3½×4½″. FRONT: Black-and-white photograph. BACK: Black printing on white cardboard. DISTRIBUTION: Cleveland area, in packages of potato chips; also issued by team.

HISTORY
Two versions of this set were issued in 1952. Cards with a one-inch coupon tab at the bottom were issued in packages of Num Num potato chips. The tabs carried a card number, and when a complete set of 20 was collected, they could be redeemed for an official American League ball, autographed by your favorite Indians player. The tab was separated from the rest of the card by a dotted cutting line. Cards without the tab were issued directly by the team. Cards with the tab are worth about 25 percent more than cards without. Card fronts have a black-and-white player photo with a white border. Backs have the card number and the player's life story.

FOR
Reasonably priced regional issue; great for team collectors.

AGAINST
Uninspired design; unpopular size.

NOTEWORTHY CARDS
The nucleus of the Indians team that took the American League pennant in 1954 is present in this set, including the team's trio of Hall of Fame pitchers: Bob Feller, Bob Lemon, and Early Wynn. Also in the Hall of Fame is manager Al Lopez. Card #16, Bob Kennedy, is much scarcer than the rest because it was withdrawn when he left the team to spend most of the season in the service.

VALUE
EX.-MT. CONDITION, WITH TAB: Complete set, $450; common card, $13.50; Hall of Famers, $20–$40; Kennedy, $150. 5-YEAR PROJECTION: Below average.

1951 BOWMAN

SPECIFICATIONS
SIZE: 2¹/₁₆×3¹/₈″. FRONT: Color painting. BACK: Red and blue printing on gray cardboard. DISTRIBUTION: Nationally, in 1¢ and 5¢ packages with bubblegum.

HISTORY
At 324 cards, Bowman's 1951 baseball card set was the largest issue up to that time. In addition to making the set larger for 1951, Bowman also made the individual cards larger, moving to a 2¹/₁₆×3¹/₈″ size that would be maintained for two years. The basic design of the set remained the same. In fact, some of the same color paintings of players that had appeared in the 1950 set were used in an enlarged version for the 1951 issue. A black panel, with the player's name in white type, was added to the front of the card. Card backs were vertical in format, but featured the same basic line-up of player personal data, a short biography, and card number. A Bowman copyright line appears at the bottom. Even in the larger format, Bowman continued to print its cards in 36-card sheets, a total

1951 Bowman, Ron Northey

of nine such sheets comprising the issue. The final 72 cards, #253–#324, are scarcer than the first 252 cards. Bowman expanded on the concept of issuing manager cards in its 1951 set, becoming the first company of the post-war era to issue a card for every major league pilot as part of the regular set.

FOR
Popular starting point for many collectors, being the first of Bowman's larger-format sets. Paintings are attractive and the set is not too tough or too expensive to complete.

AGAINST
Too many pictures shared with the 1950 set.

NOTEWORTHY CARDS
The rookie cards of both Mickey Mantle and Willie Mays appear in the high number series, and Whitey Ford's rookie card is the first card in the set. Lots of other Hall of Famers in the set. The George Kell card has a mistake on the back and reads "No. 46 in the 1950 SERIES," rather than having the correct 1951 date. White Sox manager Paul Richards' card is unusual in that it features a caricature rather than a realistic painting.

VALUE
EX.-MT. CONDITION: Complete set, $1,500; common card, #1–#252, $2.25; #253–#324, $7.50; minor stars, $4–$10; Hall of Famers, $10–$15; Dickey, Snider, Campanella, Feller, Berra, $20–$30; Williams, Ford, $55–$60; Mays, $300; Mantle, $375. 5-YEAR PROJECTION: Above average.

1951 Bowman, Roy Smalley (front)

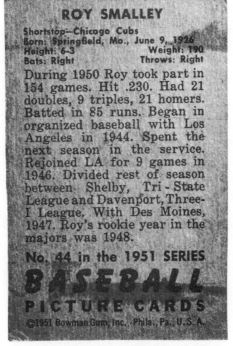

1951 Bowman, Roy Smalley (back)

1951 TOPPS RED BACKS

SPECIFICATIONS
SIZE: 2×2⅝". FRONT: Black-and-white photo on red, white, blue, and yellow background. BACK: Red printing on white cardboard. DISTRIBUTION: Nationally, two cards in package sold for 1¢.

HISTORY
The most common of Topps' five separate baseball card issues for 1951, the "Red Backs," as they are known to collectors, is a 52-card set designed to be used to play a baseball game. In addition to a player photo, the front of each round-cornered card had a game situation—out, walk, ball, double, etc.—and the cards could be shuffled, stacked, and turned over one at a time to play a game of baseball. With only 52 cards it was probably a pretty boring game, but the whole thing was just a sham to avoid court fights with Bowman, who then held what they thought was exclusive license to market current baseball players' trading cards with a piece of bubblegum. The two companies were in court constantly until 1955, when Topps bought out Bowman. It is likely that all five of the Topps issues for 1951 were available at or about the same time. It is said that the Red Backs, besides being sold two-for-a-penny in their own

1951 Bowman, Jack Kramer

"Baseball DOUBLES Playing Cards" packages, were also packed with the Connie Mack All-Star and Major League All-Star cards. The Red Backs were issued in panels of two, perforated for easy separation. A major hoard of these cards—complete in the original boxes—was discovered in a Philadelphia-area warehouse a couple of years back. Though the finder tried to "sneak" the cards into hobby channels without disrupting prices, it didn't work. Cards, wrappers, and even boxes are currently available in top condition at reasonable prices. It is interesting to note that the partner "Blue Backs" were found mixed right in with the Red Backs in this hoard, indicating that at some time in 1951 the two circulated right alongside each other.

FOR

Currently available at reasonable prices.

AGAINST

Rather unattractive. It's a good thing they have the magic "Topps" name on them; collectors in general show little interest in baseball cards that are in playing card or game card style.

NOTEWORTHY CARDS

Yogi Berra, Bob Feller, Warren Spahn, Gil Hodges, Duke Snider.

There are two variations of the Gus Zernial and Tommy Holmes cards. Zernial exists with team designations of Philadelphia and Chicago; he was traded on April 30, 1951, from the White Sox to the Athletics in a three-way deal that also included the Cleveland Indians. Tommy Holmes exists with team designations of Hartford and Boston (Braves). Interestingly, this does not appear to be a case of Topps having to create a minor league card when a player was "sent down." After a nine-year career with the Boston Braves, Holmes opened the 1951 season as playing manager of the Braves' Hartford farm team in the Eastern League. On June 20, 1951, with the Braves in fifth place in the National League, Holmes was called up to replace Billy Southworth. He continued to fill in as an outfielder while managing Boston to a fourth place finish. Holmes, in turn, was replaced as the Braves' skipper by Charlie Grimm early in 1952, and he went on to play a few games for the Dodgers before retiring.

VALUE

EX.-MT. CONDITION: Complete set, $200; common card, $2–$3; stars, $4–$8; Hall of Famers, $10–$12; Zernial, Holmes, $10; Berra, $15. 5-YEAR PROJECTION: Below average.

1951 TOPPS BLUE BACKS

SPECIFICATIONS

SIZE: 2×2⅝". FRONT: Black-and-white photo on red, white, yellow, and green background. BACK: Blue printing on white cardboard. DISTRIBUTION: Nationally, two cards in a package for 1¢.

HISTORY

Identical in basic design, set size (52 cards), and game format to the Topps "Red Backs" of the same year, the '51 Blue Backs are much scarcer. In fact, if the issue were subject to any great degree of collector popularity, it would be discovered that the Blue Backs are really quite a challenging set to complete. The warehouse hoard of Red Backs that was dumped in the collector market a couple of years ago contained only a small number of Blue Backs packaged in what appeared to be leftover Red Backs wrappers. The two sets were originally issued in different fashion; perhaps as a test, perhaps for other reasons known only to Topps' marketing people. Both types of cards were sold two to a pack for a penny. The wax wrapper for the Blue Backs says

1951 Topps Red Backs (back)

1951 Topps Red Backs, Maurice McDermott

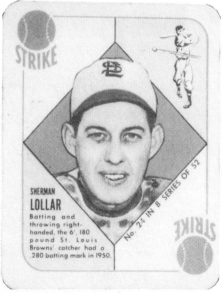

1951 Topps Blue Backs, Sherman Lollar

"Baseball Candy," while the Red Backs wrapper makes no mention of gum or candy. Some collectors say the "Candy" referred to on the Blue Backs wrapper was a piece of caramel. Others contend that it was just a legal gimmick; by calling bubblegum "Candy," Topps hoped to avoid legal troubles with Bowman, which had what they thought were exclusive rights to sell baseball cards of current players with bubblegum. The whole thing spent years in court with no satisfactory outcome; the issue was closed when Topps bought Bowman in 1955. The Blue Backs were issued in pairs, perforated for easy separation. Like the Red Backs, they have various baseball situations printed on the front to allow playing of a card game with the cards. Because the cards are printed on rather thick cardboard, and have rounded corners, they have held up quite well over the years and are often available in top grade.

FOR

Well, they *are* Topps cards; that counts for something. They may well represent good value for the money in terms of actual scarcity; but that assumes demand for the issue will someday increase.

AGAINST

They're not very attractive; they're in a funny size; and collectors don't generally care for game cards.

NOTEWORTHY CARDS

There are not as many big name stars in the Blue Backs as in the Red Backs. The only Hall of Famer in the group is Johnny Mize, though the set also contains potential Hall of Famers Enos Slaughter and Richie Ashburn.

VALUE

EX.-MT. CONDITION: Complete set, $400; common card, $5–$7; Ashburn, Slaughter, $10–$12; Mize, $17.50. 5-YEAR PROJECTION: Average.

1951 TOPPS TEAM CARDS

SPECIFICATIONS

SIZE: $5^1/_4 \times 2^1/_{16}''$. FRONT: Black-and-white photo, yellow border. BACK: Red printing on white cardboard. DISTRIBUTION: Nationally, details unsure.

HISTORY

As with Topps' four other baseball card issues of 1951, there is some question as to just how the Team Cards were distributed. They are the same size as the Connie Mack and Current All-Stars, and they were packaged in the same "Baseball Trading Card Candy" wax wrappers as the All-Star cards. Whether they were mixed into these packages with the All-Stars and/or Red Backs is not known. There is even some controversy as to whether the "Candy" referred to was caramel or bubblegum. At this late date, though, it doesn't matter. What matters is that the cards are quite scarce and among the more popular of the '51 Topps galaxy of card issues. There seem to be two or three levels of scarcity among the nine unnumbered cards in the set; prices, of course, reflect the scarcity. The idea of issuing team cards was not new to Topps in 1951; Fatima cigarettes had issued team cards in nearly identical size back

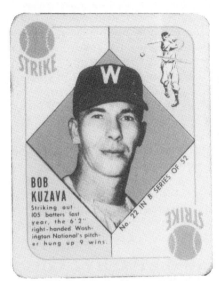

1951 Topps Blue Backs, Bob Kuzava

1951 Topps Blue Backs (back)

1951 Topps Team Cards, Brooklyn Dodgers

in 1913. Curiously, the Topps Team Cards depict just nine of the 16 major league teams of the day: the Boston Red Sox, the Brooklyn Dodgers, the Chicago White Sox, the Cincinnati Reds, the New York Giants, the Philadelphia Athletics, the Philadelphia Phillies, the St. Louis Cardinals, and the Washington Senators. The cards come in two versions, with and without the date "1950" in the black banner that gives the team name. Neither variety seems to be scarcer than the other and demand for the two is about equal, so there is no price disparity. The back of the card offers identification of the players on the front. After this issue, it would be another five years before Topps again produced team cards.

FOR

The '51 Topps Team Cards were innovative for the early 1950s, and they provide a nice large format so the players are more than just a spot of colored ink, as they are on the smaller team cards of the 1960s and 1970s.

AGAINST

The set is "incomplete," it doesn't offer all 16 teams.

VALUE

EX.-MT. CONDITION: Complete set, $650; Phils, Senators, Reds, A's, $50; Dodgers, White Sox, Giants, $75; Cardinals, Red Sox, $100. 5-YEAR PROJECTION: Below average.

1951 TOPPS CONNIE MACK ALL-STARS

SPECIFICATIONS

SIZE: 2¹/₁₆×5¹/₄". FRONT: Black-and-white photo on red background. BACK: Red printing on white cardboard. DISTRIBUTION: Nationally, details of issue unsure.

HISTORY

One of the five separate Topps issues for 1951 designed to get around

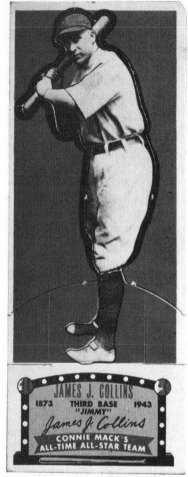

1951 Topps Connie Mack All-Stars, James J. Collins

Bowman's monopoly of issuing current players' baseball trading cards with bubblegum, the 1951 Connie Mack All-Stars are a set of 11 unnumbered, die-cut cards. Black-and-white "action" photos of the 11 Hall of Famers are printed on a red background. The "plaque" at bottom is in red, white, blue, yellow, and black. It seems that nobody remembers for sure how these cards were originally sold. The wax wrappers say "Baseball Trading Card Candy." Some sources claim this was merely a euphemism for bubblegum; others say the candy was actually a sticky piece of caramel. In addition, while there is no indication on the wrapper, it is known that these large die-cut cards were packaged with an uncut pair of the Red Backs cards also produced by Topps in 1951. It is quite likely that they were also packaged alone, one card to a 1¢ pack. Despite the fact that collectors don't usually like "retrospective" cards

issued after the playing days of the depicted player are over, the Connie Mack All-Stars are a scarce and popular issue. The fact that the set is one of Topps' first issues seems to override some of that objection. Borrowing from the "Batter Up" baseball cards of 1934–1936, the Connie Mack All-Star cards were die-cut so that most of the red background could be removed and the card folded to make a stand-up figure. Naturally, collectors today prefer to have the cards in pristine condition, with background intact. After the background was removed, the cards tended to lose various appendages such as bats, arms, and heads.

FOR

Attractive, innovative cards of baseball's greats. Quite scarce.

AGAINST

The players are not contemporary with the cards' issue. It is hard to complete a set in nice condition.

NOTEWORTHY CARDS

All are Hall of Famers: Grover C. Alexander, Mickey Cochrane, Eddie Collins, Jimmy Collins, Lou Gehrig, Walter Johnson, Connie Mack, Christy Mathewson, Babe Ruth, Tris Speaker, and Honus Wagner.

VALUE

EX.-MT. CONDITION, INCLUDING BACKGROUND: Complete set, $2,000; common card, $75–$100; Johnson, Wagner, $150–$200; Ruth, Gehrig, $400–$500. NOTE: Cards with red background removed are worth no more than half the value of a card with the background. 5-YEAR PROJECTION: Average.

1951 TOPPS MAJOR LEAGUE ALL-STARS

SPECIFICATIONS

SIZE: 2¹/₁₆×5¹/₄". FRONT: Black-and-white photo on red die-cut background. BACK: Blue printing on white cardboard. DISTRIBUTION: Nationally, details unclear.

HISTORY

This 11-card set is most often referred to by collectors as "Current All-Stars" to differentiate it from the similar old-timers issue, "Connie Mack All-Stars," also produced by Topps in 1951. Details of the issue are unclear. It is most likely that these cards were sold right alongside the Connie Mack All-Stars, probably in the same type of wrapper. Like the Connie Macks, the Current All-Stars are unnumbered, die-cut cards designed to have most of the red background removed so the card could be folded and made to stand up. At the base was a "plaque" in red, white, blue, yellow, and black with the player's biographical sketch. The idea was not new with Topps; National Chicle gum's 1934–1936 "Batter Up" baseball card issue featured die-cut, stand-up cards. Collectors today generally scorn cards that have actually been used the way they were intended; most want these cards only in uncut, unfolded form. One reason is that once the background was removed, the cards were susceptible to damage—usually heads, arms, and bats being torn off—which greatly reduces the value of the card. While the Current All-Stars set "officially" consists of 11 cards, only eight of them were actually issued in gum packs. It is quite likely that ongoing litigation between Topps and Bowman over players' contractual rights to appear on this or that baseball card set resulted in the cards of Jim Konstanty, Robin Roberts, and Eddie Stanky being withheld from circulation—all appeared in the 1951 Bowman set. The few cards of these three players which exist within the hobby—and they are among the rarest of legitimate baseball card issues, with fewer than five each being known from the current All-Stars series—are believed to have come out of Topp's back door. The rest of the set is also quite scarce, especially in nice condition with background intact, which is the way collectors want them.

FOR

These are rare cards showing mostly star players in an attractive format. On top of all that, they're from Topps.

AGAINST

Hard to find in nice condition, expensive.

NOTEWORTHY CARDS

Of the eight regularly issued cards, half are Hall of Famers: Yogi Berra, George Kell, Ralph Kiner, and Bob Lemon; Phil Rizzuto should be elected some year soon, but Hoot Evers, Larry Doby and Walt Dropo are out of luck.

VALUE

EX.-MT. CONDITION, COMPLETE BACKGROUND, UNFOLDED: Evers, Dropo, Doby, $200; Kell, Kiner, Lemon, Rizzuto, $250–$275; Berra, $350–$400; Roberts, Konstanty, Stanky, $5,000+. 5-YEAR PROJECTION: Average.

1951 BERK ROSS

SPECIFICATIONS

SIZE: $2^1/_{16} \times 2^1/_2$". FRONT: Color-tinted black-and-white photograph. BACK: Black printing on white cardboard. DISTRIBUTION: Nationally (?), two cards in small cardboard box.

HISTORY

Berk Ross traded heavily on the early success of Bowman baseball cards in its two "Hit Parade of Champions" sets in 1951 and 1952. The 1951 Berk Ross cards are the exact same size as the 1948–1950 Bowmans. Like the 1950 Bowmans, the Berk Ross cards feature no writing on the front of the card, and to cap it off, Berk Ross used many of the photos on which the Bowman paintings were based. There the comparison stops, though, for the Berk Ross cards are of very poor quality. The black-and-white photos are heavily retouched, and the added coloring can only be described as dull. Card backs contain the player's name and a few biographical and career details. The 72 cards in the 1951 Berk Ross set are numbered in four groups of 18. Cards are numbered 1–1 to 1–18, 2–1 to 2–18, 3–1 to 3–18, and 4–1 to 4–18. Berk Ross must have thought it had a better idea in terms of

marketing its cards. While the Bowman cards were sold one per package with a piece of bubblegum for 1¢ in 1950, or six cards and a piece of gum for a nickel, Berk Ross cards were sold in a small box, without gum, two for a penny. The two Berk Ross cards in each box were attached to each other and perforated for easy separation. Few collectors care whether the cards are still attached, but a small premium, 10 percent or so over the individual values of the two cards, can usually be commanded by an unbroken pair. The other Berk Ross innovation was the inclusion of many different sports stars in the 1951 set. While 40 of the 72 cards were baseball players, there were also football and basketball players, boxers, golfers, even a few women athletes. The Berk Ross cards never achieved any great response in the 1951 marketplace, and they are not particularly popular with collectors today, a result of their poor quality.

FOR

Low cost.

AGAINST

Mixing of sports in a card set is unpopular; the cards are decidedly unattractive.

NOTEWORTHY CARDS

Berk Ross scored quite a coup in 1951 by having a Joe DiMaggio card in his last season; it was DiMaggio's first card since the 1948 Leaf set. Stan Musial appeared in only two baseball card sets in 1951—Wheaties and Berk Ross. The set also features a good number of the 1950 Philadelphia Phillies "Whiz Kids," who captured the National League pennant in 1950. This was probably an effort on the part of Berk Ross to gain acceptability in Philadelphia, the headquarters for Bowman. Among the nonbaseball players in the set are Bob Cousy, Ben Hogan, Sugar Ray Robinson, Dick Button (Olympic skater, now TV commentator), and Jesse Owens.

VALUE

EX.-MT. CONDITION: Complete set, $125; common nonbaseball player, 75¢; common baseball player, $1.50; stars, $3–$7.50; Musial, $10; DiMaggio, $20. 5-YEAR PROJECTION: Below average.

1950 BOWMAN

SPECIFICATIONS

SIZE: $2^1/_{16} \times 2^1/_2''$. FRONT: Color painting. BACK: Red and black printing on cream-colored cardboard. DISTRIBUTION: Nationally, in 1¢ and 5¢ packages with bubblegum.

HISTORY

By increasing the number of cards in its 1950 baseball card set to 252, Bowman was able to print the issue in seven sheets of 36 cards each, without having to reprint cards from earlier series as had been the case in 1949. The '50 Bowmans maintained the $2^1/_{16} \times 2^1/_2''$ format of the 1948 and 1949 sets, but there was a major change in the design of the cards. Working from black-and-white photos, artists contracted by Bowman churned out color paintings of each player. The result was a far more pleasing product than the heavily retouched photos used in the 1949 set. Each card in the 1950 set is a virtual work of baseball art. Card backs were horizontal in layout, printed in red and black. A five-star circular logo of Bowman's "Picture Card Collectors Club" appears in the upper right. At left is the player's name, position, and team. Personal data appears below that, along with a short write-up on the player. The card number is at the bottom. The last 72 cards in the set can be found with or without a copyright line for the Philadelphia-based gum company below the card number, but collectors do not pay a premium for either version. Like most card sets of the 1950s through 1970s, all series of the 1950 Bowmans were not printed in equal quantity. Unlike most of the other sets, though, the scarcer cards in the set are the first 72 numbers. It is usually the higher-numbered cards, released later in the season, that are the scarce ones. Unfortunately for today's superstar collectors, most of the big names in the 1950 Bowman set appear in the first 72 cards. Overall, the '50 issue was a major step forward for Bowman. It helped them develop the type of collector loyalty they would soon need to face competition from Topps.

FOR

Extremely attractive set, and Bowman's last in the "old standard" size. The 1950 set was one of the least complicated and least expensive of Bowman's early issues.

AGAINST

It's hard to say anything bad about this set.

NOTEWORTHY CARDS

Ted Williams joined the Bowman line-up for 1950. Leaving the baseball card scene, appearing on his last card as an active player, was Hall of Famer Luke Appling. Bowman started a trend in modern cards in 1950 by including cards of selected nonplaying managers, most notably Hall of Famers Casey Stengel, Leo Durocher, and Frank Frisch. An unusual aspect and one of the few drawbacks of the 1950 Bowman set is that there are no "rookie cards" worthy of note.

VALUE

EX.-MT. CONDITION: Complete set, $900; common card, #1–#72, $6; #73–#252, $2.50; minor stars, $5–$10; Hall of Famers, $10–$20; Feller, Berra, Campanella, $25–$30; Williams, Robinson, $50. 5-YEAR PROJECTION: Average, or a bit above.

1950 DRAKE'S

SPECIFICATIONS

SIZE: $2^1/_2 \times 2^1/_2''$. FRONT: Black-and-white photograph. BACK: Black printing on gray cardboard. DISTRIBUTION: New York area, inserted into packages of bakery products and cookies.

HISTORY

The popularity of that newfangled electronic marvel—the television—especially as a medium for broadcasting baseball games, was utilized by Drake's Bakeries in 1950 as a basis for the design of its baseball card set. The cards depict a black-and-white photo of the player in a round-cornered white frame, as if being viewed on a TV screen. A white strip at the top of the black border says, "TV Baseball Series." Five years later, the Bowman bubblegum company would adapt the style for its 1955 color card set, but in 1950, the Drake's issue must have seemed quite clever. The back of the Drake's card features the usual player personal data, a career summary, an ad for Drake's Bakeries and a card number (1–36). The set is among the scarcer of the early 1950 regionals. This was Drake's only baseball card issue until 1981, when the company began annual issues of its "Big Hitters" series.

FOR

Innovative format, lots of stars from popular teams of the era.

AGAINST

The black-and-white cards seem outdated in an era when virtually every regional set was using color printing. High cost per cards make collecting a full set difficult.

NOTEWORTHY CARDS

The 36 players in the 1950 Drake's set are concentrated on the teams from New York and Boston, with lots of popular stars of the day, though Hall of Famers are not as numerous as might be expected; only five appear in the set: Campanella, Snider, Spahn, Reese, and Berra.

VALUE

EX.-MT. CONDITION: Complete set, $900; common card, $20–$25; Hall of Famers, $50–$75. 5-YEAR PROJECTION: Below average.

1950 WORLD WIDE GUM

SPECIFICATIONS

SIZE: $3^1/_4 \times 2^1/_2''$. FRONT: Blue-and-white photograph. BACK: Blank. DISTRIBUTION: Canada, in packages of bubblegum.

HISTORY

In a sense, the Canadian-issued World Wide Gum cards of 1950 are the last legacy of the Goudey Gum cards. World Wide was the brand-name under which Goudey cards had been issued in Canada in the 1930s. The 1950 set consists of 48 cards of International League players, including many future and former major leaguers. The cards are horizontal in layout, with a blue-and-white photo of the player at the left. At right is a column of type with the player's name and team. Below that, in both English and French, are the player's position, some personal data, and a career summary. At bottom is the card number and "Big League Stars." The cards are blank-backed.

FOR
Interesting multi-team Canadian minor league set.

AGAINST
Not particularly attractive.

NOTEWORTHY CARDS
Tommy Lasorda, then a minor league pitcher for the Montreal Royals, appears in the 1950 World Wide set. The most popular card, though, is Lasorda's teammate, Chuck Connors. Connors had made a single appearance for the Dodgers in 1949, as a pinch hitter (he didn't get the hit). He was traded to the Cubs organization, where he played a third of the season at first base in 1951, compiling a .239 average with two home runs. Connors moved on to the Pacific Coast League where he began acting in TV and movies. He got his big break with the series *The Rifleman*.

VALUE
EX.-MT. CONDITION: Complete set, $750; common card, $15; minor star, $20; Lasorda, $50; Connors, $75. 5-YEAR PROJECTION: Below average.

1950–1956 CALLAHAN HALL OF FAME

SPECIFICATIONS
SIZE: 1¾×2½". FRONT: Black-and-white drawing. BACK: Black

printing on white cardboard. DISTRIBUTION: Sold in sets at the National Baseball Museum and Hall of Fame in Cooperstown, New York.

HISTORY
This set of 82 small, glossy-front cards was issued over a period of seven years by the Hall of Fame. The initial group of more than 60 cards was issued in 1950. Each year, when new baseball figures were elected to the Hall of Fame, cards were issued to update the set. Besides the enshrined players, managers, executives, etc., the set included a card of then-baseball commissioner Happy Chandler (who was himself elected to the Hall of Fame in 1982) and cards picturing the interior and exterior of the building. The front of the card includes a black-and-white line drawing of the player, with a simple black frame line and white border. The back of the card has a detailed baseball biography of the player; several of the cards are known with two different versions of the back biography. The cards are unnumbered. The issue of these cards was discontinued in favor of new sets of postcards, which the Hall of Fame has been issuing over the years for sale at its souvenir shop.

FOR
The fact that the cards were issued by the Hall of Fame gives them more "legitimacy" than most old-timers baseball card issues. The black-and-white drawings are really quite excellent.

AGAINST
Their small-size has limited the popularity of the Hall of Fame set, along with the fact that it is "complete" only through the mid-1950s.

NOTEWORTHY CARDS
Since they're all Hall of Famers, there's not much more to be said. The card of Mickey Cochrane is found in two versions, one misspelling his name as "Cochran."

VALUE
EX.-MT. CONDITION: Complete set, $75; common card, 50¢; major superstar, $2–$3; "Cochran" error, $5; Cobb, Gehrig, DiMaggio, $7.50; Ruth, $10. 5-YEAR PROJECTION: Below average.

1950 REMAR BAKING COMPANY

SPECIFICATIONS
SIZE: 2×3". FRONT: Black-and-white photograph. BACK: Blue printing on white cardboard. DISTRIBUTION: Oakland Bay area, with purchases of bread.

HISTORY
The last of the Remar Baking Company issues, the 1950 set of 27 cards continued the tradition of picturing only Oakland Oaks players of the Pacific Coast League. The 1950 set also continued the Remar tradition of being confusing to collectors. The cards used the same format and, in some cases, the same pictures as the 1949 set. The only way to tell the year is to check the backs of the cards to see if the stats listed are for 1948 (on 1949 cards) or 1949 (on 1950 issue). Card fronts are the same: a photo surrounded by a white border with the player's name and position below. Card backs have the previous season's stats, some player data, and ads for Sunbeam-brand bread and the local radio station. Unlike the 1949 issue, the 1950 Remar cards seem to have been about equally distributed, with no known scarcities.

FOR
Easy set for the regional or Pacific Coast League collector.

AGAINST
Too easily confused with the 1949 set; no big name players.

NOTEWORTHY CARDS
There are no really big names in the 1950 Remar set, though Cookie Lavagetto, George Bamberger, Chuck Dressen, and Billy Herman would go on to manage in the major leagues, and Herman was inducted into the Hall of Fame in 1975.

VALUE
EX.-MT. CONDITION: Complete set, $75; common card, $2.50; minor star, $4. 5-YEAR PROJECTION: Below average.

CHUCK DRESSEN
Oaks Team Manager

1949- 1940

ENOS SLAUGHTER
Outfield, St. Louis, N.L.

1949 BOWMAN

SPECIFICATIONS

SIZE: $2^{1}/_{16} \times 2^{1}/_{2}$". FRONT: Hand-colored black-and-white photograph. BACK: Red and blue printing on cream-colored cardboard. DISTRIBUTION: Nationally, in 1¢ packages with bubblegum.

HISTORY

After its premier issue of 48 cards in 1948, Bowman really hit its stride in 1949, with one of the largest one-year baseball card issues up to that time—240 cards. The 1949 Bowmans retained the same nearly square format of the previous year's issue, but added color to the black-and-white photographs that formed the basis of the design. The color was added in a rather clumsy fashion, but most kids at that time didn't notice, or didn't care if they did notice. Instead of the stadium backgrounds of the 1948 cards, the pictures on the 1949 set were set against a solid-color background. Most of the backgrounds on the lower-numbered cards were bright colors like red, blue, and orange; the later series used pastel shades in the background. Only a few of the cards between #1 and #108 have the player's name on the front, and those that do were part of a second printing later in the year. Cards #109 to #240 all feature the player's name on the front, in a thin white strip toward the bottom of the card. On the card backs, there was also a difference between cards #1 to #108 and cards #109 to #240. All 240 of the cards featured the same basic combination of a card number, a few personal facts about the player, a short career write-up, and a premium offer, but the first 108 cards (as well as a handful of the later cards) had the player's name in printed form, while cards #109 to #240 had the player's name appearing as a facsimile autograph. The 1949 Bowman set was produced in series of 36 cards each, with the final three series (cards #145 to #240) being much more scarce than the earlier four groups. To round out the 96 "new" cards in the 5th–7th Series of 1949 Bowmans, the company reprinted a dozen cards from its earlier series, but made visible changes on each of them. Cards #4-Priddy, #78-Zoldak, #83-Scheffing, #85-Mize, #88-Salkeld, and #98-Rizzuto were printed in the later series with the names on the front of the card, while cards #109-FitzGerald, #124-Murtaugh, #126-Brazle, #127-Majeski, #132-Evans, and #143-Dillinger had the name changed on the back from facsimile autograph to print. Because these 12 cards can be found in the earlier-printed versions, the value of the later printings is not as high as the rest of the "high numbers" since the majority of collectors do not collect the variations.

FOR

The first large-scale baseball card issue of modern times. Lots of obscure players of the 1940s who don't appear in other sets.

AGAINST

The cards are really not all that good-looking; the 96 high numbers make collecting the complete set expensive; the varieties can be confusing.

NOTEWORTHY CARDS

Virtually all of the major stars of the day appear in the 1949 Bowman set, with the exception of Joe DiMaggio and Ted Williams, who were apparently under exclusive contract with Leaf gum company. The rookie cards of Hall of Fame hurler Robin Roberts and outfielder Duke Snider appear in the set. One "wrong photo" card in the set is of special interest. Card #240, "Norman 'Babe' Young," shows a head-and-shoulders portrait of a New York Yankees player. The photo actually shows Bobby Young, who was a St. Louis Cardinals rookie in 1948, but spent all of the 1949 season in the minors with Rochester. Since Babe Young's middle name was Robert, it is understandable how the mistake was made, but what is hard to fathom is why the player on the card is pictured in a Yankees uniform—neither Young ever played for the Yankees.

OUR FAVORITE CARD

Unless you collected Bowman baseball cards in 1949, it will be hard to understand the special significance of card #4, Gerry Priddy. Within a few days after the new baseball cards were issued in 1949, most of the kids who had saved their allowances all winter and those who were adept at winning big card pots in flipping contests had accumulated the first 73 cards of the set—or at least most of them. No matter how many packs of gum you bought, or how many flips you won, you could never seem to find card #4. In those days before checklist cards, nobody even knew which player they were looking for. Later in the summer, card #4 finally showed up, and nobody was particularly excited to find out it was Gerry Priddy, the second baseman of the hapless St. Louis Browns. It was only years later that the kids of '49, who had become the collectors of the 1970s, discovered the secret of card #4, Gerry Priddy. Uncut sheets of 36 cards each, just as Bowman printed them, revealed that the reason card #4 couldn't be found early in the year was that it wasn't printed until later. The spot on the sheet which would have been occupied by the Gerry Priddy card was held by card #73, Billy Cox. The folks at Bowman had not wanted it to be too easy to complete the first run of 72 cards, so they deliberately held card #4 back to keep the kids spending their pennies for baseball cards.

VALUE

EX.-MT. CONDITION: Complete set, $2,400; common card, #1–#144, $3; common high number, #145–#240, $15; stars, $5–$15; Feller, Berra, Doby, $20–$25; Musial, Campanella, Robinson, Lemon, $45–$50; Snider, $175–$200; Paige, $300. 5-YEAR PROJECTION: Average.

1949 BOWMAN PACIFIC COAST LEAGUE

SPECIFICATIONS

SIZE: $2^{1}/_{16} \times 2^{1}/_{2}$". FRONT: Hand-colored black-and-white photograph. BACK: Red and blue printing on cream-colored cardboard. DISTRIBUTION: West Coast, single cards in 1¢ packages with bubblegum; uncut sheets also sold in retail stores.

HISTORY

One of the scarcest and most expensive sets of the modern baseball card era is the 36-card Bowman issue of Pacific Coast League players in 1949. In an attempt to completely corral the baseball card market, Bowman not only issued a 240-card major league set in 1949, but also produced this separate issue of the nation's strongest minor league. In the years before the Dodgers and the Giants moved from New York to California, the Pacific Coast League was a virtual third major league populated with players who were on their way to the majors, or on their way down from the majors, or who did not want to leave California and the West Coast to play ball in the East. The Bowman Pacific Coast League set is identical in format to the "regular" '49 Bowman set. Black-and-white photos of the players were hand-painted to add color and set against a bright, solid-colored background, surrounded by a white border. There is no name or other printing on the front of the card. Backs are also quite similar to the major league Bowman set, except that the card number at top is preceded by the initials "PCL." The player's name, position, and team appear below the card number, followed by personal data and a short career summary. Nearly the entire bottom half of the card is taken up with one of several premiums which could be sent away for for a few cents and gum wrappers. The 1949 Bowman PCL cards were sold in penny packages with bubblegum, but the complete set could also be bought at candy stores and five-and-dimes as an uncut sheet. Many of the cards which survive today have ragged borders—evidence of having been cut off such sheets by youngsters who were not particularly handy with scissors yet. Strangely, not a single example of an uncut sheet of these cards is known in the hobby; perhaps this is further proof of the real rarity of this issue. Though the set is rare, it is also quite popular. Besides being collected by fans of the old PCL, the set is also popular with team collectors

because many of the players in the group had appeared, or would appear, in the major leagues, yet were never on any other baseball card. The combination of scarcity and demand leads to the high price of the cards.

FOR

Rare issue by one of the most famous baseball card companies. Lots of players not found in other sets. The ultimate modern set for collectors of minor league cards.

AGAINST

High cost of each card. Format is not particularly well done; the coloring of the black-and-white photos was pretty heavy-handed.

NOTEWORTHY CARDS

Many of the players in the '49 Bowman set played in the majors, but there are no major stars in the set.

VALUE

EX.-MT. CONDITION: Complete set, $4,000; common card, $100–$125. 5-YEAR PROJECTION: Below average.

1949, 1951 ROYAL DESSERT

SPECIFICATIONS

SIZE: 3½×2½". FRONT: Black-and-white photograph. BACK: Blank. DISTRIBUTION: Nationally, on the backs of dessert boxes.

HISTORY

The sets of baseball player and movie star cards issued on the backs of Royal pudding and gelatin dessert boxes in 1949 and again in 1951 were the predecessors to the more popularly collected Jell-O cards of the early 1960s. The Royal dessert sets were a mix of ballplayers and popular movie stars, with 24 baseball players in the group. The cards were found on the back of dessert boxes, and had to be cut off; neatly cut cards are much preferred to those with ragged edges. Some cards

have been found with an advertising message on the back; these were evidently distributed as promotional items for the set. The Royal cards were issued in two years, 1949 and 1951. The '51 set notes team changes for a couple of the players who were traded in that period. The biographies on the right side of the card were also updated and will give a clue to the year of issue. The basic format of the card includes a rather coarse black-and-white photo at the left end of the card, with a facsimile autograph across the front. There is a red strip at the top with the card number. A player biography is at top right, while the lower-right section has an ad for an album to house the cards.

FOR

Important forerunner of the more popular Jell-O cards of the 1960s. Several popular stars in the set.

AGAINST

The cards are not of very high quality and they are quite scarce.

NOTEWORTHY CARDS

Hall of Famers in the set are Stan Musial, Pee Wee Reese, George Kell, Warren Spahn, and Luke Appling.

VALUE

EX.-MT. CONDITION, NEATLY CUT: Complete set, $400; common card, $12–$15; Hall of Famers, $20–$25; Musial, $45. 5-YEAR PROJECTION: Below average.

1949 REMAR BAKING COMPANY

SPECIFICATIONS

SIZE: 2×3". FRONT: Black-and-white photograph. BACK: Blue printing on white cardboard. DISTRIBUTION: Oakland Bay area, with purchases of bread.

HISTORY

After a one-year hiatus, when the company only issued a large-format team photo card, Remar Baking Company was back in 1949 with a 32-card issue of the Oakland Oaks of the Pacific Coast League, a Class AAA team that operated independently of any major league affiliation. The 1949 set was quite similar to the issues of 1946 and 1947, but the player photo on the front was surrounded by a white border. The player's name and position are printed in the border below the photo, but the card number from previous years is gone. Card backs in 1949 changed some. Vital statistics and 1948 season performance figures replaced the biography on the back, though the ads for the local radio station and Sunbeam-brand bread remained.

FOR

Continuation of a nice series for Pacific Coast League fans; some good players on scarce minor league cards.

AGAINST

Uneven distribution of cards and consequently scarce cards make the set difficult to complete.

NOTEWORTHY CARDS

Some dozen cards are in shorter supply than the rest of the set. Billy Martin, is part of the set, as is another future Yankee, Jackie Jensen.

VALUE

EX.-MT. CONDIION: Complete set, $125; common card, $2.50; scarce card, $7.50; Jensen, $9; Martin, $15. 5-YEAR PROJECTION: Below average.

1949 SOMMER & KAUFMANN SAN FRANCISCO SEALS

SPECIFICATIONS

SIZE: 2×3″. FRONT: Black-and-white photograph. BACK: Black printing on white cardboard. DISTRIBUTION: San Francisco area, at clothing stores.

HISTORY

Almost identical to the 32-card set issued in 1948, the 1949 baseball card set issued by Sommer & Kaufmann clothing stores features only 28 cards, all members of the San Francisco Seals of the Pacific Coast League. The best way to tell the difference between the two sets is to examine the backs. The back of the 1948 issue has the words "BOYS' SHOP" above the Sommer & Kaufmann logo; the 1949 set does not have this wording. Otherwise, the cards are pretty much alike. Fronts feature a borderless black-and-white photo of the player taken at Seals Stadium. Below the photo is a white strip with the player's name, position, and card number. Besides the store ad on the back of the card, there is a short biography of the player. Like the 1948 set, the 1949 Sommer & Kaufmann issue is quite expensive on a per-card basis, and is scarce.

FOR

One of many nice regional issues of the Pacific Coast League from the 1940s and 1950s.

AGAINST

No big names in the set. Cards are easily confused with the 1948 issue. They're quite expensive for minor league cards.

NOTEWORTHY CARDS

Few of the names in the 1949 Sommer & Kaufmann set are recognizable to any but the avid Pacific Coast League fan. Exceptions are two well-known players of the 1930s: Lefty O'Doul, who managed the Seals in 1949, and Arky Vaughan, who was playing in the minors after a distinguished 14-year major league career with the Pirates and the Dodgers.

VALUE

EX.-MT. CONDITION: Complete set, $450; common card, $15; Vaughan, O'Doul, $25. 5-YEAR PROJECTION: Below average.

1948 BOWMAN

SPECIFICATIONS

SIZE: $2^1/_{16} \times 2^1/_2$″. FRONT: Black-and-white photograph. BACK: Black printing on gray cardboard. DISTRIBUTION: Nationally, one card in 1¢ packages with bubblegum.

HISTORY

The Philadephia-based Bowman gum company entered the baseball card market in 1948 with a 48-card set. Within a year, Bowman had achieved such dominance that it had the bubblegum baseball card market all to itself. An aggressive program of signing players to contracts to appear on its cards left potential competitors with little subject matter for a competing issue. The 1948 Bowman set, though, was a modest beginning. The company chose to use a small, squarish format for its cards, along the lines of the Goudey issues of the 1930s and the competing Leaf gum issue of 1948. Unlike those cards, though, which used artists' drawings or color-added photos, the '48 Bowmans presented on the front of the card a black-and-white photo of the player, with no printing or other design elements. The photo was bordered in white. The backs of the '48 Bowmans have the card number, player's name, position, and team at top, followed by the usual personal data and a short baseball biography. The bottom third of the card was an ad for Bowman's "Blony" brand gum. Because the early Bowman baseball cards were printed in sheets of 36 cards, and the 1948 issue consists of 48 cards, there is a group of 12 cards that was short-printed and is scarcer today than the other 36 in the set. This premier Bowman issue is a major baseball card milestone and many collectors consider it a perfect point at which to begin their collections, since the set features many of the players who would go on to greatness in the 1950s and even the 1960s, before entering the Hall of Fame.

FOR

Bowman's "rookie year" cards have a

simple, appealing design, using ballpark photos with no retouching. The set, with the 12 scarce cards, is challenging, but not all that expensive.

AGAINST

The black-and-white photographic design on a 1948 baseball card issue is a throwback to cards of the 1920s.

NOTEWORTHY CARDS

For a set of only 48 cards, there is a remarkably high percentage of Hall of Famers in the 1948 Bowman set. There are six Hall of Famers—Kiner, Mize, Feller, Berra, Spahn, and Musial—and three more players who probably will someday be elected—Phil Rizzuto, Marty Marion, and Enos Slaughter. The 12 short-printed cards in the set are: #7-Reiser, #8-Cooper, #13-Marshall, #16-Lohrke, #20-Kerr, #22-Bevins, #24-Leonard, #26-Shea, #28-Verban, #29-Page, #30-Lockman, and #34-Jones.

OUR FAVORITE CARD

The 1948 Bowman set contains the first baseball card of Emil Verban. It's not really his rookie card—he'd been in the National League since 1942—but it is his premier card, and it's one of the dozen short-printed cards in the set. Now, Emil Verban is not exactly a household word in the world of major league baseball though in seven major league seasons, the second baseman accumulated a respectable lifetime .272 average, and a .412 average in the 1944 World Series. No, Emil Verban is a symbol, a symbol of futility. The "official" organization for long-suffering Chicago Cubs fans is called "The Emil Verban Society," and numbers among its members President Ronald Reagan. Verban played for the Cubs from mid-1947 to mid-1950 and is representative of the suffering of fans who have been waiting since 1945 for a pennant.

VALUE

EX.-MT. CONDITION: Complete set, $375; common card, $3.50; short-printed cards, $8; stars, $8-$10; Feller, $20; Berra, Rizzuto, $30; Musial, $50. 5-YEAR PROJECTION: Average.

1948–1949 LEAF

SPECIFICATIONS

SIZE: 2⅜×2⅞". FRONT: Color-added black-and-white photo. BACK: Black printing on gray cardboard. DISTRIBUTION: Nationally, in 1¢ packages with bubblegum.

HISTORY

The premier Leaf baseball card issue was unusual in that it was issued late in 1948 and early in 1949, rather than in the spring as has become traditional with baseball cards. Because Babe Ruth, who died in August, 1948, is the only noncoaching, noncontemporary player in the set, it is assumed that the 1948–1949 Leafs were released sometime after his death. Some of the cards carry a 1948 copyright date, others have a 1949 copyright. The set is the first baseball card issue of the post-World War II era to use color in the cards, though the color was rather poor. Color was hand-added to black-and-white photos of the players, set against solid-color backgrounds. A colored strip at the bottom of the photo had the player's name in white letters. Leaf, a Chicago-based confectionery firm, chose to use the nearly square 2⅜×2⅞" format that Goudey gum cards had made popular in the 1930s. In all respects, except the inclusion of the name on the bottom of the card, the '48–'49 Leaf cards closely resembled those issued later in 1949 by Bowman. (In its later series, Bowman also added the player's name to the front of its cards.) Card backs have the player's name and card number at the top, and also include a brief baseball biography of the player and one of three premium offers. For ten gum wrappers, the collector could receive a 5×7" premium photo; for five wrappers and 10¢, a 6×12" felt pennant was available; and five wrappers and a quarter got the collector an 8½×11", 32-page album. Leaf pulled a dirty trick on bubblegum buyers in the late 1940s with its set. While the set contained only 98 cards, it was skip-numbered to #168. The deception was carried even further in the premium offer on the back of some cards, which stated that an album, "Can display 168 different Baseball cards." By not issuing those 70 cards, Leaf kept the kids spending their pennies on bubblegum looking for nonexistent cards to complete their collections—remember, this was in the days before checklists. There are two distinct degrees of difficulty within the 1948–1949 Leaf set; exactly half of the cards are considerably scarcer than the rest. A detailed checklist is necessary to tell which is which. In general, the Leaf cards are scarcer than the contemporary Bowman issue.

1948 Leaf, Bob McCall

1948 Leaf, Mickey Harris

1948 Leaf, Mizell Platt

FOR

Challenging set for the collector of modern-era cards. Lots of big stars who did not appear in Bowman's sets of 1948 and 1949.

AGAINST

Cards are really not that attractive. The 49 scarce cards are really tough and very expensive per card.

NOTEWORTHY CARDS

Leaf was able to give kids something its larger (and ultimately more successful) competitor, Bowman, could not in 1948–1949—baseball cards of Joe DiMaggio, Ted Williams, and Jackie Robinson. These were just three of the superstars who appear in the Leaf issue. Two big names among the scarce-series cards are Satchell Paige and Bob Feller. Two variation cards appear in the Leaf set. Card #102 can be found with the correct spelling of Gene Hermanski's name on the front, or an error, "Hermansk." The error card is worth $40 in top grade, while the correct spelling is an $8 card. The Cliff Aberson card (#136) can be found with blue jersey sleeves painted on all the way down his arm (worth $20 or so), or in "short sleeves" ($7.50).

OUR FAVORITE CARD

Often, when the story of the hobby's most expensive baseball card, the "T-206" cigarette card of Honus Wagner, is told in the public press, the reason cited for the withdrawal and subsequent rarity of the card is Wagner's "opposition to tobacco use." Actually, it was smoking that Wagner was opposed to (as well as not being paid royalties for use of his picture by the cigarette card company). In the 1948–1949 Leaf set, Wagner, then a coach for the Pittsburgh Pirates, is shown on card #70 stuffing his jaw with chewing tobacco.

VALUE

EX.-MT. CONDITION: Complete set, $3,750; common card, common series, $7; common card, scarce series, $45; Hall of Famers, $10–$15; Musial, Wagner, Robinson, $40–$60; Dom DiMaggio, Ted Williams, Kell, Slaughter, Doby, $75–$100; Joe DiMaggio, Ruth, $150; Feller, $200; Paige, $300. 5-YEAR PROJECTION: Below average.

1948 SWELL SPORTS THRILLS

SPECIFICATIONS

SIZE: 2½×3". FRONT: Black-and-white photograph. BACK: Black printing on gray cardboard. DISTRIBUTION: Nationally (?), one card in each penny gum pack.

HISTORY

One of a few "action" baseball card sets in which the picture is an actual game-action photo, rather than a posed portrait of a single player, the Sports Thrills set was one of two issued in 1948 by Philadelphia Chewing Gum Corporation, in packages of its Swell brand bubblegum. The set consists of 20 cards, each featuring on the front a news photo of a baseball highlight, while the back recounts the details in story form. The set mixed current and former players' activities, and leaned heavily on then-current Brooklyn Dodgers players. Many of the highlights are drawn from World Series or All-Star Games, such as Ted Williams' game-winning three-run homer in the ninth inning of the 1941 All-Star Game and Al Gionfriddo's catch in the 1947 World Series which robbed Joe DiMaggio of a three-run homer and put the series into a seventh game. Others recall earlier baseball feats like Lou Gehrig's four homers in a game and Johnny Vander Meer's back-to-back no-hitters. The set is not popularly collected, but many superstar collectors try to obtain a card of their favorite player.

FOR

The set is an interesting change from single player cards and can spice up a superstar collection. The cards are much more scarce than their prices would indicate.

AGAINST

Some collectors have an aversion to cards that don't show a simple mug shot of the player being honored.

NOTEWORTHY CARDS

Many of the plays depicted in the Sports Thrills set involve stars, includ-

1948 Swell Sports Thrills, Pee Wee Reese

ing Ted Williams, Babe Ruth, Lou Gehrig, Jackie Robinson, Pee Wee Reese, and others. Other cards in the set depict some of the national pastime's best-remembered moments and are, as such, certainly worth seeing on a baseball card.

OUR FAVORITE CARD

Card #12 in the Sports Thrills set purports to depict Babe Ruth's famous "called shot" home run in the 1932 World Series, when he supposedly pointed to the spot in the stands where he would plant the next pitch. The fact is, no photograph exists of that famous bit of baseball folklore. In fact, many of the Chicago Cubs on the field that day, as well as some of Ruth's own teammates, deny that he ever made such a gesture. Indeed, most of their contemporaries agree that if Cubs pitcher Charlie Root, a notorious "purpose" pitcher, had thought Ruth was challenging him, the Babe would have taken the next pitch in his ear. Photos of the Babe pointing—like that used on the Sports Thrills card—are after-the-fact shots recreated at the request of photographers.

VALUE

EX-MT. CONDITION: Complete set, $200; common card, $7.50; superstar card, $10–$20; Ruth, Gehrig, Williams, $25–$30. 5-YEAR PROJECTION: Below average.

1948 BABE RUTH STORY

SPECIFICATIONS

SIZE: 2×2½". FRONT: Black-and-white photograph. BACK: Black printing on gray cardboard. DISTRIBUTION: Nationally (?), one card in each penny gum pack.

HISTORY

This 28-card set was an unabashed attempt to cash in on the August, 1948, death of Babe Ruth, and the subsequent biographical movie, *The Babe Ruth Story,* starring William Bendix, which was released in 1949. The set is one of only two baseball card issues produced by Philadelphia Chewing Gum Corporation, which is better known for its football card issues of the early 1960s. Some of the cards depict scenes from the movie, while some picture the actors in photos with actual baseball players, including Babe Ruth himself, on the set of the movie before his death. The first 16 cards of the set seem to be about twice as common as cards #17 to #28. Unfortunately, of the more common first 16 cards, only one pictures the real Babe Ruth (#1). The rest of the cards picturing the real Babe Ruth (and the other real baseball players) are in the scarce higher-numbered series. Card backs have an advertisement for the movie, a "cast" of the characters and a story describing the action shown.

FOR

Babe's last contemporary cards.

AGAINST

Most of the cards show an actor portraying a baseball player. Most of the cards that picture real players are in the scarce high number series.

NOTEWORTHY CARDS

Besides those cards which have actual photos of Babe Ruth (#1, #25, #26, #27, and #28), Hall of Famers Ted Lyons, Bucky Harris, and Lefty Gomez, along with Charlie Grimm, are also pictured in the set.

VALUE

EX.-MT. CONDITION: Complete set, $250; cards #2–#16, $7.50; common high numbers, $13.50; real player cards, $15; Ruth cards, $20. 5-YEAR PROJECTION: Below average.

1948 SIGNAL OIL

SPECIFICATIONS

SIZE: 2⅜×3½". FRONT: Color added to black-and-white photograph. BACK: Black or blue printing on white cardboard. DISTRIBUTION: Oakland Bay area, with visits to gas stations.

HISTORY

Unlike its 1947 set, which included five Pacific Coast League teams, the 1948 Signal Oil Company baseball card set included only members of the Oakland Oaks team. The 24-card Signal set was different in format from the '47s, as well. The cards featured a hand-colored borderless photo of the player on the front of the card, with no writing whatsoever. Backs of the cards have the player's name and position, along with a short baseball biography and ads for Signal gas and the local radio station.

FOR

One of the more attractive 1940s Pacific Coast League regional issues.

AGAINST

You either like and collect minor league cards, or you don't.

NOTEWORTHY CARDS

A relatively large percentage of former major leaguers who would become well known as managers or coaches are assembled in the '48 Signal set. Most notable are Billy Martin and his mentor, Casey Stengel, but also included are Merrill Coombs, Cookie Lavagetto, and Ernie Lombardi. There is a card in the set for the team's radio announcer, Bud Foster.

VALUE

EX.-MT. CONDITION: Complete set, $250; common card, $9; Stengel, Martin, $35. 5-YEAR PROJECTION: Below average.

1948 SMITH'S CLOTHING

SPECIFICATIONS
SIZE: 2×3″. FRONT: Black-and-white photograph. BACK: Black printing on white cardboard. DISTRIBUTION: Oakland Bay area, with visits to clothing store.

HISTORY
The 1948 Smith's clothing store set of Oakland Oaks cards is considerably more collectible than the store's premier issue in 1947. The 1948 set again contains 25 cards, but none were withdrawn during the issue or are otherwise numerically scarce. The format of the 1948 set is pretty much the same as that of the 1947 set. A borderless black-and-white photo of the player appears on the front of the card. Beneath it is a white strip containing the player's name, position, and card number. The backs have a short biography of the player, along with an ad for the clothing store. The picture of the store and the logo in the ad are somewhat different from those used the previous year, but the easiest way to tell the two years' issues apart is the presence of a "Union-made" logo on the back of the 1948 cards, in the lower-left corner. The '48 set was also printed on much heavier cardboard than had been the case in 1947.

FOR
One of the more collectible and least expensive of the popular Pacific Coast League regionals of the late 1940s.

AGAINST
Format is too similar to several other issues in the area and the time period.

NOTEWORTHY CARDS
While there are several former and future major leaguers in the 1948 Smith's set, the only two cards with premium value are those of Oaks manager Casey Stengel and his prize pupil, Billy Martin.

VALUE
EX.-MT. CONDITION: Complete set, $200; common card, $7.50; Stengel, Martin, $25–$30. 5-YEAR PROJECTION: Below average.

1948 SOMMER & KAUFMANN SAN FRANCISCO SEALS

SPECIFICATIONS
SIZE: 2×3″. FRONT: Black-and-white photograph. BACK: Black printing on white cardboard. DISTRIBUTION: San Francisco area, at clothing stores.

HISTORY
The Sommer & Kaufmann set is just one of several baseball card sets issued in the late 1940s by California clothiers. This 1948 issue of 32 cards features only San Francisco Seals (Pacific Coast League) team members. The cards were apparently given away with visits to or purchases from the boys' department at the fashionable San Francisco and San Mateo stores operated by Sommer & Kaufmann. The cards have on the front a borderless black-and-white photo of the player. His name and position are centered in a white strip below the photo, and a card number appears in the lower-right corner. The back has a short career summary of the player and an ad for the issuer. The photos on the cards were taken at the historic old Seals stadium and give a nostalgic look at top-level minor league baseball in the late 1940s. The cards are, naturally, more plentiful on the West Coast, and they are fairly expensive.

FOR
Nice item for the Pacific Coast League collector, a challenging set.

AGAINST
The cards are hard to find in most of the country, and are quite expensive. Few names that anybody would recognize on the team.

NOTEWORTHY CARDS
Manager Lefty O'Doul is the best-known figure in the '48 Sommer & Kaufmann set. Outfielder Gene Woodling appears in this set, prior to his being called up for service with the Yankee dynasty of the late 1940s and early 1950s. Besides the players and manager, there are cards of the team's two bat boys (unnumbered) in the set.

VALUE
EX.-MT. CONDITION: Complete set, $450; common card, $15; Woodling, $20; O'Doul, $25. 5-YEAR PROJECTION: Below average.

1947 TIP TOP BREAD

SPECIFICATIONS
SIZE: 2¼×3″. FRONT: Black-and-white photograph. BACK: Black printing on white cardboard. DISTRIBUTION: Regionally, according to teams on cards, in loaves of bread.

HISTORY
While the Tip Top bread set of 1947 is collected as a complete 163-player issue, it is, in reality, a group of several regional issues, each sharing a common design. A statement at the bottom of the card back, beneath the pictured loaf of bread, indicates there were varying numbers of cards issued in each city. The entire card back is an ad for the bakery and there is no card number. Card fronts have a borderless black-and-white photo of the player, with a white strip below containing his name, position, city name, and league designation. Because the Tip Top cards were actually issued regionally, not all of the teams in the set were equally distributed. In the group of more common teams are the New York teams, the Yankees, the Dodgers, and the Giants; the St. Louis teams, the Cardinals and the Browns; and the Pittsburgh Pirates. Somewhat less common are the Boston teams, the Red Sox and the Braves; the Chicago clubs, the Cubs and the White Sox; and the Detroit Tigers. The set was actually intended to include 164 cards, but one of the New York Giants cards was not issued as advertised. The Tip Top set is significant to collectors today because many of the players depicted in it were never on any other

1947 Tip Top Bread (back)

baseball card issue. These were primarily players who had been on the team during the talent-lean World War II years, and were quickly replaced after the war.

FOR
Lots of obscure players and the regional nature of the issue make this popular with team collectors.

AGAINST
Cards are really quite scarce and expensive.

NOTEWORTHY CARDS
In addition to many of the famous players of the day, the Tip Top set also has an exclusive on many of the lesser-known players who kept major league baseball going during World War II. There are also many rookie players in the set as well as older players who were making their final appearances on a major baseball card set. Among the significant rookie cards in the set are St. Louis playground chums Yogi Berra and Joe Garagiola. One rookie that Tip Top missed was Jackie Robinson. Another major figure missing is Stan Musial.

OUR FAVORITE CARD
One of the faces on the Tip Top cards of 1947 will be instantly recognizable to fans of the TV soap opera *General Hospital* as chief of staff Dr. Steve Hardy. Few of the soap's fans, though, probably know that John Beradino, who has had the lead role in *General Hospital* since 1963, is a former major league infielder who played under his real name of Johnny Berardino (with a second "r"). Berardino played with the St. Louis Browns from 1939 to 1942 and in 1946 and 1947. Then he bounced around among the Indians, the Pirates, and the Brownies until 1952, compiling a lifetime batting average of .249 in 912 major league games over 11 seasons. Berardino appears in the 1951 Bowman and 1952 Topps set as well, and his TV star status makes his cards worth two to three times the price of "common" cards in the same sets.

VALUE
EX.-MT. CONDITION: Complete set, $4,500; common card, common team, $10; common card, scarce team, $20–$25; stars, two to three times common price on same team. 5-YEAR PROJECTION: Below average.

1947 HOMOG-ENIZED BREAD

SPECIFICATIONS
SIZE: 2¼×3½". FRONT: Black-and-white photo. BACK: Blank, or movie star photograph. DISTRIBUTION: Nationally, one card in each loaf of Homogenized Bread.

HISTORY
Several unusual features mark this 48-card set. For one thing, there are 44 baseball players and four boxers (including well-known Joe Louis and Jake LaMotta). In addition, some of the cards will be found with a photo of a movie star on the back. The set is important in the chronology of baseball card history because it was one of the first major issues after World War II, and immediately preceded the first Bowman bubblegum cards of 1948. The sets offers premier cards of soon-to-be-greats like Gil Hodges, Bobby Thomson, Yogi Berra, and Jackie Robinson. In addition, many of the game's stars from the prewar era also appear in the Homogenized Bread set: Ted Williams, Joe DiMaggio, Stan Musial, and Pee Wee Reese. There is nothing to detract from the front of the cards except a facsimile autograph. The cards are unusual among baseball cards in that they contain no statistical or biographical information, front or back. The cards feature rounded corners. Much scarcer than the early Bowman issues which followed them, the Homogenized Bread cards have not met with great collector demand.

FOR
Attractive cards, lots of superstars, low price.

AGAINST
Collectors don't particularly like round-cornered baseball cards. Ditto for sets that mix other sports or nonsports figures with the baseball players.

NOTEWORTHY CARDS
There's a very high percentage of Hall of Famers among the 44 players in the Homogenized Bread set: Yogi Berra, Lou Boudreau, Joe DiMaggio, Bob Feller, Ralph Kiner, Johnny Mize, Stan Musial, Pee Wee Reese, Jackie Robinson, and Ted Williams. In addition, Phil Rizzuto and Enos Slaughter are likely candidates.

VALUE
EX.-MT. CONDITION: Complete set, $250; common card, $3–$5; Hall of Famers, $7.50–$10; Musial, Robinson, Williams, $15–$20; DiMaggio, $25. 5-YEAR PROJECTION: Above average.

1947 BLUE TINTS

SPECIFICATIONS
SIZE: 2×2⅝". FRONT: Blue-and-white photograph. BACK: Blank. DISTRIBUTION: Nationally (?), sold in strips.

HISTORY
While this book has not generally covered the genre of baseball card

issues known as "strip cards," the 1947 Blue Tints set is a worthy exception. Strip cards were known as far back as 1910, and had their heyday in the 1920s. They take their name from the way in which they were sold—in strips of ten or a dozen or so for 1¢. The cards could then be cut apart, as they are most often found. In general, strip cards are not popular with collectors because they were cheaply made, usually with poor drawings on thin cardboard. Following World War II, when baseball cards began to make a comeback, one of the first widely issued sets was a strip-card issue which collectors today call the "Blue Tints," because of the color of the photograph on the front of the card. It is not known exactly how or where the cards were distributed, but they are somewhat popular today because of the number of then-current superstars who appeared in the set. Below the player photo on the front of the card are printed the player's name and team, with a card number in the lower right and a dark blue box around the whole. Backs are blank.

FOR
One of the earliest postwar issues, which makes it somewhat important in the scheme of hobby history. Lots of better players of the era.

AGAINST
In the true tradition of strip cards, the Blue Tints are quite cheaply made and do not have a quality appearance.

NOTEWORTHY CARDS
What Lou Gehrig is doing in the Blue Tint set is hard to say; he had died more than five years previously, and had played his last game in 1939. The Blue Tint set features the last contemporary cards of Hank Greenberg, who was finishing out his 15-year Hall of Fame career, and Mel Ott, also in his final year in 1947. There is a rookie card of Jackie Robinson, along with many other Hall of Fame players. The Leo Durocher card exists in two varieties, one picturing him with the Dodgers, one with the Giants. The Mel Ott card will be found either with or without the team name.

VALUE
EX.-MT. CONDITION: Complete set, $250; common card, $3–$4; Hall of Famers, $6–$15; Ott, Robinson, $20–$25; Williams, $40; DiMaggio, Gehrig, $45–$50. 5-YEAR PROJECTION: Below average.

1947 BOND BREAD JACKIE ROBINSON

SPECIFICATIONS
SIZE: 2¼×3½". FRONT: Black-and-white photograph. BACK: Black printing on white cardboard. DISTRIBUTION: Metropolitan New York area, with loaves of Bond bread.

HISTORY
One of few successful "one-player" baseball card issues, the 1947 Bond bread cards featured only Jackie Robinson, then in his rookie year as first baseman for the Brooklyn Dodgers. In all, there were 13 cards of the major leagues' first black ballplayer of the modern era, featuring him in a variety of portrait and posed-action photos. The cards feature nothing on the front except a round-cornered photo surrounded by a white border. Some of the pictures are horizontal in arrangement, some are vertical. One of the cards, much more common than the rest, shows Jackie in a close-up as if ready to catch the ball, and features a facsimile autograph on the front. Other cards feature a facsimile autograph on the back. Back designs vary among the cards in the set. Some have pictures of the Bond product and baker-boy logo, others have a drawing of Robinson. All backs have an endorsement of Bond bread by Robinson. The set is unnumbered. The '47 Bond cards, because they feature one of baseball's most historic and dynamic players, and because they were issued in quite limited numbers, are scarce and valuable.

FOR
An entire "rookie card" set of one of Brooklyn's best-known "Boys of Summer." Rare and valuable; unique issue on a great player.

AGAINST
Cards are extremely scarce and expensive, making assembly of a full set quite an expensive proposition.

NOTEWORTHY CARDS
Because they all feature Jackie Robinson, they're all special.

VALUE
EX.-MT. CONDITION: Complete set, $2,500; autograph-front pose, $100; all others, $200. 5-YEAR PROJECTION: Below average.

1947 SIGNAL OIL

SPECIFICATIONS
SIZE: 5½×3½". FRONT: Black-and-white drawing. BACK: Black printing on white cardboard. DISTRIBUTION: West Coast, by team areas, with purchases at gas stations.

HISTORY
Though it is one of the more unusual and challenging of the Pacific Coast League baseball card sets of the late 1940s, the 1947 Signal Oil issue is not particularly popular. The cards are horizontal in format, about postcard-size, and feature line drawings of the players on five of the six teams in the league (no San Francisco). Besides the player's portrait, there are a couple of cartoons about the player, and a small Signal gas logo. The artwork for the 89 cards in the Signal set of 1947 is the work of Al Demaree, a former major league pitcher (1912–1918) with the Giants, the Phils, the Cubs, and the Braves, who was himself on several early baseball card sets. Card backs have, on the left side, the player's personal data, a few facts about his past and ambitions, and a summary of his baseball experience. On the right is a pair of ads for Signal gas stations and the local radio stations which carried the Pacific Coast League games in each area. There are no card numbers. The '47 Signal cards were only distributed within a team's home area, and the Sacramento and Seattle cards are harder to obtain, as a whole, than the other teams. Because of cards

withdrawn when players left the teams, there are also several scarcities within some of the team sets.

FOR
Large-format cards with the distinction of having been drawn by a former major league player. Some good stars in the set.

AGAINST
In the modern era, collectors prefer photographic cards to drawn cards, and there is also a bias against postcard-size issues. A few tough cards in the set make assembling a complete set quite difficult.

NOTEWORTHY CARDS
The cards of Woody Williams (Hollywood) and Charlie Ripple (Sacramento) are much scarcer than the rest of the set. Many of the players in the set are former or future major leaguers, including Vince DiMaggio and Casey Stengel.

OUR FAVORITE CARD
One of the few baseball cards on which "The Mad Russian," Lou Novikoff, appears is in the 1947 Signal Oil set, with Seattle. In many ways Novikoff typified the war-years' ballplayer; in many other ways he was a unique figure in baseball history. Novikoff could hit the ball a mile, but couldn't field worth a darn—it's a crying shame he played in the era before the designated hitter. His manager once instructed him on the two ways he could field a ball batted in his direction: "Lay down in front of it, or wait until it stops rolling, then pick it up and throw it to third and try to keep the runner from stretching the hit to a triple." Lou's manager at Milwaukee in the minor leagues, Charlie Grimm, claimed that one time Novikoff charged into the left field corner after a hard hit ball and was gone so long Grimm came off the bench to look for him. Novikoff came wandering back from the blind corner of the field with a hot dog in one hand, a Coke in the other, but no ball. From 1944 to 1946, in between stints with the Cubs and the Phillies, Novikoff played in the minors and pitched softball. In fact, he was elected to the softball Hall of Fame.

VALUE
EX.-MT. CONDITION: Complete set, $750; common card, $5; common Seattle, Sacramento card, $15; DiMaggio, $25; Stengel, $45; Ripple, $75; Williams, $125. 5-YEAR PROJECTION: Below average.

1947 REMAR BAKING COMPANY

SPECIFICATIONS
SIZE: 2×3". FRONT: Black-and-white photograph. BACK: Blue printing on white cardboard. DISTRIBUTION: Oakland Bay area, with purchases of bread.

HISTORY
Like the company's premier card issue in 1946, the 25-card Remar set of 1947 contained only players for the Oakland Oaks of the Pacific Coast League. The cards were given away at stores with the purchase of Remar bread. The cards are identical in format to the earlier set, and many of the player photos are the same as those used in 1946. However, the 1947 cards have different card numbers in the lower-right corner of the front. The player's name and position also appear in the white strip below the borderless photo. Card backs differ in 1947 in that they are printed in blue ink. They feature a short biography of the player, a radio station ad, and a picture of a loaf of Sunbeam bread.

FOR
Good regional issue for the team or minor league collector.

AGAINST
Too similar to the 1946 cards.

NOTEWORTHY CARDS
The only famous player in the 1947 Remar set is team manager Casey Stengel. The set includes a card for team announcer Bud Foster, an unusual item in a baseball card set.

VALUE
EX.-MT. CONDITION: Complete set, $100; common card, $2.50; Stengel, $30. 5-YEAR PROJECTION: Below average.

1947 Signal Oil, Dario Lodigiani (back)

1947 SMITH'S CLOTHING

SPECIFICATIONS
SIZE: 2×3″. FRONT: Black-and-white photograph. BACK: Black printing on white cardboard. DISTRIBUTION: Oakland Bay area, with visits to clothing store.

HISTORY
One of the more challenging and expensive of the Pacific Coast League regional issues of the late 1940s is the 25-card set of Oakland Oaks cards issued by Smith's clothing store in Oakland. According to the ad on the card backs, Smith's was the "Largest men's and boy's store west of Chicago." In format the Smith's cards are very much like the Remar Bread issues of the same years and those of the Sommer & Kaufmann clothiers across the bay in San Francisco. The cards were issued over a period of weeks at the store. The front of each card has a borderless black-and-white photo of the player. In a wide white strip at the bottom of the card are the player's name, position, and card number. Card backs have a short write-up on the player's career and a large ad for the clothing store, complete with picture. The 1947 Smith's set is printed on very lightweight cardboard and the cards were easily creased.

FOR
Nice item for the minor league collector.

AGAINST
Almost complete absence of big name ballplayers. Format is too much like other issues of the era.

NOTEWORTHY CARDS
The only really popular card in the '47 Smith's set is that of the manager, Casey Stengel. The Max Marshall card is quite elusive and expensive, presumably because Marshall left the team and his card was withdrawn. To a lesser extent, the cards of Paul Gillespie, Damon Hayes, and Joe Faria are also scarce.

VALUE
EX.-MT. CONDITION: Complete set, $300; common card, $7.50; Gillespie, Faria, $15; Hayes, Stengel, $30; Marshall, $150. 5-YEAR PROJECTION: Below average.

1947 SUNBEAM BREAD

SPECIFICATIONS
SIZE: 2×3″. FRONT: Black-and-white photograph. BACK: Blue, red, and yellow printing on thin white cardboard. DISTRIBUTION: Sacramento area, given away with purchases of bread.

HISTORY
Issued in the second and final year of baseball card production for Sunbeam-brand bread, the 1947 set contains 26 cards, all of the Sacramento Solons of the Pacific Coast League. Card fronts are virtually identical to the previous year: a black-and-white photo above a white strip featuring the name, year, and position of the player, along with a photo credit. No write-up, stats, or card number appear on the back, just a color picture of a loaf of bread.

FOR
Scarce minor league issue.

AGAINST
Absolutely nobody anybody ever heard of in the set; so why are they so expensve?

NOTEWORTHY CARDS
There are none.

VALUE
EX.-MT. CONDITION: Complete set, $150; common card, $7. 5-YEAR PROJECTION: Below average.

1946 REMAR BAKING COMPANY

SPECIFICATIONS
SIZE: 2×3″. FRONT: Black-and-white photograph. BACK: Red and black printing on white cardboard. DISTRIBUTION: Oakland Bay area, cards given away with bread purchase.

HISTORY
Remar bread used an unusual method of distribution for its baseball card sets of 1946 through 1950. The cards were given to retailers who generally placed them on the shelf next to the bread, free for the taking. To say the least, this created some unusual distribution patterns. Each card features a borderless photo of one of the players of the Oakland Oaks of the Pacific Coast League. Beneath the photo is a white strip with the player's name, position, and, on some of the cards, a card number. Only 18 of the 23 cards in the 1946 issue have card numbers. When they do have them, they are in the lower-right corner. Card backs have a short write-up on the player, along with a picture of a loaf of Remar bread and an ad for the local radio station.

FOR
Nice item for team and minor league collectors.

AGAINST
Not much, unless you don't like minor league cards.

NOTEWORTHY CARDS
Casey Stengel was manager of the Oaks and appears in the set. The unnumbered Bill Raimondi card is quite scarce.

VALUE
EX.-MT. CONDITION: Complete set, $150; common card, $6; Raimondi, Stengel, $25. 5-YEAR PROJECTION: Below average.

1946 SUNBEAM BREAD

SPECIFICATIONS
SIZE: 2×3″. FRONT: Black-and-white photograph. BACK: Red, blue, and yellow printing on white cardboard. DISTRIBUTION: Sacramento area, with purchases of bread.

HISTORY
A product of the same bakery which produced the 1946–1950 Remar cards of the Oakland Oaks, the 21-card Sunbeam set featured only players from the Sacramento Solons team of the Pacific Coast League. The cards have a borderless photo at the top. A white panel below the picture gives the player's name, year, and position, and lists a photo credit. Card backs, printed in blue, yellow, and red, have a short, snappy write-up on the player, a picture of a loaf of bread, and an ad for the local radio station. The cards are unnumbered. Like the Remar cards, the Sunbeam cards were apparently distributed wholesale to grocers who handed them out to customers or left them on the shelves for the taking.

FOR
Good set for the minor league specialist. Quite scarce, but not too expensive.

AGAINST
No big name players to give anybody an incentive to collect the set.

NOTEWORTHY CARDS
Few of the players in the 1946 Sunbeam set ever achieved any measure of fame in the major leagues. Gerry Staley is the best known of the lot—and that isn't saying much.

VALUE
EX.-MT. CONDITION: Complete set, $150; common card, $7.50. 5-YEAR PROJECTION: Below average.

1941 PLAY BALL

SPECIFICATIONS
SIZE: 2½×3⅛″. FRONT: Color added to black-and-white photos. BACK: Black printing on white cardboard. DISTRIBUTION: Nationally, one card in each 1¢ package with bubblegum.

HISTORY
The 1941 Play Ball set was the last baseball card issue of Philadelphia's Gum, Inc. The intervention of World War II, which cut off paper and gum-base supplies, cut the issue short at just 72 cards. By the time the war was over, Gum, Inc., had ceased to exist, but it resurfaced in 1948 as Bowman Gum, Inc. In format, the 1941 Play Balls are quite similar to Gum, Inc.'s 1939 and 1940 issues, except that in 1941 color was added to black-and-white photos. In many cases, the same black-and-white photos that appeared in the 1940 set were used in 1941. The player's picture was framed by a colored line border. A white banner at the bottom had the player's name, often with the addition of his nickname enclosed in quotation marks. A white border surrounds the entire design. Backs of the 1941 Play Balls are almost identical to the 1939 and 1940 issues, with a card number and personal data at the top, a player biography at center, and a Play Ball/Gum, Inc. ad at the bottom. The ad reads, "Play Ball Sports Hall of Fame. Watch for other famous sports stars, famous fighters, tennis players, football heroes, etc. in this series." Those cards were never issued. For its day, the color on the 1941 Play Ball cards was not too bad, and it has contributed to the popularity of the set. Of the 72 cards in the set, cards #49 to #72 are considered somewhat scarcer than the lower numbers. Besides the normal '41 Play Balls, the designs can be found sheet-printed on thin paper.

FOR
Colorful, easy to collect; many stars.

AGAINST
You'd have to be looking pretty hard to find something not to like about the

1941 Play Ball, Chuck Klein (front)

60. CHARLES HERBERT KLEIN

Outfielder-Coach   Philadelphia Phillies

Born: Indianapolis, Ind.   October 7, 1905

Bats: Left   Throws: Right

Height: 6′   Weight: 195 lbs.

One of the most popular players ever to wear a Philadelphia uniform, "Chuck" Klein now splits his duties with the Phillies between coaching, pinch-hitting and an occasional fling in the outfield. His past playing, however, have gained him a set place in baseball annals. The quiet, personable outfielder has been one of the great hitters of modern times, boasting a .324 lifetime average. He has collected 2063 hits, including 299 home runs, and has driven across 1195 runs.

PLAY BALL
Sports Hall of Fame

Watch for other famous sports stars, famous fighters, tennis players, football heroes, etc. in this series.

©   GUM, INC., Phila., Pa.   PRINTED IN U. S. A.

1941 Play Ball, Chuck Klein (back)

1941 Play Balls. While the price per card may seem somewhat high, it should be remembered that many of these cards, like many other prewar issues, were turned in during the war-time scrap paper drives.

NOTEWORTHY CARDS

All of the big stars of the prewar game are in the set, with the exception of Bob Feller. The set contains the rookie card of Pee Wee Reese, and the 1941 Play Ball set is the only issue to contain cards of all three DiMaggio brothers, Joe, Dom, and Vince.

OUR FAVORITE CARD

Like the other Play Ball sets, the 1941 issue used a lot of player nicknames on the fronts of the cards. But really, don't you think three "Pinkies" in a set of only 72 cards is a bit much? The issue has cards of Merrill "Pinky" May, Phillies third baseman and father of current major league catcher Milt May; Michael "Pinky" Higgins, Tigers third baseman; and Franklin "Pinky" Hayes, catcher for the Athletics.

VALUE

EX. CONDITION: Complete set, $1,250; common card, #1–#48, $9; common card, #49–#72, $12; Hall of Famers, $15–$35; Pee Wee Reese, $50; Ted Williams, $175; Joe DiMaggio, $300. 5-YEAR PROJECTION: Average.

1941 GOUDEY

SPECIFICATIONS

SIZE: 2⅜×2⅞″. FRONT: Black-and-white photograph. BACK: Blank. DISTRIBUTION: Nationally, in 1¢ packages with bubblegum.

HISTORY

The 1941 issue of 33 different players' cards was the final issue for the Goudey Gum Company of Boston. The intervention of World War II caused a virtual halt to baseball card production. The paper and cardboard used to make the cards was needed for the war effort, as were the raw materials (especially rubber) from which bubblegum was formulated. While the 1941 Goudey set contains 33

1941 Goudey, George Case

different players, each player can be found with four different colored backgrounds—yellow, blue, green, and red—against which his black-and-white portrait photo is set. Beneath a black line on the front of the card are the player's name, team, and position. A card number appears in the lower-left corner, but some cards are found without the number. A white baseball design in one of the upper corners has the "Big League Gum" brand name of Goudey. The cards are blank-backed. The '41 Goudey cards are also scarce, but not that expensive, because few collectors are currently chasing them.

FOR

Last of the historic Goudey issues. The format is really not unattractive.

AGAINST

The cards seem incomplete without a back design; there are virtually no stars in the set; and the four background colors seem redundant.

NOTEWORTHY CARDS

Several players make their only baseball card appearance ever in the '41 Goudey set. By the time the war was over, they were out of major league baseball. As examples of such one-time appearances by certain players, these cards are sometimes actively sought by team collectors. The only big names in the set are Carl Hubbell and Mel Ott. Cards #21 to #25 are considered more difficult than the rest of the set.

VALUE

EX. CONDITION: Complete set (33 players, any color), $750; common card, #1–#20, #26–#33, $20; #21–#25, $50; Hubbell, Ott, $60–$75. 5-YEAR PROJECTION: Below average.

1941 DOUBLE PLAY

SPECIFICATIONS

SIZE: 2½×3⅛″. FRONT: Sepia-tone photograph. BACK: Blank. DISTRIBUTION: Nationally, one card in each 1¢ package with bubblegum.

HISTORY

One of the less-appreciated baseball card issues of the immediate pre-World War II era is Gum Products' 1941 Double Play set. The set consists of 75 cards, each with two different players' pictures, for a total of 150 player photos. The players on each card were teammates. The set combines portrait and posed-action photos, with the action pictures all appearing on cards #81-82 through #99-100, and duplicating players who also appear on portrait cards. The action cards are arranged and printed vertically, so that the players' pictures are tall and thin, while the portrait pictures are printed on horizontally arranged cards. Each half of each card had the appropriate player's name, personal data, and the previous season's batting average or win-loss record. At the bottom of each half is a separate card number. The cards are blank-backed. The card format encouraged cutting the card in half, to the detriment of the card's value. Few collectors are interested in cut halves of the Double Play set; in otherwise nice condition, the cards sell for $1 (commons) to $10 or so (Williams, DiMaggio). Cards #101-102 through #149-150 are considered somewhat scarcer than the low-numbered cards.

FOR

Interesting format, lots of lesser-known players to entice the team collector.

1941 Double Play,
Ted Williams, Joe Cronin

AGAINST

Hard to find cards in nice condition; not particularly attractive.

NOTEWORTHY CARDS

Most of the stars of prewar baseball are represented in the set; many of them appearing on both portrait and action cards. Pee Wee Reese's rookie card appears in this set.

VALUE

EX. CONDITION: Complete set, $600; common card, #1-2 through #99-100, $6; common card, #101-102 through #149-150, $9; Hall of Famers, $12-$20; Joe Cronin-Jimmy Foxx, Lefty Gomez-Phil Rizzuto, $25-$35; Ted Williams, $60; Joe DiMaggio, $75. 5-YEAR PROJECTION: Below average.

1940 PLAY BALL

SPECIFICATIONS

SIZE: 2½×3⅛". FRONT: Black-and-white photograph. BACK: Black printing on gray cardboard. DISTRIBUTION: Nationally, one card in each 1¢ package with bubblegum.

HISTORY

In its second year of baseball card production, Gum, Inc., of Philadelphia, increased the size of its set to 240 cards. Besides current players, the 1940 Play Ball set also included many cards of old-timers, making it certainly one of the earliest sets to include past players. The 1940 Play Ball cards are quite similar in design to the company's 1939 Play Ball—America set, the biggest change being that the black-and-white photo on the front of the card was surrounded by frame lines on the 1940 cards. At the bottom was a banner with the player's name, often printed as a nickname in quotation marks, along with a pair of baseballs, a bat, a glove, and a catcher's mask. Card backs in the 1940 Play Ball set were virtually identical to the 1939 effort. A card number appears in the upper left-hand corner. The top of the back has the player's personal data, and there is a Gum, Inc. ad at the bottom. In between is a well-written baseball biography. The Play Ball ad at the bottom of the card describes the cards as "A pictorial news record of America's favorite sport." A 1940 copyright line appears in the lower left. The 1940 Play Balls are divided into two degrees of scarcity, the high numbers, #181–#240, being considerably tougher to find than the lower-numbered cards.

FOR

A well-designed set chronicling baseball as it was in the pre-World War II era. Many players don't appear on any other baseball card issue.

AGAINST

Relatively high cost of the high number cards makes collecting the complete set a venture that's too costly for most collectors. Mixing of current players and old-timers has never been popular with collectors.

NOTEWORTHY CARDS

The set includes all the current stars of the day, most notably Joe DiMaggio, who is card #1 in the set, and Ted Williams. Some of the nicknames preserved for posterity on the cards are worth the price of the card: "Stormy" Weatherly, "Highpockets" Kelly, "Soup" Campbell, "Bad News" Hale, "Hot Potato" Hamlin, and "Twinkletoes" Selkirk, for example.

VALUE

EX. CONDITION: Complete set, $1,800; common card, #1–#180, $4; common card, #181–#240, $12.50; Hall of Famers, $12.50–$30; Joe Jackson, $90; Ted Williams, $125; Joe DiMaggio, $225. 5-YEAR PROJECTION: Average.

HAROLD (PIE) TRAYNOR
PITTSBURGH PIRATES

1939-1930

SPORT KINGS GUM

BABE RUTH

"BATTER-UP"
Foxx
Athletics—1st Base

No. 28

1939 PLAY BALL— AMERICA

SPECIFICATIONS

SIZE: 2½×3¼″. FRONT: Black-and-white photograph. BACK: Black printing on gray cardboard. DISTRIBUTION: Nationally, one card in 1¢ packages with bubblegum.

HISTORY

The baseball card set produced by Philadelphia's Gum, Inc. in 1939 is another of the hobby's popular starting points for collectors. After the initial bubblegum card sets of the 1933–1936 era, the Depression severely curtailed most baseball card issues until the Play Ball—America set made its appearance in 1939. One of the reasons for this set's popularity among collectors today is that a number of the players who appear in the set went on to continue their careers after World War II, and these players would form the mainstay of baseball card sets in the late 1940s. Chief among these are Joe DiMaggio and Ted Williams. The '39 Play Ball—America set is straightforward in design. The front has a plain black-and-white photograph surrounded by a white border. There is no printing on the front of the card. Card backs have a card number in the upper-left corner. At the top of the card are the player's name, team, position, and vital data, followed by a career summary. At the bottom are an ad for Play Ball—America and a notation that "This is one of a series of 250 pictures of leading baseball players. Save to get them all." The set doesn't contain 250 cards. Only cards #1 to #162 are known, and card #126 was apparently never printed. Paper conservation measures necessitated by the beginning of World War II in Europe and Asia—along with the shortage of raw materials for gum—were probably responsible for the curtailment of the set at 161 rather than 250 cards. The cards are sometimes found with the words "Sample Card" overprinted on the back. Collectors generally ascribe two levels of rarity to the set, cards #1 to #115 being the more common, cards #116 to #162 being considerably scarcer.

FOR

Popular starting point for modern baseball card collectors. Simple format and good photos of the players of the day, many of whom don't appear in other card sets.

AGAINST

There aren't any really negative factors to the 1939 Play Ball—America set; either you like it or you don't.

NOTEWORTHY CARDS

This set features the "rookie card" of Ted Williams, along with one of the more common cards of Joe DiMaggio.

VALUE

EX. CONDITION: Complete set, $1,400; common card, #1–#115, $3.50; common card, #116–#162, $12.50; Hall of Famers, $10–$20; Williams, $100–$125; DiMaggio, $150–$175. 5-YEAR PROJECTION: Below average.

1938 GOUDEY "HEADS UP"

SPECIFICATIONS

SIZE: 2³⁄₈×2⁷⁄₈″. FRONT: Hand-retouched black-and-white photo and color drawing. BACK: Black printing on white cardboard. DISTRIBUTION: Nationally, one card in 1¢ packages with bubblegum.

HISTORY

It's hard to say what Goudey Gum Company had in mind when they created their 48-card set in 1938. The set contains what are essentially two different versions of the same cards for 24 players. The first version, numbered on the back from 241 to 264, features a photograph of the player's head and cap, onto which a caricature body has been drawn. Cards #265 to #288 feature the same photo/drawing, but with a cartoon added in each corner of the card. The second type of card is considered somewhat scarcer than the first. Backs of the first group of cards mention, "This is one of a series of 288 Baseball Stars," while backs of cards #265 to #288 indicate there are 312 cards in the set. Whether Goudey meant to tie this issue to its premier set of 240 cards in 1933 is unknown, but in any case the total comes to only 288 cards for the two years. The '38 Goudey set is known to collectors as "Heads Up," and it is not particularly popular compared to the company's 1933 and 1934 issues, though the cards are quite valuable. Besides the player figure on the front of the card, only the player's name and team appear, printed in a colored strip at the bottom that rises around the drawing to form a frame. Card backs have a short career summary of the player, along with personal data, a card number, and a large Goudey ad at the bottom.

FOR

An unusual set that offers a large percentage of major stars of the late 1930s.

AGAINST

The set, with its two versions of each card, is repetitive, and, at the prices being charged for each card, it's too expensive for most collectors.

NOTEWORTHY CARDS

Of the 24 different players in the '38 Goudey set, there are seven Hall of Famers. The '38 Goudey set is the first major baseball card issue to feature cards of '40s star players Joe DiMaggio and Bob Feller.

VALUE

EX. CONDITION: Complete set, $2,500; common card, #241–#264, $25–$30; common card, #265–#288, $30–$35; Gehringer, Greenberg, Medwick, $50–$60; Foxx, Feller, $125; DiMaggio, $250–$300. 5-YEAR PROJECTION: Below average.

1936 GOUDEY

SPECIFICATIONS

SIZE: 2³⁄₈×2⁷⁄₈″. FRONT: Black-and-white photograph. BACK: Game card. DISTRIBUTION: Nationally, one card in 1¢ packs of bubblegum.

HISTORY

One of the less popular Goudey issues, the 25-card 1936 set differs from its predecessors in that it features black-and-white photographs of the players on the card fronts, rather than color drawings. The only other element on the front is a facsimile autograph. In addition to a short biographical sketch of the player, card backs contain a pair of baseball game situations that could be used to play a game with the cards. Because the set was not a great success in 1936, the cards are quite scarce today in comparison to earlier Goudey issues.

FOR

Nice actual photos of better-known players in the mid-1930s.

AGAINST

"Game" cards have never attracted much collector interest. To condition-conscious collectors, playing games with baseball cards is generally detrimental to preservation.

NOTEWORTHY CARDS

Nearly one-third of the 1936 Goudey cards are Hall of Famers: Mickey Cochrane, Kiki Cuyler, Rock Ferrell, Lefty Gomez, Hank Greenberg, Bucky Harris, Chuck Klein, and Paul Waner.

VALUE

EX.-MT. CONDITION: Complete set, $300; common card, $10; Hall of Famers, $15–$20. 5-YEAR PROJECTION: Below average.

1936 Goudey, Kiki Cuyler

1935 GOUDEY "4-IN-1"

SPECIFICATIONS

SIZE: 2⅜×2⅞". FRONT: Color painting. BACK: Black-and-white photograph. DISTRIBUTION: Nationally, one card in 1¢ packages with bubblegum.

HISTORY

The format of Goudey's third major baseball card set was a departure from anything that had been done before, and it set the stage for many similar test issues from Topps in later years. Each of the '35 Goudeys, known as "4-in-1s" to collectors, features four different players' pictures on the card front. The pictures are surrounded and separated by a red (occasionally blue) border. All of the players on any given card are members of the same team. The pictures are generally the same ones used on the 1933 and 1934 Goudey sets, in reduced size and set against a plain background. The player's last name and team nickname appear in his one-quarter of the card. Card backs are one-fourth of a large "puzzle" that could be assembled by gathering six or twelve cards with the same "Picture" number. Besides the puzzle photo on the back of the card, each card had a number identifying "Picture ___ Card ___". There were nine different back puzzles. Each of the puzzles that featured montages of players on the Tigers, the Senators and the Indians required 12 cards, lettered A–L, to complete. Each of the puzzles that featured portraits of single players—Chuck Klein, Frank Frisch, Mickey Cochrane, Joe Cronin, Jimmy Foxx, and Al Simmons—required six cards, A–F, to complete. In all, a complete set of '35 Goudeys by back/front combination would contain 114 cards. Most collectors, however, do not collect the set that way (if they collect it at all), preferring to assemble just one of each of the 36 different card fronts. The cards with blue borders are scarce, but they're not necessary to complete a set.

FOR

The idea was innovative and would be much copied in later years.

1935 Goudey "4-in-1" (back)

AGAINST

The set is far too confusing for most collectors. Not to mention the fact that most collectors don't like baseball cards with more than one player apiece.

NOTEWORTHY CARDS

Babe Ruth returned to Goudey cards in '35, his last year as a player, in combination with three of his new Braves teammates. Lou Gehrig, though, was gone.

VALUE

EX. CONDITION: Complete set (36 different fronts), $625; common card, $15; Frisch/Dean/Orsatti/Carleton, $20; Ruth/McManus/Brandt/Maranville, $100. 5-YEAR PROJECTION: Below average.

1934 GOUDEY

SPECIFICATIONS

SIZE: 2⅜×2⅞". FRONT: Color painting. BACK: Green printing on white cardboard. DISTRIBUTION: Nationally, one card in 1¢ packages of bubblegum.

HISTORY

In its second year of bubblegum gum card production, Goudey cut back its set by more than one-half—to only 96 cards—probably reflecting the depth of the Depression. Popular and durable Yankees star Lou Gehrig was promotionally tied to the '34 Goudey set. The wrappers of the "Big League" brand gum identified the cards as "Lou Gehrig Series," while 84 of the 96 cards had a small photo of Gehrig at the bottom left of the card, and the words "Lou Gehrig (as facsimile autograph) says . . . ." What Lou Gehrig "said" appears on the back of the card in the form of a write-up about the player pictured on the card, giving the impression that it had been written by Gehrig. On 12 of the cards in the scarcer high number series (#73 to #96), the photo and saying were changed to "Chuck Klein says." Klein, a Philly in 1933, but a Cub in '34, had led the National League in 1933 in hits, doubles, home runs, RBI, and batting and slugging averages. Fronts of the '34 Goudeys had a color painting of the player set against a solid-color background. On the background were silhouettes of a baseball diamond and a couple of players in action. The player's name appeared at the top of the card. Card backs had, besides the "quotation" from Gehrig or Klein, the card number and notation "1934 Series," the player's name and team, and a Goudey ad at the bottom. Collectors generally ascribe three levels of scarcity to the 1934 Goudey set. Cards #1 to #48 are the most common, cards #49 to #72 are somewhat less common, and the high numbers, #73 to #96, are quite scarce. Because the '34 Goudeys were printed on heavy cardboard, they have withstood the ravages of half a century remarkably well. As with the '33 Goudeys, many of the star cards in the 1934 set have been reproduced over the past years, but such cards are usually on thinner glossier cardboard, and most are clearly marked as reprints.

FOR

A popular set that's challenging for the serious collector.

AGAINST

The scarcer and more expensive high number cards put the '34 Goudey set beyond the fiscal reach and the patience of many collectors.

NOTEWORTHY CARDS

Only one player has two cards in the '34 Goudey set—Lou Gehrig. Surpris-

1934 Goudey, Cliff Bolton

ingly and inexplicably, there is no Babe Ruth card in the set. Many of the other Hall of Famers are present, though, along with lots of players who are obscure enough to be of interest only to the team collector.

VALUE

EX. CONDITION: Complete set, $2,000; common card, #1–#48, $10; #49–#72, $12.50; #73–#96, $45; Hall of Famers, $15–$25; Hank Greenberg, $35; Kiki Cuyler, $65; Dizzy Dean, Jimmy Foxx, $100; Lou Gehrig, $200–$225. 5-YEAR PROJECTION: Average or below.

1934–1936 DIAMOND STARS

SPECIFICATIONS

SIZE: 2⅜×2⅞". FRONT: Color drawing. BACK: Green or blue printing on white cardboard. DISTRIBUTION: Nationally, one card per 1¢ package of bubblegum.

HISTORY

While the Diamond Stars baseball card issue produced by National Chicle, Cambridge, Massachusetts, does not fit neatly into the standard hobby definition of a "set," it remains a popular favorite among 1930s sets.

Over the three-year period from 1934 through 1936, a total of 108 different card fronts was issued, for 96 different players (the last 12 cards in the set are repeats of players who had been on earlier cards). However, because many cards were issued in two or three of those years, with different backs, a total of 168 front/back combinations is available for the Diamond Stars set. The fronts of the Diamond Stars cards have a color drawing of the player, often set against a stadium or stylized ball diamond background, but sometimes just posed in front of a multi-colored background that is somewhat "art deco" in appearance. The only writing on the front of the cards is the player's name. There is a white border around this design. Cards backs were printed in either green (1934 and 1935) or blue (1935 and 1936), and contain a card number at top, a baseball playing tip by *Boston American* sportswriter Austen Lake, three or four lines about the player, and a National Chicle copyright line. There is also a notice that the card is "one of 240 major league players with playing tips." Considering the fact that a 12-card blank-backed proof sheet for unissued cards was recently discovered (and a "reprint" card set made from it), it seems quite likely that National Chicle did intend to continue the issue to 240 cards, but was probably prohibited from doing so by the economics of the Depression. The cards that were reissued in 1935 and/or 1936 were updated by changing the player's stats on the back of the card, though the copyright line remained at "1934." Luckily for collectors, the Diamond Stars were issued in somewhat logical fashion. Cards #1 to #24 comprise the original issue of 1934, with green back printing. All were reissued in 1935, along with cards #25 to #84. Of the 1935 cards, #25 to #72 are found with card backs printed only in green, while those numbered #73 to #84 can be found with either green or blue printing on back. In 1936, only blue printing was used on the backs. The '36 issue included a few of the cards from the #1 to #31 sequence, all of those from #73 to #84, and a final run of cards, #85 to #108. The last 12 cards in the set, #97 to #108, are of players who appeared earlier in the set. These "high numbers" were apparently printed in lower quantities than the rest of the set, and are quite scarce today. Despite the confusing combination of fronts and backs, the Diamond Stars set is usually collected today by trying to assemble all 108 front designs, without regard to the back variations.

FOR

Attractive cards of the 1930s, surprisingly low-priced considering they are more than 50 years old. The relatively thick cardboard on which they were printed has helped preserve many cards in higher grades.

AGAINST

The confusion about which backs were issued in which years makes the set less popular than it would otherwise be.

NOTEWORTHY CARDS

While the 1934 Diamond Stars set has many Hall of Famers and well-known favorites of the 1930s, it lacks the two biggest names of those years, Babe Ruth (then at the end of his career) and Lou Gehrig (in his prime).

VALUE

EX. CONDITION: Complete set (108 cards), $1,750; common card, #1–#84, $10–$12; #85–#96, $15; #97–#108, $40–$50; Hall of Famers, low numbers, $15–$25; Hall of Famers, high numbers, $75–$100; Rogers Hornsby, Jimmy Foxx, $40. 5-YEAR PROJECTION: Average, or perhaps a bit below.

1934–1936 BATTER-UP

SPECIFICATIONS

SIZE: 2⅜×3¼″ and 2⅜×3″. FRONT: Black-and-white or duo-tone photograph. BACK: Blank. DISTRIBUTION: Nationally, one card in 1¢ packages of bubblegum.

HISTORY

A second issue by National Chicle Gum Company, of Cambridge, Massachusetts, in the mid-1930s, the Batter-Up series of 192 cards was printed over the same three-year span (1934–1936) as the company's Diamond Stars issue. While the Batter-Up cards were not the first die-cut baseball cards, they were the first of the bubblegum card era, and were the pattern on which Topps based its 1951 and 1964 die-cut sets. Like all die-cut baseball cards, the Batter-Ups are much more desirable when intact—when they have never been punched out. Those cards that have been folded over to make the player figure "stand up" are in less demand, and cards that have had the background removed are of little interest to collectors. The Batter-Up cards feature a full-length photograph of a player, with a natural background. The cardboard has been cut almost through, to allow the background to be folded over to make the player appear to stand up in an action pose. A white box to the left or right of the player has the words "Batter-Up," the player's last name, team, and position. On cards #1 to #80, the card number is printed outside the box, while on cards #81 to #192, the card number is printed within the white box. Another major difference between these two "series" is that cards #1 to #80 are 3¼″ long, while the high numbers are just 3″ long. The high numbers are also considerably scarcer than those from #1 to #80. Each of the 192 cards in the Batter-Up set can be found in either black-and-white or as a tinted photograph in colors of blue, green, brown or sepia, red, and purple. Collectors generally assemble a set without regard to the color of the card. The cards are blank on the back. Some of the players in the set appear on more than one card.

FOR

Actual-photograph cards of a large number of the players active in the mid-1930s.

AGAINST

Hard to find cards in unfolded condition. Most of the big name players appear in the scarcer and more expensive high number series.

NOTEWORTHY CARDS

The Batter-Up set has some of the first multi-player feature cards, a trio of them in fact: Earl Webb and Wally Moses, Jim Bottomley and Paul Andrews, and Ted Lyons and Frankie Hayes. Most of the big name players of the era are included, though there are no cards of Ruth or Gehrig.

VALUE

EX. CONDITION, BACKGROUND NOT FOLDED: Complete set, $3,500; common card, #1–#80, $10; common card, #81–#192, $25; Hall of Famers, low numbers, $15–$25; Hall of Famers, high numbers, $35–$50. 5-YEAR PROJECTION: Below average.

1933 GOUDEY

SPECIFICATIONS

SIZE: 2⅜×2⅞″. FRONT: Color painting. BACK: Green printing on white cardboard. DISTRIBUTION: Nationally, one card per 1¢ package of bubblegum.

HISTORY

For many collectors, the 1933 set of 240 baseball cards produced by Goudey Gum Company, Boston, marks the beginning of the modern baseball card era. The '33 Goudey was the first major bubblegum card set, and as such is a direct ancestor of the cards being produced today. The Goudey cards feature a color painting of the player, either a full-length, partial-length, or portrait pose, set against a solid-color background. There is a red strip at the bottom with an ad for "Big League Chewing Gum," the brand with which the cards were sold. The player's name appears in one of the upper corners. The card has a white border. Card backs have a number at the top, followed by the player's name, team, and a baseball biography. An ad for Goudey appears at the bottom, with a reference to "Indian Gum," another Goudey brand, which featured cards in a similar format with American Indians on them. While there are 240 cards in the 1933 Goudey set, there are not that many different players. Several of the better-known players of the day appear on more than one card—there are four of Babe Ruth. The '33 Goudeys, and those issues that followed from the company, were printed on very substantial card-

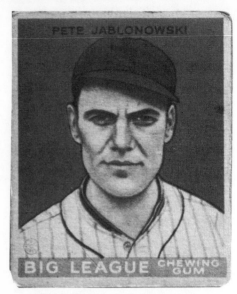

1933 Goudey, Pete Jablonowski

board, and they can often be found in surprisingly good shape today, more than half a century later. Many of the cards in the 1933 (and later) Goudey sets have been reprinted since the mid-1970s. The reprints, usually showing superstars of the era, are not all marked as such, but can usually be identified by the thinner, whiter cardboard (sometimes found with perforated edges, where the cards were torn from a book) and the glossy surface on the face of the cards.

FOR
An historically important baseball card set. With the exception of a single card (see below), the set is not too tough to accumulate, though it can be expensive. Since the '33 Goudeys came along 10 years after the last batch of major baseball card sets, there are many players who make their first and/or only appearance in this issue, making it popular with team collectors.

AGAINST
The extreme rarity of the Napoleon Lajoie card makes completing this set an impossibility for most collectors.

NOTEWORTHY CARDS
The 1933 Goudey set is a grand mix of baseball's middle years. Many of the stars of the 1920s are included in their later years, often as managers, while the young players of 1933, many of whom would remain active into the 1940s and even 1950s, are also in-

cluded. Besides the Hall of Famers, there are plenty of good, everyday players who are well-remembered by those who followed baseball in the 1930s.

OUR FAVORITE CARD
Goudey made use of a very sneaky trick in 1933 to keep kids buying penny packs of its bubblegum trying to complete the set. While the backs of the cards specified that there were 240 cards, try as they might, the bubblegum buyers in 1933 could only find 239. Card #106, Napoleon Lajoie, was not issued at all in 1933. Probably spurred by complaints by parents, Goudey issued the card the following year, but it was available only to those who wrote to Goudey complaining about not finding the card in the gum packs. An intact sheet of 1934 Goudey cards, with the 1933 Lajoie card included, is one of the great treasures of the baseball card hobby.

VALUE
EX. CONDITION: Complete set (no Lajoie), $3,500; common card, $10; Hall of Famers, $20–$45; Dizzy Dean, $75; Gehrig, $175; Ruth, $300; Lajoie, $7,000. 5-YEAR PROJECTION: Average.

1933 SPORT KINGS

SPECIFICATIONS
SIZE: 2⅜×2⅞″. FRONT: Color painting. BACK: Black printing on white cardboard. DISTRIBUTION: Nationally, one card in 1¢ packages of bubblegum.

HISTORY
While only three of the 48 cards in the Sport Kings set are baseball players, the set is included in this volume because it is popularly collected. The set's popularity stems from its issue by the Goudey Gum Company, and from the large number of famous athletes in other sports who are included in the set. The cards feature a color painting of the athlete, with a solid-color background. A black area beneath the picture has a silhouette of the sport for

which the athlete is known, along with a strip at the bottom with his or her name (the set is one of the few 20th century card issues to include women athletes). A red banner at the top of the card has the brand name "Sport Kings Gum." Card backs are quite similar to the 1933 Goudey baseball cards in format. There is a card number at top, the athlete's name, the sports in which he/she is known, a biography, and, at the bottom, a Goudey ad. The Sport Kings set features a wide range of athletic and sporting endeavors—baseball, football, basketball, hockey, swimming, aviation, riding, wrestling, and dogsledding.

FOR
An interesting set for the collector whose focus goes beyond just baseball cards. The cards are not too scarce or expensive, once you get past the baseball and football players.

AGAINST
Most collectors don't like to "mix" sports in a card set.

NOTEWORTHY CARDS
The three baseball players in the set are Babe Ruth, Ty Cobb, and Carl Hubbell. Other notable athletes in the issue include Red Grange, Jim Thorpe, and Knute Rockne (football); Jack Dempsey and Gene Tunney (boxing); Bobby Jons, Gene Sarazen, and Walter Hagen (golf); Babe Didrickson (track); and even Olympic swimming star Johnny Weissmuller in the days

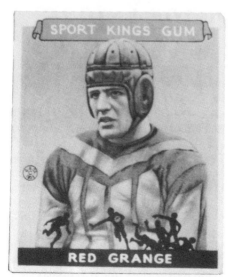

1933 Sport Kings, Red Grange

before he became famous as Tarzan in the movies.

VALUE

EX. CONDITION: Complete set, $650; common card, $8–$10; Dempsey, Grange, $30; Hubbell, Weissmuller, Didrickson, $40–$50; Thorpe, Rockne, $60–$75; Cobb, $150; Ruth, $200. 5-YEAR PROJECTION: Below average.

1933 DeLONG

SPECIFICATIONS

SIZE: 2×3″. FRONT: Black-and-white photograph and color drawing. BACK: Black printing on white cardboard. DISTRIBUTION: Nationally, one card in 1¢ package of bubblegum.

HISTORY

The DeLong Gum Company of Boston produced just one baseball card set, a 1933 issue of 24 cards. The cards have an unusual design that combines a black-and-white photograph of the player with a color drawing of a stadium scene. The player photo is superimposed over the ball diamond, making him look like a giant. A single stadium scene is used for the background of all the cards, and its vivid colors make the '33 DeLongs quite eye-catching. A yellow, blue, or red strip at the bottom of the card contains the player's name and team in a contrasting color. There is a white border around the entire card. Card backs combine a baseball playing tip aimed at youngsters with a DeLong ad. There is a card number in the upper left and, on some cards, a small drawing to illustrate the playing tip. The back write-ups have the byline of Austen Lake, baseball editor of the old *Boston Transcript* newspaper. The cards were distributed in packages of "Play Ball" gum, a brand name that would reappear often in connection with baseball cards. The unusually attractive design of the '33 DeLongs, as well as their scarcity, has made it popular.

FOR

Historically important in that, with the 1933 Goudey issue, it was one of the first bubblegum baseball card sets. Nice format, lots of stars.

AGAINST

About the only negative factor of the '33 DeLong set is that the cards are quite expensive.

NOTEWORTHY CARDS

For a set of only 24 cards, the DeLongs have a strong percentage of Hall of Famers—15 of them—led by Lou Gehrig.

VALUE

EX. CONDITION: Complete set, $2,000; common card, $50–$60; "minor" Hall of Famers, $75; "big name" Hall of Famers, $80–$100; Foxx, $125; Gehrig, $500. 5-YEAR PROJECTION: Average, perhaps a bit below.

1933 GEORGE C. MILLER

SPECIFICATIONS

SIZE: 2½×3″. FRONT: Color painting against outdoors backdrop. BACK: Checklist, premium offer. DISTRIBUTION: Nationally, one card packaged with each 1-cent piece of toffee.

HISTORY

Issued nearly five years after the last major candy card set, the George C. Miller Company cards of 1933 are contemporaries of the more common and better-known set from their Boston neighbor, Goudey. Thirty-two unnumbered cards comprise the Miller set, two representatives from each of the 16 major league teams of the era. All cards have a similar appearance, a painted head-and-shoulders color portrait set against a natural horizon of field, trees, and sky. The overall impression is visually quite appealing. There is no writing on the front of the cards. Backs offer a few biographical and statistical details, along with a checklist of the set and an offer to redeem complete 32-card sets for the choice of a "fielder's mitt, regulation American or National League baseball, or 1 Grandstand Seat to any American or National League Game (except World's Series) at any Park." The offer went on to say that the "pictures" (cards) would be returned "cancelled," with the prize. Cancelling of the cards consisted of cutting off the bottom three quarters of an inch, which contained the redemption offer, accounting for the existence today of so many mutilated Miller cards. Naturally, the Miller Company didn't want to be giving away gloves, balls, and 50¢ ballgame tickets too easily, so it appears that cards of Boston pitcher "Poison" Ivy Andrews were not distributed in the same quantity as the other 31 cards in the set. The Andrews card remains quite scarce today. Indeed, all George C. Miller Company cards are among the more scarce of the Depression-era issues.

FOR

Attractive cards in unique format. Good collecting challenge for the serious hobbyist willing to spend money.

AGAINST

Too expensive for most collectors; high-grade cards start at $125.

NOTEWORTHY CARDS

This is another set with a high percentage of Hall of Famers—60 percent—Averill, Bottomley, Cronin, Dean, Dickey, Foxx, Frisch, Gehringer, Goslin, Grove, Hafey, Klein, Maranville, Ott, Ruffing, Simmons, Terry, and both Waners.

OUR FAVORITE CARD

One more player in the George C. Miller Company set should be in the Hall of Fame, the late Charlie Grimm. Most collectors and fans today remember him as "Jolly Cholly," the banjo-strumming manager of the Chicago Cubs and Milwaukee Braves, but in a 20-year major league career he put together impressive statistics as the National League's leading first baseman. Many of his fielding records at the position remain unbroken to this day. He was no slouch with the bat, either, posting a lifetime .290 average, including a .345 season in 1923. As a manager, his winning percentage of .546 (won 1,287, lost 1,069) is far above the record of such Hall of Fame skippers as Casey Stengel (.508), Lou Boudreau (.487), Bucky

Harris (.493), Wilber Robinson (.500), and even the famed Connie Mack (.484).

VALUE

EX. CONDITION: Complete set, $5,000; common card, $125; "common" Hall of Famers, $150–$200; Andrews, $250; Dean, $300. Cancelled cards can be considered in Fair condition, at best, worth about 20 percent of the Ex. price. 5-YEAR PROJECTION: Average.

1933 TATTOO ORBIT

SPECIFICATIONS

SIZE: 2×2¼″. FRONT: Black-and-white photograph, color painting. BACK: Black printing on white cardboard. DISTRIBUTION: Nationally, one card in 1¢ packages with bubblegum.

HISTORY

You'd have to know your baseball cards to recognize this 1933 set of 60 cards at first glance. There is nothing on the cards to identify the issuer. The cards were produced by the Orbit Gum Company of Chicago, Illinois, which inserted them into packages of its Tattoo brand gum. The small, nearly square cards feature on their fronts a black-and-white photograph on which some attempt has been made to tint the skin portions a flesh color. The photos are separated from the colorful, stylized baseball park background by a black line. The red, yellow, and green backgrounds give the cards a colorful appearance that draws the eye away from the rather drab photos. There is no other printing on the front, and the cards are unnumbered. A rather wide white border surrounds the design. Card backs are extremely simple, featuring only the player's name, team, position, birth date, height, and weight. While the Tattoo Orbit cards are really quite scarce, they are not all that expensive; lack of collector demand keeps the price low. Like many of the sets in this era, the Tattoo Orbit has had some of its cards reprinted in recent years,

though reprints are usually marked as such.

FOR

A reasonably priced set for the collector who desires the cards of the 1930s. They have an unusual format and are really quite attractive.

AGAINST

The cards are quite plain, with none of the statistics and biography that most collectors seem to like so well.

NOTEWORTHY CARDS

Four of the cards are considered tougher than the rest of the set; the cards of Ivy Andrews and Rogers Hornsby (who was traded from the Cardinals to the Browns in midseason) are considered tough, but less so than those of Bump Hadley and George Blaeholder.

VALUE

EX. CONDITION: Complete set, $1,000; common card, $12.50; Hall of Famers, $15–$30; Andrews, $25; Blaeholder, Hadley, $40; Dizzy Dean, Hornsby, $50. 5-YEAR PROJECTION: Below average.

1932 U.S. CARAMEL

SPECIFICATIONS

SIZE: 2½×3″. FRONT: Black-and-white photograph. BACK: Black printing on white cardboard. DISTRIBUTION: Nationally (?), in packages of caramels.

HISTORY

In 1932 the U.S. Caramel Company, East Boston, Massachusetts, produced one of the last—and one of the rarest—of the caramel card sets that had been a baseball card staple since before the turn of the century. The baseball card market was about to be dominated by the bubblegum companies, and the U.S. Caramel issue of 31 "famous athletes" was the last of a dying breed. The set consists of 26 baseball players, three boxers, and a pair of golfers. Since the golfers and boxers are all quite well-known, they

are usually collected right along with the baseball players when the full set is collected—which isn't often, considering its rarity and high price tag. It is assumed that the rarity of the set today does not stem from the mail-in offer advertised on the back of the card, which offered a baseball for sending in one set of cards, and a baseball glove for three sets. Because card #16 (rumored to be Joe Kuhel, of the Washington Senators) is unknown today, it is quite likely that it was either never issued or issued only in severely limited numbers, thereby cutting down on the number of baseballs and gloves given away. Possibly the cards were just distributed in limited numbers from the start. In any event, they are rare and valuable today. The cards are somewhat similar to the old 1914–1915 Cracker Jack set in appearance on both front and back. The front has a black-and-white player picture set against a red background with a white border. The player's name appears in white above the picture. On back are the player's name, position, team, and league, along with a career summary. On the bottom is the redemption ad. A card number appears in the upper left.

FOR

Historically important to the hobby as one of the last of a major type of card issue. Loaded with superstars.

AGAINST

The inclusion of nonbaseball players and the absence of card #16 detract from the collectibility of this set.

NOTEWORTHY CARDS

The baseball players in the '32 U.S. Caramel set are a virtual Hall of Fame gallery, including Babe Ruth, Lou Gehrig, and Ty Cobb, even though Cobb had been out of baseball since 1928. The golfers in the set are Gene Sarazen and Bobby Jones; the boxers, Jack Dempsey, Gene Tunney, and Jack Sharkey.

VALUE

EX. CONDITION: Complete set, $3,500; common card, nonbaseball, $40; common card, baseball, $100; Dempsey, Tunney, $125; superstars, $150–$200; Cobb, $300; Gehrig, $450; Ruth, $500. 5-YEAR PROJECTION: Below average.

TY COBB
Mgr.—Detroit Americans

EDDIE COLLINS
SECOND BASE, CHICAGO AMERICANS

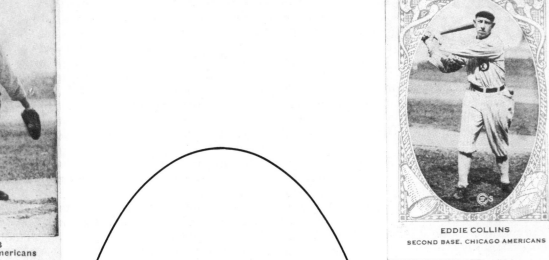

1929- 1920

1922 (E-120) AMERICAN CARAMELS

SPECIFICATIONS

SIZE: 2×3½". FRONT: Sepia or blue-green duotone photograph. BACK: Brown or blue-green printing on white cardboard. DISTRIBUTION: Nationally, in packages of caramels.

HISTORY

This is probably the most popularly collected candy card issue of the 1920s, primarily because it is one of the more attractive, even with its limited color use. With no real rarities, it presents a reasonable collecting challenge at 240 cards. The 1922 American Caramels issue is another baseball card set that is almost universally known by its catalog number—E-120—assigned by Jefferson Burdick in his early reference work, *The American Card Catalog*. This catalog designation will be used here because it will help avoid confusion with another set issued by American Caramel Company about the same time. The format of the E-120 issue features a player photo, usually posed, in an elaborate oval frame at the center of the card. The frame features drawings of baseball players and/or equipment in its corners. In the wide border at the bottom, the player's complete name is printed, along with his position, team, and league. The cards of National League players are printed in blue-green; the American League players' cards are printed in sepia. Card backs are printed in the same color as the fronts. They have the city name and league at top, followed by the team nickname, the name of the manager, and the checklist of the 15 players who appear for that team in the E-120 set. An ad at the bottom of the card includes an offer for albums to house the set. There are 15 players on each of 16 teams represented, a total of 240 cards. There is no card number on this issue. The fronts of the E-120 caramel cards were used in several other issues of the time, including a black-and-white blank-backed strip card set, and a pair of Canadian issues (each containing 120 cards from the set) advertising Neilson's chocolate bars. The E-120 cards themselves are printed on rather thin cardboard, and are usually found with creases or other apparent wear.

FOR

One of the few large-size caramel card sets of the 1920s that can be reasonably collected. Lots of stars in an attractive format.

AGAINST

E-120 pictures appeared on later caramel sets, and the entire design was used for still other sets. This lack of exclusivity diminishes demand for the E-120 cards. Large number of cards makes collecting a complete set somewhat expensive, especially in top grades.

NOTEWORTHY CARDS

All of the big stars of the early 1920s are in the set, including Babe Ruth and Ty Cobb. The name on the front of the Cobb card is misspelled "Cob."

VALUE

EX. CONDITION: Complete set, $2,500; common card, $8–$10; Hall of Famers, $12–$25; Rogers Hornsby, Walter Johnson, $50; Cobb, $125; Ruth, $150. 5-YEAR PROJECTION: Below average.

1922 (E-121) AMERICAN CARAMELS

SPECIFICATIONS

SIZE: 2×3½". FRONT: Black-and-white photograph. BACK: Black printing on white cardboard. DISTRIBUTION: Nationally, in packages of caramels.

HISTORY

The caramel card set known to collectors as E-121, a catalog identification number assigned by Jeff Burdick in his once-standard *The American Card Catalog*, is one of the most commonly encountered yet least understood candy sets of the early 1920s. For instance, it's not known why American Caramel Company chose to issue a second set of cards apparently in the same year as its E-120 set (see separate listing). It is also unknown how many cards comprise a complete set. Some E-121 cards have printing on the back that specifies, "This set consists of pictures of eighty of the leading Base Ball Stars . . . ," while others are found with backs indicating a 120-card set. Regardless, there are more than that number with each style back. Several players have more than one card, and there are many error, variation, and correction cards. In fact, there are more than 220 known E-121s. And, besides the E-121s with American Caramel Company backs, the cards are also found blank-backed and with backs of other advertisers, most often Holsum Bread. Collectors usually try to assemble a set of E-121 caramel-backs on the basis of the pictures on the front, regardless of whether the backs specify 80 or 120 cards. Design of the E-121 card is quite similar to many other cards of its era; a black-and-white photo is framed by a thin black line, around which is a wide white border. In the bottom of the border are the player's name, position, team, and league. Many of the pictures will be found in other card sets of the day. Backs have the ad for American Caramel Company. There is no card number on the E-121 issue.

FOR

A challenging set for the collector who wants to delve into the 1920s.

AGAINST

Difficulty of telling when a set is "complete" leaves many collectors frustrated. Photos shared with other card sets leave E-121 with nothing unique.

NOTEWORTHY CARDS

All the big stars are present in the set, and many of the biggest names—Cobb, Ruth, Johnson—have several different poses in the set.

VALUE

EX. CONDITION: Complete set, unknown; common card, $7; Hall of Famers, $10–$25; Rogers Hornsby, Tris Speaker, Walter Johnson, $35–$50; Cobb, $100; Ruth, $125. 5-YEAR PROJECTION: Below average.

1919-1910

1916 SPORTING NEWS

SPECIFICATIONS

SIZE: 1⅝×3″. FRONT: Black-and-white photograph. BACK: Black printing on white cardboard. DISTRIBUTION: Nationally, by mail-in offer.

HISTORY

Published then as now in St. Louis, *The Sporting News* called itself "The Baseball Paper of the World" on the backs of its two sets of baseball cards issued in 1916. Although two sets were actually issued, they are virtually identical, the only differences being the inclusion of a few different players, a few team changes, and changes of card numbers. Many of the pictures on the Sporting News set will be quite familiar to collectors; they are the same ones used in the popular American Caramel Company sets of 1921–1922 and many other regional card sets of the day. This has helped reduce the popularity and collectibility of the Sporting News issue. The cards feature a black-and-white, full-length posed or action photo of the player surrounded by a wide white border. At the bottom the player's full name, his position, team, and a card number appear. The cards are numbered alphabetically. Card backs have an ad for the paper.

FOR

Early use of actual photographs of players. Relatively inexpensive (especially for superstars) on a per-card basis.

AGAINST

Re-use of pictures in other card sets limits the popularity of this issue. The fact that two sets were issued within a year's time, with only minor changes, makes the issue confusing to collectors; the same player's picture can be found with two different card numbers.

NOTEWORTHY CARDS

Lots of the major stars of the day are featured in the Sporting News set. It is one of the few contemporary sets to have cards of both Ty Cobb and Babe Ruth.

VALUE

EX. CONDITION: Complete set (200), $1,750; common card, $8; Hall of Famers, $12–$25; Honus Wagner, Joe Jackson, Walter Johnson, Napoleon Lajoie, $30–$45; Cobb, $100; Ruth, $125. 5-YEAR PROJECTION: Below average.

1916 COLLINS-McCARTHY

SPECIFICATIONS

SIZE: 2×3¼″. FRONT: Black-and-white photograph. BACK: Black printing on white card stock. DISTRIBUTION: Northern California, in packages of candy.

HISTORY

One of the few regional sets of the early 20th century distributed on the West Coast and featuring major league ballplayers, the Collins-McCarthy "Hall of Fame" set (as they're called on the backs of the cards) numbers 200 cards. The set issued by this San Francisco confectioner is identical in make-up to several other regionally issued sets of the same year, such as those of Morehouse Baking in Lawrence, Massachusetts; Weil Baking Company, in New Orleans; and the Boston Store in Milwaukee. Each of the cards, regardless of the advertising on the back, carries the notation "This is one of a series of 200 action pictures of Major League Baseball Players, comprising Baseball's Hall of Fame." Naturally, not all the players in the set have been enshrined in the National Baseball Hall of Fame at Cooperstown, New York. In fact, the Hall of Fame wasn't established until 1936. The fronts of the Collins-McCarthy cards are identical to those issued by other companies. A black-and-white posed-action photo is surrounded by a thin black line. Beneath are three lines of type: the player's name, his position and team, and the card number. Evidently a single printer supplied the cards to all of these issuers, either selling them with a blank space on back to have their advertising message printed on or, more likely, doing the printing for the issuer and then selling them completed cards. This 1916 "Hall of Fame" series was Collins-McCarthy's only major league baseball card, but the company is well known among collectors today for being the producer of the long-running (1911–1939) Zeenut card sets.

FOR

If you live on the West Coast and want to collect the "generic" baseball card set of 1916, the Collins-McCarthy backs are the natural choice. They're a quality issue that can be assembled in a complete set with a reasonable amount of diligence and cash.

AGAINST

There's really nothing unique about the Collins-McCarthy cards except for the advertising on back.

NOTEWORTHY CARDS

There are many true Hall of Famers in the Collins-McCarthy "Hall of Fame" issue; two worthy of special note here are Babe Ruth and Casey Stengel. In this early card set, Ruth is pictured as a pitcher for the Boston Red Sox. Many of today's fans don't remember that Ruth began his career as a left-handed pitcher—and was darned good at it—before moving on to New York to become the famous Yankee home run king. Ruth had two 20+ win seasons (1916 and 1917) and in 1916 led American League pitchers with a 1.75 ERA in 40 starts. The "Old Perfesser," Casey Stengel, is pictured in the Collins-McCarthy set of 1916 as an outfielder for the Brooklyn Dodgers. Before he went on to become one of the finest and most popular managers in baseball, Stengel had a 14-year playing career in the major leagues, compiling a lifetime batting average of .284.

VALUE

EX. CONDITION: Complete set, $2,500; common card, $12; Hall of Famers, $20–$40; Cobb, $100; Ruth, $150. 5-YEAR PROJECTION: Average.

1914, 1915 CRACKER JACK

SPECIFICATIONS

SIZE: 2¼×3½". FRONT: Color lithograph. BACK: Black printing on white paper. DISTRIBUTION: Nationally, in packages of Cracker Jack (1914–1915) and by mail-in offer (1915).

HISTORY

Probably the most popular of the many pre-1920 candy card issues are the 1914 and 1915 sets issued in Cracker Jacks. The sets will be considered together here because of their similarity. The easiest way to tell the two years apart is to look at the ads on the backs of the cards. The 1914 set mentions 144 cards; the 1915 set mentions 176 cards. The sets were essentially the same, although several new players were added, trades were recognized, and a few poses were changed in the 1915 set. The 1914 Cracker Jacks were inserted into boxes of the "candy-coated popcorn, peanuts, and a prize." They are quite often found with grease stains from the candy, a factor that must be taken into consideration when grading the cards. The 1915 cards, while also found in the candy boxes, could be obtained by sending in 100 coupons from the boxes, or one coupon and 25¢. An album was also advertised for the 1915 set. Part of the popularity of the Cracker Jack sets can be traced to the fact that they are one of the few major baseball card issues of the day to include players from the Federal League, which for those two years was accorded the status of a third major league. Many of the differences between the two sets reflect movement among the American, National, and Federal Leagues. Overall, the players in the two sets were the same for the first 144 cards but 32 additional cards were added to the 1915 set. All of the 1914 players who appeared again in 1915 retained their card numbers. Card fronts were identical each year. A color lithograph of the player, in either portrait or action pose, was in the center of the card, set against a bright red background. The words "Cracker Jack/Ball Players" appear in black at the top. At the bottom, in the card's white border, are the player's last name, team, and league. Card backs have a card number at top, followed by a short write-up about the player. Separated by a line at the bottom is a Cracker Jack ad. The ad on the 1914 cards mentions that either 10,000,000 or 15,000,000 cards were being printed; while the ad on the 1915 cards offers the set and album. The Cracker Jack cards are printed on heavy paper (not cardboard), which adds to their susceptibility to damage.

FOR

Colorful cards of an important historical era in baseball. One of the few sets in which the Federal League players are found.

AGAINST

Quite expensive, and hard to find in high grades. Similarity of the 1914 and 1915 sets makes collecting both of them very repetitive.

NOTEWORTHY CARDS

All of the big stars and managers of the decade are in the set, including more than a dozen Hall of Famers.

VALUE

EX. CONDITION: Complete set, 1914, $4,500; 1915, $3,500; common card, 1914, $25; 1915, $20; Hall of Famers, $40–$100; Walter Johnson, Christy Mathewson, $125–$150; Ty Cobb, $250–$300. 5-YEAR PROJECTION: Average, perhaps below.

1914–1915 AMERICAN TOBACCO COMPANY

SPECIFICATIONS

SIZE: 1½×2⅝". FRONT: Color drawing. BACK: Black or red printing on white cardboard. DISTRIBUTION: Nationally, in different brands of cigarettes.

HISTORY

Several years after first issuing its famous T-206 set, the American Tobacco Company reissued many of the cards under three new cigarette brand names: Coupon, Red Cross, and Victory. While the same pictures are used in all sets, there are some variations in team designations among them, particularly in comparison with the T-206 issue. Players from the short-lived Federal League are included in the set. Card fronts, like the T-206 issues, have a color drawing of the player, surrounded by a white border. Beneath the border, the player's last name, team, and—sometimes—league are printed in blue or brown ink. Backs have an advertisement for one of the three cigarette brands in which the cards were packaged. Because of their similarity to the T-206 set, the ATC cards of 1914–1915 are not popularly collected; but because they are so much more scarce, they are considerably more expensive on a per-card basis, with the cards of the star players of the day bringing two to five times what the common cards bring. The cards are unnumbered and complete checklists are not known to be accurate; there are currently some 190 of the Coupon-brand cards known, the Victory cards' backs indicate there were 90 in that set, and the Red Cross set advertises 100 designs.

FOR

A real challenge for the tobacco card collector. They are among the very few issues to chronicle the brief era of the Federal League in card form.

AGAINST

Too similar to T-206; but more expensive.

NOTEWORTHY CARDS

Many of the same Hall of Famers that are in the T-206 set are also present in the 1914–1915 ATC issue, including the most popular card, Ty Cobb.

VALUE

EX. CONDITION: Complete set, unknown; common card, Coupon, $10; Red Cross, $25; Victory, $50; Hall of Famers, 2–3 times common price; Cobb, 5 times common price. 5-YEAR PROJECTION: Below average.

1914–1915 PEOPLES TOBACCO COMPANY

SPECIFICATIONS

SIZE: 1½×2⅝″. FRONT: Color drawing. BACK: Black printing on white cardboard. DISTRIBUTION: Southern U.S., in packages of cigarettes.

HISTORY

Some of the lesser-known and less-often collected of the early 20th century tobacco cards are those issued by the Peoples Tobacco Company of New Orleans with its three brands of cigarettes, Kotton (most common), Mino, and Virginia Extra (least common). The set is significant in two ways. Primarily, it is of special note because the ad on the backs of the cards notes that the company is "Not in a Trust," a reference to the American Tobacco Company conglomerate that controlled virtually the entire cigarette industry at that time. Also of interest is the fact that the pictures on the cards are the same as those used on several of the caramel card sets of the day. Indeed, the fronts of the Peoples cards are almost identical to caramel cards, featuring a color drawing of the player surrounded by a white border. In serif type beneath the picture are the player's last name, position, team, and league. Card backs, which are not numbered, have an ad for the particular brand of cigarette in which they were packaged. The set is really quite scarce, and most collectors attempt to gather one each of the 101 known designs (sometimes as many as four different poses for a player), regardless of the ad on the back.

FOR

Something "different" in a tobacco card issue. Pictures are not the same ones seen on the American Tobacco Company cards.

AGAINST

Too similar to the contemporary caramel card issues to elicit much collector interest.

NOTEWORTHY CARDS

Most of the Hall of Famers of the day, including—surprisingly—Honus Wagner, who appears in two poses.

VALUE

EX. CONDITION: Complete set, unknown; common card, $15–$20; Hall of Famers, $45–$50; Cobb, Wagner, $75. 5-YEAR PROJECTION: Below average.

1912 T-207 "BROWN BACK-GROUNDS"

SPECIFICATIONS

SIZE: 1½×2⅝″. FRONT: Color (but not very colorful) lithograph. BACK: Black printing on white cardboard. DISTRIBUTION: Nationally, in packages of cigarettes.

HISTORY

This set of 200 players is—along with the T-205 "Gold Borders" and T-206 "White Borders"—one of the "Big 3" sets of cigarette cards of the period between 1910 and 1920. It is the least popular of the trio, in part because it is the scarcest and in part because it has a large number of high-value cards, including some of the classic rarities of the baseball card field. Like the T-205 and T-206 sets, the T-207s take their "number" from *The American Card Catalog*, authored by hobby veteran Jeff Burdick. Also like those two sets, the T-207s take their nickname, "Brown Backgrounds," from the obvious physical characteristics of the cards. And, like the T-205 and T-206, the T-207 set was produced by the American Tobacco Company, which issued the cards in packages of several brands of its cigarettes: Recruit (far and away the most common), Broadleaf, Cycle, Napoleon, Red Cross, and Coupon. Card backs often include advertisements for one of these brands, though none have been found with ads for Coupon. The cards issued in the Coupon packages are sometimes called "anonymous-backs" by collectors. There are a couple of other reasons that T-207 cards have not achieved the collector popularity of their predecessor sets from ATC. The first is appearance. The cards feature a color lithograph of a player—portrait or action—set against a dark brown background. The player pictures are quite drab, with little color except for uniform details. Below the picture is a white strip with the player's last name, team, and league. A tan border surrounds the design. The design is striking in its own way, and when viewed as a set is not without appeal, but it just doesn't have the following of the more colorful T-205 and T-206 cards. Card backs have the player's full name, a baseball biography, and an ad for the cigarette brand. As with most of the sets of the day, there is no card number. Another major reason for the T-207's relative lack of collector following is that the set contains far fewer major stars of the day than do T-205 and T-206. There is another side of this coin, however, in that the larger number of relatively obscure players in the issue makes it a bonanza for the serious researcher or team collector. Many of the players who are found in the Brown Background set are not available in other card sets. As mentioned, there are 200 different players in the T-207 set. Seven major variations are generally collected to make a set "complete" at 207 cards.

FOR

A real challenge for the serious baseball card collector interested in the period from 1910 to 1920.

AGAINST

Lots of obscure players; scarce and expensive cards. Not many big stars.

NOTEWORTHY CARDS

While there are about a dozen Hall of Famers among the 200 players in T-207, the only really big names are Tris Speaker and Walter Johnson. The set does contain three of the classic rarities of the era in the form of cards that are unaccountably scarce today: Irving Lewis (Boston-Nat.), Ward Miller (Chicago-Nat.), and Louis Lowdermilk (St. Louis-Nat.). There are other Lewis and Miller cards in the set, so the collector has to be sure of the

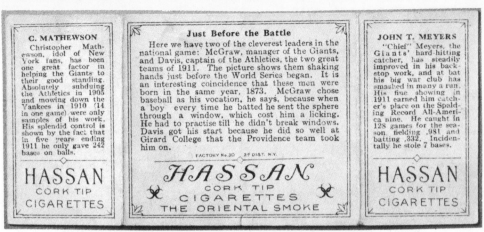

1912 Hassan Triple Folders, John T. Meyers, Christie Mathewson (back)

team to know if he has the "rare one." Several other scarce and valuable Brown Backgrounds are detailed below, but because of the number of scarce cards and the major variations, the collector should acquire a detailed checklist of this set before engaging in serious pursuit. The cards of Heinie Wagner and Bill Carrigan can be found with the correct backs and with each other's back, the latter being worth $50 or so.

VALUE

EX. CONDITION: Complete set, $6,000; common card, $10–$12; Hall of Famers, $25–$40; Johnson, $75; Speaker, $100; Ragan, Saier, Tyler, $100–$125; Miller, Lewis, Lowdermilk, $500. 5-YEAR PROJECTION: Below average.

1912 HASSAN TRIPLE-FOLDERS

SPECIFICATIONS

SIZE: 5¼×2¼". FRONT: Color lithograph and black-and-white engraving. BACK: Red or black printing. DISTRIBUTION: Nationally, in packages of cigarettes.

HISTORY

Hassan cigarettes took the concept of multiple-player cards a step further than Mecca's Doublefolder cards of the previous year. The Hassan set actually contains three baseball cards in a single panel. The center of each card is a black-and-white engraving of a baseball action scene or a player in a posed-action shot. At either side of the center "card" are the individual cards of two different players. Interestingly enough, the two smaller end cards are actually very close to being exact duplicates of the T-205 "Gold Borders" cards issued the previous year. The end cards are color lithographs of player portraits with colorful border designs. The Hassan cards are called "Triplefolders" because the two end cards are scored where they meet the center panel to fold over it into some-

thing of a booklet form. Usually, but not always, the two player cards on the ends have nothing to do with the action scene in the center panel. Currently, 74 different center panels are known in the set, some of which have more than one combination of player cards on the ends, bringing the total number of known combinations to 134. More combinations may yet be discovered. Backs of the center panels have a write-up about the action depicted on the front, while the backs of the end cards have a biography of the player. Each of the three card elements has a Hassan ad at bottom. The Hassan Triplefolders are not numbered. Value of the Triplefolders is dependent on who the featured player at center is, and whether one or both of the end cards is a Hall of Famer.

FOR

Certainly one of the most innovative baseball card designs ever made. Relatively inexpensive and a challenge to collect.

AGAINST

The large number of combinations of center and end cards is confusing to most collectors. Similarity of the end cards to the T-205 "Gold Borders" is also a negative factor.

NOTEWORTHY CARDS

Some of the most famous baseball photos of the 1910s era are reproduced as the center panel of the Hassan set. Lots of Hall of Famers. The single known combination of the card with center panel "Birmingham Gets a Home Run," is quite a bit scarcer than the rest of the set, and worth $100 or so in nice condition.

VALUE

EX. CONDITION: Complete set, $3,750; common card, $25; Hall of Famers, $30–$40; Cobb on end panel, $60–$75; Cobb as center panel, $100–$125. 5-YEAR PROJECTION: Below average.

1912 HOME RUN KISSES

SPECIFICATIONS

SIZE: 2¼×4¼". FRONT: Sepia-toned photo. BACK: Black printing on buff cardboard. DISTRIBUTION: Northern California, in packages of candy.

HISTORY

In most of the years in which the San Francisco confectionery company of Collins-McCarthy issued baseball cards, they inserted the same cards in all three of their major candy products: Zeenuts, Home Run Kisses, and Ruf-Neks. In 1912, though, the company's second year of card production, a separate set was produced for inclusion with Home Run Kisses. There are 90 cards from the six teams that comprised the Pacific Coast League in 1912: Los Angeles, Oakland, Portland, Sacramento, San Francisco, and Vernon. The cards feature a posed-action photo of the player against a blank background. To the side are the name of the candy product and the player's last name and team. The whole is surrounded by an ornate picture-frame border. Some Home Run Kisses cards have a message on back offering a premium list; most just have the small logo of the cards' photographer, "Bardell Sepia, San Francisco."

FOR

An attractive, scarce early baseball card issue from the West Coast.

AGAINST

A tough set to complete, and quite expensive. Minor league set with few big name players.

NOTEWORTHY CARDS

The Pacific Coast League enjoyed a unique status for most of its history as the highest level of minor league play. As a result many former and future major league stars will be found in most Pacific Coast League regional baseball card sets. While there are fewer such big names in the Home Run Kisses cards than you might expect, there is at least one Hall of Famer—Dave Bancroft, then with Portland, who made his big league mark as the premier shortstop in the National League over a 16-season career (1915 to 1930).

VALUE

EX. CONDITION: Complete set, $1,850; common card, $20–$25; Bancroft, $50. 5-YEAR PROJECTION: Below average.

1912 EASTERN LEAGUE

SPECIFICATIONS

SIZE: 1½×2¾". FRONT: Black-and-white photo. BACK: Black printing on white cardboard. DISTRIBUTION: Canada, Northeastern U.S. (?), in packages of cigarettes.

HISTORY

This set of 90 minor league players from the Eastern League is one of the lesser-known and little-appreciated cigarette card issues of the period between 1910 and 1920. Even the brand of cigarettes with which the set was presumably issued is unknown to to-

day's collectors. The set is generally cataloged with the Canadian card issues, and the cards are found more often on that side of the border, but it is unknown just how widely distributed the cards originally were. The Eastern League of 1912 was the predecessor of the current International League. The 90 players in this set represent two Canadian teams, Toronto and Montreal, and 6 U.S. teams: Baltimore, Buffalo, Jersey City, Providence, Rochester, and Newark. The cards themselves are well designed and attractive. Giving the overall appearance of a wooden plaque, complete with brown woodgrain-effect backgrounds, the cards feature an oval black-and-white photographic portrait of the player with the oval printed over an engraving of a baseball bat. In the upper-left corner is a baseball glove, and there is a ball in the lower right. An elongated oval at the bottom gives the player's last name. Card backs repeat the player's last name, have a short career summary, and include a card number at the bottom, an unusual feature for cards of the period. Because the set is considered "Canadian" by most collectors, even though there are more U.S. teams and players represented, it is not widely collected in the U.S.

FOR

Scarce, attractive cards in an unusual design. Relatively low price, considering scarcity.

AGAINST

Perceived "foreign" nature of the issue limits popularity.

NOTEWORTHY CARDS

While most of the players in the 1912 Eastern League set were career minor leaguers, many others had major league careers of some duration. This is one of very few sets which include cards of Hall of Fame outfielder and manager Joe Kelley and fellow HOFer "Iron Man" McGinnity, both at the end of their careers. Chick Gandil, known for his part in throwing the 1919 World Series, is included in the set, as is Luther "Dummy" Taylor, a mute pitcher in the majors from 1900 to 1908. In terms of players with only short major league careers, the set offers many opportunities for team collectors.

VALUE

EX. CONDITION: Complete set, $1,500; common card, $15; McGinnity, Kelley, $45. 5-YEAR PROJECTION: Below average.

1911–1912 T-205 "GOLD BORDERS"

SPECIFICATIONS

SIZE: 1½×2⅝". FRONT: Color lithograph. BACK: Black or red printing on white cardboard. DISTRIBUTION: Nationally, in packages of cigarettes.

HISTORY

At first inspection, the more than 200 baseball cards which collectors have come to know as the T-205 or "Gold Borders" set may appear to be more than one set, and it may well have been the intention of the American Tobacco Company trust that the cards be separate issues. Collectors, though, consider the three major groups of cards to be merely component parts to the set they have come to know as T-205, or Gold Borders. Indeed, it is the distinctive gold lithograph borders on the cards that give the set its common identity and the nickname by which it has been known to collectors for nearly three-quarters of a century. In his pioneer card catalog, Jefferson Burdick assigned the number T-205 to this set, which often leads beginning collectors to assume that it was issued before the T-206 ("White Borders") set. In fact, though, the Gold Borders cards were first issued in 1911, about the time the last of the T-206 cards were being produced, and continued to be issued into 1912. The Gold Borders were issued in many of the same brands of cigarettes that the White Borders had been packaged in, and they will be found with the following cigarette-brand ads at the bottoms of the cards' backs: American Beauty, Broadleaf, Cycle, Drum, Hassan, Honest Long Cut, Piedmont, Polar Bear, Sovereign, and Sweet Caporal. As with most tobacco card sets so issued, hobbyists collect the T-205 set without regard to which ad appears on the back; it is the front of the card that concerns them. The fronts of the T-205s are among the most striking of the era. Framed by the gold border is a color lithograph of the player, generally just a bust portrait, although the set also includes a few action pictures. The three major divisions of the T-205 set each have their own basic design. The American League cards in the set have the players pictured inside a stylized baseball diamond. A banner appears toward the bottom with the player's last name and team designation. Also at the bottom of the cards are a pair of baseball bats, a ball, a glove, and a catcher's mask. In the upper corners are a team logo and nickname. The National League cards have a head-and-shoulders portrait of the player set against a plain background. Toward the bottom is a facsimile autograph of the player (the first such use on a major baseball card set), along with the printed team name. In the upper corners are a team logo and nickname. While the National and American League cards in T-205 comprise the vast majority of the set, there are also 12 minor league players from the Eastern League (now known as the International League). Their cards have an action picture or a three-quarter-length portrait of the player, set in an ornate frame of columns and other decorative devices. The player's last name and the city for which he plays are printed in a white strip toward the bottom. Shields in the upper corners have the first letter of the minor league city's name. All of the major league players' card backs have the player's full name at the top of the card—another first for baseball cards; previous issues generally identified the player only by last name—followed by a short career summary and statistics for the 1908–1910 seasons. Minor league backs are similar, but without the seasonal stats. All of the Gold Borders have an ad at the bottom of the card for the cigarette brand in which the card was issued. There is no number on the T-205 cards. Many of the backs also have a line that reads, "Base Ball Series 400 Designs," but little more than half that number were actually issued, and just 200 different players are represented in the set. Many collectors who

specialize in T-205 consider eight or nine of the major variations in the set to be necessary for a "complete" collection. While the T-205s are contemporary with the T-206 White Borders, they are not as popularly collected. They are generally a bit more expensive than the T-206 cards, both for common cards and for star players. They are also considerably scarcer. One advantage of the T-205 Gold Borders set is that there are no super high-priced rarities in the issue, and it is one set that collectors can reasonably hope to complete—though not without challenge and a bit of cash outlay.

FOR
Striking designs. The set is collectible even now, nearly 75 years later, because of the large number of surviving cards, as long as the collector isn't too fussy about condition. Lots of big stars.

AGAINST
The three major designs of the set do not fit neatly into today's collector's idea of what a "set" should be. Condition-conscious collectors avoid the set because the gold printing on the borders tended to chip off easily, and the thin cardboard was easily creased.

NOTEWORTHY CARDS
The T-205 Gold Borders have many of the major stars of the day—including Ty Cobb, Cy Young, Christy Mathewson, and others—that bring a good price. There are also relatively scarce cards in the set that command similar prices, as do some of the variation cards. The serious collector should obtain a detailed checklist to pursue these. The minor league cards in the T-205 set are considerably scarcer than the major leaguers, and this group contains a card of Hall of Fame third baseman Jimmy Collins, who played in the majors from 1895 to 1908 and, when the T-205s were issued, was a playing manager for Providence—at the age of 41.

VALUE
EX. CONDITION: Complete set, $2,500; common card, $8–$9; common minor leaguer, $25; Hall of Famers, $15–$40; Jimmy Collins, $50; Walter Johnson, $75; Ty Cobb, $150. 5-YEAR PROJECTION: Average, or a bit below.

1911 TURKEY RED

SPECIFICATIONS
SIZE: 5¾×8″. FRONT: Color lithograph. BACK: Black or red printing on white cardboard. DISTRIBUTION: Nationally, by mail-in offer for cigarette coupons.

HISTORY
The Turkey Red set is the most popularly collected of the several major "cabinet"-size baseball card sets of the early 20th century. The hobby term "cabinet" denotes a large-size card, generally on very heavy cardboard with a wide mat around it. Many early baseball card issues offered these cabinet-size cards as premiums for wrappers or coupons; they were an added incentive to buy the product with which the card was issued. The Turkey Red series consists of 100 baseball players and 25 boxers. While the cards themselves were not numbered, the tobacco company which issued them numbered the cards in an ordering list on some card backs, while the backs of other cards carried an ad for Turkey Red brand cigarettes. Because of their large size, the Turkey Reds were not packed in the cigarette boxes themselves, but rather were obtained by mailing in coupons found in Turkey Red, Fez, and Old Mill brand cigarettes. Considering that the cost of the coupons required totaled $1—a considerable sum in 1911—it is surprising that the Turkey Red cards have survived in as great a number as they have. The Turkey Reds are the only set of baseball cabinet cards that the collector can have a reasonable chance of completing. Each card front features a large, extremely well-done, colorful lithograph of the player in an "action" pose. There is a wide gray frame around the picture and a yellow "plaque" at the bottom with the player's last name and team designation. Besides the individual player cards, there are several in the set featuring "action" plays with two players. NOTE: The 100 baseball player cards in the Turkey Red set were reproduced in a special collectors' edition in 1983. The cards are in

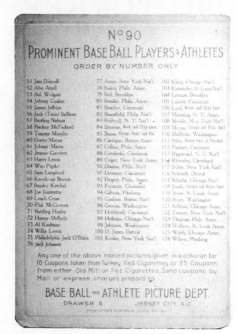

1911 Turkey Red, Michael Doolan (back)

the modern 2½×3½" size rather than the 5¾×8" size of the originals.

FOR

Attractive, affordable large-format cards from baseball's early days. Lots of stars, and popular with type collectors, as well. Because of their large size and heavy cardboard, the cards have generally survived the years well.

AGAINST

Because of the large number of cards in the set, and the relatively high cost of a common card, collecting a complete set is somewhat prohibitive. Most collectors do not collect the boxers as part of the complete set.

NOTEWORTHY CARDS

Many Hall of Famers are numbered among the 100 baseball players in the set, led by Ty Cobb, Walter Johnson, and Christy Mathewson.

VALUE

EX. CONDITION: Complete set (100), $8,500; common card, $75; Hall of Famers, $125–$250; Johnson, $350; Cobb, $750. 5-YEAR PROJECTION: Below average.

1911 MECCA "DOUBLE-FOLDERS"

SPECIFICATIONS

SIZE: 2¼×4¹¹⁄₁₆". FRONT: Color lithograph. BACK: Red printing on white cardboard. DISTRIBUTION: Nationally, in packages of cigarettes.

HISTORY

The set of 50 cards containing 100 baseball players issued by Mecca cigarettes in 1911 was probably the most innovative baseball card issue to that point in history. Each card pictured two players by utilizing a pair of matching color lithographs. When in the "open" position, the card showed a full-length picture of a player, in a stadium setting. His last name and team appeared in black script in the upper left. When the top of this card was folded over, the body of a second player appeared over the legs of the first, creating a second full-figure picture; again with the player's name and team in the upper left in black script lettering. Backs were printed in red with an ad for Mecca cigarettes at the bottom and another innovation—player statistics—at top. Mecca called these cards the "Base Ball Folder Series," and judging from the number of cards which have survived, they must have been quite popular in their day. The idea was so good that Topps swiped it in 1955 when it produced its "Double Headers" set. The 50 unnumbered cards in the set contain both major and minor league players.

FOR

Very innovative card set, relatively inexpensive.

AGAINST

The lithography of the players' pictures is a bit crude, but considering the need for the players to "share" legs, it may be understandable.

NOTEWORTHY CARDS

Many of the Hall of Famers of the day are seen in this set, including Ty Cobb. The combination card of Patsy Dougherty and Harry Lord,

White Sox teammates, is scarcer than the rest of the set.

VALUE

EX. CONDITION: Complete set, $600; common card, $9; Hall of Famers, $12–$20; Cobb-Crawford, Dougherty-Lord, $100. 5-YEAR PROJECTION: Below average.

1911 SPORTING LIFE

SPECIFICATIONS

SIZE: 1½×2⅝". FRONT: Color lithograph. BACK: Blue printing on white cardboard. DISTRIBUTION: Nationally, by mail-in offer.

HISTORY

From as far back as the 1880s, the Philadelphia-based weekly newspaper *Sporting Life* was a major source of baseball information at all levels from the minors to the majors. It was for many years a direct competitor to *The Sporting News*, which eventually won out and continues to be published today. In 1911, *Sporting Life* joined the baseball card bandwagon by beginning an issue that would eventually number 288 different cards. The Sporting Life cards were available free to buyers of the paper who sent in four cents worth of postage stamps and a coupon cut from the paper for each series of 12 cards as it was released. In all, 24 series were produced, each mailed in an envelope with the series number on it. The cards themselves are not numbered. With the exception of nine players in the later series, the players in the Sporting Life set are all major leaguers. Many of the portraits on the cards are identical to those used on the T-206 set. The set is interesting in that all of the players are featured without their baseball caps, and are set against a plain pastel background. The pictures are color lithographs surrounded by a wider white border than that found on the T-206. The player's last name, team, and league are printed at the bottom of the card. The

1911 Sporting Life, J. Frank Baker

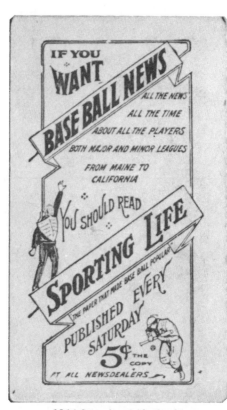

1911 Sporting Life (back)

back contains one of three different ads for the newspaper. The Sporting Life set is contemporary with the T-206 issue, but the cards are much more scarce. The price difference is not all that great, though, because there is far less demand for the newspaper card set.

FOR
Interesting set that provides real portraits of the top players of 1911.

AGAINST
Too scarce and expensive on a per-card basis to be attractive to most collectors. The pictures on most of the cards can also be found on other tobacco or candy card sets of the era.

NOTEWORTHY CARDS
The Sporting Life set has all of the major stars of the day. There are only a few collectible variations in the issue: McConnell and McQuillan, who can each be found with two card fronts naming different teams. The cards of the higher series, #19 to #24, are scarcer than the first 18 series.

VALUE
EX. CONDITION: Complete set, $3,750; common card, $10–$12; Hall of Famers, $20–$40; Walter Johnson, Honus Wagner, $50; Cobb, $100. 5-YEAR PROJECTION: Below average.

1911–1939 ZEENUTS

HISTORY
The Zeenut series was one of the longest-running and most successful baseball card issues of all time. The cards were produced by the Collins-McCarthy (later, Collins-Hencke; still later, Collins) Candy Company of San Francisco (which also produced the 1912 Home Run Kisses and 1916 "Hall of Fame" card sets). They were inserted into boxes of its three major candy products, Home Run Kisses, Ruf-Neks, and Zeenut itself. Zeenut was a direct competitor of Cracker Jack, a caramel-coated popcorn product. Priced at a penny a box in the early years, Zeenuts went up to five cents a box by the time the company went out of business in 1939. That 28-year run of continuous baseball card issue was a hobby record until 1979 when Topps began its 29th year of baseball card issue. For virtually all of the 1911–1939 period, Zeenut had a monopoly on West Coast baseball card issues of Pacific Coast League players. The first two Zeenut sets, 1911 and 1912, are sometimes found with a rubber-stamped premium offer on the back. Beginning in 1913, however, and continuing through 1937, all Zeenut cards, regardless of year, were issued with a coupon at bottom that could be redeemed for "valuable premiums" such as sports equipment, cameras, and toys. For this reason, Zeenut cards are so seldom found with coupon attached that they are always priced without the coupon. Cards which have the appendage are generally worth some 25 percent more. Cards from which the coupon has been roughly torn are worth less than those from which the coupon was neatly cut. Condition, however, is generally not a major factor for collectors of Zeenut cards—these cards are scarce in any condition. The problem of a coupon was eliminated in 1938, when the company began packaging a separate redemption certificate in the candy box along with the baseball card. The lack of coupons on most cards makes checklisting—or even identifying cards by year of issue—difficult or, in many cases, impossible. Some cards carry the year of issue as part of the printing on the front of the card. Some cards have only the last two digits of the year of issue, as "29" for 1929. Some Zeenut cards have no date at all, except on the coupon, which is usually missing. Similarly, not all Zeenut issues are identified as such. Most of the early issues have "Zeenut Series" on the front; the 1913 cards say "P. C. League Season 1913," and from 1931 on, the cards are identified only as "Coast League." Complete checklists do not exist for the Zeenut baseball cards. Diligent collectors have discovered about 3,700 different cards, but more continue to turn up every year. A few early premium lists from the company named the players to be found in a particular year's set, but whether all of them were actually released is unknown. A 1921 flier, for

instance, lists 180 cards, but collectors have so far found only 168 of them. For ease of reference, all of the Zeenut card issues will be summarized here, rather than repeating much of this information throughout the book.

SPECIFICATIONS

1911—SIZE: 2⅛×4″ (NOTE: All sizes given are for complete cards with coupon; cards which have had the coupon removed will be about ½″ shorter). FRONT: Full-length (as are all Zeenuts), sepia-toned player photo on dark brown background, surrounded by white border. BACK: Blank. SPECIAL NOTE: Some players' cards have been found with varying photo sizes.

1912—SIZE: 2⅛×4″. FRONT: Sepia photo on dark brown background, no border. BACK: Blank.

1913—SIZE: 2×3¼″. FRONT: Sepia photo on light yellow background. BACK: Blank.

1914—SIZE: 2×4″. FRONT: Black-and-white photo on dark background. BACK: Blank.

1915—SIZE: 2×3¾″. FRONT: Black-and-white photo on white background. BACK: Blank. SPECIAL NOTE: Only two players known from Vernon team.

1916—SIZE: 2×3½″. FRONT: Black-and-white photo on blue background. BACK: Blank. SPECIAL NOTE: Some cards found with 1916 date, some without.

1917—SIZE: 1¾×3½″. FRONT: Black-and-white photo on white background. BACK: Blank.

1918—SIZE: 1¾×3½″. FRONT: Black-and-white photo, white background, red border around card above coupon. BACK: Blank.

1919—SIZE: 1¾×3½″. FRONT: Black-and-white photo on gray background. BACK: Blank.

1920—SIZE: 1¾×3¾″. FRONT: Black-and-white photo against grandstand backdrop. BACK: Blank.

1921–1923—SIZE: 1¾×3½″. FRONT: Black-and-white photo on white background. BACK: Blank.

1924–1931—SIZE: 1¾×3½″. FRONT: Black-and-white photo taken in stadium. BACK: Blank. SPECIAL NOTE: Some 1927 Zeenuts cards have the "27" year designation near the player's name; on others it appears in a white circle at the top of the card.

1932—SIZE: 1¾×3½″. FRONT: Black-and-white photo on white background. BACK: Blank. SPECIAL NOTE: For the only time in the Zeenut series, the words "Coast League," the player's last name, and the team name were typeset on the 1932 cards, rather than being handlettered on the printing negative.

1933–1936—SIZE: 1¾×3½″. FRONT: Black-and-white (1933–1936) or sepia (some 1933) photo taken in stadium. BACK: Blank. SPECIAL NOTE: Collecting Zeenuts really gets tough in this era. Cards were issued all four years in identical style, a borderless photo with the player and team information in a round-cornered box toward the bottom of the card. If the card does not have a coupon (which featured an expiration date) there is no way to tell in which year it was issued, because players' pictures were repeated from one year to the next.

1937–1938—SIZE: 1¾×3½″. FRONT: Black-and-white photo taken in stadium. BACK: Blank. SPECIAL NOTE: The final two years of Zeenut cards are quite similar to the 1933–1936 series, but the black box with player data has square corners. Again, because the same pictures were used if a player appeared in both sets, it is difficult to distinguish the actual year of issue.

DISTRIBUTION: It is currently believed the Zeenuts cards were issued within a relatively small area of Northern California, centered around the San Francisco-Oakland Bay area.

FOR

The collector who wants the ultimate baseball card challenge would revel in the Zeenut series, but for most collectors, a few type cards is a sufficient sampling. The Zeenut series does fill some very important historical voids, most of the 1920s, for example, when other baseball card issues of any size were nonexistent. The set has much to offer the collector who likes to hunt out his cards and enjoys research in the relatively obscure area of baseball's minor leagues in the early days of the game. There are a lot of players represented in these sets who will be found on no other baseball cards; the problem is, because only last names are given, many of them have never been satisfactorily identified.

AGAINST

Too little is known about the range of the Zeenut series to contemplate building a complete collection. Indeed, the relatively high cost of nearly 4,000 different cards would tax most hobbyists' resources beyond the limit. The cards are not particularly attractive on the whole.

NOTEWORTHY CARDS

Because for most of its history the Pacific Coast League represented the highest level of minor league play, the make-up of its teams often reflected a strong mix of young players on their way up, older players whose major careers were through, and career minor league ballplayers. Many players will thus be found in the Zeenuts sets, as players or managers, who had made, or who would go on to make, big names for themselves in the major leagues. There are dozens of cards of players like Hall of Famer Joe Cronin and longtime Pacific Coast League manager Lefty O'Doul, but the most sought-after cards in the Zeenut series are those of Joe DiMaggio and his brothers Vince and Dom. A peculiarity of Zeenuts DiMaggio cards is that all of them misspell the family name as "DeMaggio."

VALUE

EX. CONDITION, NO COUPON: 1911–1916, $10–$20; 1917–1919, $5–$10; 1920s, $3–$5; 1930s, $3–$5; Joe DiMaggio, $50; Dom or Vince DiMaggio, $10–$20. 5-YEAR PROJECTION: Below average.

1910–1920 "GENERIC" CARAMEL CARDS

SPECIFICATIONS

SIZE: 1½×2¾″. FRONT: Color lithograph. BACK: Many styles. DISTRIBUTION: Nationally, with many brands of caramels.

HISTORY

More than two dozen sets of baseball cards—representing both major and minor leagues—were issued with various brands of caramels and other candy in the period between 1910 and 1920. It is beyond the scope of this book to chronicle all the caramel sets, especially in light of the fact that they are not widely collected. Part of the reason the caramel issues are not as popular as the contemporary cigarette cards is that many of the sets shared the same pictures. Evidently, one printing company supplied "generic" baseball cards to many different candy makers for issue in their product. Backs of some of the cards carried advertisements for specific brands of candy, while others carried checklists or simple statements such as "This card is one of a set of 50 baseball players. Prominent members of National and American Leagues." The fronts generally carried color lithographs of the players surrounded by a white border. Beneath the picture were the player's last name, position, and team. Collectors desiring to delve deeper into the caramel cards of this period should obtain detailed checklists of the many individual sets.

FOR

To the advantage of the specimen-card collector, the generic caramel cards are generally inexpensive considering their age. Individual sets can usually be collected without undue challenge or cash outlay, though some research is usually necessary.

AGAINST

The use of shared pictures within many sets makes the issues confusing for collectors. Lithographs in the caramel cards are generally not as well detailed as the cigarette cards of the same era—that accounts for the higher price of the tobacco cards.

NOTEWORTHY CARDS

Most of the major stars of the era are represented in the caramel sets.

VALUE

EX. CONDITION: Common card, $8–$15; Hall of Famers, 2–3 times common card price; Wagner, 5 times common price; Cobb, 7–8 times common price. 5-YEAR PROJECTION: Below average.

1910 OLD MILL

SPECIFICATIONS

SIZE: 1½×2⅝". FRONT: Black-and-white photograph. BACK: Black printing on white cardboard. DISTRIBUTION: Southeastern U.S., in packages of cigarettes.

HISTORY

Commonly called the "Red Borders" set by collectors, the Old Mill cigarette card issue of 1910 is the largest, yet least known, of the early tobacco card issues of the 20th century. Currently, more than 600 cards are known in the set, with more being discovered regularly. The Old Mill set covers eight minor leagues from the Southeastern part of the United States, each league being accorded its own series as designated at the top of the card back. The number of cards from each league varies greatly, with fewer than 20 known for some, and nearly 120 known for others. The circuits represented (series noted in parentheses) in the Red Borders set are: South Atlantic (1); Virginia (2); Texas (3); Virginia Valley (4); Carolina (5); Blue Grass (6); Eastern Carolina (7); and Southern Association (8). Inside the distinctive red border on each card is a black-and-white photo of the player. His last name and team name are printed in black in the bottom border. Card backs are an ad for Old Mill.

FOR

The set is a wide-open field for the baseball card researcher; collecting these cards is tough enough to keep a collector busy for years, yet they are not expensive, considering that they are three quaters of a century old.

AGAINST

Complete checklists are not currently known; the leagues and players represented are obscure.

NOTEWORTHY CARDS

The best-known card in the Old Mill set is the "rookie card" of Casey Stengel, playing at that time for Maysville, in the Blue Grass League. As for other future major leaguers in the set, more research is needed.

VALUE

EX. CONDITION: Complete set, unknown; common card, $4–$5; Stengel, $150. 5-YEAR PROJECTION: Below average.

1910 RED SUN

SPECIFICATIONS

SIZE: 1½×2⅝". FRONT: Black-and-white photograph. BACK: Red printing on white cardboard. DISTRIBUTION: Southeastern U.S., in packages of cigarettes.

HISTORY

Collectors who are looking for a challenging, but not impossible, early minor league tobacco card set might consider the 1910 Red Sun issue, produced by a New Orleans cigarette company that was part of the giant American Tobacco Company trust. The Red Sun cards have a distinctive green border around the black-and-white player photo on the front of the card, with the player's last name and team name printed in black in the green border at bottom. The backs have a flashy red design advertising the cigarettes with which the cards were issued. Like most tobacco card issues of the era, the set has no numbers. Unlike the Red Borders set of Old Mill cards, with which this issue is contemporary, the "Green Borders," as they are known to collectors, have a well-known issue limit of 75 cards (it's even spelled out on the back). All the cards in the Red Sun set are of Southern Association players.

FOR

Challenging set for the specialist; attractive cards.

AGAINST

The cards are scarce, expensive, and don't feature any real stars.

NOTEWORTHY CARDS

None to speak of.

VALUE

EX. CONDITION: Complete set, $1,500; common card, $20. 5-YEAR PROJECTION: Below average.

SPEAKER, BOSTON AMER.

COBB, DETROIT

1909- 1900

BROWN
Pitcher, Chicago N. L.

1909–1911 T-206

SPECIFICATIONS

SIZE: 1½×2⅝". FRONT: Color lithograph. BACK: Black, blue, or red printing on white cardboard. DISTRIBUTION: Nationally, in packages of cigarettes.

HISTORY

For most of the hobby's early history, this was the single most popularly collected baseball card set. Yet it is also one of the hardest and most expensive sets to complete, because it is among the T-206 cards that the famed "King of Baseball Cards," the rare Honus Wagner tobacco card, is found. Any attempt to complete a high-grade set of T-206 cards will be futile unless the collector ultimately has $20,000 or so for a Wagner card, and another $10,000 or so for the next handful of scarce cards in the set. Nevertheless, even without the "Big 3" rarities in the issue, the T-206 set is challenging enough to keep a collector busy and his hobby budget exhausted for many years. Just what is T-206 and why is it so popular? To explain, we'll have to go back to the early days of baseball card issue, to 1909, when the American Tobacco Company trust was at the peak of its dominance over the cigarette industry, having swallowed up most of the independent tobacco companies. ATC, through no less than 16 of its different brands of cigarettes, was the issuer of the T-206 cards over a three-year period beginning in 1909. The set takes its hobby name from the original catalog in the collectible card field, *The American Card Catalog,* first published by hobby pioneer Jefferson Burdick in the 1930s. In that book, which for many years was the "Bible" of the baseball card hobby, Burdick assigned catalog numbers to every known card issue. The number he gave to the massive 1909–1911 issue of the ATC was "T-206," and it has been thus known to collectors to this day. The cards are also sometimes called "White Borders," but since there are so many white-bordered tobacco cards in that era, the name T-206 is less confusing. What is confusing is the proliferation of different backs to the cards. The front of each T-206 is straightforward enough, a well-done color lithograph of a baseball player, either a portrait or action picture (sometimes both—many players appear on more than one card in the set). Around the picture is a white border. At the bottom of the border, printed in black, are the player's last name, the city in which his team is located, and, in the case of two-team cities (Boston, Philadelphia, New York, Chicago, etc.), the league designation. The lithographs are extremely well done, giving today's collector a good look at what baseball and the players were like 75 years ago. The player pictures are set against a variety of backgrounds that include plain colors, simulated sky and field, or stadium scenes. Though the small size of the cards may seem antiquated today, the 1½×2⅝" format adopted by T-206 was a standard used for many years in baseball card issue. The backs of all T-206 cards are similar in that they contain only an advertisement for one of the 16 brands of cigarettes with which the cards were issued. Some of the backs will indicate a number of cards in the issue, such as "Base Ball Series/150 Subjects," or "350 Subjects," or even, on some of the later issues, "350-460 Subjects." In fact, collectors generally accept the T-206 set to be complete at 523 cards, including major variations. It is important for collectors to know which backs are "accepted" as part of the T-206 set, because several other tobacco cards of the era, all issued by the American Tobacco Co., had an identical design. However, because Jeff Burdick—for reasons only he may have known—assigned those brand names their own catalog number, they are collected independently of the T-206 set. The most common of the 16 backs which make up the T-206 issue is far and away the Piedmont brand, followed by Sweet Caporal. Then, in approximately ascending order of rarity, there are: Polar Bear, Old Mill (not to be confused with the "Red Borders" set issued with that brand earlier), Sovereign, American Beauty, El Principe de Gales, Cycle, Tolstoi, Hindu, Broad Leaf, Carolina Bright, Lenox, Uzit, Drum, and Ty Cobb. The latter is a great rarity within the T-206 set, appearing only on the backs of some Ty Cobb cards with the red background behind his portrait. Only about a half dozen of the Cobb-back cards are known, making them far rarer than the famed Honus Wagner card, but they are currently much less expensive. In actuality, many of the front/back combinations may be rarer than the Wagner card but will never attain much value simply because T-206 is most often collected by front, rather than by back. Not all cards were issued with each of the many different backs. It is estimated that a complete collection of known front/back combinations would number some 7,500 cards. The most common method of collecting T-206 is to assemble a set of one card of each front design, regardless of the back advertisement. Some collectors, though, do attempt to collect all cards of a specific back. Polar Bear is popularly collected this way because of its distinctive format of white lettering on a dark blue background. The players (also coaches and managers) in the T-206 set include major and minor leaguers—the former having been issued first, in 1909, and the minor league players coming in the reissues of 1910 and 1911. It is these subsequent issues that account for many of the scarce and valuable varieties among T-206. Besides adding new players to the set each year, the ATC also updated the set by changing team names and uniforms, or even creating a new picture to reflect a trade. Some of the more popular players were issued in several poses right from the start. In general, the minor league players are scarcer than the major leaguers (though not in as great a demand), with those of the "Southern Leagues" (Southern Association, South Atlantic, Texas, and Virginia leagues) being the most difficult. The other minor leagues represented in T-206 are the American Association and the Eastern League (later known as the International League). In all, including variations, there are 389 major leaguers and 134 minor league players in the T-206 set, quite a formidable undertaking for any collector.

FOR

The "ultimate challenge" for the baseball card collector. A set rich in history and rarities, yet which can be collected in part by even the novice collector. For 75-year-old cards, the "common" T-206s can be surprisingly inexpensive.

AGAINST

The futility of collecting a "complete" set of T-206 is a turn-off for many collectors. Indeed, to collect the set requires much personal study and research, as a definitive history of the set has yet to be written, and even the many checklists available conflict in some details. Naturally, the prohibitively high cost of several of the cards in the set is also a drawback.

NOTEWORTHY CARDS

The T-206 set is rife with the major stars and Hall of Famers of the period, each of whom commands a pretty good premium. In addition, many of the variety cards have significant value (a detailed checklist is needed). Some of the more valuable varieties are the "Magie" error card, a misspelling of the name of Sherwood Magee, which brings $2,500 in top condition (the corrected version is a $10 card); and the "traded" cards of Demmitt "St. L. Amer." and O'Hara "St. L. Nat'l."—about $400 each. Also rare is the Washington-designated portrait card (as opposed to his fielding pose) of Elberfeld, a $150 card. The second most expensive card in the T-206 assembly is that of Philadelphia Athletics pitcher Eddie Plank. The scarcity of the Plank card is believed to have been caused by damage to the printing plate, which ruined most of the cards in production. Whatever the reason, the Plank card is very scarce, and usually commands a price tag of $5,000 or more in top condition.

OUR FAVORITE CARD

Naturally, everybody's favorite baseball card is one which is worth $20,000 or so—especially if you happen to find it in grandpa's attic. The Honus Wagner card in the T-206 set is the undisputed "King of Baseball Cards." While there are many, many cards in the hobby which are far rarer than the Wagner card, none approaches its value, simply because the Wagner card is in such demand by collectors looking to complete the popular T-206 set. There is only a single Honus Wagner variety in the T-206 set, a bareheaded portrait of the great Pittsburgh (spelled "Pittsburg" on the card) shortstop, set against an orange background. Some 40 to 50 examples of the cards are known in the hobby, but there are literally thousands of reprints and reproductions, so collectors had better know what they are looking for when they encounter a supposedly genuine Honus Wagner T-206. Collectors who find a T-206 "Wagner" card should also be aware that a second player named Wagner appears in the set. Showing Boston Red Sox shortstop Heinie Wagner both in portrait and batting poses, the Wagner "Boston Amer." cards have dashed more dreams of instant wealth than any other baseball card. They are worth at best $10 in high grade. What makes the Honus Wagner T-206 card so rare? The story goes that Wagner demanded the tobacco company cease using his picture to advertise their cigarettes because he was opposed to smoking and felt that his picture on a card would encourage young boys to smoke. There is also some evidence to suggest that Wagner's demand for withdrawal of the cards was in part due to the fact that he had not been paid for the use of his picture.

VALUE

EX. CONDITION: Complete set, $30,000; common major leaguer, $6–$7; common minor leaguer (American Assn. or Eastern League), $8–$9; common minor leaguer (Southern leagues), $20; Hall of Famers, $15–$20; Cobb, $150–$200. 5-YEAR PROJECTION: Average.

1909 RAMLY

SPECIFICATIONS

SIZE: 2×2½". FRONT: Black-and-white photograph. BACK: Black printing on white cardboard. DISTRIBUTION: Nationally (?), in packages of cigarettes.

HISTORY

Probably the most ornate and unusual cigarette card issue of the early 20th century was the 1909 set issued with Ramly and T.T.T. brand Turkish cigarettes. Since the Ramly back is the more common, collectors generally use that nickname; the cards are so scarce that nobody distinguishes between the brands on the back when building a collection. In fact, there are very few collectors trying to complete a collection of Ramlys. The cards are scarce enough and in such demand as a type card that even common players in top grade sell for $50 or more. So far, 121 different Ramly cards are known, but it is possible that additions to the set may yet be discovered. What makes the Ramly set so attractive is the border around the oval black-and-white photographic portrait of the player. The border features an ornate network of simulated vines and flowers, plus an oval frame for the photo, all of which is embossed (raised above the background surface of the card) and printed in gold. There is a gold border around the whole affair. The player's last name, position, team, and league appear in a panel toward the bottom of the card. The combination of the black-and-white photo, gold printing, and slick ivory paper stock gives the cards a unique appearance. Card backs simply give the name of the cigarette brand in which the card was found, and the address of a Massachusetts tobacco factory. As with many of the baseball card sets in the era, there are several misspelled names in the Ramly set, but that doesn't appear to detract from their collectibility.

FOR

Probably the most attractive of all early baseball cards, they are also genuinely scarce and a real challenge.

AGAINST

The Ramly set is too rich for the budget of most collectors. It lacks some of the top stars of the era, for example, Cobb and Wagner.

NOTEWORTHY CARDS

While there are no cards of Ty Cobb or Honus Wagner in the Ramly set, most of the other Hall of Famers of the era are here. Because of the high price of the common cards, the star players do not attract as great a premium as would normally be the case.

VALUE

EX. CONDITION: Complete set, $8,000; common card, $50; Hall of Famers, $100–$150; Walter Johnson, $200. 5-YEAR PROJECTION: Below average.

1909–1911 OBAK

SPECIFICATIONS
SIZE: 1½×2⅝". FRONT: Color drawing. BACK: Blue (1909 and 1910) or red (1911) printing on white cardboard. DISTRIBUTION: Western U.S., in packages of cigarettes.

HISTORY
The three sets of Obak cigarette cards issued between 1909 and 1911 are closely related to the more popular T-206 set, and in fact were produced by the Western branch of the American Tobacco Company trust that issued the T-206 and most other cigarette cards of the era. While each of the three Obak sets is easily distinguished from the others, they will be considered here together because that's how they are usually collected. All issues were similar in format: a color drawing of the player, sometimes drawn from an actual photograph of his face, appears on the front of the card, surrounded by a white border, with the player's last name, team, and, on the 1910 and 1911 cards, the league printed in black letters at bottom. Backs feature an Obak advertisement in 1909 and 1910, while the 1911 cards have a short biography and statistics along with the ad. The year of issue can be determined by the style of card back: 1909 has the word "Obak" on a slant with a "bullet" inside the "O"; the 1910 cards have the word "Obak" in straight block letters, while the 1911 cards have the backs printed in red, rather than blue. The 1909 cards feature players of the Pacific Coast League only, while the 1910 and 1911 sets have players from the Northwest League included. The 1909 issue is the scarcest, followed by the 1911. In all, there are 426 cards in the three-year Obak series.

FOR
Interesting set for the researcher; challenging to complete, but not impossible.

AGAINST
The cards are scarce in most parts of the country.

NOTEWORTHY CARDS
Between 1909 and 1911 the Pacific Coast League was the highest minor league of its day in terms of quality of play. It featured many former and future major league players. Some of these players never appeared on a major league card, which makes their cards in this set desirable for team collectors.

VALUE
EX. CONDITION: Complete set, $2,250; common card, 1909, $12.50; 1910, $4; 1911, $6. 5-YEAR PROJECTION: Below average.

1909–1911 BASE BALL CARAMELS

SPECIFICATIONS
SIZE: 1½×2¾". FRONT: Color lithograph. BACK: Black printing on white cardboard. DISTRIBUTION: Nationally, in packages of caramels.

HISTORY
Perhaps the most collectible of the caramel card issues is the "Base Ball Caramels" set issued by Philadelphia's American Caramel Company beginning in 1909. Unlike the American Caramel 1908 set (which has different players represented by the same "generic" picture), the 1909 set contains color lithographs of the players actually named on the cards. While the backs of the cards indicate there are "100 Subjects" in the "Base Ball Series," there are actually 108 players known, with several pose variations bringing the number of different cards to over 120. The basic set apparently was issued into 1911, with some of the variations reflecting team changes for traded players. The 1909 Base Ball Caramels set is quite similar in design to the tobacco cards of the era. The front features a color portrait or action lithograph of the player, surrounded by a white border. At the bottom, printed in black, are the player's last name, an abbreviation for his position, and his team designation. Backs of the cards feature at center a pair of crossed baseball bats; above them are a ball and the words "Base Ball," below them are a catcher's mitt and the word "Caramels." At top of the back is the statement, "Base Ball Series/100 Subjects," at the bottom of the card is "Mfg By/American Caramel Co./Phila., Pa." As with most of the caramel sets that would be issued until the 1920s, there is no card number. The base price of a 1909 Base Ball Caramels card is not too bad, and a fair percentage of the set can be collected for a reasonable price. But then the challenge begins, and obtaining the rest of the set can be downright difficult and expensive. There is no explanation why many of the cards in the set are scarce today; it is just an accepted fact of hobby life.

FOR
Good starting place for the collector who desires to specialize in the caramel cards of the early 20th century.

AGAINST
Fairly high number of scarce cards makes the set too challenging for most collectors, especially today's collectors who are unfamiliar with most of the names and faces on the cards.

NOTEWORTHY CARDS
Many of the game's early greats appear in the Base Ball Caramels set, including Ty Cobb, Honus Wagner, Nap Lajoie, Joe Jackson, and Cy Young. There are many scarce and valuable cards in the set, worth $20–$40 or more; a detailed checklist is necessary for the serious collector.

VALUE
EX. CONDITION: Complete set, $1,500; common card, $7; Hall of Famers, $12–$25; Speaker, Cobb, Duffy, Clarke (Pitts.), $75–$100; Sweeney (Boston), Graham, $175; Mitchell (Cincinnati), $300. 5-YEAR PROJECTION: Below average.

1909–1910 CONTENT-NEA

SPECIFICATIONS

SIZE: 1½×2⅝". FRONT: Color line drawing or black-and-white photograph. BACK: Black printing on white cardboard. DISTRIBUTION: Middle-Atlantic area, in packages of cigarettes.

HISTORY

Two distinctly different sets of baseball cards were issued in boxes on Contentnea brand cigarettes in 1909 and 1910. It is believed that they were issued together, because of the small number of the drawn cards. Sixteen of the Contentnea cards are in the style of most other cigarette cards of the era, featuring a color drawing of the player on the front, with his last name and team printed in blue in the border below. The back contains an ad for the cigarettes and the notice that the set will contain players from the Virginia and Eastern Carolina Leagues, and the Carolina Association. The other type of Contentnea cards are unusual for the time in that they depict the players (of the same leagues) in black-and-white photos. The team name and the player's last name are printed in the white border at the bottom of the card. The backs of the photo cards are similar to the drawn cards, but carry on the top the notation, "Photo Series." There are currently some 225 photographic Contentnea cards known, and new discoveries are still being made in the series.

FOR

A real research field for the specialist.

AGAINST

The cards are scarce (not particularly expensive, however) and picture obscure players, hence there is little demand.

NOTEWORTHY CARDS

Because so little research in the set has been done, it's hard to tell if there are famous big-leaguers in the group or not.

VALUE

EX. CONDITION: Complete set, unknown; common card, drawn, $20; photographic, $10. 5-YEAR PROJECTION: Below average.

1908–1910 AMERICAN CARAMEL COMPANY

SPECIFICATIONS

SIZE: 1½×2¾". FRONT: Color drawing. BACK: Black printing on white cardboard. DISTRIBUTION: Nationally, in packages of caramels.

HISTORY

While they are among the more commonly encountered caramel card sets of the early 20th century, this particular issue of "Base Ball Caramels" cards by the American Caramel Company of Philadelphia is not a particular collector favorite. The problem lies in the use of "generic" pictures for the three different series that make up the set. That is, a picture issued in 1908 with one player's name was issued again in 1910 and identified as another player. The set was begun in 1908 with 33 cards purporting to represent players of the Philadelphia Athletics, New York Giants, and Chicago Cubs. In 1910, the same 33 cards were reissued, often with different players named, thereby "adding" to the set players from the Pittsburgh, Washington, and Boston (Red Sox) teams. In all, 75 different players are named in the set, but they share just 33 pictures.

FOR

They are inexpensive examples of early candy card issues.

AGAINST

Few collectors are interested in cards that do not actually picture the player named.

NOTEWORTHY CARDS

There are lots of famous names in the set; but since the pictures aren't necessarily correct, the superstars in this set don't have the premium value usually associated with their cards in other issues.

VALUE

EX. CONDITION: Complete set, $550; common card, $5; superstar, $7–$12.50. 5-YEAR PROJECTION: Below average.

19TH CENTURY

1895 MAYO CUT PLUG

SPECIFICATIONS
SIZE: 1⅝×2⅞". FRONT: Sepia or black-and-white photo. BACK: Blank. DISTRIBUTION: Nationally, in packages of chewing/smoking tobacco.

HISTORY
The formation of the American Tobacco Company monopoly in 1890 killed off the first great era of baseball card issues. The baseball-card-issuing firms of Allen & Ginter, W. Duke & Sons, Goodwin & Co., and William S. Kimball and the nonissuing Kinney Brothers company formed the ATC and almost overnight drove nearly 250 small competitors out of business. There was virtually no competition, and thus no need to insert free cards in packages. Why the Richmond, Virginia, firm of P. H. Mayo & Brother chose to do so in 1895 is a mystery. Whatever the reason, collectors are glad the cards were produced, because they filled a gap in the issue of major baseball card sets that would have extended until 1908. Several of the players in the 1895 Mayo set appear in no other baseball card set. When the Mayo cards were produced in 1895, there was but a single major league, the 12-team National League, and this situation would persist until the American League was formed in 1901. Players from all 12 National League teams appear in the Mayo set. Perhaps the most visually striking of the 19th century tobacco cards, the 1895 Mayos feature a sepia or black-and-white photograph on a black background. Card backs are also black. The 48 cards in the set (40 different players) include 12 on which the player appears in street clothes rather than in baseball uniform. Several variations are known in the set, on which cards were reissued with new team names lettered across the jerseys or misspelled names corrected.

FOR
The only major baseball card set of the 1890s, it offers collectors a chance to complete a collection of 19th century cards at a reasonable (by comparison) price. Cards are attractive. Some players in the 1895 Mayo Cut Plug issue are not available in any other sets.

AGAINST
Variations make it tough to complete a set of all known varieties. The relatively large number of Hall of Famers means a good percentage of the cards are high-priced.

NOTEWORTHY CARDS
While the Mayo set contains 12 Hall of Famers, perhaps more significant is the fact that it contains eight players' cards which are not found in any other set: Charles Abbey, James Bannon, Ed Cartwright, Tom Corcoran, Bill Joyce, Tom Kinslow, Bill Murphy, and Otis Stockdale. None had particularly impressive careers.

OUR FAVORITE CARD
How would you like to go through a six-year major league career always pitching in the shadow of your big brother, and then, when you finally get your chance to be on a baseball card, have him usurp that, too? That's exactly what happened to Arthur "Dad" Clarkson in the Mayo set. His famous brother, Hall of Famer John Clarkson, had retired the previous year with a lifetime record of 326 wins. Mayo issued a card of "Clarkson: P." with "St. Louis" lettered across the uniform. That was Dad Clarkson, who pitched for St. Louis early that year—at least it was supposed to be Dad Clarkson; the photo was actually a picture of John Clarkson, the same portrait which appeared in the Allen & Ginter Champions set of 1887! Dad Clarkson, who had a lifetime 39-39 win-loss record from 1891 to 1896, never appeared on his own baseball card. He had some consolation, though: neither did the third pitching Clarkson brother, Walter, who compiled a 19-17 record from 1904 to 1908, just missing the dawn of the second great tobacco era.

VALUE
EX. CONDITION: Complete set, unknown; common card, $60–$75; Hall of Famers, $150–$200; Anson, $300. 5-YEAR PROJECTION: Below average.

1890 OLD JUDGE

SPECIFICATIONS
SIZE: 1½×2½". FRONT: Sepia photograph. BACK: Blank. DISTRIBUTION: Nationally, in cigarette packages.

HISTORY
Irked at the reserve clause which automatically tied a player to his team for the following season each time he signed a contract, a large number of National League players, led by John "Monte" Ward of the Giants, rebelled in 1890 and formed the Players League as an outgrowth of their union, The Brotherhood of Professional Ball Players. The Players League went into direct competition with the National League, setting up shop in seven of the eight National League cities (National League had a team in Cincinnati, Players League had a team in Buffalo). The Players League lasted only one year; there weren't enough fans to go around and the high salaries which the outlaw league had offered in order to induce players to leave their National League homes proved disastrous to management. The rebel players were allowed to go back to their former National League teams in 1891. Old Judge attempted to keep abreast of the changing baseball situation in 1890 by updating its 1889 issue, making the necessary team changes in the captions of the cards. The 1890 Old Judge cards are distinguishable at first glance from the 1889s by the initials "N.L." or "P.L." which are found in the captions or the photo area of the card. Only these two leagues were represented in 1890 Old Judges; the third major league, the American Association, was ignored.

FOR
For the collector/historian, these cards are a first-person documentary of an important year in baseball history and of the beginning of a movement which would lead in the 1960s to free agency for players.

AGAINST

The quality of the 1890 Old Judges is poor by comparison to Goodwin's early issues. Lower-grade photo materials seem to have been used, which resulted in the cards fading faster than the 1887–1889 cards. No new poses were issued, cards were just retouched or recaptioned to indicate team/league changes.

NOTEWORTHY CARDS

None that weren't in earlier Old Judge issues.

VALUE

EX. CONDITION: Complete set, unknown; common card, $20; Hall of Famers, $50–$200. 5-YEAR PROJECTION: Below average.

1889 OLD JUDGE

SPECIFICATIONS

SIZE: 1½×2½″. FRONT: Sepia photograph. BACK: Blank. DISTRIBUTION: Nationally, in packages of cigarettes.

HISTORY

The 1889 Old Judge set seems to have been something of an update set, rather than a new issue. While there are new players represented, most of the cards are merely new poses or changes in team and/or league captions. The 1889 Old Judge cards are easily distinguished from the earlier issues by the wording at bottom, "OLD JUDGE CIGARETTE FACTORY." The 1887 and 1888 cards do not have the word "factory." Again in 1889, the free and easy movement of players between teams and leagues caused Goodwin & Company problems in keeping current with their cigarette cards. Three teams had to be added to the American Association roster (St. Joseph, Sioux City, and Denver) and three teams dropped (Chicago, St. Louis, and Columbus); Cleveland replaced Detroit in the National League; and, because of movement of players who had been on earlier Old Judge cards, the company decided to issue at least a few cards for teams in

the International League, Atlantic Association, and Tri-State League. Finally, Old Judge added players from the four-team California League (Oakland, Sacramento, and two San Francisco teams) to its 1889 line-up. Only one pose each of 17 different players is currently known among the California League cards, and they make up a popular collecting specialty within the Old Judge spectrum.

FOR

The large number of new teams and wider geographic distribution of the 1889 Old Judge cards at least gives some collectors a reason to acquire a type card, if nothing else. The California League cards are a challenging and expensive, though not impossible, subset. Good value for the money.

AGAINST

The obscurity and short-lived nature of many of the teams represented in the 1889 Old Judge cards means that far fewer of the cards were saved than would have been the case for the popular National League teams.

NOTEWORTHY CARDS

At least three Hall of Famers who were not represented in the earlier issues are found in the 1889 Old Judges series. Charles "Kid" Nichols is the most difficult to find, though five poses exist with Omaha, for whom he pitched that season. In the major leagues from 1890 to 1906, Nichols compiled a 360-202 lifetime record. Similarly, Amos Rusie (243-160) pitched for Indianapolis in 1889 and went on to a 10-year major league career that led him to the Hall of Fame. Perhaps the most interesting is Clark Griffith, best known as the founder of the Washington Senators dynasty now carried on by his nephew, Calvin, as the Minnesota Twins. Griffith, who appears with Milwaukee in the 1889 Old Judges, had a major league career that spanned the 1891 to 1914 period. He won 240 games, lost 140.

VALUE

EX. CONDITION: Complete set, unknown; common card, $20; two-player card, $45; Hall of Famers, $50–$200; California League player, $60. 5-YEAR PROJECTION: Below average.

1889 HESS MAJOR LEAGUE

SPECIFICATIONS

SIZE: 1½×2¾″. FRONT: Sepia-toned photograph. BACK: Blank. DISTRIBUTION: Nationally (?), in cigarette packages.

HISTORY

Much more popular among collectors than Hess' 1888 California League issue, the Rochester, New York, firm's major league player set is another unknown quantity among 19th century tobacco cards. Twenty-one cards are known so far, of which 16 depict members of the 1889 New York Giants. The other handful of players are drawn from the rival New York Metropolitans and St. Louis Browns of the American Association, and the Detroit National League team. All of the Giants are depicted on the cards in portraits with an oval frame. Most of the other players are in poses identical to those found in the comtemporary Old Judge set. It is not known exactly which brands of cigarettes these cards were given away with; the ad at the bottom says only, "S.F. HESS & CO.'S CIGARETTES." It is not unreasonable to assume these were distributed in the Eastern U.S. in packages of the company's Creole brand while the California League cards were distributed out West.

FOR

Good set for New York Giants team collectors. Most portraits are unique to the issue.

AGAINST

Nobody knows how many cards it takes to complete a set; high value per card discourages trying.

NOTEWORTHY CARDS

The 1889 Hess set contains four Giants teammates who now are enshrined in the Hall of Fame: Roger Connor, Buck Ewing, John M. Ward, and Mickey Welch. It seems likely that someday cards of this set will also turn up for fellow Hall of Famers Jim O'Rourke and Tim Keefe, also teammates on that famous 1889 New York club.

OUR FAVORITE CARD

Although he is best remembered (when he is remembered at all) as a long-time coach of the New York Giants in later years, Walter Arlington "Arlie" Latham is pictured in the 1889 Hess Major League issue as a member of the St. Louis Browns, for whom he held down third base from 1883 to 1889. Latham had an unusual 17-season major league career that spanned nearly 30 years, beginning with Buffalo in 1880 and ending with the Giants in 1909, when, after a 10-year layoff, he suited up and played four games, starting two of them as second baseman at the age of 50. It's not as incredible as it may seem that the 50-year-old Latham stole a base in one of those games; in 1887, the first time records were kept on base steals, Latham copped 129. The following year, he led the league with 109. Latham was not only a game player during his career but a scrapper as well. In his heyday he was known as "the freshest man on earth," and his quick wit and wise mouth got him into many on-field and hotel fights. Latham was still fighting in 1909 when in spring training the 50-year-old Giants coach, standing a slight 5'8", 150 lbs., took on 6', 200 lb. Cy Seymour. Despite his reputation, Arlie Latham lived to 93.

VALUE

EX. CONDITION: Complete set, unknown; common card, $250–$300; Hall of Famers, $500. 5-YEAR PROJECTION: Below average.

1888 OLD JUDGE

SPECIFICATIONS

SIZE: 1½×2½". FRONT: Sepia photograph. BACK: Blank. DISTRIBUTION: Nationally, in cigarette packages.

HISTORY

The Old Judge cards of 1888 can be differentiated from their 1887 predecessors by the style of advertising on the card. The words "OLD JUDGE CIGARETTES" are printed at the bottom of the cards, rather than in black bands or boxes in the picture area. Additionally, the copyright date will be shown as 1888 on many cards. However, it should be noted that on Old Judge cards the copyright date refers to the Joseph Hall photograph on the card rather than to the card itself; thus some cards will carry a copyright date earlier than their actual issue. Like the 1887 issue, the Old Judges of 1888 consist of actual photographs glued to a hard cardboard backing. It is impossible to pinpoint the number of Old Judge cards issued in 1888 because new cards are being discovered every year. An estimate in the area of 400–500 is not unreasonable; quite an increase over the 117 players in the 1887 set. The increase in the number of players represented in the 1888 Old Judge set came about principally by including all the teams in the American Association and the Western Association, while adding players from the National League to the set as well. The large number of player team changes resulting from team failures, moves to different cities, contract jumping, etc., manifests itself in the 1888 Old Judge cards; many players shown with new captions or with artist-retouched photos to indicate a change of club. This, along with the several poses known for most of the players, makes it impossible for a collector to assemble a "complete" set of Old Judge cards. NOTE: It is safe to assume that all of the 1888 Old Judge cards were also issued with the Gypsy Queen designation of Goodwin & Company's other major cigarette brand. These cards are much scarcer, though, and command prices about double those for the Old Judge cards.

FOR

The larger number of players and especially of teams creates just a bit more demand for the 1888 Old Judge series. Many Hall of Famers are included, as well as players who would later become famous as managers or owners, or even in other fields. Prices are extremely reasonable, considering that the cards are practically a century old and that they are in decidedly short supply.

AGAINST

Sheer uncollectibility. Nobody can afford to complete the set.

NOTEWORTHY CARDS

Evangelist Billy Sunday appears in the 1888 Old Judge series as he neared the end of an eight-year major league career in which he was known as one of the National League's premier base-stealing threats. John Tener was a big Irishman whose mediocre pitching career was about over when he appeared on the Old Judge cards. He went on to a career in politics, as a U.S. Congressman and later as Governor of Pennsylvania. Also of special interest to collectors are the two-player cards found in the 1888 Old Judge series, usually with players from different teams posed in an "action" photo showing one tagging the other out. The set also features a few umpires and team owners, and even the young boys who served as mascots for Chicago and New York.

OUR FAVORITE CARD

Baseball was a rough game before the turn of the century, so it is not surprising that the deaf-mute William Ellsworth Hoy was universally known in the games as "Dummy." Hoy was a regular outfielder in the major leagues from 1888 through 1902, when he retired at the age of 40 after having played for six teams in the National, American, and Players Leagues, and the American Association. In his first year in the majors, Hoy led the National League with an incredible 82 stolen bases for Washington. Hoy left the game of baseball with a legacy that remains to this day; it is said that as an accommodation to the player who couldn't hear the umpires call balls and strikes and so know how to position himself in the outfield, the arbiters began throwing up their right arms to indicate a ball, their left arms for a strike. If you want a baseball card of "Dummy" Hoy, you'll have to find one of the five poses on which he appeared in Old Judge; he was never in any other set.

VALUE

EX. CONDITION: Complete set, unknown; common card, $20; two-player card, $45; Hall of Famers, $50–$200. 5-YEAR PROJECTION: Below average.

1888 ALLEN & GINTER

SPECIFICATIONS
SIZE: 1½ × 2¾″ and 2⅞ × 3¼″.
FRONT: Multi-color lithograph.
BACK: Checklist. DISTRIBUTION:
Nationally, in cigarette packages.

HISTORY
Following their initial success of the previous year, Allen & Ginter came out with a second series of "The World's Champions" cigarette cards in 1888, this time in two different sizes. The smaller cards were for inclusion in packages of 10 cigarettes, while the backs of the larger cards indicated, "One packed in every box of 20 Richmond Straight Cut No. 1 Cigarettes." Both sizes feature the same athletes, but an attractive background design pertinent to the appropriate sport has been added to the larger cards. The number of different sporting endeavors which the 1888 Allen & Ginter cards covered was expanded considerably from 1887. The line-up in the second series featured, "Cyclists, Base Ball Players, All Around Athletes, High Jumper, Pole Vaulter, Lawn Tennis Players, Wrestlers, Skaters, Pedestrians (Walkers, Runners and Go-as-you-Please), Weight Lifter, Hammer Thrower, Club Swinger, Pugilists, Oarsmen, and Swimmers." With the exception of a wrestler, Theobaud Bauer, the subjects in the 1888 A & G set are entirely different from those in the 1887 offering. Because there were so many added sports in 1888, the number of baseball players was cut back from ten to six, all from the National League. Instead of having an Allen & Ginter advertisement on the front, as in 1887, the 1888 cards feature the player's team and position under his name.

FOR
The attractive design of these cards captures the flavor of the national pastime in the 1880s.

AGAINST
Considerably scarcer than the 1887 Allen & Ginters, the 1888 series small cards are quite expensive, and the large versions are prohibitively so for most collectors. The players depicted are not as well known as those chosen to appear in 1887.

NOTEWORTHY CARDS
Of the six players in the 1888 A & G set, only New York Nationals catcher William "Buck" Ewing is a Hall of Famer. Jimmy Ryan, Chicago "centre fielder," must have seemed like a good choice back in 1888; he led the National League that season with 182 hits, 33 doubles, and 16 home runs. There are three misspellings among the six players' names: Jas. H. Fogarty, Philadelphia right fielder, actually had the middle initial "G," the card of Boston first baseman John Morrell should be spelled "Morrill," and Detroit pitcher Chas. H. Getzin should be "Getzein." There are some great nicknames here, too: Honest John Morrill, Pretzels Getzein, and Doggie Miller—who was also known as Foghorn and Calliope.

VALUE
EX. CONDITION: Complete set, unknown; common card, small size, $75; large size, $125; Ewing, small size, $150; large size, $250. 5-YEAR PROJECTION: Below average.

1888 GOODWIN CHAMPIONS

SPECIFICATIONS
SIZE: 1½ × 2⅝″. FRONT: Multi-color lithograph. BACK: Checklist. DISTRIBUTION: Nationally, in cigarette packages.

HISTORY
Issued in direct competition to Allen & Ginter's "World's Champions" cards, the 50-card "Champions" series by New York's Goodwin & Co. was inserted into packages of both the company's major brands, Old Judge and Gypsy Queen. Eight baseball players are among the 50 champions in the set, which also includes well-known names of the day in categories of: "Bicyclist, Billiards, Broadswordsman, Chess, Football, High Jumper, Jockey, Lawn Tennis, Marksman, Oarsman, Pedestrian, Pugilist, Runner, Strongest Man in the World, Wild West Hunter, and Wrestler." Some of the same athletes appear in both the Goodwin and the A & G sets, notably Buffalo Bill Cody and John L. Sullivan and, among the ballplayers, Anson, Caruthers, Glasscock, Keefe, and Kelly. Seven of the eight National League teams are represented in Goodwin's Champions cards, with only the last place Washington team omitted. The eighth card is of star Brooklyn (American Association) pitcher "Parisian Bob" Caruthers. The cards are extremely attractive lithographs with thick cardboard backing. The quality of workmanship compares favorably with the Allen & Ginter series. All of the baseball players are depicted in portraits, with the exception of Glasscock, who is shown in a fielding position.

FOR
As one of many Old Judge brand issues, the Goodwin Champions have a certain following among type collectors. The quality of the color lithography is their principal strong point. The eight baseball players in the set cannot be considered exceedingly rare—just expensive.

AGAINST
High cost on a per-card basis. Lack of demand for 19th century baseball cards.

NOTEWORTHY CARDS
Four of the eight baseball players in the Goodwin Champions set are now enshrined in the Hall of Fame: Adrian "Cap" Anson, Mike "King" Kelly, Dan Brouthers, and Tim Keefe.

OUR FAVORITE CARD
When you look at Goodwin's Champions card of Indianapolis shortstop "Pebbly Jack" Glasscock, you see baseball as it was played a century ago, with the player in knickers, striped railroad cap, long stockings, and handlebar mustache, and the game played on a field of real grass with nothing overhead but the blue sky. You'll also notice that Glasscock is playing without a glove. It makes you wonder how he managed to survive for 17 major league seasons. Glasscock twice led the National League in hits

(205 in 1889 and 172 in 1890), and was the league's batting champion in 1890 with a .336 average. He carries a lifetime .290 average.

VALUE

EX. CONDITION: Complete set, unknown; non-Hall of Famers, $100; Brouthers, Keefe, $200; Kelly, $250; Anson, $400. 5-YEAR PROJECTION: Below average.

1888 KIMBALL CHAMPIONS

SPECIFICATIONS

SIZE: 1½×2¾". FRONT: Multi-color lithograph. BACK: Checklist. DISTRIBUTION: Nationally, in packages of cigarettes.

HISTORY

In much the same style as Goodwin's and Allen & Ginter's "Champions" cigarette card series of the same year, the Rochester, New York, firm of W. S. Kimball & Company produced a 50-card set titled "Champions of Games and Sports." Only four of the 50 cards are of baseball players, the rest of the set representing a wider range of athletic activity than either of the competitors. Some of the more interesting categories of "champions" to be found in the Kimball card set include: "Checker Player, Colored Jockey, Six Days Roller Skater, Female Boxer of World, Hand Ball Player, and Cannon Ball Catcher!" Like the Goodwin and A & G cards, the Kimballs feature an engraved color portrait of the player and a small "action" scene. Like many tobacco issues of the day, the Kimball set featured an album that could be obtained by mailing in coupons found in the cigarette packages. Collectors should be aware that since the paper pages of the album contained the same lithographs as the cards themselves, it is possible that a dishonest person could have cut the pictures out of the album and pasted them onto a common (nonbaseball) card in the set, turning—for instance—a $5 swimmer's card into a $200 baseball card.

FOR

Quality of workmanship, small size of baseball players' subset.

AGAINST

High cost per card. Lack of big names among the baseball players.

NOTEWORTHY CARDS

Undoubtedly the best-known of the ballplayers in the Kimball Champions series is James "Tip" O'Neill (misspelled "O'Neil" on the card). He was certainly baseball's champion when the cards were issued in 1888. The previous year, playing for the World's Champion St. Louis Browns of the American Association, O'Neill led the league in hits, doubles, triples, home runs, home run percentage, runs, batting average, and slugging average. His batting average of .435 that year remains the major league baseball record. Actually, that .435 is a modern adjustment, because walks and hit batsmen counted as hits in 1887, and O'Neill was credited with a .492 average.

OUR FAVORITE CARD

The most interesting cards in the 1888 Kimball Champions are not necessarily the baseball players. Consider, for instance, the card of the world's champion tightrope walker, Blondin. Born Jean-Francois Gravelet in Paris in 1824, Blondin made his name and his fortune crossing a 1,100-foot-long tightrope suspended 160 feet above the waters of Niagara Falls. After his first such crossing in 1859 he repeated the feat many times, often with a new twist: blindfolded, tied in a sack, pushing a wheelbarrow, carrying a man on his back, on stilts, etc. The great acrobat performed until he was 72 years old, and died in London a year later. At a price of $5 to $7, compared to $200 for the baseball cards which were produced in equal numbers, cards like these have to be among the greatest values in the hobby today.

VALUE

EX. CONDITION: Complete set, unknown; common card (baseball), $200; O'Neill, $225. 5-YEAR PROJECTION: Below average.

1888 HESS CALIFORNIA LEAGUE

SPECIFICATIONS

SIZE: 1½×2⅞". FRONT: Multi-color lithograph or sepia-toned photo. BACK: Blank. DISTRIBUTION: California (?), in packages of cigarettes.

HISTORY

In 1888, the S. F. Hess tobacco company of Rochester, New York, became the first of many baseball card producers to tailor a set for the California market. Far removed from major league baseball, which would not venture further west than St. Louis for another 67 years, the California League (reformed in 1903 as the Pacific Coast League) became the Golden State's substitute for major league baseball. Indeed, for much of its history the league was on a virtual par with the major leagues back East, and until the Giants and the Dodgers moved West in 1958, there was a continual agitation to designate the Pacific Coast League as a third major league. Certainly Hess' inclusion of California League player cards in its Creole brand cigarettes helped boost sales on the West Coast. Two separate issues of Creole cards exist, one which pictures the players in sepia photos, a second which depicts them in color engravings, many rendered from the same photos. Both types are extremely rare; just 40 cards are known in the lithographed set, 16 in the photographed group. All four teams of the California League are represented in the issue, the Greenwood & Morans of Oakland, San Francisco's Haverlys and Pioneers, and the Stocktons.

FOR

Historical significance as the first of dozens of Pacific Coast League sets. The photographed cards give collectors an interesting perspective on how the sport "looked" a century ago.

AGAINST

A minor league set with no big name stars. High cost per card and lack of information on completeness of set makes it too challenging for all but the most avid collector.

NOTEWORTHY CARDS

The Creole set contains in its lithographed group a card of umpire J. Smith, one of very few baseball card sets to feature the arbiters.

VALUE

EX. CONDITION: Complete set, unknown; lithographed card, $200; photographed card, $300. 5-YEAR PROJECTION: Below average.

1888 YUM YUM

SPECIFICATIONS

SIZE: 1⅜×2¾″. FRONT: Sepia photo or line drawings. BACK: Blank. DISTRIBUTION: Nationally, in packages of tobacco.

HISTORY

In one of the rarest 19th century tobacco card issues, only 36 different poses are known for 31 different players. The cards come in two types, photographic portraits and full-length line engravings that seem to have been rendered from the photos used in the contemporary Old Judge cards. All eight National League teams and the Brooklyn club of the American Association are represented. Because the set was distributed with the Yum Yum brand of smoking/chewing tobacco by August Beck & Company, a Chicago firm, there are six players and seven poses representing the team then known as the White Stockings. All Chicago players are pictured in civilian clothes rather than in baseball uniforms.

FOR

Lots of well-known players of the day depicted in unique photos. Aura of true rarity. Likelihood that other cards will be discovered, worth premium money.

AGAINST

Extreme rarity and high price tag makes collecting as a set unfeasible.

NOTEWORTHY CARDS

Hall of Famers Brouthers, Clarkson, Ewing, Galvin, O'Rourke, and Welch.

OUR FAVORITE CARD

Pictured in his street clothes, Billy Sunday's card in the Yum Yum set makes him look more like the famous evangelist he became than the ballplayer he was. Sunday was a National League outfielder for eight years with Chicago, Pittsburgh, and Philadelphia, taking a modest .248 lifetime batting average with him when he left the playing field for the pulpit in 1890. In his later career, Sunday was personally responsible for "converting" fair numbers of baseball players. Less well known is the fact that he also took under his wing and financially supported many former ballplayers who were down on their luck.

VALUE

EX. CONDITION: Complete set, unknown; common card, engraving, $300; photo, $350; Hall of Famers, engraving, $400; photo, $500. 5-YEAR PROJECTION: Below average.

1888 G&B CHEWING GUM

SPECIFICATIONS

SIZE: 1×2⅛″. FRONT: Sepia photo or line engraving. BACK: Blank. DISTRIBUTION: Nationally, in packages of chewing gum.

HISTORY

Obviously linked in some way to the Chicago Yum Yum tobacco cards of August Beck are these tiny cards by the enigmatic "G&B" firm of New York City. The cards are historically significant in that they are the first widely distributed baseball card issue inserted into a product other than cigarettes or chewing tobacco. A total of 56 different designs representing 46 players is currently known, and more will surely be discovered. While the words "AMERICAN LEAGUE" appear on some of the cards, the teams and players depicted are actu-

ally members of the American Association. Those cards which have the "NATIONAL LEAGUE" designation may or may not also have the words "CHEWING GUM" printed in the bottom panel. There is much yet to be learned about this set.

FOR

Significance of being the first gum cards. Unusually small size.

AGAINST

Extreme rarity and high cost. Lack of definitive information about the set.

NOTEWORTHY CARDS

The usual gang of Hall of Famers active in the late 1880s.

VALUE

EX. CONDITION: Complete set, unknown; common card, engraving, $150; photo, $200; Hall of Famers, engraving, $250; photo, $400; Anson photo, $500. 5-YEAR PROJECTION: Below average.

1887 OLD JUDGE

SPECIFICATIONS

SIZE: 1½×2½″. FRONT: Sepia photograph. BACK: Blank. DISTRIBUTION: Nationally, in packages of cigarettes.

HISTORY

These 19th century baseball cards are actually photographic prints which have been glued to stiff cardboard backings. They served a dual purpose for Goodwin & Company a century ago; besides boosting sales of the company's Old Judge brand, the hard cardboard backing of the cards lent some rigidity to the packs of 10 cigarettes in which they were stuffed. Two distinct types of Old Judge cards were issued in 1887: script series and numbered series. The script series takes its name from the fact that players' names are printed on the cards in script lettering at the bottom of the portrait or posed-action shot. The numbered series features a penned-in card number on the negative, generally in the upper-right corner. In general, all 1887 Old Judge cards carry the wording "OLD JUDGE Cigarettes" in a curved black band at the top or bottom of the card, or in a box at the upper left. There is also an 1887 copyright date near the bottom of the card. Like all photographic Old Judge cards, the pictures for this set (with the exception of the Brooklyn players' cards, which were shot outdoors) were taken in the Brooklyn studio of Joseph Hall. Backdrop cloths and such props as baseballs hung on strings to resemble thrown or batted balls give a quaint look to this issue. Players in the 1887 series come from the eight teams that made up the National League that season, as well as the St. Louis, Brooklyn, and New York teams of the American Association (a major league at that time). Roughly half the 1887 script series Old Judge set is made up of a subset that collectors call the "Spotted Ties." These cards picture members of the original New York Mets, the Metropolitan baseball club of the American Association. Rather than being pictured in uniform, the Mets are shown in dress shirts with each ballplayer sporting a polka-dot tie, hence the nickname. Another popular subset, in the numbered series, is the 13 "Browns' Champions 1886" cards, which feature the members of the American Association pennant winner of the previous year. The distinctive striped caps and laced-up uniform jerseys and the similarity of portrait poses among the team makes them especially attractive to collectors. NOTE: Cards of the numbered series will also be found with "Gypsy Queen" advertising, rather than Old Judge, and slightly different border design. They are significantly rarer than their Old Judge counterparts and are valued at three times the Old Judge price for common cards.

FOR

There are many ways to collect the 1887 Old Judge cards. Since there are but 117 different players known, it is not unreasonable to strive to collect one card of each (though it would be virtually impossible to collect all the known poses of the various players). The popular "Spotted Tie" Mets and Championship St. Louis Browns are also reasonable, though expensive,

goals. Because of the tough cardboard with which they are backed, these cards resist creasing quite well. When compared to modern days "superstar" cards available in unlimited quantities, these Old Judge cards represent great value for the money.

AGAINST

The lack of a single, easy-to-read checklist has long hampered the collectibility of the Old Judge series. By and large, there is little collector or fan interest in turn of the century baseball or baseball cards. The fact that cards are still being discovered in this series every year means that no collector can reasonably attempt to have a "complete" set. You have to enjoy the thrill of the hunt to pursue Old Judges. Cards are prone to fading as the old photos are exposed to light; some have even turned pink.

NOTEWORTHY CARDS

There are 10 different 1887 Old Judge cards which depict Mike "King" Kelly, the premier baseball player of his day. He was purchased by Boston from Chicago in February, 1887 for the unprecedented price of $10,000, and each card in the set carries the notation "$10,000 Kelly." Kelly appears in the Chicago uniform in the script series cards of 1887, and in Boston togs in the numbered cards. Also of special interest, besides the many Hall of Famers to be found, is the inclusion of a card of St. Louis Browns owner Chris Von Der Ahe in the "Champions" subset. The Dutchman is credited with being the first ballpark owner to serve that stadium staple, the hot dog, at a baseball game. Another noteworthy Brown in the group is manager Charles Comiskey, the "Old Roman" whose name is immortalized in Chicago's American League ballpark.

OUR FAVORITE CARD

Today, when a rookie ballplayer makes it big in the major leagues he is referred to as a "phenom." The Old Judge script series of 1887 partially explains why. One of the cards in the set is of John Smith, better known to fans, as the script name on his card indicates, as "Phenomenal Smith." When the 1887 Old Judges were issued, Smith (born John Francis Gammon), had only been in the major

leagues for three years, compiling a 4-9 win-loss record—hardly "phenomenal." Playing in the majors through 1891, he retired with a decidedly mediocre record of 57-78. If the card was issued late enough in 1887, it is possible that the nickname refers to Smith's total of 55 pitching decisions that year; he was a 25-game winner with the Baltimore Orioles of the American Association—but he lost 30. Whatever the derivation of the name, it lives on today as part of baseball's idiom.

VALUE

EX. CONDITION: Complete set, unknown; common card, $30; "Spotted Ties," $150; Browns, $75; Kelly, Comiskey, $125; Von Der Ahe, Smith, $100. 5-YEAR PROJECTION: Below average.

1887 ALLEN & GINTER

SPECIFICATIONS

SIZE: 1½×2¾". FRONT: Multi-color lithograph. BACK: Checklist. DISTRIBUTION: Nationally, in cigarette packages.

HISTORY

The Richmond, Virginia, firm of John Allen and Major Lewis Ginter is often credited with being the first American tobacco company to use cigarette cards as a sales incentive, around 1885. The company's first issue of baseball cards came in 1887, when 10 of the 50 subjects in Allen & Ginter's "The World's Champions" series were contemporary diamond heroes. As checklisted on the back of each card, the remaining 40 "Champions" represented the finest "Oarsmen, Wrestlers, Pugilists, Rifle Shooters, Billiard Players, and Pool Players" of the late 1880s. Noteworthy among these non-ballplayers in the 1887 A & G set are boxer John L. Sullivan, and sharpshooters Annie Oakley and the "Hon. W. F. Cody," better known as Buffalo Bill. Collectors should note that the "Jack Dempsey" listed among the pugilists is not the "Manassa Mauler"—the champion of the 1920s wasn't even born until 1895. The 10 baseball players in the set are among the best-known of their era. Eight were from National League teams, and two from the "other" major league of the 1880s, the American Association. Both of the AA players (Charles Comiskey and Bob Caruthers) were from the St. Louis Browns, the 1886 World's Champions of baseball. Collectors should be aware that paper "cards" of the Allen & Ginter front design, but with no back printing, are sometimes found; these have been cut from an advertising poster and are worth only a fraction of the value of actual cards.

FOR

If a collector is going to own just one 19th century baseball card, it should be an Allen & Ginter. No card better captures, by means of the uniforms and poses depicted, the spirit of baseball in the 19th century. The multi-color lithography on a borderless white background, state of the art in its day, adds to the flavor of the set. Though not cheap, the complete set of 10 baseball players is a reasonable goal for the aspiring collector.

AGAINST

Modern collecting habits seem to have passed by these great old cards; there are extremely few collectors of 19th century baseball cards. Also, the per-card value is quite high.

NOTEWORTHY CARDS

Of the 10 baseball players in the 1887 Allen & Ginter set, six have been enshrined in the Hall of Fame: Adrian "Cap" Anson, John Clarkson, Charles Comiskey, Timothy Keefe, Mike Kelly, and John "Monte" Ward. The others, with the possible exception of Detroit back-up backstop Charles W. Bennett, were also major stars of the day.

OUR FAVORITE CARD

The 1887 Allen & Ginter set is one of only a handful of baseball cards to depict Charles Comiskey in his playing days. When "The Old Roman" was chosen for inclusion in the A & G set, he was manager and first baseman of the World's Champion St. Louis Browns team of the American Association. Comiskey went on to a great career as a baseball executive in Chicago, but his playing and managing

days were also impressive. In 13 seasons as a major league player (1882 to 1894) he compiled a .264 lifetime batting average. As manager of the Browns (1883 to 1889, 1891), the Chicago team in the Players League (1890), and the Cincinnati Redstockings (1892 to 1894), Comiskey compiled an 824-533 win-loss record, ranking him third in winning percentage among managers in the game's history. Perhaps the best thing about Comiskey's card in the 1887 A & G set, though, is the card itself, showing a jaunty young man in a laced-up baseball jersey with a red and white striped cap.

VALUE

EX. CONDITION: Complete set, unknown; common card, $40; Anson, $125; Kelly, $100; other Hall of Famers, $75. 5-YEAR PROJECTION: Average.

1887 BUCHNER GOLD COIN

SPECIFICATIONS

SIZE: 1¾×3″. FRONT: Multi-color lithograph drawings. BACK: Blue or black advertisement. DISTRIBUTION: Nationally, in packages of chewing tobacco.

HISTORY

With 143 cards depicting 118 different players, this is the second largest baseball card set of the 19th century. The cards were inserts in packages of D. Buchner & Company's (New York) Gold Coin brand chewing tobacco. The baseball players in the issue are really just a subset of a larger issue which, according to the wording on the backs of some of the cards, featured: "The portraits of all the leading base-ball players, police inspectors and captains, jockeys, actors & chiefs of fire departments in the country in full uniform and costume." The baseball players in the set include members of all eight National League teams of the day, along with Brooklyn and St. Louis from the American As-

sociation and Milwaukee and La Crosse of the Northwestern League. The Buchner issue is somewhat confusing in that it was apparently issued in three different printings, possibly over the span of more than one year. The first printing contains the body of the set, 76 cards; a later issue features 14 members of the St. Louis Browns; while the third group of 53 cards features 27 new players and 26 players who were in earlier groups. Among the latter 26 cards there are a few position changes or minor changes in the captions. Like many similar sets that feature variations of player cards, most collectors content themselves to collect just one card per player. There are many errors in the spellings of players' names in the set, as well as some errors that attribute players to positions that they never played. The single most notable feature of the Buchner set, though, is that the drawings on the cards are not real portraits of the players they purport to depict. Most of the "centre fielders" in the set share exactly the same picture of a player standing with hands cupped and outstretched to catch a fly ball. The only difference between the various center fielders in the set is in the color of the uniform. Occasionally a mustache will be added to a player's face, for the sake of "accuracy." This trait is especially true of the 76 cards in the first printing. The 14 cards in the St. Louis subset all have unique poses, but with the exception of President Von Der Ahe's card, which is based on a photograph, the Browns depicted in the Buchner set bear no resemblance to the actual players. There are more new poses in the third subset of 53 cards, and a few of them even seem to portray the name player. Apparently Buchner felt the average man would not realize the baseball card he pulled from his package of chaw was not an accurate representation of the player. After all, this was in the days before television or the widespread use of illustrations in newspapers. The Buchner people must have felt pretty silly, though, when the Old Judge cards—actual photographs of the players—began to circulate alongside their faked drawings.

FOR

The Buchner Gold Coin cards offer the contemporary collector a nostalgic look at baseball in the days when it was played bare-handed—some of the players are even wearing spats!

AGAINST

The generic drawings of the players are the biggest drawback of the Buchner set. Collectors want real pictures of the players on their cards. Further, the relatively high cost per card, $40 to $60, makes the prospect of assembling a complete set of 118 to 143 cards fairly unappealing.

NOTEWORTHY CARDS

Certainly the most noteworthy card in the Buchner Gold Coin set is that of Brooklyn second baseman Bill McClellan. That is, it would be noteworthy if anyone could confirm that it exists. No current collector has the card or has ever seen it. It continues to be carried on most checklists for the Buchner set because it was listed by baseball card catalog pioneer Jefferson Burdick, and he was seldom wrong. McClellan had an eight-season major league career (1878 to 1888), with Chicago, Providence, Philadelphia, Brooklyn, and Cleveland. He was not the slickest fielding second sacker in the game, however. In 1887, the year he may or may not have made his appearance in the Buchner card set, he led the major leagues in errors with 105.

VALUE

EX. CONDITION: Complete set, unknown; common card, $40–$60; Hall of Famers, $75–$125; Anson, Comiskey, Von Der Ahe, $150–$175. 5-YEAR PROJECTION: Below average.

1887 LONE JACK

SPECIFICATIONS

SIZE: 1½×2½". FRONT: Sepia-toned photograph. BACK: Blank. DISTRIBUTION: Unknown, probably only on limited regional basis in packages of Lone Jack cigarettes.

HISTORY

One of the scarcest 19th century baseball card sets, the Lone Jack issue of 13 cards was produced by the small tobacco company of that name in Lynchburg, Virginia. The Lone Jack cards are one of many sets in the era that depict the players of the 1886 World's Champion St. Louis Browns. While many baseball fans and collectors do not trace the history of the World Series beyond the first meeting between National and American League pennant winners in 1904, there were World's Championship series played between the winners of the National League and American Association flags as far back as 1884. The 1886 contest marked the first time an American Association team (Browns) had defeated the National League (Chicago White Stockings) in the post-season series. The photos which appear on the Lone Jack cards are exactly the same photos found on Old Judge's "Brown's Champions" cards of the same year. It is evident that Lone Jack acquired the photos from the Joseph Hall studio in Brooklyn. The words "LONE JACK" were written on the negatives to the left of the player's portrait, and appear in white on the cards; "Cigarettes" is on the right. The player's last name (misspelled about as often as not) is in black lettering at the bottom edge of the picture. An unproven tale often heard in collectors' circles is that the unusual name of the issuer stems from the fact that the tobacco company was once won on a bluff in a high-stakes poker game, the gutsy gambler holding nothing in his hand but a "lone jack."

FOR

Just the desirability that often attaches itself to truly rare collectibles.

AGAINST

Too expensive. The collector can find a nearly identical card in the Old Judge series for a fraction of the price.

NOTEWORTHY CARDS

Hall of Famer Charlie Comiskey (misspelled "Commisky") and Browns president Chris Von Der Ahe.

OUR FAVORITE CARD

While the Lone Jack set features the entire starting line-up, the back-up pitcher and catcher, and the team president of the St. Louis Browns, one of the most interesting characters in the set was "Parisian Bob" Caruthers. Born in Memphis during the Civil War, Robert Lee Caruthers had a nine-season major league career between 1884 and 1892, playing with St. Louis and Brooklyn in both the National League and the American Association. His lifetime 218-99 win-loss record places him third on the all-time winning percentage list at .688. In the Browns championship season of 1886, Caruthers was one of a pair of St. Louis "Iron Men" on the mound, winning 30 games. Perhaps more amazing, on the days he wasn't pitching Caruthers played left field, and in 1886 led the entire team in batting average (.334) and home runs (4). Following his playing career, Caruthers became an umpire and an alcoholic (though not necessarily in that order), and died in Peoria, Illinois in 1911 while serving a 90-day workhouse sentence for public drunkenness. Perhaps now, with his inglorious end somewhat shrouded in the mists of time, there ought to be some serious consideration given to Caruthers as a candidate for baseball's Hall of Fame.

VALUE

EX. CONDITION: Complete set, unknown; common card, $300; Comiskey, $450. 5-YEAR PROJECTION: Below average.

1887 KALAMAZOO BATS

SPECIFICATIONS

SIZE: 2¼×4". FRONT: Sepia-toned photos. BACK: Most are blank, some found with list of available premiums. DISTRIBUTION: Probably confined to New York and Philadelphia areas, inserted in cigarette packages.

HISTORY

While the bulk of the 50 known Kalamazoo Bats players cards (the brand name gets double mileage out of an 1880s nickname for a particular style of hand-rolled cigarette) can positively be identified as an 1887 issue, there is some evidence that others were issued in 1886 and 1888. Elmer Foster and Larry Corcoran, pictured as New York Metropolitans (American Association) in the set, were only with the team in 1886, and Foster only early in that year; while Lee Gibson, shown in the set as a Philadelphia Athletics (American Association) catcher, had only one game in the major leagues—in 1888. There is even one "mystery player" in the set, a fellow named Gallagher. However, nobody by that name played for Philly—or anywhere else in the major leagues—at that time. Thus, there are still questions to be answered about this rare and popular set issued by the Philadelphia tobacco firm of Charles Gross & Company. Just four teams are represented in the Kalamazoo Bats set, the aforementioned American Association teams, and their National League counterparts the Philadelphia Phillies and the New York Giants. The photographs which make up the set are most interesting; the Mets and the Giants are featured in portrait shots, the National Leaguers wearing uniform, tie, and hat, while the Mets were photographed bareheaded. The two Philadelphia teams were photographed full length in posed-action shots. The Athletics were photographed in a studio, before an artificial backdrop. The Phils were actually photographed in their home stadium, the old Baker Bowl, a unique setting for 19th century baseball cards. Besides the cards for individual players there are a number of cards featuring two players, and there is a subset of six team photo cards—the two Philadelphia teams, Baltimore, Detroit, Boston, and Pittsburg (as it was spelled in those days). For collectors of the ultra-rare, there are also cabinet-size cards, believed to be production proof cards, in player and team formats. Most of the thick cardboard backs on which the Kalamazoo Bats photos were mounted are blank, but some carry a message offering to redeem cards for premiums. The offer ranges from a 25-cent-value "plain Meerschaum cigar tube" for 50 cards, to "A very fine silk umbrella, with gold mounted handle. Value five dollars." This could be obtained by sending in 400 cards. This premium list probably accounts for the scarcity of surviving cards.

FOR
The larger size of the cards makes them more attractive to modern-day collectors. The photos, especially those taken in the Philadelphia stadium, are significant historical artifacts of the national pastime.

AGAINST
The high cost and great rarity of the cards, especially the team and cabinet issues, make it virtually impossible to assemble a complete set.

NOTEWORTHY CARDS
The Kalamazoo Bats is one of only two baseball card sets to feature Harry Wright (shown as Philadelphia National League manager, seated in the dugout). The British-born Wright (with his brothers, George and Sam) was a true baseball pioneer, whose career began as a catcher with the Boston Red Stockings of the National Association in 1871. When the National League was formed in 1876 Wright became manager for the Boston team, managing in the majors through 1893. Also worth mentioning is Harry Stowe, who played under the name Harry Stovey but appears as Stowe in the Kalamazoo Bats sets, one of just three sets in which he is featured. If ever an old-time player was unjustly passed over by the Hall of Fame, it's Harry Stovey. In his 14-year major league career he compiled a .301 lifetime average; led the league twice in hits, six times in home runs, and once or twice in most other offensive categories; he even had a .404 batting season in 1884. Other Hall of Famers found in the Kalamazoo Bats set but seldom seen in other baseball card issues are Athletics catcher Wilbert Robinson, who went on to fame as manager of the "Daffiness Boys" Brooklyn Dodgers of the 1920s; "Orator Jim" O'Rourke, the Giants' third baseman whose 19-season career spanned the period 1876 to 1904 and included a lifetime .310 batting average; and Roger Connor, the Giants' third baseman who compiled a .318 average over 18 seasons (1880 to 1897) in the majors and whose 233 triples are fifth on the all-time list.

OUR FAVORITE CARD
One of only two baseball cards on which second baseman Lou Bierbauer appeared was the Kalamazoo Bats set (actually, he appeared twice in the set, once on his own card, once on a two-player card with the mysterious "Gallagher"). Bierbauer is a little-known part of baseball lore that persists today in the nickname of a major league team. He debuted in the major leagues with the Philadelphia Athletics in 1886, but in 1890 he jumped to the Brooklyn club of the Players League, with many other union ballplayers. The so-called "Brotherhood" league broke after that single season. Under the reconciliation agreement with the National League and the American Association, players who were on the 40-man reserve lists of N. L. and A. A. teams were allowed to return to their former "homes" without penalty. Bierbauer, however, was one of a handful of players whom their former teams had not protected. He was thus free to negotiate with any team, and struck a deal with J. Palmer O'Neill, president of the Pittsburgh club. Angered by O'Neill's "theft" of Bierbauer from the Quaker City, the Philadelphia press began referring to their cross-state rival as J. "Pirate" O'Neill, and his team soon became known—and probably always will be—as the Pittsburgh Pirates. Bierbauer himself played with Pittsburgh for six years, then ended his major league career with a two-year stint (1897 and 1898) with St. Louis.

VALUE
EX. CONDITION: Complete set, unknown; common card, $250; Connor, O'Rourke, Robinson, $400–$500; Wright, $750; team card, $750. 5-YEAR PROJECTION: Below average.

1887 FOUR BASE HITS

SPECIFICATIONS
SIZE: 2¼×3⅞". FRONT: Sepia-toned photograph. BACK: Blank. DISTRIBUTION: Nationally, in cigar packages.

HISTORY
Among the rarest and most desirable of 19th century baseball cards, these

cards (large in comparison to contemporary issues) are also among the most enigmatic. It is not known who issued them or how many make up a complete set. Because of similarities in size, the *double-entendre* use of a baseball term for a tobacco product, and a couple of shared photographs, there is considerable speculation that the cards were an issue of Charles Gross & Company of Philadelphia, which produced its Kalamazoo Bats brand tobacco cards that same year. However, other collectors attribute the issue to the Chicago firm of A. Beck, because of shared photos and similarities of design and typography between the Four Base Hits cards and Beck's 1888 Yum Yum cards. Regardless of who issued them, the Four Base Hits cards are rare and valuable. Cards of only nine different players are known to exist at this time.

FOR
Rarity. Quality of workmanship. Larger size of card is closer to today's standard size and modern collectors more readily identify with the issue as a "real" baseball card.

AGAINST
High cost per card, lack of information on what will constitute a "complete" set.

NOTEWORTHY CARDS
One of the first major baseball card errors is found in the Four Base Hits cards, and it is the type of error that continues to plague card companies right up to this day—the use of the wrong player's photo. The Four Base Hits card described as that of Chicago White Stockings catcher Tom Daly (misspelled "Daily" on the card) actually features the picture of teammate (later, evangelist) Billy Sunday.

VALUE
EX. CONDITION: Complete set, unknown; common card, $450; Welch, $650; Kelly, $750. 5-YEAR PROJECTION: Below average.

1886 OLD JUDGE

SPECIFICATIONS
SIZE: 1½×2½″. FRONT: Sepia-toned engraving. BACK: Dark green. DISTRIBUTION: New York City area (?), with cigarettes.

HISTORY
This rare set is the first baseball card series produced by Goodwin & Company, the New York tobacco company, to promote the sale of its Old Judge brand of cigarettes. It differs from the better-known Old Judge cards of 1887–1889 in a number of important ways. The 1886 Old Judge cards are artists' renderings taken from woodcut portraits, rather than being actual photographs. They are printed on very thin card stock, and they are the only Old Judge cards to feature an advertisement for the cigarettes on the back—an engraving of a bewigged justice in the "O" of the word "OLD." Since all 11 of the players known in the series were members of the New York National League club of 1886, it is surmised that the series was limited to members of the team that would soon come to be called the Giants.

FOR
As the forerunner of the long and popular Old Judge card series which followed it, the 1886 issue is in strong demand by collectors of early cards. Also, it marks the start of a nearly century-old series of baseball cards for Giants team collectors. More than half of the known players in the series are members of baseball's Hall of Fame.

AGAINST
The extreme rarity of the set means that few, if any, collectors can reasonably expect to complete it. Unlike later Old Judge cards, the thin stock on which the 1886 New York Nationals were printed makes it exceedingly difficult to find cards in decent condition.

NOTEWORTHY CARDS
Hall of Famers Roger Connor (1st Base), T. J. Keefe (Pitcher). J. H. O'Rourke (Center Field), John M. Ward (Captain), and Michael Welsh (Pitcher)—the name should be spelled "Welch."

VALUE
EX. CONDITION: Complete set, unknown; common card, $200; Hall of Famers, $300. 5-YEAR PROJECTION: Below average.

HALL OF FAME

A popular baseball card collecting specialty is assembling a set of cards of members of the National Baseball Hall of Fame. While not all Hall of Famers (or HOFers, as it is sometimes seen abbreviated) were depicted on baseball cards contemporary with their playing careers (umpires, executives, and Negro leagues stars, for example), all have since been immortalized either on retrospective card issues or in the official postcards sold by the Hall of Fame. For the benefit of collectors, here is the list of players honored by being inducted into the Hall of Fame, along with the year of their enshrinement and their principal playing position.

Henry Aaron	1982	RF
Grover Cleveland Alexander	1938	RHP
Walter Alston	1983	Manager
Adrian "Cap" Anson	1939	1B
Luis Aparicio	1984	SS
Luke Appling	1964	SS
Earl Averill	1975	CF
Frank "Home Run" Baker	1957	3B
Dave Bancroft	1971	SS
Ernie Banks	1977	1B
Ed Barrow	1953	Executive
Jake Beckley	1971	1B
James "Cool Papa" Bell	1974	Negro leagues
Charles "Chief" Bender	1953	RHP
Lawrence "Yogi" Berra	1972	C
Jim Bottomley	1974	1B
Lou Boudreau	1970	SS
Roger Bresnahan	1945	C
Dennis "Dan" Brouthers	1945	1B
Mordecai Brown	1949	RHP
Morgan Bulkeley	1937	Executive
Jesse Burkett	1946	LF
Roy Campanella	1969	C
Max G. Carey	1961	CF
Alexander Cartwright	1938	Executive
Henry Chadwick	1938	Executive
Frank Chance	1946	1B
Albert "Happy" Chandler	1982	Executive
Oscar Charleston	1976	Negro leagues
Jack Chesbro	1946	RHP
Fred Clarke	1945	LF
John Clarkson	1963	RHP
Roberto Clemente	1973	RF
Ty Cobb	1936	CF
Gordon "Mickey" Cochrane	1947	C
Eddie Collins	1939	2B
Jimmy Collins	1945	3B
Earle Combs	1970	CF
Charles Comiskey	1939	Executive
John "Jocko" Conlan	1974	Umpire
Tom Connolly	1953	Umpire
Roger Connor	1976	1B
Stan Coveleski	1969	RHP
Sam Crawford	1957	RF
Joe Cronin	1956	SS
William "Candy" Cummings	1939	Executive

Hazen "Kiki" Cuyler	1968	CF
Jay "Dizzy" Dean	1953	RHP
Ed Delahanty	1945	LF
Bill Dickey	1954	C
Martin Dihigo	1977	Negro leagues
Joe DiMaggio	1955	CF
Don Drysdale	1984	RHP
Hugh Duffy	1945	CF
Bill Evans	1973	Umpire
Johnny Evers	1946	2B
William "Buck" Ewing	1939	C
Urban "Red" Faber	1964	RHP
Bob Feller	1962	RHP
Rick Ferrell	1984	C
Elmer Flick	1963	RF
Edward "Whitey" Ford	1974	LHP
Andrew "Rube" Foster	1981	Negro leagues
Jimmy Foxx	1951	1B
Ford C. Frick	1970	Executive
Frankie Frisch	1947	2B
James "Pud" Galvin	1965	RHP
Lou Gehrig	1939	1B
Charlie Gehringer	1949	2B
Bob Gibson	1981	RHP
Josh Gibson	1972	Negro leagues
Warren Giles	1979	Executive
Vernon "Lefty" Gomez	1972	LHP
Leon "Goose" Goslin	1968	LF
Hank Greenberg	1956	1B
Clark C. Griffith	1946	Executive
Burleigh Grimes	1964	RHP
Robert "Lefty" Grove	1947	LHP
Charles "Chick" Hafey	1971	LF
Jesse "Pop" Haines	1970	RHP
Billy Hamilton	1961	CF
Will Harridge	1972	Executive
Stanley "Bucky" Harris	1975	Manager
Charles "Gabby" Hartnett	1955	C
Harry Heilmann	1952	RF
Billy Herman	1975	2B
Harry Hooper	1971	RF
Rogers Hornsby	1942	2B

HALL OF FAME

Waite Hoyt	1969	RHP		Jim O'Rourke	1945	LF
Cal Hubbard	1976	Umpire		Mel Ott	1951	RF
Carl Hubbell	1947	LHP				
Miller Huggins	1964	Manager		Leroy "Satchel" Paige	1971	Negro leagues
				Herb Pennock	1948	LHP
Monte Irvin	1973	Negro leagues		Eddie Plank	1946	LHP
Travis Jackson	1982	SS		Charles "Old Hoss" Radbourne	1939	RHP
Hughie Jennings	1945	SS		Edgar "Sam" Rice	1963	RF
Byron "Ban" Johnson	1937	Executive		Branch Rickey	1967	Executive
Walter Johnson	1936	RHP		Eppa Rixey	1963	LHP
William "Judy" Johnson	1975	Negro leagues		Robin Roberts	1976	RHP
Adrian "Addie" Joss	1978	RHP		Brooks Robinson	1983	3B
				Frank Robinson	1982	RF
Al Kaline	1980	RF		Jackie Robinson	1962	2B
Tim Keefe	1964	RHP		Wilbert Robinson	1945	Manager
Willie Keeler	1939	RF		Edd Roush	1962	CF
George Kell	1983	3B		Charles "Red" Ruffing	1967	RHP
Joe Kelley	1971	LF		Amos Rusie	1977	RHP
George Kelly	1973	1B		Babe Ruth	1936	RF
Michael "King" Kelly	1945	RF				
Harmon Killebrew	1984	1B		Theodore "Ray" Schalk	1955	C
Ralph Kiner	1975	LF		Joe Sewell	1977	SS
Chuck Klein	1980	RF		Al Simmons	1953	LF
Bill Klem	1953	Umpire		George Sisler	1939	1B
Sandy Koufax	1972	LHP		Edwin "Duke" Snider	1980	CF
				Warren Spahn	1973	LHP
Napoleon "Larry" Lajoie	1937	2B		Albert G. Spalding	1939	Executive
Judge Kenesaw Landis	1944	Executive		Tris Speaker	1937	CF
Bob Lemon	1976	RHP		Casey Stengel	1966	Manager
Walter "Buck" Leonard	1972	Negro leagues				
Fred Lindstrom	1976	3B		Bill Terry	1954	1B
John "Pop" Lloyd	1977	Negro leagues		Sam Thompson	1974	RF
Al Lopez	1977	Manager		Joe Tinker	1946	SS
Ted Lyons	1955	RHP		Harold "Pie" Traynor	1948	3B
Connie Mack	1937	Manager		Arthur "Dazzy" Vance	1948	RHP
Mickey Mantle	1974	CF				
Henry "Heinie" Manush	1964	LF		George "Rube" Waddell	1946	LHP
Walter "Rabbit" Maranville	1954	SS		John "Honus" Wagner	1936	SS
Juan Marichal	1983	RHP		Roderick "Bobby" Wallace	1953	SS
Richard "Rube" Marquard	1971	LHP		Ed Walsh	1946	RHP
Eddie Mathews	1978	3B		Lloyd Waner	1967	CF
Christy Mathewson	1936	RHP		Paul Waner	1952	RF
Willie Mays	1979	CF		John M. Ward	1964	SS
Joe McCarthy	1957	Manager		George M. Weiss	1971	Executive
Tommy McCarthy	1946	RF		Mickey Welch	1973	RHP
Joe McGinnity	1946	RHP		Zach Wheat	1959	LF
John J. McGraw	1937	Manager		Ted Williams	1966	LF
Bill McKechnie	1962	Manager		Lewis "Hack" Wilson	1979	CF
Leland "Larry" McPhail	1978	Executive		George Wright	1937	Executive
Joe Medwick	1968	LF		Early Wynn	1972	RHP
Johnny Mize	1981	1B				
Stan Musial	1969	LF		Tom Yawkey	1980	Executive
				Cy Young	1937	RHP
Charles "Kid" Nichols	1949	RHP		Ross Youngs	1972	RF

GLOSSARY

ACC. Abbreviation for *The American Card Catalog*, the pioneer hobby reference by Jefferson R. Burdick. Numbers assigned in this catalog to various baseball card sets were once universally known among collectors, but are less often used today.

Advertising card. A baseball card, usually issued in panels or sheets, which has an advertising message on the back. Distributed to retail store owners to show them what the new baseball card sets would look like each year and encourage them to buy.

Advertising item. A card, sheet, magazine ad, poster, or other medium which uses the picture of a sports figure to sell a product. Popular with superstars collectors.

All-Star card. Periodically since 1958, Topps has issued as part of its regular baseball card set a group of specially designed cards depicting "All-Star" teams. In the early years, the players in this subset were chosen by the editors of *The Sporting News* or *Sport* magazine. In later years, the players were the starting teams from the annual All-Star Game.

Autographed card. A baseball card that bears the actual signature of the player depicted. Not to be confused with the printed facsimile autograph that is sometimes part of the card's design.

Back. The reverse (nonpicture) side of a baseball card. Usually contains player personal data, career information and/or statistics. Many older cards carry an advertisement for the issuer on the back. Sometimes nothing at all was printed on the back.

Back damage. Damage to the back of a card usually caused by its being mounted in a scrapbook or other display. Glue or tape remnants or stains, extra paper, or tears in the back design constitute back damage, as does extraneous writing, such as uniform numbers, etc.

Beckett or **Beckett-Eckes.** Hobby nickname for *The Sport Americana Baseball Card Price Guide*, an annual hobby reference authored by James Beckett and Dennis Eckes. Card prices are sometimes quoted as "60 percent of Beckett," meaning 60 percent of the value quoted in the latest edition of the price guide.

Bid. An offer to buy an item in a mail auction.

Blank-back. A card which, though intended to have printing on the back, did not receive it due to a printing error. A collectible type of error card.

Blanket. One of several early 20th century baseball collectibles in the form of a square piece of felt or other material. Best known are the 1914 felt blankets (ACC B-18), which are 5¼″ square, depicting one of 91 players. The term refers to the fact that these squares could be sewn together to form a quilt.

Border. The space between the picture portion and the edge of a card. Borders are usually white, but they may be other colors. Occasionally, card design didn't include a border. The condition of a card's borders in an important factor in considering its grade.

Bread label. A type of baseball collectible most often seen from the late 1940s and early 1950s. Generally these paper labels were attached to the end of a loaf of bread to seal the package. Printed in a format about 2½″ square, often with clipped corners, the labels depict a baseball player at center.

GLOSSARY

Brick. Group of baseball cards for sale as a lot, usually wrapped or sealed in plastic so the buyer can't see exactly what cards are contained, just the top and the bottom cards (which are usually the best in the brick). Unless specified otherwise, a brick will contain all cards of the same year, but they may be all different cards or assorted (not all different, possibly containing some duplicates).

Cabinet. A large-format card, usually an enlarged version of a regular-issue baseball card that was available as a premium item. Many cabinet cards are actual photographs mounted on heavy cardboard, though some have the picture portion of the card printed. They range in size from about 4½×6″ to 6×8″. Most were issued prior to 1920.

Caption. The information on the front of a baseball card, usually consisting of the player's name, position, team, and, sometimes, team insignia.

Checklist. A card or other item that lists each baseball card in a particular set and provides a space for the collector to mark whether he owns the card. Checklist cards have been issued with or as part of baseball card sets only since 1956. Checklists can also be commercially prepared books or collector-made lists for personal use.

Coin. A round baseball card, generally made of plastic or metal in the size of a silver dollar or smaller. These were popularly issued in the 1950s and 1960s as inserts in food items or in packages of baseball cards.

Collector issue. A baseball card set produced for sale solely within the hobby; that is, a set not issued as a premium with another product. Usually carries the connotation of being an unlimited edition, that is, it can be reprinted at will by the issuer.

Common card. A regular-issue baseball card of a "common" player, that is, a nonstar. Also, a card that is not scarce. Common cards are the lowest priced cards in a given set.

Convention. A sports memorabilia show where baseball cards and related collectibles are bought, sold, and traded, and other hobby activities are conducted.

Convention set. A collector's issue of baseball cards usually given away with the purchase of admission to a convention.

Counterfeit. A phony baseball card illegally printed to resemble an actual card with the intention of selling it as an original. Several of the hobby's more valuable recent cards were counterfeited in 1983, though the quality of workmanship was not good enough to fool most collectors. See **Reprint.**

Coupon. Part of a baseball card that is designed to be cut or torn off and mailed in for the redemption of premiums. A card with the coupon still attached is always worth more than a card without the coupon. See **Tab.**

Crease. A common form of damage to a baseball card caused by bending or folding the cardboard. One of the most important factors in judging the condition of a card. A card with a noticeable crease can never be considered better than Very Good in grade.

Dealer. One who buys, sells, and/or trades baseball cards and related collectibles with the expectation of making a profit. As differentiated from one who carries on the same activities solely to build a personal collection.

Die-cut card. A baseball card on which an outline around the player's picture has been partially cut through the cardboard during the manufacturing process. This allows the background to be folded away from the picture, usually creating a stand-up figure of the player. Die-cut cards are always worth considerably more when the background has not been punched out, folded, or removed.

Disc. A round baseball card made of paper or cardboard, ranging in size from the 1½″ discs of the 1910s to the 3½″ discs of today. Compare **Coin.**

Double-print. A baseball card that was printed twice as often as the other cards in the set or series, making it twice as common. Double-prints are usually created to fill out the required number of cards on a press sheet. For many years Topps double-printed a row of 11 cards on each of its 132-card printing sheets.

Error card. A card that contains a pictorial or typographic error, such as the wrong photo, a misspelled name, incorrect statistics, etc. Most error cards have no special value unless a corrected version was also issued. See **Misprint, Variation.**

Exhibit card. Large-format, generally postcard-size, card sold in arcade machines from the 1920s through the 1960s, taking its name from Chicago's Exhibit Supply Company, the principal issuer of such cards. Exhibit cards usually have little more than the player's name printed on the front, though some have a facsimile autograph and salutation, and a later series had statistics on the back. Also a generic term for any baseball picture item in the approximately 3×5″ to 5×7″ size. Many of the early exhibit cards have been reprinted in recent years by the hobby dealer who bought out the company.

Focus. The clarity of the picture on a baseball card. Few cards are blurred as the result of poorly focused photographs; more often, improper "focus" is the result of off-register printing of the four colors of ink that make up a baseball card. Generally, cards with poor "focus" are worth less than those on which the picture is printed in sharp register.

Hall of Famer. A card of a player who has been inducted into the National Baseball Hall of Fame in Cooperstown, New York.

High number. A card in the final series of a set, and thus with one of the highest card numbers in the set. Until 1974, many sets' high number cards were printed in smaller quantities than the rest of the set, and so are scarcer and usually more valuable today. Not all high numbers are scarce, and the term is also sometimes used for a scarce series within a set that is not actually the highest in card numbers.

Insert. An item included with a pack of baseball cards as a sales incentive, usually later in the year. For Topps cards in the 1960s and 1970s these included stamps, coins, posters, stickers, tattoos, specialty cards, and similar items.

Layering. The separation of the several layers of paper that make up a card. This usually occurs at the corners and is a sign of wear that should be considered in grading.

Legitimate issue. A baseball card set that is issued with another product as a sales incentive, as opposed to a **Collector issue**, which see.

Lid. A round cardboard baseball card with a picture of a player on one side, used as the top lid of a candy, ice cream, or other product. Lid issues span the decades from the 1910s through the 1980s.

Major set. Term used in connection with a nationally distributed card set, as opposed to a regional issue. Topps and Bowman were the major sets of the 1950s; today, Topps, Fleer, and Donruss are considered major issues.

Mini-card. Often shortened to "mini." Usually applied to cards from a 1975 Topps special test issue, in which the regular baseball card set was issued in certain areas in a reduced size.

Minor leaguer. A baseball card depicting a player of a minor league team, whether the set is all minor leaguers or also includes major league players. See **Pre-rookie card**.

Miscut. A card that has been improperly cut from a sheet, often severing part of the design or including parts of two cards. Miscutting decreases the value of a card.

Misprint. A card that shows the result of faulty printing. This can include cards with blank backs, wrong backs, missing colors of ink, and cards with spots or smears of ink, along with other damage. Misprints usually lower the value of a card, except to the relatively small number of error collectors.

Multi-player card. A baseball card which features two or more players.

Notching. The indentation on a card, usually at the edges, caused by rubber banding the card into a stack. Often affects the first and last cards in a set, which would be at the top and bottom of such stacks. Notching is considered damage and lowers the value of a card.

Obverse. The front, or picture, side of a card.

Panel. A strip of two or more cards, as printed and before being separated into individual cards. Also, a partial uncut sheet consisting of two or more cards. A complete panel is more valuable than the total value of the individual cards on it.

Plastic sheet. A hobby accessory for card storage, consisting of one of several plastic formulas worked into a pocketed sheet, punched with holes to fit a three-ring binder. Sometimes shortened to "plastics."

Premium. An item obtained by redeeming proofs of purchase—tabs, coupons, or wrappers—from a card. Baseball card premiums were often larger pictures of favorite players. Generally, such premiums are much scarcer than the cards themselves.

Pre-rookie card. A minor league card of a player; generally used to describe the minor league cards of a currently active player.

Rare. A term that is used to describe a card that is numerically rare—not simply valuable.

Regional card. A card issued in a limited geographic region. Also includes cards which may have been distributed nationally, but not in particularly large numbers or by a major card manufacturer.

Reprint. A reproduction of a baseball card, usually—but not always—so labeled. Generally, reprints are produced to satisfy collector demand for rare cards. Reprints are usually printed on a different type of cardboard than original cards, and without the intent that they pass for genuine. See **Counterfeit**.

Reverse. The back, or nonpicture, side of a card.

Rookie card. The first baseball card of a player upon making the major leagues. Rookie cards may or may not have been issued in the player's actual first season in the majors.

Scarce. Term used to describe a card that is difficult to find—not one that is merely expensive.

Series. A group of cards within a set that were issued together. For example, from 1952 to 1973, each annual Topps set was issued in several series over the course of each year.

Set. A complete group of cards, of identical design, issued during a single calendar year. Some collectors consider variations on the original design to be part of a set.

Skip-numbered. A set of cards that is not numbered in sequence. Sometimes numbers were skipped as cards were withdrawn due to player retirement or demotion, but sets were also skip-numbered to induce buyers to seek cards that did not exist.

Specialty card. A baseball card that pictures something other than a single player, or a card of different design or format within a set—for example, multi-player, World Series, All-Star, team, league leaders, or "In Action" cards.

Stamp. A baseball collectible in the form of a gummed

stamp with perforated edges. Often intended to be glued into a special album, but worth more if it hasn't been.

Star card. A card depicting a player of "star" caliber, as opposed to a "superstar" or "common" card. Star designation varies according to the individual collector or dealer and is often a matter of home team favoritism.

Sticker. A large stamp without perforated edges, issued with a protective backing that can be peeled off to allow the sticker to adhere to another object.

Stock. The paper or cardboard on which a baseball card is printed.

Strip card. A baseball card, usually quite small, printed and sold in long strips. Often cheaply produced and of low quality, most strip cards date to the 1920s.

Subset. A specialty run of cards within a single year's set, such as All-Star cards, Play-off cards, World Series cards, etc.

Superstar card. A card of a player who has been inducted into the National Baseball Hall of Fame, or of a current player who is virtually assured of induction when eligible. The term is often overused to describe cards of currently popular, especially new, players who may or may not someday legitimately deserve the mantle of "superstar."

Tab. A strip, attached to a card, meant to be removed from the card and redeemed for a premium. Cards with the tab intact can be worth anything from 15 to 100 percent more than cards without the tab. See **Coupon.**

Tape stain. A discolored area on a card left after the re-

moval of tape. A factor in card grading.

Team card. A card that shows an entire baseball team, rather than a single player.

Test issue. A set of cards distributed in limited numbers in limited geographic areas to test its appeal for possible mass marketing at a later date.

Trimmed card. A card that has been cut down in size from its original dimensions. Some cards were trimmed long ago to make them fit into some type of display holder. In recent years, some unscrupulous persons have slightly trimmed the edges of worn cards to make them appear Mint in condition. Trimming greatly decreases the value of a card.

Uncut sheet. A complete sheet of baseball cards as they were originally printed. Can range from 36 or fewer cards in early years to the standard 132-card sheets being produced today. The term is sometimes stretched to include partial sheets which, though cut, have not been separated into individual cards. See **Panel.**

Variation. A card that exists in two or more varieties, usually because a second version was printed to correct an error in the first. Some variations have considerable extra value, some have none.

Wrong-back. A card which, because the uncut sheet was mishandled between the printing of the back and the front, has the statistics and personal information of one player on the back, and the picture of another player on the front. Because baseball card sheets are not usually symmetrical, cards with wrong-backs usually have the back printing somewhat off-center. Wrong-back cards are slightly more valuable than their correctly printed equivalents.

INDEX

INDEX
OF
CARD SETS

INDEX OF CARD SETS

NOTES

NOTES